Lenin, Trotsky, and Stalin

Philip Pomper

LENIN, TROTSKY, AND STALIN

The Intelligentsia and Power

 Columbia University Press   New York

Columbia University Press

New York   Oxford

Copyright © 1990 Columbia University Press

All rights reserved

Library of Congress Cataloging-in-Publication Data

Pomper, Philip.

Lenin, Trotsky, and Stalin : the intelligentsia and power / Philip Pomper.

p.   cm.

Includes bibliographical references.

ISBN 0-231-06906-5

1. Heads of state—Soviet Union—Biography.

2. Revolutionists—Soviet Union—Biography.

3. Soviet Union—History—Revolution, 1917–1921—Biography.

4. Soviet Union—Biography.

5. Lenin, Vladimir Il'ich, 1870–1924—Psychology.

6. Trotsky, Leon, 1879–1940—Psychology.

7. Stalin, Joseph, 1879–1953—Psychology.

I. Title.

DK253.P65   1989

947.084′092′2—dc210

[B]

89-22138

CIP

In memory of my father

Contents

Preface

IT TAKES a certain kind of courage—perhaps not the best kind—to venture a psychobiographical study of Lenin, Trotsky, and Stalin. The late BertramWolfe produced a massive and brilliantly written book on the three figures, his deservedly famous *Three Who Made a Revolution*. But he ended his study before 1917 and never completed the projected sequel. Isaac Deutscher, who had planned to write separate biographies of the three, produced a magnificent trilogy on Trotsky's career and also wrote a provocative biography of Stalin, but never finished his biography of Lenin. Among current scholars, Adam Ulam has written penetrating biographies of both Lenin and Stalin. Robert H. McNeal and Pierre Broué have recently produced major studies of Stalin and Trotsky respectively and Robert C. Tucker's interesting psychobiography of Stalin is still in progress. Two comparative studies, E. Victor Wolfenstein's book on Lenin, Trotsky, and Gandhi, *The Revolutionary Personality*, and Bruce Mazlish's *The Revolutionary Ascetic*, which contains a valuable chapter on

Lenin, were among the first to bring a high level of psychoanalytic sophistication to the subject. One might add many other texts to this short list, but the ones mentioned are probably the best efforts at political biography, psychobiography, or both. It is appropriate to ask what there is to add in the wake of these studies.

I set myself the difficult task of integrating the psychobiographies and political careers of Lenin, Trotsky, and Stalin. To complete such a task in a single study of less than mammoth proportions, I have eschewed the monographic density practiced by Wolfe, Deutscher, Ulam, Tucker, and other biographers. To be sure, the psychological approach demands precise focus on critical moments, and here both monographic detail and documentation are called for. Scholars in the field will be aware of the emphasis placed on close study of the three families, new sources used for the sections on Trotsky in particular, and novel interpretations. I examine and interpret the formation and transformation of three personalities, first in family and school environments, then in revolutionary politics, and finally, in power. The study ends in 1924 with the death of Lenin and Trotsky's defeat in the struggle for leadership of the Communist Party.

Like other students of the Russian revolutionary movement, I have been impressed by the extent to which the Russian intelligentsia's commitments to scientific truth and social justice were transformed into something quite different in the long battle with the tsarist regime and in the internecine strife that followed the February Revolution. The story of the Russian Revolution of 1917, of the implementation of the ideas of the nineteenth-century intelligentsia, of the sacrifices of millions of lives, has been revised and retold with skill and insight by more than one generation. I in turn offer whatever insights are available through psychobiography. The encouragement of psychiatrists who have read and discussed parts of the manuscript gives me hope that despite my amateur status, I have been able to discern significant patterns in the early lives of my subjects and connected these patterns with their political achievements and failures. I therefore offer the reader a study of the lives of three men who transformed the ideals and theories of the intelligentsia in the crucibles of their psyches. Lenin, Trotsky, and Stalin carried the burdens and benefits of their pasts into each new struggle on the way to power, and each dealt with the exercise of power in his own way, with momentous historical consequences. The power of each man extends into the present. Lenin, Trotsky, and Stalin have achieved the status of symbols, and it remains to be seen whether new perspectives and political change in the Soviet Union will allow, for the first time in decades, full and frank treatment of their achievements and failures. It is not easy to deal with symbols, but it is incumbent upon us to try and to continue to hope that Soviet scholars will finally provide a fuller account of their past, an account in which all of the artificially created empty spaces are filled in. If this book helps them toward that goal, I will be amply rewarded.

Acknowledgments

THE GENEROSITY of several institutions and granting agencies permitted me to conduct the research and writing for this book in the best possible situation— one in which excellent library resources and collegial environments contributed immeasurably to the completion of my project. The research and writing was largely conducted during two years of sabbatical and leave from Wesleyan University. Wesleyan also provided support from the Jonathan Meigs Fund, for which I am grateful to my colleagues. The Wesleyan library staff eased the daily task of scholarship by routinely providing numerous valuable services and the History Department office staff, Donna Scott and Rose Marie Ingalls, responded with their usual energy to the tasks involved with the production of the manuscript. I am especially grateful to Patricia St. Clair and Janet Morgan for sharing their time and expertise generously and helping me transfer my manuscript to our mainframe computer. Long before the actual research and writing began, work with Wesleyan students over a long span of years sustained my interest in the project. Several deserve special mention: Leonard Rubenstein, Jill Bernstein, Eric Duskin, and Mitchell Briskin.

The Russian Research Center at Harvard kindly gave me the status of Visiting Scholar during 1984–85 and again in 1987–88. I would like to thank the many Fellows and Scholars there, too numerous to mention, who shared their knowledge and provided both useful criticism and encouragement. My special thanks to Nina Tumarkin, Loren Graham, Priscilla Johnson McMillan, and Adam Ulam, who helped in a variety of ways, and Mary Towle, without whom it is impossible even to imagine the Russian Research Center. I am grateful to the very capable staff at Houghton Library for facilitating my work in the Trotsky Archive.

During the summer of 1987 a grant under the Title VIII Program (Soviet-East European Training Act of 1983) permitted me to work in the Nicolaevsky Collection, Hoover Institution Archives, Stanford University. My thanks to the director, Richard F. Staar and the Fellows for their hospitality, and especially to the archivists and library staff for expediting my research. Like all scholars who have worked with the rare Russian materials in the library of the Hoover Institution, I found Hilja Kukk's help invaluable. I would like to thank Mrs. Ella Wolf for her encouragement and for generously sharing her knowledge and experience. I am deeply in debt to Charles Palm and Elena Danielson for helping me with the recently identified Trotsky materials in the Nicolaevsky Collection, and for their graciousness in sharing the riches of the Hoover Institution Archives. I also spent some time during the summer of 1986 working in the Trotsky manuscripts contained in the Manuscript Department of the Lilly Library, Indiana University. My thanks to the curator, Saundra Taylor, for her assistance.

As a Fellow of the Kennan Institute for Advanced Russian Studies of the Wilson Center for a six-month period in 1988 I enjoyed a great many privileges that made possible the completion of the writing of this book. I am grateful to Peter Reddaway and Ted Taranovsky for their collegial generosity and stimulating company, to the staff of the Kennan Institute for their many services, to Robert C. Tucker for his interesting comments on my colloquium paper at the Center, and to the Fellows who make the Wilson Center such an exciting place to work. My special thanks to Fran Hunter for her hospitality and friendship, both of which add to the appeal of the Wilson Center. I could not possibly have completed my work at the Kennan Institute without the aid of two able research assistants, Vladimir Dragunsky and Michele Kelemen.

Aside from those mentioned above, I owe a considerable debt to Paul Avrich, Terence Emmons, Leopold Haimson, William McNeill, Robert C. Williams, Drs. Robert J. Lifton, Elizabeth Hersh, Max Hernandez, and Eleanor Pringle, and Amy Bloom—whose contributions to my field, to my knowledge of history, to my understanding of psychology, or encouragement and support furthered my project. My thanks to my wife, Alice, who scrutinized the proofs, vigilantly and saved many a slip. Without her support the project would have been impossible. Only I, of course, can be held responsible for the defects of this study of Lenin, Trotsky, and Stalin, but if my book has any virtues they issue largely from my ability to use the exemplary work of others and to heed their advice. Finally, my thanks to Kate Wittenberg of Columbia University Press for helping me realize this project in the form in which I conceived it.

A Note on Dates and Transliterations

ALL WRITERS on Russian history whose studies begin before February 1(14), 1918, when the Gregorian calendar replaced the Julian, face the vexing matter of alerting readers to the calendar being used. The problem is complicated when the subjects become émigrés before February 1918. I have used the Julian calendar (twelve days behind the Gregorian in the nineteenth century, thirteen in the twentieth) throughout, although at times I alert the reader by providing the Gregorian date in parentheses, as in the above example.

Transliteration is even more vexing. It seems stilted to transliterate names with English versions quite close to the Russian or surnames with an accepted English form, such as Dostoevsky. In most cases, however, Russian names are transliterated according to the system used by the Library of Congress. If the alert reader finds exceptions either in my methods of dating or transliteration, I can only confess, as E. H. Carr did in the preface to *The Bolshevik Revolution*, that I may have even failed to achieve consistent inconsistency.

Lenin, Trotsky, and Stalin

1

The Ul'ianovs

THE EARLY lives of historical figures usually remain obscure. This is
even truer of the entire complex of family relationships that ordinarily
shapes human psychologies and individual motivation. It is not so
much lack of interest that is involved. Rather, we are faced with the usual
problems of weighing early experiences, understanding their significance for
later actions — in short, making convincing connections between the history of
a family and the achievements of a historical figure. There are other kinds of
problems as well. Tracing the history of any family that has moved swiftly
upward in society is usually difficult; it is especially difficult if the family has
achieved an exalted place. When it has nurtured the charismatic authority of a
new political system, the family, like the sacred places of some cultures, can
only be approached ritualistically. The more ordinary forms of censorship and
embellishment give way to myth and archetype. Of course, in this particular
case the charismatic authority is the founder of the dictatorship of the proletar-

iat, and the mythology tends to invert the usual stories about the hero's birth and perilous passage. Instead of a connection with the gods or a noble blood line only later discovered, the humbler aspects of his origins are stressed. If the hero is saved from drowning, for example, it is duly noted that a factory worker or some equally exploited representative of the working classes pulled him from the water. Moreover, all connections, however tenuous, between family members and the revolutionary movement are recorded.

The family history constructed around Vladimir Il'ich Ul'ianov, however, should be seen less as fabrication than as selective remembering. When a political culture, still in its own childhood, tells the story of its founder's childhood, it does so in a consciously didactic manner. Posterity should therefore be grateful to Lenin's older sister, Anna, for providing, along with the mandatory lessons about the development of the leader of the proletariat, memories less disciplined and more revealing. If one reads all her available memoirs attentively, it turns out that Vladimir, later to be Lenin, rates perhaps fifth place in her personal ranking of family heroes and heroines. In first place stands Alexander (Sasha, in the diminutive), the eldest son. From Anna's memoirs we learn that Alexander was the son chosen to further the family honor by his achievements.

The special role of the eldest son was marked out first of all by the culture in which the Ul'ianovs lived. The eldest son had strong responsibilities as mediator of the father's dread authority. Of course, in enlightened families one need not necessarily speak of dread paternal authority, but even in such families fathers could be intimidating, and the eldest sons in such cases might alleviate the inequality of generations by providing a less threatening version of authority. Il'ia Ul'ianov, the father, had his own particular reasons as well for giving Alexander a special role—indeed, a special burden. Il'ia's older brother had martyred himself in order to help Il'ia in his career. Even if Il'ia did not tell Alexander that he too must become a martyr for the sake of his younger siblings, he extolled the virtues of self-sacrifice and duty. This was the burden passed on to Alexander—an ethic of duty, a sense that he owed a debt. Despite human failings that probably affected Alexander more than the other children, Il'ia provided a vivid model of dutifulness. In turn, Alexander was expected to be a model for the younger siblings, a moral authority in his own right. Il'ia, however, died before Alexander reinterpreted the family imperative by becoming a revolutionary terrorist. He was hanged for his part in a conspiracy to assassinate Alexander III in 1887.

Not Vladimir but Alexander played the pivotal role in family history, although he was only twenty-one at his execution in May 1887. In some families, the child who is chosen to carry the family's honor and to perform great deeds perishes prematurely; the worthiest and most beloved family members suffer harsh fates; and a survivor, perhaps one not especially promising at first, or even lovable, changes history in ways unforeseen. Two martyred eldest brothers in two successive generations stand prominently in the family history behind one of the outstanding political careers in modern history.

IL'IA UL'IANOV was the last of four children born to Nikolai Ul'ianov and his wife, Anna (earlier, Smirnov). Nikolai had married late, in 1812, when he was over forty years old.[1] When Il'ia was born in 1831, his father was well into his sixties; and when Nikolai died in 1836, he left behind not only a five-year-old child, but the eldest son, Vasilii, about eighteen years old, and two daughters, Maria and Fedosiia, ages thirteen and eleven respectively, in addition to his wife. Nikolai had worked as a tailor and achieved the status of *meshchanin* (generally, a lower middle class urban dweller) in the census of 1835. He possessed a modest house in a poor section of the city of Astrakhan, at that time a busy port on the delta of the Volga River. The purchase of a two-story house of stone and wood, the first floor occupied by his shop, in the slums of Astrakhan, which were filled with ethnic minorities, runaway or freed serfs, retired soldiers and sailors who did not return to their villages of origin, tradesmen, craftsmen, and stevedores, nonetheless probably signified a move upward for the Ul'ianov family, which was of serf origin. Even marginal families can put down roots, and evidently Nikolai's son Vasilii was determined to sustain the family's position.

Like many other things about the family, Vasilii's heroism remains a bit mysterious. We can infer from his actions, at least, that he understood the importance of education and made it a central and guiding value for his younger brother, Il'ia. It is also likely that Vasilii detected in Il'ia the ability that eventually won him a silver medal in a gymnasium in Astrakhan. As family legend has it, Vasilii neither pursued education himself nor even raised a family. He began his career in 1841 delivering salt at a salary of fifty-seven silver rubles a year and eventually achieved the status of clerk in a large and successful Astrakhan mercantile firm, the Brothers Sapozhnikov. In order to became a clerk, he had to be more than marginally literate, and he had completed elementary school. His many responsibilities suggest a considerable degree of ability and energy. What little we know of him reveals at least modest upward mobility.[2] A photograph of Vasilii shows a balding man with a mustache, dressed up for his sitting in a checked vest and modish frock coat. He posed with his arms folded, starched cuffs and cufflinks protruding elegantly. His hair is trimmed, heavily pomaded, and curled at the temples. Vasilii's nephew Vladimir bore a distinct resemblance to him. Photographs of Il'ia show a much more imposing figure, although rather small of stature, sometimes with a hand thrust under his coat in the Napoleonic manner, but Il'ia too wore his hair curled at the temples. He was a homely man, with a narrower skull, broader cheekbones, and more slanted eyes than Vasilii, and he was pock-marked, according to the medical report issued on the occasion of his application for the gymnasium in Astrakhan. Il'ia achieved hereditary nobility during Vasilii's lifetime, in 1874, for Vasilii died of tuberculosis in 1878 at the age of about sixty. This chronology creates a small family puzzle. Why didn't Il'ia share his good fortune with his family?

In Anna Elizarova-Ul'ianov's memoirs, not a single visit by Uncle Vasilii or any other member of the Astrakhan family is mentioned, even though Il'ia's family after his marriage in 1863 continued to live in cities on the Volga. On April 4, 1866, Il'ia asked the director of the gymnasium in Nizhnii Novgorod for a leave to visit Astrakhan, presumably to see his family.[3] This is the last record of any real or intended trip by Il'ia himself to see his family in Astrkahan. Anna remembered only one visit to Astrakhan, which occurred when she was a child of about four, and her memory of it was so dim (writing as she did in 1927) that it is not entirely clear whom she met beside her grandmother and uncle. She, her brother Sasha, nineteenth months her junior, and her mother took a trip on a Volga steamer from Nizhnii Novgorod in 1868 or 1869, not long before they moved to Simbirsk. Of the trip Anna could only vaguely recall: "a little house, the old grandmother and uncle . . . who treated us as specially favored guests and, as mother saw it, quite spoiled us."[4] The grandmother, Anna Ul'ianov—her namesake—was roughly eighty at the time, and it is likely that the family planned the trip to permit her at least one glimpse of her daughter-in-law and grandchildren before her death. For reasons not altogether clear, Il'ia had decisively separated himself and his second family from his relatives in Astrakhan soon after his marriage. In doing so, he left behind not only his mother and sisters, but a man, still in his forties, who had been the real founder of the historical family through his willing self-sacrifice and sponsorship of Il'ia. Yet the separation apparently gave the older brother a stronger mystique, for Il'ia never tired of telling his children about Uncle Vasilii's sacrifice. To the children he must have been less a human being of flesh and blood than a moral monolith.

The social and cultural superiority of Maria Alexandrovna's family may explain some of the distance between Il'ia and his past. In fact, his wife's background could not have been much more different from his. The north German and Swedish Lutheran culture in which she grew up showed strongly in several ways: in her taciturn, restrained manner; in the way she raised children; in her spirit of organization and work ethic; and at the Christmas holiday, when the family had a Christmas tree. But her background was not typically north German or Swedish either, for she belonged to an ethnic minority in the Russian empire. Like Il'ia's family, hers was marginal in some sense. Furthermore, other family eccentricities make it difficult to present any neat social or cultural formulation. Even if one could produce a general statement about the transmutation of northern Protestant culture in a Russian setting, one would have to explain Maria's choice of a Russified Kalmyk—Il'ia's likely ethnic origins. Another fact needs clarification. At the time of her marriage in 1863 Maria was twenty-eight and verging on spinsterhood, given the norm for that era, and we must speculate why. A photograph of Maria taken in 1863 shows a proud, erect woman with dark wavy hair, strongly etched eybrows, and an imperious look. Later photos (perhaps less judiciously doctored) show a prominent upper lip and slightly protruding upper teeth, but in a face with otherwise attractive features. Homeliness or physical deformity are not the answers.

The Blank family was large, but not unusually so. It consisted of Dr.

Alexander Blank, his wife Anna, who died in 1840, and six children. Anna Blank's family originated in the north-German trading center, Lubeck, and continued its mercantile activities in St. Petersburg after emigration in 1790. Johan Grosschopf, her father, had married a woman of Swedish origin, Anna Ohrstedt. The Swedish family was also mercantile, for Karl Ohrstedt was a goldsmith.[5] While the Grosschopf family continued to rise in business, government, and the military, this family, like the one in Astrakhan, receded from view, perhaps because of some sort of estrangement, and like the tiny home in an Astrakhan slum, the spacious mansion of the Grosschopf family on Vasilevskii Island in St. Petersburg remained a distant outpost of Ul'ianov family culture. There is no evidence of any significant connection with the Grosschopf and Ohrstedt branches of the family.

To learn more about Maria Blank's background, we must examine her father's career. Although Alexander Blank was responsible for a relative lowering of the social position of his wife, he somewhat elevated himself in the process. His origins are mysterious. The name "Blank" suggests German or Jewish ethnic background. We know that he was born in 1799 and that his family was urban but not wealthy, given its *meshchanin* status. If born Jewish, Dr. Blank must have been baptized at some point. Like his son-in-law Il'ia Ul'ianov, Alexander Blank used ability, ambition, and education to make his way, first in St. Petersburg, where he studied in the Medico-Surgical Academy and practiced medicine. Dr. Blank also became a hospital administrator and later held positions in Smolensk, Olonetsk, and the Urals. After his wife's death he purchased the estate of Kokushkino in Kazan province on the Volga and, after retiring in 1847, lived there for the last twenty-three years of his life. Given his urban background and cultural level, Dr. Blank's choice of provincial life far from his early centers of activity suggests some sort of rejection of his past milieu. He evidently chose to raise his six children (five of them daughters) in a healthy rural setting according to a very definite regime he had formulated on the basis of medical science and his experience of life. Dr. Blank's little nest at Kokushkino was one of the interesting variations in the life of the rural gentry, which admitted a multitude of eccentricities.

Maria Blank, born in 1835, grew up in a largely feminine milieu. (Her brother, Dmitrii, died in 1850.) Although her mother died when Maria was still a child, she, like her future husband, had a substitute parent, an aunt, Dr. Blank's sister-in-law, Ekaterina Essen, who was ten years older than her brother-in-law. However, beginning in the 1840s there was no lack of male company in the Blank household. Dr. Blank's estate became a gathering place for a circle of young men who quickly discovered the charms of his daughters (Anna, born in 1831; Liubov, in 1832; Ekaterina, in 1833; Maria, in 1835; and Sofia, in 1836.) All five of the daughters married men who at some time in their lives were teachers or school administrators or both. Maria first met her future husband in Penza in 1861, while visiting her sister Anna, who was married to Ivan Veretennikov, a school inspector at the Institute for the Nobility, where Il'ia taught physics and mathematics. Dr. Blank's choice of male companions no doubt played a significant role in the fate of his daughters, but he and Ekaterina Essen had made intellectual and cultural values central in the upbringing of the five girls.

According to family lore, Dr. Blank was a cultivated if eccentric man who had travelled widely and held "progressive" ideas. His medical views, however, are not advertisements for his good judgment. He believed in the curative and bracing powers of water applied to the body in either sickness or health and became known for hydrotherapeutic compresses and wraps. Dr. Blank's children received many such treatments, and the daughters, at least, thrived. Tea and coffee were *verboten*. Dr. Blank did not believe in heavy clothing, and dress was plain. Although hair styles are not mentioned, one may guess that in childhood the girls' hair was cut short. Childhood pictures of Maria's own daughters, Anna and Olga, show them with severely short haircuts as children, whereas their brothers have hair down to their shoulders—probably a continuation of the family custom. The word "austere" clearly describes the Blank regime. Maria had been raised in an atmosphere of Aunt Ekaterina's Germanic puritanism and her father's "progressive" rigorism in the sheltered setting of Kokushkino for most of her unmarried life. Domestic instruction, in her case, consisted largely of music and foreign languages, and she learned enough to pass qualifying examinations in 1863 that certified her to teach French and German (as well as Russian, Bible, and arithmetic) at the primary level.[6]

It should be added that Dr. Blank was not a humorless individual and was even capable of childish pranks. He probably was sufficiently attractive as a person to inspire his daughters—at least one of his daughters—to look for a man of similar qualities. There are interesting parallels between Dr. Blank and his son-in-law, Il'ia. Both began as *meshchan'e*, educated themselves, entered demanding professions, married women higher in the social scale, and became members of the gentry estate. Perhaps her ties to her father are sufficient to explain Maria's delayed marriage. A Soviet writer hypothesizes that Maria was Dr. Blank's favorite, closest to his austere ideal of young womanhood. One might also speculate that the aging widower detected in Maria both the strength of character and self-sacrificing characteristics she later showed in great abundance in her marriage and thus chose her to take care of him in his old age. Perhaps Maria made the choice herself. There is usually complicity in such arrangements. Maria's fondness for Kokushkino is attested to by the Ul'ianov family's annual summer vacations there. For the Ul'ianov children departure for Kokushkino signified liberation from school examinations and the companionship of their cousins (Maria's sisters' children) in a setting of fields, forests, and rivers.

The adjectives liberally applied to Maria by memoirists—gentle, yet firm, restrained, devoted, patient, supportive, courageous—all suggest not only a good mother and wife but a natural pedagogue. Surely, in other circumstances she might have pursued that calling, but instead she used her talents in a domestic setting. One senses, too, that her intense devotion and unusual success with her children caused a variety of problems. Initially, it created an ordinary family problem, in which two individuals with deep convictions pursuing the same end with different methods come into conflict. An intervention, in which Il'ia took control of the boys' education, is noted in Anna's memoirs. More will be said about this later, but it is important to note here that even if Maria opposed her husband at times, she submitted to Il'ia's demands. Disagreements about child-rearing were settled behind the scenes, and the parents presented a united front.

Not suprisingly, eight known pregnancies (two children died in early infancy, Olga in 1869 and Nikolai in 1873), a perilous family budget, and continuous domestic responsibilities during Il'ia's long professional absences are sufficient to account for the rapid loss of looks recorded in photographs. After fifteen years of marriage the proud fiancée of the instructor of physics and mathematics looked matronly, subdued, and perhaps was prematurely gray. An acquaintance in Simbirsk said of her: "She looked much older than her age."[7] Yet Maria showed unusual longevity in an era when women were literally used up in the process of reproduction. She reached the age of eighty-one.

Il'ia must have detected in Maria a natural partner in the projects forming in his mind during the early 1860s. They were in fundamental accord about the conduct of a virtuous life—one of unremitting labor, of duty to one's calling. Education was Il'ia's calling, perhaps his obsession. Education had permitted him to escape from the slums of Astrakhan, to obtain a Master's degree at the University of Kazan, to move in the company of colleagues who valued him and helped him rise even higher in his chosen profession. Il'ia and the age of Russian Enlightenment were in singular accord, too. Educated commoners had seized the new opportunities available to them during the era of Great Reforms to become a cultural vanguard (whether one disagreed with their version of culture or not) in the 1850s and 1860s. Although themselves men of letters, they promoted study of the natural sciences as the key to the future of humankind. They did not always agree about strategies for achieving a just society, but the leaders of the movement called "nihilism" (a label popularized through Turgenev's novel *Fathers and Sons*) shared a naturalistic outlook on the human condition. Despite their atheism and materialism, they called for dutiful social commitments on behalf of human progress on utilitarian and self-interested grounds, which presumably were also scientific. They believed they had found in socialism a scientifically based ethic. Il'ia departed from the radical wing of the Russian Enlightenment. He remained devoutly Christian until his death—more devout than his wife or children—while also dedicated to the natural sciences.

Il'ia's career has only superficial resemblances to those of the radical intelligentsia, although every effort is made to connect him with their movement. He acted, above all, like a person grateful for having had the opportunity to study, who wanted to give others the same opportunity. But the zeal with which he inflicted education upon his own children sometimes had less salutary effects than his professional efforts on behalf of the peasants and culturally deprived ethnic groups of Simbirsk province and Kazan district. This cavil aside, Il'ia's career dramatically illustrates the spread of enlightenment in

Russia. Inaugurated in the eighteenth century, the great movement for secular learning had suffered partial reversals during xenophobic reactions, reaffirmations of "traditional" values and teachings (themselves imported doctrines of earlier periods), and censorship. Il'ia had the good fortune, the talent, and the energy to exploit the period of relative liberalism during the reign of Alexander II, and reform-minded bureaucrats used men like Il'ia to further their projects. This was especially true following the Crimean War and Alexander II's realization that without ambitious reforms Russia would continue to fall behind the Western powers. Reform meant not only liberating the serfs but educating them as well. Nikolai Pirogov, a surgeon who in 1856 initiated the discussion of the educational reform, was one of the prominent enlighteners behind the education statute of 1864; Il'ia's professional advancement coincided with the era launched by the reform.

A short survey of Il'ia's career reveals a truly impressive rise. His gifts were recognized early. Otherwise, a child of his background would not have attended a gymnasium, a demanding form of secondary education that prepared young men for universities or technical institutes. When he graduated in 1850, he won a silver medal—a level of achievement quite unprecedented in the Astrakhan gymnasium. With a career in the civil service in mind, Il'ia decided to apply to Kazan University, north on the Volga. Despite a recommendation from the director of the gymnasium, Il'ia's background prevented him from receiving a stipend from the university. At this point, his brother Vasilii's material support became crucial. Vasilii made it possible for Il'ia to board a steamboat for Kazan in July 1850. Kazan University, the frontier post of higher education in the eastern part of the Russian Empire, did not have the academic wealth of St. Petersburg or Moscow. The university did not have a good law faculty, but it did boast one of the great mathematicians of the age, Nikolai Lobachevsky. Thus, instead of pursuing a career in law—his first choice— Il'ia studied mathematics and physics, specializing in astronomy and meteorology, and received his degree in 1854. Although we know the subject of Il'ia's Bachelor's thesis, "Olbers' Method for Calculating the Orbit of the Comet Klinkerfuss," it is difficult to determine the extent of his scientific talent. In 1855 with Lobachevsky's help—the latter played an administrative role in Kazan's school system—Il'ia received the position of senior teacher of physics and mathemtics in the advanced classes of the Penza Institute for the Gentry, located in the capital of the Volga province. He taught the children of the social estate whose elite privileges had put obstacles in the way of his own career. For eight years he remained at the Penza Institute and for four years was in charge of meteorological observations at the station there.

Il'ia married Maria Blank in 1863 and then moved to the city of Nizhnii Novgorod, where he took a position in the gymnasium. The young science and mathematics teacher and his wife enjoyed the lively cultural life available to them in the commercial city located at the confluence of the Oka and Volga. Their family grew, first with Anna's birth in August 1864, then with Sasha's, nineteen months later in March 1866. An assassination attempt against Alexander II during that year by a student, Dmitrii Karakozov, was the most dramatic manifestation of revolutionary discontent with the Great Reforms within the radical subculture of nihilism—another byproduct of the era of reform. The child born to Il'ia and Maria in 1866 would make an attempt on the life of Alexander II's son in 1887. However, the world of politics, the reactions following radical moves in the 1860's, did not immediately affect the Ul'ianovs. Rather, the first event to disturb the young couple was the death of a third child, Olga, in early infancy in 1869.

Although the development of the revolutionary movement in Russia during this period affected the government's attitude toward control of the curriculum and administration of the expanded system of local education, the Ministry of Popular Enlightenment nonetheless hired a cohort of dedicated school inspectors to establish model schools throughout the empire in 1869. Il'ia received an offer to assume one of the newly created posts of school inspector for the province of Simbirsk, whose capital was a Volga town of roughly 40,000. Although the seat of an episcopal see, with a cathedral rising from the area of the city known as the Crown because of its elevation 560 feet above the Volga, Simbirsk was known for its slow pace of life. Il'ia accepted the post, and when he and his family boarded the steamship on September 22, 1869, Maria was already pregnant with their fourth child, Vladimir. He was born in the city of Simbirsk, now Ulianovsk, on April 10, 1870, now celebrated on April 22, because of the change from the Julian to Gregorian calendar in February 1918.

Il'ia had become the representative of an understaffed, underpaid (and thus corruptible), but reform-minded state bureaucracy, subject to the vicissitudes of politics. He was relatively young when he assumed his position, but given his poor health (about which details are lacking) and the travel involved, it was taxing work. There were only thirty-four inspectors in 1871. They had wide discretionary powers, and much depended upon their initiative, energy, and imagination.[8] By 1874 three inspectors were designated for each province, and one of them was to be made Director of Schools in the province. In Simbirsk province, with a population of somewhat more than 1 million in 1870, 460 public elementary schools served 1,546 settlements of various sizes, and each school had an average of twenty-one pupils. A staff of 526 poorly qualified teachers included 294 priests and three mullahs. Only 19 percent of the schools functioned normally. To diagnose the school system's deficiencies, Il'ia had to travel about the province. He also had to discuss his plans to increase budgets, build schools, train and hire competent teachers, buy textbooks and equipment, raise salaries, and other diverse matters with villagers, officials of local zemstvo boards, and his own ministry.

Il'ia's work entailed long absences and physically trying conditions as well as the pressures of administrative responsibilities. On the other hand, it offered the excitement of working on the frontier on a heroic scale. Simbirsk province was as large as a small European nation, even if its roads were of Asiatic character. Among Il'ia's many achievements were the creation of a Pedagogical Institute, schools for backward ethnic groups (Chuvash, Mordvinian, Tatar), and a large increase (more than double the original 9,000) in the number of students. To be sure, during an era of expansion Il'ia's personal achievement may not have been extraordinary, but his dedication and energy cannot be doubted. For his efforts, Il'ia was made Director of Schools in Simbirsk in 1874 and was simultaneously ennobled. His rank in the civil service—actual state councillor—carried with it hereditary nobility.

Notwithstanding all the print spent trying to connect Il'ia with Russian radicalism by way of his literary tastes (for example, his favorite poet, Nekrasov, was of the *narodnik* school), some personal contacts with radicals, and the affinity for scientism he shared with the nihilists, Il'ia Ul'ianov remained a loyal citizen and official with a passion for education. He responded heroically to the call for teachers and administrators willing to work for popular enlightenment at the very edge of European culture in a province and city made famous (or infamous) by the novelist Ivan Goncharov. Simbirsk was the stagnant environment responsible for the somnolent antihero, Oblomov, in Goncharov's novel (1859) of that name. Il'ia and his entire family were the very antithesis of Oblomovism (Oblomov's state of indolence had been interpreted as a sign of social malaise and elevated to an "ism" by the radical publicist Nikolai Dobroliubov). They must have had a great deal of fun over Oblomov, whose name and patronymic were Il'ia Il'ich. From all the evidence, the family fit badly into the environment of Simbirsk. Il'ia's zeal and his frequent and long absences no doubt played some role. So did the backwardness of the city, for the Enlightenment had spread unevenly, and gentry society in Simbirsk simply did not have a niche for culturally advanced families with odd genealogies.

The Ul'ianov family became rather isolated, one might even say introverted, perhaps mainly out of choice. Whatever the reasons, the Ul'ianov children remained distinct from their peers throughout their school careers. Aside from the annual summer outings to Kokushkino, where they had cousins on Maria's side of the family as playmates, the children seem to have had few close friends. Even the family conclaves at Kokushkino must have been like miniature teachers' conventions. In short, the Ul'ianov family had closed in upon itself, and educational values permeated every aspect of its private as well as public life. This is the environment in which Vladimir Il'ich Ul'ianov spent roughly one third of his life.

The morally strenuous and professionally dedicated director of schools in Simbirsk had found an ideal partner in his wife. She regretted openly to the children that she had been denied the opportunity to advance her own education. Theirs became her central concern. Her children wrote glowing reports about her pedagogical methods. She made both learning and household tasks enjoyable by adding an element of play. The children were rewarded with chocolate, trinkets, music, and carefully measured praise. Yet this relative idyll of learning had a major drawback. It had to end. Il'ia grew anxious about the effects of Maria's methods upon the boys, in particular, and intervened. According to Anna, "He was afraid of the effeminizing effects of this domestic pampering and found it expedient to place the boys as early as possible under masculine influence."[9] Perhaps Il'ia had noticed things that Anna, as a girl, would not have. Maria had been educated at home by her Aunt Ekaterina; she had grown up in the company of four sisters; and there is no evidence that she treated her sons and daughters differently. All were taught the same lessons; all performed the same tasks. However, according to Anna, Maria was sensitive to her children's distinct personalities and their varying needs for rewards and encouragement. This is implicit in Anna's comments about her father's views:

> Father believed in earlier entry into school so that the children, especially the boys, would be habituated to work and learn discipline. . . . Father was against "showering people with praise," as he put it, considering it extremely harmful for people to have high opinions of themselves. Now, as I look back at our childhood, I think that it would have been better for us if this generally applied pedagogical line had been applied less strictly. It was fully correct only for Vladimir, whose vast self-confidence and constantly distinguished achievement in school called for a corrective. In no way affecting his accurate self-assessment, it undoubtedly reduced the arrogance, which children with outstanding abilities are prone to . . . and taught him, in spite of all the praise, to work diligently. For the rest of us—especially for the girls, who were suffering from lack of confidence, small doses of praise would have been useful.[10]

Anna's complaint, muted though it may be, suggests (as do other comments in her memoirs) resentment at the psychological harm caused by Il'ia's excessive strictness. But not all were harmed equally, and Vladimir apparently thrived. Not only the girls but Alexander (Sasha in the diminutive) suffered from Il'ia's methods, as Anna indicated: "Of course, Sasha did not suffer from lack of confidence in his abilities, but he was by nature very modest and self-disciplined anyway, and since a sense of duty dominated his character . . . more approval and more of everything that would have increased his *joie de vivre*, would have been only useful for him. But in child-rearing, just as in a melody, one note usually dominates."[11] Maria accepted Il'ia's authority and even formed a united front with him, but the children already knew of a paradise lost. Perhaps Maria was resented too, for having given in.

The nature and effects of Il'ia's intervention in Sasha's case deserve special attention. Speculation about the family tragedy comes from an unexpected source. Trotsky, who had experienced patriarchal severity in his own childhood and adolescence and was guilty of similar mistakes with his own sons, supplied what he believed Anna had left out. He tried to imagine the probable failures of a man who had risen from the slums of Astrakhan and who officially deplored the use of physical chastisement in pedagogy but who (we know from Anna) was capable of outbursts of temper. Thus, Trotsky was led to ask:

> Did Il'ia Nikolaevich's system, together with abstention from praise, comprise abstention from punishment? . . . Did he, as a father, follow his own pedagogical rules? There is no direct testimony on this score. Recollections by members of the family, without ever minimizing or holding back anything, emphasize in everyway the even temper and restraint of the mother—which suggests that things were different with the father. The authoritarianism of Il'ia Nikolaevich and his quick temper also serve to reinforce this assumption."[12]

Something had stifled Sasha's spontaneity. In the quotation from Anna's memoirs, the phrase "joie de vivre" is used to translate *zhizneradostnost'*, a Russian word for which it is difficult to find an English equivalent. Alexander's grimness shows clearly in several photographs. Even if we take into account the solemnity of photographic sessions in that era and the Russian and Soviet practice of touching up photos to the point of altering basic features, every photo of Sasha shows a face whose eyes and and set of the mouth suggest more than a hint of anger, but mainly sadness. Although one memoirist who knew him at the university describes him as being of medium height, in the graduation photo for his gymnasium class in 1883 he seems to be the smallest boy in his row. As eldest son, this small, angry, and sad boy was chosen to play a central role in the Ul'ianov family. A family photo taken in 1879 has Alexander in the place of honor, between Il'ia and Maria.

Alexander Ul'ianov, Terrorist

ALEXANDER'S FATE is a matter of historical record. He was hanged in May 1887 for his part in a plot to assassinate Alexander III. His younger brother, Vladimir, who had shown no inclination during adolescence to follow in his brother's footsteps, almost certainly became a revolutionary because of Alexander's execution. The rest is history. It is therefore important to learn as much about Sasha as we can. The Ul'ianov family configuration had historical consequences, and Alexander was the pivotal figure in it. Although the reconstruction of Alexander's path to terrorism and martyrdom involves psychological hypotheses, in this case failure to speculate would leave a promising pattern of evidence unused.

Seen in the light of later events, the first piece of evidence comes from Anna's report of a nearly fatal illness in 1870—the very year of Vladimir's birth. Sasha was four years old when he contracted an "inflammation of the stomach." Diagnoses of this sort were very common, like reports of "catarrhs" and at this point in medical history of several varieties of typhus. Symptoms such as fever, bowel ailments, weight loss, and weakness tended to be grouped under such general diagnoses. Later reports of illness in the family diagnosed as typhus or catarrh suggest breakdowns from academic stress and pressure to achieve. It is possible that nineteenth-century sanitation had less to do with Sasha's illness in 1870 than the changes in the family situation. The Ul'ianovs had moved to Simbirsk less than a year earlier. Within a few months a new son had been born. Il'ia's new position called for greater time away from the family. The last two years had placed unusual strain on Maria, and this must have affected her relationship to the children. The changes taking place might easily produce a variety of symptoms in a sensitive child. The following is Anna's narrative of a critical moment during Sasha's illness:

> I remember his only dangerous illness—inflammation of the stomach—when he was four years old. I remember how mother's despair astonished me: she fell on her knees before the icon, and whispered to me. "Pray for Sasha." I remember how she tore howling Volodya from her breast, thrust him toward the nurse, and threw herself toward Sasha, who had taken a serious turn at that moment. . . . I remember mother's glowing face, when she guided and supported him during his convalescence—when he had to be taught to walk all over again.[1]

Anna adds another bit of information that leads to questions about the age differences between children in the family and the effects upon the older children of the loss of Maria's highly prized attention. Sasha had been born nineteen months after Anna, Volodya a little more than four years later, and Olga less than nineteen months after him. The first four siblings divided neatly into two opposite gender pairs, quite close in age. Even the two pairs were not far apart. In such circumstances, the older children (particularly those with a very close younger sibling) might easily regress. Volodya did not learn to walk until he was about three. He began walking simultaneously with his younger sister, Olga, and they also learned to read together. The parents worried that Volodya might be retarded, but no organic cause is indicated, and it seems likely that the problem was jealousy and imitation of Olga in order to compete for Maria's attention. Perhaps, given the circumstances mentioned above, Sasha regressed too, for even a convalescent four-year-old does not ordinarily have to be taught to walk again. The relative positions of children in the family probably temporarily slowed down the development of the first child and accelerated that of the second in each pair. Sasha and Olga were at first the brilliant children, although Volodya soon caught up.

Sasha was evidently both the father's and mother's favorite. He resembled his mother both physically and temperamentally, but paternal influence was too powerful to ignore, and Sasha soon decided upon science as his calling. Il'ia pushed his son into the Simbirsk gymnasium at the early age of eight. Entry into a masculine world forcibly severed his close ties to Anna and his mother. All of this had a devastating effect upon Sasha. The women in the family suffered anxiety about his wounded spirit, but nothing seemed to mitigate his depression. He became increasingly taciturn and withdrawn, even within the family circle. Although to all appearances he remained the dutiful child and excellent student, rebellion quietly incubated in Sasha.

The picture of an ideally integrated, progressive family is not an invention, pure and simple. Anna's memoirs also describe a family working, studying, enjoying music and games, and engaging in a variety of outdoor sports. The children made runs for their sleds in the winter. They skated and skied. During the summer they gardened, swam, boated, played croquet, and collected natural objects in the woods around Kokushkino. For a while (in 1878 or 1879) they created their own journal, "Subbotnik" (Saturday). Each child had a humorous pseudonym. All of them looked up to Sasha, who led them in their games in early childhood. Family unity rested on the bedrock of shared values. The children were successfully taught the supreme values of learning and methodical work. They were urged to seek ever higher levels, no matter what their level of achievement. Even the boisterous Volodya learned the family ethic. Il'ia and Maria might have differed about methods, but they agreed about learning and hard work. Sasha offered the younger children a more accessible model. Volodya learned soon enough that he should imitate Sasha if he wanted approval and attention, and he did so with such childish pedantry that it became a source of amusement to the entire family. All seemed well in the Ul'ianov family, even if it lived an isolated life.

It is possible to construct another picture of the family, one of a dangerously escalating rigorism, in which Sasha became the first victim because of birth order, gender, and possibly, his own propensities. Whatever his ability—and it was considerable—Sasha had to achieve more than his father and be more virtuous than Uncle Vasilii. This was his interpretation of the family imperative. A silver medal would signify academic failure; ordinary virtue, moral sloth. Anna pictures a boy whose conscientiousness gradually overcame his spontaneity, his spirit of play. As editor of "Subbotnik," Sasha (age twelve or thirteen) was responsible for the game column, for which he constructed rebuses and puzzles under the pseudonym "Vralman," a Russian-German hybrid signifying "liar," evidently taken from the name of a character in a satire by Fonvizin. During his late teens, Sasha withdrew into his studies and a home laboratory. The boy who had enjoyed word games spoke less and less, and his written communication became laconic and businesslike. His love of nature also underwent a transformation, with nature becoming less a playground than a workshop. Sasha collected insects in order to dissect them and prepared himself to became a scientist—all quite normal for an ambitious adolescent of this era and certainly in keeping with his father's wishes. Sasha also seemed to be following the utilitarian prescription of the influential nihilist ideologue, Dmitrii Pisarev, who admonished the intelligentsia to leave their literary culture of "rosewood and satin" for the laboratory. But in spirit Sasha most clearly resembled the ascetic branch of nihilism, represented by Nikolai Chernyshevskii and Nikolai Dobroliubov. His dutifulness and martyrlike qualities were akin to theirs. Maria was the source of this quality in the family. Trotsky, like most students of the Ul'ianov family, deduced from Anna's memoirs that Maria was a "moral genius." One senses that all the children paid a price for her gift of making duty seem a matter of life and death. Anna would have us believe that Sasha surpassed his mother—that he was a transcendent moral genius possessing "the same rare combination of extraordinary firmness and serenity, tenderness, and fairness; but he was more austere and singleminded, and even more courageous."[2]

Other memoirists add detail to this picture, as if intent on making Alexander into an icon. One protested that the police photograph of Alexander, in which he looks "dull and even somber, a wretched character," did not do him justice: "His clear and open face, on the contrary, always radiated his youthful charm through an unusually intelligent expression. It was a face which we generally describe as exalted."[3] The only available photographs show a grim face, and other memoirists describe an introverted and sometimes anguished person. Alexander's self-judgment may be the most reliable guide to his personality. In January 1887, just a few months before his arrest and execution, he wrote a long, critical letter to his cousin Maria about a mutual friend. He also characterized himself:

> I am not in any way deceiving myself about the effect that this letter will have on our relations, but perhaps it will be less harsh if you believe me when I say that the latter failing issues exclusively from the severity of my character and an inclination to see first of all and more clearly than everything else the bad sides of a person."[4]

The above description of himself, written when Alexander was twenty, adds a psychological dimension to an essay written five years earlier for a gymnasium class, "What We Must Do in Order to Be Useful to Society and the State," in which Alexander extolled the virtues of duty, love of hard work, and labor for the good of society.[5] He emphasized subordination of individual egoism to social utility even more strongly in the letter to his cousin. If anything, Alexander had become more rigorous—more demanding of himself and critical of others.

Alexander's sensitivity showed itself in his understanding that it was unreasonable to expect of others his level of achievement, his sense of duty, and the demands he made upon himself. He found himself in a bind: he could neither tolerate lower standards, nor was he willing to enforce higher ones on those close to him. Thus, he did not like to be held up as a model to his siblings.[6] Yet he could not forgive others their sins. By a strategy of withdrawal he signified both his intolerance and his desire to avoid harming others. He seemed hypersensitive to any form of physical or verbal aggression. Yet this outwardly shy, withdrawn boy would help prepare dynamite bombs to take a human life. Like all moralists, Sasha had a dark side. When he was twelve or thirteen, he puzzled Anna by choosing as his favorite character in Tolstoy's *War and Peace* the roguish Dolokhov, who seemed to be his own antithesis.[7] Beneath Alexander's spare "scientific" logic, an overly scrupulous conscience worked its way toward a simultaneously murderous and suicidal conclusion. His psychology demanded that he himself pay the full price for his intentions, even though the conspiracy was discovered before a serious attempt could be made to assassinate the Tsar. An admirer of Turgenev's fictional hero Bazarov, Alexander Ul'ianov shared the view of the radical critic Dmitrii Pisarev: The "new people" could not endure any disharmony between their reason and their feelings, between their convictions and their actions.

The story of Alexander's evolution into a terrorist need not be told in full. Hundreds of similar stories might be told for the young men and women of the revolutionary intelligentsia. The conspiracy Alexander joined toward the end of this four years at the university was, despite its extremism, in keeping with the mood of the radical students there.[8] The most radical among them obeyed the merciless logic that led to terrorism and martyrdom. Officially tolerated student groups, *zemliachestva*, based upon regional and ethnic origins, would create libraries where students could educate themselves in radicalism, or even establish ties with the revolutionary underground. A core of activists might form and declare affiliation with *The People's Will*, the terrorist organization that had assassinated Alexander II in 1881 and had subsequently been shattered. This was the route taken by Alexander and his coconspirators. The conspiracy was well underway when he joined, but he assumed an active role when the real leader, Petr Shevyrev, became ill. Trotsky, a man sensitive to the travails of adolescent commitment, pictures Sasha as struggling until almost the very end against the turn to terrorism.

For much of 1886 and 1887 Alexander was busy conducting research on freshwater annelids and isopods, but by January 1887 the decision had been made, and he turned his knowledge of chemistry to the manufacture of dynamite. (Anna had no idea that he had been fully radicalized, even though Alexander used her to receive a coded telegram, thereby implicating her in the conspiracy. She too was arrested and imprisoned for a short time.) When explaining the factors leading to his radicalization and the events that precipitated his crucial decision, Alexander proclaimed the inevitability of his intellectual and moral commitment to progress and social justice. He professed above all a desire to propagate enlightenment among the people, which meant propaganda for a social revolution. Terror was a means, a way of forcing concessions from the government and raising the morale of the people. During a session of the trial on April 18, 1887, when Alexander was cross-examined, he outlined his rationale for terror:

> I say that an intellectual feels the urge to exchange views with intellectually less developed people so strongly, that he finds it irresistible. . . . Our intelligentsia is physically so weak and so unorganized that it is incapable of waging an open struggle at present and can only defend its right to think and to participate intellectually in public life through a terrorist form of struggle. . . . Among the Russian people one will always find a dozen persons, who are so dedicated in their ideals and take their country's plight so much to heart, that they readily sacrifice their lives for their cause."[9]

At the end of a long statement, Alexander characterized his analysis as "an objective scientific appraisal" of the causes of terrorism in Russia, rather than an expression of personal indignation.[10] Throughout he expressed self-effacement, as if not he, not Alexander Ul'ianov, but a disembodied intellect and conscience had spoken.

Students of the Russian revolutionary intelligentsia need not look farther than some of the more perceptive members of the movement for insights into the psychological background of such statements. Trotsky found in the revolutionary intelligentsia mood swings reflecting its long history of failure to attract mass support. He put it succinctly: "The whole history of the intelligentsia develops between . . . two poles of pride and self-abnegation—which are the short and long shadows of its social weakness."[11] But Rosa Luxemburg's fuller statement of the problem suggests pathological forms of self-affirmation and self-repudiation: "It is amusing to note the strange somersaults that the respectable human 'ego' has had to perform in recent Russian history. Knocked to the ground, almost reduced to dust, by Russian absolutism, the 'ego' takes revenge by turning to revolutionary activity. In the shape of a committee of conspirators, in the name of a nonexistent Will of the People, it seats itself on a kind of throne and proclaims it is all-powerful."[12]

The pole of pride could and did lead to aspiring dictators, those who thought that they knew more and could see farther than anyone else. The more ruthless of them would use any means possible to secure power over the movement, but before 1917 their careers cast short shadows in the history of an essentially self-effacing intelligentsia. Those who wanted above all to fulfill their duty to the people in a redemptive act of self-sacrifice stood shoulder to shoulder with the few who aggressively sought power. Such is the chemistry of conscience that the polarities pride–power and humility–self-sacrifice, can exist simultaneously in one and the same mind. Alexander claimed proudly that he had deduced terrorism with scientific rigor. The critically thinking minority (as Petr Lavrov, the leading *narodnik* theorist, had labeled it) had to spread progressive ideas to the less privileged working classes because developed people owed a debt to those who had supported them by physical labor. Like other *narodniki*, Alexander had concluded that if propaganda activities were thwarted, terror inevitably followed. A developed person had to take action, even if it meant taking another's life. "Scientific" pride authorized this kind of power; and even if martyrdom should be the outcome, one still acquired the enduring form of power associated with martyrdom—symbolic power.

Some of Alexander's last actions, although belonging to the history of the revolutionary movement, still had connections with family history. He made the final break with the family ethic of academic achievement with another inspired symbolic gesture. Its symbolism cannot be denied, even though Alexander treated it as a practical matter. During the trial interrogation of April 15 Alexander was asked how he could afford to pay for a coconspirator's trip to Vilno to purchase nitric acid for the bombs. He replied: "I raised [the money] by pawning my gold medal, which I received at the University for my essay."[13] The medal had been awarded for his thesis, "Segmental and Generative Organs of Freshwater Annaluta," and had been granted on February 3, 1886, less than a month after the death of his father. Il'ia had died suddenly after a stroke on January 12, and Alexander, who continued to work on his thesis during the winter break, was the only family member absent from the funeral. In Alexander's mind the medal symbolized parental values, but the connection of the award with the violation of the ritual of mourning must have created an interesting constellation of feelings.

Il'ia's death profoundly affected the entire family, but the behavior and feelings of the older children was most dramatic. Anna had a psychological breakdown accompanied by strong suicidal urges and was unable to stay in school. Alexander's reaction was recorded by his friend, Ivan Chebotarev: "Alexander was completing his paper at the university when he suddenly received news of his father's death. He dropped everything and for a few days kept pacing his room as though he were wounded. I called on him on the second or third day and found him still striding back and forth with a listless faraway look in his eyes. I became frightened for him. . . . After a week, he pulled himself together . . . and took up his paper again and completed it, and even appeared at our study circles." [14] During his last summer at home Alexander gave no indication that he would abandon his scientific career.

Duty to education and intellectual achievement overrode all other values and activities in the family. Just as Alexander completed his thesis and earned a gold medal during the family crisis of Il'ia's death, Vladimir earned a gold medal at the Simbirsk gymnasium during the tumult over Alexander and Anna in the spring of 1887, when Olga also received one as the outstanding graduate at the Mariinskaia women's gymnasium. Anna, meanwhile, suffered extreme guilt because of her inability to carry on in school. The children knew that Maria, as well as Il'ia, wanted them to sustain the family ethic in any extremity. When Maria vainly petitioned the tsar for mercy, she seemed to believe that the tsar, too, would recognize academic excellence:

> The distress and despair of a mother urges me to appeal to Your Imperial Majesty, to the only one who can give us protection and help.
> It is mercy, Your Majesty, mercy for my children that I beg of you.
> My eldest son Alexander, a gold-medal graduate of the gymnasium, has been awarded a gold medal at the University as well. My daughter Anna has been studying successfully at the St. Petersburg High Courses for Women. Just when both were on the verge of completing their full courses—within two months—I suddenly find myself deprived of both my elder children. . . .
> Words cannot describe my awful grief and suffering" [15]

In a revealing remark to his mother during her first visit to him during his imprisonment, Alexander might have been saying obliquely that the gold medals had become more important to her than life—or death. According to Anna, he reminded her that Vladimir and Olga would surely win gold medals too and that this would be a consolation to her after his death. [16] But a different message was contained in one of Alexander's last requests to his mother. He asked her to redeem the gold medal he had pawned for 100 rubles, to resell it at its real value, which he calculated to be 130 rubles, and to give the remaining 30 roubles to one Tulinov, to whom he owed that sum. [17] The commission, whether consciously or not, seemed designed not so much to console Maria as to tell her that what she valued so highly as a symbol of

achievement was for him associated with debt, or duty, and that he had found a duty higher than the family imperative of academic achievement. At another level, almost certainly unconscious, Alexander cruelly denied his mother the symbol of his achievement, as well as his very life. During his last weeks he had punished her by refusing to petition the tsar on his own behalf, and when he had at last given in, his plea for clemency had been half-hearted and insufficiently contrite. Alexander's behavior raises many questions about the family configuration that cannot be answered here. Suffice it to say that his martyrdom shook the surviving family members as profoundly as if he had thrown his dynamite bombs in their direction.

Maria survived the blow and kept the other children studying, but the foundations of the original Ul'ianov family project had been destroyed. Vladimir would pursue the goal of revolution as dutifully and resolutely in the face of every calamity as he had been taught to pursue education. Eventually, he would pull the entire family onto the path marked out by Alexander's self-sacrifice. Family history repeated itself in an odd but momentous fashion.

Vladimir Ul'ianov, Substitute Revolutionary

ALTHOUGH IN childhood Vladimir had imitated his older brother, when he reached adolescence, he became aware of profound differences between himself and Sasha. This was a mutual awareness. Alexander had told Anna in so many words that he disliked his younger brother, even though he recognized his ability.[1] On his part, the younger brother had as much reason to resent as to admire Alexander, for Volodya was odd man out in the family romance. Olga, the sibling closest to him and his childhood playmate, looked up to Alexander and, after a period of resembling the livelier Vladimir, developed Sasha's austerity and ferocious dedication to work. She also preferred the natural sciences and, with Sasha, seemed to be the embodiment of the family's values and ambitions. Although she had planned to become a physician, Olga had mastered several languages. Dmitrii too imitated Sasha, accompanying him on his field trips to collect specimens. Although Dmitrii became involved in revolutionary work, he also realized his ambition of becoming a physician. The youngest child, Maria (born in 1878), was paired with her near sibling, Dmitrii, but of all the children she was Vladimir's closest associate in his adult years. She also showed the family's ability and pertinacity as a student of languages. Although Alexander's death did bring the younger children under Vladimir's tutelage to some extent, he was clearly only a substitute for Sasha. He most certainly had not had the central or favored position in the family constellation during most of his childhood and adolescence, but this was not without its advantages.

Volodya had been spared the pressures that had fallen on the first pair of children. During their early childhood, Maria had run the household without any domestic help, but after the move to Simbirsk, Il'ia's new position and higher salary permitted them to hire a nurse and a cook. Alexander's illness diverted Maria's attention from him during his early infancy. Perhaps the nurse's care had a salutary effect on Volodya, her favorite. Volodya's probable regression after the birth of Olga, his slow development, and the parents' fear that he was abnormally slow might have led them to expect less of their second son. The rapidity of his development afterwards suggested to them that he had been merely lazy, but his relationship to his parents had already been formed. It was less intense than that of Il'ia and Maria with the older children. Unfortunately, the role of Varvara Grigor'evna Sarbatova, the nurse who served the Ul'ianov family for approximately twenty years and died in the Ul'ianov household in 1890, cannot be established precisely. Most students of Ul'ianov family history are intent upon showing the influence of family members upon each other. One wonders, though, how much her care influenced the development of the four younger children.

Aside from the delegation of some aspects of the care of the younger children to the nurse, the influence of the parents was mediated in another important way. Il'ia had quite consciously apprenticed his younger son to Alexander, but the two nonetheless diverged in both academic interest and general orientation. By refusing to imitate Il'ia's deputy, Volodya seemed to be rejecting Il'ia's general preferences, but things were more complicated. Volodya benefitted from Sasha's unwillingness to inflict his own authority aggressively on the other children, but he also felt the sting of Sasha's usually unspoken criticism. Alexander withdrew from Volodya's boisterousness, his intrusiveness, and his mockery, whereas the younger brother showed no inclination to collect and dissect insects or imitate Alexander's austere and dutiful behavior. He did not have a martyr's character. Furthermore, Alexander's mediation lessened Volodya's resentment towards Il'ia's severity and, possibly, increased it against Maria Alexandrovna, for the older brother's moral qualities and methods of criticism resembled hers. There is no indication that Vladimir suffered from Il'ia's strictness, but throughout his life Lenin showed little affinity for the subdued temperament, the restrained, persistent kind of moral authority embodied in Alexander and Maria Alexandrovna. Quite the contrary, it seemed to infuriate him.

Volodya was clearly not Maria's favorite; Sasha was. Anna notes that Volodya was capable of treating his mother rudely and that Alexander had to reproach him for it. Paradoxically, even though Alexander was the eldest son and the primary carrier of Il'ia's values and ambitions, Volodya resembled his father much more both physically and temperamentally. Such resemblances are ordinarily the source of strong bonds in families. One observer, a frequent visitor in the household beginning in 1880 through her professional connection with Il'ia, noted the affinity between Il'ia and Vladimir.

At the dinner table Il'ia was swiftly transformed and became a completely different person, quite unlike the one in his study. He made witty comments, joked, laughed a great deal, and did not talk about official matters at all. Generally it was always merry, cozy, and relaxed during dinner at the Ul'ianovs. Volodya and Olia, the gymnasium students, were at the forefront, with their ready wit. Il'ia Nikolaevich loved most of all to joust [*pikirovat'sia*] with Volodya. Joking, he cussed out the gymnasium, gymnasium instruction, and had plenty of fun at the expense of the instructors. Volodya always very successfully parried his father's blows and in turn mocked the people's schools [the schools created by Il'ia to spread enlightenment], sometimes cutting his father to the quick. . . . Alexander Il'ich always came late to the table, and they always had to call him down from upstairs, where he lived and worked. Il'ia Nikolaevich also liked to joke about Alexander's erudition [*uchenost'*] but the latter only kept silent and sometimes smiled. Generally, Alexander always seemed reserved [*zamknut*] and cold.[2]

Although Il'ia had first worried about Volodya's work habits, he learned soon enough that his younger son had superior abilities and that he would sustain the family honor. Perhaps Il'ia had also come to recognize that his younger son had qualities he himself admired, even if they departed from his austere official position. Perhaps he realized the huge emotional distance between himself and his older son. But if he resembled his father in his vigorous and sometimes explosive behavior, Volodya's interests were closer to his mother's — languages and literature — and like her, he loved music. The mixture of paternal and maternal characteristics in Alexander and Vladimir is not unusual; nor is it unusual for ambivalences and tensions to appear in such intensely bonded families. What is important is that at the time of Alexander's execution the two brothers were not close. Vladimir, against his own plans, was forced upon a path different from his chosen one and closer to Alexander's. During the first few years after Alexander's death he evidently felt that he had to try to be Alexander.

Vladimir's place in the family changed dramatically after the deaths, in rapid succession, of Il'ia and Alexander. He became the responsible male, his mother's support in most respects, although Il'ia's pension kept the family solvent. He also had to revise his image of Alexander, for the entire affair had been a complete shock to the family. It was almost unbelievable that the shy, withdrawn Alexander, who of late had spent all of his vacation time with those accursed worms, had also made dynamite to kill the Tsar. Alexander had become a heroically mysterious figure, and Vladimir was forced to study the movement to which his brother had given his life. Although he had moved to the center of the family in some sense, he remained in Sasha's shadow, as did the entire family. They suffered first of all from the disgrace of having nurtured a terrorist, for most citizens of the empire were still loyal subjects of the Tsar. Although reports that the family was suddenly shunned by fair-weather liberal acquaintances may be exaggerated—the family had always shunned Simbirsk society, except for Il'ia's professional associates—its isolation did increase. Further, Vladimir's own identity was temporarily obliterated, for he not only had to take Sasha's place in the family but he could not escape being identified as the younger brother of a revolutionary celebrity. During his schooldays, he had to follow in Alexander's footsteps as a gold-medal student. Now, as the brother of an executed terrorist, certain things were expected of him. The authorities, of course, were especially alert to any misbehavior on the part of an Ul'ianov. Ironically, in childhood Volodya had been deliquent compared to Alexander; now his brother's crime had made any conventional career problematic for him.

The change in Vladimir's behavior was dramatic, even taking into account all of the upheavals of 1886–1887. Dmitrii's description of his older brother suggests that Vladimir had at least temporarily acquired Alexander's manner of expression:

> Everyone closely acquainted with Vladimir Il'ich understood how his frame of mind had changed: The jolly person, with his infectious, childlike laughter, roaring until the tears came, who could in conversation transport people with his swiftly moving ideas, now became grimly restrained, strict, closed up in himself, highly focussed, commanding [*vlastnyĭ*], issuing curt, sharp phrases, deeply immersed in the solution of some sort of difficult, important problem.[3]

The descriptions of Vladimir in 1887–1888 call to mind many descriptions of Alexander, except for the part about commanding behavior. To be sure, Vladimir had more than enough reasons to be gloomy, even depressed, but his systematic program of reading in areas of Sasha's interest suggests that he was trying to become more like his dead brother, to rethink his thoughts and understand the reasons for his commitment. Vladimir, who had hitherto shown no special interest in social and political issues, now studied avidly and systematically in these areas. But he showed a rather healthy opacity to the central psychological message in much of the literature. He never acquired a martyr's mentality. His renunciation of his previous commitments, like his refusal to continue his piano lessons when he enrolled in the gymnasium because it was not a properly masculine activity, was symptomatic of a conscious choice of role rather than unconscious repression leading to self-abnegation.

Vladimir had long ago accepted the discipline expected of him in the family, and he had equipped himself for the kind of career expected of an Ul'ianov. However, unlike Alexander, who had complained to Anna that he could study and work in the laboratory only sixteen hours a day, Vladimir had shown no love of surplus repression. He became a revolutionary ascetic by conscious design rather than inclination. Later, he preached discipline precisely because he knew that it was not a natural inclination for most, and he believed that the discipline associated with the role of revolutionary was particularly demanding. Alexander could not bring himself to demand of others what he demanded of himself. He had none of Vladimir's commanding character. He believed that he deserved to die and seemed to pursue punishment. Before his execution he told his mother: "I wanted to kill a man . . . I too may be killed."[4] Martyrs attract others to their cause by their example, but few among their followers share their "moral genius." Vladimir could acquire the heroic discipline taught by the exemplary figures, the precursors of Bolshevism, but its meaning for him was different. It did not signify a will to a symbolic act of self-sacrifice but was rather a means to a concrete end. He placed it in the service of an essentially commanding personality. Heroic discipline signified for Vladimir a will to power.

When Vladimir first heard that his brother had been sentenced to death, according to Maria Il'inichna, who was nine years old at the time, he said: "No, we won't take this path. This is not the path to follow."[5] These Delphic words, if they were uttered at all, have generally been interpreted to mean that Vladimir would take a different *revolutionary* path and that he would avoid Alexander's fate. Even if the alleged utterance is not a product of a faulty memory or myth-making, other interpretations are possible. Trotsky, for example, took a highly skeptical approach to Maria's report and later variations. By Trotsky's test of psychological verisimilitude the words, if uttered at all, probably signified despair:

> All the laws of human psychology are here trampled on. Volodya is not thrown into despair upon receiving the dreadful news, does not grieve for the irredeemable loss, but wipes his brow and announces the need to find a "more effective road." To whom were these words addressed: The mother was in Petersburg, Anna was still in prison. Evidently Vladimir imparted his tactical discovery to the thirteen-year-old Dmitrii and the nine-year-old Maria. . . . In these conditions, what could the words attributed to him by the younger sister mean? In any case, not an opposition of the revolutionary struggle of the masses to the terror of the intellectuals. Even if one were to assume for a moment that a similar phrase was actually uttered, then it could not have expressed a program but only despair. Sasha should not have embarked on that path! Why did he not devote himself to science? Why did he doom himself?[6]

Trotsky's skepticism is warranted, but his broader psychological interpretation of the reversal of Vladimir's attitude toward Alexander is more to the point. Trotsky supposes a welter of feelings—grief, bitterness, remorse, guilt, hatred, desire for revenge. Despite the power Alexander had gained through martyrdom, his behavior must have embittered the entire family. In the course of mourning, survivors reflect on all of their sins, the injuries they have inflicted upon the deceased. Although as a child he had imitated his older brother, of late Vladimir had mocked Alexander, rejected him. But then a different Alexander, a mysterious figure had suddenly appeared, and just as suddenly vanished from view. How much guilt did Vladimir feel? It is quite likely that he had resented Alexander's ability to command the attention and love of the women in the family, chafed at the role of second son (although this was mitigated by the bond between him and Il'ia), and experienced the usual, murderous, repressed wishes. There is more than enough here for inspiring powerful feelings of guilt, from a psychoanalytic point of view. Revenge inflicted upon tsarist authority would simultaneously be atonement for his sins against Sasha.[7] But Vladimir still could not escape the Ul'ianov family imperative—study. His rebellion would have to express itself in his choice of an academic path.

Until 1887 Vladimir had shown little or no interest in the kinds of subjects and books that ordinarily shaped revolutionary commitments. He had shown great promise as a student of Latin and Greek and seemed spontaneously to love language. But now the study of philology was out of the question. An instructor at the University of Kazan who had long discussions with him during the summer of 1887 thought that he showed promise as a mathematician, but Vladimir rejected mathematics and the natural sciences decisively during the summer of 1887. Law was closest to his growing interest in the social sciences, which had given Alexander the "scientific" basis for his commitment.

By enrolling in the faculty of law, Vladimir reluctantly fulfilled his obligation to his mother and to the family project—academic achievement—but simultaneously drew nearer to Alexander's path. The reasons for his enrolling in Kazan are not entirely clear. Perhaps he was prohibited from enrolling in universities in St. Petersburg or Moscow because of Alexander. But were the authorities or Maria Alexandrovna the real source of the prohibition? Enrollment in Kazan also made it easier for her to live with him and prevent a repetition of Alexander's and Anna's fates. Maria Alexandrovna, almost shattered by Alexander's death, clung more fiercely to her remaining offspring. Her petitions and promises as well as Il'ia's reputation and her children's earlier achievements sustained the family's position. Anna was able to continue her education at home, under police surveillance; Vladimir entered the University of Kazan, with a strong recommendation from Fedor Kerensky, the director of the Simbirsk gymnasium; and the two youngest children, Dmitrii and Maria, continued to study as before, but now in Kazan. The move to Kazan in the autumn of 1887 signified the family's flight from the bitter memories associated with the last period of their life in Simbirsk. At first, Maria only sold the family home in Simbirsk and kept her share of Kokushkino, where she and her children spent the summer of 1887. In the autumn she rented an apartment in the city of Kazan.

Unlike Alexander, Vladimir lived at home while attending the university. His brief career at Kazan ended at the beginning of December 1887, when he joined a demonstration against university regulations prohibiting autonomous student organizations and activities. The regulations of 1884 were designed to suppress radicalism and to restrict admission, and, like earlier regulations of this sort, they provoked angry demonstrations in 1884 and again in 1887, when the Ministry of Popular Enlightenment issued a circular affecting enrollment in gymnasiums. Demonstrations in Moscow in November 1887 led to the deaths of two students. In Kazan on December 4, 1887, ninety-nine students protested by returning their matriculation tickets; among them was Vladimir

Il'ich Ul'ianov. He even spent a night in the local jail and was expelled with thirty-eight others for his role in the demonstration. On December 7 he departed for Kokushkino, where his real revolutionary apprenticeship began.

Vladimir had attended lectures for only one month before his protest and explusion. The police report on his unseemly and suspicious behavior is based upon trivia.[8] Joining a student protest did not necessarily signify a firm revolutionary commitment. In Vladimir's case it was symptomatic of a smoldering hatred of tsarist authority and, very likely, increasing dissatisfaction with the first compromise he had made to satisfy his mother's wishes. Other compromises would follow. It would take him years to work up the courage to make a clean break. He entered into an extended moratorium, in which he made half-hearted commitments to everything except an apprenticeship for a revolutionary career. He prepared for that as diligently as if he were a student striving to win a gold medal. A close cousin, N. Veretennikov, provides an interesting description of Vladimir during the beginning of his long moratorium, the summer of 1887:

> From earliest childhood, every year, from year to year, I saw Volodya, and his physical and moral changes were barely perceptible. During the preceding winter Volodya abruptly changed: He became restrained, laughed more infrequently, was stingy with words—he had grown up. All at once he became an adult, a serious person, but in appearance he remained just as before. Volodya's seriousness was deep down, not affected. There wasn't a bit of gloominess or depression in Volodya's seriousness. He now showed a reserve I hadn't seen in him before, I'd say—a conscious, willful closing off. A feature of subtle irony began to show up, especially clearly expressed at first by an oblique glance, with somewhat narrowed eyes, and turns of speech.[9]

His noisy mockery was transmuted into subtler gestures and curt, ironic remarks. Unlike Alexander, he withdrew not so much to avoid hurting others as to concentrate his attention. Veretennikov aptly noted that Vladimir did not appear to be genuinely depressed. He enthusiastically applied himself to the classics of Russian nihilism and populism, the texts that for almost three decades had inspired the revolutionary subculture. Less than three years earlier, when Alexander had pored over the same texts, Vladimir had not shown the slightest interest in them. His new attitude toward Alexander gave the texts an added significance. He had also taken his first step toward the revolutionary movement by his first gesture of rebellion, his first arrest. Now, somewhat belatedly, it was time to lay a firm ideological foundation for his commitment, to be no less "scientific" about it than his brother had been. The emotional charge behind Vladimir's transformation preceded any program of reading and gave "science" an instrumental status at first. The classics would provide theoretical rationalization for his commitment and heroic models of revolutionary behavior. Chernyshevskii's novel, *What Is to Be Done?*, affected him the most. A kind of revolutionary bildungsroman, it offered more stimulus for self-transformation and commitment than the more abstract and theoretical works.

The youth who had whiled away days reading Turgenev, the embodiment of gentry sensibility compared to the *raznochintsy* of the 1850s and 1860s, now studied Chernyshevskii and Dobroliubov whom Turgenev had called a snake and a cobra, the way a person longing for conversion reads religious texts.

Conversion

LENIN'S STUDY of Chernyshevskii and Dobroliubov, the enormous impression they made on him, and the consequences for his revolutionary career have led some students of Lenin to conclude that he was a product far more of the Russian revolutionary subculture than of European Marxism. The reasons for this are not always disinterested. Even those who reject Marx recognize his stature as a thinker, whereas Chernyshevskii is regarded as a somewhat vulgar materialist, an inverted Christian ascetic—a symptom of the transmutation of Western theories in a still immature intelligentsia subculture. According to this view, the mediation of Russian thinkers not only vulgarized or simplified the original doctrines but infused them with a Russian spirit, which in turn implies the most extreme forms of self-sacrifice, authoritarianism, and violence in the service of an eschatology. However, if both Marx and Chernyshevskii are seen as branches on the same tree, much of the difficulty disappears. Lenin found in both Chernyshevskii and Marx a sense of intellectual superiority, impatience with sloth or compromise, elitism, and a spirit of uncompromising struggle, all of which were already native to him.

The issue of the *quality* of Chernyshevskii's materialism or depth of understanding of the Hegelian dialectic is hardly important if we keep in mind that we are examining the initiation of an angry, vengeful, eighteen-year-old into a revolutionary subculture. The Russian revolutionary subculture had a sectarian, ascetic character partly because of its perilous, underground existence and partly because some if its most prominent figures carried Christian symbolism (not always consciously) and morality into their presumably scientific, secular commitment. This was not a uniquely Russian practice, given the clerical origins of many leading intelligentsia thinkers in western Europe and the continuing power of Judeo-Christian visions of chosen people, redemption, social justice, and history. New chosen groups appeared, identified by "scientific" sociologies; new victimized collectivities were assigned heroic roles in historical dramas of redemption; new ideologues translated into modern terms the wish and prophesy that the last would be first, that rulers and ruled would change places.

Secularized variations of Judeo-Christian eschatology circulated among a pan-European socialist intelligentsia. Although national hostilities and stereotypes affected the attitudes of ideologues of different nationalities towards each other, a shared culture of radical ideologies, strategies, and techniques makes it impossible to draw a hard line between "native" Russian socialism and imported variations. However, in Russia the peasants were designated the chosen vehicle of historical salvation, whereas in western Europe, the industrial workers were assigned a similar role. Like prophets of religious sects, the intelligentsia ideologues often assigned themselves and their followers crucial roles in bringing the word to those who, in being saved, would themselves become saviors. Many "developed" people expressed ambivalence toward the victims of social injustice and a variety of psychological strategies for resolving it. Fear, contempt, doubts about the capacity of the masses to achieve development, and feelings of guilt accompanying such unworthy attitudes toward the people were often resolved by the strategy of reversal. The people became the real carriers of virtue rather than objects to refashion and lead. The revolutionary intelligentsia exaggerated the value of indigenous communal institutions and the peasants' innate socialist and revolutionary tendencies. Not only would the last be the first, they would be first sooner than anyone had thought. The doctrine of revolutionary *narodnichestvo* (usually translated as "populism") assuaged a sense of national inferiority and placed Russia in the progressive vanguard.

The romantic mood was the spiritual essence of *narodnichestvo*, and like most forms of romanticism it was imbued with the idea of the virtue of the primitive and spontaneous. But the peasants—the supposed carriers of primitive virtues and spontaneity—refused to play their role as violent savior. While professing the leading role of the peasants, the *narodniki* formed conspiracies and used any means to incite them to rebellion. Thus, the strategy of enlightenment gave way to cults of revolutionary violence and adventurism. The types of leaders who were attracted by romantic rhetoric were often morally and intellectually quite distinct from the shapers of *narodnik* doctrines, for the latter often had arrived at their romantic ideas only after long study and disappointment. Their converts tended to be impatient for the revolutionary upheaval and were more likely to use terrorism to hasten its arrival.

Stubborn pursuit of the intelligentsia's original project, the achievement of social justice by way of enlightenment, yielded a cyclical pattern of doctrinal modification and strategic change. The enlighteners were frustrated in their hopes of either converting the rulers to the doctrine (the strategy of revolution from above, enlightened despotism) or spreading their ideas to the victims. Strategic adaptations of the doctrine deemphasized the role of enlightenment and shifted hope from the intelligentsia saviors to the *narod*, then back again to the intelligentsia, now emphasizing the need for new revolutionary techniques in order to destroy the obstacles between the leaders and their ideas and the people. Clashes with the tsarist police, attrition among the revolutionary circles, self-defense and revenge, and finally, the idea of striking at the very top were common to each cycle. To be sure, during every given phase of a cycle, there were proponents and practitioners of alternate strategies, but in each phase one strategy was relatively dominant. Terrorism was the outcome of the failures of earlier strategies in both the nihilist and populist cycles of the revolutionary movement. After each phase of terrorism (1866–1870 and 1878–1883) doctrinal as well as strategic modifications occurred.

Nihilism, populism, and Marxism were the doctrines inspiring the three cycles, although the first two blended into each other imperceptibly. The initial phase of each cycle was dominated by the idea of enlightenment itself; the second by the idea of making contact with the victims of oppression and exploitation; and the third by the professionalization of revolutionary practice, the formation of a revolutionary underground, conspirators using more advanced techniques of struggle—and terrorism. Doctrinaire Marxists repudiated the long tradition that had stressed the peculiar fitness of the Russian peasants and their institutions for socialism. By the end of the nineteenth century the leading members of the Russian intelligentsia accepted the idea that progress would occur only through a massive growth of industrial technology and production. Nonetheless, Marxists, like nihilists and populists, experienced the kinds of frustrations over several decades that yielded a pattern of strategic change similar to that of their forerunners.

The Bolshevik emphasis within Marxism in many respects corresponded to the strategies and moods of the third phase of the previous two cycles, even though the appearance of mass constituencies complicated the dynamics of the intelligentsia subculture. Although Marxism taught that the historical dialectic worked implacably, it, like all doctrines pointing toward salvation, inspired its followers to intervene in the process in some fashion. Marxists in different national revolutionary subcultures supplied their own blueprints for revolution, their own timetables, and since dialectics is not an exact science, their "scientific" conclusions were strongly affected by a great many factors, including their own personalities. In time, Marxists reproduced all of the earlier variations of revolutionary strategy, even though they generally rejected terrorism. The impatient, all-or-nothing mentality characteristic of the terrorist phase, the odd combination of optimism and pessimism, the emphasis upon revolutionary leadership and will, on organizational technique, the Jacobin approach—all of this the Bolsheviks shared with the terrorists of the nihilist and *narodnik* periods.

Whether professing nihilism, *narodnichestvo*, or Marxism, the leading theoreticians demanded that their followers understand the scientific basis of their commitment. The initial phase of every cycle had a distinctly rationalistic and scientistic character, in which the leading theoreticians acquired powerful mystiques. Students would form study circles and puzzle over every nuance of the works of the *teoretiki*, yet they themselves would control the dynamics of the movement by interpreting the ideas, trying to put them into practice, and influencing the *teoretiki*. A very rich history of theory and practice, this highly developed revolutionary subculture attracted young people from all social strata and with every kind of temperament. The role of revolutionary was both venerable and honored among Russian youth by the 1880s. Initiates would typically study the entire history of the movement and read its enduring classics. They would usually find more than a little inspirational material and an abundance of models to imitate.

Chernyshevskii and Dobroliubov had more of the prophet and martyr in them than the professional revolutionary. Like most prominent intelligentsia leaders, they found socialism attractive because it fused in one great doctrine moral and intellectual, ethical and scientific currents and permitted them to express their already formed Christian morality. One could preach atheism and still *feel* Christian. Chernyshevskii prophesied the emergence of a new kind of revolutionary hero. Dobroliubov used literary criticism as a vehicle for his moralizing. Both demanded great rigor of their converts. A true Russian revolutionary had to be an autodidact, for control over education and censorship made it impossible to learn about socialism otherwise. Having acquired enlightenment, the convert would then find a way of spreading it.

Revolutionism was actually an extension of enlightenment, and it could spread only through the actions of an elite. The most rigorous individuals, "the salt of the salt of the earth," in Chernyshevskii's words, would lead the revolutionary movement. He provided an enormous service to the revolutionary subculture by sketching a true "rigorist" the distilled essence of practical enlightenment and revolutionism. Rakhmetov is a secondary character in the plot structure of *What Is to Be Done?*, Chernyshevskii's novel of 1862, and although his revolutionary behavior is described only obliquely, he captured the imagination of those seeking models of revolutionary behavior. Rakhmetov's practical acumen and physical prowess made him quite different from his creator, Chernyshevskii. A forceful man of action and practical learning, a widely-traveled and bountiful aristocrat, a physical paragon, Rakhmetov gave up the ordinary indulgences (except for cigars) in order to reach the heights of rigorism. He probably succeeded as a character because he was sufficiently robust, modern, and adventurous to attract many for whom asceticism had no deep appeal. To be sure, Chernyshevskii could not resist a note of heroic asceticism now and then. He had Rakhmetov sleep on a bed of nails to prepare himself to resist torture. But on the whole, his rigorism was worldly and progressive — not the moralism, asceticism, and self-sacrifice of the *raznochinets* saint and prophet. In fact, he was a perfect model for a young man who had been preparing himself for a professional career.

Lenin was following thousands of others who had sought guidance and found it in Chernyshevskii, Dobroliubov, Pisarev, and other masters of the radical branch of the Russian enlightenment. But, as with all prophetic teaching, disciples drew different conclusions from the masters. Although Chernyshevskii was mainly an enlightener, he preached at a time when frustration with the Great Reforms forced him and others to seek radical solutions to Russia's ills. The discontented students of the reform era quickly outpaced their teachers in radicalism. Within a few years, the moralistic, ascetic posture of the teacher-martyr (Chernyshevskii had been arrested in 1861 and sent to Siberia in 1863) had been pushed into the background by a new kind of elite, equally rigorous, equally self-sacrificing, but terrorist. The most radical students decided that political assassination might help further Chernyshevskii's program. They interpreted the meaning of Rakhmetov's rigorism in their own fashion.

Alexander Ul'ianov embodied the spirit and doctrines of the 1860s and 1870s and had already encountered Marxism. He was a "harmonious" product of the Russian revolutionary subculture. Like Chernyshevskii and Dobroliubov, he was a martyr by inclination; he had followed Pisarev's prescription to study the natural sciences; and he had accepted the idea of the intelligentsia's "debt to the people," a message contained in the writings of the 1860s and best formulated in Peter Lavrov's *Historical Letters* (1868–1869). Sasha had begun by joining a self-education circle typical of "developed" Russian students and discovering the brutality of the authorities in the course of student demonstrations and had ended by joining a terrorist conspiracy. In his brief career he had recapitulated much of the intellectual and strategic development of the Russian revolutionary intelligentsia during the three decades before his death. Like many others, he had read Marx as an authority in the area of political economy, but believed that Russia had unique problems calling for distinctive strategies. Although Marxism became a dominant doctrine by the end of the 1890s, it was merely another aspect of "scientific" preparation for many young intellectuals during the 1880s. Neither his ideas—which were typically eclectic—nor his choice of terror distinguished Alexander. His martyrdom did, and even in the act of martyrdom he showed a well-hidden allegiance. Of the five young men who were executed, only Sasha kissed the cross offered by a priest.

Lenin brought his own inclinations to his reading of Chernyshevskii and later of Marx. He had less of Sasha's scientistic rigidity (although no young Russian intellectual of that era was free of scientism) and none of his brother's morbidity and therefore must have found other elements of Chernyshevskii's and Dobroliubov's nihilism more appealing: the superior, ironic tone of their moralizing, their mockery of moral, physical, and intellectual sloth, their harsh critique of compromise, their elitism—their apparent hardness. He did not sense their awkwardness, their pathetic and ridiculous sides, which Nabokov at several decades' distance tried to capture in *The Gift*; and he apparently missed the thinly disguised spirit of martyrdom behind the militancy. Vladimir's temperament and mood permitted him to be a rigorist like Rakhmetov but not an ascetic and martyr. Lenin's rigorism was based upon Rakhmetov's revolutionary professionalism, his disciplined preparation for struggle. Rakhmetov's *methodical* approach could be read as more military than monkish in spirit, and his self-denial need not be seen as that of a self-punishing ascetic. Lenin's own statement of his reading of Chernyshevskii's corpus reveals that Chernyshevskii gave him a total outlook and code of conduct from epistemology to ideas about physical preparation for revolutionary action. In 1887–1888 Lenin was seeking a blueprint for a new way of life, and he found it in Chernyshevskii. Recalling his formative years as a revolutionary in 1904, he acknowledged his debt to Chernyshevskii:

> Chernyshevskii was my favorite author. I read everything in *Sovremennik* [The Contemporary], every line of it, and more than once. Thanks to Chernyshevskii, I was first acquainted with philosophical materialism. He first showed me Hegel's role in the development of philosophical thought, and from him came the concept of dialectical method, after which it was much easier to master Marx's dialectic. . . . Chernyshevskii's encyclopedic knowledge, the clarity of his revolutionary views, his merciless polemical talent—captivated me. . . . There are musicians of whom it is said they have perfect pitch, there are others about whom one can say that they possess absolute revolutionary flair. Marx was like that, and so was Chernyshevskii. . . . Until my acquaintance with the writings of Marx, Engels, and Plekhanov, only Chernyshevskii had a major, overpowering

influence on me, and it began with *What Is to Be Done?* . . . He not only showed that every clear thinking and genuinely decent person had to be a revolutionary, but what rules he ought to follow, how he has to pursue his goals, what methods and means to use to realize them. In view of this service all of his errors fade; furthermore, he was not so much guilty of them as were the undeveloped social relationships of his time.[10]

Lenin's *reading* of Chernyshevskii's hero Rakhmetov and of Chernyshevskii himself gave Lenin an image of revolutionary action and encouraged him to develop qualities he already sensed in himself. He would be a student of revolutionary theory and technique and would avoid his brother's fate. An eighteen-year-old already converted to a revolutionary outlook in principle could hardly have found a better book than *What Is to Be Done?*. Not least of all, Chernyshevskii's rigorism found perfect soil in a youth whose family had already joined the broad current of enlightenment in Russia and which already practiced its own kind of rigorism. The words with which Lenin describes Chernyshevskii's impact — "captivated," "overpowered," and, in another context, "plowed over" — surely give an authentic rendering of his response to the single most inspirational writer of the revolutionary subculture.

At first Vladimir had probably wanted to share Alexander's fate out of guilt. Several of his actions during 1887–1888 suggest this: his effort to make contact with the most radical elements of the revolutionary subculture; his participation in an illegal *zemliachestvo* at the University of Kazan; his role in the student demonstration; after his arrest, his impulsive desire to send a letter that would have compromised both him and the recipient (an incident reported by Anna in her memoirs); his actual dispatch of a letter to his idol, Chernyshevskii, in 1888. Lenin's reckless and impulsive side — hardly a recessive part of his personality — was quite prominent in this period of his life. But a remark he made to a fellow protestor during his brief incarceration in December 1887 implies a feeling that his fate had already been determined. When asked by E. Foss what he thought he would do after being expelled from the university, he had replied: "What is there to think about . . . the trail has been blazed for me by my older brother."[11] But his actions in imitation of Sasha during 1887–1888 remained within limits. The most important consequence was a stricter type of police surveillance. He probably was spared further arrest during 1887–1892 because he was not closely tied to any revolutionary circle, even though he had befriended a number of active revolutionaries and former members of conspiracies of the 1860s and 1870s. The reputation of the People's Will still dominated the imagination of revolutionary youth. Conspiratorial circles were not difficult to find and join — but they were extremely fragile. They performed the service of transmitting to a new generation the techniques and lore of the revolutionary underground.

Lenin did not make himself over all at once. The famous remark he made to N. Valentinov (Volsky) about being "plowed over" completely by *What Is to Be Done?* — his acknowledgement of a sort of conversion experience — must be read in the light of the situation in 1887. Vladimir was already in the rebellious mood of the superior adolescent student. The series of shocks of 1886–1887 made him review his commitments even more radically, but when he emerged from his long house arrest, so to speak, he was recognizably the person he had been before his brother's execution and his new reading of Chernyshevskii.[12] He could not sustain his imitation of Sasha, even at the superficial level of manner of expression, but he would pursue Sasha's and Chernyshevskii's project in his own manner. Valentinov is quite correct, though, in calling Chernyshevskii the John the Baptist of the revolution. By proclaiming and sketching a new man and a total way of life, including a rosy vision of the socialist future, he gave Lenin the opportunity to express more fully elements already formed in his own personality, although in a different idiom. He settled Lenin on the profession of revolution and gave him something that he especially needed at a moment of personal devastation, though it is what most superior adolescents need—a sense of a future worth living and fighting for. But Lenin, still adolescent, had to live through yet another phase of family life.

His status in the family had undergone a number of dramatic changes. As the cadet son, he had begun life in Sasha's shadow. Worse still, his slowness compared to his younger sister, Olga, had caused worry in the family. When Vladimir finally had shown that he was a match for his most gifted siblings, a new anxiety arose: Il'ia and Maria thought that he was lazy, for he showed less aptitude for relentless work than Sasha and Olga. Il'ia, who recognized in the boy a version of himself, had made incessant demands on him but had liked him better than Sasha. Maria Aleksandrovna had not tolerated his boisterousness and impudence and clearly had favored Sasha. Of all the children, only Maria seems to have genuinely liked him. After Il'ia's death, he had behaved arrogantly and rebelliously. There had been serious tensions between him and Maria Alexandrovna and, through her, with Il'ia's substitute and her protector, Alexander. Then, after Alexander's death, Vladimir became the responsible male, the head of the family. Perhaps his expulsion from the university gave him some of Sasha's heroic aura. Maria Alexandrovna's efforts to protect her second son from Sasha's fate also made his welfare central to the family's plans. The household was rearranged for his benefit. Undoubtedly deriving some psychological benefit from his promotion, Vladimir in time began to show some signs of healthy adolescent experimentation.

The young man did not leave his family and try to disappear into the revolutionary underground. However, he did begin to smoke cigars, presumably in imitation of Rakhmetov (a man who would not deny himself small pleasures), but possibly because he wanted to imitate his student friends and acquire a more masculine air. (A rosy-cheeked youth, the first-year student had struck one of his new acquaintances at the university as somewhat effeminate.)[13] Maria Alexandrovna soon curtailed this habit of the "new man."[14] Lenin submitted to Maria Alexandrovna's wishes out of the same sense of guilt that motivated many of his actions during this period of his life. He owed a debt to her as well as to Sasha. They had both shown extraordinary strength and courage. He now felt obliged to be more like Sasha, more dutiful, although he clearly suffered from the strain. The hefty Volodya lost weight as well as hair during his first year in domestic exile.

Lenin would gladly have reentered the university had the authorities permitted it. An isolated regime of study in a domestic setting was not intolerable for an Ul'ianov, but the family educational imperative made him feel incomplete without a university degree. It still took precedence over the revolutionary imperative. While Maria Alexandrovna conducted the struggle on the educational front with petitions and visits to officialdom, Vladimir studied revolution and awaited the results of her efforts. Overt rebellion was impossible.

Moratorium and Apprenticeship

LENIN'S LIFE from 1888 to 1893 was devoted to half-commitments under-taken out of concern and respect for his mother, intensive study of revolutionary theory, and reconnoitering of the revolutionary move-ment. During this period he became a Marxist, but exactly when and how are a matter of historical dispute. The family moved from Kokushkino to the city of Kazan in August 1888 and to Samara province in May 1889. At first, Maria Alexandrovna repeatedly and unsuccessfully petitioned the authorities to relent and permit her son to return to his studies. Lenin read intensively and made contact with the local intelligentsia. According to Anna, he began to read the first volume of *Das Kapital* during the winter of 1888–1889 and frequently visited the apartments of individuals with ties to revolutionary circles. It is not certain that Lenin knew about the activities of the central circle led by N. E.

Fedoseev at the time, but in any case, he moved to Samara province with his family before arrests were made in July 1889.

According to the standard Soviet account, Lenin had been fully converted to Marx during the Kazan period and became one of Russia's first Marxists. Even at the age of eighteen, it is proposed, Lenin had grasped the leading revolutionary role of the industrial workers. However, as noted earlier, interest in and admiration for Marx at this time rarely signified commitment to the idea of the supremacy of the proletariat or to the long-term strategy of propaganda implied by Russia's stage of economic and social development. Attempts to interpret Lenin's own connections as primarily Marxist at this time are refuted by Trotsky, among others. Trotsky, who had had to make some difficult adolescent choices during his own revolutionary career, understood that a hard line between supporters of the People's Will and admirers of Marx simply did not exist in 1888. One could fraternize with people who called themselves *narodovol'tsy* and others who called themselves social democrats and adherents of Marx without feeling any sectarian pull during the late 1880s. Attempts to emphasize Lenin's indirect connection with Fedoseev have no cogency. Trotsky's argument that Lenin still sought to carry on in his own way Alexander's commitment rings true.[1]

Maria Alexandrovna had hoped to make a farmer out of her son and with this in mind had sold her share of Kokushkino and the property in Simbirsk and purchased an estate near the village of Alakaevka in Samara. She was the quiet force working in the background throughout this period. It is easy to forget that Lenin had been only seventeen when expelled from Kazan University and like all the Ul'ianov children was socially underdeveloped—*dikii*, primitive, in Anna's colorful way of putting it, *zastenchiv*, shy, in Maria Il'inichna's. His dependence upon his mother for material support closed the protective circle around him, but, of course, by submitting to her wishes, he was supporting her as well. Thus, he tried farming and waited for her petitions to bear fruit.

A studious, brooding nineteen-year-old preparing himself for a revolutionary career is an unlikely candidate for the role of estate manager. Lenin learned a great deal about Russia's agrarian economy during this period from books, but his first surviving piece of serious writing, "New Economic Movements in the Life of the Peasants" (1893), owed nothing to any practical farming experience in Alakaevka. Perhaps, as Anna claims, he did glean some knowledge from acquaintances there, particularly from the brother of Mark Elizarov, a former student of peasant origins, whom she had married in 1889. Maria Alexandrovna had purchased the 220 acre farm, replete with a mill, at Alakaevka with Elizarov's advice and help. However, only one cryptic remark about Lenin's experience managing the property has survived, and it comes by way of Nadezhda Krupskaia, Lenin's comrade and wife, who heard it from him. According to her, Lenin said:

> Mother wanted me to get involved with agriculture. I had made a start, but I saw it was an impossible situation. My relations with the peasants were becoming abnormal.[2]

In the absence of any but the slightest autobiographical remarks on Lenin's side, it is the laconic reports of police spies and memoirs of members of discussion and study circles in the province and city of Samara (now Kuibyshev) that give us most of our knowledge of his activities. Anna's remarks about this period suffer from vagueness, and the family memoirs as a whole reveal more about domestic life and Lenin's daily routine than his efforts at farming or his revolutionary apprenticeship. The memoirs of A. A. Preobrazhenskii, a *narodnik* who tried to sustain an agricultural commune in Samara province near Alakaevka, are one of the fullest nonfamily sources for 1889. Lenin was recommended to him by D. A. Goncharov, one of Lenin's classmates from Simbirsk, who had also been expelled from Kazan University in 1887.

According to Preobrazhenskii, Goncharov described his young friend as a budding "genius" at statistics. Goncharov evidently had in mind Lenin's already developed interest in the socio-economic data about broad issues of political economy, the development of capitalism in Russia, social stratification among the peasants, the fate of peasant communal institutions, and other matters that were being debated by the increasingly divided socialist factions. He introduced Preobrazhenskii to the Ul'ianovs in the winter of 1889–1890. Although eight years older than Ul'ianov, Preobrazhenskii felt that his interlocutor was mature beyond his years intellectually, as well as in appearance. (Lenin had grown a thin beard and mustache, as if to compensate for his rapid loss of head hair.) Preobrazhenskii had arrived at a rather pessimistic view of the peasants' communal characteristics, and Lenin agreed with him, possibly because of his own "abnormal" relations with the peasants. Whatever the peasant commune was, it was not the embryo of a future communist society. But the new friends quarreled about the extent to which capitalism had made inroads in the countryside, and Preobrazhenskii claims that Lenin had already concluded that the factory workers and not the peasants would be in the vanguard of the revolution. In addition, Lenin referred to Marx.[3] It is likely that Preobrazhenskii telescoped more than three years of Lenin's development in his account, which refers to the period between the winter of 1889–1890 and the summer of 1893. Thus, like other accounts that suggest that Lenin had become a doctrinaire Marxist by 1889, this one is probably misleading.

Non-Soviet historians tend to emphasize Lenin's interest in revolutionary technique and organization during this period, his contact with political exiles, some of whom had been connected with the Jacobin trends of the early 1860s and Nechaev's conspiracy, and *narodovol'tsy*. They are no doubt correct in this emphasis. Once again, Trotsky, who had no interest in retrospectively hurrying Lenin along the road to Marxism (he himself had been a populist until 1897), recognized Lenin's strong connection with the terrorist element in the revolutionary subculture. Young Lenin's commitment to follow the trail blazed by Alexander but not Alexander's fate inclined him toward the members of the exile community in Samara who could teach him how to engage in revolutionary conspiracy without being apprehended.

The crushing victory of the tsarist police over the revolutionaries had made advanced techniques of organization imperative, and despite their failures, the

Jacobins and terrorists were the old hands and the Marxists the novices in this area. If the word "apprenticeship" is taken its usual sense, then Lenin was more an apprentice to the *narodovol'tsy*. There were no Marxist veterans of revolutionary organization, struggle, and defeat on Russian soil—only the émigré *teoretiki*, Plekhanov, Aksel'rod, and Zasulich, who had been voices crying in the wilderness since 1883. Surely, Trotsky, who had an excellent sense of the history of the Russian revolutionary movement, is correct in his statement about the conversion of a significant part of the intelligentsia to Marxism:

> Capitalism had to achieve significant successes; the intelligentsia had to exhaust completely all other alternatives—Bakuninism, Lavrovism, propaganda among the peasants, colonizing in the villages, terror, peaceful educational activities, and Tolstoyanism. The workers had to launch their waves of strikes. The Social Democatic movement in the West had to assume a more active character. Finally, the catastrophic famine of 1891 had to lay bare all the sores of Russia's national economy.[4]

Even the most coldly calculating rigorist would find it difficult to break with a tradition both heroic and optimistic. Lenin's impatient revolutionary temperament would have made it painful for him to accept a doctrine that put revolution far off into the future, even though the early Russian Marxists did not abjure political struggle. He quickly showed that he would be a most impatient kind of Marxist, having strong affinities with the more sanguine representatives of the revolutionary subculture of the earlier decades. In any case, he was not ready to make a full commitment, given his family responsibilities and Maria Alexandrovna's plans.

Maria Alexandrovna was more successful at petitioning than her son was at farming. During the spring of 1890 she prevailed in her efforts to enroll Vladimir in a degree program at St. Petersburg University. He became an external student, with the right to take examinations in the faculty of law. After a visit to St. Petersburg in August–October 1890, Lenin returned to Samara to prepare himself for the examinations. Olga Il'inichna, meanwhile, had enrolled in the Bestuzhev higher courses for women, and she was able to help her brother by sending information about his law program. Lenin's extraordinary self-discipline and academic ability revealed themselves dramatically during 1890–1891, for in April 1891, less than one year after he received permission to become an external student, he took a series of law examinations and passed them at the highest level.

While the examinations were still in progress, Olga became ill with enteric fever *(briushnoi tif)*, and Vladimir had to hospitalize her. At the beginning of May he wrote home that Olga's condition had deteriorated and suggested that Maria Alexandrovna come to St. Petersburg, but Maria arrived to no avail. Olga died on May 8, 1891, the fourth anniversary of Alexander's execution, of typhus complicated by erysipelas, and was buried on May 10 in St. Petersburg. The impact of this tragedy on the family can only be imagined. Most sources note only Lenin's ability to continue his work successfully (just as he had done during Alexander's incarceration) and Maria Alexandrovna's strength and courage, but it is more important to try to understand how Olga's death affected Lenin's revolutionary career.

In all likelihood, it reinforced the survivor guilt Vladimir already felt in connection with Alexander's execution. She had been his closest sibling, his constant companion during early childhood. As she grew up, she came to resemble Alexander, and this must have affected Vladimir's attitude toward her. There is no indication that she and Lenin were especially close during the Samara period. During her illness, he had been responsible for her care, and Anna's memoirs observe that the hospital in which he placed her was a very poor one. In the absence of more information, we can only speculate about the extent of Vladimir's feelings of guilt—assuming that he had any at all—in connection with his responsibility for Olga's care. However, there is no evidence that Olga's death precipitated any self-defeating or self-destructive behavior, or even depression. Lenin returned to his studies in Samara, completed them, took his remaining exams in St. Petersburg in September–October 1891, and received the highest marks. In November 1891 he was awarded a first class degree.

Olga's death was the last in a series of family disasters, beginning with Il'ia's death in 1886 and Sasha's execution in 1887. Lenin's favorite cousin, Anna, one of Russia's first woman doctors, died of tuberculosis at Kokushkino in 1888; his nurse, who had loved him more than the other children, died in Samara in 1890. Maria Alexandrovna demanded that like her, the children carry on in the face of every obstacle or tragedy. She had not called Alexander home from school to attend Il'ia's funeral—a terrible mistake; she had expected the other children to perform while Sasha awaited execution; she expected no less of Vladimir in 1891. By putting their studies and academic achievement before everything else, she had intruded in the process of mourning and burdened her children with an excessive amount of guilt. Vladimir may have disposed of his survivor guilt and dealt with the loss of his siblings by taking over parts of their identities and suppressing parts of his. Sasha had been a revolutionary, an admirer of Chernyshevskii; Olga had been notable for her extraordinary capacity for work. No one would work harder at revolution than Vladimir. But he mutilated the self-identity he had been preparing before their deaths. How much of himself he suppressed in the process of expiating his guilt toward his dead siblings is impossible to measure. Perhaps Lenin actually relieved some of the guilt he felt by achieving what he was supposed to. It all makes much more sense psychologically if the gold medals and first class degree are seen as sacrifices as well as triumphs, marks of duty and ways of honoring the dead rather than as symptoms of self-centered behavior, of hard and ruthless pursuit of personal gain in the face of family disaster.

Lenin's suppression of himself probably lay behind his instrumental approach to revolutionism. He had suppressed part of himself and converted the remaining part into an instrument by taking over Alexander's project and seeking revenge for him and the family. He would treat others as instruments as well—as if they had no personal existence aside from their revolutionary profession. Lenin did have an almost touching concern for the physical health of his comrades, but even then he acted as if it was his duty to preserve them for the cause. Once one could no longer serve the cause, life lost its meaning. The acquisition of a law degree, in terms of the known future, appears to be an act of filial piety. Lenin had satisfied the family imperative. The law degree became his passport to an independent life.

Second Conversion

THE VERY year of Lenin's strikingly successful performance as an external student of law proved to be a kind of test for the revolutionary subculture as well. The Russian state had demonstrated a ruthless will to survive: It had upgraded its internal security measures against terrorism to the point of creating a variety of police state during the 1880s, and it had made the decision to modernize its economy, which it did equally ruthlessly under the economic regime of Count Sergei Witte. The efforts of Alexander III's government to manage the dual threat of a revolutionary subculture and a weak economy seemed to be succeeding, but in fact the state had only bought some time at the expense of increasing the alienation of the young and aggravating the precarious position of the lower strata of the agricultural population. When an acute famine followed the poor harvest of 1891, both the government and the revolutionaries found themselves in an odd quandary. The government, which had tried to avoid any initiatives from the educated and oppositional public, now found that it had to appeal to that very public for help. The agricultural catastrophe of 1891–1892 proved to be too great for the government's resources, and it sanctioned the mobilization of private philanthropic aid to the famine-stricken countryside.

Meanwhile, in those years the still vaguely divided groups within the revolutionary subculture were faced with a calamity that was simultaneously an opportunity—a large mass of starving peasants and villages invaded by typhoid and cholera epidemics. The intense pressures of the situation forced many green revolutionary recruits to face larger strategic issues as well as immediate philanthropic ones. The famine and the government's appeal evoked a variety of "hard" and "soft" responses. The former involved rejection of any cooperation with the tsarist regime but took varying positions, from the deterministic, long-term strategic outlook of the Marxist émigrés that economic ruin of the mass of the agricultural population and inevitable economic misery would ultimately create the basis for revolution to the more immediate concern of the politically oriented *narodniki* that their revolutionary struggle against the regime would be compromised.

Lenin unambiguously opposed joining the local committee for aid to the famine-stricken peasants of Samara, which suffered more than most provinces. Only he and M. P. Golubeva, one of the political exiles of the Jacobin persuasion (she was a disciple of P. G. Zaichnevskii) in Samara, refused to join the vast majority of the local intelligentsia in volunteer work in emergency canteens and medical facilities.[5] His lack of sentimentality in revolutionary behavior was not an artificially cultivated political trait but an expression of his overall psychology: a low tolerance for compromise, for palliatives, for "soft" approaches that blunted the edge of commitment. Furthermore, he already exhibited a lifelong political characteristic in his contacts with the Samara exile circles. After a period of relative respect for an opponents' position, he would engage in intellectual jousting, then ironic dismissal or vehement condemnation.

At an early point in their relationship, Lenin's wife, Nadezhda Konstanti-novna Krupskaia, noted his "malicious and cold" laughter when she recom-mended work in committees of literacy during 1894 in St. Petersburg. In Samara Lenin had already taken a position against philanthropic activity, against palliatives. It signified his rejection of liberal *kulturträger* solutions and his seeming repudiation of his family's way of life, particularly his fa-ther's.[6] Thus, his political hardness, which he developed during his long moratorium and apprenticeship in Kazan and Samara, made him reject his family's orientation. Like most youthful rebellions against deeply internalized values, it called for cruelly uncivil expression.

Despite the efforts of numerous "memoirists," some of them obviously carried away or pushed by circumstances to the point of falsifying incidents in Lenin's life during the crucial years 1888–1893, we know very little about this period. The most egregious falsification is the story of Lenin's alleged meeting with a leading theoretician of Russian *narodnichestvo* who was simultaneously Russia's best known literary critic, N. K. Mikhailovskii. The meeting was supposed to have taken place at the end of May or the beginning of June 1892, in the chronology of A. Ivanskii, who relies upon the memoirs of A. Beliakov. The very vagueness of the dating of the incident is itself telling, for according to the account, twenty-two people attended and, given the importance of the figures involved, it is astonishing that more precise information about it did not appear until 1960, when Beliakov's memoirs were published. In his memoirs, Beliakov characterized the incident as a meeting of "two mutually exclusive world views, sharply contradictory to each other."[7]

Mikhailovskii presumably appeared in Samara at the invitation of V. V. Vodovozov, a local *narodnik* who invited Lenin as well as the other local politicals, mainly *narodniki*, with the knowledge that Lenin's strong advocacy of the Marxist point of view would provide an interesting stimulus for discus-sion. Mikhailovskii was supposed to present a talk on the *narodnik* path to socialism. Both the scene at Vozovozov's *dacha* and the alleged presentation are described in detail as is Lenin's response to Mikhailovskii. The argument presented by Lenin in Beliakov's memoirs is a concise statement of Lenin's Marxism and his reasons for rejecting the *narodnik* point of view in 1892, but they are probably a product of Beliakov's imagination or someone's prompting.[8] In addition, there is no mention of the incident in the very thorough, twelve-volume biographical chronicle devoted to Lenin's life, which began to appear in 1970. Thus, we cannot rely on the most dramatic rendering of Lenin's position in 1892 in the absence of any of his own writings, which began to appear in print only in 1893.

Lenin's conversion to an orthodox, social democratic brand of Marxism was gradual and undramatic. During 1888–1893 he was clearly a rather cautious, studious young man. Trotsky, whose efforts to rethink Lenin's path to Marxism were far more strenuous and empathic than those of Soviet hagiographers, pays tribute to Lenin's caution and shrewdness and suggests that 1891 is the definitive moment of Lenin's turn to social demoracy. He does not believe that Lenin read Plekhanov before that time and doubts that Lenin could have become a social democrat without the help of Plekhanov's brilliant polemics.[9] He systematically disposes of all efforts to hasten Lenin's conversion.

The establishment of the precise moment when Lenin became a Social Democrat as such, rather than merely a species of *narodnik* who tried to incorporate Marxist "science" into a preeminently political vision, is only a tertiary concern. It becomes clearer with the passage of time that Lenin's orientation or *style* of politics is more important than Marxian doctrine in the long run. Thus, it is more crucial for understanding his development to know why he converted to Marxism, and then to grasp what kind of Marxist he became than it is to establish the precise moment of his conversion. At this particular moment in the development of the revolutionary subculture, Marxism was establishing itself as a competitor with populism. The tragedy of the famine and epidemics of 1891–1892, in which starving and sick peasants turned against the well-meaning doctors and their helpers who came to inoculate them and showed no inclination to become a revolutionary force, even in their desperate situation, convinced many aspiring young revolutionaries to turn elsewhere. A young person could snatch some hope and a sense of vitality from a new doctrine, even though the current situation seemed hopeless. The psychology of "the worse, the better" consoled "hards" like Lenin, who now saw the ruin of the peasants as a positive sign that capitalism was creating a landless proletariat. This, in turn, heralded the growth of a new revolutionary force, the urban working class.

By converting decisively by 1892, Lenin established an important continuing element of his identity. A Marxist in 1892 in Russia felt himself to be the vanguard of a vanguard. He claimed to superior "scientific" understanding of history and of the current historical moment. Lenin rejected sentimental attachments to a species of revolutionary theory that had dangled false hopes about the peasants as socialists *avant la lettre* and masked a great deal of nationalistic feeling. On the other hand, he was slower to reject the *methods* developed by the *narodovol'tsy* than other Marxists. Lenin, too, was prone to wishful thinking about Russia's readiness for revolution. An exceedingly impatient man, he sustained his illusions by means of misreadings of "hard" data about economic, social, and political phenomena rather than sentimental attachment to the notion that Russia had some special historical grace. He showed his conservative side by remaining a loyal Marxist for the rest of his life. But in his conversion he had already shown a remarkable ability to reject sentimental attachments, to sever ties to the past. This proved to be a central characteristic of his mature political style.

A review of the circumstances of Lenin's conversion to a revolutionary career reveals how undramatic, careful, and dull it was compared to those of many of his predecessors in the movement. All of the efforts to dramatize it remain unconvincing. Aside from a brief period of reckless and self-defeating behavior during his adolescent conversion in 1887–1888, Lenin settled down to bookish, careful study. It is difficult to establish boundaries within this period because we have no decisive moments, no signposts other than Lenin's reading and contacts with political exiles of varying stripes, but mainly within the *narodnik* tradition. When he did emerge as an orthodox Marxist, it was as an expert on economics, and this he had probably done partly as expiation for his sins against Sasha, whose interest in questions of political economy and social issues he had not shared and perhaps even ridiculed. Even if Lenin's rejection of his early love of language and belles lettres was at first a form of self-punishment, an expression of survivor guilt, his conversion was thorough and authentic. He remained at his post through thick and thin for thirty years. Thus, after an initial, doctrinally superficial adolescent conversion, when he was "plowed over" by *What Is to Be Done?*, Lenin systematically reviewed his commitment, tried two careers half-heartedly, and made a whole-hearted, adult commitment to a more "mature" and promising doctrine.

Trotsky, so convincing in his general assessment of Lenin's apprenticeship and moratorium, puts off Lenin's final decision to enter the field for Marxist orthodoxy until August 1893, when Lenin actually left his family and moved to St. Petersburg. But he underestimates Lenin's concern for his mother after Olga's death. Lenin's family situation slowed down his revolutionary career in this case, just as it had precipitated it in 1887. By the end of 1892 Lenin felt smothered in a half-hearted and unrewarding legal career and a domestic situation in which he painfully played the role of dutiful son. At last, Lenin found an end to his long moratorium. Just as Chernyshevskii had given him the positive emotional charge for his revolutionary conversion and a positive identity in the figure of Rakhmetov, Chekhov gave him an image of his possible ruin, a negative identity in the character of Dr. Ragin in his story, "Ward No. 6." It is also possible that the story also reactivated the trauma and guilt he had experienced because of Olga's death, for Ragin ruminates on the awful conditions of the provincial hospital in which "There was never a shortage of erysipelas in the surgical division." Lenin had placed Olga in what proved to be a second-rate hospital, and in her weakened condition she had contracted a skin infection.

The doctor's stoic acceptance of the misery and injustice around him, his flight into a world of books and elevated ideas, must have seemed akin to Lenin's own position in Samara. To be sure, he did aggressively pursue one scoundrel in a law suit, but on the whole his year as a legal defender for a well-intentioned liberal lawyer must have seemed as meaningless as Ragin's medical practice. Chekhov was a master at showing how the conditions of provincial life gradually destroyed people of high mind and delicate spirit. Aside from Dr. Ragin, Lenin might also have identified himself with Gromov, the paranoid former court clerk, a resident of the psychiatric ward in the hospital—ward number six. Like Lenin, he was the son of a civil servant whose brother and father died in rapid succession. Both Gromov and Dr. Ragin, the two most educated people in the town, were helpless in the face of the world's irrationality, cruelty, and injustice. Unlike Gromov, the healthy Ragin had ended up in the psychiatric ward because of his laziness and passivity, which, followed by impotent rage, proved to be his undoing.

The detestation of laziness and passivity already instilled in Lenin by his upbringing and reinforced by his reading of Chernyshevskii, Dobroliubov, and Pisarev now became a more conscious part of his mature identity. Chekhov added to the others a grim vision of the inevitability of the decline of a person's intellectual and psychological strength in a provincial Russian environment. Lenin told his sister Anna toward the end of 1892 that he felt as if he were in ward number six.[10] Chekhov's story thus had the impact of a literary shock treatment. It forced Lenin to review earlier traumas and painfully negative aspects of his identity, to reject these traits decisively, and to gather all of his will power for a leap out of the provincial mire. Although he had hardly been inactive throughout this period, Lenin could no longer equate activity in the circles of political exiles in Samara with a full-blooded revolutionary career. Throughout his life Lenin reacted to defeat and depression with similar mobilizations of energy and a will to victory, but he evidently decided to keep a reminder of his negative identity as a psychological spur by eventually settling on the ironic pseudonym "Lenin," derived from *len'*, laziness.

Lenin's long regime of study and rumination in Kazan and Samara, although claustrophobic by 1892, proved useful in several ways. It gave him considerable background and momentum for his new career. He felt himself to be fully ready, without doubts or anxieties about the correctness of his course. It also gave him a useful experience in survival in conditions of relative isolation. He would have to endure doldrums more than once, but Lenin did not have to spend too long in St. Petersburg without excitement. First of all, it was a period of theoretical controversy between *narodniki* and Marxists. Gray veterans and green novices, proponents of the two schools entered the field, and Lenin, armed with a vast array of statistics taken especially from V. E. Postnikov's study of the peasants of south Russia, impressed his new colleagues. He also benefited from the Ul'ianov name. Alexander's reputation as a revolutionary martyr guaranteed a friendly reception for his younger brother. Although we may doubt memoirists who claim that Lenin immediately galvanized the St. Petersburg Marxists to action, his formidable abilities were quickly recognized.

The tendency to hasten Lenin's preeminence as a leader is accompanied by an equally strong inclination to impute to him immediate and striking success in areas where he did not have experience, such as organizational work among disparate Marxist circles or spreading propaganda among workers' groups. Lenin impressed his new comrades mainly as a surprisingly (given his youth and provincial background) erudite Marxist theoretician and devastating polemicist. It is difficult to guage the effects of his propaganda activities among the workers' circles of St. Petersburg, but the descriptions of his polemics with *narodniki* have a ring of authenticity. Lenin's sarcasm, his scornful manner, his methods of devastating his opponents are all continuous with his last years in Samara. In two of his major works of 1893–1895, one of which circulated in the form of notebooks ("Concerning the So-Called Question of Markets") and the other in hectographed form *(What the "Friends of the People" Are and How They Fight Against the Social-Democrats)* Lenin proved himself to be an able disciple of the leading Russian Marxist theoretician, Plekhanov, astutely applying Marxian theory to Russian statistics and providing a socioeconomic map of the native terrain as well as a critique of the major *narodnik* theorists. The attack on the *narodniki* is remarkable for its breadth, ranging from epistemology to revolutionary strategy, and even more so for its sustained vehemence. Lenin offered Wilhelm Liebknecht's prescription for Social Democrats: Study, Propaganda, Organization. He devised his own description of a leader, which coincided with what he was already doing in St. Petersburg:

> You cannot be an ideological leader without the above mentioned theoretical work, just as you cannot be one without directing this work to meet the needs of the cause, and without spreading the results of this theory among the workers and helping them to organise.[11]

Granting the impressive erudition of his lengthy blast at the *narodniki*, Lenin's pamphlet also exhibits a naive faith in the power of Marxist dialectical method, its ability to describe reality and to convince the real representatives of the proletariat of its accuracy:

> There can be no dogmatism where the supreme and sole criterion of a doctrine is its conformity to the actual process of social and economic development; there can be no sectarianism when the task is that of promoting the organization of the proletariat, and when, therefore, the role of the "intelligentsia" is to make special leaders from among the intelligentsia unnecessary. Hence, despite the existence of differences among Marxists on various theoretical questions, the methods of their political activity have remained unchanged ever since the group arose.[12]

Lenin would find himself engaged in a lifelong struggle against a series of "petit-bourgeois" heresies precisely because of his enduring belief that only one correct position could be derived from Marxian analysis. As he matured as a politician, he would admit to mistakes, but this did not trouble him a great deal. Even dialecticians erred. When he began to berate fellow Social Democrats in terms no less vehement than those devised to destroy liberals and *narodniki*, he contributed to the very sectarianism whose disappearance he had predicted. In Lenin's version of dialectics, history would not tolerate more than one leading doctrine or group. Those who failed to grasp social "reality" at any given moment of the dialectical process became representatives of the bourgeoisie, whatever their subjective beliefs or goals. So long as they remained in error, they would be subject to merciless attacks, even if they had been close comrades in the struggle. Any critical reader of political rhetoric must take into account the polarizing effect of political debate and the mobilization of passions for struggle, but in view of Lenin's lifelong mobilization for struggle we find no other style of expression in his entire corpus. The features already present in Lenin's earliest works persisted to the very end of his life. They were completely appropriate for a man who wanted not merely revolution but victory.

Like all militants, Lenin believed that he who is not with us is against us. Marx provided a supporting "scientific" sociology for a militant psychology and a method for applying it flexibly. Dialectical flexibility proved useful politically in that it sanctioned the identification of not one but a whole series of enemies, while keeping the practitioner focused upon a social "reality" that would yield only one true position, one leading group. To be sure, Lenin did recognize that Marxists would have to ally themselves with contingents of the enemy forces, but from the very outset of his activity he made it clear that he felt unenthusiastic about alliances with the dialectically deficient. He already viewed such allies as tools, to be used and discarded. In short, he already exhibited the attitude of a ruthless variety of politician. However, this characteristic apparently existed side by side with the mentality of a species of dogmatic scholar-thinker, totally absorbed in his work and wholly convinced of the rectitude of his "science." Finally, Lenin had the burning spirit of the youthful convert. Without the last, it is impossible to explain Lenin's apparent belief in 1894 that Marxism could avoid the kinds of defections and splits that had characterized all other doctrines. Lenin's "scientific" travails do not in the least hide the lineaments of a moralist—a moralist descended from Russian nihilists and German Left-Hegelians, who despised piety in others but created new devotional idioms for themselves and their followers.

Despite his detestation of liberalism in 1894, Lenin tried to place his article, "New Economic Movements in Peasant Life," in the liberal journal, *Russian Thought,* but it was rejected. Although he must have derived some satisfaction from the distribution and reception of his underground works in 1894–1895, he no doubt longed to see himself in print in substantial legal publications. The brief period of "Legal Marxism," when both émigrés and home based theorists were able to publish their works, enticed him as well. Lenin no doubt envied his fellow Marxist Peter Struve's success in this period, but it was not merely out of envy that he criticized Struve's *Critical Remarks on the Question of the Economic Development of Russia* (1894). As a historical source, his review of Struve's book reveals Lenin's already developed political instincts, his ability to detect the *political* tendency of a theoretical position, which, in the case of Struve, he read as an insufficiently firm commitment to Marxian orthodoxy.[13] Published legally in a collection of Marxist writings, Lenin's voluminous review, along with the other essays in *Material for a Consideration of Our Economic Development,* (1895) did not reach a wide public. The tsarist authorities confiscated the printing and only a few copies of Lenin's first legal publication survived.

On balance, it is correct to see adumbrations of the later Lenin in his vehement criticisms of any tendencies toward liberalism or reformism in 1893–1894, but it would be wrong to ignore the strong elements of continuity in Lenin's identity and activity. He probably longed for a major publication that would be the equivalent of a dissertation in that it would establish him as a master of Marxian "science." Furthermore, Lenin did not at first abandon his professional status. He enrolled in the St. Petersburg bar as M. F. Volkenshtein's assistant, but practiced only as a legal defense lawyer with no real income. He also sustained his family ties and the rhythms of student life, to the point of leaving St. Petersburg in June 1894 to stay with his family until late August in their *dacha* near Moscow. Even the fully converted Marxist enjoyed summer vacations.

After months of exhausting work at his tirades against populists and his criticism of Struve, Lenin fell ill in early 1895 with a respiratory infection. With the help of the Ul'ianov family doctor he recovered in the spring of 1895, in time to embark on a pilgrimage to the centers of Marxism in Europe. Travel abroad permitted him to make direct contact with the leaders of the socialist movement, not to speak of some of the great libraries of Europe. Lenin was in Switzerland in May 1895 and later during that spring and summer in Paris and Berlin. Life for a militant young Marxist was not without its pleasant interludes, its moments of excitement.

Most important of all, in Switzerland Lenin met the founders and theoretical lights of Russian Marxism, the Group for the Liberation of Labor (Gruppa Osvobozhdenie Truda), a small band of middle-aged émigrés who had abandoned *narodnichestvo* when still young and provided the first powerful arguments in favor of Marxism beginning in 1883. Even the supremely confident Lenin could not at first hold his own against the urbane, rapier-like intellect of George Plekhanov, the avuncular kindness of Pavel Aksel'rod, and the revolutionary mystique of Vera Zasulich, who, like his brother Alexander, had engaged in an act of terror but had been acquitted and escaped abroad. After abandoning *narodnichestvo* Plekhanov, Aksel'rod, and Zasulich had virtually singlehandedly sustained Russian Marxism through lean years. Plekhanov in particular had inspired a handful of converts with his early works, *Socialism and the Political Struggle* (1883), and *Our Differences* (1885), and had given Russian Marxism a respected voice in the Second International during and after 1889. When these venerated figures met Lenin in 1895, they could feel secure in their position as the most exalted theoreticians of Russian Marxism.

Lenin first went to Geneva to meet Plekhanov and then to Zurich, where Aksel'rod was living. They both criticized Lenin's attitude toward liberalism in Russia, Plekhanov wittily and Aksel'rod in his gentler, pedagogical manner. Lenin showed a capacity for deference to authority at this stage in his life, and, with his straightforward, businesslike manner, which indicated absorption in his cause rather than vanity or personal ambition, he made an excellent impression. Aksel'rod spent a few days with him in the countryside near Zurich. He not only backed Plekhanov's criticism of Lenin's position but disabused him of any idea that Social Democracy in Russia would be able to avoid sectarianism and factionalism.[14] After years of experience in the revolutionary movement both in Russia and abroad, Aksel'rod had acquired a certain worldliness, which, however, did not in the least diminish his own faith in Marxism. He emphasized the need for an eagle-eyed detachment of Social Democrats who could stand safely outside the fray and guide the movement's general strategy, if not its day to day struggle.[15] This detachment, of course, would be the Group for the Liberation of Labor.

Although Lenin accepted the advice of the elders of Russian Marxism, he was constitutionally incapable of ridding himself of his hatred of liberalism. He also interpreted Aksel'rod's idea of a guiding group from his own character-istically dogmatic point of view, but none of this was apparent in 1895. To the delighted Aksel'rod, he was one of the signs of a growing Social Democratic army in Russia, a young man who would serve as a capable field officer. Later, Aksel'rod learned that the field officer had higher ambitions. At the end of September Lenin returned to St. Petersburg after a tour that included meetings with Paul Lafargue, Marx's son-in-law, and Wilhelm Liebknecht, one of the founders of the German Social Democratic Party. He brought with him a trunk with a compartment containing illegal literature. All of this could only strengthen his authority and give additional cachet to the prematurely bald young man already known as *starik*, "old one," in his own group, the leading group in St. Petersburg, whose members were called *stariki*. However, the group assumed a new title at the behest of their leaders abroad. They united the Social Democratic circles under an umbrella organization officially designated "The Union of Struggle for the Liberation of the Working Class" in December 1895.

Lenin quickly established himself as a leading figure in the Union, but not all of his early colleagues appreciated his aggressive, commanding style of leadership. This can be readily seen from oft-quoted remarks by defectors from Marxism and ill-wishers like Peter Struve and inferred from memoirs by fellow Bolsheviks like P. N. Lepeshinskii. When Lepeshinskii first met Lenin in Siberia toward the end of 1898, he had already formed an image of him based upon contact with Lenin's St. Petersburg colleagues:

> When I first met Il'ich, all of my ideas of him as a "general," as a mocking, arrogant, and cruel person vanished after the very first moments of my acquain-tance with him. None of us was distinguished by such a naturally simple, sweet [*milyi*], good relationship to those around him, such tact, such delicacy, and such respect for the freedom and human dignity of each one of us, his com-rades.[16]

The thoughtful, tactful Lenin did indeed exist intermittently, but Lenin did not make his reputation on tact and courtesy.

The work of study, propaganda, and organization proceeded apace. Contact with other Social Democratic groups in the industrialized western part of the Russian Empire, particularly with the one in Vilno through the arrival of a young Jewish Marxist, Iulii Martov (Tsederbaum), led to a change of tactics. The Marxists of Vilno had discovered that Jewish workers responded to agita-tion on behalf of their own economic demands. Martov, who had begun his revolutionary career in St. Petersburg at the tender age of eighteen, was arrested in 1892, became a convert to Marxism, and during his exile in Lithuania learned the new tactics. The Social Democrats had created clear distinctions between propaganda (many complex ideas for the few) and agita-tion (a few simple ideas for the many). Martov had engaged in both tactics and carried the main progammatic document of the new strategy, *On Agitation*, to his comrades in St. Petersburg in October 1894. When he completed his term of exile a year later, Martov became a member of a group of Social Democrats known as "the young ones," who soon entered the umbrella organization created by "the elders," and then he joined Lenin on the committee of five leading the organization.[17] They immediately established a close political friendship, but their first period of collaboration ended rather suddenly in December 1895.

5

Exile and Emigration

LENIN'S ARREST on December 8, 1895, when the workers of St. Petersburg were just beginning a long period of labor unrest, could only strengthen his commitment. Two years after his arrival in St. Petersburg, he had seen dramatic results. On the very eve if his arrest, he and his group were preparing the first issue of The Worker's Cause, designed to be the agitational journal of the Union of Struggle for the Liberation of the Working Class, but the issue was confiscated by the police. Even if it is difficult to measure precisely the impact of either his organization's or his own propaganda and agitation on the proletariat of St. Petersburg, there can be no doubting the beliefs of the young revolutionaries in the efficacy of their work. Arrest and imprisonment did nothing to lower Lenin's morale. To the contrary, his first real imprisonment (the brief detention in Kazan hardly counted) served as a relatively painless rite of passage and simultaneously gave him the opportunity to pursue his study of Russian economic and social conditions. The most assiduous student of conspiratorial methods among the Marxists, Lenin sustained a lively correspondence with both fellow prisoners and the outside by means of legal communications and secret messages written with milk or lemon juice and even played chess by code with nearby cellmates. The authorities permitted the prisoners visits, gifts, and, most important of all, books and writing supplies. Lenin's family played a major role in the transmission of both legal and illegal materials. Anna was now a willing rather than unwitting accomplice, and the entire family aided and abetted him. Both before and after his arrest, Lenin lived largely on the funds supplied by his mother. During his "preliminary detention" of more than fourteen months, Lenin suffered neither psychologically nor materially and was able to lay the groundwork for a major study, *The Development of Capitalism in Russia* (1899), thanks to Anna's foraging through the libraries of St. Petersburg for vast quantities of books.

Lenin left St. Petersburg in February 1897, but before his departure for Siberia he was able to sit for a now famous photograph with his comrades in the Union of Struggle for the Liberation of the Working Class. In the photo both his physical location and the intense expression on his face distinguish him from the others and project him as a leader. The gathering suggests the high morale of the group as they prepared for Siberian exile. As Anna Elizarova noted in her memoirs, the political prisoners of Marxian persuasion generally did not lose morale. Their detention coincided with a surge in the labor movement of 1896–1897, of which they were fully informed. Their sacrifice was not for nought.

From the moment of his earliest steps as a Marxist Lenin combined the revolutionary, Jacobin spirit of Marx in his most militant phases and the later scientism of Engels. In Siberian exile Lenin strengthened his skills, as he would repeatedly as an émigré, updating the scientific (deterministic) side of Marxism while sustaining the impatient, uncompromising, Jacobin (voluntaristic) spirit that distinguished him in the long run among leading Russian Marxists of his generation. A reader plowing through the dense pages of *The Development of Capitalism in Russia* might not picture the author as an impatient sort of revolutionary Marxist, but in its historical context Lenin's socioeconomic analysis was a highly militant work.

In the major work of his period of Siberian exile (1897–1900) Lenin was trying to finish off the major *narodnik* proponents (V. P. Vorontsov and N. F. Danielson) and their theory that Russia could not develop a sufficient internal market for advanced industrial capitalism. He tried to bury his opponents under an avalanche of data and argumentation. As a Marxian scientist applying the methods and findings of *Das Kapital* to Russia, he showed a characteristic tendency to rush things, in this case to exaggerate the extent of capitalism's triumphal march in Russia. He was later (1916) to make the same mistake for world capitalism, arguing that it had reached its zenith and was on the verge of collapse. In 1899, however, he had only to show that capitalism had already proleatrianized a majority of Russian peasants—those very peasants whose stubborn communal institutions the *narodniki* believed gave Russia a special advantage over the developed capitalist nations in the movement toward socialism. They also believed in the virtues of small-scale units of production. To Lenin and to other Marxists the *narodniki* did not understand either the Russian peasants and their institutions or economic laws. Although Lenin was correct about *narodnik* illusions, his own sociology of the peasants was based upon a theory that looked forward to the disappearance of peasant cultivators as well as agrarian capitalists and to their total absorption into large-scale agricultural units, the rural equivalent of socialized labor in huge factories.

The *Development of Capitalism in Russia* is an impressive book, but its long-term legacy, an illusion that the peasants were well on the way to class polarization and would soon struggle amongst themselves as proletarians and bourgeoisie, proved to be positively harmful. Alliances with the peasants were necessary, but orthodox Marxists—Lenin, Karl Kautsky (who also published a book on agrarian issues in 1899), and the Russian émigrés among them—did not view the peasant smallholders as a genuinely revolutionary class. Rather, they were petty bourgeoisie clinging to their economically irrational bits of land. The failure of the peasants to behave as they were supposed to and disappear was a major embarrassment to Russian Marxists and the source of a human catastrophe of vast dimensions more than thirty years later, when the Soviet Union was ruled by an equally impatient, though more brutal man than Lenin.

But in 1899 Lenin's historical sociology did not have to be correct. Russian Marxism flourished at a moment when the tsarist regime, having experimented with social engineering in the 1860s, was now taking even greater risks by subjecting the peasants to extraordinary fiscal pressures and encouraging investment in heavy industry. In view of increasing mass misery and social unrest, Marxists and *narodniki* alike could find "scientific" support for their positions. The preeminence of Marxism in the mid-1890s among the revolutionary intelligentsia quickly faded. Marxists later had to struggle with a revived *narodnichestvo* in the form of the Socialist Revolutionary Party after major peasant rebellions in 1902. Red-blooded revolutionaries of both camps responded to the opportunities available to them, and liberals leaned to the left. To be sure, no one's prophesies were exactly fulfilled, and all revolutionary parties would have to reexamine their strategies during the first years of the twentieth-century, but mass constituencies had appeared and challenged the adaptability of leaders.

Narodniki continued to go to the villages and the factories, but they revised their attitude toward large-scale industry. Marxists continued to concentrate their efforts on the factory proletariat, but were forced to devote greater thought to a program for the peasants. Liberals welcomed revolutionary violence in all forms, for both *narodniki* and Marxists believed in a liberal, constitutional phase of historical development. For the first time oppositionists did not have to rely mainly upon students as shock troops of the movement against autocracy. Social unrest in factories and villages in the period 1899–1905 developed faster than the supply of revolutionary agitators. Professional unions with both urban and rural constituencies spearheaded the liberal opposition. The politically astute learned how to adapt themselves, how to be flexible, but revolutionary leaders did not abandon their "scientific" doctrines, their attitudes toward the peasants or to the factory proletariat, their "subjective" or Marxian sociologies. An image of the special virtues of a favored group suited the psychology of the leaders. It inspired them to concentrate their efforts in a certain direction, even if their political methods often led to joint ventures in revolutionary practice.

Resemblances between the Jacobin brand of Marxism and the conspiratorial branch of *narodnichestvo* made it seem puzzling that Marxists should polemicize so strenuously against the heirs of the People's Will. Both *narodovol'tsy* and Jacobin Marxists emphasized political goals and struggles in the near future and wanted to use liberal institutions as means to further their long-term anarcho-communist aims. The most radical and impatient, like Lenin and Trotsky, gladly dispensed with liberal forms when historical circumstances gave them the opportunity to do so, and they were joined by the left-wing heirs of the *narodnik* tradition. But it would be fallacious to assume that resemblance implies continuity, even though Lenin clearly had studied the *narodovol'tsy* and knew what he found useful in their tradition. He admired their hatred of the Russian autocracy, an emotion he shared, but passionate motives behind political attitudes were not sufficient to bridge the abyss separating Marxists and *narodovol'tsy*. Lenin believed throughout his revolutionary career that the urban proletariat would take the lead in the political struggle against the autocracy. He refused to accept the *narodnik* distinction between political conspiracies designed to destroy the autocracy, the major obstacle to the spread of socialist ideas, and the politics of mass movements. To be sure, within three years after his release from Siberian exile he would promote a form of leadership and a party organization quite distinct from the broad labor movement and a few years later he would fight to sustain the conspiratorial type of underground revolutionary party. Yet he refused to give up his belief in the special historical role of the urban proletariat in Russia as elsewhere.

Lenin's analysis in *The Development of Capitalism in Russia* is a kind of *profession de foi* in a new and powerful idiom. To appeal to the intelligentsia, modern doctrines must combine faith and realism, or science, and Lenin's faith in the correctness of his "science" sustained him through lean years. The notion of faith raises the vexing issue of resemblances between Marxism and earlier Judeo-Christian traditions.

A rough human sense that there will be justice, that wrongs will be righted, that sufferings and humiliations will be revenged, that the rich will not enter either a heavenly kingdom or earthly socialist paradise, underlies a great many religious and secular doctrines, expressed in a variety of "sacred" and "scientific" idioms. Another common denominator of such doctrines is their identification of victims who are chosen to be saved and oppressors who are doomed, whether by God's love and justice or history's dialectic. Needless to say, this kind of hopeful and militant vision, when sustained over a long period of time, yields a history of struggle, frustration, adaptation, sectarianism, and defection. Like their religious predecessors, the new secular movements spread out

over a spectrum of positions reflecting defeated expectations, changed historical conditions, and the psychologies of individuals creating the movements'
doctrines and strategies.

Lenin shared the familiar orientation described above with Russian nihilists
and *narodniki* as well as a great variety of European Left-Hegelians and
Marxists, but his own peculiarly aggressive personality affected his prosecution
of the cause. No one can read *The Development of Capitalism in Russia* without
feeling that it was informed more by Lenin's passion for humiliating his
intelligentsia opponents and his hatred for political enemies than his compassion for those who were undergoing proletarianization. Lenin concentrated his
fire in his "major study" *(boPshaia rabota)* on those who still defended the old
Russian socialist faith—the *narodniki*—all the while receiving disquieting
news of heresies arising within social democracy, especially "critical" neo-
Kantian approaches to Marxism signifying a loss of the fighting political mood
of the mid-1890s. It must have been dismaying for him to see Aksel'rod's
predictions come true so quickly. Legal Marxists like Struve and S. N. Bulga-
kov drifted into liberalism. Eduard Bernstein's revision of Marxism soon tainted
the militant spirit of early Russian Marxism, and "economism," a native heresy
conceding the leading role in the political struggle to liberals while limiting
Marxists to the struggle for economic benefits, alarmed both the older generation of Marxists and young militants like Lenin. Lenin's hatred and contempt
for liberalism, held in check after his trip abroad in 1895, burst out again.

Lenin's difficulty with Marxian revisionism and those who accorded an
important role to liberals is symptomatic of a doctrinal and psychological
problem peculiar to Marxism and absent in the old *narodnik* creed. Marx had
revealed the systemic necessity of class exploitation. Capitalism was by its
very nature savagely unjust. Since most revolutionaries were not simply thinking machines looking for the most rational foundation for production and
distribution but possessed of "religious" attitudes, or, in any case, of a sense
of mission, they found in Marx and Engels the description of a morally
intolerable system in which the wealth of the few could only be gotten at the
expense of the poverty of the many. On the other hand, Marx posited the
necessary contribution of each historical phase to economic and social progress.
The bourgeoisie and their liberal institutions could not disappear from history
until they had developed the forces of production as far as they could, when
the onset of the inevitable and fatal crisis of capitalism would occur. Capitalism was a necessary evil on the way to socialism. But Marx had no blueprint
for its many historical variations, only his laws of capitalism and their consequences. Neither he nor Engels had a revolutionary timetable either, and it
was possible for their followers to lapse into a purely "scientific" and morally
slothful type of Marxism, an academic Marxism without a sense of urgency
about revolutionary tasks to be performed. On the other hand, the most morally
mobilized would find ways to hasten capitalism's final hour, even while separating themselves from the *narodniki*, whose revolutionism was "unscientific."
Thus, during a period of mainly doctrinal debates and sectarianism, revolution-

aries who were temperamentally quite close to each other engaged in combat; but when the real revolutionary moment arrived, they often found themselves working together.

Marx and Engels had issued confusing signals to Russian and other Marxists during their lifetimes, for they had welcomed revolutions in situations "scientific" Marxists might see as "premature" and also suggested that in some advanced nations socialism might be achieved peacefully through the political structures created by liberal governments. The founding fathers were impatient for socialist revolution, but hardly dogmatic about the means for achieving socialism. Since interpretations of the historical moment by individual Marxists (not to speak of Marx and Engels themselves) in any case differed greatly on the basis of a great many factors, including individual psychology, the doctrine of socialism by the end of the nineteenth century had become richly varied. When Lenin entered exile, he had no inkling that orthodoxy would be challenged so vigorously. At the end of his three years in Shushenskoe he mobilized himself to take arms against revisionism and economism, and within three years of emigrating to Europe he found that he and he alone had the vigilance, the theoretical background, and the strategic and tactical knowledge to save Russian Marxism from its own heresies. He soon attacked his revered older colleagues, Plekhanov, Aksel'rod, and Zasulich, as well as those members of his own generation who refused to see the light. One wonders what would have happened had Marx and Engels survived into the twentieth century and encountered the intense young man from the Volga region of Russia—and disagreed with him.

Lenin's seeming break with the past and full mobilization in a new cause sometimes obscures the extraordinary continuity of his style of life as well as his basic morality. Lenin's personal conservatism showed in his dress (white shirts, ties, three-piece suits), his attitudes toward the arts, and his lifelong commitment to the career he had chosen while still a teenager—that of a professional revolutionary—a career preferred by some of the most respectable people in the Russian empire in that period. While in exile he married Nadezhda Konstantinovna Krupskaia, and his choice of a life companion reveals how powerfully he had been shaped by his family. The marriage, which took place on July 10, 1898, did not represent a new stage in Lenin's transformation. Had Krupskaia changed her political views, one can be certain that a divorce would have followed. A professional pedagogue, Krupskaia exhibited an Ul'ianov-like dutifulness and was devoted to revolutionary work.

To someone who had been surrounded all his life by teachers and then revolutionaries, she offered a familiar way of life and shared values. Like Lenin's sisters, Anna and Olga, his bride had attended the Bestuzhev higher courses for women in St. Petersburg. Krupskaia (who was ordinarily addressed after her marriage by her maiden surname) was also of gentry background, but like Lenin's family, hers was hardly one of the standard sort. Krupskaia's biographer astutely notes the similarities of character shared by her mother, who had also taught, and Maria Alexandrovna.[1] She accompanied her daughter to Shushenskoe, one of the most pleasant and climatically tolerable of the exile communities. It was a relatively comfortable arrangement, the closest thing to a continuation of Lenin's own family atmosphere.

The marriage itself arose out of a typical ruse—revolutionaries often entered into fictitious engagements and marriages for a variety of conspiratorial reasons and in order to join comrades in exile. Although libidinal motives may have been involved as well, they were apparently not as strong as political ones in the case of Lenin and Krupskaia. Malicious comments about Krupskaia's piscine appearance punctuate discussions of her probable relationship with Lenin. A thyroid condition caused her eyes to bulge. During the greater part of her adult life she could hardly be called physically attractive, but when she was a young woman (she was actually a little older than Lenin, having been born in 1869), Lenin might have been impressed by her high cheekbones and full lips and the subtle slant of her eyes. Krupskaia, who had known and admired Lenin as a comrade since 1894, assumed some of the secretarial services with which he ordinarily burdened his sisters. The eight-rouble subsistence stipend given each of them by the government, plus substantial family resources and money earned from writing and translation, permitted them to hire a maid. Lenin's Siberian existence had many of the amenities to which he had long been accustomed—winter sports, chess, hiking—and he even kept a bird dog for his hunting excursions.

Whatever the romantic aspects—or lack thereof—in their marriage, Lenin and Krupskaia formed an ideal working team. She pursued her interest in women's issues from a Marxian point of view, but devoted herself mainly to supporting her husband's unrelenting political labors, whether literary or organizational. The two exiles, who had left St. Petersburg encouraged by the apparent success of militant Marxism, both waxed indignant at the signs of weakening political commitment that reached them in a conspiratorial letter sent by Lenin's sister Anna in July 1899. Anna had transmitted in secret chemical writing the economist heresy embodied in E. D. Kuskova's "Credo." Lenin responded angrily. The "young" Marxists in St. Petersburg were threatening the movement created by the "elders," who had designed all of their propaganda and agitational activities in support of the workers' economic demands with political goals in mind. The author of the "Credo" made politics the main business of liberals, not Marxists, and asked her fellow Marxists to follow the path of least resistance by supporting the workers' instincts to form organizations to improve working conditions and wages. The following lines must have received particular attention:

> Intolerant Marxism, negative Marxism, primitive Marxism (whose conception of the class division of society is too schematic) will give way to democratic Marxism, and the social position of the party within modern society will undergo a sharp change. The party *will recognize* society; its narrow corporative and, in the majority of cases, sectarian tasks will be widened to social tasks, and its striving to seize power will be transformed into a striving for change, a striving to reform present-day society on democratic lines adapted to the present state of affairs, with the object of protecting the rights (all rights) of the laboring classes in the most effective and fullest way. The concept "politics" will be enlarged

and will acquire a truly social meaning, and the practical demands of the moment will acquire greater weight and will be able to count on receiving greater attention than they have been getting up to now.[2]

One can only imagine Lenin's rage at reading the above lines. To a Marxist of sectarian temperament who believed that the proletariat would have to be the vanguard of all democratic forces in the Russian empire, the "Credo" could only be infuriating. Lenin wrote a protest, quite free of invective (he saved that for his correspondence), presenting the orthodox line in the name of Russian Social Democrats, after having discussed it with seventeen fellow exiles and signatories.[3] It was the beginning of his open war with heretics within his own camp, a struggle he waged while simultaneously drawing up plans for unifying the movement though the creation of a party newspaper and theoretical journal. During the last half of 1899 a number of characteristically Leninist themes appeared repeatedly in his efforts to formulate a program for Russian Social Democrats: insistent pleas for the professionalization of political organization; a call for a unified party with a central organ published abroad; persistent attacks on revolutionary provincialism, on petty, amateurish forms of political activity, summarized under an opprobious term signifying parlor politics, *kruzhkovshchina;* surprising flexibility about tactics, including recognition that terror might at times be both inevitable and useful; expressions of concern about the role of revolutionary elements within the peasantry; and ambivalence about the concessions a Marxist party could make to peasants. The essential leader had been formed by the end of his period of exile in late January 1900.

Although Lenin learned to be flexible in his Marxism, during his years as a revolutionary he bent only in the service of his *political* goals; and after the revolution, while he experimented with economic and social programs, he refused to compromise his party's leading role. He consistently rejected any tactic that would put Social Democrats at the "tail" of a larger democratic movement led by "bourgeois" parties; and by a rather loose application of the label "petty bourgeois," he reserved for himself the right to decide who objectively served the party of the proletariat. Furthermore, believing that any complication of the Marxian class schema tended to blur the battle lines, he defended what Kuskova called "primitive" or "schematic." Lenin reacted with alarm at new-fangled approaches to social analysis. A firm party line and militant organization were of the utmost necessity at a time when the intelligentsia showed alarming signs of its vacillation, its logorrhea, its tendency to import dangerous new ideas rather than adhering to the *correct* ideas (imported a bit earlier) that had converted him.

Lenin was already conservative in his own way, defending his vision of a political vanguard tenaciously, and already suspicious of the intelligentsia's ability to play a proper political role. The intelligentsia's very fascination with new ideas, its alertness to historical shifts, its openness to new ways of looking at things, its *intellectual* vanguardism, gave it the wrong kind of flexibility. He called it "opportunism." His flexibility he called "dialectics." Lenin's labels "amateurism," "opportunism," and "petty bourgeois" signalled his mistrust of the old intelligentsia and the beginning of the political movement that destroyed it. While the intelligentsia critically examined the validity of Marxian ideas in the light of new developments and ideas, Lenin was acquiring the skills and techniques of a political leader. But he was not alone. He had borrowed much of his rhetoric from orthodox Marxists abroad and was supported by many of the exiled veterans of the period 1883–1896.

The theoretical leader of German Social Democracy, Karl Kautsky, had already leveled his fire at Bernsteinism; the Group for the Liberation of Labor in Switzerland published its own blast, Plekhanov's collection, *Vademecum*, against the heretics who had seized control of the Russian Social Democratic organ, *The Worker's Cause*. The collection appeared shortly before Lenin's emigration. The forceful Plekhanov, who had been responsible for many of the positions that had inspired Lenin during his conversion to Marxism and whose invective continued to nourish his disciple, had helped to create a force he himself was not able to control. Like exiled *teoretiki* before him in the history of the Russian revolutionary movement, he watched with alarm the deviations of the young. The small band of Marxists who had founded the movement had enjoyed a few short years of unquestioned authority, and responded bitterly to the events of 1898–1899. They contributed to a split within Russian Social Democracy that they themselves could not heal and sought help from younger colleagues whose loyalty to them seemed unquestionable. Plekhanov, Aksel'-rod, and Zasulich only later understood how much they would have to pay for promoting their young field commander, Vladimir Ul'ianov.

Lenin had put himself in the forefront of orthodoxy with his "Protest" and had spent his last months in Russia reestablishing ties with orthodox comrades like Martov and A. N. Potresov and even waverers like Struve, all the while feverishly planning and promoting the new organs of Social Democracy and a party congress. His sometimes incautious movements attracted police attention, and his illegal visit to St. Petersburg on May 20, 1900 (he was prohibited entry to the capital) led to his arrest on May 21. After ten days under arrest he was released to his mother's custody in Podol'sk, south of Moscow. Undaunted, he resumed his organizing activities until July 16, when he left Russia. He planned to join the elders of the movement as a colleague in exile. The decision to emigrate signified not only Lenin's desire to serve the movement but his sense of his own stature and his eminently practical conclusion that a leader should not be vulnerable to arrest.

6

Lenin and Plekhanov

B Y 1900 Lenin's ability, energy, loyalty, practical experience, and the work he had already done in the service of a new party organ made him a logical candidate for the editorial board and a leading organizational role. He had been blooded, served time in prison and Siberia.[1] He was now impatient to serve with the other orthodox leaders, who, like him, apparently wanted a solidly professionalized political organization combining the best features of German Social Democracy and the Russian revolutionary underground. (At the time, and until 1914, he assumed that leaders of the Second International had one loyalty — to the working class — and that all of their work had aimed at the conquest of power by the proletariat.) With other Russian Marxists, Lenin assumed that Russia faced unique problems, and the strategy and tactics for solving them set the agenda for the new party organ, *Iskra (The Spark).*

Russian Marxists had long assumed that the proletariat would have to play a leading revolutionary role in the conquest of bourgeois liberties, in view of the relative weakness of the Russian bourgeoisie. Moreover, the Russian autocracy had proven its ability to suppress political activity. Underground conspiracies by pathetically small socialist parties had presented the greatest challenge to tsarist power, but all had been crushed. The Social Democrats had failed in their first effort at an all-Russian party congress. When the delegates met in Minsk in 1898, they were quickly arrested. Although the labor movement itself had won a major battle in 1897, when an eleven and one half hour limit to the working day had been decreed, the workers showed no strict ideological loyalty or political discipline. They were more than willing to take the path of least resistance, and many Social Democrats were happy to follow them along that path. To the orthodox all of this signified lack of control over the movement, "bourgeois hegemony," and declining militancy. Even though the proletariat would triumph in the end, if properly led by Social Democracy it could cut short the period of subjection to bourgeois hegemony and its own suffering. Thus, leadership and organization of a party that had both mass characteristics and conspiratorial qualities (given Russian conditions) were crucial. Russian backwardness called for special forms of struggle.

Lenin's hopes and plans yielded immediate results. The older émigrés sat down to talks with the young collaborators (Lenin and Potresov) from the St. Petersburg Social Democratic organization. They were defying the lessons of the past, for earlier efforts at collaboration between *teoretiki* of an older generation and *praktiki* of a younger one had yielded misunderstandings, acrimony, and divisions and had rarely endured for more than short periods. Alexander Herzen had found the *raznochintsy* who came abroad insufferable. Bakunin and Ogarev had welcomed them but had become embroiled with Nechaev. Lavrov had succeeded at holding together his revolutionary journal for more than three years, but that too had foundered. The problem of guiding a movement from afar, of raising material support for émigré journals and party leaders safely ensconced abroad, of coordinating the programmatic work of the émigrés with that of the revolutionaries engaged in the day-to-day struggle at home were formidable structural problems. Resentments over this division of labor and disputes over the use of funds recurred throughout the history of the revolutionary movement, and the Marxist émigrés suffered from more than a few scandals.

The clash of personalities played an equally significant role.[2] The *teoretiki* of the Group for the Liberation of Labor were celebrities who had lived through the heroic stage of the Russian revolutionary movement and had been present at the dawn of Marxism. They knew the great figures of the Second International. Plekhanov in addition had a reputation as a theoretician of pan-European stature, a brilliant stylist, and a man of devastating wit. He was not simply first among equals. At times he brutally demanded of his closest allies, Aksel'rod and Zasulich, unquestioning subordination to his policies. His need to assert his preeminence, his dogmatism and belligerence, and his hazing of younger recruits crippled efforts at expansion and unification. Despite the efforts of Zasulich to mediate controversies, Plekhanov seriously alienated a series of collaborators. On the other hand, younger leaders often displayed insufferable arrogance themselves and showed insensitivity to the position of the émigrés. Even Aksel'rod and Zasulich, far more tolerant and friendly to the young than Plekhanov, found it difficult to sustain friendly relations with the younger generation. The relationships of the older émigrés were complicated by tiffs with each other's protégés. Yet they had no choice but to make the effort at sustained collaboration with younger émigrés. Isolated work had little appeal, even though personal wounds sometimes called for therapeutic withdrawals and geographic dispersion of the leaders themselves.

The interrelationships of the members of the editorial board of the new Russian Social Democratic journal, *The Spark*, and its theoretical counterpart, *The Dawn*, testify to the role of personal and generational loyalty, egoism, insecurity, and ambition in the next crisis of Russian Marxism, the emergence of "hards" and "softs," Bolsheviks and Mensheviks. The first personality clash involving Lenin occurred at the end of July and the first half of August 1900. He arrived when Plekhanov's rage at the affronteries of the younger generation was at its height. He now saw heresy everywhere, and refused to make the slightest concession to another point of view. The *Vademecum* had carried polemics to an unprecedented extreme, for in his unmasking of his young opponents, Plekhanov had used evidence appearing in personal letters to Aksel'rod, with the latter's assent.

Lenin and Potresov had presented the draft of the programmatic editorial for *The Spark* and *The Dawn* to Plekhanov in a spirit of loyal coworkers submitting their work to the master. Although they already expected to play an important role, they were still somewhat reverent. To their great consternation, Plekhanov condemned their efforts on behalf of unification and conciliation, which included an invitation to Peter Struve to participate on the new journal. The very Lenin who had reluctantly submitted to Plekhanov's and Aksel'rod's calls for tolerance toward liberals now found himself listening to the most extreme invective in the spirit of *Vademecum* hurled against "spies," "swindlers," "traitors" who "deserved to be shot." Plekhanov accused Lenin of *opportunism!* It was a bitter lesson and one that Lenin did not forget. Respected, trusted (even beloved) leaders could change positions and leave their followers in the lurch. Lenin's own efforts at moderation and compromise now seemed to be timid, passive, and politically naive. Probably wondering if he had gone too far in his zealous support of orthodoxy, he became determined not to be outflanked by Plekhanov or anyone else. Plekhanov had taught him that will power was more than half the battle. The leader of Russian Social Democracy had no compunctions about precipitating crises or about splitting a still small and embattled party; and, if nothing else worked, he used threats of resignation to bring his opponents into line. From all of this Lenin learned another lesson about leadership, a rather unpleasant one for a young man in a position of subordination, but ultimately quite useful: A real leader could use such tactics successfully. An apt pupil, Lenin applied what he had learned with surprising speed.

Plekhanov's handling of the draft of a lead editorial with programmatic content, written in the spring of 1900 before Lenin's emigration and transmitted to Plekhanov by Potresov before Lenin's arrival, shocked him even more than *Vademecum* had. It revealed to Lenin that he had not pleased Plekhanov, that he was not one of Plekhanov's favorites, that he was just another upstart to be put down. The newly arrived émigré had been warned about Plekhanov's suspiciousness and belligerence, but these traits in themselves would not have disturbed him had they not been directed against dutiful field officers. Nor was Lenin prepared for an outburst of anti-Semitism against the Bund, a Jewish Marxist labor organization within the movement. Martov, the Jewish member of the trio of young collaborators, had not yet arrived abroad, and Lenin and Potresov listened in disbelief to Plekhanov's tirade. In the course of the August meetings Plekhanov was transformed from a revered leader into an ogre, and Lenin and Potresov yielded point after point, revealing themselves to be easily intimidated political tyros.

Lenin's description of his and Potresov's feelings after Plekhanov's browbeating is the most extended self-revelation of his emotional life in his entire corpus. It sheds much light on psychological antecedents and on Lenin's future career. The traumatic episode with Plekhanov had revived earlier traumas. Lenin's language in "How *The Spark* Was Nearly Extinguished," written on August 20, reveals this vividly and deserves lengthy quotation:

My "infatuation" with Plekhanov disappeared as if by magic, and I felt offended and embittered to an unbelievable degree. Never, never in my life, had I regarded any other man with such sincere respect and veneration, never had I stood before any man so "humbly" and never before had I been so brutally "kicked." That's what it was—we had actually been kicked. We had been scared like little children, scared by the grown-ups threatening to leave us to ourselves, and when we funked (the shame of it!) we were brushed aside with an incredible unceremoniousness. . . . And since a man with whom we desired to co-operate closely and establish most intimate relations, resorted to chess moves in dealing with comrades, there could be no doubt that this man was bad, yes, bad, inspired by petty motives of personal vanity and conceit—an insincere man. This discovery—and it was indeed a discovery—struck us like a thunderbolt; for up to this moment both of us had stood in admiration of Plekhanov, and, as we do with a loved one, had forgiven him everything; we had closed our eyes to all his shortcomings. . . . Our indignation knew no bounds. Our ideal had been destroyed; gloatingly we trampled it underfoot like a dethroned god. . . . We did not dare undertake the editorship *ourselves*; beside, it would be positively repulsive to do so now, for it would appear as though we really coveted the editor's post, that we really were *Streber*, careerists, and that we, too, were inspired by motives of vanity, though in a smaller way. . . . [Lenin's ellipsis] It is difficult to describe adequately what our feelings were that night—such mixed, heavy, confused feelings. It was a real drama; the complete abandonment of the thing which for years we had tended like a favorite child, and with which we had inseparably linked the whole of our life's work. And all because we had formerly been infatuated with Plekhanov. Had we not been so infatuated, had we regarded him more dispassionately, more level-headedly, had we studied him more objectively, our conduct towards him would have been different and we would not have suffered such disaster, in the literal sense of the word, we would not have received such a "moral ducking," as Arsenev [Potresov] correctly expressed it. We had received a painfully bitter, painfully brutal lesson. Young comrades "court" an elder comrade out of the great love they bear for him—and suddenly he injects into this love an atmosphere of intrigue, compelling them to feel, not as younger brothers, but as fools to be led by the nose, as pawns to be moved about at will, and, still worse, as clumsy *Streber* who must be thoroughly frightened and quashed! An enamoured youth receives from the object of his love a bitter lesson—to regard all persons "without sentiment," to keep a stone in one's sling. . . . Blinded by our love, we had actually behaved like *slaves*, and it is humiliating to be a slave.[3]

Lenin went on to describe their decision to terminate the project, Aksel'rod's efforts to mediate, and the latter's expression of the fear that Zasulich, who had threatened dire things over such schisms any number of times, would commit suicide. Aksel'rod's remarks and a meeting with Zasulich triggered another emotional response:

I shall never forget the mood in which we three [Lenin, Potresov, and Aksel'rod] went out that morning. "It's like going to a funeral," I thought to myself. And indeed we walked as in a funeral procession—silent, with downcast eyes, oppressed to the extreme by the absurdness, the preposterousness, and the senselessness of our loss. As though a curse had descended upon us! Everything had been proceeding smoothly after so many misfortunes and failures, when suddenly, a whirlwind—and the end, the whole thing shattered again. I could hardly bring myself to believe it (as one cannot bring oneself to believe the death of a near one)—could it be I the fervent worshipper of Plekhanov, who was walking along with compressed lips [erroneously translated as "clenched teeth" in text], a devilish chill in my soul [translated "heart"] intending to hurl cold and bitter words at him and almost to announce the "breaking-off of our relations"? Was this but a hideous dream, or was it reality?[4]

They involved Zasulich in the discussion and found her admirably self-possessed, despite the anguish their remarks caused her:

It was extremely painful to listen to the sincere pleadings of this woman, weak before Plekhanov, but absolutely sincere and passionately loyal to the cause, who bore the yoke of Plekhanovism with the "heroism of a slave" (Arsenev's [Potresov's] expression). It was indeed so painful that at times I thought I would burst into tears. . . . [Lenin's ellipsis] Words of pity, despair, etc., easily move one to tears at a funeral. . . . [Lenin's ellipsis][5]

The young men had still another meeting with the three veterans, with all parties on a different footing. While Lenin and Potresov were aware that Plekhanov had been in far greater struggles, that this must have seemed like a mere skirmish to him, they now refused to be intimidated. Lenin had learned to see all of Plekhanov's behavior in a new light, as maneuvers in a battle, and he shifted into a new mode of behavior himself: à la guerre comme à la guerre. To conduct a war effectively, one had to subdue one's emotions, listen to threats and ultimatums, and sometimes suffer such behavior with "compressed lips." When threats failed, Plekhanov shifted to a different tactic, suggesting that it was not any deficiency in *them*, that they were the best colleagues he could hope for, and that if the enterprise collapsed, he would leave the political arena. Lenin read this maneuver as base flattery. He and Potresov left without having come to an agreement with Plekhanov.

After having slept on it (or having spent a sleepless night), Potresov produced a compromise, a different sort of publication, to begin with. This he and Lenin presented to Plekhanov, but they still could not resolve all the issues separating them. In the course of discussions the bitter feelings eased, war became diplomacy, and Lenin had discovered that it was possible to carry on without love, without comradely feelings, and to collaborate with someone, all the while preparing for war with him: si vis pacem, para bellum.[6] After all, *The Spark* was not extinguished.

During a period of less than two weeks—between the meetings of August 11–15 and his composition of "How *The Spark* Was Nearly Extinguished" about a week later—Lenin had achieved a new level of consciousness as a political actor. He could not have achieved it had he not been the sort of person with a vocation for politics. Undoubtedly, he himself had many of Plekhanov's propensities but probably needed to see them displayed in a context where *family* feelings were involved. Plekhanov had forced him to the conscious realization that one had to give up affective ties in order to be a successful political actor; that one had to see people as pawns; that sentimental attachments led to defeat and slavery; that passions had to be transformed into cold calculation in politics, as in war.

Ul'ianov Becomes Lenin

NO ONE with any claim to psychological acumen has failed to notice the importance of the episode with Plekhanov in August 1900, and the extraordinary amount of narrative dramatization and self-revelation in "How *The Spark* Was Nearly Extinguished." Yet even the most superficial student of Lenin quickly realizes that much of the behavior ascribed to Plekhanov was already at least incipient in Lenin and later appeared in extreme form. It is easy to conclude that much of what Lenin attributed to Plekhanov involved projection of his own attitudes and ambitions as well as accurate assessments of Plekhanov's motives. After all, Lenin and Potresov were plotting to control the journal, to insulate it from the intolerant and unreliable elders by moving the editorial office to Germany. They had even discussed the matter in Geneva with some of Plekhanov's own younger comrades. It is unlikely that the threat to his position could have escaped Plekhanov or that he would have acquiesced without a struggle. He had already revealed that in his split with the younger Social Democrats in the Union. But Plekhanov had not really used the word *Streber*, "careerist," to describe Lenin and Potresov. Lenin had introduced the word into his dramatization later. Lenin believed the accusation was implicit in Plekhanov's response to their proposals, but clearly Lenin had a guilty conscience, and this only inflamed his resentment. Even though Lenin's own account reveals his ambition to take over some of Plekhanov's authority, he could not see in himself what he saw in Plekhanov. Rather than admit to his own ambitions, *his* maneuvering, he projected them onto Plekhanov. This permitted him to heighten his indignation against Plekhanov and to see himself and Potresov as innocent victims. Only *after* Plekhanov had displayed his ruthlessness would Lenin and Potresov respond in kind—with cold calculation rather than "loving" familial attitudes. Lenin regretted, above all, their complicity in their own victimization. First they had failed to see through Plekhanov, and then they had cowered before his threats like frightened children. Too late, they learned to control their comradely feelings and face him coldly.

The struggle with Plekhanov presumably evoked memories of earlier attachments, conflicts, humiliations, and losses. To Lenin, he probably had some of Illia's traits and some of Alexander's. Zasulich's torn loyalties (both to the "father" and the "children" or to the children competing for her love) and her profound grief contemplating the loss of a "family" member no doubt reminded Lenin of Maria Alexandrovna. Lenin could identify himself with Zasulich, Plekhanov's "heroic slave," through partial identification with his mother. Thus, the threat of a sudden break, the loss of the head of the family, the death of their "favorite child," *The Spark*, revived images of unexpected deaths, funerals, his mother's victimization, and his own grief.

The document, aside from containing a *cri de coeur*, announces Lenin's determination to become a leader rather than a follower, a master rather than a slave. However, it is a *dramatization* of a *conscious* aim rather than a signal of a dramatic change of behavior. Lenin had reacted to earlier traumatic conflicts and losses in his life aggressively, by mobilizing his energy and assuming some characteristics of loved ones who had threatened him and whom he had lost. He had simultaneously suppressed any of his own characteristics that he believed could hinder him in the achievement of an identity *superior* to the figures whom he had loved and admired. Unlike them, he would not become a victim. In all likelihood, until the traumatic conflict with Plekhanov he had not been able to formulate any of this consciously.

Il'ia, Alexander, Chernyshevskii, and Plekhanov all belonged to the series of those whom Lenin had loved, albeit ambivalently, but lost. He had discovered them to be flawed. Il'ia's commitment to *kulturträger*, liberal solutions had to be decisively repudiated. Alexander had been his childhood model, but they had been mutually estranged in adolescence. Then Alexander's death had forced Lenin to revise his attitude and led Lenin toward Chernyshevskii and his first conversion. After study and reflection, he had rejected both Alexander's and Chernyshevskii *narodnik* beliefs and retained useful aspects of their revolutionism. The pattern of Lenin's formation of a new identity emerges clearly: first, love, admiration, and imitation, mixed with criticism and negative feelings for those with whom he had personal contact; then disenchantment and partial rejection of the ambivalently loved person. In Lenin's family history, losses occurred through death rather than merely rejection. In either case, Lenin built his identity through retention of some of the rejected or lost person's characteristics and through *decisive* repudiation of others.

Lenin's ambivalence led to *aggressive* rejection as well as to zealous imitation of the lost (or rejected) person. He seems to have mobilized himself dramatically at moments of loss, for he had to prove to *himself* that he was indeed superior to the lost (or rejected) person, possibly to escape a survivor's ordinary feelings of guilt. Lenin evidently had very little tolerance for feelings of guilt. The defense mechanism of projection helped him deal with his own aggressive feelings. In August 1900 this permitted him to place all of the blame on Plekhanov. But by making Plekhanov the aggressor and himself and Potresov the victims, he revived images and feelings of earlier victimization. He then mobilized even greater aggressive energy to fend off passive acceptance of victimization, slavishness of the sort exhibited by Zasulich (and, earlier, his mother), and their psychological effect, immobilizing depression and thoughts of suicide. Lenin still needed to hide from himself his own desire to replace Plekhanov, but he dramatized his refusal to be a victim, to be a slave.

The traumatic encounter with Plekhanov, and Lenin's writing of "How *The Spark* Was Nearly Extinguished" not only revived Lenin's emotional strategies for dealing with "loved" authority but permitted him to formulate a political modus operandi. The document also reveals that aside from being able astutely and realistically to grasp some of his opponents' motives, Lenin defensively distorted them as well. He transformed opponents into bad people (deceivers, self-promoters, traitors) to achieve the kind of mobilization of aggressive energies that he typically deployed in political struggle—hence, his indignation, angry intolerance, and ruthless treatment of close colleagues once they become opponents.

In "How *The Spark* Was Nearly Extinguished" Lenin describes his project as "a favorite child." He saw himself as a good father and Plekhanov as a bad one (also, as a bad older brother) who had to be replaced. The Social Democratic Party had become Lenin's family, and families could have only one head. He knew that it was out of the question for him and his young colleagues to assume full control. Plekhanov had to be at least the titular head of the enterprise; Lenin had to bide his time, gather strength, and assert his preeminence when the time was ripe. Now, Lenin consciously recognized that in order to acquire mastery over others, one had to have a high degree of control over one's own feelings, especially feelings that made one submissive or passive. He learned how to collaborate coldly with people whom he neither trusted nor wholly respected, so long as they were useful to the cause.

There is a kind of epilogue to "How *The Spark* Was Nearly Extinguished," another dramatic document, this one describing a negotiation between Lenin, Potresov, and Zasulich on one side, and Peter Struve and his wife on the other. Lenin wrote his thoughts down shortly after the meeting of December 16, 1900, on December 17 at two A.M., which suggests he had to get it off his mind. Although much briefer than the narrative of the meetings with Plekhanov, it is another story of maneuvering, in which Struve, like Plekhanov earlier, perceives Lenin and his associates to be powerless and tries to dictate terms of surrender to them. Lenin describes Potresov as a victim of wishful thinking and himself as fully up to the task to see through Struve's deceit. Again, although perfectly aware of the maneuvering and political behavior within the

Social Democratic camp itself, Lenin condemns Struve for revealing himself to be a "politician" and is outraged that Struve should try to bargain with them. In Lenin's narrative it is Struve who loses control of himself and shows anger and Potresov and Zasulich who quarrel with the Struves. Lenin himself is alert to all of the "twins' " ploys, direct and calm in his questioning, and precise and clear in his presentation of his own ideas. While the others quarrel, Lenin for the most part remains silent but expresses his contempt by laughing openly.

Although his indignation at having to maneuver with a comrade still appears in the "Note of December 17, 1900," it is far less dramatic than the story of Plekhanov's behavior and its impact. Yet Lenin claims for this meeting greater significance than the lesson learned during the earlier meeting with Plekhanov. In the "Note" he puts it this way:

> It was a meeting, significant and "historic" in its way . . . at least historic in my life, a summing up of a page of my life, if not an entire epoch, and determining for a long time my conduct and life's course.[7]

One wonders why the discovery of Struve's duplicity should have been more important for Lenin's life history than disenchantment with Plekhanov. What new lesson did Lenin draw from the clash with Struve? In each case, there is an unmasking, with the clear inference that you cannot trust anybody to behave properly; in each narrative, once you see through people and learn how to control your "soft" feelings about them, you can best them in a struggle. Lenin expressed not only his sense of moral superiority but a new sense of his growing ability at political maneuvering. The "epochal" change probably had nothing to do with Struve as such but rather involved Lenin's discovery that he had suffered in *each* conflict because he had left the main initiative for maneuvering to his "brother," Potresov. There is an implicit accusation in each story. Lenin had wanted to approach Plekhanov differently, but had yielded to Potresov's more "friendly" approach. In the negotiations with Struve it had been Potresov once again who had misread Struve's intentions and put Lenin off balance at the outset. So, the historic lesson appears to be about alliances: If you ally yourself with "softs," they'll carry you to defeat with them; they'll convert you into someone else's tool. Henceforth, Lenin would seek out other "hards" as allies. They would bridle under dictation, just as Lenin had in relation to Plekhanov. Their self-subordination, like Lenin's, would tend to be tactical, and intraparty rebellions would punctuate the history of Bolshevism.

Very quickly after the terrible scenes with Plekhanov, Lenin discovered how much closer he was to him than to Potresov, Aksel'rod, and Zasulich. In subsequent negotiations with Struve in January 1901, against Lenin's wishes, Potresov, Aksel'rod, and Zasulich acceded to Struve's demands. Plekhanov, who, of the older exiles, showed more toughness against the Revisionists and greater alertness to their perfidy, had convinced him of the deceitfulness of the young Economists and of the correctness of his position in *Vademecum*. On January 17(30), 1901, Lenin wrote a bitter letter to Plekhanov, now his ally, referring to Struve throughout as "Judas." "Love" was no longer important; a person's political correctness and usefulness was. Lenin now identified himself with Plekhanov at his most intolerant and domineering. Painful though Plekhanov's ruthlessness had been when inflicted on Lenin's "hide," he had given Lenin a politically useful lesson. Lenin would repeatedly inflict similar lessons on his colleagues.

Throughout his career Lenin lost control over his rage and vented it against a vast array of "fools," "opportunists," "deceivers," "hucksters," "politicians," and "Judases," who threatened to destroy *his* project. Although the project became increasingly ambitious—first a party newspaper and journal, then a party, then a revolution, and finally the conservation of all that he had won—the familiar cast of bad characters appears in each crisis. On their side, the "soft" colleagues soon noticed certain repellent features in their fiercely industrious and reliable, but dogmatic and domineering coeditor. To be sure, Lenin remained sufficiently politically domesticated to establish himself as one of the ranking figures in the movement. He was able to tend his "child," *The Spark*, and then to nourish a party. But the humiliations he inflicted on his comrades created the conditions for repetitions of "family" dramas. Although Lenin had learned lessons very useful for a revolutionary politician in an era of ruthless political behavior, he did not really practice the "cold" ruthlessness sometimes attributed to him. His inability to control his rage against both opponents and colleagues who crossed him lay at the source of an especially vindictive political culture.

More important, Lenin's repudiation of a traditional *structure* of authority did not go as far as that of most Russian revolutionaries. Instead of desiring to replace the old authorities, to become "fathers," most of the *narodniki* had simply wanted to destroy the structure of authority itself. They were all anarchists as to ends, as was Lenin himself. However, Lenin's acceptance of Marx's scientific authority and then his ruthless and dogmatic defense of it in the face of his own "dialectical" flexibility were symptomatic of a fundamentally authoritarian outlook.

Even before Lenin had arrived upon the scene, Bakunin had astutely forecast the possible consequences of "scientific" authority in revolutionary movements. Although acceptance of scientific authority in itself did not necessarily signify a commitment to political authoritarianism, in Lenin's case it was clearly symptomatic of a deeply conservative political *psychology*. He would destroy the old political forms and symbols and attempt to put "scientific" authority in their place, but in his control over his party he reproduced a variation of hierarchical authority and tight organization of the sort he had experienced in his family. "Science" became an appendage of that type of political authority and organization.

Oddly enough, Lenin's authoritarianism and drive for power did not signify any megalomaniacal tendency. His self-irony saved him from that. He had retained an element of his negative identity as a child, and he made that element central to his identity as a revolutionary leader. The choice of an ironic pseudonym based on the word "laziness" no doubt signifies Lenin's striving for mobilizing himself against his own weaknesses, his tendency toward inactivity and depression. It is a sort of banner of struggle. One conquered one's negative identity by consciously exposing it, keeping it out in the open as a constant reminder of one's weakness, like Sasha's earlier use of the pseudonym "Vralman" (liar) when they were children writing for the "Subbotnik." But conscious choice of a negative identity as one's public (though pseudonymous) self also signifies an element of self-repudiation in Lenin's style of leadership. Throughout his career, despite his drive for power and control, Lenin did not seem to act in a spirit of self-aggrandisement. Simple admission of fallibility, a sense that no one was without sin, including himself, saved Lenin from some of the worst extremes toward which "hard" leaders drift.

7

The Emergence of Leninism

LENIN'S WRITINGS and actions during 1900–1903, before the convening of the Second Party Congress of the RSDRP in July, should have revealed that he stood outside the usual generational affiliations. In most respects he was conservative in that he rejected new ideas that appealed to the younger Economists and Revisionists in 1898–1903. Until 1903 his strongest ties were still with the members of his generation who sustained the "orthodoxy" of the founders, Plekhanov and the Group for the Liberation of Labor. Thus, he, Potresov, and Martov formed a kind of triumvirate that allied itself with the older generation doctrinally but showed an understandable drive for autonomy as well. The ambivalence of the younger men and Plekhanov's authoritarianism created friction but did not prevent three years of successful collaboration. However, Lenin very quickly emerged as the one figure among the junior triumvirate with a genuine passion for organization, a ferocious capacity for work, and an authentically "hard" mentality—a hatred for compromise and alliance with any but the faithful.

On the basis of his past research and writing, Lenin became the expert on agrarian matters and policy for *The Spark*, but this was only one aspect of his broader role. Increasingly, Lenin took upon himself the main burdens of editorial and organizational work connected with the biweekly. By far the most punctual, organized, industrious, and fully mobilized member of the editorial board, he outstripped his colleagues by a significant margin. Lenin naturally tended to seek alliances with Plekhanov as a fellow hard-liner, but the two of them were so autocratic and tactless that it was difficult to keep them in harness together, even at a distance. However, Plekhanov was less of a problem than the other middle-aged émigrés. At least he did his share of the work by assuming virtually the total burden of theory in his contributions to *The Spark's* theoretical sister journal, *The Dawn*. Lenin found Aksel'rod's, Potresov's, and Zasulich's lack of productivity insufferable and began looking for a way to remove them from the editorial board. Distinctly a product of the Ul'ianov family ethic, Lenin followed the principle of "from each according to his ability, to each according to his work" when it came to editorial authority and believed that he, Plekhanov, and Martov deserved the leading role. Somewhat thoughtlessly, he planned to reduce the editorial board to a triumvirate at the Second Congress, assuming that he would be able to control the triumvirate because Martov would be closer to him than to Plekhanov on issues where Lenin and Plekhanov clashed.

Lenin had also done most of the groundwork for the Congress and engineered a solid bloc of supporters for the editorial board. Given all of the above, it was perfectly reasonable for Lenin to believe that he would soon become first among equals in the circle of émigré leaders, just as he had been among the *stariki* (elders) in St. Petersburg; and in view of the activities of the *The Spark's* agents under his guidance, Lenin could picture himself as the moving force of Russian Social Democracy. Plekhanov would be titular head as the party's leading *teoretik*, but Lenin would control the organization. It was Lenin who designed the party regulations in preparation for the Congress. He was a political engineer creating a machine with his own purposes in mind. However, his plan for the Congress itself had several failings. Lenin had carefully martialed the hards but had not taken into account the impact of his tactics upon his colleagues. Matters that he thought had been settled well in advance did not turn out as planned. Furthermore, what had appeared to be primarily organizational matters proved to be grounded in assumptions with implications reaching far beyond mere political gadgetry.

One revealing moment occurred on July 29, 1903, at the fifteenth session of the Congress, when a majority of the program commission decided to change the eighth paragraph of the program by adding the words "and consciousness" after "solidarity" to the phrase describing the growth in the size and solidarity of the proletariat as a consequence of the contradictions of the capitalist system. Lenin objected on the grounds that the addition gave the impression that proletarian consciousness grew spontaneously and said: "In international social democracy there is no conscious activity of the workers aside from the influence of social democracy."[1] This brief statement encapsulates Lenin's belief in the crucial role of the leadership, a conscious vanguard with the responsibility for organizing less conscious workers and guiding their political activity. Lenin's correction was voted down.

In the course of the lengthy Congress, which met first in Brussels on July 17–24 and completed its work in London on July 29–August 3 (Old Style), Lenin's preliminary efforts at organizing *The Spark*'s bloc of delegates did have the effect of expelling unwanted elements (that is, unwanted by the orthodox) from the party and yielded victories. However, all of this was trivial compared to the storm provoked by Lenin's behavior during and after the Congress. Lenin's initiatives forced confrontations, splits, and personal acrimony. What had begun as a drive to consolidate *The Spark*'s leadership over the Russian Social Democratic movement ended as a struggle against Lenin's control over the party, and chronic factionalism. Lenin's appropriation of the term *Bolshevik* (majoritarian) for those members of the bloc who remained stably committed to his initiatives was not merely a clever ploy. He had created a majority and watched it snatched away, largely because of Martov's defection. Martov, it turned out, was soft.

From the perspective of political history the crucial struggle between Lenin and Martov at the Second Party Congress occurred over the issue of party membership. Lenin's formula for membership called for "personal participation in one of the party organizations," whereas Martov's welcomed as members those who gave "regular personal assistance under the guidance of one of its organizations."[2] Lenin, of course, consistently tried to trim down to a hard core of committed revolutionaries. However, his *behavior* played as great a role as his aims and perhaps was decisive in turning Martov against him. It now became as much a matter of opposing the person, Lenin, as fighting for programmatic or constitutional matters in the creation of a Social Democratic Party.[3] The turning point in the history of the party coincided with the emergence of a new attitude towards Lenin. Heretofore he had been seen as a kind of zealot — impatient, uncompromising, hotheaded, but enormously useful to the party. Now, with cold calculation and remarkable effectiveness, *The Spark*'s hired gun was in the process of staging a coup within the party, or subjecting it to a "state of siege," as it was put. What is more remarkable, although several members of the Congress and later other Social Democrats applied faultless logic, ancient political wisdom, and rhetorical brilliance to an unmasking of Lenin, they found it impossible to stop him.

If we view the situation at the Congress from Lenin's standpoint, the Mensheviks (minoritarians) now led by Martov and Aksel'rod, threatened his plan to build a technically competent, centralized, and disciplined organization. All of this struck Lenin as personal betrayal as well as politically retrograde behavior, for he assumed that everything had been settled but a few secondary details. Lenin's support at the center disintegrated before his eyes. Enraged and embittered, Lenin caucused the hard core of his supporters for another assault. The mutual intransigence of the new factions converted the

Second Congress of the RSDRP into a disaster for Russian Marxism at a time when militant liberals, a new generation of revolutionary populists, and even police-sponsored labor organizations were threatening to gain hegemony over an increasingly politicized labor movement.

Lenin's drive for authority was not limited to political and organizational matters. It eventually became clear that he had only provisionally yielded preeminence on basic theoretical issues to the veterans of Russian Social Democracy. He looked to German Social Democracy and Karl Kautsky for support for his positions. His theorizing began to take its peculiarly Leninist turn when in the voluminous pamphlet *What Is to Be Done?* (1901–1902) he added to his chronically impatient posture the uncompromising demand that the Social Democratic Party be, above all, a revolutionary *organization* comprised of professionals. Lenin had always been the most conspiratorially minded of all Russian Marxists, but he now elevated revolutionary method to a position of dominance in theory as well. Organizational strategy encroached upon territory that had been occupied previously by social theory.

Instead of seeking authorization in spontaneous mass movements, Lenin located authority in the "conscious" elements of social democracy, the organization of professional revolutionaries. The indisputably practical side to Lenin's vision obscured for a while the larger social and political implications. Russian revolutionaries, after all, had suffered numerous defeats. Like his brother Alexander, they had taken the duelist's approach to struggle and perished. On the other hand, a mass party could be easily infiltrated. Instead of a broad, diffuse, and vulnerable mass party, Lenin wanted one limited to theoretically advanced, technically competent revolutionaries enrolled in and working for a party organization. But he added a crucial dimension to their role. They would be the conscious vanguard, and by this he meant not just the technical organizers of the political struggle, the "midwives" of revolutionary process, but the guardians of scientific authority and makers of policy.

As students of revolutionary history, all Marxists, including Lenin, understood the implications of Jacobinism. Furthermore, when Lenin was still an infant, Bakunin had seen in Marx's claim to scientific authority dangers of the emergence of a new kind of political priesthood. The "harder" the organization and the more sectarian the attitude of its leaders, the more likely it was to detach itself from mass movements and set itself up as a distinct authority. This elementary wisdom, of course, is not limited to revolutionary undertakings, but it made the Jacobin form of Marxism especially suspect in a movement presumably dedicated to mass initiative. Lenin, of course, asserted democratic aims and claimed attachment to a proletarian constituency. He seemed to believe that everything except organizational matters had already been settled, but his "soft" colleagues easily pointed out the implacable logic of his organizational emphasis and his ideas about the "conscious" vanguard. Lenin's blueprint laid the basis for the dictatorship of a single person.

Thus, in 1903–1904 Lenin already looked like both a heretic and a candidate for dictatorship, for he had transferred his faith from the revolutionary proletariat to an organization, to cadres of professional revolutionaries, and it was quite easy to question his motives for doing so, as well as his judgement. Long before he actually had political power, Lenin was recognized as an aspiring Robespierre and a potential Bonaparte. But, just as his opponents showed basic political wisdom about the implications of "hardness," Lenin understood what was needed for victory in conditions of struggle. In chaotic revolutionary situations organizational discipline (indeed, dictatorship) guaranteed responsiveness to events, quick mobilization, tactical flexibility. In battlefield conditions, long-standing theoretical formulas and popular moods might both be dangerous. Only a disciplined party with a spirit of subordination to its leaders could rectify mistakes, change course if necessary, strike when the moment demanded, and both adjust to popular movements and acquire hegemony over them. In practice membership in the Bolshevik Party signified subordination to Lenin and his surprising maneuvers. Lenin simply split (or later, purged) the organization when some of his staff officers failed to follow him. He was already acting in this spirit at the Second Party Congress.

From the very outset, Bolshevism took on both anti-intelligentsia and anti-popular characteristics. Lenin's fighting organization, like a two-edged sword, cut at the intelligentsia's and the workers' ways of life, transforming its members into preeminently political actors, into disciplined troops of a militant party. The intelligentsia had to give up the "bell jar" atmosphere in which they had flourished and their insubordinate mentality; they had to suspend their habit of criticism and accept party discipline. The workers had to exchange their habitual drive for mere trade unionism and short-term benefits for far-sighted party programs, for political struggle led by officers who knew better than they did the aims of the war and the strategies and tactics to be used. In short, Lenin was recruiting an elite that would be capable of turning against both the intelligentsia and the proletariat, if necessary. His critics immediately noticed the "bureaucratic centralism" implied in the approach—the tendency to create an organization that would transfer its members' loyalties from a cause to the organization itself and subordinate them to a hierarchical command structure.

Thus, despite its elitism, Leninism contradicted the modus operandi of the intelligentsia. Lenin did not have to invent his critique of the intelligentsia. Marxian theorists had difficulty settling upon a class definition for the intelligentsia. There was room for only two struggling classes in Marxian theory of the day; all ambiguous social groups (such as the intelligentsia) were either called "bourgeois" or thrown into the petit bourgeoisie. These facile resolutions of complex sociological issues were less important than the confused and contradictory efforts to characterize the groups and their mentalities. Aksel'rod, in his attack upon Bolshevism, showed that the intelligentsia were inclined to be elitists and chronic centralists. Kautsky, on the other hand, emphasized the intelligentsia's individualism, and Lenin used Kautsky in support of his position.

Lenin, no less than other Marxists, appropriated the "scientific" authority the intelligentsia had claimed for itself, but he repudiated the intelligentsia's mentality, which, by definition, could not be proletarian. In the second quarter of the nineteenth century, the dialectical approach had at first strengthened the idea of permanent criticism—a permanent revolution of the mind and spirit—but Marxism had increasingly emphasized the "scientific" authority of the dialectical "method," something Marx himself had encouraged and Engels had developed after Marx's death. Furthermore, Marxism tried to locate the dialectic in a world of "material" relationships. The relationship of thought to action, of theory to practice, was also called "dialectical," but in the real world of struggle, theory became a series of ad hoc rationalizations, informed as much by individual temperament and political infighting as anything else. Thus, by 1903 there was an extraordinary amount of diversity among the leaders of the Marxian movement, dialecticians all. They could not agree about the most basic issues, including that of the social psychology of the intelligentsia, but unlike the disputes of earlier intelligentsia critics or scientists, their debates had life-and-death significance. The self-repudiation of the intelligentsia, indeed, its self-destruction, was one quite logical product of Marxian dialectics, but it took an individual who was quite consciously repudiating his own past, his own "bell jar" existence, to give the intelligentsia's drive for self-destruction a particularly vehement character.

Lenin was no less adept than his colleagues at constructing theoretical rationalizations for his policies in dialectical language, and he was far more original than many of them, but he never changed his essential approach. He was engaged in a struggle for control of the Social Democratic movement. During the course of the struggle he elaborated an organizational weapon that could function in a great variety of conditions. As has been noted often enough, Lenin exuded the militant spirit of Marx in his early Jacobin phase, the Marx of the period 1847–1852 and the Marx who later in life praised the Paris Commune of 1871. No less than his opponents, Lenin had assiduously studied revolutionary history, particularly the French revolutionary era. However, unlike most of the leaders of Russian socialism, Lenin looked to the risk-taking leaders of earlier, failed revolutions and believed that armed now with the correct *theory*, with the force of history behind him, he would be able to avoid their mistakes.

This faith in Marxian theory, combined with Lenin's organizational realism, gave him all of the psychological confidence he needed to take great risks. Marx had issued no timetables, no organizational blueprints, but he had inspired militancy. Lenin quite reasonably read Marx as someone offering not patience but a sword, and he proceeded to amend Marxian theory to take into account organizational imperatives in his immediate context of struggle. He then made ad hoc adjustments to battlefield conditions in a vast array of theoretical writings in areas as diverse as epistemology, political economy, and historical sociology. Neither dialectical "method" nor Marxism had solved the puzzles of history, but they had inspirational value. Lenin had to convince himself that his actions were in accord with Marxism. He convinced himself that in order to be a good Marxist one had to have a disciplined organization.

AFTER *What Is to Be Done?*, whose full theoretical significance became apparent only at the Second Party Congress, Lenin's next major statement came in his analysis of the split in the party *One Step Forward, Two Steps Back* (1904). During 1903 and 1904 he suffered devastating (and prophetic) attacks from the non-Bolshevik press. Aksel'rod pinned the label "bureaucratic centralism" on Lenin's design, a label that Trotsky, who was quite close to Aksel'rod at the time, later used against Stalin. In *One Step Forward, Two Steps Back* Lenin gave his version of the history of the Second Party Congress and its aftermath. Here and in other writings it is clear that his self-image was changing. He chafed at his dependency upon other Social Democratic leaders and implicitly saw himself as the only one with the will to organize a party safe from either the intelligentsia's or the workers' tendencies to disorganization and opportunism. In retrospect, he understood that he had misjudged his closest colleagues and suffered the consequences. Warning signals had gone unheeded on both sides of the conflict. Furthermore, during the post-Congress stages of his struggle with other Social Democratic leaders, he carried his organizational dictum to a point where, instead of flexibility, it inspired rigidity. His organization was too new, too diffident either to adapt itself to mass initiatives or to assume leadership over a broad oppositional front. Thus, 1903–1905 were years of disarray and defeat.

The Emergence of Bolshevism

THE LEADERS of Russian Social Democracy had themselves to blame for the sickliness of their party during 1903–1905. If Lenin was some sort of monster, they had nurtured him. Granting the correctness of the Mensheviks and other softs about Lenin's intentions, it was also true that Lenin had by dint of hard labor and the appeal of his public positions created a following for himself. He had achieved his majority at the Second Party Congress by playing within the rules of the game, but no one before him had played the game so hard. It *seemed* like a different game; even Plekhanov was surprised. Lenin's opponents mobilized themselves too late and engaged in a series of frantic maneuvers to take back the ground that he had already won in a fair fight. The vendettas and escalating intrigues that led to Lenin's virtual isolation in 1904 need not be examined in detail. Although they temporarily upset his plans and caused him severe personal distress, he responded to the traumas of defeat and political isolation by redoubling his efforts. An apt Bolshevik political cartoon of the period shows Lenin as a tomcat playing dead and the Mensheviks as mice celebrating his demise—until he turns upon them ferociously.[4] Lenin's political gifts were formidable, more than a match for his opponents' in the long run.

Months of vituperation, vain efforts at reconciliation, airing of dirty linen in open debate, accusations of unscrupulous behavior, plus the effort of chewing over the Congress, of explaining and justifying his position brought Lenin to a near breakdown. Little knots of factional loyalists tightened around the chief figures. Palpable ill will ruined even the ecumenical celebrations that, at least physically, brought all Russian socialists together. One such occasion was the thirty-third anniversary of the Paris Commune, which for Lenin and others was the harbinger of the dictatorship of the proletariat. There are several accounts of Lenin's speech on March 9(22), 1904 in Geneva, but one of the more interesting ones is by a foreign agent of the Okhrana:

> Lenin starts his speech quietly, confidently, with full consciousness of his powers, begins with a description of the heroic exploits of March 18, 1871, but gradually the speech turns into open agitation, producing an awesome effect on his listeners. No one utters a word. There is complete silence in the hall. Only Lenin's vivid words with total enthusiasm ring out and beat like a hammer on taut nerves. His cries, long live Russian Social Democracy, are drowned out by thunderous applause. The applause goes on for a minute. But involuntarily people shift their glances from Lenin to another group, in the corner, standing off by themselves: the kindly, elderly Vera Ivanovna Zasulich; L. Martov [sic!], with a pleasant, gentle, and highly sympathetic face; glib and self-confident Trotsky and other chiefs of "the minority." Then you notice that they do not join in with Lenin and the others. It is a bit clumsy, offensive . . .[5]

In their memoirs Lenin's adherents attest to the inspirational power of the speech. P. N. Lepeshinskii, one of Lenin's closest allies, who preceded him on the rostrum, recollected that, as they filed out of the packed hall, he heard some of the lesser Mensheviks remark, "Now that's a real leader *[vozhd']*! If we only had one like that!"[6] Even if the story is the product of Lepeshinskii's imagination, it reveals a psychological truth: Lenin acted like a leader, sounded like one. However, these moments when Lenin projected a positive image were obscured in 1903–1904 by his rage against his former colleagues and apparently destructive maneuvers.

Throughout 1904 the Menshevik faction had more of the literary celebrities of Russian Social Democracy and more supporters among the émigrés. Plekhanov, still the symbolic head of the movement, had reluctantly come over to the Mensheviks after the Second Congress of the Foreign League of Russian Revolutionary Social Democrats in October 1903, where they had a clear majority and were able to block Lenin's maneuvers. Other Bolsheviks lost faith in Lenin and became "conciliators" during 1904. Lenin lost control not only of the party organ but over the party council and central committee as well. He could not even rely upon formerly trusted field officers to execute his maneuvers to regain control. Like Plekhanov's *Vademecum* of 1900, the intransigent tone of Lenin's *One Step Forward, Two Steps Back* and his frenzied calls for a new party congress repelled many of his own followers. Party history was repeating itself, with Lenin now playing Plekhanov's former role.

Words lost their meaning as each faction attacked the other: Now the Bolsheviks used the epithet "Bonapartism" to describe Menshevik methods of control; each side accused the other of reviving the old *kruzhok* mentality and perpetuating the intelligentsia's control over the movement. Lenin's willingness to carry on by pamphleteering in 1904[7] without a single ally from the established leadership signified a new stage in his development. It showed more clearly than ever before his ability to break old ties and create new ones.

Both Krupskaia and Valentinov testify to his psychological and physical exhaustion—the latter probably related to depression. After a year of futile struggle with the Menshevik "disorganizers," defections from his own Bolshevik committees, and failure to force a new party congress, he resorted to the therapy of isolation. Accustomed in the past to restorative summer vacations in the countryside, he returned to this method at the end of July 1904. He and Krupskaia loaded rucksacks and spent the next few weeks hiking in the mountains. Nerves restored, Lenin began to recruit literary collaborators for the new organ of the Bolshevik faction with his usual zeal. Berating, pressuring, he promised his followers that they would sentence their cause to "certain, inglorious death" if they tarried.[8]

According to the Bolshevik line, Lenin's faction carried the banner of *partiinost'*, signifying more advanced forms of party organization and discipline appropriate to a genuine workers' movement. The Mensheviks, on the other hand, represented the primitivism of *kruzhkovshchina*, spontaneity, and the anarchy of intelligentsia individualism. They attracted to their ranks all of the elements that Lenin's *Iskra* had repudiated—and did not represent so much the new, massing proletarian forces as decrepit émigré circles. In short, Lenin warned his followers of a regression to the disorganized state of affairs before 1900. Was this merely the rhetoric of factional strife, or did Lenin genuinely believe in the labels he pinned on his opponents? All of the evidence points to a chronically sectarian vision: One was either saved or damned; all of the Social Democrats who were damned, whatever their personal and political history before they fell into error, assumed the characteristics of the old demon of opportunism. It was as if nothing had changed between 1898 and 1905. But the Russo-Japanese War and internal events connected with the crisis of the regime revealed otherwise.

The New Years (Old Style) 1905 issue of the new Bolshevik central organ, *Vpered* (Forward), exulted over the fall of Port Arthur to Japanese armies. The military catastrophe could only hasten the fall of the autocracy. Liberal campaigns, labor unrest, the strike of the Putilov factory, and the demonstration of January 9(22), 1905, yielded Bloody Sunday. In his initial responses to these dramatic developments, Lenin showed a genuinely internationalist spirit:

> The catastrophe of our bitterest enemy signifies not only the approach of Russian freedom. It also heralds a new revolutionary upsurgence of the European proletariat.[9]

> The proletariat of the entire world now looks at the proletariat of all Russia with feverish impatience. The overthrow of Tsarism in Russia, heroically begun by our working class, will be the turning point in the history of all countries, will ease the cause of the workers of all nations, of all states, in all corners of the globe.[10]

On the other hand, when he faced the Russian empire and its explosive internal politics, Lenin showed a dismally sectarian spirit. He seemed to be more intent on sustaining the purity of his faction than joining a revolutionary front and fought any signs of inappropriate blurring of the theoretical and tactical lines separating the Bolsheviks from Social Democratic "opportunists," bourgeois liberals, and neo-*narodniki*. Lenin repeatedly showed his willingness to build an organization from the ground up and to do what none of the other émigré leaders had done—to keep his party free of "soft" alliances and ruthlessly to discipline or expel a series of schismatics. This, rather than any special theoretical acumen, tactical adaptability, or farsightedness, was the key to his success in the long run. In the short run, it led to political isolation.

By 1905 Lenin had become a kind of outcast among the leaders of the Russian Social Democratic movement. Furthermore, despite numerous testimonials to Lenin's personal charisma, it is quite clear that he was as often repellent as attractive. It is impossible to find a single person of stature in the party who did not rebel repeatedly against Lenin between the founding of bolshevism and his death. He succeeded not by dint of his personal magnetism but through his tenacity and orientation toward a goal—by showing decisiveness and a will to control a sometimes broken down and pathetic, but always functioning political machine and by transferring his drive for control to the revolution itself. However, in 1905 Lenin was not ready to play a major role. The situation lent itself to brilliant improvisers rather than to dogged machine politicians.

8

1905

DURING THE period 1905–1097 an explosive revolutionary situation in Russia appeared, yielded a genuinely threatening mass upheaval, and was suppressed by the tsarist regime after limited concessions. Revolutionaries in 1905 faced all of the major issues they would confront a second time in 1917. The revolution of 1905 occurred during an unsuccessful war, which had to be explained in Marxian terms. Party organizers had to adapt themselves to a fluid situation, to a broad revolutionary front stimulated in 1905 by the Russian government's failed experiments with "police socialism" in the labor movement and its untimely concessions to the right wing of the liberal opposition. Not only a new militant liberal party, the Constitutional Democrats, and the revived *narodnik* revolutionary party, the Socialist Revolutionaries, but other sociopolitical forms had emerged spontaneously: unions of workers and professionals and, most important of all, an offshoot of the massive strikes in major industrial centers, workers' councils, soviets, whose deputies often elected members of the revolutionary intelligentsia to their executive committees.

Social Democratic *teoretiki* produced a wealth of tactical responses to the upheaval of 1905. For the first time revolutionaries had to hold up their party banners and programs and collaborate with "class enemies" in the open air of mass meetings instead of the sectarian atmosphere of the underground; they all had to take into account the leftward movement of liberal educated society, the emergence of liberal organizations and a party led by militants who, for the moment, saw no enemies to the Left. The class nature of the peasants was still troubling, the fate of the peasants in the programs of Marxist factions still problematic, but the revolutionary weight of the peasants had to be taken into account. Finally, Social Democrats had to react to the regime's belated political manipulations and concessions and face its still-intact instruments of force.

The impressive range of the responses of Social Democratic leaders and theoreticians reveals once again how doctrines are transformed by both circumstances and individual temperament. The proliferation of new "isms" often signified moves in the game of power among rival sects rather than theoretical illuminations or tactical adaptations to new situations. Lenin's success as a leader depended not only upon personal qualities but upon his ability to project theoretical stature; to attend to the details of organization and jealously guard the autonomy of his party; to distinguish (however artificially) his party from contending groups by carefully crafted theoretical formulations, rhetoric, programs, slogans, and, not least of all, terms of opprobium; to appropriate from others and modify "dialectical" extrapolations of "scientific" Marxism; and to elaborate (now in conjunction with his own "committeemen" and coeditors) the organizational dogmas, which, of course, he believed were already outlined or implicit in Marx and Engels. All of the major actors assiduously studied earlier critical moments in revolutionary history—1793, 1848, and 1871—and sought counsel in the interpretations of Marx and Engels. The leaders of Russian Social Democracy argued like Talmudists over the correct reading of the fathers. As is always the case, they found what they needed, given their patience or impatience, "softness" or "hardness," cautiousness or adventurousness.

The maximalists within the Social Democratic movement revealed themselves to be ready to abandon the orthodox Marxian formula of a two-phase revolution, first bourgeois and then socialist. The two-stage formula had always been problematic, for it assumed that the bourgeoisie were both weak and terribly dangerous, when in fact they were simply weak and dependent upon the military and police force of a quasifeudal regime. It was the regime that was dangerous. But should it lose control over the army and other instruments of internal security, it would collapse—and no significant barrier would stand between the owners of estates and factories and impoverished millions. This stark truth was continually rediscovered by tacticians during the long history of the Russian revolutionary movement. Theoretical formulations calling for a halt at the bourgeois-democratic phase of the revolution and for deference to an admittedly weak class enemy seem, in retrospect, completely unconvincing.

They were emotionally lame as well. How would one go about telling workers that they were not ready for a regime of socialist justice and equality, that more capitalist accumulation would have to occur at their expense before they would be ready for socialism? Workers might notice the implication: They were cannon fodder for the bourgeoisie. What was needed was theoretical justification for having a revolution against both tsarism and the "bourgeoisie" immediately—for that was the only emotionally acceptable revolution, once socialist agitators reached mass constituencies. At first, only the most adventurous—Trotsky and Parvus—would take the leap and call for a socialist revolution. Lenin's compromise in *Two Tactics of Social Democracy in the Democratic Revolution* reflected his doctrinal conservatism as well as his maximalist temperament.

Lenin's shift of focus to the "bourgeois" peasants, as opposed to the educated urban enemies of the tsarist regime, did not remove the awkwardness of the two-phase formula, for Marxian goals of modern, technically advanced, large-scale production could not be achieved if a vast multitude of land poor peasants were to realize their aims—the acquisition of a few more acres for technically backward family cultivation in a communal context. Nonetheless, Lenin seriously revised his peasant policy in view of the increasing importance of the peasants as a revolutionary force since 1902. His willingness to study the peasants' aspirations and to find a way to satisfy their land hunger in 1905 foretold his adoption of the Socialist Revolutionary land program in 1917. Lenin also made hesitant steps toward the idea of permanent revolution, which will be discussed in detail below, but in other ways he was the most conservative of the Social Democratic leaders in that he was still obsessed with the issues of 1900, still focused upon building an organization and guarding the autonomy of the party. Nor did he ever abandon his assumption that the urban proletariat would be the leading force in the revolution.

IN 1905 Lenin, still not fully recovered from the trauma of 1903, had too much of his attention focused on the power struggle within the Social Democratic Party and was too dedicated to his principle of a narrow party to take immediate advantage of the opportunities that emerged. He remained true to his detestation of alliances with soft groups not subordinated to party discipline, and so did many of his field commanders. Bolshevik committeemen also showed a certain inflexibility about enrolling large numbers of workers in their committees, so deeply had they internalized Bolshevik organizational thinking and ideas about leadership. However, here Lenin's sensitivity to Menshevik accusations that the Bolsheviks represented the old intelligentsia elitism and *kruzhkovshchina* evidently affected his policy. He called for the enrollment of workers in the committees in a ratio of four workers to one *intelligent*. In this and other issues Lenin found himself fighting the majority of committeemen—and sometimes losing to them.

Had he been completely inflexible in 1905–1906 and not given in on some issues, Lenin would have failed to sustain and expand his following. He learned that one had to join other organizations even if they were filled with "opportunists" and class enemies and then find a way to use, control, or subvert them. Lenin and his own followers were sometimes out of phase, as first the *praktiki* and then he, the *teoretik* distant from the battlefield, responded to new developments. Now experiencing the difficulties previous generations of *teoretiki* had faced, Lenin showed that for all his similarities to his mentor, he was not simply a clone of Plekhanov, who had become overadapted to émigré life and could not adjust to the new and more complex revolutionary situation.

The unfolding of the revolution of 1905, its failure, and the long and painful aftermath all revealed Lenin's ability to expand his repertoire of political skills. One source of his flexibility, his lack of strong ties of friendship to any group of executives within his own party, had its drawbacks as well as its advantages. He was not the sort of machine politician who operates through a powerful group of cronies. When opportunities or crises arose, his lack of such ties would permit him to bring new blood into the party and to bypass or suppress the opposition of loyal but less flexible party leaders. However, at moments when rapid tactical adjustments had to be made, a hierarchical, narrow, and rule-bound party could as easily turn against him as it could serve him as an obedient instrument. He then had to use bitterly divisive tactics (for example, splitting his opponents, purging, finding new allies) in the struggle against the top- and middle-level executives within the legal structure created by him at party conferences and congresses. And when nothing else worked, he resorted to Plekhanov's methods: He threatened to resign from his posts and searched for alternative instruments, for cadres who would obey his will. In the party crisis created by his decision to seize power in 1917 he threatened to go to the streets and find his support there. In short, Lenin would bind others to party discipline but would not submit to it when he thought himself right and the party wrong.

Lenin's methods permitted him to make adaptations and recruit talent, but he could not foresee all of the consequences of overriding and bypassing long-term loyal executives and putting former opponents or people without reputation in the party into high positions. These battlefield promotions ultimately created insecurities, frictions, jealousies, intraparty bickering, and resentment. Long-term loyalty and service to the party organization meant less to Lenin as a measure of one's standing than one's present usefulness and adherence to the current party line. Those who failed to follow his line became persona non grata—or were purged. He was particularly brutal with the most theoretically talented recruits working for the Bolshevik party organ, once they began to take novel approaches to Marxian theory. Here, Lenin's dogmatic behavior resembled Plekhanov's when the latter had confronted an earlier wave of neo-Kantian deviations from Marxian orthodoxy. Even when less equipped to deal with certain areas of theory than those whom he attacked, Lenin stubbornly asserted his preeminence as party *teoretik*.

The first exclusively Bolshevik congress in April–May 1905 clearly exhibited Lenin's modus operandi in both its strengths and its weaknesses. All of the major ideas, which he developed at great length during the summer of 1905 in *Two Tactics of Social Democracy in the Democratic Revolution,* were already present. A predacious student of the publications of his Social Democratic opponents, Lenin appropriated from them what suited him and held up for ridicule before his followers those theoretical or programmatic positions that made them heretics. For example, in a lengthy speech on April 18 (May 1), 1905, on the position of Bolsheviks toward a provisional government, which would presumably create a new republican state after the overthrow of the tsarist regime, he derided Alexander Martynov's timidity. Martynov, the former leader of economism and one of Lenin's bêtes noires, had candidly and prophetically set forth the peculiarly Marxian dilemma facing a party of the sort created by Lenin. Lenin responded:

> Martynov contends that if we play a decisive role in the insurrection, we face a great danger, that the proletariat will force us to seize power. . . . *Vpered* asks Martynov and L. Martov, what are we talking about: a socialist or democratic dictatorship? . . . The issue of a revolutionary democratic dictatorship has meaning only in the case of the complete overthrow of the autocracy. It is possible that we will repeat the events of 1848–50, that is, the autocracy will not be overthrown but limited and converted into a constitutional monarchy. In that case, it is useless to talk about any sort of democratic dictatorship. But if the autocratic government will indeed be overthrown, then it must be succeeded by another one. And this other one can only be a provisional revolutionary government. . . . It can base itself only on the revolutionary people, that is, on the proletariat and peasants. It can only be a dictatorship, that is, not the organization of "order," but the organization of war. Whoever goes out to storm a fortress cannot refuse to continue the war once he captures the fortress. One of two possibilities: either we take the fortress in order to hold it, or else announce that we are not going to attack, that we only want to occupy a little area near the fortress.[1]

Lenin's subsequent discussion reveals his lack of anxiety about his troops going too far. Quite the contrary, he seemed more anxious that they would not go far enough, that without constant pressure from below the bourgeoisie might yield to counterrevolution. Without the proletarians and peasants (the latter themselves divided into proletarian and bourgeois strata), the bourgeoisie proper might not settle accounts with the tsarist regime; they might not resort to the necessary "plebian" method—revolutionary terror against counterrevolutionaries. Furthermore, like Trotsky and Parvus, Lenin had begun to entertain the possibility of permanent revolution, the notion that a socialist revolution, and not merely a "democratic" one, would catalyze the world proletariat and signal the end of the rule of the bourgeoisie. In this case, the Russian proletariat would not be trapped in its fortress, surrounded and isolated in a world of hostile bourgeois-imperialist powers; it would be the first outpost of the world revolution. The provisional government would give way to a socialist republic and after the export of the revolution (here again, the history of the French Revolution of 1789 instructed Russian Marxists) would be nurtured by more economically developed, fraternal socialist powers.

As all careful students of Lenin have noted, he was temperamentally inclined toward Trotsky's idea of permanent revolution long before he abandoned the notion of a revolutionary-democratic regime of indeterminate tenure. But, unlike Trotsky, he commanded an organization that would, however balkily, follow him in his adventures. In 1905 the idea of permanent revolution, like all of the formulas about provisional governments and the nature of the new state, proved to be academic; in 1917 it became the theoretical justification for Lenin's use of his organizational weapon in a revolutionary seizure of power.

Lenin's future problems with his party were prefigured by his experience at the Third Party Congress in April–May 1905. He had to face once again the old problem of the relationship of the intelligentsia and the workers, now within his own party committees. Here Lenin showed incipient faith in the ability of a disciplined organization to educate and control large numbers of proletarian recruits. The *komitetchiki* need not fear an influx of workers. Lenin had long felt that the intelligentsia were by nature divisive and that not only were the workers by "instinct" more socialist, but they were by nature more subject to organization and discipline. Thus, a ratio of four workers to one *intelligent* in a committee would be salutary.[2] He and Bogdanov introduced a resolution without this rather optimistic formula, but the resolution was designed at least to promote the electoral principle and greater intraparty democracy. A majority of *komitetchiki* opposed it as superfluous.[3]

Krupskaia, the editor of the minutes of the Congress, describes in her memoirs the characteristics of a committeeman:

> The "committeeman" was usually a rather self-assured person. He saw what a tremendous influence the work of the committee had on the masses, and as a rule he recognized no inner-Party democracy. "Inner-Party democracy only leads to trouble with the police. We are connected with the movement as it is," the "committeemen" would say. Inwardly, they rather despised the Party workers abroad, who, in their opinion, had nothing better to do than squabble among themselves. . . . The "committeemen" objected to the overruling influence of the center abroad. At the same time they did not want innovations. They were neither desirous nor capable of adjusting themselves to the quickly changing conditions.[4]

The emergence of the *komitetchiki*, with their own brand of professionalism, their camaraderie, and their resentment of the center, was a fateful development in the history of the Bolshevik Party and possibly the most interesting aspect of the events taking place in London in April–May 1905. The authority of the center was bound to diminish at a time when those on the scene had to make quick decisions themselves. Their self-image changed and confidence grew with each new stage of the revolution of 1905, and they deeply resented the damage done by the conflicts among the *teoretiki*.

Lenin did not escape the criticism of delegates to the Congress, despite his already immense authority among the Bolsheviks. Indeed, the veteran M. G. Tskhakaia was already sensitive to the growing cult of Lenin at the Third Party Congress:

During discussions here I have repeatedly heard in connection with one or another issue: "leninism," "the spirit of the leninist [party] rules," etc. And one orator even threatened to fight against Lenin in the name of "the spirit of Leninism," as if the orator understood it better than comrade Lenin! . . . In free countries, like Germany, I hope there are comrades, no worse than our comrade Lenin, like Kautsky, Bebel, and even one of our teachers, Engels, who don't have "isms" appended to their names, but who enjoy great popularity and standing. We are only s.-d., revolutionary s.-d., scientific socialists, Marxists, like respected comrade Lenin. Our method, like our teaching, is revolutionary; it is our tool; we must use it and not get petrified or ossified in different sorts of "isms."[5]

The delegates opposed Lenin on important organizational matters where they felt that their experience was superior to his. There were disagreements both about the ratio of workers and intellectuals in committees and the relationship of the center to the periphery. Some *komitetchiki* showed suspiciousness of the tendency of the *teoretiki* to subordinate real needs to rhetoric dictated by debates with the rival Mensheviks. Others were sensitive to the danger of losing constituencies to their rivals. Close votes at the Congress, such as the one on intraparty democracy (for example, Lenin and Bogdanov's resolution lost by a vote of 9½ to 12), revealed lack of monolithic unity among both *komitetchiki* and *teoretiki*, although it would be misleading to draw a neat dichotomy. In any case, Lenin remained in control of the party organ and the Bolshevik Party's organization and sectarian spirit remained firmly Leninist.[6] This sectarian spirit turned against Lenin after 1905, when he himself seemed to retreat, to make "soft" adaptations. He lost his position as unquestioned leader of his faction and had to fight in order to regain it.

LENIN'S ROLE as battlefield leader in 1905 was limited by his initial distance from the action and his late arrival. He was far too careful to risk arrest. He contributed nothing of note to the fate of the St. Petersburg Soviet or the soviet movement. Neither he nor his party felt comfortable about working with a mass, open body side by side with figures like Trotsky. It was Trotsky who showed the greatest dynamism, the greatest confidence that he was fitted for leadership in the whirlwind of the Revolution of 1905, and he, not Lenin, became the hero of the moment.

9

The Bronsteins

ALMOST EVERYTHING we know about Trotsky's family comes from his autobiography, but the basic facts are not in dispute, even if an astute reader can sense Trotsky's occasional efforts to appeal to heroic archetypes. For example, it is a propitious accident that his birthday fell on October 26, which in the old style is the anniversary of the October Revolution. No one, least of all Trotsky himself, has suggested that he decided to have the revolution on his birthday, but he does note the coincidence and leaves it to the reader's superstitiousness to do the rest. There is something of the heroic about Trotsky's name, too. The police bureaucracy usually recorded the Hebrew or Yiddish versions of slavicized Jewish names. According to the reports of the Okhrana, David Leontevich Bronstein's real name was David Leib Bronstein.[1] Trotsky was named for his paternal grandfather. The name "Leib" in Yiddish ("Löwe" in German) means "lion." "Lev" is the Slavic version, whereas "Leon" is a Latinate variation on the leonine theme. The prefix "lev-" sometimes means "left," but this too is a happy coincidence.

Trotsky's Jewish origins made a heroic identity at least problematic. During the reign of Alexander II Jews found themselves faced with far more options than had been available to earlier generations and with them more painful choices. The stubborn struggle to maintain Jewish identity in a hostile environment existed side by side with equally strenuous efforts to embrace secular enlightenment. The more secular-minded elements of the Jewish community greeted every sign of liberalism and tried to exploit opportunities for assimilation or integration. By the 1870s many Jewish students had moved beyond gratefulness for the expanded opportunities available to them and joined the revolutionary movement. One of the five members of the People's Will hanged for the assassination of Alexander II was Jewish, and she was only one of a growing number of Jewish revolutionary actors. In the eyes of the Third Section and later the Okhrana Poles and Jews were especially suspect because of the Polish struggle for independence and the deep mistrust and hatred of the two nationalities among government officials charged with internal security. The concentration of Jewish settlements in border areas of the empire gave Jews the opportunity to engage in the smuggling of all kinds of contraband, including revolutionary literature, and gave the authorities more reason to mistrust them. Anti-Polish and anti-Semitic attitudes among officials were supported by popular opinion and even by literary giants like Dostoevsky.

A centuries-old constellation of stereotypes, anxieties, and phobias about Jews survived with undiminished vitality in the Russian empire. One need not dwell on the religious differences, the distancing of Jews from the community at large because of different beliefs, festivals, ceremonies, and other obviously distinguishing features. Jews were seen as having a tribal loyalty stronger than their commitment to any other collectivity. They were plagued by the tendency to be seen simultaneously as cowardly and bloodthirsty; as diabolically able yet parasitic; as city people or bookish people who avoided dirty work and physical labor. The ancient stereotype of the Jew as huckster and money-grubber, of course, was very strong. Odd though it may seem, Jews even paid a price for their tradition of sobriety. Despite numerous lapses, on the whole Jews avoided the more stupefying forms of inebriation practiced in the larger community. This was seen as a sign of rejection, of inhumanity, and, most important of all, of diminished masculinity, although the practice of circumcision had much more direct implications for masculinity. One could go on: Jewish use of the uvular "r" in speech was seen as a symptom of a physiological defect; common Jewish physical characteristics were caricatured and depicted in satanic and monstrous forms; bloody images surrounding Jewish rituals became the basis for hysterical accusations; dark fears about Jewish cruelty and desires for revenge against the gentile community had practical consequences for the treatment of Jews both before and after the revolution.

Long after the initial conditions (aside from the inescapable religious ones) fostering anti-Semitism had changed, alarming new reasons for suspicion appeared, such as the prominence of Jews in a variety of commercial and industrial activities, and reinforced the persistent, old anti-Semitic attitudes. The participation of Jews in the new forms of urban industrial life now permitted anti-Semites to associate Jews with the ills of modernization. Whereas earlier they had represented a dark past, Jews now heralded an anarchic future. Jews were convenient projecting screens for anxieties and could be used as scapegoats by unscrupulous politicians of all persuasions, although the reactionary right—devoted to tradition, chauvinistic, fearful of the changes around them—most frequently exploited folk attitudes in anti-Semitic pogroms.

Despite the enormous contribution of Jews to the development of Russian revolutionary parties over the course of several decades, their strong presence in leading roles in all revolutionary parties, and Lenin's own lack of overt anti-Semitic attitudes, once the revolutionary subculture came into contact with mass constituencies, anti-Semitism emerged in virulent forms. When the Bolshevik faction became a governing party, folk prejudice served the careerism or political opportunism of some Communist leaders and officials or else gave them the occasion to vent their own latent anti-Semitism. To be sure, in a revolutionary subculture and later, a ruling party in which anyone might be suspected at any moment of being corrupted by "bourgeois" influences, ideological heresies, or other ethnic loyalties—including Great Russian chauvinism—suspicion of Jews might be seen as only a special case. But it was a particularly virulent case, even in a multinational empire with a variety of ethnic and social hostilities.

All of these aspects of Jewish identity in the Russian empire played more than a small role in Trotsky's political career as well as in his childhood and adolescence. His mature commitment to a universalistic secular doctrine made any strong assertion of the importance of Jewish identity in his earlier life difficult. In his autobiography he tends to stress his family's departures from the stereotypes and in this way reveals his own rejection of Jewish identity, even though he recognized the evil of anti-Semitism. Trotsky himself cannot be accused of anti-Semitism, but he clearly wanted to put as much distance between himself and a traditional Jewish milieu as he could, mainly by selective remembering.

The family in which Lev Bronstein, later to be known as Leon Trotsky (or, less frequently to the English-speaking world, Lev Trotsky), spent his early childhood had none of the heroic features of the Ul'ianov family. Nonetheless, his parents had more than enough ambition, pride, and resources to develop his gifts. Unlike most Jewish families in the Russian empire, the Bronsteins had chosen agriculture as their way of life. Originally from Poltava, Leib Bronstein, Trotsky's grandfather, joined a group of Jewish farmers belonging to the agricultural colony, Gromokla, which took advantage of the opportunities for commercial farming in Kherson province, in the southern part of the Ukraine. They were the beneficiaries of the Russian empire's vast steppe spaces and the government's desire to fill them with agriculturists. Even Jews were encouraged to colonize these areas and were given the right to acquire land, at least until the reaction in 1882 following the assassination of Alexander II once again took this right away. Jews typically did not farm. Ukrainian Jews connected with agriculture were usually middlemen in the grain trade or estate managers rather than cultivators. David Bronstein confounded the stereotype even more by becoming a successful farmer. He acquired not only the estate of Yanovka, but additional land and herds. By settling on Yanovka, about four kilometers away from Gromokla, the closest town with a *cheder* and synagogue, in 1879, David Bronstein put a geographically slight but culturally important space between himself and the closest Jewish community.

David and Anna Bronstein evidently did not speak Yiddish at home, for Trotsky claims that he, unlike the children who lived in Gromokla, could not speak Yiddish. This in itself is odd. David Bronstein spoke a mixture of Russian and Ukrainian, was fluent in neither, and was illiterate for most of his life. If he had any native tongue, it surely was Yiddish. Perhaps he was determined to assimilate himself and his children to his new millieu and forbade himself and his wife, whose speech habits are not discussed by Trotsky, to speak Yiddish at home. Unless Trotsky has stretched the truth beyond recovery, we must picture the family as marginal to both the Jewish and non-Jewish communities, but more closely tied to the former. Neither David Bronstein nor his wife were religious, and according to Trotsky, his father was not a believer. The family traveled to Gromokla for Rosh Hashanah, but as time went on, they kept fewer and fewer rituals. All of this was by choice, given the trivial distance between Gromokla and Yanovka. Yet David's ties to his family were close enough for him to ask his brother and sister-in-law to house his son during the school sessions, and he wanted his son to have a Jewish education.

All of these puzzles and inconsistencies reveal, more than anything else, the complexities and tensions of cultural assimilation. Of course, it was not necessary to move to the steppe in order to fall under the sway of secular, non-Jewish culture. Deconversions similar to Trotsky's were happening in cities and *shtetels*. One should not make too much of the fact that Trotsky grew up on a farm for the first nine years of his life. It certainly did not inspire in him any deep admiration for the peasants, even though in his autobiography he advertises his compassion for them during his childhood. Lyova's life on the farm was a mere sojourn. He is candid about it. In all of his stories about his efforts to do farmwork, he describes himself as clumsy, inept, and far inferior to his father. The Bronsteins were only lightly rooted in the soil of Kherson province.

David Leontevich's extended family is treated only in passing by his son. The words "father and his brothers his sisters" are crossed out in a manuscript page of a draft of his autobiography, as if his father's relatives were too unremarkable for separate treatment.[2] Descriptions and anecdotes concerning uncles, aunts, and cousins do appear though, usually in connection with Trotsky's schooling. David Leontevich's family was evidently culturally more backward than his wife's, even though she herself was poorly educated and whispered when she read. When he began school at the age of seven, Trotsky stayed in Gromokla with his paternal Uncle Abram and Aunt Rachel. But he was withdrawn from the school there after two years and sent to live with his mother's family in Odessa in 1888. Somehow, he lived in Gromokla, studied Hebrew, but did not learn any Yiddish, even though it was being spoken all around him—and he, a child of extraordinary ability. One senses more than a little memory loss about this period of his life in a man inordinately proud of his powers of recall.

There is also remarkably little about Trotsky's siblings in the autobiography. We know that he was the fifth child of David and Anna, who bore eight children in all, and that four died in infancy of diphtheria and scarlet fever. As a small boy he had seen his younger sister, Rosa, die of diphtheria. Trotsky had an older brother Alexander, an older sister, Elizaveta, and a younger one, Olga.[3] He provides no character sketches or any systematic information about them, although he does mention his brother and sisters occasionally. The young Trotsky also had a nurse, Masha, but she too is only vaguely sketched. Evidently, she was not so much a nurse as a babysitter, for Trotsky remembers that she was only sixteen or so when he was two or three. She is described as his "former nurse" in 1886 or 1887. In his sketches of her, she is a simple girl. The dearth of memoirs about the Bronstein family and Trotsky's status (only now changing) as either demon or nonperson in the Soviet Union make it almost impossible to find out even the most elementary facts about the family aside from those provided by Trotsky himself. We are led to assume that sibling relationships were not significant for Trotsky's development, although we can infer that Olga was his closest companion. Differences in age among the children are not specified, but Alexander and Elizaveta were several years older than Lyova and Olga. They were already adolescents and away at school during Trotsky's early childhood. Trotsky's stories about the relationships of parents and children in his family yield a picture of neglect and lack of affection on the one side and failure to fulfill parental expectations on the other.

In his autobiography Trotsky describes his mother as a capricious person. She did not always submit readily to her husband's demands, there were quarrels, and Anna sometimes shut herself in the bedroom for an entire day. One comes away with the impression that he respected his father more than his mother from early childhood.[4] Trotsky relates how he and his sisters, Elizaveta and Olga, suffered from Anna's temperamental outbursts. She vented her frustrations with life on the farm on the children, meting out punishments unevenly. David showed greater tact and more patience and judiciousness. He showed his stern and autocratic side later, when the children were older.[5]

Trotsky goes to some pains to give the reader a picture of Anna Bronstein's neglect of the younger children. Never forgetting his Marxian orientation, he attributes Anna's neglect of the children and lack of affection to her duties on the farm and in general to the unaccustomed burdens placed upon her, a town-dweller before her marriage. The mother only resentfully accustomed herself to life on the farm, and probably wished her children to live differently. Nonetheless, she shouldered the burden, managing the mill, the household, and even the entire farm when David made trips to town to take care of the commercial side of his business or to buy goods and equipment.

Although David is described as even-tempered compared to his wife, we know from Trotsky's own testimony and from that of others that he had an explosive temper and strong will. In one scene in the autobiography, he administers two slaps to his son for the boy's misadventure with a carriage.[6] One assumes that these were not the only ones Trotsky received during his childhood. David Bronstein's domination within the family had its counterpart in his relations with the local peasants and agricultural laborers who, when confronted with David's superior power, protested by sit-down demonstrations. In Trotsky's stories of David's dealings with his agricultural workers, he describes himself as taking the side of the underdog, even when a little boy. As for his own dealings with his father, his accounts show no affection and imply that David did not understand his sensitive, precocious son. When David demanded that Leva recite his poetry for guests against his will, the child resorted to his mother's style of protest, fleeing in tears, but would finally have to submit. Trotsky often depicted himself as a victim who identified himself with other victims—those who were dependent upon the bounty of their sometimes unjust superiors or were forced to perform under duress. In this last respect he might have had a closer identification with his mother, but it is far more likely that he could not identify himself strongly with anyone in his immediate family.

Even though he describes his homesickness for Yanovka after being sent to school in Odessa, most of the stories dealing with nature and farm life make them sound dangerous—as places where he often suffered hurt or humiliation. In several stories the boy contrasts his father's physical masterfulness to his own weakness and incompetency. Another masterful figure, the mechanic Ivan Vasilevich Greben, was far more attractive to the boy, but the world of the farm and its machines was not for him. Trotsky could impress others, even his father, with his mastery of the world of letters, the one area where he excelled, but when it came to that world, Anna's family had the upper hand, and the young boy left his father's tutelage to live with her nephew when he was nine, before those crucial years in adolescence when he might have formed a strong identification with David. Instead, the cultural gap between them widened, they never really developed a close bond, and they clashed when the father tried to enforce his will on a youth who had chosen another path. Trotsky later forgave David, who outlived his wife (Anna died in 1910 or 1911) and maintained contact with his son until his death in 1922, at the age of eighty-three. After taking Marxian imperatives and David's cultural deficit into account, Trotsky portrayed his father as a hard worker with considerable natural gifts, who played the economic and family role demanded of him surprisingly well.

David's illiteracy did not prevent him from appreciating the need for technical competency. The Bronstein farm boasted a ten-horsepower steam engine for milling and threshing, evidently the best source of mechanical power in the locale, for peasants came from miles around to avail themselves of the Bronstein's milling services for a small fee. Trotsky's narrative makes family life an extension of the farm's economic activity. The family seems to be relatively without boundaries, merging not only with David's relatives at Gromokla and

Bobrinets but with the world of servants and workers living at Yanovka and that of the local peasants and merchants whose economies are connected with it. Ivan Vasilevich, the mechanic, dined with the family. In the machine shop or yard Leva was exposed to ideas and language that children in families like Lenin's could only encounter on the street or in the schoolyard.

David Bronstein's probes into the world of commerce and industry extended far beyond Yanovka. He often withheld his grain in hopes of taking advantage of a seller's market, but sometimes competition forced prices down, and the illiterate second-generation farmer understood that grain from the Argentine had been responsible for his losses. European technique also affected the family's economic life. Trotsky's older brother, Alexander, and his Uncle Brodsky, who had studied brewing in Munich, set up their own brewery in Bobrinets. David envisioned some such fate for his younger son, perhaps as an engineer, and tried to accustom him to the world of business. When Leva was still only a child of seven and later, during his summer vacations, he kept accounts for his father and performed other secretarial services. David had nothing against education. Quite the contrary, he valued it highly, but mainly for its economic utility. All of the father's efforts pointed in the same direction: to a practical career for his younger son, probably a technical one, and the upgrading of the family enterprise.

Unlike the young Lenin, who spent his childhood and adolescence in the hot-house environment of an extremely close and culturally intense family, Trotsky grew up in a relatively loosely integrated family in a culturally indistinct environment. However, the Bronsteins did show vigilance about their children's academic gifts (a vigilance, no doubt, born of both Jewish and late-nineteenth century Russian values as well as practical concerns for upward mobility) and zeal at finding a way to develop them. When Trotsky was a small boy, his parents preferred that he stay away from the farm or the fields surrounding it. He spent many hours on the sofa in the dining room, drawing or, after he acquired literacy at the age of seven, reading and writing. A cousin, Senia Zhivotovskii, who was a year and a half older than Leva and lived in Yanovka at the time, collaborated with him on a journal filled with verses and drawings. Senia, a gifted artist, was his first cultural model. As a child, Leva took great pains with his draftsmanship.[7]

Perhaps the most significant moment in the boy's cultural development occurred during Christmas week, 1886, when a group of mummers came to the farm. They played "Tsar Maximilian" for the Bronsteins. More than forty years later he recorded the impact of that event: "For the first time a fantastic world was revealed to me, a world transformed into theatrical reality." The rhymed speech inspired the boy to try his hand at verse, an activity that at first seemed to incite David but later became a source of paternal pride.[8] Even more important, the performance of the mummers may have inspired the love of the theater that the mature Trotsky exhibited in his revolutionary career. No one in the movement would have a surer sense of revolution as theater than Trotsky; and no one would have quite the gift for transforming imagined revolutionary scenarios into historical reality.

When Leva's love of learning and unusual gifts became clear, he was sent in 1888 to live with Anna's relatives in Odessa. He was the child who carried the family hopes. Although Trotsky says little about them, he reveals that his older brother, Alexander, and sister Elizaveta had not distinguished themselves as students. He too was already at a disadvantage when he arrived in Odessa because he had learned the Bronstein Russian-Ukrainian jargon (if, indeed, no Yiddish was spoken at home) rather than pure Russian, but the Shpentsers belonged to the Russified Jewish intelligentsia of Odessa and were up to the task of remedying Leva's lacks. Moisei Fillipovich, in his late twenties at the time of their first encounter, was already a family celebrity— the only real *intelligent* they had produced. He had been denied a university education because of his political offenses in high school but had nonetheless acquired sufficient background to make his way in the world of publishing. In 1887 he had not gotten his venture on its feet, yet he was about to marry, and the Bronsteins evidently offered him a decent sum to board their son. Moisei Fillipovich spent the summer of 1887 in Yanovka, partly for reasons of health but also to prepare his cousin for city life. One summer in his cousin's company was sufficient to make the boy aware of Yanovka's primitiveness.

10

The Impostor

DURING THE years when Trotsky lived with Moisei Fillipovich, his wife, Fanny Solomonovna Shpentser, was the family's real provider. She was the headmistress of the State School for Jewish Girls and gave birth to a daughter, Vera, shortly before Leva's arrival. Although both of the Shpentsers left short memoirs of Trotsky's life with them in Odessa, they reveal little and, given the importance of his six years in their household, Trotsky has surprisingly little to say of them in his autobiography. Yet they transformed him from a country boy to a city boy, changed his mode of dress, his manners, and his grooming, and set him up to enroll in the St. Paul's *realschule*, a highly regarded secondary school in Odessa. In their home he was exposed to the culture of the world of publishing, met middle-level intelligentsia figures, and, most important of all, began to develop a sense of style. Although Trotsky expresses respect and gratefulness to both Shpentsers and affection for Fanny Solomonovna in his autobiography, conflicts are also indicated. Their more liberal regime later permitted forms of adolescent rebellion that would have been ruthlessly crushed in his own family setting, but for a country child the standards of behavior demanded by the Shpentsers caused friction at first and inspired nostalgia for Leva's first family.[1]

Although Leva returned to Yanovka for his summer vacations, he immediately sensed the cultural gap. Not only did he see things differently, he was treated differently. The boy's princely status in his family grew apace. At first only carrying the family's hopes, he soon became the repository of their pride. Once fully prepared for school (he had to spend a year in a preparatory course after passing the admissions examination at an insufficiently high level, given the standards and quotas set for Jewish applicants), he quickly rose to the top of his class. His certificates of merit graced the entrance hall of the Bronstein house. And the boy looked the part. Handsome, with thick dark hair, clear blue eyes, and prominent dimples, he exuded brightness and confidence. No longer neglected and humiliated, Leva commanded everyone's attention. Indeed, he became the perfect child—too perfect.[2]

During his transformation from country boy to city boy he paid special attention to his language and appearance. Any criticisms were engraved upon his memory, and, probably by way of overcompensation, he took great pains crafting his writing and perfecting his penmanship. In dress he became so fastidious that Fanny Solomonovna remembered his anxiety about the smallest bit of lint on his clothing.[3] Trotsky himself recalls a traumatic incident. The nine-year-old student set out for school on the first day of classes, decked out in the full regalia of St. Paul's *realschule:* cloak, jacket with golden buttons, belt with gleaming buckle, peaked cap with a medallion inscribed with the school insignia, intertwined leaves surrounding a monogram. Leva carried a new leather bookbag and exuded self-importance.[4] On Uspenskii Street, however, he was confronted by a street urchin who

> . . . stopped, looked me up and down, hawked deeply, and spat on my sleeve. It was as if a lightning bolt had struck from a clear sky and reduced me to ashes. It seemed especially unfathomable, that he could spit on this wonderful new uniform, which signified a profound change in my life.[5]

Struck dumb for a few moments, he gathered some chestnut leaves from the street and wiped the spit off his uniform. In recounting the incident, Trotsky expresses his sympathy for the insulter, whose entire humiliated existence justified the attack. The story, perhaps unwittingly, foretells the resentment and similarly untoward behavior of future colleagues, whom Trotsky found more difficult to forgive.

Still another humiliation awaited Trotsky when he arrived in St. Paul's yard. The school monitor told him that students in the preparatory class did not have the privilege of wearing the medallion, the buckle, or the buttons. If he had been reduced to ashes on the road to St. Paul's, he was now utterly annihilated. When a man of fifty recounts such an early traumatic episode (especially if he is a man with Trotsky's remarkable penchant for analogies), one suspects that the message extends beyond the particular event. It is the story of an unwitting impostor who suffers a double humiliation, first for his pride and then for his transgression. Perhaps in summing up his career about forty years later in 1929, Trotsky unconsciously sensed the connection between this incident and another one that occurred in Paris in 1902, when he was allied with Lenin on *The Spark*.

> Once we decided to take Lenin to the opera. . . . An utterly unmusical reminiscence is always associated in my mind with this visit to the opera. In Paris Lenin had bought himself a pair of shoes that had turned out to be too tight. As fate would have it, I badly needed a new pair of shoes just then. I was given Lenin's, and at first I thought they fitted me perfectly. The trip to the opera was all right. But in the theatre I began to have pains. On the way home I suffered agonies, while Lenin twitted me all the more mercilessly because he had gone through the same thing for several hours in those shoes.[6]

Although Trotsky's identification with Lenin (they both had experienced the same suffering) is central to the telling of the story, it nonetheless suggests that he should not have tried to step into Lenin's shoes—and that Lenin had derived a certain pleasure from Trotsky's pain. Trotsky, like Lenin in 1903, was later accused of Napoleonic ambitions. His relationship with Lenin—as Lenin's ally during the heyday of *The Spark* and later as Lenin's partner and possible heir after 1917—led to both triumph and disaster. Trotsky was seen as a Judas figure by Lenin after his "defection" at the Second Congress in 1903 and then as a Menshevik masquerading as a Bolshevik after 1917. Finally, he was depicted as a betrayer of Lenin and the party after Lenin's death. Stalin and his henchmen falsified history to strip Trotsky of his real achievements in the October Revolution and the Civil War. The drama first presented in homely form in the story of the school uniform recurs as the tragedy of his political career: Trotsky aspires to an exalted role, acquires the regalia of a position, provokes the resentment of others, and then is labeled an impostor.

Despite his inauspicious beginning at St. Paul's, Leva flourished there. The curriculum of the *realschule* emphasized mathematics and the natural sciences rather than the humanities, and the students did not have to take Latin and Greek. The scientistic spirit of the times favored the *realschule* and made it seem progressive relative to the gymnasium, but the regime had made the latter the preferred preparatory school for the gentry, and enrollment in the *realschule* usually signified either a progressive point of view or plebian status. St. Paul's had its own special characteristics. At first a Lutheran institution serving Odessa's German colony, it had become Russified without, however, completely losing its Germanic character. The strictness of schedule and demands for accuracy suited Trotsky. Dutiful, precise, and equally talented in verbal and mathematical disciplines, he quickly gathered his rewards: the highest grades, general recognition of his abilities, and the resentment that accompanies such distinction among fellow adolescents.

The boy was otherwise undistinguished, resembling somewhat a character in the tales of his younger contemporary, Isaac Babel, whose pale, studious Odessan Jewish boys shun the sea, do not learn to swim or fish, and fare badly in encounters with rougher sorts. Although he was well built and of medium height, Leva was neither athletically gifted nor robust. He suffered from "chronic catarrh of the digestive tract"—perhaps what would be diagnosed as colitis in a modern medical idiom. The symptoms were connected with "nervous shocks." In the fourth class, when he was fourteen, he had to be sent to Yanovka to recover.[7] As an adult, Trotsky also suffered from debilitating illnesses, mysterious fevers that appeared when he was under extreme nervous tension and that, like his childhood "catarrh," incapacitated him for long periods.

Although resented for his academic feats, his dutifulness, and fastidiousness, Leva was not unpopular in St. Paul's. Alongside a certain kind of moral courage, he carried the weapon of a competitive person who is diffident about physical encounters—a deadly wit.[8] He also carried with him from Yanovka a strong feeling for underdogs, a trait that almost foreshortened his career at St. Paul's. In the second class (Trotsky was twelve) his intimidating French instructor cruelly victimized one of the poorer students, for which all the others in the class arranged a "concert," a howl in unison as the instructor left the classroom. When only some of the boys were selected for punishment, they soon betrayed others—including Trotsky—and one obviously resentful classmate began to dredge up some of Trotsky's previously undetected sins against the school authorities. Trotsky was expelled for the remainder of the school year, although he was permitted to return to take his final examinations.[9]

According to the memoirs of Skorcheletti, a fellow student at St. Paul's, Trotsky had confronted the instructor, Burnande, and directly insulted him. Skorcheletti relates another incident involving a student inordinately proud of his gentry background—one Kologrivov, who habitually boasted about the role of the gentry in Russia. Once, when Kologrivov, Trotsky, and other students were walking together, this proud scion of the gentry said, "The *dvorianstvo* [nobility] are the legs which support a gigantic Russia." Trotsky allegedly replied, "Perhaps, but they have feet of clay—they are crumbling and then all of Russia will go to the devil."[10] Although the last incident (if, indeed, it really happened) would nicely endow Leva with social and political consciousness as well as wit, in his autobiography Trotsky only narrates the one incident with Burnande, and in such a way that he can quite consciously connect it with his later career:

> What had happened? Had I come too rashly to the aid of an injured boy who was not my friend and for whom otherwise I had no feeling of sympathy? Or had I placed too much confidence in the united support of the class? . . . I was admitted to the third grade. There I met most of the boys who had either betrayed me, or defended me, or had remained neutral. This determined my personal relations for a long time. . . . Such, one might say, was the first political test I underwent. These were the groups that resulted from the episode: the talebearers and the envious at the one pole, the frank, courageous boys at the other, and the neutral vacillating mass in the middle. These three groups never quite disappeared even during the years that followed. I met them again and again in my life, in the most varied circumstances.[11]

The incident at St. Paul's probably called to mind (among other political fights) the struggle between Trotsky and the party *apparat* that began in 1923. Lenin had given Trotsky writings that he could have used against Stalin and others in the fight over the Georgian affair in 1922 and the handling of the nationalities in general. After Lenin's serious stroke in March 1923 Trotsky had withheld the materials and refrained from attacking Stalin. The move proved to be a mistake. Instead of being rewarded for protecting Stalin and trying to be a good comrade, he was accused of delinquency. Trotsky became involved in a series of attacks and counterattacks in which he and his opponents smeared each other for earlier sins. Naturally, he saw himself as the envied one, the one whom the dying Lenin had chosen as his ally. He and his fellow left oppositionists were the frank, courageous faction. The triumvirate of Zinov'ev, Kamenev, and Stalin at first led the resentful tale-bearers, and the great mass of the party wavered for several years before Stalin and the *apparat* gained control.

Another incident, in which Trotsky supported a classmate's protest against an irresponsible instructor, marred Trotsky's record in the fifth class, but the remainder of his career at St. Paul's was uneventful. Trotsky did not feel any nostalgia for St. Paul's. To be sure, in his autobiography he recognizes that in the course of seven years the school had trained him well, but he gives no indication that he found there either models, inspiration, or a path in life. Rather, the cowardly behavior of most students in the face of arbitrary and unjust authority and the authorities' lack of dignity gave him negative models and lessons. His own success as a student had made him a leader in the eyes of some students, like Kostya Rozenshtein, his closest friend, but he had made enemies too. At first, he had made every effort to please everyone with his appearance, manners, and achievements, but he was often repaid with envy, resentment, and unjust treatment. Although self-critical, he did not shed his sense of superiority. Self-criticism only spurred him to higher levels of achievement and greater pride; the envy and resentment of others did not shake his self-confidence. He left St. Paul's in 1895 at the age of sixteen with his pride and ambition intact but with incipient rebellion in his soul.

The same sensitivity to inequality and injustice that Trotsky had shown at St. Paul's as well as a growing urge to protest showed up particularly strongly during summers at Yanovka in his relationship with his father. He found it more difficult to endure David's stinginess with workers and service people. By his late teens he knew what he did not want to be: petit bourgeois, official, or servile. He did not have a positive sense of Jewish identity to fall back on. Although he mentions Hebrew lessons beginning in 1890, he does not say whether they were in preparation for his ritual passage into manhood, his Bar Mitzvah. He made up for his lack of religious feeling or strong ethnic identity by yearning for a progressive, rational identity as citizen of an advanced society.

Trotsky's rejection of everything but academic achievement and progressive values inspired in him an overvaluation of the "scientific" approach to reality: the search for general laws. In this respect he was a fairly typical young *intelligent*. Like many young perfectionists, he found his immediate milieu, town and country, family and nonfamily, both oppressive and backward. Unlike the young Lenin, who entered his seventeenth year with a solid positive identity grounded in his family and school experiences and showing only the usual adolescent rebelliousness against school authorities, at the same age Trotsky had only his own gifts and the vague longing to escape to some better world—to the United States or to western Europe. He had been alienated from his family by town life, higher culture, and his growing perception of the Bronsteins' mean, petit-bourgeois spirit; and he had been alienated from St. Paul's by its cruel authoritarianism, formalism, and injustice. He entered his seventeenth year with an inchoate spirit of opposition. In his own words:

> During my school years I held no political views, nor for that matter had I any desire to acquire them. At the same time my subconscious strivings were tinged by a spirit of opposition. I had an intense hatred of the existing order, of injustice, of tyranny. . . . It came from the conditions existing during the reign of Alexander III [1881–1894]; the high-handedness of the police; the exploitation practiced by landlords; the grafting by officials; the nationalistic restrictions; the cases of injustice at school and in the street; the close contact with children, servants and laborers in the country; the conversations in the workshop; the humane spirit in the Shpentser family; the reading of Nekrasov's poems and of all kinds of other books, and in general, the entire social atmosphere of the time. . . . One thing is certain: even then life stored within my consciousness a considerable load of social protest. What did it consist of? Sympathy for the down-trodden and indignation over injustice—the latter was perhaps the stronger feeling.[12]

The young graduate of St. Paul's had the temerity to mention his democratic hopes to his father in the summer of 1895 but received no support from him. Quite the contrary, David Bronstein warned his son that dreams of a constitution were futile. The reign of Alexander III had created in the older generation, at least, the illusion that the tsarist regime could stand for hundreds of years.[13] Nor did Trotsky receive any stimulus for his new political and social interests from his older siblings. In any case, he had to return to school for an additional year in order to prepare for higher education. St. Paul's only offered six grades —one year less than the usual preparatory curriculum. Thus, in the autumn of 1895 the sixteen-year-old set out for another Black Sea port, Nikolaev. There he met young people his age who did have progressive views.

When Trotsky entered the Dikshtein household as a boarder in 1896, his landlady's daughter, a Marxist and friend of Alexandra Sokolovskaia, Trotsky's future wife, noted how perfect his manners and appearance were. He dressed like an Odessan dandy and wore the stylish cap of his new *realschule* over a smooth, short haircut.[14] Had David Bronstein known that he had entrusted his son to a household with young radicals in it, he would no doubt have made other arrangements. But it would be a mistake to see this accidental living arrangement as the source of Trotsky's radicalization in 1896. The young Trotsky would have encountered the political and social movements developing in southern Russia at the turn of the century in one way or another. At first, he

was reluctant to break with his past at St. Paul's or his central purpose—
academic achievement in preparation for higher education in mathematics or
some technological speciality.[15] During his first month in Nikolaev he prepared
as assiduously as ever for his classes and rejected the socialist ideas pressed
upon him by the younger Dikshteins, who were somewhat older than he.

11

Lev Bronstein's Two Conversions

TROTSKY HELD out for only a few months before the influence of the members of a study circle located in Nikolaev converted him. He does not narrate any distinct moment of conversion, but the memoirs of those close to him in 1895–1896 describe a radically transformed person, and the chapter that tells about the change in his autobiography is entitled "The Break." When drawn into the debates between *narodniki* and Marxists, he found his knowledge deficient and resorted to the usual remedies — plunging into books and exploiting the knowledge of those already initiated. Trotsky gained access to forbidden pamphlets and books with the help of a leftist bookseller named Galatskii[1] and received his education in socialism in the pleasant setting of Franz Shvigovskii's study circle. Shvigovskii, Czech by origin and a gardener by profession, lived on the property of one Lanovskii and maintained his own orchard and vegetable and flower gardens on the plot of land around his cottage.[2] Shvigovskii himself and the majority of the approximately thirty young people who frequented the circle and sometimes lived in the cottage for short periods were inclined to the *narodnik* point of view. Two Marxists, Alexandra Sokolovskaia and G. A. Ziv, always found themselves on the defensive.

At first, the *narodnik* school of subjective sociology founded by Lavrov and Mikhailovskii in the late 1860s strongly attracted Trotsky.[3] Starting with the idea that "critically thinking individuals" owed a debt to society, Lavrov demanded that they repay it by embodying their ideals of truth and justice in a new social order. Even though Lavrov's ethical approach was basically Kantian, the subjective sociologists' "scientific ethic" intersected with Chernyshevskii's and Pisarev's equally "scientific" nihilist ethic of rational egoism, which held that it was also pleasurable and utilitarian (Jeremy Bentham and John Stuart Mill had also directly influenced Trotsky) to sacrifice oneself or work unremittingly for the general good. All of them proposed not just study but action in the service of one's ideals. The moral and intellectual heroism demanded of the young *intelligent* as well as the exalted role sketched in Lavrov's *Historical Letters* and the vision of the trajectory of human development in Mikhailovskii's *What is Progress?* appealed directly to Trotsky's emerging self-identity. The subjective school of sociology made the socialist intelligentsia the vanguard of progress in human history, but according to its major theorists, Russian socialists had to assume a *narodnik* position, given the particular economic, social, and political situation in the Russian empire. This, of course, was the position Lenin had assailed in his earliest works.

Trotsky's claim that he experienced a vivid new feeling of "joining a great chain as a tiny link"[4] might seem less than authentic, or at the very least, a poor description of the appeal of the *narodnik* movement to him, given the attractiveness of the heroic element of the "critically thinking individual's" identity. However, the idea of self-sacrifice and loss of his unsatisfying identity as a lonely young *intelligent* of petit-bourgeois Jewish background must have had equally strong appeal. Lavrov (among others) had called for subordination to the discipline of an organized party in *Historical Letters* and in the late 1870s both Land and Freedom and its offshoot, the People's Will, had responded by teaching their members how to fade into the underground. In short, the theoreticians of populism had united in one doctrine an appeal to the adolescent *intelligent's* ambivalent desire for both heroism and service to the people, self-affirmation and self-effacement, rebellion and self-subordination, detachment from one milieu and absorption into another one. The story of Alexander Ul'ianov is as good an illustration as any.

None of this was achieved painlessly. Nikolaev was close enough to Yanovka for frequent visits by David Bronstein. Indeed, that was one of the reasons for the choice of Nikolaev. The elder Bronstein kept a close eye on his son and grew alarmed when he saw the visible signs of his transformation during the winter of 1895–1896. The landlady's daughter provides a vivid picture of David rudely berating his son and her mother as well.

During this period he often visited. He is more accurately described as a tall person than one of average height—bearded. He had an intelligent face, an imperious character, stubborn. Given his total lack of education, he could even be called coarse. Noticing the change in his son, he hurled sharp reproaches at my mother, accusing her of failing to look after Trotsky vigilantly. The father's conversations with Trotsky were carried on in a harsh tone of voice. Trotsky decisively refused to study in a university or institute, although the father said he would pay for everything. Later he refused his father's money and help and broke with him completely.[5]

David Bronstein had decided that his son would be an engineer and advance the family fortunes by building sugar refineries and breweries.[6] The sixteen-year-old just as vehemently demanded his right to decide his own fate. However, Dikshtein was wrong in her belief that Trotsky had broken with his father completely in the spring of 1896. The struggle did not end when Trotsky moved out of the Dikshtein house, nor did his relations with his family.

The *realschule* in Nikolaev presented less of an obstacle to Trotsky's new interests than his stubborn father. It was an easier school and less strict than St. Paul's. He could coast on what he had already learned and even miss classes without relinquishing his position as star pupil. During the latter part of the winter and spring of 1896 he spent long nights in Shvigovskii's cottage or garden discussing social issues around the ever-present samovar with other members of Rassadnik (the Seedbed), as they called their circle. In the spring of 1896 Trotsky and Shvigovskii's younger brother, who had befriended him in the *realschule* in Nikolaev, planted flowers in the garden in the form of the initials "S R", signifying "Social Revolution."[7] This was indeed the springtime of Trotsky's career as a revolutionary socialist. Like the young Lenin in Samara, Trotsky encountered older mentors, exiled veterans of the *narodnik* movement in Nikolaev. (The tsarist regime's habit of exiling political criminals to provincial towns was still a boon to the political education of the locals.) Franz Shvigovskii, who had never been involved in actual revolutionary activity, was a young man of twenty-eight to thirty in 1896,[8] more like a kindly older brother than a substitute father.

At the time of Trotsky's rejection of his father's plans for him, probably near the end of the school year in 1896, Shvigovskii moved to a larger house on the outskirts of Nikolaev, and Trotsky moved in with him.[9] Trotsky, Ziv, Alexandra Sokolvskaia's two brothers, and the Shvigovskii brothers formed a kind of commune. Each contributed eleven rubles per month, a quite modest expenditure, but in view of Trotsky's rejection of parental support, he had to scrape the sum together by tutoring.[10] David Bronstein, who refused to give up his son without a fight, on one occasion stormed into the house, almost tripped over Vegman, one of Shvigovskii's guests who was sleeping on the floor, and shouted at him: "So you've run away from your father too?"[11] The emotional strain of the break no doubt affected Trotsky as well, but he held out against family pressure for some months. With some coaxing from Shvigovskii, however, he decided to return to Odessa.[12]

Trotsky, like Lenin, tended to lapse into depression when not fully mobilized; he could not sustain half-hearted commitments. During the period of struggle beginning in the spring of 1896 and ending in the late autumn, when he was torn between his father's demands and his own, Trotsky showed serious signs of psychological distress. His ordinary high spirits gave way to gloom. He deeply doubted his own will power, his capacity to make decisions. Like all those actively seeking faith—in this case a rational faith—he sometimes despaired of achieving it. Trotsky was even more intense than Lenin, less patient, and this led to frequent physical breakdowns as well as an accelerated career. During the spring he had a fainting spell in the course of one of his bouts of, probably, psychosomatic illness.[13]

What is notable about Trotsky by comparison with Lenin is the rapidity with which he broke with the past. Within two years he made the shift from apolitical student to full-time revolutionary. Instead of studying systematically, cross-examining both books and people at length, Trotsky jumped from one book to another feverishly and launched into debate with little or no preparation. This did not at all resemble the Ul'ianov modus operandi. To be sure, Lenin had gone through an early crisis and a sudden transformation precipitated by Sasha's death, but it was followed by a long period of rustication and backbreaking study. Trotsky's first conversion, to populism, occurred in early 1896, his arrest, signifying a final break with a legal existence, in January 1898, and his second decisive conversion, to Marxism, no later than 1899. He thus had traveled his path from populism to doctrinaire Marxism in roughly three years, or even less if one takes into account his transition to Marxism in 1897–1898. It had taken Lenin roughly five years (1887–1892) to complete the same journey, his apprenticeship having lasted roughly eight years, if one adds his first efforts at propaganda and agitation in St. Petersburg before his arrest. Even a brief overview suggests that Lenin's preparation for a revolutionary career had a systematically professional character about it compared to Trotsky's.

Although less systematic in his preparation, Trotsky was no less zealous in his desire to find a "system" to which he could devote himself—a scientific doctrine he could serve wholeheartedly—and Shvigovskii's commune permitted him to do this. Despite his initial lack of background, from the beginning Trotsky was an impressive figure in Shvigovskii's study circle. He summoned up intuition, improvised, and, once settling upon a position, used his impressive debating skills to subdue an opponent. Although this suggests superficiality and dilettantism, Trotsky had one of those remarkable minds that could anticipate intermediate steps and whole arguments and dispose of them instantaneously. With his opponents often providing the facts and figures, he could swiftly see structures and patterns in data and construct convincing arguments around them with iron logic. (Given his superficial knowledge, Trotsky found it expedient to appeal to logic.) In our current idiom, he was a quick study. Trotsky not only outshone his opponents in logic and debating skills, he devastated them with his sarcastic wit. The handful of memoirists who describe the impression he made do not mince words: He was arrogant, supremely confident, boastful, insolent, and proud.[14] He did not stop at wounding and humiliating opponents. Aleksandra Sokolovskaia, his future wife but at the time his ideological opponent, was angered by his successful effort to exclude the journal *New Word* from the public library in Nikolaev when it changed from a *narodnik* to a Marxist orientation.[15] As the youngest member of the group and already recognized as their ablest recruit, Trotsky was given special license.

The characteristics described by Trotsky's comrades of 1895–1898 did not disappear. The boastfulness noted by his earliest comrades is confirmed by Skorcheletti, who maintained contact with Trotsky during the revolution of 1905 and lived near him in Finland when Trotsky was in hiding in Usiriko between trips to St. Petersburg. According to Skorcheletti:

> At the time he was completely convinced that a Russian revolution would happen during his lifetime, and would always say, "I'll be Danton." We therefore called him "Danton."[16]

Of course, it would be good to know Trotsky's tone of voice when he said such things and whether he had a smile on his face, but there are other indications that even if he was joking, he was also asserting an important part of his self-identity. Ziv and Skorcheletti claim that Trotsky had studied techniques of debate, that he consciously crafted his oratorical skills and modeled himself on the great socialist tribune, Ferdinand Lassalle. There are also suggestions of a grandiose self-image—an adolescent one, to be sure. His youthful conspiratorial name L'vov was simply the genitive plural of his first name and signified descent from the king of beasts. In a police photo of the period Trotsky actually does faintly resemble a lion, but the studiedly leonine look in those days easily gave way to grins and clowning, according to friends like Shatunovskii, who saw only in the later Trotsky what Ziv claims to have seen in the earlier one. One cannot rule out at least some backward projection, but it is impossible to deny Trotsky's later high-handedness and need for self-display. Elements of grandiosity in his self-image outlived adolescence and were reinforced by historical reality.

G. A. Ziv, the only eyewitness to Trotsky's performances in Shvigovskii's garden to publish his memoirs, believed that it was an intense desire to demonstrate his superiority rather than devotion to scientific truths and dedication to a cause that drove Trotsky to out-perform and humiliate his comrades. A physician in 1921, when he published his memoirs, Ziv was evidently also an amateur psychologist and succinctly presented his view of Trotsky's personality:

> Bronstein's actual individuality lay neither in cognition nor in feeling, but in will; his individuality resided entirely in his activism *[aktivnost']*. To actively display his will, to raise himself above everyone, to be everywhere and always the first—this was always the basis and essence of Bronstein's personality; the remaining aspects of his psyche were only auxiliary superstructures and exten-

sions. . . . The workers interested him as necessary objects of his activism, his revolutionary activity *[deiatel'nost']*; comrades interested him as means, through which he displayed his revolutionary activism; he loved the workers, loved his comrades in the organization, because he loved himself in them.[17]

Trotsky's first biographer, Max Eastman, had access to this and other unflattering assessments, and although obviously ambivalent toward his subject from the very beginning, he found a way to put the above traits in a different light:

> The Russians, whose language often shows a better psychology than ours, have a special word for this quality, distinguishing it on the one hand from ambition, and on the other hand from self-conceit. . . . He was exceedingly *samoliubiv*, and you have to know what that word means if you want to understand him and appreciate the difficulties that he must have had, or life had, in disciplining his nature. It means a fierce eagerness to excel others, and an intemperate sensitiveness to a challenge, or to the presence of a challenging personality. It . . . might be called in English an instinct for rivalry. . . . It involves an alert awareness of self, and is upon the whole a very disagreeable trait—especially as it appears to those horses who were not bred for speed.[18]

Although Trotsky's attitude and methods divided his colleagues into two camps—the admiring and the resentful—both were galvanized by his presence. One of the witnesses to his early activity, a machinist named Shatunovskii who worked in a boiler factory in Odessa, while admitting that Trotsky made enemies, claimed that his personal magnetism won over even opponents.[19] Trotsky's need for action had the effect of setting other people into motion. His motto of the time was: "Faith is dead without action."[20] With the other members of Rassadnik he decided to organize a free university. They would educate each other. After two lectures on sociology by Trotsky, the enterprise collapsed. A successful struggle against an increase in fees levied by the public library in Nikolaev occupied some of his time and energy, but triumph left him idle again. He then turned to writing as his major outlet and coauthored a play in which an older *narodnik* courts a young Marxist woman, who rejects him (and his populism) mercilessly. On behalf of the latter creative effort, he even rented a room in another house with his coauthor, Il'ia Sokolovskii. This feverish product of teenage political bohemianism failed to see the light of day. It does, however, suggest that Il'ia's sister, Alexandra Sokolovskaia, the probable inspiration for the woman in the play, had begun to wear away at Trotsky's *narodnik* faith.[21]

He began vacillating in other ways as autumn approached. Schools, after all, were the sites of his major triumphs, and despite his idyll in Shvigovskii's garden, Trotsky found it difficult to break all at once the rhythms of student life. Although he changed into the costume of the Rassadnik group, blue workers' blouse and straw hat (they also carried distinctive black canes),[22] stopped shining his shoes, and let his neat haircut grow into a disheveled mop, Trotsky could not suppress the effects of seven years in the Shpentser household and St. Paul's. When Vegman saw him for the first time, he noted that Trotsky's scruffy appearance formed an odd contrast with his lordly ways.[23]

Trotsky himself understood that his transformation was incomplete, that he needed more time to ponder his fate. Sometime during the summer of 1896 he compromised with his father: He would return to Odessa and investigate the possibility of becoming a mathematician. While there, he would live with an uncle, Krakovshchinskii, who owned a boiler factory in the city and would explain the business to him.[24]

Trotsky attended a few lectures in mathematics at Odessa University during the first semester, evidently as an auditor, discussed economics with his uncle, and, finding no inspiration in either, began instead to propagandize Krakov-shchinskii's employees.[25] He took a position teaching the second class in a secondary school, but spent most of his time organizing a workers' circle and debating tactics with the leader of a competing group. By his own assessment, his propaganda among the workers yielded insignificant results,[26] but it affected his other commitments. He often came late to work, had several tiffs with the school administration, and when asked to cut his hair, abandoned the position.[27] After being warned that he might be arrested, Trotsky took a steamboat to Nikolaev in the late autumn and returned to Shvigovskii's, where he resumed his self-education in socialism and, like Lenin in 1887–1892, prepared himself for a decisive moment.[28] Alexandra Sokolovskaia claims that while in Odessa Trotsky read works by Plekhanov, Struve, and Marx.[29] Evidently, what he read only incensed him. According to his own testimony, Trotsky had read *The New Word*, the organ of legal Marxism, which inspired him to write an adolescent blast (rejected by the Odessa journal, *Southern Review*) against Peter Struve entitled "The Reptiles on the Pages of a St. Petersburg Journal."[30]

Trotsky remained an adolescent in most respects. He arranged a cruel trick on Alexandra Sokolovskaia that was probably a symptom of his infatuation with her. One member of the circle remembered her as "slender, well proportioned, with excellent features, feminine, intelligent, gentle." He added that they were all in love with her.[31] Toward the end of 1896 Shvigovskii told her that in Odessa Trotsky had become a Marxist, a piece of news that could only hearten her, until now one of only two Marxists in Nikolaev. At a New Year's Eve party at Shvigovskii's she greeted Trotsky, and he enthusiastically confirmed that he had indeed become a Marxist. Just as the merry crowd began to toll off twelve to greet the New Year, Trotsky rose and toasted: "Let all Marxists be cursed— all who bring aridity and hard-heartedness to all aspects of life."[32] Sokolovskaia would not accept Shvigovskii's apology and explanation that it was all a joke. Her relations with Trotsky were mended during a campaign to democratize the membership of the library in Nikolaev and to put Shvigovskii and another member of the circle on the board of directors. Trotsky both organized the campaign and donated money to the cause. Sokolovskaia, with misgivings, renewed comradely relations.[33]

Within a few weeks after returning to Nikolaev, an abrupt shift in mood in socialist circles cut short Trotsky's period of revolutionary dilettantism. Students from the major industrial and university cities (some of them expelled for participating in demonstrations) brought vivid news about the large-scale strikes in St. Petersburg, the upsurge in the student movements in Kiev and Moscow, and, most dramatic of all, the disturbances triggered by the self-immolation of a woman student in February 1897. The extraordinary act of self-sacrifice must have seemed like a reproach to the half-committed. This was the signal Trotsky had been waiting for. Formerly absorbing *kruzhok* conversations ranging from Darwinism to preparation for conspiratorial work now seemed effete. He and other in Shvigovskii's circle went over to propaganda and agitation.

Grigorii Sokolovskii made the first contacts with workers in Nikolaev which within a short time led to the organization of systematic propaganda sessions.[34] A rapidly growing industrial center with roughly 10,000 workers, benefiting from the economic boom in the Ukraine connected with the industrialization program inaugurated by Sergei Witte, Nikolaev provided the young agitators with an excellent field for their activity. Local sectarians with antistate beliefs had eased the task by their gospel-inspired appeal to egalitarianism and social justice. Within a short time the young *narodnik* propagandists replaced the language of the Bible with a modern socialist idiom:

> The workers streamed toward us as if they had been waiting for this. . . . We never sought them out; they looked for us. Young and inexperienced leaders that we were, we were soon overwhelmed by the movement we had started. Every word of ours met with a response. As many as twenty and twenty-five or more of the workers gathered at our secret readings and discussions, held in houses, in the woods, or on the river. The predominant element was composed of highly skilled workers who earned fairly good wages. They already had an eight-hour day at the Nikolaev ship-building yards; they were not interested in strikes; what they wanted was justice in social relations. . . . During the first weeks of our conversations, some of them still used sectarian expressions, and often made comparisons with the period of the early Christians. But nearly all of them soon dropped this way of speaking when they found that they were only a laughing-stock for the younger men.[35]

The immediate and enthusiastic response of the workers, especially the younger, more literate ones, created a euphoric mood among Trotsky and his comrades. They soon began to produce their own literature on a hectograph in the form of a journal, *Our Cause*. The painful, time-consuming method of hand-producing the journal did not deter them. Trotsky spent entire days writing out the texts of proclamations and articles for copying on the hecto-graph. Printed propaganda and agitation quickly took precedence in his eyes. He began making weekly trips to Odessa by steamer and received help from groups forming there. The supply of literature expanded. Trotsky tells very little about its character in his autobiography, but in reply to questions and comments by Max Eastman (who evidently had seen copies of the journal and proclamations) in 1923, he tried to clarify its tone.

> You completely correctly point out that our proclamations had an economic rather than a revolutionary character. Social-Democratic work in Nikolaev had just begun. In the upper stratum of skilled workers there was a significant number of political oppositionists, issuing from both social and religious soil (sects). But beneath them there were broader masses of very backward workers.

Our journal ("Our Cause") and our booklets were for the better prepared, more cultured workers and were distributed individually. The proclamations, on the other hand, were spread in the factories and pasted on their walls. If we had started in right away with the Tsar and revolution, it might have frightened the mass. But we had in view mass political agitation. We did not reach that point because of the arrests. . . . Later an entire doctrine, so-called economism, came out of agitational work focused on economic issues. . . . But when we worked in Nikolaev this doctrine still didn't exist; in any event, we had no conception of it.[36]

Trotsky and his comrades evidently understood the familiar distinction between propaganda and agitation, but other doctrinal nuances of the period escaped them. Still involved in the debate between Marxism and Populism, they were probably unaware of the schism developing in Social Democracy. They were provincials, educated and adapted to local conditions, and lagged behind the more advanced centers of intelligentsia activity, like St. Petersburg and Moscow. When Ziv, well read compared to the others, but a bit lame in discussion, was asked about the debate between Struve and the *narodniki*, he was unable to give them a useful account.[37] Trotsky began his career in a theoretical backwater compared to Lenin.

Trotsky's group was decidedly eclectic in approach. In the boil of active work and expanding opportunities doctrinal quarrels temporarily dissolved. The Odessans translated the *Communist Manifesto* and the Nikolaevans circulated one precious copy. Sokolovskaia and Vegman claim that in Odessa they had read Plekhanov's *Development of a Monistic View of History*, a book that attacked the favorite theorists of the *narodniki* and that, when introduced to the circle in Nikolaev by Sokolovskaia, was literally thrown to the floor in disgust.[38] According to Vegman,

The greater part considered themselves *narodniki*, and there was an amusing contradiction between our activity and our convictions. . . . Believing that the peasantry had to be the main factor in the liberation movement and that it was necessary to go to the peasants, to enlighten them, at the same time, living in the cities and not seeing a single peasant—we encountered only workers and worked among them.[39]

Vegman's retrospective view should be balanced by the knowledge that not only Marxists appealed to factory workers, who themselves had frequently been born and raised in villages and whose families often still lived in those villages. This was as true in 1905 and 1917 as it was in 1897.

A sizable but short-lived organization of propagandists and workers, the South Russian Workers' Union, emerged out of the initial *kustarnichestvo* (cottage industry) of the Nikolaev group. It embraced groups in nearby Odessa and Ekaterinoslav. Alexandra Sokolovskaia played a central role, second only to Trotsky's. By virtue of his enormous energy, organizational zeal, and work on the creation and procurement of literature, rather than superior knowledge or theoretical acumen, Trotsky quickly assumed a position of preeminence in the Union. The proclamations had a simple, direct appeal, making use of inside information and focusing the workers' resentment on especially obnoxious individuals in the factory management or other hated authorities. Trotsky also drafted a set of rules and what he describes as a Social Democratic program for the Union, although he still had not accepted Marxian theory.[40]

After an unsuccessful maneuver to avoid detection, Trotsky was apprehended outside Nikolaev on an estate where Shvigovskii worked as gardener. He was taken to a prison in Nikolaev, where he had a single cellmate, and then transferred after three weeks to solitary confinement and physical misery in the Kherson prison. There he suffered for three months, until the Bronsteins succeeded in bribing the warden and smuggling in provisions and clean clothes. He moved to his next place of incarceration, the Odessa prison, in May 1898. Although placed in solitary confinement there too, he could communicate by tapping codes. Those in adjoining cells could even exchange their prison writings by a clever system made possible by open outside windows.

In one of his replies to Max Eastman's questionnaires in 1923, Trotsky described the jail in Odessa as "the last word in American technology." Ziv's memoirs provide additional detail. There were four wings, each with four floors, and each floor had a metal gallery. It was a panopticon, the four wings arranged radially, with a viewing place at their juncture. The corridors and floors were linked by metal bridges and staircases. The wardens signaled each other by striking their keys against the railings. Every footfall, every communication resounded throughout the prison. However, as the foregoing account suggests, even the best prison technology could not overcome Russian slackness—and bribetaking. Subordinate wardens could easily be persuaded to wink at the rules, and when the windows to the cells were opened in the spring, the prisoners stood on stools and shouted to each other or else exchanged manuscripts. Interestingly, Trotsky mentions the easygoing warden overseeing the political section of the prison and the gendarmes who interrogated him, but not the chief warden. We are indebted to Ziv for a description of the latter: "On my walks, visits, etc., I saw each time the mighty figure of the chief warden leaning on a long sabre, with the eagle eye of a field marshal surveying his possessions and feeling like a little Tsar; and he truly was a little Tsar. The surname of this chief warden was—Trotsky."[41]

IT IS interesting that both Lenin and Trotsky chose pseudonyms with such strongly negative associations. Neither of them liked to talk about the origins or meaning of their pseudonyms. In Lenin's case, the name signified a self-irony whose origins in his childhood experience he did not want to explain to anyone. Lenin had a strong need for privacy, and this was a private matter.[42] Although Trotsky admitted that the chief warden of the Odessa prison was the source of his pseudonym, he never gave very convincing reasons for choosing the name. Even a biographer as sympathetic as Isaac Deutscher found it odd that Trotsky, before his escape from exile in Irkutsk more than two years after leaving the prison in Odessa, should select the name of the chief warden. Deutscher, referring to this escape, asked: "In this hazardous escape did the identification with his jailor perhaps gratify in the fugitive a subconscious craving for safety?"[43]

A psychological approach is warranted, although Deutscher's speculation seems far-fetched. A more psychologically penetrating biographer noted: "It was almost as if Trotsky had unconsciously taken into himself a part of that power he was fighting against."[44] He also astutely notes that *Trotz* is the German word for defiance. The joining of an image of oppression and a word for defiance in a name that on the surface is Slavic but hides within it a foreign word suggests a complex play of emotions and ideas.

Trotsky told Max Eastman that he chose the name because it was non-Jewish. Jews were barred from Siberia, and he had to have a non-Jewish name in his false passport. Furthermore, he liked the name.[45] Trotsky's partial rejection of his Jewish identity for practical reasons is certainly involved, but nothing is more Jewish than defiance and stubbornness in the face of oppression (or even divine command), and behind the superficial repudiation of Jewish identity lies a hidden affirmation. Someone with Trotsky's linguistic background and love of irony could easily have managed this play with words and meanings. Although he might be accused of falsification in his story to Eastman, it is more accurate to describe Trotsky's account as misleading.

Throughout his life Trotsky was more inclined to concealment or to misleading partial revelations than to outright lying. A Jewish identity was much more than merely a minor obstacle in the path of a revolutionary trying to forge a new kind of human identity, for in Trotsky's historical environment Jewish identity signified an odd mixture of contradictory ideas: narrow, exclusive loyalties and worldwide designs; seclusion in ghettos and *shtetels* and cosmopolitan wandering. Christians had long seen Jews as a stubborn people who chose to live in darkness, who rejected divine grace; yet Jews played a major new prophetic role as chief dispensers of a bright new faith—socialism. Someone with Trotsky's intelligence surely understood all of this, and Trotsky himself chose to be the new kind of secular Jew. The old Jewish identity had to be repudiated insofar as it signified victimization and ethnic provincialism. The new Marxian secular prophesy still had lurking within it the idea of a chosen people and a division of humanity into the saved and the damned, but it promised to transcend, finally, all tribal and invidious identities.

If we are to believe Trotsky, he had become a Marxist in practice during 1897, even before his imprisonment and recognized his conversion during the first days of his confinement.[46] The process of conversion to Marxism is not carefully recorded by Trotsky himself, but Deutscher's description of Trotsky's earlier conversion to socialism serves equally well, and in this case, the psychological observations are unimpeachable:

> Again and again we shall see this psychological mechanism at work in him: He is confronted with a new idea to which up to a point he is conditioned to respond; yet he resists at first with stubborn haughtiness; his resistance grows with the attraction; and he subdues incipient doubt and hesitation. Then his

defences crumble, his self-confidence begins to vanish; but he is still too proud or not convinced enough to give any sign of yielding. There is no outward indication yet of the struggle that goes on in his mind. Then, suddenly, the new conviction hardens in him, and, as if in a single moment, overcomes his spirit of contradiction and his vanity.[47]

Deutscher's description bears a strong resemblance to Trotsky's vision of dialectical change, recorded in notes written during 1933–1935. In his notebooks of that period he revealed a strong penchant for catastrophism in his general vision of dialectics, and he evidently modelled his theory of cognition upon his own transformations and conversions:

Everything flows, but not outside [its] banks. The world is not "fluid," there are changes in it, the crystallization of durable (congealed) elements, although indeed not "eternal" ones. Then life creates its own banks for itself in order later to wash them away. The quantitative changes of matter at a given stage push against these congealed forms, which sufficed for its previous state. Conflict. Catastrophe. Either the old form conquers (only partially conquers), necessitating the self-adaptation of the conquered (partially) process, or the process of movement explodes the old form and creates a new one, by way of its new crystallizations from its wombs and the assimilation of elements of the old form. . . .

Thus, in the domain of thinking (cognition) as well, the quantitive changes lead to qualitative ones, and then these transformations haven't a [steady] evolutionary character but are accompanied by *breaks in gradualness*, that is, by small or large intellectual catastrophes.[48]

The emotional components of Trotsky's *narodnik* outlook lived a kind of subterranean existence after his conversion to Marxism. The populists' stress on the role of the individual in historical change, on heroism, and the impatient optimism that had made Marxism seem barren and heartless at first still satisfied some of Trotsky's emotional needs. Although Marxism "exploded the old form," it left behind the emotional core of Trotsky's original commitment. Unlike Lenin, who repudiated the romantic outlook of the duelist, Trotsky retained too much of it for his own political good. He could not forego self-display. Like the defiant and stubborn Jewish identity concealed behind "Trotsky," a heroic, romantic identity, an affirmation of the individual's contribution to history, clung to Trotsky's Marxian identity. He would never be able the sink silently into the revolutionary underground or dutifully submit to the organizational imperative demanded of a good Leninist.

TO TROTSKY'S good fortune, the prisoner in the adjoining cell was Il'ia Sokolovskii, who, he soon learned, had also converted to Marxism. They discovered that the construction of the cells permitted them to remove a brick under their common ventilation duct and communicate directly. Not only could they exchange notes and books (once the binding had been removed), they could even shake hands! Although the prison authorities discovered their arrangement and transferred Trotsky to a different cell after about two months, his new neighbor proved to be another fellow Rassadnik—and Marxist—Ziv. In addition, Trotsky still had library privileges and could receive visitors. It was a tolerable situation, one in which an eighteen-year-old revolutionary apprentice could fill in some of the gaps in his education.

Trotsky spent much of the time studying languages (German, French, Italian, and English), but following the prescription, "Know thine enemy," he took advantage of the prison library's conservative publications, very often theological journals, to study arguments against various non-Orthodox Christian and progressive doctrines. These were the only books available during his first period in prison, but he soon began to receive books from friends and relatives in Odessa. Unlike Lenin, who had grounded himself in Marxian economics and was already working upon *The Development of Capitalism in Russia* in Shushenskoe in 1898–1899, Trotsky was still searching for basic theoretical knowledge and learning the doctrine of historical materialism from the elegantly concise works of Antonio Labriola. In the Odessa prison he also deepened his understanding and appreciation of Darwin's theory of evolution. Throughout his life he found support for his dialectical vision in an unorthodox interpretation of Darwin.

In order to put his newly acquired Marxism to the test, he began to write a study of freemasonry from the Marxian point of view—the materialist conception of history. Had the work survived, it might have played the same role for Trotsky that *The Development of Capitalism* had played for Lenin, permitting him to show, both to himself and to the world, his mastery of Marxian doctrine in an original work. In his autobiography Trotsky wrote of his voluminous (though thinly researched), unpublished history of freemasonry with some pride and regretted its loss. It gave body to the theory of dialectics he had learned from Labriola and deepened by studying the classics of historical materialism during his years in exile.[49] Moreover, Labriola's essayistic approach suited him well, and in future projects Trotsky showed little inclination to write heavy Marxian treatises. His most successful works are about events in which he himself participated or about historical processes connected with them. As a writer of Marxian historical drama, Trotsky remains unsurpassed.

12

Leon Trotsky, Romantic Exile

THE OTHER notable event of Trotsky's prison years was his marriage to Alexandra Sokolovskaia. Aside from Trotsky's own rather politically tinged account of this change in his life (no doubt downplaying the romantic interest because of his relationship with Natalia Sedova at the time of its composition), there are Sokolovskaia's and Ziv's memoirs. Hers fill only fifteen pages (double-spaced typing) of legal-size paper and, echoing Trotsky's version in his autobiography, express above all appreciation of her husband's dedication to revolution. Considerably older than Trotsky, she came from the struggling lower urban stratum.[1] Sokolovskaia does not specify her father's work, but he was evidently from the *meshchanstvo* rather than the proletariat. An autodidact and lover of learning, Lev Sokolovskii introduced his daughter to the books that converted her at first to the *narodnik* point of view. She herself discovered the writings of Marx, Plekhanov, Struve, and Lenin through contacts with students in Odessa, where she was studying to be a midwife.

Like Trotsky and the others, she was swept up in the police dragnet of January 1898 and put into solitary confinement in the Odessa prison. During their second year, when prisoners were permitted visits and able to borrow books, Trotsky managed to smuggle notes to her in the backing of book covers. They saw each other for the first time after their arrest in the late autumn of 1899 and wanted to marry immediately in Odessa, but were prevented from doing so by David Bronstein. They were married in a transit prison in Moscow in the spring of 1900 by a "rabbi-chaplain" shortly before their departure for Siberia.[2]

Trotsky and his bride, like many political exiles, married to avoid loneliness in Siberia and to sustain political collaboration, but they were probably also in love. Ziv, who travelled in the same convoy to Siberia, noted the affectionate behavior of the newlyweds. In their relationship politics evidently acted as an aphrodisiac.[3] Within two years of their arrival in Ust-Kut in the early autumn of 1900, Sokolovskaia gave birth to two daughters, the first, Zina, sometime during the winter or spring of 1901 and the second, Nina, about a year later, in Verkholensk, where they had moved when Zina was ten months old.[4]

THE STORY of their Siberian exile and their family reveals how totally the two of them subordinated personal matters to politics. Neither of them mentions the names of their daughters or even when they were born. Sokolovskaia supported without complaint her husband's decision to escape in the summer of 1902, even though he left her with two small children, the younger only four months old. In fact, when she completed her four-year term of exile, she left her daughters with Trotsky's parents and traveled to Switzerland, where she received a posting from the Social Democratic Party's central committee. Although she met Trotsky in Switzerland and then again in Berlin (probably in 1904), she mentions only that she consulted with him about her posting. Trotsky had already established a new and permanent relationship with Natalia Sedova, whom he met in Paris in the autumn of 1902. Legally he remained Sokolovskaia's husband.

Sokolovskaia's continuing respect and loyalty can be inferred not only from her memoirs, but from the tragic denouement of her revolutionary career. During 1905 and 1917 Trotsky reestablished contact with his first family and received both love and adulation from his daughters. Sokolovskaia supported her husband's politics in the 1920s and became an oppositionist leader in Leningrad. Her younger daughter, Nina Nevelson, to whom she was closer,[5] married an oppositionist. Suffering from tuberculosis and separated from her husband, Nina collapsed during the spring of 1928 and died on June 9. The older daughter, Zina (Zinaida) Volkov, had been raised mainly by Trotsky's parents, but had maintained contact with her sister and was at her deathbed. Zina, who also suffered from tuberculosis, left the Soviet Union with her son,

Seva, and joined Trotsky in exile on the island of Prinkipo, but she soon showed signs of mental instability and went to Berlin for psychiatric care. Psychoanalysis failed to arrest the progress of her illness—something Trotsky had predicted, given the circumstances—and she committed suicide in January 1933, shortly before Hitler assumed power. Sokolovskaia sent a bitter and reproachful letter to her husband when she learned of the death of her only surviving child.[6]

The family tragedy is too complex for adequate treatment here, but a few remarks are warranted. It reveals that Trotsky created powerful double binds for his children. Like many impressive but somewhat distant parents, he inspired both awe and resentment. He could be tender and affectionate, attentive and helpful in a fatherly or comradely fashion, but only episodically. He was too involved in his political work to tend to their emotional needs. Furthermore, he could be both cold and explosively critical—not always justly. He never really knew his younger daughter; his younger son, Sergei, fought with him and went his own apolitical way, only to fall victim to Stalin during the purges; his older son, Leon, became his trusted helper in the 1930s, but incurred his father's wrath when he failed to fulfill his commissions in minute detail and according to strict schedules. Like the other children, he predeceased his father. Trotsky's failings in his family relations mirrored his political faults, and the two families, like his political project, perished from his own mishandling as well as Stalin's revenge.

DURING SIBERIAN exile Trotsky began to realize his talents as a political journalist. Although censorship restricted him to literary and philosophical essays, mainly reviews, he managed to sustain a Marxian point of view in his criticism. Trotsky's extraordinarily fluent, confident style conveyed to the reader the impression that the author had mastered almost all of human learning. His penchant for bringing together insights and information from different areas of learning into a single text and a liberal sprinkling of mostly Latin, German, and French maxims and terms give his essays a learned quality. They were designed to be both intimidating and entertaining, with elements of ex cathedra gravity alongside feuilleton lightness. No one would mistake the author writing under the pseudonym Antid Oto for a graduate of *realschule* without any higher learning. Trotsky took his non de plume from an Italian dictionary. It is simply the word "antidote" split in two. Under this pseudonym, signifying his practice of Marxian medicine against liberal and *narodnik* quackery, Trotsky gained an instantaneous reputation, mainly as a contributor to *The Eastern Review*.

Trotsky's excellent grasp of both Russian and world literary culture, prefigured here and demonstrated even more impressively twenty-two years later in *Literature and Revolution*, and his *talent* distinguished him from Lenin. Although Lenin read widely and was well-equipped linguistically, he was hardly a literary critic, and he eschewed the niceties of literary style in favor of a sledgehammer approach to criticism. This probably signified renunciation of something that he had earlier loved in favor of his new calling, but Lenin, one senses, did not have great gifts as a writer. Vera Zasulich compared Lenin to a bulldog and Plekhanov to a greyhound with their political qualities in mind. According to Trotsky, she said of Lenin, "his was a 'deadly grip.' "[7] On the other hand, Plekhanov shook and shook his opponent, and then let go. The image might be transferred to Lenin and Trotsky with the aesthetic side of the comparison in view. Lenin seems to have had one goal in mind when he wrote: to smash his opponent into smithereens. Trotsky was a conscious stylist. Literary style, like sartorial elegance and studied oratory, was an aspect of Trotsky's self-display. If his youth shows at all, it is in his recourse to parenthetical asides and exclamation marks to devastate his opponents, stylistic extravagances that eventually disappear from his writing.

Several repeating themes—the individual and society, the dying out of the old gentry world and the illnesses of bourgeois culture, the social meaning of fin de siècle decadence and pessimism, and the need for faith, hope, and optimism about the dawning twentieth century—emerged from essays on such figures as Nietzsche, Schnitzler, and Ibsen as well as Russian authors and intelligentsia figures like Gogol, Belinsky, Herzen, Dobroliubov, and Berdiaev. It is a testimony to the richness of the culture of the old Russian intelligentsia and the latitude permitted by censorship that a political exile writing as a critic for a Siberian daily could both earn a modest supplement (four kopecks a line) to the subsistence given by the authorities and become a popular writer. Writing became the vehicle of Trotsky's optimism, his affirmation of the future, and in his autobiography, when he describes the suicides among the political exiles who did not understand the art of self-therapy, one senses that his pseudonym might also have signified another central function of writing: It was an antidote against depression and despair.

Trotsky's need for a rational faith in progress played a greater role in his psychological economy than Lenin's did in his. Although he yielded little to Lenin in combativeness, Trotsky's investment in his utopian vision made compromise extremely painful for him. At no point in his career did he abandon his faith in human progress. He expressed it grandiloquently in an essay, "On Pessimism, Optimism, the Twentieth Century, and Much More," appearing in *The Eastern Review* of February 17, 1901:

> —*Dum spiro, spero!* Where there's life, there's hope!—exclaims the optimist about the future.—If my life were that of the heavenly bodies, I would show complete indifference to a pitiful lump of muck lost in the infinite universe, I would with equanimity shine on both evil and good. . . . But I am—*a person!* And "universal history," which to you, dispassionate priest of science, bookkeeper of eternity, seems but an insignificant instant in the temporal budget, is for me—everything! And while I still breathe—I will struggle for the sake of the future, that radiant and bright future, when humanity, strong and excellent, controls the spontaneous current of its history and directs it to a limitless horizon of beauty, joy, happiness! . . . *Dum spiro, spero!*[8]

The change to a Marxian idiom did not alter Trotsky's initial inspiration. The above lines express Mikhailovskii's anthropocentric vision as well as Marx's aim to end the chaos and slavishness of human "prehistory." Trotsky gave his Marxism the voluntaristic coloring that many former *narodniki* carried to their new commitment. Clearly, he had assured himself that Marxism would permit him to carry on as a passionate tribune of humanity with undiminished energy and optimism. The function of ideology as substitute religion and therapy is clearer in Trotsky than in Lenin. However faintly, Trotsky's remark about humanity controlling the "spontaneous current of history" foreshadows his acceptance of Bolshevism, his enthusiastic fulfillment of his role as organizer of the Red Army, his fascination with military methods and Taylorism in the organization of labor, and, generally, his sponsorship of "administrative" methods. Nonetheless, he managed to infuse his love of order and machine culture with religious feeling.

The article, "Poetry, the Machine, and the Poetry of the Machine," appearing on September 8, 1901, shows that David Bronstein's intention to make an engineer of him and Trotsky's exposure to the world of machines in his uncle's boiler factory in Odessa had not turned him from engineering in a more exalted sense. In the course of rejecting John Ruskin's romanticism and all species of mysticism, Trotsky affirmed Marxian Prometheanism:

> We are deeply convinced that the machine, as the symbol and embodiment of the indefatigable struggle of human genius for liberation from nature, must become the object of high—to be sure, realistic, and not mystical—inspiration! . . . The task of the present moment consists in liberating people from the domination of others, without again subjecting them to the uncontrolled power of nature. Lifted up by an endless series of human waves to the heights of contemporary social needs and ideals, the proud and refractory son of nature, having savoured the satanic dream of subordinating nature to the power of his brain and making a captive of it, like a beautiful slave girl—humanity will not renounce the machine, for we can ascend to the mountainous kingdom of freedom only on a mighty locomotive, and not on a winded, exhausted old nag.[9]

Syntax and florid style aside, in these ideas and images we see the Trotsky of *Literature and Revolution* and many other works. By the age of twenty, Trotsky had found both his ideological inspiration and his voice. In the process of rejecting other varieties of romanticism, however, he became a romantic of the machine and machine production—a Marxian romantic.

Trotsky and *The Spark*

DURING HIS roughly two years in Siberia, Trotsky encountered anarchism, Tolstoyanism, neo-Kantianism, "bourgeois" pessimism, Nietzschianism, and other old and new "isms" without wavering from his commitment to Marxism. He witnessed the revival of revolutionary populism, signaled by the assassinations of two government ministers by the Fighting Organization of the Socialist Revolutionary Party and furthered by widespread peasant rebellions in the Ukraine in 1902. He knew of the struggle between Kautsky and Bernstein in the German Social Democratic movement, but gives no indication that he was aware of the fight of the Iskraites against heresies in Russian Social Democracy before 1902. Like others, he responded to the call for a centralized Marxian revolutionary organization. Shortly before his decision to escape, he learned of *The Spark* and read Lenin's *What Is to Be Done?* The prospect of collaborating on a venture of this sort, plus Alexandra L'vovna's encouragement, decided the matter. Escape from a Siberian village was quite commonplace; the real trick was surviving the hazards of the journey back to European Russia.

After a long, jolting ride in a peasant cart under a load of hay and matting, Trotsky reached the city of Irkutsk, on the new Trans-Siberian railway. Friends there gave him what he needed for his trip to the Volga region—to Samara. In Samara he contacted Krzhizhanovskii, Lenin's former colleague in St. Petersburg. Now chief organizer for *The Spark* in Russia, Krzhizhanovskii gave Trotsky his first party duties in the Ukrainian cities of Poltava, Kharkov, and Kiev, but decided that the new recruit's talents as a journalist (which earned him the party sobriquet "Pero," "pen" in Russian) would be wasted in organizational work and sent him to Zurich to introduce himself to Aksel'rod. This decision, which Krzhizhanovskii later tried to reverse, may have been an important turning point in Trotsky's career. Had he stayed on at organizational work, it is likely that Trotsky's political education would have been far more complete, his perspective different. Instead, he went right to the top, and in 1902–1903 experienced a dizzying reversal of sudden elevation and disappointment. At a stopover in Vienna, thanks to his status as Siberian escapee and his host's Russian daughter-in-law, he inveigled a stay at the home of Austria's leading Social Democrat, Viktor Adler. From Vienna he went to Zurich and introduced himself to Aksel'rod, who was to become his mentor, and then, after a stopover in Paris, he went to London, the real command center of *The Spark*, sometime in the autumn of 1902.[10] Shortly after Trotsky had brushed the hay from his clothes, he found himself debating with the leaders of Russian socialism.

He arrived at Lenin's and Krupskaia's London apartment at dawn and thought nothing of waking them up. Trotsky's penchant for arriving at inopportune times (he had invaded Adler's home on a Sunday in Vienna and rousted Aksel'rod out of bed at 2:00 A.M. in Zurich) suggests more than a little immaturity and a most intrusive form of self-centeredness. After debriefing him about his experience in Siberia and the Ukraine, Lenin and Krupskaia extended his tour of revolutionary celebrities. He met Zasulich and Martov of the Iskraites and Nikolai Chaikovskii and Varlaam Cherkezov, veterans of the movement of the 1860s and 1870s. As one would expect of a young man not used to civilized ways (by his own admission), he argued heatedly with these unrepentant relics. Of his new acquaintances, one, at least, did not forgive him his youth and lack of manners. Plekhanov, a man of miniscule tolerance, found him insufferable. Lenin, on the other hand, forgave him his bad manners and florid style. In his search for allies for the struggles that lay ahead he saw Trotsky as a valuable recruit.

Despite Trotsky's efforts to distance himself from his Jewish past, aside from Lenin (and the alliance with Lenin lasted for only a few months), he found his closest friends among the Jewish émigrés—Lev Deutsch and Aksel'rod. Deutsch, one of the earliest members of the Group for the Liberation of Labor and currently business manager of *The Spark*, recognized Trotsky's talents and, when Krzhizhanovskii decided to call him back to Russia for organizational work, interceded for this "Benjamin." Lenin evidently endorsed Deutsch's view.[11] Trotsky himself no doubt wanted to stay abroad and work with the leadership of *The Spark*. In his own words: "I actually fell in love with *Iskra*, and was so ashamed of my ignorance that I strained every nerve in my effort to overcome it."[12] Aside from writing for *The Spark*, Trotsky became a lecturer on the Social Democrat circuit, first in London and then in Brussels, Liège, and Paris.

NATALIA IVANOVNA Sedova, a young art student and *Iskra* agent, who first met Trotsky when she was commissioned to find a room for him in Paris, fell in love with him instantaneously, and the twenty-two-year old émigré reciprocated. Unlike Sokolovskaia, who was Jewish and a *meshchanka*, Sedova was of noble birth. She had become a rebel at an early age and converted to Marxism in Geneva under the influence of the Group for the Liberation of Labor. After the split in Russian Marxism she remained faithful to the founders and worked for *The Spark*. In Paris, where she studied art at the Sorbonne, Sedova arranged lodgings for new arrivals and oriented them to the city. Although like Trotsky's wife she was self-sacrificing in her relationship with him, the two women differed in most respects. Unlike Lenin, who chose as his life companion a woman who might have been a member of his own family in her values and character, and with whom romance had been either ephemeral or nonexistent, Trotsky chose a woman from another world whom he loved deeply. By linking his life to that of such a woman so quickly, Trotsky revealed not only youthful impulsiveness but a preference for deracination and a new identity. The relationship with Natalia Sedova must have made it even more difficult for him to return to Russia to do organizational work.

TROTSKY'S LECTURES were evidently quite a success. His career as an orator on the larger stage of émigré politics began in London, in Whitechapel, where he devastated the elders of the Russian revolutionary movement who still clung to their old faiths. The sheer mental agility and arrogance that had permitted him to crush his opponents in Shvigovskii's garden were intact, but Trotsky's learning had advanced sufficiently to give him cogency among the leaders of Russian socialism. He continued his triumphal tour on the continent and dutifully took the *Iskra* line, supporting the Guesdists in their demonstrations against the government of Waldeck-Rousseau. Lenin arrived in Paris on February 10(23), 1903 and gave his own series of lectures. During this visit Trotsky, Sedova, Lenin, and Martov made the memorable trip to the Opéra Comique mentioned earlier, with Trotsky suffering in the shoes he had borrowed from Lenin.[13]

Thoughout the autumn and winter of 1902–1903 Trotsky observed the relationships among the editors of *The Spark*. His remarks, first written twenty-two years after the events, by his own admission may not be altogether accurate,[14] but they are doubtlessly valuable. Zasulich's strong dislike for Lenin impressed him the most, and he attributed it to "organic incompatibility," deep personality differences. She preferred Plekhanov's dogmatism to Lenin's "death grip," and despite her friendliness to young recruits, she usually supported Plekhanov in internecine strife. Although Martov was seemingly Lenin's natural ally, Trotsky noted Lenin's critical posture toward his "soft" colleague, but this observation might easily be the product of looking backward from the Second Party Congress. Furthermore, Trotsky believed that Zasulich had influenced Martov's attitude toward Lenin. Plekhanov, Aksel'rod, and Potresov were more distant because the former two lived in Switzerland and Potresov spent much of his time on the Continent, but Aksel'rod, like Zasulich, tended to support Plekhanov.

The complexities and confusions of émigré politics issuing from personal and generational affiliations, psychological factors, and even ethnic tensions are nowhere clearer than in an incident of early March 1903. Lenin tried to coopt Trotsky to the editorial board of *The Spark* and was blocked by Plekhanov, who forced him to put off the decision until the party congress. According to Trotsky's version, Plekhanov recognized Lenin's effort as a maneuver to give the younger Iskraites a majority (Lenin, Martov, Potresov, and Trotsky) against the older ones (Plekhanov, Aksel'rod and Zasulich).[15] But there was more to it. Much remained unspoken and unwritten, probably even unthought. Perhaps Trotsky was not able to face up to some of the harshest truths: Plekhanov's anti-Semitism was a factor in his rejection of Trotsky, whose Jewish background probably made him attractive to Deutsch and Aksel'rod. More important still, Trotsky's need to excel and his penchant for self-display affronted Plekhanov, who must have seen in Trotsky not only an arrogant upstart but a caricature of himself. In the end, P. N. Krasikov, a veteran party worker close to both Plekhanov and Lenin, was temporarily coopted instead.[16]

It is difficult to say a great deal about Lenin's attitude towards Trotsky as a person, because in the only correspondence in which he discusses Trotsky he does so only from the point of view of his usefulness to the cause. Trotsky reproduced Lenin's letter of March 2, 1903, to Plekhanov in his autobiography, so important was it to him in 1929 to display a token of Lenin's approval of him at the beginning of their political relationship. Honestly appraising Trotsky's strengths and weaknesses, Lenin did indeed want to coopt "Pero" to the editorial board. There is mainly praise for Trotsky's energy, his "remarkable" ability, and his skill as a lecturer in Lenin's letter to Plekhanov, and only mild criticism of his stylistic excesses. Lenin saw an opportunity to coopt a willing and able ally, someone to shoulder part of the burden of the editorial work,[17] but nothing like a strong personal relationship developed between the two men. Events at the Second Party Congress cut short their first period of collaboration.

At first a strong ally, Trotsky underwent an extraordinary transformation into a bitter opponent during the Congress. In the course of the debate and the machinations behind the scenes, Trotsky's attitude toward Lenin changed dramatically. He had served as one of Lenin's "cudgels" until the fateful turning point in the Congress, on August 2(15), 1903. The record of the Congress shows Trotsky at first confidently fighting the Bund and other opponents of *The Spark* line and provoking both ovations from the Iskraites and protests from their opponents. Now he took Martov's side and became embroiled in debate with both Plekhanov and Lenin. To Trotsky's surprise, Lenin was allying himself with Plekhanov and destroying the unity of *The Spark*. Even worse, Lenin tried to pressure him with a real cudgel, the thuggish Krasikov,[18] an early warning signal of the rough types Lenin would promote in his party and the very man Lenin and Plekhanov had agreed to coopt temporarily to the editorial board instead of Trotsky. Even a political novice like Trotsky could hardly fail to see that he himself was only a tool, and an expendable one at that, in Lenin's eyes. Lenin's unsentimental approach, his disregard for Trotsky's self-esteem, undoubtedly played as great a role in Trotsky's defection to the softs as the reasons given in Trotsky's autobiography:

> How did I come to be with the "softs" at the congress? Of the *Iskra* editors, my closest connections were with Martov, Zasulich and Aksel'rod. Their influence over me was unquestionable. Before the congress there were various shades of opinion on the editorial board, but no sharp differences. I stood farthest from Plekhanov, who, after the first really trivial encounters, had taken an intense dislike to me. Lenin's attitude toward me was unexceptionally kind. But now it was he who, in my eyes, was attacking the editorial board, a body which was, in my opinion, a single unit, and which bore the exciting name of *Iskra*. The idea of a split within the board seemed nothing short of sacrilegious to me. . . . My whole being seemed to protest against this merciless cutting off of the older ones when they were at last on the threshold of an organized party. It was my indignation at his attitude that really led to my parting with him at the second congress.[19]

Trotsky's emotional shock was equal in magnitude to Lenin's surprise at the defection of people close to him. Trotsky did not grasp the complicated pattern of affiliations on *Iskra* or the emotional structure that permitted Lenin to maneuver around Plekhanov and simultaneously sustain an alliance with him. Plekhanov's stunning performance at the Second Party Congress, his unwavering hard line, had revitalized their alliance. But in Trotsky's eyes, association with Plekhanov now made Lenin a villain too: He did not really care about Trotsky but only wanted to use him; he did not really want to keep the *Iskra* family together but only wanted power for himself. Trotsky could not tolerate the humiliation of people close to him and the ruthless transformation of an organization he "loved" into the instrument of Plekhanov and Lenin.[20]

This was the first blow to Trotsky's revolutionary romance. Like Lenin in August 1900, Trotsky learned bitterly that there was no place for love in politics. Of course, Trotsky's ambition (here too, he resembled Lenin in 1900) might have played more than a small role in his defection. On the verge of becoming an editor of the organ of Russian Social Democracy and, at the age of twenty-three, a leader of the party, he felt himself a victim of the division of the party into hards and softs. For a short time he was also a beneficiary. After Plekhanov's reversal of his position, reconstitution of the old editorial board, and Lenin's resignation, Trotsky's Menshevik allies fought to keep him as a contributor to *The Spark* and succeeded for a short time, but they were not strong enough to protect him from Plekhanov.

PLEKHANOV HAD been the key figure in the intraparty struggles of 1898–1904. The wounds he inflicted on the hides of his comrades played more than a small role in their political hardening, but in the end he found himself unable to sever his ties with his old colleagues and to cause an irreversible split in the party over what still seemed to be an organizational dispute. The Plekhanov who had inspired Lenin at the Third Party Congress with the ringing slogan "The good of the revolution is the highest good" (delivered in Latin, oddly enough, to the champions of the proletariat) revealed that he was less ruthless than his words. Lenin was the only genuine "hard" on the editorial board of *The Spark*. At the second congress of the Foreign League of Revolutionary Social Democracy in mid-October 1903, the newly formed Mensheviks began their coup against the Bolsheviks. Plekhanov, in the unaccustomed role of mediator, found Lenin to be irreconcilable. By the end of October the split had become final, and Lenin resigned from the editorial board of *The Spark*. Lenin was the only leader of the original *Iskra* whose psychology permitted him ruthlessly to sever ties not only with close colleagues, but with the organ that symbolized the success of the movement. The others, including Plekhanov, learned the limits of their own "hardness" in 1903–1904.

The confrontation of hards and softs inspired both intemperate political rhetoric and profound political prophesy. Personal ambitions and grievances lay behind much of this outpouring, but this did not limit the value of the pamphleteering or lessen the wisdom of some of the utterances. Trotsky's turgid outrage probably signified a number of things: the transference of his anger against Plekhanov to Lenin; his desire to ingratiate himself with his new allies; and genuine insight into the dangers of Lenin's position. Even in this environment of mutual recrimination Trotsky's performance stood out. It was an early sign of his tendency to escalate conflict in the service of his personal fortunes under the guise of principled struggle. In this last respect he was no different from many political egoists, who are quite good at hiding their personal ambitions under rationalizations and projections that parade as support for "principled" positions and struggle against dangerous power seekers.

13

Trotsky Against Lenin

TROTSKY'S COMPULSION to excel and his combativeness underlay many of the difficulties he experienced in the period after 1903. Those who earlier forgave him his youthful arrogance and excess soon found him intolerable. Plekhanov's reaction to him in 1902 was simply an early warning signal. It is difficult to sustain personal relations, much less political ones, with someone who has a way of letting you know that you are intellectually inferior to him. His speeches at the Second Party Congress show how readily he got his opponents' backs up. Lenin took the floor several times immediately after Trotsky when the latter began opposing the hard-line position. However, Trotsky was not the main enemy. Lenin pinned the label "Balalaikin" on him, a name borrowed from the gallery of the satirist Saltykov-Shchedrin's grotesques, suggesting that Trotsky resembled a shyster lawyer. It was hardly a threatening image.

Lenin's analysis of alliances and tabulation of votes at the Second Party

Congress yielded not only political groupings but a rather striking statistic: Jews controlled twenty-one of the forty-three casting (as opposed to consultative) votes at the Congress.[1] It was also rather obvious that the Mensheviks were misproportionately Jewish, even though they had stood firm against the Jewish nationalist group at the Congress, the Bund. Although the association of Jewishness, the "minority" position, and softness never became a significant part of the record, it was an insidious part of the consciousness of both factions after the split, expressed usually in sly jokes. Lenin characterized the position of the group of nine Iskraites who had split off as a " 'soft, zigzag line' (or a feminine line, as some wisecrackers quipped, and not without reason)."[2]

Trotsky seemed to be particularly sensitive to these invidious distinctions, even though he rejected them at a conscious level. As noted earlier, those closest to Trotsky, the Social Democrats who had befriended and helped him, were mainly Jews: Aksel'rod, Deutsch, and later, Parvus. There are some interesting similarities in his later characterizations of the leading Mensheviks, Aksel'rod and Martov. In 1924, when describing the old *Iskra*, he wrote of Aksel'rod:

> He was a homeopath of prerevolutionary politics. He applied the procedures and methods of a laboratory; he dealt with minute quantities; he observed the smallest groups; he weighed everything on a chemist's scale. Not for nothing did L. G. Deutsch consider Aksel'rod as belonging to the same type as Spinoza. It is not without significance that Spinoza was a diamond cutter.[3]

Perhaps not fully consciously, Trotsky began to associate Jews with small-scale, domesticated forms of political activity rather than more masculine, battlefield forms. He revealed this again in his remarks about Martov in notes written approximately thirty years after the *Iskra* period: "Martov's delicate, fragile thought halted, powerless in the face of major events. . . . Martov's intellect, psychology [was] feminine. . . . Martov's thought was the thought of a watchmaker in politics."[4] Although it is impossible to say precisely when he began to associate Menshevism with softness (signifying for Trotsky mainly indecisiveness and timidity), Jewishness, painstaking but unheroic activity, and femininity, in his autobiography Trotsky suggests that October 1905, when he recognized how different he was from the Mensheviks, was a turning point for him:

> In October I plunged headlong into the gigantic whirlpool, which, in a personal sense, was the greatest test of my powers. Decisions had to be made under fire. I can't help noting that those decisions came to me quite obviously. I did not turn back to see what others might say, and I very seldom had the opportunity to consult anybody; everything had to be done in such a hurry. Later, I observed with astonishment and a sense of estrangement how every event caught the cleverest of the Mensheviks, Martov, unawares and threw him into confusion. Without thinking about it—there was too little time for self-examination—I organically felt that my years of apprenticeship were over, although not in the sense that I'd stopped learning.[5]

In the year following the Second Party Congress Trotsky gave no indication that he perceived any lack of combativeness, of the will to leadership in his colleagues. Young, inexperienced, he attached himself at first to Aksel'rod, who became his mentor. By the standards of the revolutionary subculture, Aksel'rod was already a venerable figure. In his early fifties when Trotsky arrived in Zurich, Aksel'rod had faded into the background until the Congress, partly because of his own illnesses (both physical and psychological), partly because of his wife's. His inability to work systematically had been one of the factors working in Lenin's favor during 1900–1903. Aksel'rod's complaints about some of Lenin's policies—his agrarian policy and attitudes towards liberals, for example—had small effect. When faced with bitter conflict, Aksel'rod was prone to flight. He had in abundance the kindly, tolerant characteristics of Shvigovskii, Trotsky's first mentor.

Given the fierce struggles developing among Social Democrats, Aksel'rod seemed doomed to extinction as a political factor. During moments of significant change in political subcultures, most of the actors responsible for the modus operandi at a given phase find themselves disoriented. Like Plekhanov and Martov, Aksel'rod had discovered too late that Lenin was a new phenomenon, or, more accurately, an old one in a new context. After recovering from the shock of the Second Party Congress, they all vied with one another at finding theoretical formulations for the Bolshevik heresy, and Aksel'rod experienced something like a political resurrection. During this phase of Aksel'rod's long career, he powerfully influenced Trotsky.

Aksel'rod analyzed the Social Democratic political machinery that had been created in an ad hoc manner and that Lenin was now trying to turn into an elaborate apparatus with a central control mechanism. In social terms this apparatus signified the hegemony of the intelligentsia over the proletariat. Like other Marxists, Aksel'rod could not free himself from the two-class approach to social analysis. The intelligentsia had to be classified as bourgeois or petit-bourgeois; thus, in order for the working class truly to liberate itself, it would have to assume responsibility for its own political life. In essence, Aksel'rod called for an end to the period of intelligentsia hegemony and apparatus-building and envisioned in due time the absorption of the Social Democratic intelligentsia into a self-activating and self-governing proletarian party. Aksel'rod's Menshevism was still another expression of the intelligentsia's ambivalent attitude toward its own role, an attitude that came to the fore at moments such as 1903.

To Trotsky and others all of this was an illumination. That is not to say that Aksel'rod was correct. Rather, he had created a new perspective and a new set of terms that permitted a portion of a political community in distress to overcome a crisis and renew its activity. Like the other future leaders of Menshevism, Trotsky accepted Aksel'rod's version of the troubles with Russian Social Democracy and avidly took up the idea that the crisis signaled the dawn of a new period in the movement. In view of the parallel crisis of the Russian autocracy in 1904, it was implausible to Marxian dialecticians that they were indeed witnessing the beginning of a new epoch. Thus, Trotsky joined others who wishfully perceived Lenin and the old *Spark* as a necessary but passing phase of Russian Social Democracy. He had already attacked Lenin vehemently in his "Report of the Siberian Delegation" after the Second Party Congress, and he developed many of the ideas presented there at greater length in 1904.[6]

When he resumed his attack on Lenin in the summer of 1904, Trotsky decided to display the full virtuosity of his polemical technique. His voluminous pamphlet, *Our Political Tasks*, contains not only a straightforward critique of Lenin's *One Step Forward, Two Steps Back*, but a Socratic dialogue between a Bolshevik and Menshevik and an imaginary exchange of letters between party workers. Rather than merely expose Lenin's errors, Trotsky tried to humiliate him in a dazzling display of superior understanding of Marxian theory and revolutionary history, to turn Lenin's own authorities, including Kautsky, against him, and to show the dreadful flaws in Lenin's logic. Most interesting of all, Trotsky showed where Lenin's position led. The pamphlet began with some halfhearted concessions to Lenin's usefulness during 1900–1903, but moved to an attack upon Lenin's failure to emphasize sufficiently revolutionary will and the need to stimulate the collective will of the proletariat. Like the other Mensheviks, Trotsky perceived Lenin as a symptom of the intelligentsia's need for control and a proponent, above all, of the harmful domination of *consciousness* over *spontaneity*. For Trotsky, this approach would act as a brake upon collective action rather than a stimulus.

Trotsky's enduring contribution—and it should be taken into account that he was still only twenty-four—was the term "substitutionism" to describe the consequence of Lenin's political blueprint: the substitution of the professional revolutionaries for the proletariat in the political arena. Trotsky counterposed substitutionism to a form of leadership in which the intelligentsia "nurtured" (he used the term *vospitanie*) the will to action of the proletariat. Lenin's initially useful efforts to avoid "tailism" and to raise the political consciousness of the proletariat had degenerated into bureaucratic formalism and centralism, which Trotsky also referred to as "Asiatic" centralism. In Trotsky's famous statement, "In the party's internal politics these methods lead, as we shall further see, to this: the party organization 'substitutes' itself for the party, the C.C. [Central Committee] 'substitutes' itself for the party organization, and, at last, a 'dictator' substitutes himself for the C.C."[7]

The idea of "substitutionism" is itself meaningful only if one begins with Marxian assumptions about the self-activity of a proletarian party and its historical role, assumptions that can be rejected. But Trotsky's description, both as an empirical observation and prophesy, is flawless. It became something of an embarrassment, particularly during Stalin's dictatorship, when European Marxists, disillusioned with the fate of the revolution, held up, among others, Trotsky's and Rosa Luxemburg's warnings of 1904. Needless to say, the same wisdom can be found abundantly in the writings of numerous anarchists and liberals, as well as other Social Democrats. Like Trotsky, Luxemburg had sensed that a deadly choking off of initiative and spontaneous growth would follow from Leninist methods. Trotsky's predatorily searching intellect yielded political wisdom that transcended Marxian doctrine and dialectical "method." However, his commitment to Marxism was too strong for him to explore the full implications of his discovery. He did not grasp that extended revolutionary crises and the vicissitudes of postrevolutionary politics themselves tended to promote the type of Jacobin-Blanquist leadership against which he inveighed; and he could not abandon his romantic vision of the creativity of the revolutionary masses.

Political wisdom informs both Trotsky's observations about Lenin's organizational methods and Jacobinism as a revolutionary phenomenon. He noted that Lenin's "organizational algebraic formula" might be detached from the Social Democratic movement and used in different situations.[8] Furthermore, Trotsky explored political psychology and emerged with a reasonable connection between dictatorship and a paranoid style of politics. Although Trotsky presented Lenin as a caricature of Robespierre and although the latter had acted in a different kind of historical drama, the fate of the French Jacobins was still instructive. Trotsky divined both the "detachability" of certain kinds of political technique (in particular, Jacobin-Blanquist) and the psychology of a revolutionary dictatorship, which would devour its children. He even discovered the Protean characteristics of his own species, the intelligentsia, whose doctrinal commitments changed with the seasons. His foresight, however, could prevent neither the growth of Bolshevism nor his own "Blanquist opportunism"—a category of political behavior he explored in *Our Political Tasks*. His own passion for revolution, his own impatience, and, no doubt, personal ambition later converted him to the Bolshevik variety of Blanquism.

One of the most devastating blows delivered against Lenin by Trotsky in 1904 came in connection with Lenin's notion that factory work disciplined the proletariat for party activity. Lenin had counterposed intelligentsia individualism and anarchism to proletarian discipline and, in fending off Menshevik charges of elitism, had somewhat overstated the case: The proletariat would *teach* the Social Democratic intelligentsia political discipline! With malicious delight, Trotsky turned Marx against Lenin. The conditions of factory work deadened the proletariat, destroyed the natural rhythms of human creativity. One had to get workers to rebel against the barracks discipline of the modern factory, not try to import it into the party. "The barracks regime cannot be the regime of our party, just as the factory cannot be its prototype."[9] Lenin, of course, had a greater aversion to parliamentary talkshops or, more to the point, to the coffeehouse, the scene of the infuriating rambling and tergiversation of his colleagues, than to the compulsory rhythms of the modern factory. In fact, he later became fascinated with time-motion method of factory organization, the infamous (to most socialists) Taylorism.

Trotsky, like Marx, had been inspired more than a little by the romantic rebellion against the modern division of labor, the vision of a liberated, integral human personality. The idea of the whole being, freed from the too-specialized work of the modern era, had been central to the *narodnik* vision of Mikhailovskii, Trotsky's former mentor. But Trotsky, like any consistent Marxist, also believed in the ultimately liberating effects of modern factory production. Like Lenin, he later found Taylorism a useful method for raising production. Trotsky's antifactory rhetoric in 1904, was mainly rhetoric. However, the hollowness of the rhetoric (especially when measured against his romance of the machine and later espousal of the "militarization" of labor) does not diminish the value of his critique. In the course of attacking Lenin, Trotsky had stumbled upon a problem in Marxism, but his commitment had prevented him from pursuing it. Lenin did not understand the psychology issuing from factory conditions, but did Marx?

The Marxian intelligentsia assumed that workers, miserable to the point of rebellion and ready to express explosively "plebian" forms of vengeance against their oppressors, would somehow emerge from the revolution with the right psychology for socialist self-discipline. They would submit themselves to factory discipline, now that they owned the factories, and accept the most advanced forms of the organization of production, because they would see that it was to their benefit. However, according to Trotsky, they would only do so under the correct tutelage—that of the socialist intelligentsia. One could not avoid the role of the intelligentsia. Rather, the outcome depended upon the intelligentsia's ability to remain the teachers of the proletariat without becoming their rulers. Lenin's methods would clearly lead to the latter outcome, the betrayal of Marxism, and to a false revolution made in the name of proletarian liberation—of human liberation.

WHEN LOOKING back at his prophesy of 1904 from the distance of over three decades, Trotsky recognized its correctness, but admitted only that it described the "process of degeneration" in the Communist Party *after* Lenin's final illness and death. He applied the label "revolutionary centralism" to Lenin's approach in order to distinguish it from Stalin's bureaucratic centralism.[10] This seems intellectually dishonest, for in 1904 Trotsky had predicted that a revolution led successfully by a Jacobin or Blanquist style of leadership would have a rotten foundation, that it would inevitably degenerate. In 1917 Trotsky failed to heed his own warning that impatience leads to the use of harmful revolutionary methods. His own impatience and bolshevization took such extreme forms that many of the reproaches hurled by him against Lenin were, in only slightly different form, later turned against him. Reviewed with utter honesty after 1917, Trotsky's insights of 1904 would have alerted him to the hazards of his position. Instead, he rationalized his betrayal of his views with a politically expedient (given his fidelity to Marxism and his ambitions) explanation for the "betrayal" of the revolution and the emergence (as he erroneously saw it) of a dictator for the bureaucracy, rather than a dictatorship of the proletariat.

14

Trotsky in 1905

D URING THE year between the Third Party Congress and the attenuation of Trotsky's relationship with the Mensheviks in Geneva,[1] he found both a new mentor and a style of political behavior more congenial to him. The sectarianism now exhibited by both Bosheviks and Mensheviks repelled him. On their side, his comrades were at first inclined to protect him from Plekhanov, but soon found his extravagances annoying. It is not surprising that Trotsky was attracted to the one figure in the movement whose daring and independence matched his own. Shortly after the appearance of *Our Political Tasks*, he established a brief but important collaboration with Alexander Helphand, better known by his pseudonym, Parvus. In September 1904 Trotsky and Natalia Sedova traveled to Munich and moved in with Parvus, who often extended a helping hand to itinerant comrades. The odd contrast of Aksel'rod, Trotsky's avuncular guide in 1903–1904, with his picaresque new mentor, twelve years his senior, suggests how volatile he was. "Parvus,"

Helphand's Latin pseudonym, formed an ironic contrast with his real surname, derived from "elephant," and with the physical reality as well. His nickname, "Fatty," reflected a Churchillian, bulldog physiognomy and build. Trotsky was later to call him the Falstaff of the revolution. Nonetheless, it was not difficult for the younger man to form at least a temporary and partial identification with him.

Like Trotsky, Parvus had spent part of his childhood and adolescence in Odessa. His family had moved there after a pogrom in their village in Minsk province. As a teenager, Parvus had sampled the literature of revolution, gone through a *nardonik* apprenticeship among the artisans of Odessa, and emigrated at the age of twenty. He had become a Marxist during his years as a student in Switzerland and traded his earlier identity for a pan-European Social Democratic one. Parvus exhibited the virile political qualities admired by Trotsky. He had both a powerful global vision and vivid historical imagination and relied upon them to a fault. He developed positions whose boldness and originality made him a popular revolutionary journalist, but got him into trouble with his German and Russian Social Democratic colleagues. An accomplished (despite his third class degree) student of political economy with a doctorate from the University of Basel, Parvus' global outlook permitted him to identify trends and make timely predictions about approaching conflicts. Although the savage jockeying among the great powers and shifts of economic strength made such prophesy a far from arcane art—one did not even have to be a Marxist to understand the relationship among global political, social, and economic trends—Parvus differed from others in the nature of his commitment. He placed large wagers on war and revolution with more than just ideals of social justice in mind. More adventurous than most, he tended to migrate to the site of the most promising action. He had a flair not only for sensing impending conflicts among states and revolutionary developments but for taking advantage of war and revolution for his own pecuniary gain. His biographers appropriately titled their book *The Merchant of Revolution.*[2]

Parvus' odd morality ultimately repelled Trotsky, who at first found his revolutionary nomadism and entrepreneurial qualities an attractive contrast with the increasingly sectarian, routinized behavior of the Geneva émigrés. A man of learning, a provocative revolutionary journalist, a daring (though not always successful) businessman, who knew how to start from scratch and build publishing ventures, an optimist of inexhaustible energy, Parvus at first seemed to be the antithesis of the "homeopaths" of revolution with whom Trotsky had been associating in 1903–1904. Parvus urgently predicted an imminent Russian revolution and a global crisis and war, and he reproached the fractured Social Democratic movement for its inability to unify itself in order to take advantage of the situation.

In 1905 both Parvus and Trotsky showed their loyalty to revolution as such rather than to party sects neither of them found congenial. Parvus had established his reputation in the German Social Democratic movement. An early opponent of Bernstein and a vigorous proponent of an independent proletarian party, his "orthodoxy" had brought him close to Plekhanov's group. Parvus, already a veteran by the standards of Russian Social Democracy, had been influential during the first years of *Iskra*, when it was published in Munich. When the movement split, he continued to contribute to *The Spark* and, like Trotsky, was closer to the Mensheviks but not comfortable with mere Menshevism. He offered Trotsky not only a place to stay in Munich and intellectual companionship, but the opportunity to form a strong association with someone of influence who was not bound to a self-defeating sect and a rigid party line. Finally, the two men shared a belief in the imminence of socialist revolution and were less inclined than other Social Democrats (here they resembled Lenin) to seek cooperation with liberals or tolerate a phase of bourgeois rule.

Trotsky and Parvus greeted Bloody Sunday with a pamphlet, *Before the Ninth of January*, which Trotsky had begun in the autumn of 1904, inspired by the upsurgence of liberal opposition, the so-called "banquet campaign," and completed after the massacre of January 9(22), 1905. Parvus composed an introduction for the pamphlet, whose content owed a great deal to the impact of his intellectual exchanges with Trotsky and his own series of articles, "War and Revolution," which had appeared earlier in *The Spark*. Although Parvus, like his disciple Trotsky and, later, Lenin, mistakenly believed that the fates of the imperial powers and the entire capitalist system were closely linked (the false assumption underlying the theory of permanent revolution), he presented Social Democrats with a realistic picture of the crisis of the Russian imperial regime. He saw the Russo-Japanese War as the beginning of a period of global crisis among competing industrial states. The antagonisms of the new, imperialistic, industrializing nations with the established ones were no secret. It took a mind trained up in both political economy and Marxism to predict a total systemic crisis and greet it with revolutionary jubilation.

WRITTEN SHORTLY after *Our Political Tasks, Before the Ninth of January* marks a far more important turning point in Trotsky's career than his better-known work. It contains Trotsky's vision of the Russian Revolution and, like Lenin's *Letter to a Comrade*, presents in brief compass and precise terms a revolutionary modus operandi. Much of the pamphlet is devoted to an attack on the liberal "political eunuchs," like Struve, and advocacy of an independent proletarian revolutionary vanguard. Trotsky's savage attack upon the liberal elements in the developing revolutionary front alienated the Mensheviks, who delayed publishing the pamphlet. It brought him, at least in this respect, closer to Lenin, who despised liberal frailty and demanded that the proletariat put pressure upon liberals by assuming leadership of the revolutionary front. In any case, aside from contributing to his break with the Mensheviks, Trotsky's assault on the liberals is far less significant than the last part of the pamphlet, which exhibits Trotsky's emerging revolutionary style. Whereas Lenin devoted his greatest efforts to building and sustaining a party organization, the officers' corps that would lead the revolutionary forces, Trotsky concentrated instead on the disposition of forces in a fluid revolutionary situation, most important of all, the attitude of the tsarist army toward the revolutionaries. When Lenin, with his organizational emphasis, and Trotsky, with his mastery of the psychology and leadership of crowds, finally joined forces in 1917, they formed a historically momentous revolutionary partnership.

Trotsky's essential vision in the pamphlet is that of an open, fluid, mass movement. He counterposed his and Parvus' image of leadership to the traditional one, most clearly embodied in Bolshevism. What was needed was "freedom from the organizational routine and pitiful traditions of the conspiratorial underground; a broad vision; bold initiative; the ability to evaluate the situation; once again, bold initiative."[3] Like Parvus, Trotsky advocated the tactic of the general political strike. The workers would involve the entire population in a massive demonstration against the government. The city would be the main arena of revolutionary events. Trotsky had studied the revolutions of 1848 and, like other Russian Marxists during this period, pondered the art of insurrection. He had examined descriptions of the behavior of troops sent to suppress recent mass strikes and rebellions in the south of Russia. On this basis, he portrayed that crucial moment in revolutionary uprisings when unarmed masses confront armed soldiers. In his later history of the Russian Revolution, he showed his skill as a dramatist of such confrontations and shifts of mood in both troops and insurrectionists.

Trotsky's lyric description of the concentration and deployment of revolutionary forces in *Before the Ninth of January* seems more like the work of a gifted dramatist imagining a mise-en-scène than that of a sober tactician:

> Tear the workers away from the machines and the workshops; lead them through the factory gate out into the street; direct them to neighboring factions; proclaim a stoppage there; and carry new masses into the streets. Thus, moving from factory to factory, from workshop to workshop, growing under way and sweeping away police obstacles, haranguing and attracting passers-by, absorbing groups that come from the opposite direction, filling the streets, taking possession of the first suitable buildings for public meetings, entrenching yourselves in those buildings, using them for uninterrupted revolutionary meetings with a permanently shifting and changing audience, you shall bring order into the movement of the masses, raise their confidence, explain to them the purpose and the sense of events; and thus you shall eventually transform the city into a revolutionary camp—this, by and large, is the plan of action.[4]

This passage reveals an improvisational approach to revolution, a sense of dynamism, of the changing chemistry of mass action. It expresses the confidence of a young man whose power with words and sensitivity to the needs of his audience would make him one of the charismatic figures in revolutionary history. The words seem inspired, prophetic, for they describe with considerable precision the scenes to come in both 1905 and 1917. Yet for all its power, *Before the Ninth of January* sounded a bit feverish and lacked cogency at the time of its publication. It called for an eight-hour day, a general political strike, an end to the war, and the convocation of a constituent assembly. Parvus predicted that the provisional revolutionary government would be Social Democratic, for the workers would be the vanguard of the movement. Such ideas in 1904 and early 1905 were as wild and provocative to Russian Social Democrats, both Mensheviks and Bolsheviks, as Lenin's April Theses would be in 1917.

The partnership of Parvus and Trotsky 1905 in many ways prefigures that of Lenin and Trotsky. In each case, the senior partner ran the "business" end of the operation (in 1905, an extraordinarily successful revolutionary newspaper), while the younger man worked mainly up front, in the midst of the revolutionary throngs. For all his ability, Parvus had no personal charisma—indeed, he was somewhat repellent. But he knew how to organize a publishing venture. Trotsky projected revolutionary fervor and utter devotion to the cause, but his exhibitionism, his need to be at the center of the stage before a mass audience, made him dependent upon others in crucial organizational matters. Although he understood the importance of organization, he stressed organizational flexibility. Like Lenin, Trotsky was learning his profession, but he could not be a professional in the same way that Lenin was. In 1905 Lenin's organization could not be the framework for Trotsky's career. The man who had split the party in 1903 and championed the methods of the underground could not be his ally. Only Parvus offered optimism, liberation from the morass of émigré politics, and gifts that both reinforced and complemented his own. History obliged with the Russo-Japanese War and a massive strike movement. The dreariness of the split, the depressing year of factional intrigue, gave way to the exaltation of 1905.

Trotsky at Center Stage

TROTSKY'S WILLINGNESS to take risks and impatience to join the fray distinguished him among the leading émigrés. He and Sedova left Parvus and Munich, took counsel with Viktor Adler in Vienna, and departed for Kiev in February 1905. In the Russian Empire the divisions of Social Democrats into sects affected but did not completely inhibit collaboration. Thus, Leonid Krasin, a Bolshevik conciliator in politics and engineer by profession, ran a secret printing press in Kiev that served as the initial outlet for Trotsky's pampleteering after his return. As the party's premier technical expert, Krasin furthered Trotsky's education in the weapons of insurrection. He also helped Trotsky make connections in St. Petersburg. Trotsky claims in his autobiography that he influenced Lenin and the Bolsheviks through Krasin, who proposed Trotsky's theses about the nature of a provisional government at the Bolshevik congress meeting in April.[5] Lenin backed Krasin, thus indirectly supporting Trotsky's line. When he wrote his autobiography, Trotsky hurled this fact at the Stalinist falsifiers, who denied his priority in any "correct" tactical formulation. Even more important, he asserted a tie with Lenin they denied. The convergence of Lenin's and Trotsky's tactical views is important for the long run, but in 1905 any theses about a provisional revolutionary government remained academic. The regime could still fight back.

The calendar of Trotsky's revolutionary odyssey in 1905 bears some superficial resemblances to Lenin's in 1917. Like Lenin in 1917, Trotsky arrived in

1905 soon after the revolution had gotten underway; like Lenin, he had to flee St. Petersburg and hide in Finland during the summer; and like Lenin, he only returned in October for one of the decisive battles of 1905 in St. Petersburg. Trotsky returned under the stimulus of the great October general strike, and none too soon for him. He was alone—Natalia Sedova had been arrested on May Day—and he felt his vitality crushed by underground existence and routine activity. Trotsky's description of his stay in Finland is full of bleak imagery: "A heavy snow fell. The pine-trees were wrapped in a white shroud. The *pension* was like death."[6] (Death, in fact, was nearby. The landlord's wife died shortly before his departure, and Trotsky found himself in the company of a real corpse.) When he received word that the general strike planned for January 1906 had prematurely begun in October, he joyfully bolted for St. Petersburg and returned in time to play a major role in the St. Petersburg Soviet of Workers' Deputies.

Although spontaneous in some sense, the Soviet movement did not spring up from the October general strike alone. It had some of its origins in Zubatov's police unions, others in Gapon's St, Petersburg Assembly of Factory Workers, and still deeper roots in older traditions of labor organization.[7] More important, after the disaster with Gapon and Bloody Sunday, the government still tried to exploit the workers' desire to vent their grievances and to find legal outlets for their incipient labor organizations. This last experiment, the Shidlovskii Commission, provided the workers with experience at organizing elections. Functioning between January 29 and February 20, 1905, the commission played into the hands of socialist and liberal agitators and furthered the politicization of the workers.[8] Thus, the regime laid some of the groundwork for the labor movement and its most radical expression, the soviet. The radical parties, particularly Menshevik Social Democrats, did the rest. Soviets appeared in every major city in the empire and eventually represented the vast majority of Russian industrial workers.

Although in retrospect the most significant sociopolitical institutions to emerge in 1905, soviets were only one of several vehicles for the expression of social and political discontent. Legal and illegal professional and trade unions, an All-Russian Peasant Union, the *zemstvo* movement, nationalist movements, student demonstrations, mutinies in the army and navy—all these played a role in the revolutionary front. Already infiltrated by intelligentsia and worker members of the revolutionary parties, mobilized groups looked to them for leadership, but did not always back radical political slogans. They often resented efforts by the Social Democrats in particular to assert hegemony over them and set a political agenda. Social Democratic agitators did indeed begin to assert their leadership over some unions and soviets, but events prevented the crystallization of political control. By late October, it was a vast, kaleidoscopic movement no single party, liberal or radical, could dominate. The chemistry of the movement changed from day to day, sometimes from hour to hour.

IT WAS the sort of situation that could encourage and simultaneously mislead an adventurer like Trotsky, a gifted improviser, who believed that the chaotic eruption of 1905 contained within it a new order. Two passages in his autobiography reveal with striking clarity Trotsky's faith in both the rational dialectic of revolutionary process and his own fitness for leadership at the moment of revolution:

> Revolutionary chaos is not at all like an earthquake or a flood. In the confusion of a revolution, a new order begins to take shape instantly; men and ideas distribute themselves naturally in new channels. Revolution appears as utter madness only to those whom it sweeps aside and overthrows. To us it was different. We were in our own element, albeit a very stormy one. . . . No great work is possible without intuition—that is, without that subconscious sense which, although it may be developed and enriched by theoretical work, must be engrained in the very nature of the individual. Neither theoretical education nor practical routine can replace the political insight which enables one to apprehend a situation, weigh it as a whole, and foresee the future. This gift takes on decisive importance at a time of abrupt changes and breaks—the condition of revolution. The events of 1905 revealed in me, I believe, this revolutionary intuition, and enabled me to rely on its assured support during my later life.[9]

This confession of his peculiar fitness as a leader implicitly refers to Trotsky in 1917 as well as 1905, although for political reasons he felt safer making such claims in connection with 1905. No one would question his preeminence as a leader in the St. Petersburg Soviet of 1905. Trotsky felt he could indulge himself by quoting Lunacharskii's memoirs:

> "I remember somebody saying in Lenin's presence: 'The star of Khrustalev [Nosar] is setting. Today the strong man in the Soviet is Trotsky.' For a moment Lenin's expression seemed to darken; then he said, 'Well, Trotsky has won this by his tireless and striking work.' "[10]

Trotsky in 1905 felt that his revolutionary apprenticeship had come to an end. Even more important, he sensed that he was organically suited for life at the edge, for leadership at those catastrophic moments when others, like Martov, hesitated and drew back. In short, Trotsky discovered within himself the capacity to gain control over masses of people in a fluid situation, something he had visualized and sketched out in his addendum to *Before the Ninth of January*. He was like an artist who had imagined a work and then embodied his vision in his chosen medium. Trotsky achieved one of the pinnacles of his career in 1905, but the temporary success of an improvisational and charismatic style of leadership deluded him into believing that he was the *natural* leader of the revolution—that he was a man of destiny. Trotsky's sense of organic fitness for the job contrasts with Lenin's grudging explanation, which Trotsky quoted in his autobiography without understanding its significance. Lenin believed that Trotsky had succeeded in 1905 because he had *worked* hard, not because of a natural gift of intuition. Hard work was Lenin's way. It was the way of a revolutionary toolmaker, rather than that of a revolutionary artist playing a role in a Marxian drama. The imaginations of the best extemporaneous artists are nourished on models. Perhaps Trotsky remembered at some level of his mind that his models, Danton and Lassalle, had ended tragically and, even if unconsciously, had a tragic end in mind for himself. A man with Trotsky's imagination would hardly create a pallid ending to his own career.

PERHAPS TROTSKY believed so intensely in the triumph of the revolution that he could take risks that Lenin, for example, would not; perhaps he irrationally believed himself to be invulnerable; or perhaps, like his hero Lassalle, he had too much of the duelist in him. Of course, confrontations with authority and getting arrested are the stock-in-trade of the professional revolutionary. But do *mature* leaders put themselves in the way of arrest? Certainly, they frequently do so in movements of civil disobedience in political cultures where a certain modicum of trust, of belief in the clemency of the ruling authority warrants such risks. One wonders if the tsarist regime's wavering in 1905 warranted the risk of arrest, trial, imprisonment, and exile. It is difficult to avoid the conclusion that arrest and trial were part of Trotsky's script. He needed to confront the tsarist hangmen in a dramatic courtroom scene, to accuse his accusers before a national audience. Trotsky would not be denied an opportunity to take the stage in the last drama of 1905, the trial of the soviet leadership. His theatrically defiant behavior in the soviet might easily have led to his martyrdom.

THE PARALYSIS caused by the general strike forced the government to concede the Manifesto of October 17, 1905. After decades of struggle with the autocracy, the combined forces of liberalism and socialism seemed to be on the verge of winning a genuine constitutional system. However, the left wing of the revolutionary front continually had before it the lessons of 1848 and desperately sought to keep alive the pressure from the left. Anything less than that would permit the tsarist regime to recover and to consolidate its position as a still powerful and repressive constitutional monarchy supported by conservative landowners, businessmen, bureaucrats, and professionals. Trotsky put himself at the forefront of the left opposition. On October 18 he joined several other speakers at St. Petersburg University addressing a huge crowd from a balcony. It was an interesting task for a radical orator. On the one hand, he could not deny the euphoria caused by the Manifesto; on the other, he had to display its inadequacy and point to the dangers ahead. He called for the removal of all troops from St. Petersburg and then, waving a copy of the October Manifesto, shouted:

> Citizens! Our strength is in ourselves. With a sword in hand we must stand guard over our freedom. As for the Tsar's manifesto, look, it's only a scrap of paper. Here it is before you—here it is crumpled in my fist. Today they have issued it, tomorrow they will take it away and tear it into pieces, just as I am now tearing up this paper freedom before your eyes![11]

Lenin was never capable of such grandiloquent gestures. Trotsky followed his oratory with a stirring article in *Izvestiia*, in which he reiterated the Soviet's slogans for a constituent assembly, amnesty, the eight-hour workday, the removal of troops, and, not least of all, the creation of a militia. Trotsky's urgency about the formation of a workers' militia in 1905 foreshadows his role as the head of the military committee of the Petrograd Soviet in October 1917.

Other émigré leaders returned after Nicholas II granted an amnesty to political criminals on October 30, 1905. Parvus, however, left before the amnesty and arrived in St. Petersburg toward the end of October. He and Trotsky stole a march on the others in the area of revolutionary journalism by purchasing a small-circulation (30,000) liberal newspaper, *The Russian Gazette*. Within less than two months they were selling 500,000 newspapers daily, at one kopeck a copy. When Martov and Zasulich returned in November to represent the more moderate Menshevik line in their newspaper, *The Beginning*, they were able to establish a modus vivendi with Trotsky and Parvus. Even though the Mensheviks believed a socialist government would be premature, given Russia's stage of development, they stood with those who worked for an insurrection. Furthermore, they were closer to Trotsky and Parvus in their views on organization than they were to the Bolsheviks. In 1905 Trotsky's ambiguous stance worked to his advantage. He was more radical than the Mensheviks in his goals for the revolution and more flexible than the Bolsheviks about organization. This gave him a voice on the board of *The Beginning* and an additional outlet for his ideas. Even the Bolshevik journal, *New Life*, published his articles. Finally, he wrote for the organ of the St. Petersburg Soviet, *Izvestiia*, which, of course, is still the title of the official newspaper of the Soviet government. The soviet and socialist press became the rallying point for those who wanted to bury the old regime in a revolutionary insurrection. Their newspapers and journals achieved huge circulation during the "days of freedom," the period between the granting of the October Manifesto and the suppression of the soviets by the regime in December.

Trotsky's behavior as one of the leaders and for a short time, Chairman of the Presidium of the St. Petersburg Soviet's Executive Committee, foreshadowed his role in 1917. His greatest strength was also his most profound weakness. Trotsky's revolutionary faith inspired others, but it led to reckless behavior. To be sure, such faith at first seemed wed to realism in October 1905. It is difficult to understand Trotsky's actions without grasping the magnitude of the labor movement and the drama of the Soviet in the seven weeks of its existence. The first meeting of the St. Petersburg Soviet preceded the October Manifesto by four days. On October 13, 1905, a meeting of thirty to forty deputies, all of them elected by their factory constituencies, convened in an assembly hall of the Technological Institute in St. Petersburg. The founders of the Soviet endorsed the idea of a general strike and called for all factories to send deputies, one for each 500 workers. From its modest beginnings, mainly based in one district of St. Petersburg, the Soviet grew until it represented roughly 200,000 workers. As its height it had 562 deputies. Although not the first soviet to appear in 1905, the St. Petersburg Soviet was the most influential one in the Russian empire—and Trotsky, who celebrated his twenty-sixth birthday during the second week of the Soviet's existence, was indeed its Danton.

In his autobiography Trotsky hints that only his sojourn in the woods in Finland permitted G. S. Nosar (Khrustalev), a radical lawyer and leader in the labor movement, to become president of the Soviet. In any case, Trotsky and others provided the real leadership.[12] Trotsky's influence in the Soviet grew apace after his oratory of October 18, and the Soviet's defiant gestures often seemed to be an extension of Trotsky's personality, his revolutionary faith and will. The Soviet refused to accept meekly what the regime had given and precipitated the days of freedom by decreeing an end to censorship. Even more important, workers were told to legislate a de facto eight-hour workday by laying down their tools at the end of eight hours of work. But within a short time, the Soviet had to rescind the eight-hour day in the face of lockouts. Hopes of a united front of workers, peasants, soldiers, and sailors faded. All of Trotsky's feverish hopes and the agitation inspired by them yielded before the reality of the shifting morale of the revolutionary forces and the failure of the revolutionaries to bring the troops over to their side in sufficient numbers. The regime arrested Nosar on November 26, and, rather than seek safety, Trotsky seemed to look forward to an even more grandiloquent gesture of defiance.

The regime never lost control over its instruments of force. To be sure, mutinies in both the army and navy warned of things to come, but the disintegration of tsarist authority and the control of the officers' corps had not advanced to a critical point; links between the revolutionary parties and military units were still frail; and, not least of all, the revolutionary movement had not reached a point where a single leader would pursue power ruthlessly for his own party. The mass rebellion took diffuse forms; the strike paralyzed the country and thus threatened the regime; but the St. Petersburg Soviet, in the fifty-two days of its existence (October 13 through December 3, 1905), had not developed to the point where it would be dominated by a single determined party, which in turn would control its military arm, as it would in 1917. Thus, when the regime decided to arrest Nosar, resistance was impossible; and when the time came for Trotsky, the head of the Soviet presidium after Nosar's arrest, on December 3, 1905, he and the other members of the Executive Committee counseled nonresistance to the members of the Soviet who carried arms. The St. Petersburg Soviet was abolished for the time being. The regime began to isolate segments of the revolutionary front and dispose of them piecemeal with its troops.

Exeunt

A FTER THE arrests on December 3 it fell to Parvus to fill in for Trotsky. Parvus had authored the Soviet's famous financial manifesto of December 2, which he hoped would drain specie out of the banks, bankrupt the government, discourage foreign loans, and, possibly, channel some gold in his direction. Parvus' manifesto, in fact, had precipitated the government's decision to crack down on the Soviet. Although the rump of the St. Petersburg Soviet still had sufficient authority to call another (the third since early October) general strike to begin on December 8, the Moscow Soviet now seized the initiative and established its own timetable. The strike began in Moscow on December 7, 1905. In Moscow, the Soviet decided to use the strike as the trigger for armed insurrection. Until this time the government had treated massive urban demonstrations with relative restraint, doing everything possible to avoid a repetition of the massacre of January 9, 1905. Now it faced the left wing of the revolutionary front, those who would not be satisfied with anything less than the complete overthrow of the regime in an armed insurrection. The unreliability of the troops in the Moscow garrison, open preparation for an insurrection, and the breakdown of authority in several areas of the empire, forced the government's hand. The fall of Moscow would be a staggering symbolic and strategic defeat to the regime. On the other hand, the defeat of the Moscow insurrectionaries would demonstrate the weakness and isolation of the most radical elements of the revolutionary front. On December 15–16 the elite Semenovskii regiment of the imperial guards and other units arrived in Moscow. The rebels were subdued with the help of artillery barrages, and the strike halted on December 19.

FOR ALL intents and purposes, the destruction of the Moscow Soviet ended the threat to the regime. The government survived the crises of 1905, thanks to the diplomatic and financial skills of Witte, the ruthlessness of Minister of Interior Durnovo, and the brutal determination of Witte's successor as prime minister, Peter Stolypin. Throughout 1906 the regime sent out punitive expeditions to the countryside and the rebellious nationalities. The army and Okhrana crushed a campaign of terror and expropriation organized by the Socialist Revolutionary Maximalists and participated in by the Bolsheviks. The resources of the state proved adequate to the threats mounted against it. The reform program and parliamentary system installed by Stolypin in his famous "coup d'état" of June 1907 were, on the one hand, a belated attempt at social engineering and, on the other, a last effort to organize a bloc of support to keep the regime functioning until the ongoing program of industrial development brought more strength than instability to the empire. Stolypin's famous wager on the social and economic transformation of the peasantry through dissolution of the old communal structures depended on decades of relative stability. The assassination of Stolypin in 1911 was one of the signals of a new era of social and political disequilibrium. History, alas, is not a laboratory in the true sense and does not permit us to know what would have happened had Stolypin's system been given the several decades it needed. In any case, from the perspective of the revolutionaries, even the brief stabilization of the regime after the turmoil of 1905–1906 was terribly demoralizing.

Until the outbreak of the first global war, the one predicted by Parvus and eagerly awaited by Russian Marxists, revolutionaries could not fail to feel moments of despair. They had studied the lessons of history; they had known about 1848, about the pitfalls of revolutionary situations. But they had come away almost empty-handed, and it was still painful. Armed insurrection had failed. Instead of being replaced by a democratic republic or, according to the theory of permanent revolution, a socialist republic signaling the end to the global bourgeois order, the ruling regime had emerged intact. By 1907 it had installed a Prussian-style system with massive conservative underpinning in a curial system of elections, bicameralism, and other constitutional measures to protect the autocrat's and old elite's power and image. Yet even within that political context all groups enjoyed new freedoms. Political parties functioned, and the opposition, some of it loyal, some of it revolutionary, openly assailed the regime's most heinous behavior. Many former radicals became more domesticated, confident that things were changing. They lost their revolutionary edge. Furthermore, the chaotic last phases of 1905–1906 had thrown a fright into educated society. Many, like Peter Struve, began to feel that the old structure afforded them some protection from the uncivilized left. The liberal slogan, no enemies to the left, lost numerous adherents. The period 1907–1912 was one of loss and defeat for revolutionaries.

TROTSKY'S IMPRISONMENT, trial, and escape from exile were a fittingly dramatic denouement to 1905. His year in prison formed a striking contrast with his earlier incarcerations in Nikolaev and Odessa. Like Lenin in 1896, he was given access to books, conducted research, wrote articles, and even completed a major theoretical work on rent and the history of social relations in Russia. Oddly enough, this work suffered the same fate as his history of freemasonry written in the Odessa prison. He lost it. He was more fortunate with his articles on the revolution of 1905, which were converted into a brilliant history of the revolution, *1905*. Trotsky was one of many Russian revolutionaries who found imprisonment an excellent environment for intense study and writing. At its best, political imprisonment was more like a monastic retreat than a punishment. So it was during Trotsky's solitary confinement in the Peter and Paul fortress. Trotsky must also have felt that his stay in the fortress was a token of his celebrity, for most of the illustrious martyrs of the revolutionary movement had served time there. After transfer to preliminary detention in preparation for his trial, Trotsky was able to rejoin his comrades Parvus (who had been arrested roughly a month after Trotsky), Deutsch, and others, not all of whom were tried publicly. Trotsky and those arrested on December 3, 1905, were brought to trial on September 19, 1906.

An unexpected contest developed during the course of the trial. The accused leaders of the Soviet, several of whom were Jews, did not merely defend themselves against the government's charge of conspiracy to organize armed insurrection. They in turn accused the government of complicity in the organization of pogroms. The pogroms were only part of a broader reaction, the attacks of the "Black Hundreds" that developed in counterpoint to the revolution of 1905 and the emergence of the proto-Fascist Union of the Russian

People. The most reactionary elements continued to believe that the revolution was a Jewish and Polish conspiracy. Although the defendants of course failed in their efforts to turn the tables on the prosecution, they did have the satisfaction of being declared not guilty of the charge that they had armed the workers for the purpose of insurrection.

Trotsky's mother and father attended the trial. They witnessed their son transform the courtroom into a classroom, a seminar on the nature of socialist revolution and the place of insurrection in it. They watched with pride a handsome, lean young man with a mustache and small goatee and a wavy mass of dark hair, which stood out like a lion's mane. He wore pince-nez for his myopia, attested to by perceptibly protuberant eyes. Impeccably dressed in a frock coat, high starched collar, and bow tie, he might easily have been mistaken for one of the lawyers at the trial, and he had the manner of a theatrical species of professor. At one session, perhaps the day of his speech, he posed for a group picture with a portfolio stuffed with papers. He was so convincing, so *respectable* when he delivered his long speech on October 4, 1906, that his mother could not believe that they would send him to Siberia. Surely he deserved some sort of reward. When Trotsky recounted the scene in his autobiography, he expressed openly what many who have rebelled against their parents feel but do not offer to a reading public. His trial afforded him a brilliant opportunity to show his worth, to justify himself to his doubting parents:

> It was now impossible to explain away my conduct as a boy's foolishness, as they had in my Nikolaev days when I lived in Shvigovskii's garden. I was an editor of newspapers, the chairman of the Soviet, and I had a name as a writer. The old couple were impressed by all this. . . . My mother was sure that I would not only be acquitted, but even given some mark of distinction. I tried to persuade her to prepare for a sentence of hard labor.[13]

Trotsky tried to give the prosecuting attorney a lesson in law and logic, to show that the St. Petersburg Soviet had more claim to state authority than the Tsar's minions, that it represented a new order. The Soviet had failed only in that it could not protect the people from the illegitimate force of the tsarist state. Trotsky possessed a rare ability to assume the mantle of authority, to look morally and intellectually superior to those who claimed authority.

Similar scenes recurred throughout Trotsky's life. He would face superior force armed with nothing but words and logic; he would vindicate himself and his cause, accuse his accusers, defy and humiliate his antagonists in a hopeless struggle; and although he might awe spectators and win sympathy by his performances, he would only bemuse or infuriate his opponents. The unequal courtroom duel with the tsarist regime in St. Petersburg, the diplomatic duel with the Germans and Austro-Hungarians at Brest-Litovsk in 1918, and the one with Stalin in Mexico at the sessions of the Dewey Commission in 1937 all displayed Trotsky's moral superiority. In the end he could not avert defeat— and death. Trotsky had been prepared for death in 1905. He liked to quote the old French revolutionary saying about having made a pact not with victory but with death. Although martyrdom had been an acceptable part of his scenario, Trotsky came away from the experience of 1905 feeling as if he had a charmed life.

AFTER BEING sentenced to Siberian exile in Obdorsk on December 5, 1906, Trotsky and the others spent a few more weeks in prison. They were transferred to a transit prison and from there to a train on January 10, 1907, when they began their long trip to the Arctic Circle. During the journey Trotsky kept a diary. At a village stopover on January 16 the convoy of fifteen exiles, crowded into a single room in a peasant hut for the night, cast lots for the privilege of sleeping on the one divan. Trotsky won, which prompted him to write: "I'm always lucky in life." [14] His luck continued. He decided to feign illness when he reached Berezov, on the Ob River, still more than three hundred miles away from their final destination. At the end of February 1907 Trotsky left Berezov hidden in a sleigh pulled by three reindeer and driven by the tradition-ally skilled but chronically drunk driver. In about a week they reached the Urals, and shortly thereafter Trotsky sent a telegram to Natalia Sedova to meet him in Samino. From there they went to St. Petersburg, where they stayed for a short time before departing for Finland. Trotsky had the distinct pleasure of selling the account of his Siberian odyssey. In April 1907 he left Finland by steamer for Stockholm, London, and ten years of exile.

15

Lenin at Loose Ends

LENIN REACTED ambivalently to the hurly-burly of 1905. The awesome scale of the nonsectarian mass movement marching under mainly liberal slogans at once excited his revolutionary hopes and worried him. How could one march at the head of this vast, spontaneous movement? How would his organization be able to retain its boundaries? How could the Bolsheviks avoid contamination by collaboration with despised liberals and *narodniki*, with Social Democratic softs and opportunists? European Social Democratic leaders urgently advised the split Russian Social Democrats to heal themselves, to unify. Lenin's maneuverings to make the Third Party Congress a source of legitimacy in the eyes of leading European Social Democrats failed. The resolutions orchestrated by Lenin lost whatever authority they had possessed when questioned by such august figures as Kautsky. In view of the magnitude of the events of 1905 sectarian maneuvering seemed increasingly petty and self-defeating, the atmosphere of the underground stale. During

1905 Lenin was under enormous pressure to change course—something already apparent at the Third Party Congress—and very quickly, he did, but without abandoning his basic vision and goals.

WHILE TROTSKY chafed in hiding in Finland, waiting for his moment to return to St. Petersburg, Lenin in Geneva, aided by able field commanders like Krasin, Bogdanov, Lunacharskii, and S. I. Gusev shouldered a mass of party affairs. He edited the new Bolshevik central organ, *The Proletarian.* During the summer he worked on his voluminous pamphlet, *Two Tactics of Social-Democracy in the Democratic Revolution,* his definitive theoretical work of the period. Characteristically, Lenin took part in every possible aspect of party life: smuggling literature, procuring weapons, establishing ties with newly erupting areas in the Russian Empire, scrutinizing foreign responses to the revolution. But he remained a chateau general, surveying the battlefield from afar in Geneva, and still expended considerable energy on the sectarian struggle with his Menshevik opponents.

The management of party affairs and literature took precedence over all else. Only repeated pleas from the Central Committee and Lenin's certainty that he had made suitable arrangements in Switzerland for carrying on in his absence convinced him at the end of September that he could leave. Even then, his fear of arrest made him request Sweden rather than Finland as a meeting place. If they were all arrested, the party would fall prey to the Mensheviks. Lenin hoped that the insurrection would not take place until the spring. But the situation in Russia kept outstripping the expectations of the revolutionaries. Although he sent detailed instructions about how to conduct the military side of the struggle, Lenin's modus operandi and sense of priorities had been formed before the experience of October 1905, and he was extremely cautious. Meanwhile, the Mensheviks were making themselves dominant in the labor movement, whether expressed in the form of illegal trade unions or the soviets, and, thanks to Trotsky's affiliation with them, dominated the deliberations of the St. Petersburg Soviet. When he at last began making final arrangements for his departure at the end of October, Lenin tried to convince Plekhanov to join the editorial board of the new Bolshevik legal newspaper published in St. Petersburg. The plea to Plekhanov, just before his departure, suggests not only a shrewd move on Lenin's part to enhance the prestige of the journal, which was competing with *The Russian Gazette* and *The Beginning,* but a gesture in the direction of the reunification of the party. Plekhanov never replied.

Lenin wrote his first response to the soviet movement shortly after his arrival in Stockholm in early November. It expresses more diffidence than one usually finds in Lenin's writings. He still felt distant and partially informed about events. Intended for *New Life,* for an unknown reason his article was not published there, but was "found" and first published thirty-five years later, on November 5, 1940, in *Pravda.* (The date of publication, just before the anniversaries of the Revolution of 1917 and the writing of the article seems hardly accidental.)[1] With remarkable accuracy the article, "Our Tasks and the Soviet of Workers' Deputies," previews Lenin's approach to the soviets in 1917. Lenin was writing in reply to the hard Bolshevik approach expressed in the fifth issue of *New Life*, where it was assumed one could not belong both to the soviet and the party.

> I may be wrong, but I believe (on the strength of the incomplete and only "paper" information at my disposal) that politically the Soviet of Workers' Deputies should be regarded as the embryo of a *provisional revolutionary government*. I think the Soviet should proclaim itself the provisional revolutionary government of the whole of Russia as early as possible, or should *set up* a provisional revolutionary government (which would amount to the same thing, only in another form). . . . We have been speaking all the time of the need of a militant alliance of Social Democrats and revolutionary bourgeois democrats. We have been speaking of it and the workers have actually done it.[2]

Foreseeing the objections of his own followers, Lenin reassured them repeatedly that the proletarian movement was strong enough to sustain its identity and that all elements of the revolutionary front could agree upon a program that included, in brief: full civil liberties; the convocation of a constituent assembly; the arming of the people; freedom for oppressed nationalities in the Russian empire; the eight-hour working day and the curbing of capitalist exploitation; and, not least of all, transfer of all the land to the peasants. The democratic elements in the revolutionary movement of 1905—meaning the vast majority of the population—already supported this program, claimed Lenin. All that remained was to unify the movement around the program, to organize the revolutionary forces through the soviets, and to guide them toward an armed insurrection. Speeding up his timetable for insurrection by several months, Lenin called for the overthrow of tsarist rule by January 9, 1906, the first anniversary of Bloody Sunday. Yet Lenin admitted at the beginning of the article that he had had only second-hand information, much of it evidently gleaned from the press, and he left it to the discretion of his fellow editors to decide whether to publish it. Either he thought better of sending the article, or else they decided not to publish it.

Lenin soon tested his Stockholm illumination about the Soviet against reality. He attended two sessions of the St. Petersburg Soviet, those of November 12 and 13, 1905. Party history credits him with the Executive Committee's resolution of November 14 on the conduct of the struggle with lockouts, although the editors of Trotsky's collected works included it in the second volume.[3] Trotsky claims that Lenin never spoke at the Soviet and "took no active part" in its work.[4] Perhaps Trotsky meant full sessions of the Soviet, for there is a vivid description of Lenin's presentation of his putative resolution on the lockouts at a session of the Executive Committee of the St. Petersburg Soviet on November 13(26), 1905.[5] M. Essen's description of the reception of Lenin's speech sounds suspiciously stylized. The speech supposedly electrified the audience and provoked a "rumble of approval which grew into a stormy ovation." Yet this was presumably only a speech to the Executive Committee. There is a similar ending to a description of Lenin orating by Krzhizhanovskii.

It was a speech about participation in the Duma and took place on May 9(22), 1906. The description, after making Lenin out to be a man of granite, ends: "He left the rostrum to the thunder of applause, changing into an ovation."[6]

Krupskaia is probably the most reliable source on Lenin as an orator in this period. She refers only to the speech of May 9 described above:

> On May 9 Vladimir Ilich, for the first time in Russia, addressed a huge mass meeting at Panina's People's House under the name of Karpov. The hall was packed with workers from all districts. . . . I was standing among the crowd. Ilich was terribly agitated. He stood silent for about a minute, very pale. All the blood had flowed to his heart. You could sense at once that the speaker's agitation was communicating itself to the audience. Then all of a sudden a burst of hand-clapping swept through the hall—the Party comrades had recognized Ilich. . . . A hush descended upon the hall. A wave of extraordinary enthusiasm swept the audience after Ilich's speech.[7]

Krupskaia describes a man unaccustomed to addressing a huge audience of unfamiliar faces. Lenin had to overcome a moment of stage fright. It seems unlikely that he had had any practice addressing the five hundred odd delegates of the Soviet of Workers' Deputies in St. Petersburg.

Although Lenin did have contacts with members of the St. Petersburg Soviet's Executive Committee, there is no further indication that he warmed to the Soviet after his arrival in St. Petersburg. It is altogether likely that he felt disoriented or ill at ease in a body in which others, Trotsky in particular, had seized the initiative. Lenin's first publication mentioning the Soviet in *New Life* on November 15, 1905, calls the party to support the Soviet during the period of lockouts, but contains nothing about the Soviet as the basis for a provisional government. Several other articles that refer to the soviets, among them, "The Dying Autocracy and the New Organs of Popular Power" contain ideas similar to those in his unpublished article.

> For the socialist proletariat, for the revolutionary peasantry, and for all those who are resolutely and irrevocably taking a stand with them in the struggle for liberty, the establishment of a provisional revolutionary government is a great and extremely important task, which becomes more pressing with every day. The October revolution, together with the military risings which followed it, has so weakened the autocracy that the organs of a new power—that of the people— have begun to spring up spontaneously, on the ground ploughed up by the political strike and fertilised with the blood of the champions of liberty. These organs are bringing about in practice the alliance between the socialist proletariat and the revolutionary petty bourgeoisie. . . . For us representatives of the socialist proletariat the forthcoming democratic revolution is only one of the steps to the great goal, the socialist revolution. Bearing this in mind, we shall never merge with the petty-bourgeois parties or groups, however sincere, revolutionary or strong they may be; we know for certain that on the road to socialism, the ways of the worker and of the petty proprietor will very often inevitably diverge. But it is in the interests of socialism that we shall now do our utmost for the democratic revolution to be accomplished as speedily, as fully and as resolutely as possible. With this end in view, we shall conclude, and are concluding, a temporary alliance with all the revolutionary democratic forces to

attain our common immediate political aim. It is to this end that, while strictly preserving our Party identity and independence, we enter the Soviets of Worker Deputies and other revolutionary associations.[8]

By "other revolutionary associations" Lenin meant the soviets of soldiers' deputies, railwaymen's, peasant, and town revolutionary committees, and other spontaneous forms of popular organization, which he called "embryonic forms" of revolutionary power. Lenin's continual refrain, the strict preservation of the party's autonomy, always appears alongside pleas for joining the broader movement. On the other hand, it would be wrong to underestimate the great departure Lenin had taken from his original Bolshevism and that of many of his followers. The term "spontaneity" had shed its negative connotations; organs created by spontaneous popular initiative now had great political potential. Observing the spontaneous popular organs at first hand convinced him that they could be controlled. He had faith in his organization's ability to exert that control. Lenin expressed confidence that Social Democrats had already laid a solid foundation in the organizational experience, programs, and tactical rules of the preceding years. The party could absorb large numbers of new members without fearing loss of its sharply defined character or its leading role. At moments, Lenin used rhetoric sufficiently "soft" to cause those who had studied his previous writings to gape:

> The working class is instinctively, spontaneously Social Democratic, and more than ten years of work put in by Social Democracy has done a great deal to transform this spontaneity into consciousness. . . . Don't forget that in every live and growing party there will always be elements of instability, vacillation, wavering. But these elements can be influenced, and they will submit to the influence of the steadfast and solid core of Social Democrats. . . . Our Party has stagnated while working underground. As a delegate to the Third Congress rightly said, it has been suffocating underground during the last few years. The "underground" is breaking up. Forward, then, more boldly; take up the new weapon, distribute it among new people, extend your bases, rally all the worker Social-Democrats round yourselves, incorporate them in the ranks of the Party organizations by hundreds and thousands. Let their delegates put new life into the ranks of our central bodies, let the fresh spirit of young revolutionary Russia pour in through them.[9]

This burst of revolutionary optimism and plea for renewal shows that Lenin himself had become infused with the spirit of 1905, although his style of leadership still differed radically from Trotsky's. Lenin spent no time at all trying to establish himself as an orator. Rather, he expended his best energies within his own organization and sized up the broader organizational possibilities before him, like a general assessing the available forces before a battle. His rhetoric about the soviets shifted. During 1906 Lenin's struggle with the Mensheviks and Plekhanov over participation in the Duma created by the tsarist government led to modifications in his views of the soviets. Whereas at first he seemed to stress its potential as the embryo of a new government, later he began to emphasize a more limited use for it: "The Soviet of workers' deputies is not a workers' parliament and not an organ of proletarian self-rule, in general, not an organ of self-rule, but a combat organization for the achievement of definite goals . . . a broad military alliance of socialist and revolutionary democrats."[10] He needed to distinguish *their* notion of the soviets as organs of local self-government from his. To those fainthearted liberals who welcomed the suppression of the organs of popular power, Lenin held up the soviets as a true expression of the creativity of the masses.

Lenin's assessment of the soviets was intimately bound up with his goal of an armed uprising. Had the uprisings of 1905 succeeded, the soviet might have become more than merely an "organ of mass, direct struggle." For Lenin, the end was more important than the means. The means, in this case, the soviets, would acquire their final significance once the end—armed insurrection—had been achieved. But armed insurrection would be impossible unless the soviets created military organizations. The soviets would be able neither to defend themselves (this had been amply demonstrated in Moscow in December) nor go on the attack. As the revolution of 1905 lost momentum, Lenin continued to call for an armed uprising, for the formation of small armed bands, *druzhenniki*. His instructions are nothing less than a call to a desperate guerrilla war, the plea of a professional revolutionary watching the greatest opportunity in decades of struggle with the autocracy slipping away:

> The masses must know that they are setting out on an armed, bloody, desperate struggle. Victory demands widespread contempt for death. The attack on the enemy must be the most energetic; attack, and not defense, must become the slogan of the masses; merciless annihilation of the enemy must become their task.[11]

Like revolutionaries before him, and like Trotsky, Lenin called for a pact not with victory but with death. The Bolsheviks who responded to his call in 1905–1907 included committeemen who had fought in the underground for years and who found demobilization intolerable. The most disparate talents joined in a desperate effort to regain revolutionary momentum after the Moscow uprising was crushed. Urbane professionals and intellectuals like Krasin, Lunacharskii, and Bogdanov joined with picaresque figures like S. A. Ter-Petrosian and one of his mentors, a rising young committeeman from Transcaucasia known in the underground as Koba, whose real name was Iosif Vissarionovich Dzhugashvili.

16

Iosif Dzhugashvili Becomes Koba

IT IS difficult to avoid the worst pitfalls of biography when investigating Stalin's childhood. Unlike Lenin, he had no siblings and no life companion to write memoirs about him. Unlike Trotsky, he did not write an autobiography. Furthermore, most of the memoir material about his childhood and youth was written at a time when he had achieved a dread form of power. His daughter's memoirs contain very important information but are tantalizingly fragmentary. The only material worthy of serious study is sparse and tempts biographers to reduce Stalin to one or another type: the Georgian mountaineer with revenge encoded in his psyche; the gifted son of a drunken and brutal father and protective, self-sacrificing mother; the brilliant but disadvantaged boy with a deep, terrible grudge. What is worse, the meager written sources are contradicted by oral tradition in areas crucial for an understanding of Stalin's psychological development.[1] Did he sympathize and identify himself primarily with a supportive mother victimized by a putatively brutal father or with a father who was not at all brutal, but a gentle, pathetic lonely man victimized by circumstance and by a shrewish wife? Whatever the truth about the elder Dzhugashvilis, the poverty of models for a positive identity is striking. Stalin was undoubtedly a compound social victim: a member of a humiliated minority in the Russian Empire; a boy whose father was a failure by most measures and whose mother did domestic work; a dutiful and gifted child subjected to the stultifying regime of a claustrophobic seminary; a romantic youth looking to the past for his values who was forced, ultimately, to choose the future.

STALIN WAS victimized by both nature and circumstance. The second and third toes on his left foot were joined in a congenital deformity. Pock-marked since the age of seven, his left arm visibly shorter than the right and weakened as the result of an accident when he was ten or eleven,[2] Stalin was not a physically impressive figure and tales of his childhood prowess cannot be trusted. Thus, even though he is described as a skillful swimmer, far ahead of his age group, his daughter claimed that her father never learned to swim. When he achieved full stature he stood about five feet four inches tall.[3] The only surviving child in his family, he was the sole bearer of his parents' hopes and an object of contention between his father, Vissarion Dzhugashvili, and his mother Ekaterina, née Geladze.[4] Despite all of these deficits, he was able to find what he needed to create a strong, albeit problematic, identity for himself.

Stalin's social origins are not a matter of dispute. His father's ancestors were serfs who lived in a fertile, clement, wine-making region south of the magnificent Caucasus range. Their ethnic background (Georgian, Ossetian, or some mixture) is uncertain, but Vissarion Ivanovich Dzhugashvili spoke Georgian and could declaim by heart the great Georgian epic poem, Rustaveli's *Knight in the Panther's Skin*. At the time of Vissarion's birth his parents lived in the town of Didi-Lilo. If any family attitudes or traditions survived and were passed on to his son through him, they were not recorded. We do not know any other useful facts about Vissarion's family, except that his father died before he left Didi-Lilo. Neither his mother nor any siblings are mentioned. Stalin's seemingly uncharacteristic love of gardens, noted by his daughter in her memoirs, suggests that he had received something from generations of viticulturists and gardeners.[5] So far as class consciousness is concerned, no Soviet student of the Dzughashvili family would fail to note that Stalin's paternal great grandfather, Zaza, had been arrested for participation in a serf rebellion. However, there is no evidence that Vissarion himself exhibited any dissident social consciousness. In fact, in the only bit of family history transmitted to us directly by Stalin (setting aside a remark in an interview with the psychobiographer Emil Ludwig), albeit in flimsy camouflage, he does not even attribute to his father a genuinely proletarian consciousness. Rather, he pictures Vissarion as a man of petit-bourgeois mentality, and this is no doubt as accurate as that expansive sociological category permits.[6]

His exact birthdate is unknown, but Vissarion Ivanovich Dzhugashvili was probably born around 1850, in the era of serfdom, which was abolished in Georgia in 1864. He left his lord's estate when quite young, but there is no way of knowing for certain whether he did it out of ambition or necessity. After learning the shoemaking trade in the capital city of Georgia, Tbilisi, he moved to the town of Gori. A city of eight thousand on the Kura River and a short trainride from Tbilisi, it was in the area of Didi-Lilo. Vissarion Dzhugashvili first worked as one of the master shoemakers in Baramov's shop and then tried to maintain his own in the basement of his home, but failed. He married in 1874 while in Gori, but by 1884 gave up his shop, left his wife and five-year-old son, and went to work in the Adelkhanov shoe factory in Tbilisi. The practice of leaving the family behind in a village or town while working in a nearby urban center was very common during the early stages of industrialization, although one can well imagine its effects. It is not known if Vissarion established a regular schedule of visits to Gori. However, when his boy reached the age of nine or ten, he decided to make an apprentice shoemaker of him and, against his wife's wishes, took him to Tbilisi. The boy wound thread and helped in a variety of ways.[7] Ekaterina intervened and took the boy back to Gori. This struggle probably marks the low point in family relations. Vissarion was allegedly stabbed fatally in a quarrel in Tbilisi in 1890, shortly after the struggle with Ekaterina over Soso.[8]

Ekaterina Georgievna Geladze was born in the village of Gambreuli, in the area of Gori, in 1859, if her memory can be trusted. She too came from a serf family. They had worked as gardeners when serfs, but had chosen urban life after the emancipation of 1864. Ekaterina's father had died when she was young, leaving her, two brothers, and her mother, Melaniia. They made their living as potters.[9] Although her mother and brothers taught her how to read and write, Ekaterina was evidently barely literate at the time of her marriage and never advanced farther. According to Stalin, she could hardly write her name.[10] The young woman suffered the deaths of three infants (it is not clear whether they all died in childbirth or during infancy) before the birth of her son Iosif, known by the diminutive, Soso, on December 9 (21), 1879. There is no record of any pregnancy after that. Either the record is flawed, or else the Dzhugashvilis practiced a very disciplined form of birth control.

One should not rule out abstinence, given what little we know of Ekaterina's personality. This might explain some of the problems with the marriage as well. To all indications, Vissarion became a burden to her. Once she had a son, Ekaterina could satisfy her deep and probably superstitious religious feeling and at the same time elevate their social status by sending him into the priesthood. All sources agree that her son's career became the major focus of her energies. Without his mother's ambition and self-sacrifice it is unlikely that Soso would have had the enormous pride and need to excel that he exhibited in both academic and physical activities as a schoolboy. She worked in the house at her sewing machine, took in wash, and did domestic work in other households in order to supplement the family income, much of it evidently sacrificed to Vissarion's drinking habit. Ekaterina stood up to Vissarion when he tried to make a shoemaker of her only son. It seems likely that she treated her husband as a failure and humiliated him in the boy's presence. Not at all a meek person, she did not submit passively to beatings by her husband, but struck him back, and we know that Soso witnessed such scenes.[11]

The boy grew up in an atmosphere of mutual humiliation, lack of respect, and brutality, but he had every reason to prefer his mother to his father. We know, however, that Stalin had little direct contact with her after he became a professional revolutionary, and no correspondence between them has been preserved, despite the fact that she lived to ripe old age.[12] He later praised her strictness and strength of character, but this positive assessment possibly belonged to a later time, when he himself had to raise children. From his daughter's memoirs it sounds as if he was justifying his own strictness by pointing out the value of his mother's. Stalin eventually learned to appreciate her strength of character and native intelligence and in 1935 was amused by her expression of regret that he hadn't become a priest.[13] Ekaterina never lost her provincial, petit-bourgeois outlook. What amused him later in life probably felt less pleasant when he was a child and adolescent, and he could easily have carried a grudge against his mother as well as his father for a long time. One should therefore exercise great caution when using the aging Stalin's retrospective assessment of his family to judge how he felt about his parents when he was a child or adolescent.[14]

It is difficult to trust any sources about the family, whether primary or conveyed through oral tradition. Iosif Iremashvili, a friend of Stalin during his school years who knew the family well, drew the dichotomy of an ideal Georgian woman and a coarse, brutal Ossetian man in his description of the two parents. It has the ring of both dramatization and ethnic stereotyping, but Iremashvili's version is the generally accepted one. An antithetical version is preserved in oral tradition and presented in Anatolii Rybakov's novel, *Children of Arbat*. Rybakov pictures the father as a victim of Ekaterina's domineering character, the son as a sad observer of his affectionate but ineffectual father's plight. Vissarion is a Chaplinesque little man, and Stalin identifies himself with this lonely victimized figure. Which version shall we believe? Was the father a petty, jealous man trying to prevent his wife from elevating his son above him by making a priest out of Soso? Was he violent and brutal, hated by his son? Or was he a helpless, lonely man trying to protect his son from a shrewish, ambitious wife who wanted to emasculate both of them? The entire family history seems to reach a kind of tragic climax in 1890. We do not know if Vissarion really died in that year. We can only be certain that the family split at that time. Iremashvili reports that Vissarion's alleged death didn't affect Soso at all, but one cannot rest with such a superficial assessment of the loss, whether through death or departure, of a father. If the rest of Iremashvili's account is correct, Soso should at least have felt a sense of liberation.

It is not easy to sort this out. Most family tragedies have stages, complexities, and lack the stark simplicity of mother and child versus father, with the child always taking one side. We can be certain about the following: Vissarion had lost the respect of his wife, and she in turn communicated her disdain to Soso; Vissarion did not submit to this situation passively, but struggled to win his son back; the two parents fought and struck each other; at least once, in coming to his mother's aid, Soso actually threw a knife at his father.[15] Ekaterina won the struggle over the boy's future, possibly before Vissarion's final death, and the evidence strongly suggests that Soso finally sided with her. With the father absent most of the time beginning in 1884, the son acquired the status of the man in the household. But it was an ambiguous status, for in a male dominated culture he was subjected to a woman's sole authority—and her physical punishment. We do not know of any male relatives who might have served as models for him, except for Ekaterina's brothers, who probably played some role in his upbringing. It is also likely that they interceded on Ekaterina's behalf in her struggle with Vissarion. Finally, we know that Stalin often spent summers in the village of Tsroma, near Gori, in the home of his friend Misha Davitashvili, although it is impossible to know how that might have affected him. If one is to speculate, then speculations about the boy's relationship to his father are the ones most likely to yield fruit.

The picture of his father as a drunken and violent man who could also play upon the boy's sympathies is not at all unlikely in such relationships. Although Stalin must have feared and often hated his father, Iremashvili's dramatic version of the father-son conflict and its consequences is on its face problematic, for it made Stalin's excellent socialization at school incomprehensible.

> Undeserved dreadful beating made the boy as hard and heartless as the father himself was. Since all people in authority over others owing to power or seniority seemed to him to be like his father, there soon arose in him a vengeful feeling against all people standing above him. From childhood on the realization of his thoughts of revenge became the aim to which everything was subordinated.[16]

Iremashvili's account suggests that Stalin would have difficulty learning from male teachers. This was not at all the case. Stalin must have established good relationships with his teachers in order to graduate at the top of his class. It is more important to speculate about the impact of Soso's possible *identification* with someone like Vissarion. The psychological strategy of identification with the aggressor was clearly part of the mature Stalin's repertoire and not inconsistent with his relationship to his father. One of Stalin's pseudonym's was "Besoshvili," derived from his father's name, "Beso" being the diminutive of "Vissarion." However, the identification with Vissarion (and later aggressors) was overlaid by an ideal self-image, about which more will be said later.

One cannot take Iremashvili's picture of a domineering, unfeeling boy and adolescent uncritically. Even if we assume, as Iremashvili did, that Soso had become cold and unsympathetic as a result of Vissarion's beatings, there is more to it than that. The picture is complicated by passages describing their friendship, their walks hand in hand along mountain paths, and their discussions of literature. What emerges is a more complex image of a childhood and adolescence whose miseries were mitigated by success in school and dreams of heroism. Soso only gradually suppressed his soft feelings and cultivated hard ones. Vissarion's beatings no doubt played a role, but they did not destroy the boy's drive for a positive identity. Once free of his father's threatening presence, Soso thrived. Only a sensitive, gifted, and idealistic boy would trouble to make a noble profession of hard feelings, of a deep need for revenge.

Although one can only speculate about such things, Soso's aggressiveness and drive for domination among his school friends might have issued partly from Ekaterina's threat to his masculinity. He could not endure defeat and did not scruple about the means to gain victory. Reliable accounts about his childhood behavior are rare, but Iremashvili describes their wrestling match in the schoolyard of the theological school in Gori in 1890. Iremashvili, the undisputed wrestling champion, had to take on Soso, who was still new to the school but already had established a reputation as a tough fighter.[17] Although Iremashvili had given up the match as a draw and started to walk away unguarded, Soso grabbed him, threw him to the grass, and pinned him.[18] Once Soso had established his dominance, Iremashvili became his good friend and possibly the only one who frequented the Dzhugashvili household.

Soso had a great many reasons to fight for his dignity. We do not have precise information about his social status relative to his schoolmates, but all accounts suggest he was at the bottom of the scale.[19] Ekaterina did domestic work for the theological school in which he was enrolled, another possible source of humiliation, another reason vehemently to assert his own dignity.[20] On the other hand, his aggressive behavior might have been overcompensation for his physical deformities and size. He was evidently small for his age group, if we can trust a school photograph. Stalin's bearing, head tilted slightly back and nose elevated (accurately described by Iremashvili as well as captured by the camera), is that of a boy trying to be as tall as possible, as proud as possible. Assertion of one's dignity is not mysterious or unexpected, but there is no pat explanation for the need to *dominate* in any person, much less in a child about whom we know so little. Threatened masculinity, resentment over social status, and overcompensation for physical defects are often components of a drive for domination—the examples in modern politics are legion—but they are surely not the whole story. Without some sense of his own natural gifts as well as his mother's ambition and methods of rearing him, it is unlikely that Soso would have had the enormous pride and confidence he exhibited as boy and man. During his school years the conviction grew in him that someday he would be a hero.

The Construction of a Heroic Identity

THE APPROVAL of his teachers—Soso graduated at the head of his class in 1894—must have played some role in shaping the boy's sense of himself. However, the school regime incited rebellious attitudes. Beginning in 1890, Alexander III's policy of Russification made Russian the language of instruction. Georgian was taught as a minor language in the church school in Gori. Soso undoubtedly shared the general resentment against the oppressor, but it is difficult to determine just how defiantly he behaved. On the one hand, he is described as a leader in the revolts against school authority; on the other hand, memoirists depict a model student who graduated with a certificate of honor and recommendations strong enough to win a scholarship at the seminary in Tbilisi. More generally, Soso is described as diligent and well behaved, yet exuberant and mischievous. Svetlana Allilueva supports the latter view with an anecdote told to her by her father: "The son [Ekaterina's] was an ordinary village boy, who fought, played naughty tricks. One day he dropped a brick down a chimney into an open hearth, frightening and burning the owners of the house."[21]

None of this is incongruous with what we know about Stalin. We needn't choose between the defiant and mischievous boy and the dutiful one. They both existed in the same person. Soso had learned to live with oppression, even though he flared up against it. The mature Stalin, who usually coldly hid his feelings, sometimes vented them explosively. The art of dissimulation, which became central to his political modus operandi, was an important survival mechanism for a boy in his circumstances. The capacity for subordination shown in Soso's behavior in school, the camouflaging of feeling, is not inconsistent with the boy's situation at home with a drunken and violent father and a strict, demanding mother. Soso Dzhugashvili showed some of the typical stigmata of the gifted child of a lower class family, which, in addition, belonged to an "inferior" minority.

Soso Dzhugashvili is an instructive case and a historically momentous one. Although it is not easy to measure such things, he was a gifted adolescent and in his own way self-assured. As noted earlier, he had a small scholarship while still in Gori, three rubles a month, something his mother still remembered and thought worthy of mentioning to a correspondent from *Pravda* who interviewed her in October 1935. Both his achievements in the church school in Gori and his performance on the entrance examination won him a boarding scholarship to the Tbilisi Theological Seminary.[22] One can be certain that Ekaterina Georgievna had impressed upon Soso the value of the scholarship and the need to continue unwaveringly on his course. Failure as a student would make her sacrifices—and his own—meaningless. However, once free of his mother's surveillance and subjected to the charms of life in the seminary, Soso rebelled. Like Trotsky in Nikolaev, he began to neglect his official studies and devote his main energies to self-education. In a process not at all unusual for teenagers of that period, he underwent fairly rapid induction into the subculture of rebellion existing within the Theological Seminary and the city of Tbilisi.

The regime in the seminary seemed designed to produce rebels, and it did, in abundance. Although Stalin in his usual laconic manner commented only on the system of spying to Emil Ludwig in the interview cited earlier, Iremashvili, among others, provided an eloquent description in his memoirs:

> Life in school was sad and monotonous. Locked in day and night within barracks walls, we felt like prisoners who must spend years there, without being guilty of anything. All of us were despondent and sullen. . . . When, from time to time, youthful temperament did break through, it was immediately suppressed by the monks and monitors. The Tsarist inspection of schools forbade us the

reading of Georgian literature and newspapers. . . . Even the few literary works the lay authorities allowed us to read were forbidden to us by the church authorities because we were future priests. The works of Tolstoy, Dostoevsky, Turgenev and other classics remained inaccessible to us.[23]

Rather than passively accepting this dual tyranny, the boys took to reading by candlelight in their rooms at night, sacrificing their sleep, ruining their health, and accumulating black marks when discovered by the monitors. Soso and his friend Iremashvili continued their self-education in romantic nationalism, studying Georgian classics and writing Georgian poetry. Soso's mastery of the poetic idiom of romantic nationalism and his gifts were confirmed by I. Chavchavadze, editor of *Iveria* (Iberia), a Georgian nationalist journal, who published several of Soso's poems in 1895–1896.[24] The poems reflect not only Georgian national feeling, communion with the nation's sacred places, the burial ground of its heroes of the past, but strong religious feeling, expressed in natural imagery. The moon is presented as a tender, maternal deity to whom the poet bares his breast in a grandiloquent gesture. He expresses less bitterness than hope in stylized, bookish images. At the age of sixteen, Soso evidently identified himself with the poets who sang not only of fallen knights but of oppressed peasants. He dedicated one of his poems to the populist poet, R. Eristavi. Although it is not easy to connect these poems with the adolescent who joined the Marxist organization in Tbilisi three years later, their publication strengthened the identity that Soso was creating for himself out of books. Later, he identified himself with the heroes and victims rather than with the poets who sang of them.

The tsarist regime's censorship had long inspired in Russian students a craving for forbidden socialist literature. On the periphery of the empire, the intelligentsias of national minorities tried to preserve their national culture, although they read the literature of social injustice, first *narodnik* and then Marxist, as well. The national movements in the borderlands gathered strength alongside the socialist movement and complicated it. Idealistic young Georgians, like members of other nationalities, faced a difficult choice: Should they affirm, above all, the autonomy of their nation, or should they subordinate national aspirations to the general drive for socialism? Soso did not have to face that problem immediately. The regime gave young intellectuals a reason to band together, to study their own cultural heritage and read their nation's literary masterpieces with a special hunger.

The erosion of values and inversion of identity experienced by subjugated peoples or minorities can be transmitted vividly in literature and profoundly affect the formation of individual identity. Georgian literature paraded old values and images of knightly heroism alongside images of contemporary oppression, degradation, and rebellion. The chivalric ideal of Georgian men, expressed by Rustaveli in an epic poem of the late twelfth or early thirteenth century, became transformed into the glorification of the outlaw, the *abrek*. In *The Knight in the Panther's Skin*, the heroes sacrifice everything for love, fealty, and other knightly virtues and values. The knights live sorrowful lives. Three of them, notable for their unearthly beauty as well as Herculean strength, form an invincible band. They are united with equally effulgent consorts after a series of trials. All major figures in the poem, whether male or female, are Homeric in their stylized grandeur and simplicity. Iremashvili recounted in homely fashion in his memoirs the impact of the poem: "Soso and I often talked about Georgia's tragic fate. We were inspired by the works of the poet Shota Rustaveli, who already in the twelfth century . . . glorified friendship and sang of love of one's wife and mother and homeland."[25] These ideal, chivalric images, when placed alongside images of heroism of a different sort in modern texts, brought home to sensitive readers the disenchantment of their world.

Idealistic Georgian adolescents, including young Stalin, read Rustaveli's poem side by side with the contemporary romantic literature of rebellion. Iremashvili testifies to the powerful, formative influence of a single work, a novel published in 1882, *The Patricide*, by Alexander Kazbegi. The story of love, treachery, and vengeance is set in the mid-1840s at the time of a major Chechen rebellion in the Caucasus. The character in the novel who impressed Stalin the most was a taciturn young man named Koba, who expressed knightly Georgian virtues in a nineteenth-century context. According to Iremashvili:

> Soso's model and dream-image was Koba, the hero in Kazbegi's novel "Nunu" [sic]. . . . Koba became Soso's God, gave his life meaning. He wanted to become a second Koba, a fighter and hero as celebrated as he. The figure of Koba would live again in him. From this time on he called himself "Koba" and wouldn't tolerate being called anything else. His face glowed with pride and joy when we addressed him as "Koba." For many years Soso kept this name, which was also his first pseudonym, when he began his career as a Social Democratic writer and propagandist.[26]

Strange though it may seem, Stalin still clung to the Koba pseudonym well into his thirties. It was a durable part of his identity. Like Lenin, who received initial inspiration from Chernyshevskii's hero, Rakhmetov, Stalin tried to live according to a model taken from literature. It was not difficult to construct and sustain a socialist version of the Koba identity.

In Kazbegi's novel, personal virtue exists in inverse measure to social position and political power. The central figures, Iago and Nunu, are doomed lovers, temporarily saved and united by Koba. A mysterious young man who appears suddenly in the novel, Koba has some of the primitive strength and moral simplicity of Rustaveli's knights. Like Tariel, the knight in the panther's skin, Koba and other virtuous young men cannot act within the existing order. They become rebels and join forces with Shamil, the Moslem leader who welded together a powerful multiethnic coalition with striking, though temporary, success against Russian forces in 1845, a historical event fictionalized in the novel. Rebellious Moslems, oppressed Georgians, the poor—victims of Russian oppression and of inequality—transmute into modern form the virtues of Rustaveli's knightly heroes. Not the knight, condemned to weeping and wandering until he gains his rightful place and rescues his bride, but the outlaw, the *abrek*, who lives by raiding the herds of the wealthy and occasionally ambushes a Russian convoy, becomes the heroic figure. The central image in both cases is the rescuer, who defends helpless women, unites separated lovers, and creates a band of brothers bound by intense loyalty.

Although the emotional scale is different, the simplicity of emotions is repeated. Koba says little, but occasionally instructs Iago in masculine virtue: "It's unbecoming for a man to grieve for nothing."[27] This is a rejection of the emotionalism of Tariel, whose uncontrollable grief when absent from his loved one triggers the action of Rustaveli's epic. Koba expresses little emotion, is laconic, and prefers swift and decisive action. Equally important, it is hard to discern the real feelings of others. The modern heroes know that not only laws and authorities but values have changed—people have lost a sense of honor, cannot be trusted to behave properly according to ancient codes: "The times have changed. Brother betrays brother, sister—sister."[28] The code of loyalty of the outlaw band of brothers must replace that of the legal order: "Let my hand serve yours, my eyes, yours, my legs, yours, and let Lomisa [a sacred mountain chapel] punish traitors!"[29] When at the end of the novel, the band of brothers has been betrayed and destroyed in an ambush and Nunu falsely accused of killing her father (from which she dies of grief and shame), Koba miraculously survives. His code, the code of the *abrek*, demands vengeance. Alone, he ambushes the villains and fades away into the forest. For the sake of vengeance lonely survival is acceptable. It betokens loyalty and honor. In a topsy-turvy world in which the legal authorities were the real outlaws, virtuous men could only band together and take whatever revenge they could. Soso, like other young rebels, had to submit, biding his time and cultivating vengeful feelings.

THE KOBA identity prepared Stalin for a revolutionary career. He substituted the proletariat for the national and ethnic victims of tsarism and the party for the band of brothers. When the Bolsheviks engaged in the tactic of armed robbery and raided convoys, the "expropriations" of the period 1906–1908, Stalin naturally was its ardent proponent. Life and fiction merged. However, during the long period of decline after the defeats of 1905–1908, Stalin gradually shed his romantic identity. The images of the small band of brothers and the sole avenger were replaced by that of the disciplined member of the party apparatus and the mass movement. As Stalin's national feeling faded and he became a party functionary, he found that the arts of dissimulation and intrigue served him better than Koba's primitive code and direct approach to problems. However, the later paranoid Stalin regressed to a degraded version of the Koba identity. In his most paranoid phase, the larger world, including the party itself, was full of traitors, of treachery and double-dealing. He always had a small circle of cronies, who became his band of brothers. To be sure, even among them (if not them, perhaps their wives) there might be betrayers. He might have to go it alone.

Even at the summit of power, Stalin still *felt* like a cunning outlaw, a man evading traps, a sole survivor. He became the paranoid survivor-ruler, described by Elias Canetti in *Crowds and Power* as "mankind's worst evil, its curse, and perhaps its doom." The Koba image, etched into his memory during adolescence, was still the core of Stalin's later dread identity as General Secretary. Institutions such as the party purge became an instrument of Stalin's private code, now no longer that of an idealistic adolescent but of a pathologically suspicious ruler. Those who saw Stalin as a typical committeeman before the October Revolution, a "grey blur" in 1917, and a faceless bureaucrat after could hardly understand this. The Koba identity, which had given a poor, oppressed adolescent the inspiration to choose and sustain a revolutionary career, had undergone a transmutation in the course of that career into one of the ingredients of a paranoid political style.

The boy had found what he needed: the elements of a positive identity, heroic models. But gradually, he replaced the poetic, nostalgic Georgian identity of his adolescence with a Russian one. Stalin eventually identified himself with past Russian rulers and military heroes. In his official ideology and public persona he became a Russian. He could reinforce his identity as heroic victim and survivor through Russian national symbolism as well as Georgian and simultaneously acquire the superior identity of a conqueror and cultural hegemon. He also preserved a private, "low" Georgian identity, expressed in heavy drinking and feasting and vulgar behavior with his cronies. We find in the development of Stalin's political psychology reversals and confusions typical for marginal groups. A member of an oppressed or "inferior" nationality or ethnic group becomes an oppressor and yet still feels like a victim. When added to the unusual anxiety of revolutionary power in a context of continual instability, the psychology of victim-survivor-conqueror is fertile soil for paranoid politics and cultural disaster. Stalin's political psychology is a variation on a theme all too familiar in the twentieth century.

IN TELLING the story of unusual lives and careers, there is a tendency to rush things along. Trotsky, a man especially sensitive about revolutionary pedigrees, carefully avoided this biographical sin. He derided the story that Stalin had studied Darwin and become an atheist at the age of thirteen. Moreover, Trotsky believed that Stalin remained obedient to authority for some time during his teens. After he entered the seminary, Stalin studied theology, logic, Greek, Latin, Church Slavonic, history, and literature without any overt rebellion. Very soon, however, he began to lead the double life of many gifted students living under tsarist rule. According to Iremashvili, the authorities at the seminary began to persecute the students suspected of subversive activities, Stalin prominent among them. His grades suffered, but this only encouraged him to rebel overtly. He quickly sank to the bottom of his class.

The intellectually inquisitive and rebellious students fell under the tutelage of radical older seminarians and graduates or expelled students who had joined revolutionary circles in Tbilisi. The new students were furnished with reading lists in every area of interest. Soso voraciously read European classics of social protest in Russian translation and the literature of the Russian revolutionary subculture. Although he must have been exposed to *narodnik* ideas, Stalin did not go through a lengthy struggle with the *narodnik* heritage. The Social Democrats who established their domination in Tbilisi decisively during his years at the seminary had already done that, and he had accepted their point of view by 1898.

In a familiar psychological process, Soso hardened as he became more committed to rebellion. Descriptions of the grim adolescent, sarcastic, contemptuous of the feelings of others, and closed up in himself, call to mind those of Lenin after Sasha's death. Iremashvili, who had observed him both in Gori and Tbilisi, may even have projected some of Stalin's later hardness and domineering characteristics to the earlier period. However, there is no doubting the accuracy of observations about Stalin's hardness and unpleasantness during his years in the seminary and afterwards. Some of his traits were typical behavioral symptoms of a rejection of poetic "soft" feelings, the outward signs of an inner determination to prepare for a struggle to the death. Ordinary human problems and failings had to be pushed aside cruelly. In Stalin's case, crudeness of manner and overt contempt for others made him a particularly unsympathetic figure. He tended to polarize his fellow students into two groups: those who accepted his leadership and those who were repelled by him.

Openly contemptuous of school authority, by the school year 1898–1899 he was threatened with expulsion. Ekaterina claims she intervened and withdrew him from school because of his bad health. Although most biographers of Stalin have rejected her story as a symptom of her stubborn pride and sense of decorum (it would be unseemly if the General Secretary of the Communist Party of the Soviet Union had flunked out of school), it should not be dismissed out of hand. Iremashvili's memoirs tell us that Soso's late-night reading had undermined his health, but he could not have been very ill, for ill health did not prevent him from remaining in Tbilisi and becoming a professional revolutionary after leaving the seminary in 1899. More likely, Stalin found it extremely difficult to face his mother, and he may have used a chronic but minor illness as an excuse for his failure in school. Ekaterina believed her son and conveniently ignored what followed—which is history.

17

Koba: From Apprentice to Journeyman

DURING HIS five years at the seminary, Stalin completed his metamorphosis from adolescent romantic nationalism to Marxism. By 1898 he had decided to quit school and join the incipient Social Democratic organization in Tbilisi, Mesame Dasi (the Third Group). Stalin's rapid progress from the study of theology to Marxism may seem somewhat odd, but it was not that at all. The absence of a university in Tbilisi made the Theological Seminary the focus of activity for propagandists. The founders of Georgian Social Democracy had been students at the seminary, and they continued to recruit there despite the efforts of the seminary authorities. The Georgian Social Democratic organization boasted a legal Marxist journal, *Kvali* (The Furrow), and several impressive leaders: Noi Zhordania, a founder of the Mesame Dasi, editor of *Kvali*, and later president of the Georgian Republic formed in 1918 and suppressed in 1921; several other figures who became prominent Mensheviks and Bolsheviks (N. Chkeidze, S. Dzhibladze, F. Makharadze, M. Tskhakaia, A. Tsulukidze); and most important of all for Stalin, V. Ketskhoveli, a native of Gori and brother of one of Stalin's schoolfriends, who probably played the largest role in sponsoring Stalin in the movement and setting him on a definite path.

Unfortunately, Stalin's collected works contain very little mention of his early comrades. Ketskhoveli's relationship with Stalin must be inferred from the accounts of third parties. Official biographers evidently thought it unseemly to dwell too much on the connection between the leader of the Soviet Union and a tertiary figure, who figured only in the history of Georgian Social Democracy for about a decade and then died in prison in a quixotic gesture in 1903. The historical literature about Stalin is patently designed to create parallels between him and Lenin and, whenever possible, links. Thus, Stalin had to be no less a leader in Tbilisi than Lenin had been in St. Petersburg. In the official version Stalin is already first among equals in his relationship with the central figures of *Brzdola* (The Struggle), the underground Georgian Marxist organ. But by his own admission, in 1898 he was still an apprentice seeking sponsorship and advice from the leaders of Georgian Marxism. In a speech of June 8, 1926, to the railway workers in Tbilisi, he referred to this period with becoming modesty:

> I recall the year 1898, when I was first put in charge of a study circle of workers from the railway workshops. . . . I recall the days when in the home of Comrade Sturua and in the presence of Dzhibladze (he was also one of my teachers at that time), Chodorishvili, Chkeidze, Bochorishvili, Ninua and other advanced workers of Tbilisi, I received my first lessons in practical work. Compared with these comrades, I was then quite a young man. I may have been a little better-read than many of them were, but as a practical worker I was unquestionably a novice in those days. It was here, among these comrades, that I received my first baptism in the revolutionary struggle. It was here, among these comrades, that I became an apprentice in the art of revolution. As you see, my first teachers were Tbilisi workers.[1]

Having neglected his studies in favor of clandestine self-education and propaganda among Tbilisi's railway workers, the nineteen-year-old seminarian had to make a painful decision. Against the advice of Iremashvili and the older Zhordania, he decided to drop out of school (this was a less painful alternative than waiting for expulsion, by now a foregone conclusion) in May 1899.[2] Given Stalin's lack of financial means, he became a professional revolutionary in the truest sense. Both Lenin and Trotsky had family support to fall back upon in time of need. Stalin could rely only on his corevolutionaries. With their help and part-time employment he lived a hand-to-mouth existence beginning in 1899.

Soon after he joined the movement, *Iskra* made its impact upon Georgian Social Democrats. Under Ketskhoveli's leadership and with the help of Viktor Kurtanovskii, a former *narodovolets* who had encountered Lenin in Siberia and become one of the early links with *The Spark*, the future Georgian Bolsheviks began to publish *Brzdola* in 1901 (only four issues were published in 1901– 1902). Two unsigned articles, attributed to Stalin by the editors of his collected works, appeared in the first three issues. "From the Editors" (September 1901) and "The Russian Social Democratic Party and Its Immediate Tasks" (November and December 1901), although not literary masterpieces, are still too fluent to be Stalin's work. More likely, he was involved in the discussions leading to their composition and obviously shared their tactical line. The policies were clear, the goals well-defined: The Georgian movement belonged to the larger Social Democratic movement; the *Iskra* line against revisionism and economism and for political struggle was the correct one. Stalin surely endorsed the tactical emphasis upon the role of students and street demonstrations. *Brzdola's* tactics reflected the events of 1899–1901, when students had played the role of vanguard and triggered workers' demonstrations with their own.

After joining *Brzdola*, Stalin was elected to the Social Democratic committee in Tbilisi in November 1901[3] and became a strong advocate of what became the minority view in Georgian Social Democracy, that of the tight, conspiratorial type of committee structure advocated by the Iskraites. In Tbilisi they debated the inclusion of workers on the committee, and Stalin, who opposed inclusion, lost. In Trotsky's ungenerous interpretation, the young apprentice was already a creature of the party *apparat*, fearful of grassroots participation.[4] Although it is impossible to determine exactly what he did after the vote went against him, Stalin evidently assumed the sort of stubborn, aggressive posture that he had cultivated during his last years in the seminary. His obstreperous behavior created friction between him and other members of the committee, particularly Dzhibladze. Stalin was transferred to Batum, a small industrial town on the eastern coast of the Black Sea, very shortly after his election.

The departure from Tbilisi signified a kind of turning point. Instead of remaining in the capital with the more worldly *teoretiki* of Georgian Social Democracy, Stalin went into the trenches, now with the workers in the oil and tobacco industries of Batum. He helped organize and participated in the large-scale street demonstrations of 1900–1902, early warning signals of the massive upheavals of 1905. His putative leading role in the street demonstrations has been subjected to critical scrutiny. Did he really march at the head of the May Day demonstration in 1901 in Tbilisi, the first of its kind in the history of the workers' movement in the Russian Empire? Did he organize and lead the massive workers' demonstrations in Batum that led to the use of troops, the arrest of hundreds of demonstrators, and the massacre of March 9, 1902, when fifteen workers were killed and fifty-four injured? The historians serving the cult of Stalin did their best with scanty material. Two agitational proclamations, written in Georgian and printed on June 10 and 19, 1902, under the imprimatur of the "Batum Social-Democratic Group," are considered to be his work, but they contain nothing noteworthy.[5]

To their credit (it must have taken at least a modicum of penetration of Stalin's psyche), the official historians captured the epic spirit of Stalin's inner world and the Koba identity and, at least in this respect, serve us well. Stalin is presented the way he liked to see himself: as a decisive leader of few words who appeared suddenly at the scene of action to do his revolutionary work. We are told, accurately, by his first worshipful, official Western biographer that he grew a beard, wore a red-checkered scarf, and looked like "a romantic art student."[6] But on the whole, when we delve for a more complex image of Stalin in the memoirs and reconstructions of his early career, we encounter highly unsatisfying poster images, like those of the paintings of socialist "realism," in which workers with bull necks, bulging forearms, and clenched fists strike heroic postures, and leaders have aureoles.

Psychological verisimilitude suggests that an apprentice to Ketskhoveli who was also nurturing a Koba identity would seek the main action in 1901–1902. Stalin may have even been a bit intoxicated by his initial experiences under fire in street demonstrations and developed a dangerous sense of invulnerability. He recalls more of Trotsky than Lenin in his romantic posture as a fighter taking risks, with these extremely important differences: Stalin's Koba identity and his apprenticeship to Ketskhoveli put a premium on the arts of *conceal-ment*, and, red-checkered scarf aside, he tended to keep out of sight. Stalin's curt manner of expression, his modest literary output, and his seeming lack of ambition to produce a theoretical master work, marked him off from the two men who would overshadow him during the revolutions of 1905 and 1917 and the Civil War. Trotsky, a bit maliciously but not without accuracy, observed:

> The boy studied Russian speech only in school, where again the majority of pupils were Georgians. The spirit of the Russian language, its free nature, its inherent rhythm, Joseph never acquired. Moreover he was called upon to study the foreign language, which was to take the place of his native tongue, in the stilted atmosphere of a theological school. He imbibed the turns of Russian speech together with the formulae of churchly scholasticism. He learned the speech itself, not as a natural and inseparable spiritual organ for the expression of his own feelings and thoughts, but as an artificial and external instrument for transmitting a foreign and hated mysticism. In later life he was even less able to become intimate with or to assimilate the language, to use it precisely or to ennoble it, because he habitually employed words to camouflage thought and feeling rather than to express them. Consequently, Russian always remained for him not only a language half-foreign and makeshift, but far worse for his consciousness, conventional and strained.[7]

His assessment of Stalin's deficit contained an implicit, perhaps not fully conscious, affirmation of his own achievement relative to Stalin's. It also contains the snobbishness of the literatus and *teoretik* and the bitterness of a man bested by an "inferior" opponent notable only for his arts of concealment. It is important to note that Stalin's poverty of expression and stylizations issued as much from his choice of identity as the limitations of his background. Stalin, who spoke Russian with a Georgian accent all his life, never learned to write Russian artfully and developed a defensive contempt for the *teoretiki*. But so far as *he* was concerned, *they*, not he, were the scholastics, seeking ever more elaborate ways to understand and express what he understood simply and expressed artlessly. He reserved his ingenuity for the struggle itself; his identity was that of a cunning fighter who knew how to survive.

The twenty-two-year-old apprentice was not sufficiently artful to avoid arrest on April 5, 1902, in the Okhrana crackdown after the events in Batum in March 1902. However, he did try to avoid prosecution by smuggling notes out of prison. One of them, to Iremashvili, contained instructions that would have helped Stalin establish an alibi. He wanted his mother to say that he had been in Gori during the events in Batum. The notes were intercepted by a prison guard. Trotsky's remarks about the episode reveals how differently they approached their roles as revolutionaries.

> The deception of gendarmes was a rule in that very serious game which was called revolutionary conspiracy. However, one cannot help pausing with amazement at the carelessness with which Koba [Trotsky uses Stalin's well-known pseudonym] subjected two of his comrades [Iremashvili and Elisabedashvili] to danger. The purely political aspect of his act merits no less attention. It would be natural to expect a revolutionist who had helped to prepare a demonstration that had ended so tragically to desire to share the prisoners' dock with the rank and file workers. Not for sentimental considerations, but in order to shed political light on the events and to condemn the behavior of the authorities — that is, in order to utilize the tribune of the courtroom for purposes of revolutionary propaganda. Such opportunities were not any too frequent! The absence of such desire in Koba can be explained only by the narrowness of his outlook. It is quite evident that he did not understand the political significance of the demonstration and that his chief aim was to escape its consequences.[8]

Trotsky, of course, had in mind his own behavior during the trial of the Executive Committee of the St. Petersburg Soviet in 1906. What is even clearer, Trotsky did not understand Stalin's mentality. The assumptions behind the tactic of massive street demonstrations dominated Stalin's thinking. Cossack whips and sabers would revolutionize the demonstrators. Casualties were inevitable, but the revolutionary accounts would show a plus. The image of the orator in the dock, so appealing to Trotsky, held no allure for Stalin. He was a poor public speaker with no sense of how to project his voice, which fell faintly from the rostrum even when he achieved a far more exalted position than revolutionary apprentice. To escape the battlefield, to return, to win the next time — these were Stalin's goals. He was preeminently a man of the underground.

Stalin spent twenty-two months in prison and Siberian exile before escaping from Novaia Uda, in the province of Irkutsk. After a little more than a year in Batum he was transferred to Kutais, northeast and somewhat inland, where he remained incarcerated until he was taken back to Batum. His convoy left for Siberia in the late summer of 1903 and arrived in Novaia Uda on November 27, 1903. He escaped from Novaia Uda on January 5, 1904, and made his way to Tbilisi.[9] These two years remain something of a blank in Stalin's life. He continued his self-education, but evidently wrote little or nothing. Not a single document survives, despite the fact that his first imprisonment and exile coincided with some of the most dramatic moments in the history of Russian Social Democracy.

We do not really know much about Stalin's reaction to the events of the period, although we are assured that he had always admired Lenin and was a

Bolshevik avant la lettre. The official record shows that Stalin received a letter from Lenin in December 1903, but no such letter has surfaced in Lenin's corpus. We have to rely upon Stalin's vaunted memory:

> I first became acquainted with Lenin in 1903. True, it was not a personal acquaintance, but was by correspondence. . . . I was in exile in Siberia at the time. . . . At the time I did not regard him merely as a leader of the Party, but as its actual founder, for he alone understood the inner essence and urgent needs of our party. . . . Lenin was not just one of the leaders, but a leader of the highest rank, a mountain eagle, who knew no fear in the struggle, and who boldly led the party forward along the unexplored paths of the Russian revolutionary movement. This impression took such a deep hold of me that I felt impelled to write about it to a close friend of mine who was living as a political exile abroad, requesting him to give me his opinion. Some time later, when I was already in exile in Siberia—this was at the end of 1903—I received an enthusiastic reply from my friend and a simple, but profoundly expressive letter from Lenin, to whom, it turned out, my friend had shown the letter. Lenin's note was comparatively short, but it contained a bold and fearless criticism of the practical work of our Party, and a remarkably clear and concise account of the entire plan of work of the Party in the immediate future.[10]

It is more than a little unlikely that a young, provincial revolutionary like Stalin would have placed Lenin above Plekhanov as a leader at that time. As for the letter itself, Stalin claimed that he had acted according to conspiratorial habit and burned it. The above "facts" were presented in a speech of January 28, 1924, a week after Lenin's death. The struggle for authority in the party had already begun, and all of the candidates for leadership searched their memory for their earliest connections with Lenin, who acquired far more respect from his close colleagues in death than he had in life. Stalin probably telescoped events of his first exile in Novaia Uda with those of his party work in September–October 1904 in Kutais, when he wrote two letters to a comrade in Leipzig in which he mourned the end of Lenin's *Iskra*, bluntly criticized Plekhanov, and championed the Leninist position—that leadership of the socialist movement had to come from outside the spontaneous working-class movement. We can be certain that Stalin had become a follower of Lenin by the autumn of 1904.[11]

A NEW phase of Stalin's life began in 1905. He married Ekaterina Svanidze and they lived as man and wife until her death in October 1907.[12] Shortly before her death Ekaterina bore a son, Yakov. The virtual silence in the sources about the marriage is not mysterious if one keeps in mind that unless family members were party functionaries, they rarely appear in the official record of the lives of the leaders. Ekaterina's father was a railroad worker and her brother an *intelligent*. Both were Social Democrats. There is little to record, except that for a short time Ekaterina kept house for Stalin, although he was absent much of the time on revolutionary duties, shared his bed, and bore him a child. We know too little about their living conditions in Tbilisi to reconstruct the family milieu. It is likely that the young woman lived near relatives in order to get the sort of support a woman in her situation needed. The most psychologically astute biographer of Stalin, relying upon Iremashvili's account, plausibly suggests that he chose someone like his mother—indeed, someone with his mother's name—and that Ekaterina Svanidze provided the kind of adulation and concern that Ekaterina Dzhugashvili had earlier.[13] Iremashvili's account of Stalin's behavior at his young wife's funeral has a mythic air about it:

> He was extremely downcast, but he met me in the friendly manner as of old. This hard man's pallid face reflected the heartfelt anguish caused by the death of his faithful companion. At the cemetery gate, Koba firmly pressed my hand, pointed to the coffin and said: "Soso [Iremashvili's name was also Iosif], this creature softened my stony heart. She is dead and with her my last warm feelings for all human beings have died." He placed his hand over his heart: "It is all so desolate inside, so unspeakably desolate!" From the day he buried his wife, he indeed lost the last vestiges of human feeling. His heart filled with the unalterably malicious hatred which his cruel father had begun to engender in him while he was still a child. Ruthless with himself, he became ruthless with all people.[14]

One is reminded of the story of Ivan the Dread's reaction to the death of his young wife and other stories of the origins of cruelty in loss of love. Granting the accuracy of Iremashvili's rendering of Stalin's words and gestures, at the very most he reveals that Stalin was still capable of stylized romantic gestures at ceremonial occasions. Even assuming that Stalin experienced real grief, Iremashvili's interpretation is unconvincing and sounds mythic because Stalin did not show any more tenderness between 1905 and 1907 than he had before or after that time. Rather, he showed the same extreme militancy and casualness about lives expended in revolutionary struggle that he would exhibit on an epic scale after he had assumed supreme power.

Stalin's biographers have accurately noted the appeal of Lenin's militancy, indeed his militaristic imagery. When the struggle between Mensheviks and Bolsheviks heated up and with it the rhetoric of struggle occasioned by the revolutionary events of 1904–1905, Stalin quickly learned the Bolshevik idiom. He saw the party as a vanguard, not just a body of conscious leaders but a kind of officers corps of the proletarian army. In his first articles after his return from Novaia Uda he put his gift of simplification—and it was a genuine gift—to good use in explaining the Bolshevik policy on party organization. He caught the spirit of organization in Lenin and drove it home in typical fashion —by monotonous repetition.

However, Stalin's rhetoric heats up when he describes the proletariat's physical sacrifice, the soldiers' suffering, their losses in the Russo-Japanese War, their duty to avenge their fallen comrades. He uses stock images of enslavement and cruelty: whips, chains, beatings, mockery. The counterpart of this can be found in earlier revolutionary pamphlets, usually those of the extreme wing of the movement, but stylized expression does not necessarily suggest lack of authentic feeling. The decisive assault against the supposedly tottering autocracy is announced in the name of popular revenge for past humiliations and for the deaths of comrades already fallen in the struggle. Stalin entitled a manifesto of January 8, 1905, "Workers of the Caucasus, It Is Time to Take Revenge!" It is tempting to see Stalin crafting his rhetoric of revenge for Caucasians, given the code of mountaineers, but Stalin was expressing his true feelings.

By February 1905 Stalin had begun directing his fire against tensions and conflicts among the nationalities, warning that the tsar was pursuing a policy of divide and conquer. Working in an area of the Russian empire noted for ethnic division and strife, he had accepted the internationalist position of the party. Once again, his rhetoric appeals to the feelings of those who had lost comrades or loved ones, this time in pogroms against Jews, Tatars, and Armenians. The brief manifesto, "Long Live International Fraternity!" inconspicuous among his collected works, is the earliest production in the area of his later speciality, the nationalities problem. By far his longest article of 1905 (published as a pamphlet in May 1905 and occupying roughly forty pages of the first volume of his works), oddly entitled "Briefly about the Disagreements in the Party," contains all of Stalin's stylistic sins in abundance. Aside from a reluctance to give Stalin any credit for his gift at simplifying complicated ideas and positions—a gift not alien to Trotsky, but in his case allied with remarkable literary talent—Trotsky's remarks about Stalin's productions of 1905 are unerring:

> His writing revealed an attempt to attain a systematic exposition of the theme; but that effort usually expressed itself in schematic arrangement of material, the enumeration of arguments, artificial rhetorical questions, and in unwieldy repetitions heavily on the didactic side.[15]

Trotsky's general depreciation of Stalin's role in 1905 might be seen as a backward projection of his assessment of Stalin's performance in 1917. Stalin remained a secondary figure, virtually invisible in 1917. Trotsky claims that Stalin's relatively minor importance in 1905 was not just a matter of the weakness of his revolutionary journalism. Grudgingly admitting that Stalin's feeble productions were grist for the revolutionary mill, Trotsky then parades before the reader a list of the revolutionary celebrities in the small Caucasian Bolshevik faction, among them Leonid Krasin and Lev Kamenev (who married Trotsky's sister, Olga). Stalin simply did not measure up:

> Most of the committeemen proved themselves not big enough for the period of endless meetings, of stormy strikes, of street demonstrations. Revolutionists must harangue crowds in the public square, must write on the spur of the moment, make grave decisions instantaneously. Neither the first nor the second nor the third is a gift of Stalin's: his voice is as weak as his imagination; the gift of improvisation is alien to this plodding thinker, who ever gropes his way.[16]

Of course, one recognizes in Trotsky's otherwise astute characterizations an element of self-promotion. Trotsky had a certain possessiveness about both 1905 and 1917, when he had occupied center stage. They were *his* and Lenin's moments, and no mediocrity of a committeeman would usurp his glory by falsifying history. This proprietary interest in the great moments of the Russian revolutionary process complicates historical study. It is difficult to begrudge Trotsky a certain measure of pride—and malice—and the above lines are not his most malicious ones about Stalin. However, Trotsky did credit Stalin with a certain candor when the latter in a speech made on January 28, 1924, designated 1907–1908 as the years when he achieved a new level of revolutionary competency. Even in these years he worked from behind the scenes. What Trotsky did not understand was Stalin's *pride* in concealment. Nor did Trotsky recognize that his own actions had played more than a small role in provoking the falsifications of history in which Stalin's sycophants rewrote the stories of 1905 and 1917.

Even if, with Trotsky, we assume that Stalin was unsuited for leadership in a turbulent revolutionary situation, we still need to investigate the qualities of leadership Stalin did possess. Although Koba-Stalin preferred to remain hidden, he was an active party functionary. Furthermore, when the main action had died down, Stalin's peculiar skills showed to best advantage. Given what we know of Stalin's later leadership, it is not enough simply to label him "creature of the party machine" and leave it at that. Trotsky, projecting backward a situation that only came into existence after 1917, was unable to rest his case with a sociology of the *apparat* and had to explore Stalin's modus operandi. This entailed psychological observations that deserve scrutiny:

> In a complex situation, when confronted with new considerations, Koba prefers to bide his time, to keep his peace, or to retreat. In all those instances when it is necessary for him to choose between the idea and the political machine, he invariably inclines toward the machine. The program must first of all create its bureaucracy before Koba can have any respect for it. Lack of confidence in the masses, as well as in individuals, is the basis of his nature. His empiricism always compels him to choose the path of least resistance. That is why, as a rule, at all the great turning points of history this near-sighted revolutionist assumes an opportunist position, which brings him exceedingly close to the Mensheviks and on occasion places him to the right of them. At the same time he invariably is inclined to favor the most resolute actions in solving the problems he has mastered. Under all conditions well-organized violence seems to him the shortest distance between two points. Here an analogy begs to be drawn. The Russian terrorists were in essence petty bourgeois democrats, yet they were extremely resolute and audacious. Marxists were wont to refer to them as "liberals with a bomb." Stalin has always been what he remains to this day— a politician of the golden mean who does not hesitate to resort to the most extreme measures. Strategically he is an opportunist; tactically he is a "revolutionist." He is a kind of opportunist with a bomb.[17]

This odd mixture of unconvincing sociological and political judgments, sound psychological insights, and accurate observations about Stalin's way of maneuvering reveals why Stalin is such a difficult case. If Trotsky had more sensitively taken into account Stalin's bitter experiences with street demonstrations during his revolutionary apprenticeship—experiences that antedated Trotsky's encounters with the masses in 1905—he might have read Stalin's behavior differently. The impatient young man of 1901–1902 painfully learned to wait, to avoid pitched battles when uncertain of the disposition of forces. His cautious "empiricism" proved to be a strength in the long run compared to Trotsky's intuitive leaps. What Trotsky acutely captures is the contrast between Stalin's "grey" modus operandi and his radical aims, between his cautious behavior in the initial phases of a struggle and his resolutely violent actions at points farther along, when his enemies had either exhausted themselves or he had found the field open for a decisive maneuver. Trotsky's reluctance to credit Stalin's left position is, of course, understandable because he had marked out that territory for himself. A man who gloried in his own gift of swift, intuitive responsiveness to complex situations and his role at the center of the stage could feel only contempt for this colorless little man who spoke his lines so badly and faded into the scenery. At the time he was writing his biography of Stalin, Trotsky could not afford to remember that some of the things that he said of Stalin he had said in somewhat different words about Lenin.

In recently published excerpts from the memoirs of F. M. Knuniants, who met Stalin during this period, some of Trotsky's observations are supported. She had been warned in advance that Stalin was a "dried-up seminarist," a "talmudist," and with some apprehension obeyed her party assignment and went to their first meeting in Tbilisi.

> And now I've arrived at comrade Koba's. He is small, skinny, dark, speaks barely audibly. Looking me over from head to toe, he asks why I've come, what I want of him. I hand him Mikha's note. He reads it and again looks me over from head to toe.

> —You? A propagandist? [18]

Knuniants further describes Stalin's interrogation of her, his condescension and lack of tact, but she had to swallow her pride and submit to party discipline. Her memoir supports the descriptions of Stalin in émigré writings. Stalin was not the kind of man who could command center stage. Indeed, he was somewhat repellent. Others put up with him because he was a dedicated party worker, a resourceful operative in the underground of the Caucasus, now in Tbilisi, now in Baku, or another revolutionary area. Even more important for his political future, Stalin was a Bolshevik in an area of the empire where the Mensheviks had made the greatest headway. It is possible to read this as a sign of ambition—he could rise to the top more quickly in a smaller faction with few established leaders. Stories of Stalin's envy of established, gifted, and beloved party leaders, including Bolsheviks, also ring true, although conjectures that he sometimes denounced rivals to the Okhrana have never been verified. [19] What is more likely, in a psychological strategy shared by many who combine romantic visions with vindictive personal agendas, Stalin hid his envy and ambition from *himself*. He always attacked his opponents in the party as incompetents, delinquents, or traitors. The process that led to Stalin's emergence to prominence is the usual one: party work in the underground, widened contacts, and elevation to greater responsibility as leaders of the first rank became casualties of the intense struggle of 1904–1905.

Stalin and Lenin

A T THE end of 1905 Stalin had his first direct contact with Lenin. He went to the Bolshevik conference at Tammerfors, Finland, under the pseudonym Ivanovich as a representative of the Caucasian Union of the party in December 1905. Until that time the venerable Tskhakaia had been the Bolshevik mainstay from the Caucasus at overseas conferences. Unfortunately, little is known about the Tammerfors Conference. Stalin's own description of his first sighting of Lenin at Tammerfors on December 12, the opening day of the week-long conference, is perhaps the most interesting document connected with it, for it has served as the point of departure for speculation about Stalin's attitude toward Lenin and, even more important, his identification with him.[20] Stalin's remarks are quite revealing, but exactly of what is a matter of interpretation.

> I first met Lenin in December 1905 at the Bolshevik conference in Tammerfors (Finland). I was hoping to see the mountain eagle of our Party, the great man, great not only politically, but, if you will, physically, because in my imagination I had pictured Lenin as a giant, stately and imposing. What, then, was my disappointment to see a most ordinary-looking man, below average height, in no way, literally in no way, distinguishable from ordinary mortals.[21]

First of all, our credulity is strained when we are told that Stalin did not even know what Lenin looked like before he attended the conference. If he had been an ardent Leninist since his Siberian exile and had contacts with people who had seen Lenin, it is improbable that he would have relied solely upon his imagination for a picture of Lenin. Stalin goes on to describe Lenin's lack of ceremony, his modesty and simplicity, his efforts "to remain unobserved, or, at least, not to make himself conspicuous."[22] Stalin's "reminiscences" were probably designed to make a point about *himself* rather than about Lenin. He was saying, "Don't be disappointed with me. Although physically unprepossessing and 'grey' in style, I'm really a powerful leader." In his effort to establish his own fitness for leadership in 1924, Stalin presented an image of Lenin quite close to his own persona. When he enumerated several of Lenin's important qualities of leadership, Stalin implied that he had learned them from the master. Here, Stalin's remarks sound authentic. He was undoubtedly grateful to Lenin for providing a model of leadership from which he had indeed learned a great deal by 1924. However, Stalin no doubt had a quite different attitude toward Lenin in 1905–1906.

In all likelihood Stalin, like other committeemen, resented Lenin more than a little in this period. He was disappointed not so much by Lenin's appearance but by his policies. The Lenin who had inspired him in 1903–1904 did not always live up to his expectations. Like other committeemen he had probably found it difficult to follow Lenin's softening position on the inclusion of workers in party committees and then Lenin's movement toward the Menshevik position on participation in the Duma. It is beyond question that Stalin opposed Lenin's agrarian policy at the Fourth Party Congress in Stockholm only a few months after Tammerfors.[23] Stalin's dissatisfaction with the agrarian program of the party, including that of the Bolshevik faction, is well documented. Lenin, in fact, lost on both issues. He was forced to accede to the Bolshevik majority at Tammerfors, and even at Stockholm Lenin could only muster sixteen supporters for participation in the Duma. At Stockholm Stalin and fifteen other Bolsheviks abstained and eleven voted against Lenin's position on the Duma. Even more important, in Stockholm on April 13, 1906, Stalin took the floor against both the Menshevik policy of municipalization and Lenin's agrarian policy of nationalization. One can discern a certain amount of tact in his short speech, in that he began by attacking Plekhanov and Peter Maslov, both Mensheviks, but did not actually speak against Lenin or any other Bolshevik. In public, at least, his *partiinost'* (party loyalty) was beyond reproach. Like Lenin and Trotsky, Stalin was one of those men of deep conviction who do whatever is necessary to achieve their ends. But unlike them, he had to develop the skills of a lower-level functionary. He learned to avoid pitched battles with his superiors even when he opposed them, but in 1905–1906 he was already capable of opposing the Bolshevik leadership.

Stalin showed his preference for direct, simple, and unambiguous solutions to problems. In 1905–1906 the simplest solution was to give the peasants what they wanted above all—the landlords' property—and to encourage them to dispose of it as they saw fit. Competition with the Socialist Revolutionary Party for the allegiance of the peasants forced the hand of the Bolsheviks in 1905–1906, as it would again in 1917. Lenin, the agrarian expert of the Social Democratic Party had to yield to his committeemen, whose contact with the peasants and their demands made land seizure and redistribution by peasant committees the most logical revolutionary slogan. There is no need to review Stalin's efforts to make his agrarian policy conform to Marxian strategy.[24] Here, he was caught in the same dilemma as any Marxian revolutionary in a nation where the peasants were an overwhelming majority. While extolling the leadership of the proletariat, the Bolsheviks had to woo the peasants and then deal with the economic and social consequences of land redistribution after the revolution.

NONE OF Stalin's behavior in 1905–1906 is especially surprising, given the likely consequences of factional politics, the shifting revolutionary battlefield, feverish expectations, and crashing disappointments. However, Stalin did whatever he could to erase from history his earlier quarrels and dissatisfactions with Lenin. What is worse, this practice did not cease after Stalin had destroyed his opponents. When it was impossible to hide the record, as was the case with his opposition to Lenin's agrarian policy in Stockholm, Stalin made the best of a bad situation. In his preface to the first volume of his collected works in 1946, Stalin felt obliged to apologize for not fully grasping Lenin's prescience, although the reasoning is so tortuous that the only precise thing communicated is the apology itself. What is more important, Stalin showed himself capable of joining with other party workers against the leadership. He was a consistent radical during this period—one of those who desperately tried to keep the revolution alive, to find the correct slogans, and to engage in the most desperate tactic of all, expropriations. Stalin was more than willing to take a position against the majority (although in the debate over agrarian policy he was with the Bolshevik majority), and the idea of intriguing against the decision of the Menshevik-dominated Stockholm Congress, which voted overwhelmingly against expropriations, seemed especially appealing. Here he was also a good student of Lenin, who never permitted himself to be bound by formal votes when he *knew* he was right. Subversion of his opponents' policies was a skill Stalin cultivated throughout his apprenticeship.

Journeyman

IN HIS speech of June 8, 1926, to the railway workers of Tbilisi, Stalin remembered 1907–1909 as the period when he ceased to be an apprentice *(uchenik)* and moved up a level to "journeyman" *(podmaster'e)*.

> Three years of revolutionary activity among the workers in the oil industry steeled me as a practical fighter and as one of the local practical leaders. Association with such advanced workers in Baku as Vatsek, Saratovets, Fioletov, and others, on the one hand, and the storm of acute conflicts between the workers and the oil owners, on the other, first taught me what it means to lead large masses of workers. It was there, in Baku, that I thus received my second baptism in the revolutionary struggle. There I became a journeyman in the art of revolution.[25]

We, however, do not have to accept Stalin's periodization of his metamorphosis uncritically or the homely metaphor designed to evoke his kinship with the railway workers. A study of his works suggests that toward the end of 1906 he tried to add some of the authority of the *teoretik* to his identity. He wrote a series of articles under the title "Anarchism or Socialism", in which he discussed, among other matters, weighty theoretical issues of dialectical method. Stalin treated dialectics with the same simplicity and impatience with subtleties, the same thumping logic, that he applied to political matters. He shared with Lenin the habit of misrepresenting or reducing to absurdity the position of his opponents.[26] In a fashion typical for the Marxian intelligentsia, Stalin covered himself with the mantle of authority by liberal reference to the fathers of socialism, sprinkling quasi-academic documentation through the articles ("see K. Marx" or "see F. Engels" with a work, but with no edition or page cited).

IT IS difficult to read Stalin's essays without feeling a mixture of admiration for his autodidactic achievement and embarrassment for the confidently asserted but simplistic statements about the evolution of human consciousness and the development of social consciousness culminating at last in the proletariat. After disposing of criticism of the dialectical method, passing judgment on

Cuvier's catastrophism, Darwin's gradualism, and the relative virtues of neo-Darwinism and neo-Lamarckianism, Stalin moves on to the relationship of consciousness to being and to the stages of development of human consciousness—all of this and much more in articles adding up to less than one hundred pages. The central problems and solutions had been worked out mainly by Plekhanov and rendered into an intellectual pabulum by Marxian instructor-propagandists. Absorbed by avid young men like Soso Dzhugashvili, the ideas were further simplified and transmitted in numerous underground publications, where they contended with the equally derivative ideas of intelligentsia thinkers of other parties and sects—in this case, the followers of Kropotkin. One wonders if Stalin, who repeatedly attacked Plekhanov in articles and in his statements from the floor at the Stockholm Congress, fully understood how much he owed to Plekhanov's mentorship, mediated by others.

Despite the abstract, philosophical character of "Anarchism or Socialism," it contains passages revelatory of Stalin's personal development. Perhaps he had himself in mind in the following passage:

> That in life which is born and grows day after day is invincible, its progress cannot be checked. That is to say, if, for example, the proletariat as a class is born and grows day after day, no matter how weak and small in numbers it may be *today*, in the long run, it must triumph. Why? Because it is growing, gaining strength and marching forward. On the other hand, that in life which is growing old and advancing to its grave must inevitably sustain defeat, even if *today* it represents a titanic force.[27]

Stalin had a personal stake in the ancient faith, now presented in a socialist idiom, that the last would be first. He had himself gathered strength, always moving forward. No defeat would ever shake his faith in himself or his chosen people—the proletariat.

AS THE mass movement subsided and the government's boldness increased, only the most faithfully militant revolutionaries, who included in their ranks those most disposed to carrying on the struggle by means of violence, remained on the battlefield. Aside from Bolsheviks like Stalin, this category embraced SR Maximalists and Anarchists. The Bolsheviks, theoretically opposed to terrorism, in fact engaged in it during the last phases of the revolution of 1905. In a process familiar to students of political conflict, Stalin attacked at a theoretical level revolutionaries who were quite close to him in practice. As Trotsky noted, acts of terror grew in inverse ratio to mass action, such as strikes. At its peak in 1906–1907, political terrorism resembled guerrilla warfare, given the level of casualties on both sides. The terrorist phase began earlier and ended later in Transcaucasia, where Stalin operated. The conspiratorial qualities he had cultivated in the "deep underground" of Batum and Tbilisi made him a valuable operative in the "Black City," the oil center of Baku.

The extent of Stalin's activities during this period are difficult to determine, precisely because of his conspiratorial acumen. He did very little in later years to bring them to light and biographers have imaginatively filled in the blanks. Those disposed to see Stalin as a double agent, simultaneously working for the Bolsheviks and the Okhrana (using the latter to rid him of opponents), interpret the absence of information as confirmation of his double dealing.[28] On the other hand, Trotsky uses it to depreciate Stalin's role as a leader and to relegate him to a secondary, unheroic role behind the technical organizer of the expropriations, Krasin, and the executor of the most daring one, S. A. Ter-Petrosian, better known as Kamo. Other prominent Bolsheviks, Maxim Litvinov and A. A. Bogdanov, also overshadowed Stalin.[29] Nonetheless, despite the absence of any solid evidence, Trotsky believed that Stalin helped plan the Erevan Square expropriation of June 7, 1907.

Trotsky credits unreliable sources in supposing that Stalin met Lenin twice during 1907, once in Berlin a few weeks before the Erevan Square "ex" and once after it. If such meetings did occur, they were never entered into any official record and do not appear in any chronologies of Lenin's or Stalin's activities. Trotsky believed that Lenin could have had only one purpose in meeting Stalin: arranging the "ex" and disposing of the booty. Given the notoriety of the Erevan Square "ex," in which innocent bystanders were killed and wounded, and its denouement, in which the unpassable money brought only misfortune to the Bolsheviks, Trotsky speculates that the planning of the event was even murkier. Whatever the value of his conjectures about the planning of the Erevan Square "ex," Trotsky's remarks about the origins of Lenin's admiration for Stalin are noteworthy.

> If the assumption is warranted that Lenin had previously made arrangements with Koba about plans for the Tiflis expropriation, then it was quite natural for him to have been filled with admiration for the man he regarded as organizer of that coup. It is likely that upon reading the telegram about the seizure of the booty without a single loss of life by the revolutionists, Lenin exclaimed to himself, or he might have told Krupskaia, "Splendid Georgian!" These are the words we shall find in one of his letters to Gorky. Enthusiasm for people who showed resoluteness, or were simply successful in carrying out an operation assigned to them, was highly characteristic of Lenin to the very end of his life. Above all, he prized men of action. Basing his judgment of Koba on the latter's vaunted record in the Caucasian expropriations, Lenin apparently came to regard him as a person capable of seeing things through or of leading others unflinchingly. He made up his mind that the "splendid Georgian" would be useful.[30]

Lenin's admiration for revolutionary men of action in general is well established. It was the natural by-product of his loathing of intelligentsia word-mongering and vacillation. He was personally acquainted with and admired Ter-Petrosian. Whether or not Lenin had any direct contact with Stalin in connection with the Erevan Square holdup, Trotsky is probably correct about his attitude toward those who planned and executed it. If Stalin had indeed been involved in its planning and organization, he undoubtedly would have attracted Lenin's attention and approval. Lenin had written an appreciative review summarizing one of Stalin's articles written in August 1905 attacking the Mensheviks. However, one searches in vain for any other signs of recognition in Lenin's writings, and even the official chronology in Stalin's works yields nothing for the years when Stalin became a "journeyman for the revolution."[31]

Stalin gives little indication in his writings of any change in attitude toward Lenin from the Stockholm to the London Congress. He was clearly elated that the Bolsheviks had turned the tables on the Mensheviks and had lost only one vote—the one in which guerrilla actions (including expropriations) were condemned. There is good evidence that Stalin was acutely conscious of the difference between his revolutionary constituency (including not only Georgians but Armenians, Tatars, and many other relatively small ethnic groups compared to the Russians and Ukrainians) and the world in which Lenin moved. He came away from the Fifth Congress of the RSDRP, held in London during April–May 1907, with the sense that the Bolsheviks had forged ties with the "purely" Russian industrial proletariat working in large-scale industry, whereas the Mensheviks (and Bund) relied upon minor nationalities (Georgian, Jewish) in areas where handicraft production, peasant semiproletarians, "semibourgeois" elements dominated. Stalin increasingly rejected his own (and his father's) background, but unlike Trotsky he did not begin to develop a cosmopolitan identity. He seemed to be striving for an unambiguous, pure identity and found it in an idealized image of the Russian proletariat and its vanguard, the Bolsheviks. A few weeks abroad in 1906 and 1907 did not develop in Stalin a taste for European culture.

During Stalin's last years, the phrase "rootless cosmopolitan" carried deadly anti-Semitic connotations. This attitude is already perceptible in Stalin's "notes of a delegate" to the London Congress, originally published in the first issue of *The Baku Proletariat* in June 1907 and reprinted in 1935 as the foreword to the minutes of the Congress.

> The figures showed that the majority of the Menshevik group were Jews (not counting the Bundists, of course), then came Georgians and then Russians. On the other hand, the overwhelming majority of the Bolshevik group were Russians, then came Jews (not counting Poles and Letts, of course), then Georgians, etc. In this connection one of the Bolsheviks . . . observed in jest that the Mensheviks constituted a Jewish group and, therefore, it wouldn't be a bad idea for us Bolsheviks to organize a pogrom in the Party. It is not difficult to explain the composition of the different groups: the main centres of Bolshevism are the areas of large-scale industry, purely Russian districts with the exception of Poland, whereas the Menshevik districts are districts with small production and, at the same time, Jewish, Georgian, etc., districts.[32]

According to one memoirist, who witnessed Stalin's performances at meetings with Georgian and Russian workers, Stalin repeatedly said: "Lenin is upset because God sent him comrades like the Mensheviks! What kind of people are they! Martov, Dan, Aksel'rod—are sawn-off [no doubt a reference to circumcision] Yids. . . . Just try and work with them. You can't rely on them in a fight or have any fun with them at a feast."[33]

Stalin evidently found it difficult to take Jewish revolutionaries too seriously.

He had more than one reason to feel contempt for Trotsky. A small dismissive reference to Trotsky in his "notes of a delegate" expresses Stalin's immediate dislike for Trotsky's efforts at reconciling the factions. He called Trotsky a "beautiful irrelevancy."

AFTER THE Congress and his posting to Baku Stalin seemed all the more determined to bring matters to a head, to sharpen the struggle, but he did it clandestinely, as Koba. The only things we know for certain about Stalin during the Baku period are the following: He arrived there in June after the Fifth Congress; he worked with able leaders, notably Stepan Shaumian, with whom he had a serious falling out; as a *komitetchik*, undergrounder, and leftist, he had difficulty adjusting to the mass, open trade-union movement in Baku. Stalin still showed a penchant for exacerbating conflict rather than resolving it. This had been his approach in March 1902 in Batum, at a time when the revolutionary movement was still gathering force. The Bolshevik resurgence, for which he was partly responsible, only heightened his militancy. Participation in trade-union activities went against the grain for someone who tended to use bargaining only as a means to heighten the struggle. At first he fought any sort of discussions with the factory owners. Stalin wanted to recapture the mood of 1905, to revive the tactic of the general strike, but he found himself too extreme for the majority of Baku Bolsheviks. Between the autumn of 1907 and January 1908 Stalin changed his position and recognized trade union bargaining as a legitimate expression of the movement. This is perhaps the clearest signal in the early part of his career that he knew how to retreat, to bide his time, without abandoning his radical aims. He was arrested on March 25, 1908, a few weeks before the government cracked down on the labor movement in Baku, but even in the face of the failure of trade unions to achieve their aims Stalin did not renew his call for a general strike. He called for individual strikes at individual firms, but described this as an "expedient form of retreat."[34] Despite his tactical adaptations, Stalin remained on the left of the RSDRP's left wing and waited for the next opportunity for an attack.

18

The Travails of Russian Social Democracy

HE EVENTS of 1905 had generated widespread support for a reconciliation of the warring factions in the Social Democratic Party. The two
factions had united at the committee level in several theaters of revolution without receiving the blessing of the Central Committee (since the Third
Congress orchestrated by Lenin, all-Bolshevik), which itself began to take
initiative in unification. The pressure on the émigré leaders of the factions to
cease their bickering increased. The Bolshevik and Menshevik leadership had
responded to the call for unification, both at their separate congresses (the
Mensheviks had called theirs a "conference") in the spring of 1905 and on
several occasions after that. Everyone recognized the need for reunification,
but temperamental differences among the leaders, the momentum of factionalism, and the actions of the tsarist government in 1906–1907 foredoomed the
unification congress. When the 114 delegates (sixty-two Mensheviks and forty-
six Bolsheviks among them) convened in Stockholm on April 10 (23), 1906,

they still believed the revolution to be alive and were willing to try to act like statesmen instead of factional leaders for its sake. But if ever a group lacked the quality of statesmanship among its leaders, the Russian Social Democrats did. Although Lenin was as irenic as he could be in Stockholm and submitted formally to the will of the real majority, he had no intention of subordinating himself or his organization to the Mensheviks. In the midst of struggle, one sometimes had to bivouac with people whom one did not really trust as fighters. Stolypin's campaign to subdue the Duma and crush the guerrilla war waged by the irreconcileable left tested the alliance. At the first signs of Menshevik softness, Lenin would lead his followers from the camp.

THE APPARENT nearness of victory and the sheer growth of the Social Democratic movement had raised the stakes for all the leaders. The Social Democratic Party had enrolled roughly 70,000 members, and the national Social Democratic groups (the Jewish Bund, the Poles, and the Latvians) taken together doubled that figure. Lenin's modest behavior at the Fourth Congress reflected his position: The Bolsheviks were decidedly a minority. The Mensheviks controlled the new party newspaper, *Social Democrat*, and elected a majority to the new Central Committee. They graciously accepted Lenin's definition of a party member, the formal source of the split of 1903. Events had outdistanced the terms of the earlier debates; the positions of the leaders had changed.

In 1906 Lenin could no longer feel (as he had in 1903) that he had been betrayed. Like Trotsky, the Mensheviks had earned their position by their work on the battlefield. Indeed, they had become de facto Trotskyists for a brief period, joining the van of the revolution. Lenin looked forward to new battles ahead and could more readily join with fighters who thus far had proven themselves. Neither group had any illusions about real solidarity, but they had to make some effort at joint action against their political opponents in the revolutionary movement: the liberals and non-Marxist parties of the left, the Socialist Revolutionaries and the Anarchists. The effort failed. The revolution of 1905 created a tension between those who, like Marx in 1848, would not be satisfied with half-measures and those who feared a "premature" attack upon the emerging bourgeois order. In 1905 in Russia the revolutionary, militant spirit of Marx and Engels in the struggles of 1848 confronted their later scientism.

The tactical formulas of the different factions did not reflect just the "correlation of forces" in society. The formulas also reflected the transformation of theory by personality, the reactions of individual leaders in the course of struggle, and the ongoing contest among the leaders for preeminence in the movement. The theoretical idiom with which they justified themselves or attacked their opponents could not give significant weight to their own leadership as a separate factor. However, in private communication, and all too often in public, they would pin derisory labels upon each other that had little to do with Marxian sociology; and in later histories of the revolution, participants like Trotsky would struggle with the problem of Lenin's role and, by implication, his own. Most certainly, the diverse reactions of the leaders of Social Democracy to 1905 would play an enormous role in 1917. Attitudes formed in the period 1905–1907 survived with undiminished strength until the next revolutionary upsurge.

After 1905 the Mensheviks began to lose their militancy. Like the liberals, they realized that the still frail basis for orderly progress might be swept away by another revolutionary whirlwind. Trotsky soon became uneasy with them, even though his personal affiliation with leading Mensheviks made it difficult for him to break with them. So far as Lenin was concerned, they became a class ally of the bourgeoisie. The dialectic did not offer the luxury of compromise. If you supported the Kadets, objectively you supported the bourgeoisie. Yet the Mensheviks (however much they were divided) remained faithful to the Marxian orthodoxy of the late nineteenth and early twentieth century. Their support for the Kadets followed logically from the Marxism of that era; their models, the German Social Democrats, had acquired their character during that time. Order was essential. One had to stop the revolution at a predetermined point. But this was more than a little problematic after the Russian Revolution of 1905, which showed how difficult it was to make masses of mobilized people behave according to a theory. Although they showed the courage of their convictions, to leaders like Lenin and many younger revolutionaries, the Mensheviks *appeared* cowardly, fearful of a new kind of proletarian spontaneity with which they could not identify themselves.

The Mensheviks showed that their commitments as a Marxist intelligentsia to an orderly *vision* of development were stronger than their desire for leadership. They could not preside over an unruly movement that overflowed the boundaries set by the Marxian theory of development. Spontaneity should not be disorderly. It should not threaten the liberal movement, for a liberal regime was needed as a framework for the further development of capitalism in backward Russia. The Mensheviks began to regret their temporary intoxication with the atmosphere of the soviets and Trotsky's influence on their line in *The Beginning*. They longed for a civilized constituency of the German Social Democratic type and watched with alarm the volcanic character of the Russian labor movement.

Trotsky's doctrine of permanent revolution, above all a sign of revolutionary optimism and militancy, was also an ingenious "solution" to the terrible problems faced by Marxian revolutionaries in a backward nation. Compared to its competitors, Trotsky's was the most internally consistent theory, given the initial premises of Russian Marxists: If the workers were indeed the revolutionary vanguard and if the bourgeoisie were indeed weak, then the revolutionary government would be dominated by workers once the tsarist state apparatus had been destroyed. The peasants would have to be the junior partner in this alliance, even if they were the vast majority of the population. The workers would not stop at half-measures, but would create a socialist dictatorship. They would call for socialist revolution everywhere. Backward Russia would lead the world socialist revolution and then become integrated into a system of socialist states. The doctrine of permanent revolution had an all-or-nothing character and would not tolerate the isolation of the Russian revolutionary proletariat in a capitalist world. Most important of all, it was founded on false premises. The idea that a Russian socialist revolution would trigger a global revolution performed the function of a revolutionary narcotic, which deluded the leaders into taking great risks, into gambling on a revolution in a relatively backward nation. The painful costs of the doctrine would be felt during periods of defeat.

After having played a heroic role at the center of Russian Social Democracy during the autumn of 1905, Trotsky experienced the bitterness of being treated, once again, as a junior partner, a politically somewhat naive and annoying young man. The Mensheviks now questioned the wisdom of his tactics in the St. Petersburg Soviet, and he returned the compliment by questioning their tactic of "untying" the proletariat. He had felt betrayed by the Mensheviks in 1904, superior to them in 1905, and in 1906 would not submit to their new tactical formulations. Although he shared with the Mensheviks an intense dislike for Lenin, he sought to reconcile the two factions. Trotsky's continuous call for unity reflected not only good intentions but his inability to work with either faction. In a word, Trotsky went his own way. By 1906 it is appropriate to use the term "Trotskyism," although after 1905 he sustained personal ties with the Mensheviks, particularly his old mentors, Aksel'rod and Parvus. These were not strong ties. He was more revolutionary than the Mensheviks. In any case, given his temperament, Trotsky could not remain very long in any organization. He had learned that he could operate very well in the chaos of revolution as a freelance leader, attach himself to one of the factions, and steer them toward his position. Faith in his own intuition and charisma gave Trotsky enormous strength in some situations, but proved in the end to be a political liability.

Lenin developed tactics no less revolutionary than Trotsky's, but given the psychology of political leadership and combat, he could not openly accept the Parvus-Trotsky approach. He continued to call for a revolutionary democratic dictatorship of the proletariat and peasantry rather than a socialist dictatorship. Lenin's doctrine was based upon the questionable premise that his dictatorship of proletarians and peasants would sponsor capital development. The proletariat would not do anything to impede capital growth and industrial production, and the peasants would not reduce agriculture to petty production and consumption. But Lenin had entertained the idea of "uninterrupted revolution" and, however much he tried to distinguish himself from Parvus and Trotsky, was equally impatient for a socialist dictatorship. Lenin would use any means to keep the revolution alive, and although he was not ready to say it, he would not at all regret a revolution that disposed of the bourgeoisie as well as the old regime. Lenin's later theory of imperialism would permit him to call for a socialist dictatorship of the proletariat and poor peasants in 1917. But in 1906 the enmity between Trotsky and Lenin remained strong, and Lenin steered clear of permanent revolution.

The lessons of 1905–1906 were vivid to leaders with a fierce will to master the art of revolutionary combat. Once a revolutionary surge gained momentum, it was difficult for the leaders to stop it. They had to move to the front and lead the charge. Slogans and resolutions had to burst forth in battlefield conditions like artillery salvoes. The revolutionary masses did not ordinarily ask themselves whether their demands would be good for future capital development. They rallied behind slogans that could benefit them immediately, and it did not matter a great deal whether the slogans issued from Social Democrats, Socialist Revolutionaries, Kadets, or anarchists. Lenin quickly grasped that leadership over an ever-expanding revolutionary army required stealing the thunder of others. Furthermore, like troops in any battle, the revolutionary masses would stop fighting if led into impossible situations. The exhaustion of the St. Petersburg workers in a series of strikes and the crushing of the Moscow uprising in December were very instructive. Although the futile soviet campaigns of 1905 had to be affirmed as exemplary acts of revolutionary will and courage, they revealed that the revolutionary energy of the masses could be depleted. They would not act as mere cannon fodder, not even for the most correct Social Democratic leadership. One had to be realistic and know when to retreat in the face of superior force. These lessons were etched into Lenin's memory. He did not forget them in 1917 or later.

Lenin's relaxation of his sectarian zeal in 1906 showed a significant growth in confidence and revealed that his orientation toward his goal, destruction of the tsarist regime, was stronger than his identity as a member of a faction or party. Lenin already knew that it was possible to survive a long period of revolutionary unemployment. To the resigned, dogged mentality of the revolutionary émigré he added the outlook of a revolutionary condottiere. Another moment of opportunity would come. The officers corps had been trained, the masses had shown their revolutionism. The revolutionary army had to be gathered, disciplined to storm positions designated by the correct leadership —Lenin.

The experience of 1905 had infused Lenin with some of the spirit of improvisation Trotsky already possessed. Lenin's view of spontaneity accordingly changed. It no longer signified trade-union compromise, "tailism," opportunism, softness, and sloth but revolutionary aggressiveness and energy, combativeness, mobilized masses looking for leadership. Now Lenin could identify himself wholeheartedly with the mass movement, for his own strategies of self-mobilization involved a release of aggressive energy. Now that the masses acted like extensions or objective correlatives of his own aggressive energy, Lenin could welcome mass recruitment. He no longer sounded like the old, conspiratorial Lenin of *What Is to Be Done?* All of this proved to be extremely useful, indeed crucial, for the conditions of party life after 1906 made it impossible for any of the leaders to sustain a stable following. The extreme disarray in the party might have been totally demoralizing had Lenin not acquired the conviction that a revolutionary officers corps had already been trained and that soon enough he would have another revolutionary army in the field.

THE IMPERATIVES of struggle brought the leaders together for a brief moment in 1906. The temporary strength of the Mensheviks was illusory, for it had been nourished by their ties with Trotsky and Parvus and their role in a spontaneous upsurge that they now regretted. Trotsky, whose Siberian odyssey prevented him from participating in the Fourth Party Congress, was temperamentally incapable of joining either faction. Lenin would join in alliances for purposes of combat, but could never really submit to the leadership of others. The old intrigues and enmities returned with redoubled force. Lenin quickly resumed his role of wild man at the Fifth Party Congress.

The Fifth (London) Congress

THE UNIFICATION congress of 1906 had generated some good will, but political developments in Russia quickly precipitated new splits. The existence of a Duma was itself a source of division. Neither the Mensheviks nor Bolsheviks knew at first quite how to deal with the situation. The Bolsheviks had entered the Fourth Party Congress with a unified position in favor of boycotting the elections, but the ongoing electoral returns revealed far greater strength on the left than had been anticipated. In the absence of organized participation by either the Social Democrats or the Socialist Revolutionaries, the Kadets and a new agrarian party, the Trudoviks (Laborites), became the parties of choice for dissatisfied urban and rural constituencies in the First Duma. This gave many Mensheviks, Lenin, and some of his followers second thoughts. Lenin offended the majority of his own faction by voting with the Mensheviks to end the boycott, but this was only one aspect of a long internecine struggle, of which more will be said later. Lenin's Bolshevik field commanders yielded nothing to him in all-or-nothing radicalism. The RSDRP sustained a mere masquerade of formal unity, and even the factions increasingly showed fissiparous tendencies. Disappointment with the quality of leadership exercised by the émigrés affected the party particularly strongly after the defeats of 1906–1907.

The struggle between the radical wing of the Duma and the tsarist government led to the former's dissolution in June 1906 and a new election. During the course of the second electoral campaign, Bolsheviks and Mensheviks collaborated harmoniously in many areas, but in St. Petersburg the factions came to blows. Lenin's blistering accusations provoked the Menshevik Central Committee of the party to call him before a party tribunal, where he refused to recant. The Mensheviks outnumbered the Bolsheviks by a ratio of two to one in the Second Duma, which contained sixty-five Social Democrats. They pursued a tactic of pushing the liberals to the left when possible, but joining with them in order to isolate the right, and this did not satisfy the left wing of the party. Meanwhile, liberals had lost confidence and the regime had gained it. Prime Minister Stolypin seized the first opportunity to dissolve the Duma again. The government decided to rid itself of the disloyal opposition by an illegal maneuver and issued new electoral laws in June 1907, shortly after the Fifth

Party Congress in London. The accompanying crackdowns against the left opposition finally achieved what Stolypin had been aiming for—a period of quiescence.

At the Fifth Party Congress, the largest in party history, Lenin recovered some of the ground lost to the Mensheviks in 1906 by achieving a Bolshevik plurality on the new Central Committee, now containing official representatives of three nationalities: Jewish, Polish, and Latvian. The Mensheviks and a majority of the Bund formed a kind of bloc (highlighting the "Jewish" character of Menshevism), whereas a majority of the Poles and Latvians usually voted with the Bolsheviks. However, in many disputes the nationalities, in the interest of party unity, blurred factional division rather than accentuated it. The Bolshevik success in numerous votes at the Fifth Party Congress did not compensate Lenin for the failure of the united party to make armed insurrection part of its program, and, most important, the party in strong terms reaffirmed its stand against the Bolshevik tactic of expropriations and partisan actions. To Lenin and his militant faction, this was cowardice, even though a continuation of the call for armed insurrection and Bolshevik participation in expropriations and armed attacks with the SRs seriously damaged the Bolsheviks in the eyes of European Social Democrats. The militant Bolsheviks still believed that a final confrontation with the regime was imminent. They would not abide by any meaningless legalities when engaged in battle.

Trotsky arrived in London with a small coterie and asserted his independence. He showed poor political sense in lecturing both factions on their sins, accusing his former Menshevik allies of being hopeless formalists in their notions of historical development. On the other hand, the Bolsheviks were equally formalistic in their "rigorism" and "intransigence." Trotsky had divined the logic of sectarian political struggle and justly pointed out that a Bolshevik tactic would often simply be the "naked antithesis" of the Menshevik one. During the fourteenth session he fired away in a long speech at both sides. At one point he asked the Bolsheviks to withdraw their resolution attacking the Social Democratic deputies in the Duma and to introduce a resolution that would inspire unity instead. Lenin shouted from the floor, "You introduce it!" Trotsky seized the opportunity to make an ad hominem attack and simultaneously preach:

> You want to wrangle over every word spoken at a Congress consisting of 300 persons instead of making a sincere effort at an agreement in the commission. You want me, comrade Lenin, to introduce a compromise proposal, and I want you yourself to understand and recognize the necessity of such a resolution and introduce it instead of me. Without recognition of a compromise the compromise itself becomes a source of new conflict and demoralization. [1]

At the twenty-third session of the Congress on May 13(26), 1907, Trotsky presented his own position at considerable length. He postured a bit by quoting Miliukov, the Kadet leader, on the militant mood generated by Trotskyism in the last months of 1905 and saying: "Mister Miliukov, as you see, does me too much honor, connecting my name with the peak period of the revolution." [2] Of course, Trotsky hoped that all present would see the truth in Miliukov's observation. More important, he expressed views about the natural alliance of the proletariat and revolutionary elements of the peasantry against the bourgeois liberals and the old regime, which brought him close to the Bolshevik tactic. Although Lenin would not make any new concessions to the idea of "uninterrupted revolution" (a phrasing he preferred to "permanent revolution"), he recognized on the floor of the Congress that Trotsky had drawn near to his position.[3] However, he wounded Trotsky's vanity by suggesting (at least, so it seemed to Trotsky) that Trotsky had shifted his position under Kautsky's influence; Trotsky corrected him by citing some of his own earlier statements about the relationship of the proletariat to the peasants. A number of subsequent remarks at the Congress made it perfectly clear that Trotsky had no warm feelings for Lenin or the Bolsheviks.

The Mensheviks' traditional support for broad bodies of workers, now expressed in Aksel'rod's call for a workers' congress, accorded well with Trotsky's own ideas about making contact with broad masses of workers. The Bolsheviks attacked it as anarchosyndicalist in tendency and in doing so, expressed their usual attitudes toward nonparty organizations. Trotsky compared a Bolshevik resolution denying party members the right to agitate for a workers' congress to Bismarck's Exceptional Laws against Socialists—it was a futile, despotic measure. Many of the old wounds were reopened in the debate over the workers' congress at the thirtieth session of the Congress. Despite his closeness to Bolshevik tactical ideas about class alliances and his repudiation of Menshevik "formalism" about historical stages, Trotsky became enraged at Bolshevik organizational despotism. He was caught in a double-bind: The Mensheviks could not satisfy his radicalism, and Bolshevik-style Jacobinism repelled him.

THE DEBATES at the Fifth Party Congress seem hopelessly academic and futile in retrospect. The regime consolidated its position; the revolutionary movement disintegrated. From an influential, mass party, with an enrollment of roughly 150,000 (counting the nationalities) the Russian Social Democratic Workers' Party, after 1907 became once again a weak, splintered organization of underground revolutionaries, infiltrated by the Okhrana. The process of polarization catalyzed by Lenin in 1903 and only temporarily arrested in 1905–1907 proceeded apace. The insights of 1903–1904 proved to be the crucial ones in the long run. Lenin was right about the organizational imperative in revolutionism; the Mensheviks, Trotsky, and Rosa Luxemburg were right about the consequences of Lenin's organizational model. But Lenin had shown himself sufficiently flexible to welcome a broad, spontaneous revolutionary movement and was determined to be ready to organize whatever parts of it he had to when it appeared, whereas the leading Mensheviks had drawn back. Maximalists like Trotsky and Luxemburg were attracted by Bolshevik revolutionary élan but repelled by Lenin's dogmatism and ruthless intrigues. The most talented leaders in the party remained at odds.

In London the three men whose collaboration and conflict would have the most momentous consequences for the course and outcome of the October Revolution shared the same hall for the first time. Lenin's and Trotsky's mutual antipathy was strong. In London in 1907 Lenin perceived Trotsky as a *poseur*,[4] yet less than a year later he was willing to use Trotsky's pen in the service of his cause, whereas collaboration with Lenin remained unthinkable for Trotsky. At that time Stalin did not even exist for Trotsky, who in his biography somewhat maliciously noted that Stalin was such a nonentity in 1907 that he had voice but no vote in London and, notwithstanding his right to speak, did not take the floor on a single occasion.[5] Stalin in 1907 dismissed Trotsky as, again, a "beautiful irrelevancy," and, as noted earlier, he was hardly worshipful of Lenin.

Lenin remained fully mobilized. For him the period 1906–1907 resembled 1899–1900 and 1903–1904. In each case Lenin had encountered unforeseen opponents and, instead of losing heart, had begun a furious campaign to overcome them. His attacks, at first expressed in choice political epithets and earthy forms of vituperation, had taken increasingly concrete forms: control over party organs, savage political infighting, clandestine maneuvering, and now, guerrilla warfare against both the government and the party. Lenin refused to submit to party discipline. The Fourth and Fifth Party Congresses demonstrated, above all, that the Mensheviks had neither the will nor the ability to control the radical wing of the party. The tension between the spirit and the letter of Marxism rendered them helpless, capable only of resolutions and meaningless legal measures against Lenin. The psychology of revolutionary politics gave the advantage to the Bolsheviks. However, by 1908 Lenin began to repeat an already familiar pattern of political behavior. His tactical improvisions and theoretical dogmatism split the Bolsheviks and created acute problems with his own faction. The years ahead would be lonely ones.

19

Philosophical Interlude

IN THE years 1908–1913 the old regime recovered its confidence, and, as a corollary, the revolutionary parties experienced a loss of morale and strength. The celebration of the tercentenary of the Romanov dynasty in 1913 symbolized the regime's durability. In retrospect the tsarist regime's period of recovery seems akin to that moment in Greek tragedy when the gods befuddle the tragic hero, inducing a state of blind ambition that leads to a reversal of fortune and his ruin. But it is difficult to cast Nicholas II as a tragic hero, given his puny moral dimensions and mainly uxorious virtues. The prime minister who seemed most capable of saving the Russian empire, Stolypin, had been assassinated in 1911 as his reward for his brutally successful policies. He is a more attractive candidate for the role. However, in the end, the scale of the tragedy, in which tens of millions eventually died, dwarfs traditional dramatic subjects. While the dynasts, their civil servants, police agents, and military men worked to restore Romanov imperial dignity, foreign and native financiers, industrialists, and engineers created the bases for greater wealth and power.

The regime's last effort, like its earlier attempts to combine social engineering with repression, failed. It could not even count on the loyalties of the very bourgeoisie whom the revolutionaries had designated the class enemy. A surprising number of them supported the revolution and contributed funds to revolutionary parties. The regime's stabilization was fragile, its destabilizing elements too numerous to suppress. In fact, it was forced to contribute to its own disequilibrium by hastening the process of modernization with Stolypin's agrarian reforms. These experiments in large-scale social and economic engineering were desperate gambles, first by Witte and then by Stolypin, that the regime's instruments of force could cope with the disturbances generated by social change until such time when a prosperous middle class would emerge and generate stable progress. Both the revolutionaries and the economic and social engineers serving the regime understood how precarious the situation was; and the perceptive among them knew that another experience like the Russo-Japanese War would almost certainly end the old regime. World War I far outdid their expectations.

Masses of peasants crowded into cities and factories during the Russian imperial regime's drive to catch up with the more advanced industrial nations. The celebration of the Romanov tercentenary occurred at a time when labor was being radicalized anew after a short period of quiescence. The brief moment in 1905, when the revolutionary intelligentsia, the educated public, factory workers, peasants, and dissatisfied servants of the autocracy all joined in a broad and unified revolutionary front had passed. Liberal slogans of a constitution and democratic elections according to the famous "four-tail" formula—free, equal, secret, and direct—had held the disparate elements of the front together in 1905. After 1905 most liberals had lost confidence in the slogan "no enemies to the left." The labor movement, affected by changes in the factory labor force, by more than two decades of propaganda and agitation, and by the intransigence of owners and the repression of the regime, resurrected itself after a series of defeats and moved even farther to the left. The villagers left behind suffered from the chronic land hunger of an overpopulated countryside. Industrial growth and migration did not drain off enough of the excess population in the heartland to mitigate the villagers' poverty. Social change and progress in agricultural technique and economic organization did not occur quickly enough either to raise the standard of living in the countryside significantly or to defuse the resentments of former serfs who believed that landlords' estates should be parceled out to them. Peasant soldiers became more open to socialist agitation, despite the power of traditional symbols and the fever of nationalism accompanying war efforts.

Meanwhile, the intelligentsia had begun to question some of the foundations of its radical style of thought. The symbolic moment occurred in 1909, when several brilliant representatives of the Russian intelligentsia, including former Marxists, issued a symposium, *Signposts*, in which they analyzed and rejected the mentality of the revolutionary intelligentsia. The materialistic doctrines of the mid-nineteenth century had lost much of their inspiration. After the turn of the century more sophisticated epistemologies, ethical visions, and religious doctrines responded to the growing need of many members of the intelligentsia for something beyond self-sacrifice for the *narod,* the proletariat, or, more generally, the cause of socialism and the symbolic immortality conferred by participation in material progress. Although the new currents of thought served some members of the intelligentsia well, the ambiguous cosmology emerging from the new quantum physics and relativity created anxiety among those who still derived their essential inspiration from the old materialist metaphysics. To the stalwarts, Lenin among them, changes in styles of thought and other cultural innovations seemed to be refuse deposited by the receding revolutionary tide.

The critics of materialism benefited from the findings of the natural sciences —ironically, the very source of confident, mid-nineteenth century materialism. The study of matter itself had yielded surprising results. Once thought solid and durable, matter had become porous and mutable and finally nothing but an aspect of energy. The stuff of the universe became increasingly like the shapes in the clouds viewed by Hamlet and Polonius—a function of the observer's position and imagination. To be sure, many dialecticians found the mutability of matter and even of our conceptions of time and space quite in keeping with dialectical theory. It was not a dynamic vision of reality or even the notion that science and scientific ideas changed that threatened dialectical materialists. It was the notion of what exactly was out there and how it was related to the human mind. The attack upon the solid universe existing independently of the human mind and containing it became an attack upon the "scientific" Marxian notion of history to the less imaginative and adaptive members of the socialist community.

Marx had already given matter mental attributes by maintaining Hegel's dialectic in history, and Engels had found it in nature as well. Although the more complex neo-Kantian vision of reality was also dynamic, it did not necessarily give the universe the inexorably progressive character imparted by Hegel. Laws became probabilistic, and what "laws" there were—particularly those of thermodynamics—suggested a dissipation of energy and a bleak cosmological future. The new physics also brought with it increasingly sophisticated thought about the role of the subject in producing order. Philosophers of science made the shaping of subjective experience central to our relationship to the external world. Neo-Kantianism gave the mind an active role—it was impossible simply to talk about it as if it were just a brain, matter in motion, reflecting the interaction of its own material structure with that of matter external to it. Hegelians had long derided Kantianism for its supposedly static vision of the human mind. However, the Kantian vision of a mind with its own distinctive attributes, playing an active role in cognition, had long nurtured progressive visions, including Kant's own.

The mind could be seen in historical perspective as an agent responding appropriately to changing environments and producing new visions of progress. It did not merely passively reflect an "objective" reality. For many Marxists the new emphasis upon the mind as agent played a role similar to that played by materialism for earlier generations. It gave human beings an active, shaping role in the universe. However, for others it threatened the inevitability of the progress conferred by the law-bound world of matter, in which human beings expressed their freedom by cooperating with orderly and benign material processes. Neo-Kantianism had already played a role in the deconversion of several leading Marxists around the turn of the century. Both Lenin and Plekhanov had witnessed that dismal phase of Social Democracy. Now, to their dismay, a new epidemic of "idealism" began to influence members of the Bolshevik faction by way of the philosophy of science.

Other philosophical currents emphasizing the role of religious inspiration and myth in binding and mobilizing human communities became increasingly attractive. Here, too, Marx had already provided nurturance for his followers by incorporating into his vision of historical change a vision quite consonant in its way with Judeo-Christian soteriology. Instead of individual salvation he had offered collective progress toward human liberation made possible by the grace of the dialectic of history. Individual revolutionaries could salve their consciences by knowing that the Marxian salvation could not be achieved without struggle and self-sacrifice. By choosing both, they *actively* and voluntarily served human salvation, even though the larger process was determined. Now, more sophisticated thought about religion and myth encouraged some members of the intelligentsia to use the inspiration conferred by religious modes and myths in the revolutionary cause. Conscious manipulation of the psychological need for symbolic immortality existed side by side with scientific utopianism, which emphasized the satisfaction of immediate human needs and the extension of human life.

A split opened up between Marxists more prone to experiment with new trends in philosophy, religion, literature, the fine arts, and morality, and cultural conservatives like Lenin, who were quite experimental in the political arena but would brook no changes in the settled (as they saw it) canons of Marxism. Lenin, in lawyer-like fashion, had it both ways. He did benefit intellectually (although this might not be apparent in his magnum opus of 1908, *Materialism and Empiriocriticism*) from a reading of his opponents' works. But in 1908 he read them with only one thing in mind: preparing a philosophical brief against them and pinning the usual array of derogatory labels on heretics. He would later do the same for other "liberating" cultural currents. The philosophical disputes among the Marxists were a small part of the general efflorescence of culture occurring during Russia's "Silver Age," all of it threatening to someone like Lenin—all of it apparently symptomatic of the general decline of the movement. Lenin's intolerance for heterodoxy revealed not so much a man incapable of learning as one who for whom political orthodoxy implied orthodoxy in other areas as well—an ominous posture with fateful consequences for Soviet culture.

The experiments of the top layer of Bolshevik leaders with new ideas seems in retrospect both natural and necessary. They may have played a therapeutic role during a period of defeat, but they were surely a sign of continuing intellectual vitality. The efforts of Bogdanov, Lunacharskii, Gorky, and others to add new spiritual and scientific dimensions to the body of doctrine handed to them by (mainly) Marx, Engels, Kautsky, and Plekhanov produced a response in Lenin that foreshadowed his later treatment of what he considered to be dangerous deviations within the party. Lenin devoted much of his time in 1908–1911 to thundering against the new trends. He was going against one of the natural tendencies of his faction, for during 1904 he had attracted the most adventurous and in some respects most experimental figures in the Social Democratic movement—men like Bonch-Bruevich, Lunacharskii, Bogdanov, and Krasin. Although all of them participated in the "underground" aspect of Bolshevism and engaged in a variety of party activities, they represented the culturally advanced layer in an organization with an increasingly anti-intelligentsia tendency. In due time, though in prison and Siberian exile for much of the period, the pedestrian and dogmatic Stalin found himself promoted at least partly because Lenin had rejected the more culturally experimental leaders in his faction. Even though Stalin had found the disputes over philosophy a "tempest in a teapot," he had remained loyal to Lenin's basic line.

Meanwhile, Trotsky absorbed the cosmopolitan culture of prewar Vienna in particular and Europe as a whole. He was more like Lunacharskii and Bogdanov in his appreciation of new cultural trends and incorporated neo-Kantian elements in his vision of science—without ever acknowledging a debt to Kant. Trotsky's later published writings and notes on such complex matter as the philosophy of science and the relationship of consciousness to being, although quite brief, reflect the influence of the Viennese intellectual milieu in which he lived. Unlike Lenin's lieutenants during the period of revolutionary doldrums, Trotsky did not cross swords with Lenin over these kinds of issues. In fact, during this period of dissension Trotsky was courted by both Lenin and his opponents. On his side, Trotsky found both Lenin and the Bolshevik schismatics little to his liking, yet he increasingly rejected the Mensheviks as political partners.

The Mensheviks were strongly drawn to the path of European Social Democracy and distressed by the traditional Russian revolutionary style: conspiratorial, underground, prone to terrorism. The "liquidators" increasingly controlled the tone of the faction. They staked their hopes on a legal labor movement and participation in a coalition of progressive forces in the Duma. Trotsky longed for a unified Social Democratic Party and was deeply angered by Lenin's maneuvering, but his radical vision brought him closer to the Bolsheviks than to the Mensheviks. He maintained friendships with leading Mensheviks, with whom he shared a fear and loathing of Lenin. However, whenever he tried to work with them against Lenin, he found them unreliable as partners and insufficiently militant. After all of his efforts at unifying the party failed, Trotsky gravitated toward the more militant Bolshevik faction.

KRUPSKAIA CONVENIENTLY divided the events of 1908–1917 into three periods. In 1908–1911 she and Lenin returned to Geneva during a period of "rampant reaction" and philosophical deviations, which had to be crushed. Lenin had to fight against the Menshevik "liquidators" to preserve the underground organizational forms painfully built up over the years. He had to struggle against philosophical and tactical deviations within his own party: god-seeking and god-building; recallism and ultimatism. Then, in the second period, 1911–1914, Lenin and the party revived with the renewal of labor militancy and an explosive strike movement. The Bolsheviks gained relative to the Mensheviks as the chemistry of the workers' movement worked in their behalf. During this period Lenin became increasingly involved with the question of the fate of nationalities under imperial control in the event of war. Later, in 1914–1917 he had to divine the significance of the war for world revolution. He did everything in his power to turn the war into a vast uprising against its imperialistic perpetrators—to make it the catalyst for civil wars and socialist revolutions. In the course of this last period Lenin rejected the authority of the Second International. He became a renegade in the Social Democratic movement. Finally, he and Trotsky converged in their views and joined forces in 1917. Lenin had adopted the theory of permanent revolution.

The years 1907–1917 reveal more than anything else Lenin's tenacity. They show how he cultivated a style of leadership that permitted him to alienate the first-rank leaders in his faction, promote people without names, and then win back those he had driven out—and more. He survived a period of defeat, schism, and near disintegration of the revolutionary movement without abandoning either his revolutionary faith (although at moments he pessimistically extended the timetable for revolution) or his confidence in his own fitness to lead the revolutionary forces.

Lenin as Philosopher

O DDLY ENOUGH, at a time when the revolutionary intelligentsia most assiduously questioned its own commitments and practices, even its Bolshevik wing continued to act according to a traditional pattern of behavior. Self-criticism simply yielded new variations on old themes. What is most striking, much of the "new" thinking issued from already mature members (ranging in age from the mid-thirties to mid-forties) of the movement reflecting upon their commitments and achievements rather than from a new generation of thinkers. In this period of self-examination and rethinking Lenin reasserted his sectarian stubbornness, and it took familiar forms. He not only evoked the classic authors of early Russian Marxism but expanded his own authority as a *teoretik* to new areas. However much he repudiated what he considered to be the intelligentsia's way of life, Lenin implicitly accepted the intelligentsia's approach. He believed that it was necessary to have thought through "scientifically" and to be ready to argue persuasively every aspect of Marxian doctrine, from epistemology to political tactics. Lenin assumed that his own stature as a leader depended upon his ability to understand and present the philosophical arguments in support of a tactical position, however frail the connections between, for example, the theory of cognition and the tactic of participation in the Duma. Lenin operated under this theoretical imperative throughout his life, revealing himself to be an unrepentant *intelligent* in his own fashion. At first mainly a Marxian economist and expert on agrarian matters, Lenin now issued pronouncements on every area of theory.

Lenin's tendency to draw a sharp line between the "correct" position and all others issued both from his personal intolerance and the polemical style developed by the founders themselves. At the age of thirty-eight Lenin had lost none of the pugnacity encouraged by the style and native to him personally. It was reinforced by his loss of respect for others in the movement. He leaned less on Plekhanov, who had already launched the attack against the heretics. Lenin treated him condescendingly in *Materialism and Empiriocriticism* and relied heavily upon Engels, who had written more on philosophy and the natural sciences than Marx in the years of their collaboration and after Marx's death. For Lenin, Engels had said the last word about epistemology and the philosophy of science. Engels, like Marx, had found in materialism liberation from the ghostly world of idealism and from the "opiate" of religion. Their common contempt for idealism issued from their generation's struggle for a philosophy of action. The rebels of the 1830s and 1840s believed that idealism in philosophy, like belief in god, justified the existing order and encouraged passive submission to oppression and exploitation. Despite its mechanistic and deterministic features—which seemingly undercut both moralism and activism —they infused materialism with a revolutionary spirit and made it a banner of struggle. Lenin sustained the traditions of that period of rebellion in philosophy. He sought answers to all of his questions about epistemology and the philosophy of science in the works of the founders of dialectical materialism.

Lenin lumped together under the label "idealism" (showing equal contempt for skepticism and agnosticism) all philosophies that took the psyche rather than matter (physical, objective reality) as their point of departure. He derided any effort to distinguish collective forms of cognition from individual ones, given this essential blunder: "To think that philosophical idealism vanishes when the consciousness of mankind is substituted for the consciousness of the individual, or the socially organized experience for the experience of one person, is like thinking that capitalism vanishes when one capitalist is replaced by the joint-stock company."[1]

Time and again he showed the inaptness of the heretics' use of Plekhanov's works not because they had been unjust to Plekhanov but because Plekhanov himself had left the correct path. The correct path went from Feuerbach (despite his errors) through Marx, Engels, and Joseph Dietzgen, the worker autodidact (who also got muddled at times). Later in 1914–1915, when Lenin took voluminous notes on Hegel, he showed much greater appreciation for Hegel's contribution to dialectical materialism. In 1908, however, he mobilized himself to sunder any connections between idealism and the *correct* point of view. Whatever concessions he made to Hegel came by way of Engels.

The center of Lenin's position and the refrain of *Materialism and Empiriocriticism* is: "The world is matter moving in conformity to law, and our knowledge, being the highest product of nature, is in a position only to *reflect* this conformity to law."[2] Lenin's allegiance to the highly optimistic reflection theory of knowledge brought down on him all the difficulties faced by previous generations of materialists. He had to reconcile its seeming rigidities with the historical and relativistic point of view that had made Marxism seem sophisticated compared to earlier and later varieties of "vulgar" materialism. For Lenin, Engels had solved all of the basic problems. He had emphasized the "dialectical" in the term "dialectical materialism." Lenin had no difficulty with the notion that every scientific theory had an approximate, "relative" character. By this he meant that at any given moment in history our knowledge was imperfect but always improving. The surest test of progress in scientific knowledge was *practice*—increasing mastery over nature. The successes of engineering and of laboratory scientists synthesizing new substances or analyzing and reproducing known ones had especially impressed nineteenth-century materialists. Lenin believed that they were either explicitly or implicitly guided in their praxis by materialistic assumptions. But even steady progress toward "objective, absolute, and eternal truth" fell short. Human knowledge never quite yielded a totally accurate reflection of the reality external to the knower. Lenin boldly issued the apparently contradictory statement that the external world and its laws are "fully knowable to man but can never be known to him *with finality*"—*do kontsa*.[3] A bit farther in the text he writes:

> For Engels all living human practice permeates the theory of knowledge itself and provides an *objective* criterion of truth. For until we know a law of nature, it, existing and acting independently of and outside our mind, makes us slaves of "blind necessity." But once we come to know this law, which acts (as Marx repeated a thousand times) *independently* of our will and our mind, we become the masters of nature. The mastery of nature manifested in human practice is a result of an objectively correct reflection within the human head of the phenomena and processes of nature, and is proof of the fact that this reflection (within the limits of what is revealed by practice) is objective, absolute, eternal truth.[4]

In short, Lenin was not comfortable with relativism. He believed in the steady progress of human knowledge through greater familiarity with the stuff of the universe. Lenin's point of view was probably closest to that of the most utilitarian, empirically grounded, and unimaginative laboratory workers and engineers and farthest from the physicist-mathematicians who worked mainly with highly imaginative, abstract mathematical models of reality and invented such things as n-dimensional space. In this respect, he differed radically from Bogdanov and other Bolshevik heretics. Lenin had a utilitarian rather than an aesthetic approach to the natural sciences and had neither curiosity about nor insight into the nature of scientific creativity. In fact, he was a philistine.

Lenin never really came to grips with the vexing issue of proletarian versus bourgeois science and culture. Throughout his life he showed contempt for this type of relativism. One either treated the world from a materialist point of view, or one did not, whatever one's class affiliation; one was either a cultured person or not in one's conduct. Despite his frequent carping at bourgeois philistinism, Lenin generally accepted given forms of culture and morality, unless it seemed to him that they impeded revolution and the victory of the proletariat. In any case, his attack upon Bogdanov, Lunacharskii, Gorky, and others is more readily assigned to his peculiar political modus operandi, his personal inflexibility and need to assert his authority. It is difficult to see how their epistemological views threatened the revolution or indeed why disagreements about such issues should matter a great deal to a political leader. During the course of dealing with the problem of the philosophy of science Lenin could see that scientists were themselves divided about the nature of scientific knowledge and its progress. But Lenin's Marxism and his notion of science did not allow the existence of more than two camps (feudal remnants aside), and it followed that there was only one true and progressive position. Lenin thus felt constrained to assign all forms of idealism, agnosticism, and skepticism to the bourgeoisie. Their espousal delivered one over to the enemy.

When dealing with the ambiguities of the emerging new cosmology based upon the observation of the mutability of matter (radium) and quantum mechanics, Lenin could fall back upon that all-purpose tool for dealing with change and boundary problems—the dialectic. Engels and Lenin believed that matter itself had a dialectical character. Thus, its mutability, manifested in radioactive decay, and "the absence of absolute boundaries in nature" caused no problems whatsoever. Rather, it corroborated dialectical materialism. Lenin, to be sure, never came to grips with the more general problem of energy dissipation promised by the principle of entropy in thermodynamics. He fled the pessimistic implications of the new physics and concentrated only on its consonance with dialectics and its progressive character. In this respect, he differed little from his opponents, for whom the centrality of energy in the new cosmology provided inspiration for new holistic visions. Lenin's irritation with the new terminologies they invented for their visions of the socialist future showed both personal conservatism and snobbism of the culturally "solid" person for upstarts. He acted a great deal like a Plekhanov with a club rather than a rapier.

Lenin used dialectics to resolve ambiguities and to focus himself in a process of *struggle*. His emphasis upon one of the three laws of dialectics (according to Engels) in his outline of the elements of dialectics in his philosophical notebooks on Hegel's *Wissenschaft der Logik (Science of Logic)* reveals this quite dramatically. For Lenin, the law of dialectics announcing the unity of opposites was the crucial one. It confirmed his political experience and his expectations. The moment of unity was fragile and passed quickly into struggle. As he confronted an endless series of problems, Lenin had to struggle with his own settled positions. Self-movement, itself difficult enough, was complicated in political work. One would inevitably be yoked together with future renegades, people who would not be able to see the need to change or the correct path. Their sheer inertia would pull the party in the wrong direction. The notion of the dialectic signified for Lenin mainly perpetual struggle, constant movement from one position to another, from one battlefield to another, with a small group of "conscious" comrades in tow.

For Hegel and many other idealists engaged in theoretical work, dialectics often signified not only the spiritual character of reality but both personal psychological development and a constant critical alertness—a readiness to embrace permanent revolution in the world of knowledge rather than in the world of politics. Hegel himself was to blame for the confusion of spiritual, psychological, logical, and theoretical processes with natural and historical ones. His left-wing disciples and reinterpreters varied a great deal. Lenin's real métier was politics, and, in sharp contrast to his cultural philistinism, he found creative, indeed daring uses for the dialectic in politics. But permanent revolution in theoretical matters is far less painful than permanent revolution in politics. Moreover, after 1917 "dialectical" politicians decided what theoretical changes were permissible. Stalin, whose philistinism was of a different order, demonstrated this quite dramatically.

The crux of the matter for Lenin lay in the resolution of the problem of the relation of social consciousness to social being. Just as the world of inorganic nature produced first of all organic life and then its higher product, the human brain, social being preceded social consciousness and was not identical with it, as his opponent Bogdanov assumed. Lenin's argument about social being and consciousness exactly paralleled his theory of cognition:

> Social consciousness *reflects* social being—that is Marx's teaching. A reflection may be an approximately true copy of the reflected, but to speak of identity is absurd. Consciousness in general *reflects* being—that is the general thesis of *all* materialism. It is impossible not see its direct and *inseparable* connection with the thesis of historical materialism: social consciousness reflects social being. . . . Historical materialism recognizes social being as independent of the social consciousness of humanity. In both cases consciousness is only the reflection of being, at best an approximately true reflection of it. From this Marxist philosophy, which is cast from a single piece of steel, you cannot eliminate one basic premise, one essential part, without departing from objective truth, without falling a prey to bourgeois-reactionary falsehood.[5]

The consequences of this approach need not be pursued in depth. One need only mention the plurality of social being, the Kautsky-Plekhanov-Lenin theory that consciousness could only come to the proletariat from the outside, and the splits among students of social being—among Marxian social scientists themselves—and a host of problems appears. As happens too often in the history of social thought, the interesting perspectives stimulated by a theory had quite startling results when translated into practical politics. By the twentieth century, the expansion of vision provided by Hegelianism and early Marxism had been replaced by the dreadful simplifications of revolutionary politics. In the period after 1917 new generations of Marxian thinkers grappled with the problem of the relationship between social being and consciousness—and even with the role of the unconscious mind. Lenin, however, was far from this. During his sojourn in Freud's Vienna Trotsky came into contact with psychoanalytic ideas about the unconscious, but theoretical mixing of Marx and Freud could barely emerge, much less survive, in a party dominated at first by a man who described Marxism as a philosophy cast from a single piece of steel and later by a man appropriately named Stalin.

Lenin Against the Bolsheviks

LENIN'S SAVAGE attack on the philosophical currents that had gained a deserved popularity among European Social Democrats and his own faction added to his status as a renegade within the Social Democratic movement. He looked increasingly dogmatic, petulant, and self-serving. To his fellow Bolsheviks he had abandoned the true revolutionary line and its advanced currents of thought. To the Mensheviks he remained a disruptive force within the party. During the first years of revolutionary decline after 1907 all of the leaders acted as if they were more concerned with their standing and reputation than with reviving the revolution. To be sure, the issue of money complicated things, and this was not a trivial factor. As the party contracted and funds became scarcer, squabbles over money and access to printing presses became ever more bitter. But scandals concerning the acquisition and control of funds were only the diapason to other squabbles of the most academic sort. The quarrels, in retrospect, seem petty and malicious. A kind of routinization of conflict took place, expressed in the overproduction of labels for new heresies. Any student of the émigré politics of the period comes away bemused and, like Stalin, inclined to see it all as a tempest in a teapot. During 1908–1911 the worst ills of emigration and political schism came to the fore.

Within this atmosphere the leaders of the movement wrote partisan histories, organized competing party schools, continued old journals and founded new ones, and republished their own most important works. From the perspective of several decades, the more interesting ideas issued from the left-wing Bolsheviks, whose leader, Bogdanov, for a while overshadowed Lenin in the faction.[6] Lenin's conflict with Bogdanov, which reached its crisis in June 1909, when Lenin expelled Bogdanov from the Bolshevik center, probably had its roots in 1905. At that time, Lenin had lost influence compared to Bogdanov due to his distance from the revolutionary action and his concern with the preeminence of *The Proletarian* as the organ of the Bolshevik faction.[7] While *The Proletarian* in resurrected form continued to be the official organ of the Bolshevik faction and Lenin's main project in 1908–1910, the new "faction" created its own journal, *Vpered* (Forward), thereby signaling that it was the true continuator of the Bolshevik tradition. Lenin's hostility to his former colleagues is well illustrated in a letter of September 1909 to one of his followers:

> Keep in mind that I am writing an article for *The Proletarian* where I openly treat Maksimov [Bogdanov] and Co.'s band of swine like *canailles.* . . . I would advise everyone either not go to Bogdanov's lecture—or to give him the sort of rebuff that would once and for all finish off his desire to butt in. . . . Nothing would be more harmful right now than sentimentality *[mindal'nichan'ia]*. A *complete break* and war *stronger than with the Mensheviks.* This war will quickly educate the fools, who haven't yet "examined things."[8]

Lenin had declared war on those scoundrels who were enticing unsuspecting workers, the cadres of the future, to the pleasant isle of Capri to bombard them with recallism, ultimatism, god-building, empiriomonism, syndicalism, and other heresies. Although he was able to exploit a division among the students at Capri, Lenin derived little satisfaction from the strife. Krupskaia describes in her memoirs one of the low points of the interfactional struggle. She and Lenin were in Paris, where they had settled in December 1908 after a stay of not quite a year in Geneva. Some of his former supporters, like the irascible Aleksinskii, were not averse to physical brawls. Aleksinskii decided to give the Bolshevik center, as it was called, a lesson.

> Aleksinskii's group once broke into a meeting of the Bolshevik group, who had gathered in a cafe in Avenue d'Orleans. Aleksinskii sat down at the table with an insolent air and demanded to be given the floor. When this was refused he gave a whistle, and the *Vperedists* who had come with him attacked our comrades. Two members of our group, Abram Skovno and Isaac Krivoi, were about to hurl themselves into the fray, but Nikolai Sapozhkov (Kuznetsov), a man of tremendous physical strength, snatched Abram up under one arm and Isaac under the other, while the proprietor of the café, an experienced man in the matter of brawls, turned off the lights. The fight was thus nipped in the bud. But Il'ich roamed the streets of Paris almost all night after that, and when he came home, he could not fall asleep.[9]

Despite it all, Lenin could recall all of the earlier splits and defections, the seeming disintegration of orthodoxy in the late 1890s—inspired at that time too by accursed neo-Kantianism—and remind himself that he had been able to reinvigorate the movement and create a powerful party organ. And then the revolution of 1905 had come. Moreover, the revolutionary tide would rise again; he would sustain himself, rebuild the general staff of the party from whatever materials were at hand. Let Bogdanov, Lunacharskii, and other party chiefs of 1905 defect. Lenin had already been schooled in political survival. He would do what Plekhanov had done in 1900: find new allies and keep whatever old ones he could. Lenin might take some solace in the knowledge that the Mensheviks too had splintered. Plekhanov, like Trotsky, had detached himself from the Mensheviks in 1909. Lenin's attitude toward Trotsky in particular clearly reveals his political modus operandi.

Lenin's correspondence illustrates once again his utter inability to see anyone who opposed his initiatives as having good intentions. In a letter to M. P. Tomsky of September 30, 1909, he stated that *The Proletarian* had offered Trotsky "the most advantageous conditions" and in the most "sincere" way (Lenin underlined "sincere" in the letter) had proposed an alliance ("bloc"). The Bolshevik center would cover the budgetary deficit for his journal *Pravda;* he would have an equal role on the editorial board in Paris. This depended upon his relocating from Vienna to Paris. But, according to Lenin, Trotsky wanted a majority on the editorial board (two Trotskyists to one Bolshevik) and would bring his own coeditors from Vienna. In an earlier letter of August 18, 1909, to Zinov'ev Lenin had written blisteringly of Trotsky: "Trotsky behaved like the basest careerist and factionalist. The scoundrel wanted to 'set up' his whole cozy *Pravda* crowd at our expense."[10] To Lenin this could mean only one thing: Trotsky was an ambitious man trying to build his own faction. The parallel with Lenin's position vis-à-vis Plekhanov in 1900, when Lenin had fulminated in "How the Spark Was Nearly Extinguished" that Plekhanov had treated him and Potresov as *careerists*, is very instructive. Lenin simply put himself in Trotsky's shoes. Like Lenin, Potresov, and Martov in 1900, Trotsky wanted to be master of the premier party organ. In concluding his letter to Tomsky about the affair, Lenin uttered a prophesy:

> Trotsky does not want to build a party together with the Bolsheviks, but to create *his own* faction. What of it—let him try! He'll make "his own" faction by taking a few from the Mensheviks, a few from us, but in the end inevitably will lead *[privedet]* the workers to Bolshevism. [11]

This prophesy, which clearly implied that Trotsky's militant, revolutionary spirit would make him a de facto ally in the long run, created such cognitive dissonance in the editor of Lenin's correspondence that he felt constrained to interpret it in a footnote. The workers would see Trotsky's antiparty position and as a reaction to it would arrive at Bolshevism! [12]

BY 1910 things had reached rock bottom both for Lenin and the RSDRP. Negotiations with Trotsky and Plekhanov yielded little. Plekhanov seemed to be more concerned with the version of party history being produced by the Mensheviks than with building a unified organization. A dispute with Potresov over his description of Plekhanov's role in the history of the movement precipitated the break with the Mensheviks. Trotsky would have nothing to do with anything that smacked of schismatic behavior. He shied away from commitments to either faction and took an irenic, suprafactional position in *Pravda*. He seemed content to preach unity and establish his position as a cosmopolitan socialist by forming ties with the Austrian, German, and Polish parties from his base in Vienna. Plekhanov and Lenin could unite only temporarily, apparently mainly out of wounded vanity, a sense of isolation—and hostility toward Trotsky. Lenin increasingly relied upon figures of the second rank, like Zinov'ev, Kamenev, and Stalin.

The lowest point occurred after the plenary meeting of the Central Committee of the RSDRP in Paris January 2(15)–23(February 5), 1910 when Lenin lost his organ, and was forced to surrender the ample resources the Bolsheviks had accumulated by fair means and foul. The funds were placed in the hands of three trustees, all members of the German Social Democratic party: Kautsky, Franz Mehring, and Clara Zetkin. As one historian has aptly put it, the plenum left Bolshevism "in receivership." [13] All of this was symptomatic of the RSDRP's frustration with the acquisition and distribution of funds and use of resources by the Bolsheviks, themselves split about such matters. Furthermore, the plenum voted to subsidize Trotsky's journal. The flow of resources to Trotsky and away from Lenin symbolized, however temporarily, a reorientation of the party toward the unifiers. Trotsky, mistakenly as it turned out, saw the January plenum as a major turning point in the history of the party. [14] However, once

Trotsky's *Pravda* became a popular and subsidized journal, it also became a target for Lenin, whose tremendous will to victory made the struggle with Trotsky's journal a foregone conclusion. Lenin began scheming during 1910–1911 to deprive Trotsky of the subsidy and to attract his readership to a new Bolshevik publication, *Rabochaia gazeta* (Workers' Journal). He not only defeated Trotsky by 1912 but stole the title of Trotsky's journal for the Bolshevik newspaper established in 1912 in St. Petersburg. He was aided in his campaign by Trotsky's lack of political judgment.

Using the German Social Democratic press to attack the schismatic tendencies of the RSDRP, Trotsky managed at least temporarily to alienate both Bolsheviks and Mensheviks. The occasion was an article published in *Vorwarts* (Berlin) on August 28, 1910, just before the Copenhagen Congress of the Second International.[15] Conflict over the article escalated on September 2, 1910, when Lenin, Plekhanov and Adolf Warski, a Polish Social Democrat and coeditor of *Social-Democrat*, protested to the German party chiefs and attacked Trotsky at the Congress. However true his comments and however widely known the party's difficulties, Trotsky had commited the cardinal political sin of calling down a plague on all houses (except his own) in print in a nonparty newspaper. It was clearly a play for sympathy for his suprafactional position, for which there was indeed considerable sympathy. Few of Lenin's followers had a stomach for his incessant mobilization against deviations from his party line. His ardent supporters of one moment became "conciliators" at another. But the logic of the situation simply made Trotsky another contender for leadership, and his error permitted Lenin to brand him both a factionalist and a Judas figure in the party, whose main appeal was to traitorous conciliators. It is symptomatic of Trotsky's poor sense of timing as a politician (although the German party chiefs evidently wanted it that way) that his article appeared in a ceremonial context—the Congress of the Second International. Instead of appearing to their colleagues as leaders, the members of the Russian delegation were made to feel like delinquent children. Only later did Trotsky discover that he had played to the wrong audience. In his autobiography he probably exaggerated his sense that one could not trust the revolutionary commitments of either the Austrian or the German Social Democrats at that time. In any case, Trotsky did not deny that he was "under the spell" of German Social Democracy in the years before World War I.

Despite his rejection of both factions, Trotsky undoubtedly remained *personally* closer to the Mensheviks, particularly to Aksel'rod. In 1910–1911 the two of them courted Kautsky, still the most prestigious figure in the Social Democratic movement, mainly with funding in mind.[16] Kautsky and the other trustees of the fund set up by the January–February plenum were beset by demands for money by both Mensheviks and Bolsheviks. But dealings with the German Social Democrats aside, Trotsky during 1911–1912 devoted most of his efforts to moving the Mensheviks toward his position rather than trying to win over the Bolsheviks. Lenin remained his bête noire. Perhaps his hostility toward Lenin made some slight collaboration with Lenin's intrafactional rivals attractive to Trotsky. He had lectured for the Bogdanov faction on the Austrian labor movement after it transferred its operation from Capri to Bologna in November 1910, but his brief contact with it did not lead anywhere. He later characterized his participation in the Bologna school and his defense of *Vpered* in *Pravda* as an evenhanded approach, a way of showing support for a group that had been persecuted by Lenin unjustly.

20

The Death and Rebirth of Bolshevism

T HE CONFLICTS of the years 1908–1911 demonstrated that Lenin's tenaciousness at political infighting was superior to that of his opponents. Ruthlessness alone was not the determining factor, for the left-wing Bolsheviks had shown no lack of it. Bogdanov, despite his control of considerable resources, was unable to hold his group together, and the Bologna school followed Capri as a failed experiment. The *Vpered* group gradually disintegrated. In 1911 Lenin organized his own school at Longjumeau, a Parisian suburb.[1] No one felt comfortable with the absurd situation of those years, yet neither the Mensheviks nor Bolsheviks seemed capable of uniting the party, much less their own factions. Martov showed fatal political weaknesses —irresoluteness and dreadful timing. Trotsky during 1910–1912 made a supreme effort at unification, but in view of Lenin's immovability as well as his own preferences, it continued to be mainly in conjunction with the Mensheviks and Bolsheviks who were alienated from Lenin. Trotsky's task was to capture

Menshevism, as he had done in 1905, revitalize it, render it more militant, and attract to it those Bolsheviks who had tired of Lenin's "Nechaevist-Bonapartism," as Aksel'rod described it. Trotsky's efforts yielded the so-called "August Bloc" of 1912, an unstable political grouping that could not survive its own divisiveness and Lenin's relentless machinations. Lenin, on the other hand, had to make his leadership credible again. He was up to the task. No one—not even Plekhanov—so successfully combined ruthlessness with righteousness, chicanery with legalism, and slander of others with self-justification. No one showed the same capacity to mobilize energy and intelligence continuously for the sake of his goal and to acquire layers of political toughness in behalf of domination of the party.

Lenin showed an extraordinary capacity for picking out the "soft" tendencies of his opponents' positions. To the Mensheviks the Russian proletariat was "immature," the peasants still needed the school of capitalism, and the revolutionary intelligentsia had problems adapting itself both to parliamentarism and to leadership of the proletariat. For Lenin these signified liberal rather than truly Marxist positions. Menshevik and Trotskyist arguments about Russia's relative backwardness now smacked of opportunism. Lenin too had fears about backwardness, but they revolved around the weakness of the liberals in their struggle with feudal "remnants." He paraded the cowardice of the German liberals in 1848 and Russian liberals in 1905. History taught that liberals had never liberated the proletariat and had often betrayed the peasants. In Russia they impeded the overthrow of tsarism and gentry power. For Lenin the question now was whether Russia could avoid establishing a Junker-style monarchy—that is, a conservative constitutional monarchy of the Prussian sort—during the continuing process of its bourgeois revolution. The slogan of a dictatorship of the proletariat and the peasantry became a crucial issue. The confiscation of gentry land associated with this slogan would put Russia on the "American" path of development by creating a "peasant bourgeois-democratic republic." According to Lenin's anlaysis, the Mensheviks led by Martov would yield to the liberals, who in turn would give in to the Russian *dvorianstvo* version of Prussian Junkerdom. Thus, Lenin's slogan linking the proletariat with the peasants rather than liberals signified his campaign for a "higher" form of democracy, whereas, the politics of his opponents linked the workers with the liberals and, through them, with the Russian gentry and monarchy. Of course, even if Lenin's political analysis were correct, the problem of economic backwardness would still remain.

Although Lenin tried to assert his superiority as a Marxist analyst by showing that his position rested upon economic, social, and political realities, he had been quite exercised by Trotsky's accusations that the Bolsheviks were sectarian and could not adapt themselves to the proletariat. The sectarian label had been pinned on Lenin long before 1910, and, of course, it was quite appropriate. Trotsky's reproach revived the trauma of 1905, when Trotsky and the Mensheviks had, however briefly, led the labor movement and Lenin had been eclipsed; and the assessment about the dismal state of affairs with respect to the Duma and the contemporary workers' movement could hardly be faulted.

Lenin here took his rock-bottom Leninist approach. The proliferation of factions did not signify a fatal disease of the party. At one of the low points in his
revolutionary career, after the virtual capitulation of the Bolshevik faction at
the January plenum of 1910, Lenin wrote to Gorky:

> Important, profound factors led and still lead to unification of the party: the
> necessity of a purification *[ochistki]* of social-democracy, of liquidationism, and
> recallism in the intellectual area; the terribly difficult position of the party and
> all s.-d. work and the maturing of a new type of s.-d. worker, in the practical
> area. At the plenum of the CC ("the long plenum"—three weeks of agony,
> everyone's nerves were stretched to the limit, one hundred thousand devils!) to
> these important and profound factors, which far from everyone understood, were
> added petty, trivial ones, were added the mood of "conciliationism in general"
> (without a clear idea of with whom, for what, and how), was added hatred of the
> Bolshevik Center for its merciless ideological war, was added squabbling and
> the Mensheviks' scandal-mongering—the baby was born with abscesses. Now
> we are still agonizing. Either things will end well—we'll lance the abscesses,
> drain the pus, the baby will be cured and grow. Or—at the worst—the baby
> will die. Then we'll be childless for a while (that is: we'll restore the bolshevik
> faction), and then we'll give birth to a healthier infant.[2]

Lenin simply refused to recognize any faction but his own as truly representing the proletariat. The others served the bourgeoisie and Russian tsarism.
Lenin prescribed the only true medicine: a purge, renewal, and unification on
the basis of a narrower but healthier faction led by him, of course. This
intolerance and self-assurance, which maddened his opponents, had great
survival value for Lenin. However, after the January plenum the momentum
for a time seemed to lie with Trotsky and his approach to unification.

Trotsky's rhetoric and style of politics, which provoked Lenin's contempt,
had essential weaknesses. Although he acquired a handfull of loyal collaborators on the bimonthly Viennese *Pravda*, he remained a popular political
journalist rather than a political leader of the first rank in the party. His
articles for the German Social Democratic press, however infuriating to Lenin,
presented a rather straightforward account of the splits and positions of the
factions within the RSDRP, all couched, of course, in a Marxian analysis of
the reasons for the party's decline and presented in a reproachful tone. *Pravda*
modelled itself on the German Social Democratic Party press. Neither Trotsky
nor his colleagues signed their articles. Furthermore, *Pravda* studiously avoided
invoking any of the leading theoreticians of the RSDRP or citing their works.
The authorities to which *Pravda* referred its readers were Marx, Engels,
Lassalle, and Kautsky. Thus, *Pravda* made every effort to stand above Russian
émigré squabbling, but even though supported by the private funds of its
coeditors, A. A. Ioffe and M. I. Skobelev, it could not survive without party
subsidies.

After the January plenum in 1910, Trotsky's brother-in-law, L. B. Kamenev, was posted to the editorial board of *Pravda* by the Central Committee of
the RSDRP as a condition of its subsidization. Trotsky soon fell out with
Kamenev, who left *Pravda* after a few months of collaboration. Kamenev's

departure permitted Lenin to assail *Pravda*'s right to a subsidy or its claim to be anything but a factional organ. Trotsky found it easier to break decisively with Bolsheviks than Mensheviks and would not tolerate any Leninist agents in his operation. For a time, at least, Trotsky managed to occupy a centrist position around which both Mensheviks and Bolsheviks who wanted to avoid the "liquidationist" or the "recallist-ultimatist" extremes might rally. However, Trotsky's centrist position proved to be a political liability in the long run. On the one hand, he attacked the Mensheviks for protecting their "liquidators" and tried to keep them in harness with elements of the party that the Menshevik leaders considered to be unruly and destructive. On the other hand, he alienated the Bolsheviks by demanding that a conspiratorial faction yoke itself to one that might render its modus operandi ineffective. Given the de facto continuation of the Mensheviks as an underground party, the crucial factor during this period, liquidators aside, was Trotsky's obvious preference for the Mensheviks as allies. He simply trusted them more than he did the Bolsheviks, even though in his autobiography he emphasized the differences between them. Like all other non-Leninists, Trotsky suffered Lenin's repeated slanders. Difficulties with the Russian party made the German one all the more attractive. Given these circumstances, one can appreciate Trotsky's efforts to ingratiate himself with the leaders of German Social Democracy. His efforts succeeded to the extent that they valued his views and published his articles in their leading organs. However, World War I destroyed the authority of the leading German Social Democrats, and Trotsky's career as an international socialist developed in a far different context.

THE OKHRANA agent who reported on émigré politics during 1911 was sufficiently astute (notwithstanding his misjudgment about the durability of the Lenin-Plekhanov alliance) to understand the weakness of the Menshevik position and the advantages of Lenin's aggressiveness. His prediction of social unrest accompanying industrial recovery also proved to be correct. He wrote in his report of January 24, 1911:

> One must surmise that Lenin and Plekhanov will ultimately prevail, and bring their opponents to heel, particularly the most stubborn ones, whom they will try to neutralize or altogether exclude from the party. Moreover, the industrial upsurge has caused a new wave of strikes, and that will certainly stimulate as well some degree of revival of the party's local underground activity, and this is no weak card to play in the struggle with the liquidators, who thrived only during a period of disintegration in the party and a lessening of the proletariat's energy.[3]

The liquidators wanted, of course, to put an end to underground activity. The Mensheviks around *The Voice of the Social-Democrat*, the *golosovtsy*, recognized the need for both legal and illegal activity, but preferred the former. In the center the Plekhanovites also believed in both, but preferred the latter. The Trotskyists seconded them in this. The Bolshevik-conciliators wanted to unify all the groups who believed in illegal activity. On the Left, the group around *Vpered* were close to the Bolshevik-conciliators, whereas the Leninists wanted not only to sustain the underground but to professionalize it even more, get rid of soft elements, and reduce it to a hard core of tempered revolutionaries.[4] Add to this the politics of the Bund and the Latvian, Polish, and Caucasian Social Democrats, and one has some sense of the complexity of revolutionary politics in this period.

Although the above police summary is a schematic way of looking at the movement and neglectful of the personal rivalries among the leaders, it captures the mood of 1910–1912. Lenin's furious rhetoric against the other factions and his accusations against Trotsky in particular once again suggest that in 1910–1912 he was reliving the trauma of Potresov's wavering and Struve's "betrayal" in 1900 and repeating the strategy that had served him then. Now, as then, he formed an alliance with Plekhanov against the "softs." Potresov became for him the arch liquidator. Behind the Vienna Club's and *Pravda*'s calls for unity, he saw "little Judas" Trotsky (the label Lenin had pinned on Struve in 1900) forming an alliance with Potresov on the right and Lenin's intrafactional opponents, Bogdanov and the *Vpered* group, on the left. Lenin almost certainly believed these accusations, no doubt because he saw the actors of 1908–1912 playing roles in a contest of hards and softs, real party types against anti-party types. He found himself fighting the old demons of 1899–1903 in new garb. He did not make this comparison unconsciously. Quite the contrary, he saw his opponents as camouflaged revisionists—they were too cowardly to admit it—and made the comparison with Struve openly in the party press. Armed with the "wisdom" he had acquired in earlier struggles, Lenin would not ally himself with any softs; nor would he be caught lagging. Rather than permit his enemies to betray him at a conference, he would move first.

The struggles of 1908–1911 came to a head in January 1912, when Lenin simply acted as if his faction were the party at the Prague Conference engineered by him and his followers. He infuriated his opponents by organizing an almost exclusively Bolshevik conclave of eighteen delegates under the guise of an all-Russian conference of the RSDRP, presumably the Sixth All-Russian Party Conference, in Prague. The conference took place between January 5 (18) and 17 (30), 1912. Having decided to split formally with the other factions, Lenin now did not hesitate reading the liquidators out of the party and creating an all-Leninist Central Committee. It featured the new Bolshevik staff officers. Among its original full members were Zinov'ev, Kamenev, and Sergei Ordzhonikidze. Stalin was later coopted. Lenin seized the party's organizational commanding heights, repudiated the subsidy granted to Trotsky by the old Central Committee, and then expropriated the title of Trotsky's popular workers' periodical, *Pravda*. All of this was part of Lenin's two-prong approach, in which he hardened the party organization while softening his tactics. That is, he moved into areas of activity where the Mensheviks and Trotsky had created a ready constituency, but on Bolshevik terms. His organization would use all of the legal opportunities for agitating among the workers to the fullest. They would strenuously campaign in the workers' curiae for seats in the fourth Duma; Bolshevik cells would take an active part in the burgeoning strike movement of 1911–1914 and in trade union organizations; they would infiltrate other legal organizations and institutions; they would even support the campaign to help the peasants suffering from famine and use it to advertise the failure of Stolypin's policy; and, of course, illegal work in all areas would be strengthened. In short, while pursuing his traditional reliance upon an illegal and disciplined party organization, Lenin prepared to steal the thunder of his opponents.

Lenin in 1912 believed that the RSDRP had evolved to the point where it resembled the German Social Democratic Party during the period 1878–1890, when it had operated under Bismarck's antisocialist laws and yet grown into a powerful parliamentary bloc. Lenin's new emphasis upon flexibility, upon a less tightly bounded party, surprised and alarmed some of his fellow Bolsheviks, including Zinov'ev. The new formula called for "illegal cells surrounded by a network of legal cells." One of the delegates suggested that Lenin's new organizational dicta might make it difficult to conduct an effective struggle against the liquidators. Aside from facing criticisms of this sort for softening organizational boundaries, Lenin had to fend off attempts to replace the practice of cooptation to the party center by election and to reply to Ordzhonikidze's attack upon the émigré organization.[5] The Prague Conference did not yield a docile group of delegates. In the end, however, Lenin had his way.

After the Prague Conference, in the March 14 (27), 1912, issue of *Pravda* the editors predicted that whoever dared to oppose the urge to unite "would be cast aside, as a vestige of a regrettable past." In a long attack, "To All Members of the Party," Trotsky characterized Lenin's tactic as a symptom of émigré malaise, which could not affect mature party members, but might breed confusion in less developed minds. All groups, including liquidators, might be brought back to the fold. But the Leninist "circles" or "sects" were afraid to be dissolved in a real party and mass movement. Trotsky accused Lenin of "*kruzhok* vengefulness and arbitrariness," but above all of impotence. The Prague Conference only demonstrated the isolation and lifelessness of Lenin's faction. Lenin repelled the mature, first-rank figures in the movement, including the Bolshevik-conciliators belonging to the older generation of *praktiki*, and surrounded himself with a few hundred nonentities:

> This is the task: to gather "a crowd" around the "hero." . . . The doom of Leninism issues from its opportunistic and unprincipled subordination of the needs of the movement to the needs of the self-preservation of a circle, which renders it organically unable to unite around itself elements possessing serious party experience. Around the "hero" there can only be a "crowd"; any barrier is impermissible.[6]

To be sure, Lenin's actions finally provoked his opponents into forming the August Bloc in response to Trotsky's call for a unity conference. However, the inability of the other groups to create a stable coalition once again suggests how difficult it was to assert leadership over the RSDRP. The August Bloc entered party history as a dismal failure over which the Bolsheviks could gloat in years to come.

In 1912, in time to exploit the revival of the labor movement, Lenin once again established his faction as both the hardest and most dynamic one after being challenged by the *Vpered* group on the left. Lenin showed quite clearly that he himself would decide exactly who belonged in the party. His decision to move to a formal split seemed to be more madness than method, given the tiny basis of support left to him in the early part of 1912. The party membership had shrunk to about 10,000 by 1910, and, if Trotsky's figures are correct, Lenin had no more than five hundred supporters at the time of the Prague Conference. Lenin chose to operate from this small base, so long as it was sufficiently hard—and obedient. But Trotsky was mistaken about the political impotence of the type of organization Lenin was building and about Lenin's rigidity. Lenin's willingness to follow his own prescription of lancing the abscess and killing the child was a symptom of unusual political will and risk-taking; and the types of people who were attracted to Lenin were not without their own kind of will and initiative. Obedience to Lenin's party line did not mean slavish subordination to a hero figure. Trotsky would have to repent of many of his judgments about Lenin and his followership and nonetheless end by paying dearly for them.

Among the Bolshevik "crowd," one undergrounder, described as a "marvelous Georgian" by Lenin in another letter to Gorky, emerged from provincial obscurity into the first rank. He had spent much of the period of émigré squabbling in Russian prisons. Like many *praktiki* he had developed a measure of contempt for the behavior of the splintered émigré community, its meaningless theoretical debates, and its mismanagement of the funds he and his comrades had obtained for them. Despite moments of doubt and open criticism, he remained loyal to Lenin at a crucial moment in party history, when Lenin promoted the faithful.

SURVIVAL DURING the period of revolutionary decline called for considerable powers of psychological endurance on the part of even the most professional of revolutionaries. In view of the fact that between March 25, 1908, and March 8, 1917, a period of almost nine years, Stalin enjoyed less than two years of freedom, his qualities of survival in prison and exile are of no small interest. In the safe havens of political emigration revolutionaries had to fend off depression and despair in the face of scandals, splits, and savagely uncivil forms of political behavior among nominal comrades. Undergrounders like Stalin had to survive the loneliness of their work, the trials of imprisonment and exile, the disappointment of defeat, the melting away of the party, and, not least of all, their own anger and irritation with the conduct of party affairs by the émigrés. Even the most loyal Leninists tired of émigré squabbling. Stalin would have been rather odd had he not vented his feelings from time to time. What is most surprising to a historian, a few documents revealing his opposition to Lenin during 1908–1912 survived and got into print, and, rather than making Stalin seem disloyal, they reveal hints of political maturity and independence of mind. Furthermore, the ambivalent memoirs of a prisonmate, which were designed to cast Stalin in a sinister light, reveal grudging admiration for Stalin's physical courage and psychological toughness. The Stalin of 1908–1912 does not emerge as a despicable sort. Rather, he appears to be a dedicated revolutionary with unusual stamina.

The prisonmate, S. Vereshchak, an SR, described Stalin's seeming inhumanity—his shutting out of the sufferings of his fellow prisoners, his apparent indifference to violence, his deviousness (using innuendo and slander) in carrying out vendettas against his enemies, his consorting with common criminals in the Bailov prison. All of this tends to support the standard picture of Stalin's cruelty and perfidy and casts doubt on the nature of his commitment. Vereshchak suggests that Stalin's behavior was noteworthy, unusual, but aside from the cruelty—which is undoubtedly there—it seems well adapted to the circumstances. His contacts with criminals can be read in the light of his Koba identity: One learned what one could about survival, and criminals had valuable experience in areas of interest to underground revolutionaries.

Despite his obvious distaste for Stalin's ability to close himself off and his apparent penchant for intrigue, Vereshchak testified as well to Stalin's remarkable memory, which permitted him to impress his fellow inmates during tutorials on the Marxian classics.

> Koba's appearance and his vulgarity in argument always made his sallies unpleasant. His speeches were always devoid of wit and had the character of straightforward exposition. But what was perpetually astonishing was his machinelike memory. When you stared at his poorly developed forehead and small cranium, it seemed like you could puncture it like a cylinder of gas, and all of Marx's *Kapital* would hiss out noisily. Marxism was his element; in it he was indomitable. There was no power that could budge him from a position. . . . He knew how to place any phenomenon under an appropriate Marxian formula.[7]

Vereshchak also recounted an event that Stalin's later sycophantic biographers did not fail to exploit fully. A regiment of soldiers forced the political prisoners at Bailov to run a gauntlet: "Koba walked, his head unbowed, under the blow of rifle butts, a book in his hands. And when the free-for-all was let loose, Koba forced the doors of his cell with a slop bucket, ignoring the threats of bayonets."[8] It is not surprising that by 1912 he had begun to use a new pseudonym—not just Koba, but K. Stalin, signifying both Koba's skill in the underground and Stalin's qualities as a tempered revolutionary fighter.

Even more important for students of Stalin's political character, he remained throughout the period a Bolshevik loyalist and, like others, learned to survive Lenin's capriciousness. Lenin had not made it easy for his followers during 1908–1912. At the beginning of the period he had seemed to the undergrounders to be leaning too far towards the Mensheviks and legal activity. Then he raised a silly fuss about philosophy and expelled Bogdanov and his group. Not only Stalin but other Caucasian Bolsheviks felt that he had treated Bogdanov too harshly. Furthermore, Stalin had his own mind about philosophical matters. Far from being a cringing subordinate, in the theoretical area he had written about dialectical materialism in "Anarchism and Socialism" and, in commenting on the Bogdanov-Lenin controversy, had taken an independent position, seeing virtue in Machism and in Bogdanov's criticisms of Lenin's *Materialism and Empiriocriticism*. It is reasonable to conclude that in 1908–1909 Stalin was not a strict Leninist.[9] He, like many others, was at least ambivalent about Lenin's leadership.

Of all students of Stalin's behavior between 1908 and 1912, Trotsky was most ferret-like in finding disloyalty to Lenin and signs of conciliationism in Stalin's ambiguous positions. Given Trotsky's struggles during this period precisely in behalf of conciliation, his retrospective condemnation of Stalin for leaning in that direction seems particularly unconvincing. Trotsky seized upon any evidence that Stalin was disdainful of Lenin's leadership or deviated from Lenin's line, permitting him to develop his general thesis about Stalin. Even in 1908–1912, when Stalin was supposed to have been one of Lenin's stalwarts, he had wavered. On the one hand, Stalin wrote a letter on December 31, 1910, in which he praised the Lenin-Plekhanov line, credit for which he assigned mainly to Lenin, and condemned Trotsky's efforts to create a bloc. Trotsky interpreted this and other parts of the letter as Stalin's effort to ingratiate himself with Lenin (who would presumably be apprised of the contents of the letter) and advance his candidacy for the Central Committee. On the other, less than a month later, on January 24, 1911, Stalin wrote to Vladimir Bobrovskii about the "tempest in a teapot," this time referring not to the debate over philosophy, but to the blocs that had formed among the émigré leaders and to the workers' disdain for the emigration.[10]

Not only Trotsky but Soviet historians writing after de-Stalinization began to take note of Stalin's disagreements with Lenin. Furthermore, they took more careful measure of Stalin's role during 1908 and his last arrest in February 1913. Instead of having him guiding the movement in short bursts of activity while at large or from afar while in prison and exile, they demystified his role. At the height of Stalin's cult, hagiographers had given Stalin a leading role in founding and guiding *Pravda* in 1912. Now it was pointed out that Stalin had been in St. Petersburg and attended a meeting on April 10, when the first issue of *Pravda* was planned, but that in all he had spent twelve days there before being arrested again.[11] Indeed, the conciliationist tone of Stalin's article, "Our Goals," published in the first (April 22, 1912) issue of *Pravda*, was duly noted. Although he did gravitate toward the *Vpered* group for a time and even toward conciliationism,[12] Stalin was one of those chronic hard-timers who responded enthusiastically to Lenin's decision in 1912 to draw a sharp boundary separating the party, the insiders, from a great variety of deviations. For a brief moment this bold act of leadership removed the ambiguities Stalin found so difficult to tolerate. Even more important, Lenin emerged as the most stalwart champion of illegal, underground party activity—to which Stalin had devoted his life. Yet, as the signs of resurgence in the labor movement increased dramtically in 1911–1912 and the election campaign to the Fourth Duma drew near, Lenin decided to transfer the party's main centers of activity away from the maddening émigré centers and to launch a new legal newspaper in St. Petersburg. By focusing upon these legal activities, Lenin exposed his followers to the conciliationist mood among many workers and activists.

It was difficult to do precisely what Lenin intended: to engage in activities similar to those of the Mensheviks and to make inroads into their constituency and yet to wage war to the death with them at the same time. At later stages in his political career Lenin would behave in a similar fashion: He would apparently shift his line closer to that of his latest bitter opponents, yet, instead of uniting with them, he would find other grounds for struggle. By maneuvering in this manner, Lenin would avoid being outflanked by those in his faction who might accuse him of going soft, but he would also pay a price. Many loyal Bolsheviks found his dual-track approach impossible to follow.

When Lenin moved to a formal split, he seemingly strengthened the commitment to the underground; yet he simultaneously thrust his faction into the legal arena with the launching (from Trotsky's point of view, piratical boarding) of *Pravda* and the campaign for the Fourth Duma. In this new setting some of the Bolsheviks in St. Petersburg were unable to sustain Lenin's militant line, whose real intention was to destroy the Mensheviks, not collaborate with them. Even dedicated undergrounders like Stalin found it prudent in such circumstances to make concessions to the mood in the capital. Whenever Lenin's lieutenants in St. Petersburg showed any inclination to be seduced by the Mensheviks or the *Vpered* group, he unleashed his full rage. Lenin clearly felt subverted by the staff of *Pravda* and the deputies to the Duma and tried to find a way of gaining greater leverage over them. He demanded unreasonable compliance with a line that, in the context of 1912–1913, seemed increasingly difficult to implement. Lenin's correspondence and Krupskaia's memoirs reveal his frustration, but it does not follow that Lenin's followers were at fault. Efforts by Trotsky and Soviet historians during the period of de-Stalinization to make Stalin look like something less than a true disciple hardly put Stalin in a bad light relative to Lenin during this period.

A student of the relations between the two men quite naturally asks at this point: Why did Lenin start relying upon Stalin more heavily during this period? Evidence of Lenin's attitude toward Stalin is slim, but Lenin was hardly blind to either his ambitions or his criticism.[13] However, he had confronted far more serious deviations from his line, and men like Stalin had proven their value and loyalty. In Lenin's correspondence one begins to find direct reference only after Stalin's cooptation to the Central Committee in 1912 and his posting to the editorial board of *Pravda*. The few comments are on the whole quite positive, but this is hardly significant. Lenin developed rapid enthusiasms for new people—"infatuations"—but they could just as instantaneously fall from grace. What is more significant in this case is the category to which Lenin assigned Stalin. Trotsky astutely noted that "the element of primitiveness undoubtedly attracted Lenin."[14]

Lenin's penchant for undergrounders and men of action like Kamo had not abated despite the apparent move toward legal activity. The promotion of toughs rather than just political "hards" to the first rank of the Bolshevik leadership was especially clear by 1912. Not only Malinovsky but other members of the new Central Committee had decidedly pugnacious characteristics. Sergo Ordzhonikizde, like Stalin a Caucasian, tended to express himself with his fists when provoked. The need to find sufficiently tough allies in his campaign led Lenin to Stalin. However, not even Stalin could follow his line, and Lenin resorted to a variety of methods for bringing pressure and the authority of the Central Committee to bear on his recalcitrant followers in St. Petersburg.

Party history had made it quite clear how difficult it was to remain in Lenin's good graces. Membership in the Central Committee and a position on the editorial board, while a major promotion for Stalin, also made him a target for Lenin's criticism. A perusal of Lenin's correspondence with his editors reveals what a harsh taskmaster he was. Within a short time after its inception in April 1912, Lenin found fault with *Pravda*'s line. Despite all of his efforts, Lenin could not keep his faction (which he had designated the party) disciplined and pure. Lenin's successful campaign to get his candidates elected to the Fourth Duma carried the split in the party into a new arena, and this created new sources of tension. The reaction against Lenin's splitting tactics affected both *Pravda* and the Duma faction.

Lenin suffered not only from deviations from his militant line but from censorship of his views. The editorial board of *Pravda* sometimes felt that Lenin's blasts were harmful and tried to tone them down or delay publication. He brought relentless pressure to bear on them and, in doing so, used trusted underground organizers like Iakov Sverdlov. It seems hardly accidental that Lenin later used Sverdlov and Stalin in similar roles in the party after the revolution. Lenin's formal victories in votes were not always accompanied by the enthusiasm of his browbeaten colleagues, who could not be relied upon sedulously to carry out his directives. Stalin, although pleased at his promotions to the Central Committee and the editorial board of *Pravda*, continued to show a stubborn streak of independence. After the elections to the Duma (in which the Mensheviks won seven seats to the Bolsheviks' six) Lenin and the Bolshevik Central Committee demanded equality for the two Duma factions, despite the Menshevik majority. Stalin was one of those who opposed Lenin's strong-arm tactic of forcing the Mensheviks to accept the equality of the Bolshevik faction in the Duma. He did so despite the decision of the Central Committee, for which he had voted.[15] Like others who had direct contact with the workers and lower-level party members, Stalin knew that the spirit of conciliation was pervasive and that strong-arm tactics might alienate the very constituency to which the Bolsheviks appealed.

Balky behavior and passive subversion of policy is a common strategy of subordinates serving under someone like Lenin. The first sign of it had appeared during the split of 1903, when Lenin's "majority" was subverted by his erstwhile allies. Subversion of legally orchestrated policies plagued him not only in 1912–1913 but during 1917 and after. Even recently promoted hired guns like Stalin could not follow Lenin's twisting line and incessant calls for battle. The Bolshevik center executing (or sabotaging) Lenin's policy in *Pravda* and in the Duma in 1912–1913 would act similarly in February–April 1917, when Lenin would drive them to break with all the riff-raff of the Provisional Government. By 1912 Lenin surely knew that his war upon a variety of opponents would alienate many previous followers, yet he always reacted furiously to deviations. Lenin's saving grace as a leader was his confidence that he could rebuild after a purge and his willingness to take back earlier heretics—even bitter opponents. Lenin would read them out of the party repeatedly if he thought it necessary. For their part the "heretics" would not forget Lenin's harsh behavior. They would be ready to oppose him if he appeared to be on a really destructive rampage. The events of 1908–1913 created in Lenin's followers chronic wariness about his judgment as a leader, wariness that never really disappeared. These years prefigure the later struggles of 1917–1922.

Years of Ambiguity

ENIN'S SPLITTING tactics made him an especially attractive target for the secret police. Roman Malinovsky, the leader of the six Bolsheviks in the Fourth Duma and one of Lenin's closest collaborators on the Central Committee and *Pravda*, proved to be a police spy—the most effective of several who had infiltrated the party.[16] Malinovsky, who helped Lenin win over the Metalworkers' Union for the Bolsheviks and establish a strong base in St. Petersburg, had been strengthening the Bolshevik faction because the Okhrana had identified Lenin as a destructive force in the party. Thus, Malinovsky was elected to the Duma with police help and his union-organizing tolerated. When rumors began to circulate widely in 1914 that Malinovsky was an Okhrana agent, Lenin defended him zealously against what he thought were merely slanders dreamed up by the Mensheviks. In 1918 irrefutable evidence was produced, and Malinovsky was executed. The Okhrana's success in infiltrating Lenin's organization and playing a significant role in party affairs was only one aspect of the continuing malaise of the RSDRP. Lenin's new baby was hardly without blemishes. His major ally in sustaining the split in the party was a St. Petersburg metal worker with a criminal record, who turned out to be a police agent.

Bolshevik victories during 1912–1914 therefore have a singularly ambiguous character. On the one hand, the Bolsheviks had formally designated themselves the party in Prague; they had established a legal daily, *Pravda*, which successfully competed with its Menshevik counterpart, *The Ray*, they had (with Malinovsky's help) Bolshevized the St. Petersburg Metalworkers' Union, formerly a Menshevik stronghold; they had penetrated other legal unions and had begun to turn them into their own instruments for revolution by creating illegal party cells in them; they were working assiduously in all the legal arenas available to them; they had successfully campaigned against their opponents in workers' curiae in the major industrial centers in the elections to the Fourth Duma; they had carried the split in the party into the Duma. However, as noted above, Lenin had to fight his own lieutenants and could not always rely on Central Committee members to act as his obedient instruments, even after getting them to vote his way. In June 1912 he and Krupskaia moved to Cracow, closer to the Russian border, in order to exert more control as well as to be ready for the next revolutionary upheaval.

Some of Lenin's victories were illusory. Even while carrying out Lenin's orders, Malinovsky was betraying high-ranking party members, including his own colleagues on the Central Committee, to the Okhrana. In February 1913 Lenin's main agents on *Pravda*, Stalin and Sverdlov, were both victims of Malinovsky's double-dealing. The regime could strike down the top Bolshevik leadership (and did so with greater zeal as the Bolsheviks looked more threatening) with relative ease. More important, the Bolshevik successes, which undoubtedly signified their ability to capture the more militant mood of the labor movement, did not necessarily signify support for all of Lenin's policies. According to a recent study:

> Worker support for Bolshevik leadership dramatically increased in 1913–14, but did not reach the proportions Lenin claimed. Nor did labor support for the Bolsheviks represent an endorsement of Lenin's position on all of the controversial issues that were debated at the time. Indeed, contemporary Social Democrats were careful to draw a distinction between "Bolsheviki" and "Pravdisty." The latter term applied to strict followers of Lenin who adhered to his pronouncements on the subject of party unity, whereas "Bolsheviki" accepted the general tactical approach prescribed at the Prague Conference but rejected Lenin's position on the issue of intraparty unity and cooperation with the Mensheviks. A majority of the Moscow party followers, including a number of leading trade unionists, were "Bolsheviki." In June 1914 they explicitly repudiated Lenin's policy on factional struggle and endorsed a resolution calling for a general party congress of the RSDRP, including all factions willing to accept both legal and illegal methods of struggle. . . . The premise that pro-Bolshevik unionists were followers of Lenin cannot be maintained in view of the strong conciliationist tendency in Moscow."[17]

Given Lenin's ongoing struggle with "conciliationism" on his own editorial board, the solidarity of even the Pravdisty with their leader was somewhat illusory. His style of leadership created perpetual tensions and conflicts. Moreover, the shift into legal activities created even more opportunities for divided loyalties. Party members serving a trade union constituency began to see things from a grassroots point of view—and that point of view did not always coincide with Lenin's. The ongoing expansion and differentiation of party activities laid the ground for future disagreements among subgroups of the party, disputes that played a significant role in the postrevolutionary period.

Thus, on both accounts, control over the heights of the party and a loyal grassroots following, Lenin's gains have to be weighed carefully. By proclaiming his faction the party, he showed boldness, a will to political power, and a good sense of timing in his effort to catch the crest of the new upsurge of labor militancy. Lenin showed that he would not be remote, overly cautious, or laggard as he had been in the early phases of 1905. However, the methods he used caused confusion in the very constituency he was trying to capture, alienated him from the rest of the RSDRP, and made him the bad boy of the party in the eyes of the leadership of the Second International. Lenin had experienced moments of deep exhaustion and defeat without succumbing to despair. At a poignant moment recorded by Krupskaia he had responded to the double suicide of Laura (née Marx) and Paul Lafargue in October 1911 by saying: "If you can't do any more work for the Party you must be able to face the truth and die like the Lafargues."[18] As the above quotation suggests, he saw *himself* as an instrument too—something to be cast aside if proven useless for the task ahead. However, as was his habit, Lenin reacted to thoughts of passivity, defeat, and death with a furious mobilization of aggressive energy. Despite the frustration of intraparty squabbling and intrafactional disobedience Lenin felt himself gaining control.

THE VITALITY of the working class movement during the period 1912–1914 issued from several factors: First, the economic revival and new conflicts with employers affected the mood of labor; second, after Stolypin's assassination in 1911 the government mixed repressssion with an extension of legal rights, permitting at least a partial revival of the trade union movement; third, the government's handling of the elections to the Fourth Duma in 1912 expanded the opportunities for propaganda and agitation; fourth, the celebration of the Romanov tercentenary in 1913 (which included amnesty for political prisoners) created a false atmosphere of clemency, which only embittered those struggling for real economic, social, and political gains. In short, the government tried to head off social discontent by a number of psychological and political ploys. However, in counterpoint with these measures in 1912–1913 the regime showed its brutal and reactionary character dramatically. The most dramatic moment came on April 4, 1912, when tsarist troops fired upon Russian workers in the Lena goldfields, triggering a strike movement reminiscent of the reaction to Bloody Sunday. Then in 1913 the muckraking connected with the trial of Mendel Beilis, an alleged ritual murderer, in which anti-Semitism in high places played a significant role, scandalized educated Russian society, already affronted by the ongoing relationship of the royal family to Rasputin. In short, during a moment of extreme nationalism in a prewar atmosphere, when the symbols of national strength and survival were being paraded, the regime was discrediting itself. Meanwhile, the events of 1912–1914 pushed the European powers towards war.

The Nationalities Problem

LENIN NOW had to confront complex issues connected with the emerging nationalities, not only those adjacent to the Russian empire on its western and southern border, but those to the east as well. A global change was occurring, as imperial powers confronted the aspirations of oppressed nationalities and those recently liberated but still unsatisfied with their place in the sun. Lenin's relative reticence about the momentous issues around national independence testifies, perhaps, to his high intelligence. In the period before the war he wrote only two major pieces on the issue of national autonomy, although he referred to it frequently in smaller articles. The nationalities problem fit ill with Marxism. It was perhaps even more puzzling than the peasant problem. One could at least delude oneself into believing that the peasant problem was soluble in Marxian terms by extrapolating from economic data, constructing Procrustean sociologies, and predicting the inevitable splitting of the peasants along class lines. But how did one fit nationality into the Marxist scheme? Of course, according to Marxian theory national boundaries created superficial divisions compared to economic forces and the relations of production, but nationalist passion seemed to inflame people and mobilize them even more than their class interests. World War I would show how ready people were to make sacrifices for the sake of the national or imperial dignity or, in the case of the Slavs of the Russian Empire, for related ethnic groups and coreligionists. Even the discredited Romanov dynasty would be able to rally its people around the war effort—at least at the outset. This was a complication—indeed, as history has showed, a fatal one—for a Marxian socialist with a genuinely internationalist orientation. But in 1914–1916 it was a spur to theoretical creativity. Lenin would have to unmask the real meaning of war in the twentieth century and turn it to advantage.

In the immediate prewar period Lenin seemed concerned that the imperialist wars and the enthusiasms associated with them might divert attention away from organizational tasks, from the burgeoning labor movement, and from his specialty, the peasant problem. Krupskaia noted that during the Cracow period, when the nationalities problem assumed vast importance, Lenin wrote over forty articles on the peasant question.[19] However, consummate politician that he was, Lenin would not rest long without converting the nationalities issue into an instrument of struggle. Lenin had to deal with aspirations that ran counter to a Marxian notion of progress, for concessions made to national autonomy might easily impede economic development and the unification of the world proletariat around a single socialist program. On the other hand, so long as a popular struggle could be turned against the remnants of feudalism and the bourgeois order, it could be a useful tool in the struggle for socialism. Lenin dealt with the nationalities problem in the way that he dealt with the peasant problem. He chose a short-term instrumental solution, which in the long run proved to be so costly as to make the achievement of his long-term goal problematic. In retrospect, it seems especially ominous that Lenin should turn to Stalin as his hired pen. Stalin, of course, inherited both the peasant and nationalities problems after Lenin's death, and his "solutions" are models of the style of politics practiced by the terribles simplificateurs of the twentieth century. But why did Lenin commission Stalin to write a major *theoretical* piece for him on the nationalities problem in 1912?

Trotsky, who must have been truly puzzled by Lenin's choice, suggested that Lenin's commission issued from a sense of tact. For all of his relentless pressure on his lieutenants, Lenin had learned that they needed encouragement and, when vanquished, an "honorable retreat." The situation in 1912–1913 was still not so lavish that he could afford to alienate seasoned people like Stalin.[20] He dealt with recalcitrant subordinates like Stalin (whose sins, after all, were far less serious than those of others) by giving them face-saving tasks precisely when they had just been disgraced. Trotsky inferred from the available evidence that Lenin knew that Stalin had mishandled his assignment on *Pravda* and that by putting him to work in Vienna and Cracow on the nationalities issue, he was simultaneously sidelining him and softening the blow.[21] On the other hand, there is a remark in Krupskaia's memoirs suggesting that Lenin and Stalin saw eye to eye about *Pravda:* "Il'ich was worried about *Pravda*, and so was Stalin. They discussed ways of putting it right."[22]

One of the closest and most thoughtful Western students of this moment in party history, Bertram Wolfe, suggests that Stalin's background and the happenstance of his availability played the crucial role in Lenin's choice. Lenin had not chosen Stalin in particular. Rather, he had chosen someone from the Caucasus. Georgians and Armenians played roles out of proportion to their numbers in the Russian Empire in the Bolshevik hierarchy, as did members of other minority nationalities. Lenin highly prized the Transcaucasian Bolsheviks for their services in an area of the Empire where Mensheviks dominated. As the nationalities issue assumed more prominence, he naturally turned to them to fight his battle against new menaces—the Jewish Bund's policy of national-cultural autonomy and the Austrian socialists' concept of federation. Although Stalin served him well, he would have been just as content to use the pen of another high-ranking Transcaucasian Bolshevik, a person of greater stature than Stalin, Stepan Shaumian.[23] In any case, Stalin had proven himself as a journalist in Lenin's eyes and (at least in person) seemed malleable and in tune with Lenin's wishes. One can be certain that in face to face contacts Stalin had impressed Lenin as an obedient disciple who would present his line faithfully. That is evidently the import of Lenin's statement in a letter to Gorky written during February 1913:

> With regard to nationalism I fully agree with you, that it is necessary to get involved with the issue a bit more seriously. We have a wonderful Georgian who set to work on it and is writing a big article for *Enlightenment*, having collected *all* of the Austrian and other materials. . . . Also, in the Caucasus s.-d. Georgians + Armenians + Tatars + Russians worked *together*, in a *single* s.-d. organization *for more than ten years*. This is not just a phrase, but a proletarian solution of the national problem.[24]

Lenin's approach to nationalism was that of a convinced Marxist having to separate out the "progressive" and useful aspects of nationalism from its retrograde and harmful ones. One biographer has claimed that Lenin was unconsciously a Russian nationalist.[25] There is only the thinnest evidence for this view, and it is mainly of a negative sort. Lenin never seemed to have developed much fondness for things non-Russian, never had been dazzled by the achievements of the nations to the West or seduced by their culture or political institutions. But he showed the same sectarian attitude toward things Western that he did toward those Russian: He admired what promoted the socialist revolution and would be useful for the socialist future and despised what impeded the march to socialism. Lenin's *conscious* aversion for Great Russian chauvinism can hardly be doubted. He expressed it frequently and vehemently. Members of oppressed nationalities played a misproportionately large role in his central committees and later in the Politburo. A stronger argument can be made for his conscious identification with the victims of dominant nationalities—and a desire to rectify the indignities they had suffered. Given Lenin's own mixed origins, nothing would appear more natural to him.

On the other hand, to rule out unconscious identification with the oppressor would be unwise, given the role it has played in political history. But we have a great deal of evidence that Lenin was quite sensitive to the presence of Great Russian chauvinism in those who had suffered from it. He waged his last struggle in 1922–1923 against precisely that syndrome at a critical moment in the history of the party. Lenin's worst sin was his insensitivity to early warning signals of Great Russian chauvinism in his hired guns. It would have taken unusual insight to find anything of the sort in Stalin in 1912–1913, when Lenin commissioned him to work on the nationalities issue and then published the finished product, "Marxism and the National Question," in the Bolsheviks' theoretical organ, *Enlightenment*.

Stalin and Lenin on the Nationalities

HISTORIANS HAVE long known Lenin's part in the formulation of "Marxism and the National Question" and discovered Stalin's debt to Kautsky as well, but in the end the work is Stalin's and expresses his views.[26] Both Lenin and Stalin saw the nationalities problem as a divisive force, which also diverted attention and strength from the main battlefield. National oppression confused things, created the illusion of a common cause between the bourgeoisie and proletariat of persecuted nationalities. In a revealing statement, which almost certainly reflected Lenin's view in 1912, Stalin wrote:

> [T]he hub of the political life of Russia is not the national but the agrarian question. Consequently, the fate of the Russia problem, and accordingly, the "liberation" of the nations too is bound up in Russia with the solution of the agrarian question, i.e., with the destruction of the relics of feudalism, i.e., with the democratization of the country. That explains why in Russia the national question is not an independent and decisive one, but a part of the general and more important question of the emancipation of the country. . . . It is not the national, but the agrarian question that decides the fate of progress in Russia. The national question is a subordinate one.[27]

In short, Stalin reflected Lenin's concerns of the moment and his reluctance to devote a great deal of attention to the nationalities problem. But Lenin could not leave it alone either. To do so would leave the field open to the proponents of national-cultural autonomy and federalism. Once forced by the logic of political struggle to clarify his views, Lenin—and Stalin—advocated national self-determination, a regional approach, and democratic centralism.

The term "national-cultural autonomy" signified a self-administered cultural life for groups of people with distinct linguistic and ethnic heritages. By making common culture rather than a common homeland the basis of a federal approach to socialism, this solution to the nationality problem would not threaten territorial integrity. However, it would destroy administrative centralism and open the way to much mischief. Lenin's strong centralist bias contended with his indignation against the domination of weak nationalities by strong ones. The Marxian vision, after all, was a unifying one, and Marx himself had been a centralist. How could one rectify the injustices done to oppressed peoples and simultaneously avoid the perpetuation of divisions among peoples — the formation of new obstacles to a unified socialist humanity? How could one encourage the international culture of socialism and distinguish it from the "bourgeois" culture of nationalism? Lenin had a more immediate anxiety: the destruction of a unified socialist party organization by a federation of autonomous national party groups along the lines of the Austrian Social Democratic Party. Stalin presented Lenin's solutions to all of these problems and anxieties in "Marxism and the National Question" in 1913.

Ambivalence toward *any* kind of national divisions shows through quite clearly in a series of propositions about Social Democracy and nationalism. Each positive statement about a nation's rights is followed by a cautionary, "this, of course, does not mean . . ." Thus, Social Democracy asserted the right of nations to preserve their culture against forcible interference by a hegemonic power, but it would agitate against "harmful customs and institutions." Social Democrats would support the rights of nations to secede from established multinational states, but they would measure those rights in any given case in the light of the interests of the proletariat and act accordingly.

The determination of the interests of the proletariat, as we know, fell to the Leninist vanguard, which also claimed to know the dialectic of history better than its opponents in the socialist camp. What is crucial, the party could label any given manifestation of nationalism "feudal" or "bourgeois," "reactionary" or "progressive," depending upon the views of the Bolshevik leadership. Furthermore, the repeated promise of the treatise, the right of nations to self-determination, was overshadowed in the end by the assertion of a *regional* approach, which would bind different nationalities together in economically rational groupings. The regional approach did not sufficiently take into account the traditional enmities of the ethnic groups (Azeri Tatars and Armenians, for example) in a given area. They often despised each other more than they resented the hegemonic power that bound them together. Stalin and Lenin presented "democracy" as a universal cure for all of the ancient grievances, enmities, and mutual suspicion of national groups: "Give the country complete democracy and all grounds for fear will vanish. [28]

The generous and optimistic vision suggested above did not survive the struggles of the Civil War of 1918–1921. The nationalities problem persisted in both forms: the hegemony of a dominant nationality over all the others; the enmities of minor nationalities bound together against their will in administrative regions of the Empire. "Democratic" centralism on a multinational scale became something of a fiction, but both Stalin and Lenin evidently believed in it on the basis of the presumed successes of the party in the Caucasus.

The entire theoretical construction and its hopes rested upon Lenin's faith in organization—in *his* organization. During 1912–1914, when the nationalities problem forced him to confront cultural issues as well, Lenin emphasized the *educational* role of proletarian internationalism. Stalin faithfully mimicked him.

THE POLITICAL culture of Social Democracy, which Russians had learned mainly from their German Social Democratic mentors, taught Lenin the rudiments of machine politics, which had to be amended along conspiratorial lines in a Russian political environment. The political culture that emerged—and attracted men like Stalin—demanded renunciation of old loyalties, criticism of everything that did not serve the victory of the proletariat and the international order of the future. One's native culture had to be subjected to the test of proletarian internationalism. Somehow, Stalin, who as a youth had worshiped Georgian poets and shown clear signs of the most romantic sort of nationalism, had detached his affections from his native culture and its past. Such severances are not easy to achieve—something always persists and lives a subterranean life. The process of conscious renunciation may distort early influences, but they express themselves somehow. By 1912 Stalin had apparently put his early romantic nationalism behind him. He had studied the international language of the future, Esperanto, while in prison. To all appearances, he took internationalism seriously. It is important to establish this for Stalin—it is hardly in doubt in Lenin's case—in view of his later behavior. As one views Stalin's progress, one is struck by his adaptive powers. However, the psychological need for heroic stature never left him. It became transmuted into a new idiom—not that of romantic nationalism but proletarian internationalism. It was the Koba part of his identity in a new form: Koba-Stalin.

The continuous process of transmutation is not easy to track, but Stalin provided a number of clues to his self-image during this period. The most striking ones are found in his references to other heroic figures. In February 1910 he wrote a short pamphlet praising August Bebel on the latter's seventieth birthday. Clearly, Stalin aspired to be a Bebel of Russian Social Democracy. Bebel had risen from the depths of working-class poverty. It had not destroyed his "striving toward the light" or diminished his will. He had been tempered in the struggle, sought knowledge, attended workers' meetings, joined workers' organizations, and "fighting and winning, step by step surmounting the obstacles that surrounded him, Bebel at last rose from the mass of the workers and became the leader of the militant workers of Germany."[29] When he eulogized Bebel, Stalin's inverted romanticism played a crucial role. Stalin had transformed Koba into a dutiful but nonetheless heroic proletarian leader. Stalin undoubtedly had himself in mind when he wrote that "Bebel, the faithful guardian of the interests of the proletariat, appeared wherever the fight was hottest, wherever his seething proletarian energy was needed."[30]

As he rose in the party, Stalin increasingly thought of himself as a leader—not someone like Lenin but like the Bebel of his pamphlet. Stalin's identification with men who had risen from "the depths" could only complicate his relationship with Lenin. Lenin clearly had the aura of distant authority that surrounded the émigrés and undoubtedly piqued the committeemen. Lenin did not fight in the trenches but directed the battle from afar. They, not he, suffered the dangers of arrest when he called them abroad in order to straighten out their line. When face to face with Lenin, Stalin did not see someone like himself, or his image of Bebel, but a man in a three-piece suit, wearing a tie, an authoritative person. Furthermore, Lenin's domestic life had nothing in common with anything Stalin had experienced. During his last Siberian exile Stalin fathered a child by a peasant woman and left them to their fate. He had none of the civilized way of the devoted family man. Lenin and Stalin were worlds apart culturally. Lenin might go to the opera in Trotsky's company. It is hard to imagine Stalin as a companion on such an outing. Rather than seeing Lenin as a hero, it is more likely that he saw him without any sentimentality, as an authority, an important figure in Social Democracy, and sometimes a harmfully meddlesome person.

Lenin, on the other hand, had a weakness for tough proletarian types—the "primitive" as Trotsky put it—especially when they served his line energetically. Thus, Stalin, although serving under Lenin and fully understanding his subordination, had a certain psychological advantage in the relationship. Perhaps he sensed this when he met Lenin in Cracow and carried on extended discussions with him during his last trip abroad (early November 1912–mid-February 1913). On his side, Lenin had a remarkable gift for sensing the political tendencies of the positions of his opponents in the intelligentsia. He seemed to know where they were heading before they themselves did and roundly assailed them as soon as the slightest signal of "opportunism" appeared. However, he seemed to suppress whatever warning signals he picked up from people like Stalin. When it came to perceptions of the oppressed, Lenin suffered from some of the same romantic distortions as other intelligentsia thinkers. Hence, Stalin became a "wonderful Georgian."

21

Lenin in Isolation

LENIN'S STRUGGLES of 1912–1914 yielded in the end his complete political isolation within the Russian Social Democratic Workers' Party. He had affronted the other leaders of the party by his unscrupulous methods of fundraising, blasted them in the area of theory, pinned misleading labels on them, undermined their attempts at unity, created splits in every major arena of party work. All efforts to chain him had failed. However, the impulse toward unity and conciliation remained both among the leaders and the rank and file of the party.[1] In July 1914 Lenin faced a united front, a coalition of the most respected figures in the party, who had succeeded in convincing the leaders of the Second International to place unification of the Russian branch of the movement on the agenda of the Tenth Congress of the International planned for August 1914. It was clear to everyone that something had to be done about Lenin. Against Lenin's wishes, eleven groups (including his own and his Latvian filial) assembled in Brussels in July for a conference under the sponsorship of the International Socialist Bureau. Lenin, who had been setting in motion the machinery for a sixth party congress, was furious. He faced a coalition broader than the August bloc, now convening under the auspices of the Second International.

Nine Social Democratic groups voted for unification. Among those in attendance were Plekhanov, Martov, Aksel'rod, Trotsky, and Rosa Luxemburg. By refusing to attend and instead sending Inessa Armand as his mouthpiece, Lenin put himself at an immediate disadvantage. However, given the alternative—a likely outburst on his part—he had chosen the lesser evil. It was, in any case, a matter of avoiding a total loss of face, since defeat (anything other than acceptance of his conditions) was a foregone conclusion. Lenin's brief, which Armand delivered on July 4(17), the second day of conference, if read in its entirety, would have taken over two hours. (The chairman forced her to condense it.) The resolutions passed by the nine groups (with the Latvian delegation and the Bolsheviks abstaining) had been designed to satisfy both he Menshevik desire to prevent Lenin from representing his faction as the party and to put to rest Lenin's fear of liquidationism. At the foundation of Lenin's brief for his faction was his argument that a fully functioning party already existed and could only exist by virtue of its underground organization in the conditions of tsarist Russia. The resolution passed by the conference contained a clause affirming the need at that time for an underground party organization. Thus, had he opposed the resolution, Lenin would have appeared to be nakedly power seeking—or simply unreasonable. Clearly, even before World War I and the schism in the International caused by the German Social Democratic Party's voting credits for the German Empire's military budget, relations between Lenin and the International were breaking down. One can only speculate about Lenin's reaction had the Vienna Conference of the Second International ever convened and put its force behind the resolution passed in Brussels.

The document Lenin had prepared for the Brussels Conference is an advertisement for the achievements of Bolshevism. A typically Leninist exercise in political indignation and intransigence, it contained the arguments Lenin had been drumming into the heads of his followers in the pages of *Pravda* and *The Enlightenment*. Lenin divided the party into true members (Pravdisty), liquidators, and defenders of liquidators. He proudly proffered Bolshevik tactics and currents slogans, all of which were designed to combat reformism and inspire revolutionism; he presented his version of party history; he extolled Bolshevik successes and ridiculed the pitiful backing and resources of his opponents; he paraded their sins; he sought not compromise but total surrender on his terms, fourteen conditions so detailed as to make discussion impossible. It took extraordinary insensitivity on Lenin's part to pressure Inessa Armand, reputedly his paramour, to mouth his words (translated by her into French) and make his case.

Possibly the truest comment in his communication to the Brussels Conference came at the very end of the prepared speech. Lenin claimed that his opponents were incapable of creating either a party or an organization. The latter was the crux of the matter. He had created the most viable organization in the conditions of 1912–1914. Although he himself had been more than a little responsible for the factionalism in the party, he was only one symptom of the divisions in the socialist camp—divisions that existed in European Social Democratic parties in different ways. The other factions were incapable of uniting—the August bloc had demonstrated that. In view of his successes in 1912–1914 he thought it reasonable that he should demand unification on his terms. However, he had shown anxious vigilance throughout the period, for he knew from past traumas how easily one could fall. He had already experienced several moments of seeming victory. After each one, the legions of evil had appeared: revisionism and economism, then Menshevism, then the Bolshevik heresies of boycottism, recallism, and ultimatism, and god-building. Now he had to fight the liquidators and their defenders. As always, Lenin believed that unification on his enemies' terms—an alliance with soft-liners—would open the way to the collapse of a genuinely revolutionary Social Democracy and the hegemony of the liberals.

In 1914 Lenin still found it somewhat intimidating to face the authority of the Second International alongside a solid array of opponents within the RSDRP. The fourteen conditions for unification contained in his address to the conference were also a stalling tactic. In the absence of surrender (highly unlikely) Lenin had hoped that his opponents would offer counterresolutions permitting his delegation to promise to put them before the Sixty Party Congress, which of course would be heavily Bolshevik.[2] It was a familiar drama: a split party, Lenin in control of the official party organ, his organization busy rounding up a majority for a party congress. He had every reason to expect victory and the authority conferred by an all-Russian congress. His opponents did not rise to the bait, but it did not matter. World War I intervened. The Brussels Conference, whose resolution would very likely have been validated by the Vienna Congress in August, passed into history as a might have been.[3]

TO LENIN, Trotsky, the most consistent critic of factionalism and sectarianism in the party throughout the period 1903–1914, was the embodiment of intelligentsia duplicity. In a typical locution Lenin called him an "arch-*intelligent*." When Trotsky began publishing *The Struggle* in 1914, Lenin leapt to the attack. With more than a little glee in several articles he paraded his achievements and Trotsky's impotence. Lenin, in fact, had done precisely what Trotsky had said he could not do. He had plunged into the mass movement of 1912–1914 and provided it with revolutionary slogans: an eight-hour working day, confiscation of landlords' estates, and the creation of a democratic republic. He had created a legal mass-circulation newspaper and penetrated the workers' legal organizations. Lenin had seized opportunities while his opponents had remained virtually paralyzed. Their passivity signified only one thing to him: They were not true representatives of the advanced revolutionary workers but bourgeois intelligentsia. Lenin began lumping all of his opponents' factions together under the term "intelligentsia currents."[4]

It did not matter if you thought you were a Marxist or a champion of the proletarian cause or even if you had been a professional revolutionary for forty years, as some of his factional opponents had been. The dialectic of history would select only one vanguard, and only it was worthy of the designation "Marxist" or "proletarian." Lenin had carried this view faithfully for twenty years, had acted upon it consistently—and had identified his own positions as the correct ones. His success in 1912–1914 confirmed him in the view that he was in step with history.

The artificial polarizations that occur during political struggle and his own need for power and control undoubtedly played major roles in determining Lenin's maneuvers and shaping his extreme rhetoric. Lenin had become a consummate student of techniques of political struggle and knew precisely what he was doing when he pinned outrageous labels on his opponents. However, his personal motives were opaque to him. They may as well have not existed. Lenin saw himself as an agent of the dialectic, and the dialectic called for incessant struggle. During 1914–1915, after massive arrests, the shutdown of *Pravda*, and the repression and temporary diversion of the labor movement due to war, Lenin channelled some of his energy into a study of dialectics. He took voluminous notes on Hegel's *Science of Logic*. They reveal the intelligentsia side of Lenin—his continuing need to inquire into the foundations of a theory that had become his lifeblood. It is typical of Lenin that at a time when his rhetoric had become vehemently anti-intelligentsia, he reaffirmed his own roots, as it were. His notebooks reveal that all of the struggles of the preceding years—and those he anticipated—were made meaningful by a study of theory and by his interpretation of dialectics.

Lenin's particular interpretation of dialectics centered on the "law" (according to Engels) of the unity and interpenetration of opposites. Given the resonance of this law with psychological ambivalence, it probably appealed to unconscious currents as well as to conscious recognition of political processes. Reviewing the past in the light of the law of the unity and interpenetration of opposites, Lenin found justification for his maneuvers, for his role in the precipitation of chronic division and endless struggle. His enumeration of the "elements" of dialectics is quite revealing, particularly the following ones. The unity being discussed, the "thing in itself," is probably unconsciously self-referential as well as consciously a description of the party and movement to which Lenin had devoted his life—and with which he completely identified himself.

2) the complete totality, the many-varied *relationships* of this thing to others.
3) *the development* of this thing . . . , its own motion, its own life.
4) the internal contradictions of *the tendencies* . . . in this thing.
5) The thing . . . as the sum *and unity of opposites.*
6) *the struggle*, the respective [the preceding word in English in Lenin's text] unfolding of these opposites, contradictory strivings, etc. . . . .
9) not only the unity of opposites, but *the transitions **of every** determination*, quality, feature, aspect, characteristic and *every* other [into its opposite?] [The preceding brackets are Lenin's.]

10) the endless process of uncovering *of new* aspects, relationships, etc. . . .

13) the repetition at a higher stage of given features, characteristics, etc. of a lower and

14) the apparent turning back to the old one (the negation of the negation) [5]

Lenin's faith in Marxism and dialectics was a living faith, which he reinvigorated by studying the classics. He undoubtedly justified all of his political machinations by means of dialectics. But at a more mundane level Lenin, like most politicians, derived justification for his maneuvers from immediate encounters with the dirtiness of the world around him. The non-Marxist world, of course, wallowed in wickedness and corruption, but intraparty and intrafactional struggle had provided the most painful encounters. Lenin had survived repeated "kicks" from comrades and would administer even harder ones himself. Shades of earlier struggles reappeared in every new one, in a dialectical spiral. Lenin carried the memories of the old struggles with him into every new one, and emerged from each with an updated arsenal of labels, slogans, and organizational weapons. Those who had to deal with him either kept pace or fell by the wayside. Dialectics validated Lenin's sense of perpetual tension, struggle, and victory.

Renewed contact with dialectical theory in 1914–1915 no doubt helped Lenin to move beyond the struggles within his own party and toward a more global vision. Lenin's most influential revision of Marxian theory, *Imperialism, the Highest Stage of Capitalism*, probably owed something to the inspiration of dialectics as well as to an intensive reading of modern political economists. Even more important, the global war forced all self-respecting Marxian theorists to explain the political struggle by means of economic and social data. Lenin was up to the task. When the Cracow period came to an end in August 1914 (after Lenin's brief incarceration on suspicion of being a Russian spy!) and Lenin arrived in Switzerland early in September, he had made a momentous decision to unmask not only the imperialist powers but the leaders of the Second International. The dialectic of struggle now forced him to break with all of the revered authorities of his youth. Kautsky, mentor to all leading Russian Social Democrats, had shown his true face as an agent of the German bourgeoisie—an opportunist. Lenin's first model, Plekhanov, was advocating defense of the Russian homeland. World War I forced Lenin beyond another major psychological threshold: He would be ready to stand alone, if necessary, not just against the Russian Social Democratic Workers' Party but against the Second International. But he did not have to stand alone. Some of his old comrades in arms—Trotsky and Rosa Luxemburg prominent among them—came to conclusions similar to his own, as did a number of other radical Social Democrats.

Lenin showed the dialectician's capacity to see beyond the breakdown of the Second International and the catastrophe of global war to the imminent victory of socialism. Over a period of fourteen years as an émigré he had become a masterful revolutionary politician. There was more than a little truth in Trotsky's angry accusation of April 1912, after he had suffered the theft of the title of his journal, that Lenin nourished himself on discord and chaos.[6] But so did all revolutionary politicians, for revolutionary changes issue from profound crises. The bloody trenches of World War I created an enormous, new revolutionary constituency, and only those leaders who knew how to exploit it would be prepared for the struggles that lay ahead.

22

Lenin, Trotsky, and World War I

LENIN'S THEORETICAL work and practical maneuvering during World War I show how important theory was for him. It gave him the confidence to take bold and unpopular positions—quite dangerous positions. First of all, he preached defeatism and civil war—class war—at a time when to all appearances the vast majority of the populations of belligerent nations, including his own, supported the war effort with patriotic enthusiasm. He genuinely believed that proletarian brethren in the trenches would stretch out their hands in friendship to each other and then turn their bayonets against the bourgeoisie. By preaching civil war, Lenin found some new "friends"—namely, those Germans crafty enough to realize that the return of revolutionaries of Lenin's ilk to Russia might seriously disrupt the Russian war effort. On the other hand, he exposed himself to charges of treason, indeed of being in the pay of the Germans. But the suspicions of treason issuing from his defeatist position and cry for class war proved to be a temporary (though for a time, dangerous) factor compared to those connected with his prediction of the collapse of capitalism. The gamble associated with that prediction was vastly more harmful to his cause in the long run. Lenin's diagnosis of the crisis of imperialism became both his hope and his snare.

The phenomenon of imperialism, political and economic, had been well studied by astute thinkers of various nationalities. Rudolf Hilferding, an Austrian Marxist, one of the leading theoreticians of Social Democracy, and author of *Finance Capital* had analyzed monopolistic capitalism, J. A. Hobson, an English political economist, had written an influential study of imperialism, and Lenin's young colleague, Nikolai Bukharin, had written *The World Economy of Imperialism* in 1914. With his usual thoroughness, Lenin scoured these and a great many other works for perspectives, arguments, and statistics. His notebooks and research apparatus, faithfully preserved and published in his collected works, are impressive indeed.[1] Lenin brought together a vast array of data—economic, social, and political—and produced an essay of great power and influence. Although labeled a "popular essay," *Imperialism, the Highest Stage of Capitalism* is designed for a highly literate audience. It is a "scientific" Marxian treatise.

Lenin's dialectical vision of the interpenetration of opposites served him well. Capitalism's impressive expansion, its superficial robustness, could not mask its internal contradictions. It was decayed, parasitic, and self-destructive. On the one hand, the bourgeoisie of developed nations were living unproductively, by clipping coupons. On the other hand—and this was his crucial position—Lenin argued that despite the triumphs of the huge monopolies and finance capitalism, competition among monopolists guaranteed a fatal outcome. The diminishing space for expansion into foreign markets and competition for new areas of investment with cheap labor and sources of raw material would inevitably lead to wars among the imperialistic powers. Lenin thus presented a dual image of bloated, parasitic accumulation and consumption and uncontrollable predatory activity, leading to the final crisis of capitalism. Equally important, he explained why the workers' aristocracy of the dominant powers supported their nations' imperial activities: They themselves received higher wages and benefits because the monopoly capitalists were exploiting an external proletariat—the proletariat of the colonial peoples. It now became perfectly clear how the leaders of the Second International had become chauvinists and opportunists, why they voted military budgets. They were linked to a social stratum that had been bought off by the super-profits of colonial exploiters. The implications were clear: The proletariat of the imperial powers had to throw off the leadership of the Second International, which had objectively become an ally of the bourgeoisie; colonial peoples had to rise up against their exploiters. A global revolution was in the offing.

Imperialism, the Highest Stage of Capitalism explained why working people were shooting at each other rather than their oppressors. It predicted that they would soon be transforming imperialist war into socialist revolution in the advanced industrial nations and into wars of national liberation in colonial areas. Lenin had shown early in his career how well he could make statistics serve his campaign of the moment. *The Development of Capitalism in Russia* had exaggerated the extent of Russia's socioeconomic progress and justified a struggle against the assumed hegemony of the bourgeoisie. Now *Imperialism, the Highest Stage of Capitalism* justified an immediate socialist revolution and an all-out attack on the bourgeois order. Lenin had remained a revolutionary optimist. Behind the Marxian conceptualizations and statistical tables one finds his characteristic revolutionary impatience. Nonetheless, it is difficult to imagine him sustaining his drive to revolution without his faith in the correctness of the theory behind his tactics—as well as the "Bakuninist" recklessness that was obvious to other revolutionaries of the Marxian persuasion. In his mid-forties, he understood that this might be the last chance for revolution in his lifetime.

While working on his treatise on imperialism, Lenin began to review the prospects for revolution in different areas. His efforts to deal with the enormous problems of global "uneven development" from the point of view of revolutionary Marxism yielded one formulation that at the time attracted little attention. All socialists, of course, were aware of differing degrees of global economic development. Any serious consideration of the spread of revolutionary socialism had to take it into account. Lenin addressed the issue of uneven development in August 1915 in the process of distinguishing his position on the idea of a "United States" of Europe, a notion popular among revolutionary socialists, from the formulations of those whom he was unmasking (particularly Trotsky) at that time.

> The unevenness of economic and political development is an absolute law of capitalism. From this it follows that the victory of socialism is possible at first in a few or even in one capitalist country, taken by itself *[otdel'no vziatoi]*. The victorious proletariat of this country, having expropriated the capitalists and organized socialist production, would stand *against* the remaining capitalist world, attracting to itself the oppressed classes of other countries, stirring them to insurrection against the capitalists, if necessary even coming out *[vystupaia]* with military force against the exploiting classes and their states. The political form of the society, in which the proletariat conquers, overthrowing the bourgeoisie, will be a democratic republic, centralizing all the more the strength of the proletariat of a given nation or given nations in the struggle against the states, which still have not gone over to socialism. The destruction of classes is impossible without the dictatorship of the oppressed class, the proletariat. The free unification of nations in a socialist order is impossible without a more or less lengthy, stubborn struggle of the socialist republics with the backward *[otstalymi]* states.[2]

Lenin reasserted his notion of uneven development and socialism in one or a few countries again a year later. While arguing against disarmament and for certain kinds of war in an article written in September 1916 (but only appearing in September–October 1917 in the youth journal of the International), he stated:

The development of capitalism is achieved in an extremely uneven manner in different countries. Things could not be otherwise under commodity production. From this issues an indisputable conclusion: socialism cannot conquer simultaneously *in all* countries. It will conquer at first in one or a few countries, but the remaining ones will remain bourgeois or prebourgeois for some time *[v techenie nekotorogo vremeni]*. This must call forth not only friction, but the direct efforts of the bourgeoisie of other countries to defeat the victorious proletariat of a socialist state. In these cases war from our side would be lawful and just. This would be war for socialism, for the liberation of other peoples from the bourgeoisie.[3]

Lenin apparently had in mind the victory of socialism in the most developed capitalist nations (one or a few of them), those in which the forces and relations of production made them ripe for socialist revolution. Given Marxian assumptions, it would appear likely that a more developed nation or a group of developed nations with large, well-organized, class-conscious factory workers would lead the way. However, they might not be the first to have a revolution. As for the Russian Empire, in 1915–1916 Lenin foresaw only the overthrow of the "military-feudal" yoke of tsarism by a "revolutionary-democratic dictatorship of the proletariat and peasantry." This would still be only a "bourgeois-democratic" revolution. As the imperialist war continued, it would yield civil wars, socialist revolutions—and the victorious socialists (whether in one or a few countries) would proceed to help their more backward brethren. But Lenin guessed wrong; things happened in quite a different way. The problem of uneven development and socialism in a single country would be addressed by Lenin's heirs, with momentous consequences.

Trotsky, of course, also guessed wrong. However, he never denied that revolution would occur in one nation first. Quite the contrary, he called for intense struggle on national soil with the hope that the Russian Revolution would trigger revolutions in the advanced industrial nations. But one had to be vigilant and fend off any "national revolutionary Messianism" which might grip a revolutionary movement. *"The revolution must begin on a national basis, but, in view of the economic and military-political interdependence of the European states, it cannot be concluded on that basis."*[4]

AFTER HE completed it in June 1916, Lenin tried to sneak *Imperialism, the Highest Stage of Capitalism* past tsarist censors. He did not succeed, but his correspondence for the period provides some unexpected confirmation for the view that Vladimir Il'ich Ulianov's pseudonym, Lenin, signified "laziness." Lenin's agent for the project was M. N. Pokrovsky, a talented historian who later became the leading figure in the new Communist regime's historical profession and still later, a victim of Stalin's wrath. In the summer of 1916 Lenin conspired with him about getting his manuscript published in Russia. Pokrovsky suggested a new pseudonym (rather than "V. Il'in," which Lenin had used when he wrote *The Development of Capitalism in Russia* and which he still used for his legal writings), and Lenin replied: "With reference to the author's name, I would of course prefer my usual pseudonym. If that is inconvenient, I propose a new one: N. Lenivtsyn."[5] The new pseudonym is, of course, his standard party pseudonym slightly altered. Instead of turning the noun *len'*, laziness, into a surname, he now used the short form *leniv* of the adjective, lazy. In the midst of a momentous new campaign, a furious new mobilization, marked by a major new theoretical work, he still chose to keep before him the negative identity of his childhood. It also signified the strength of his overall identity, his will to combat—and victory.

Lenin showed the same intransigence within the international movement that he had within the Russian one. He went into one of his familiar rages not only against those Social Democrats who supported their nations' war efforts (the "defensists") but against those who took a pacifist position, merely calling for peace without any gains, territorial or monetary, to any of the belligerent powers. The only correct position was defeatism and a call to class war. Lenin now tried to do on an international scale what he had done continuously since 1903 in the Russian movement: He tried to split off the healthy revolutionary elements from the diseased "opportunistic" ones. Here, on a European stage, he again encountered the principle of unification in the person of Trotsky, who now tried to do for the Second International and Europe as a whole what he had unsuccessfully tried to do for the factions of his own party. The arch splitter faced the arch unifier on an international stage.

FOR TROTSKY, as for the Mensheviks, Lenin remained the bogey of the party. Trotsky had expressed his attitude toward Lenin's behavior quite vehemently and publicly (although in an unsigned article, as was his habit in the Viennese *Pravda*) in April 1912, when after the Prague Conference, Lenin had seized the title of Trotsky's newspaper. "Lenin's circle, the incarnation of factional reaction and schismatic willfulness, has not only tried, by seizing the Party's resources, to deprive us of fire and water, but has done everything possible during the last two years to smear and make hateful in the eyes of the working class the name *Pravda*."[6]

Trotsky's views were widely shared among non-Bolsheviks. They never forgave Lenin for his fundraising techniques or for his seizure of the "firm name" in 1912. Their bitterness, as well as Trotsky's, is well documented, but Trotsky's is most interesting in view of his later affiliation with Lenin. Trotsky's correspondence with leading Mensheviks often contained disparaging remarks about Lenin. In a letter to Aksel'rod he wrote:

> Lenin's history [referring to Lenin's appeal to the new generation of workers] shows that in the near future political development can actually proceed more violently and catastrophically then it seemed to many—and it is all the more important to heighten the energy of the Mensheviks and their power to fight back, otherwise precisely Lenin will prove to be the parasite benefiting from this "catastrophism."[7]

The apparent rejection of catastrophic change sounds odd, given Trotsky's own embrace of it both in his style of revolutionism and his later formulation of dialectics, in which he took a distinctly catastrophic approach. Affiliation with the Mensheviks and adoption of a European attitude towards the immature Russian labor movement at least partly explains Trotsky's attitude at this particular moment in his career. As noted earlier, there is precedent in Trotsky's development for a vehement rejection of something followed by surrender and a dramatic change of affiliation—his personal catastrophism. However, the time scale here is far more extended than that involved in his earlier conversion from *narodnichestvo* to Marxism. Trotsky's hostility toward Lenin extended through the period 1903–1917 without any apparent diminution of intensity.

One eloquent letter to the leader of the Menshevik Duma faction, N. S. Chkeidze, was intercepted by the Okhrana. It was discovered after the revolution in the Okhrana files and later used against Trotsky by his opponents in the Communist Party. Trotsky's letter of April 1, 1913, to Chkeidze once again expresses not only his own views but those commonly held by leading Mensheviks about Lenin and his faction. Lenin led the immature, uncivilized elements of the proletariat:

> Yes . . . one's spirit is gladdened to read the speeches of our deputies, the letters of workers to the editorial board of *The Ray*, or your recording of the facts of the workers' movement. And how senseless . . . seems the wretched squabbling, systematically inflamed by Lenin, this professional exploiter of any sort of backwardness in the Russian workers' movement, a master at this kind of thing. Not one intellectually sound European socialist will believe that a split is possible on the basis of those margarine [artificial] disagreements that Lenin fabricates in Cracow. Lenin's "successes" in themselves, no matter how much they look like an obstacle, do not inspire any great fear in me. Now it is neither 1903 nor 1908. Lenin supports his organ with the "dark money" he has grabbed from Kautsky and Zetkin . . . and having made "unity" . . . its banner, attracted a worker readership, which, naturally saw the very appearance of a daily worker's newspaper as its own great achievement. And then, when the paper got firmly established, Lenin made it a tool of circle intrigue and unprincipled splitting. However, the spontaneous craving of the workers for unity is so irresistible that Lenin has to play hide-and-seek systematically with his readers, to speak of unity from below, while conducting a split from above, subjecting the concept of the class struggle to circle and factional definitions. In a word, Lenin's entire edifice at this moment is built on lies and falsifications and contains the poisonous principle of its own disintegration. There is no doubt that if the other side acts intelligently, a most severe disintegration will begin in the very near future precisely over the question: unity or split.[8]

Trotsky's optimism, of course, was ill-founded, although there was an element of truth in his observation that Lenin's "edifice" might easily disintegrate. The urge toward conciliation and unity was indeed powerful. However, Trotsky had underestimated Lenin's capacity for bringing the Bolsheviks to heel, on the one hand, and the tendency of the larger socialist movement to split, on the other. In April 1913 it would have taken a prophet indeed to foresee the extent of Bolshevik success.

In retrospect, one can find signs of Trotsky's later attraction to Bolshevism in his condemnation of *kruzhkovshchina* and the Russian intelligentsia's political impotence. Trotsky took his cue from Peter Chaadaev and produced one of the more eloquent condemnations of the Russian intelligentsia, also revealing along the way some of the psychological meaning of his attack—a repudiation of his own weaknesses.

> Before it [the Russian intelligentsia] there was always a vast selection of ready-made literary schools, philosophical systems, scientific doctrines, political programs. In any European library it could observe its spiritual growth in a thousand mirrors. . . . This habituated it to self-observation, the cultivation of intuition, pliancy, receptivity, sensitivity, feminine features of the psyche, but at root level trimmed away the physical power of thought.[9]

The theme of practical impotence *(bessilie)* and intellectual flightiness is central to the essay. Trotsky's own sensitivity to issues involving decisiveness and full manhood, his search for political virility, eventually led him to Bolshevism and forced him to abandon his earlier animus towards Lenin's modus operandi. He later had to choose between Lenin's form of substitutionism, in which the party organization and possibly a dictator of the party's central committee would usurp power, and the intelligentsia's traditional situation in which:

> The intelligentsia substitutes itself for parties, classes, the people. The intelligentsia experiences cultural epochs—for the people. The intelligentsia chooses the paths of development—for the people. Where indeed does all of this titanic work occur? Precisely in the imagination of the intelligentsia itself! . . . At first the aristocratic intelligentsia substituted itself for the "mob", then the *raznochinets-narodnik* substituted for the peasants; subsequently, the *intelligent*-Marxist substituted for the proletariat. . . . Even in the event that the [leading] idea moved in the same direction as general historical development, under the influence of the West it so far surpassed this development at the time that the carriers of the idea, the intelligentsia, were tied to the political life of the country not through the class, which it wanted to serve, but only through "the idea" of this class. So it was with the first circles of the Marxist intelligentsia. Only gradually the spirit became flesh.[10]

Trotsky's fear of being part of an impotent, disembodied intelligentsia separated from the world of the flesh rather than a genuine leader in a flesh and blood movement expressed itself in his repeated attacks upon *kruzhkovshchina* and his striving for unification. At the time (March 1912) he still believed that Lenin embodied the sectarian spirit of *kruzhkovschina*.

DURING 1913, when Stalin was abroad working on his treatise on nationalities, Trotsky had his first face-to-face encounter with him, an accidental meeting that at the time meant nothing but that Trotsky described toward the end of his life. He noted Stalin's rudeness and unattractive appearance.[11] It is unlikely that Trotsky knew that this man had described him as a "noisy hero with fake muscles" in an article appearing roughly at the time of their encounter.[12] Stalin, of course, believed that a real hero acted not noisily but stealthily. To Stalin, the fact that Trotsky was a Jew no doubt strengthened his conviction that this word monger would never do well in a real fight.

Meanwhile, Trotsky's allies proved to be hopelessly inept. He inveighed against their liquidationist leanings, tried to move them to the Left, but failed. Like Lenin and his followers the Menshevik leaders saw in Trotsky an ambitious man who used the rhetoric of unity for his own ends. Even without the sectarianism native to Marxism and the complications of World War I, the chronic jealousy and lack of mutual trust among the leaders of the RSDRP, their stubborn sense of hierarchy, along with Trotsky's infallible ability to antagonize, made his striving for a unified party utopian. Trotsky then staked everything on the forces of the larger European socialist community, an even more futile hope. His reliance upon the Second International's durability and power to curb divisiveness proved equally utopian.

TROTSKY'S QUIXOTIC behavior as a political unifier should not overshadow his achievements during the period of the Balkan Wars and World War I. He fully realized his talents as a journalist during the years 1912–1917, first as a correspondent for the journal, *Kievan Thought*, then as a coeditor of the Parisian newspapers *The Voice* and its successor, *Our Word*, and finally as a member of the editorial board of *The New World* in New York. The first, a legal journal of Marxian orientation, permitted Trotsky to eke out a living. Unlike Lenin, whose income from party and family sources and writing for the legal press yielded a tolerable income most of the time (although the years 1912–1917 were difficult ones for him and Krupskaia), Trotsky lived mainly by his pen. Furthermore, he had a family. Natalia had given birth to two sons, Lev in 1906 and Sergei in 1908. In his autobiography he describes a life of contrasts. On the one hand, he and Natalia enjoyed a rich cultural and political life in Vienna during 1907–1914; on the other, they raised two small sons without domestic help and had to live through financial crises and trips to the pawnshop. It was a hand-to-mouth existence. Trotsky's correspondence with Aksel'rod in 1912 expresses deep gratitude for financial help at a time when he was without money to pay for medical treatment. There are indications, however, that he still received funds from his family. His parents traveled to Europe, and, on at least one occasion, Trotsky's father helped him with medical bills in 1912. The year 1912 was evidently a low point, when an abscessed jaw, hernia, and frayed nerves connected with the campaign for and denouement of the August bloc plagued Trotsky.[13] He must have felt revived by the opportunity to travel to the Balkans as war correspondent in the autumn of that year.

The Balkan Wars saved Trotsky from the despair of petty émigré politics but plunged him into the unrestrained brutality of the era. The emerging nations gave free reign to their genocidal impulses. Modern weapons, imperial politics, and traditional enmities combined to cheapen the lives of vulnerable minorities in any theater of war. The mindless violence of the period repelled Trotsky and evoked his compassion for victims, but it also eventually steeled him for the violence of revolution and civil war. Rather than make any concessions to Slavophile chauvinism, he had the courage to expose the atrocities of the Slavic nationalities against Moslem victims. In the end, the death immersion he experienced had the effect of justifying revolutionary violence for Trotsky in a new way. His experiences as a war correspondent gave him a very concrete grasp of the magnitude of the disaster.

Forced from Austria to France after the outbreak of the war, Trotsky joined forces with the group of talented socialist publicists who edited and contributed to *The Voice* (1914–1915) and *Our Word* (1915–1916). Here he and Martov had their final falling out over editorial policy. Like all members of the Second International Trotsky had to work out a socialist strategy for dealing with war, and this provided the occasion for still another political battle with Lenin. In September 1915, when thirty-eight delegates, members of the disintegrating Second International, gathered at Zimmerwald in Switzerland, Lenin and Trotsky were still antagonists. Lenin actively campaigned for the creation of a new International and presented his slogans of defeatism and civil war. He stood on the extreme left, often alone (although usually with Zinov'ev, who had become his faithful factotum during this period). As was his political habit, when faced with a riven body, Trotsky sought to create a consensus and ended by playing the major role in drafting a centrist manifesto.[14] The Zimmerwald Manifesto demanded only peace without annexations or indemnities—hardly enough to satisfy the Zimmerwald left. Lenin's desire to abuse the opportunists in no uncertain language met with little sympathy, and his tactic of turning imperialist war into civil war repelled most Zimmerwaldists. Unlike Lenin, they could not easily break with the past.

Lenin's extraordinary ability to dissolve ties with both individuals and symbols of authority stood him in good stead during the catastrophic changes of 1914–1918. It was as if he had cast overboard all of the emotional ballast that sustains most people and retained only Marx, Engels, and his revolutionary drive. Kautsky, until recently for Lenin the single most authoritative figure in the Second International, now became "the renegade Kautsky." The Second International had revealed its ideological and moral bankruptcy. After the German Social Democrats voted the military budget, Lenin had allegedly said on July 23(August 5), 1914: "This is the end of the Second International. From this day forth I am no longer a Social Democrat and will become a Communist."[15] According to the same source, Lenin withdrew into himself for a few days in order to complete the "inner work" involved in such a momentous decision. However, one may surmise that Lenin's inner work had more to do with his political plans, his mapping out of the tactics he would employ during 1914–1917, than with the resolution of any emotional turmoil connected with the break. Lenin, like all Russian Social Democrats, had been caught by surprise, but he responded with his usual self-mobilization for battle.

Krupskaia noted in her memoirs the depression and accompanying fatigue experienced by Lenin in the wake of Zimmerwald—a sure sign that he felt defeated. At a follow-up conference in Kienthal in April 1916, attended this time by forty-four delegates, Lenin, now leader of the "Zimmerwald left," continued his attack upon any solution but defeatism, civil war, and a new International. Trotsky did not attend. Lenin's persistent efforts to push the delegates to the left succeeded to the extent that he captured a few more votes for his positions, although he did not win majorities for any one of them, and affected the tone of the resolutions adopted at Kienthal. The extremist tactic of splitting and starting anew still attracted few adherents even on the Left. Although some European socialists could muster up the courage to oppose their nations' war efforts, it was beyond the moral and emotional capabilities of most to break with the Second International. Even Lenin sustained his tie to the Second International as an institution by affixing his signature to documents issued by a small militant group trying to change the International rather than destroy it. Lenin was not quite prepared to go it alone.

Lenin retained his instrumental, utilitarian outlook. As was his habit, during this moment of rupture he sill sought talented allies. When Martov, for example, struck the right chord in the early moments of the war, Lenin complimented his work on *The Voice*. The two would never become fully reconciled, but it is important to note Lenin's recognition of Martov's political usefulness. Of course, he remained at odds with Trotsky, whose accursed ability with words seduced others into vague centrist positions. As Lenin saw it, Trotsky was especially dangerous because, although really a Kautskyan and opportunist, he sounded like a leftist and might steal the very constituency Lenin sought to capture.

Trotsky, on his side, had a particular phobia for Lenin's faction. He rejected an invitation to collaborate on the Bolshevik organ *Communist* in 1915. Despite the letter to Chkeidze in which he wrote that Lenin's organization contained the "poisonous principle of its own disintegration," Trotsky feared Lenin. Indeed, his fear must have grown during the war, for, as noted above, he also believed that Lenin's success was parasitic, that it depended upon "catastrophic" conditions. The two men remained embittered toward one another, each holding to the image that he had formed during the long years of exile and squabbling. It seems extraordinary in retrospect that Trotsky could distinguish the kind of "catastrophe" that would serve Lenin's "parasitism" from the kind that would serve him. Indeed, Trotsky would appear to be the "parasite" to the Old Bolsheviks after 1917.

Lenin saw in all of Trotsky's maneuvers for unification a de facto capitulation to the Right. Of course, Lenin typically believed his opponents were opportunists of one or another species, that they were *all* capitulating to the Right, but he showed special contempt for Trotsky. In a letter to Inessa Armand of February 1917 he revealed his disdain in colorful terms. Trotsky at that time was in the United States and writing alongside Bukharin and Kollontai on *The New World* in New York City. Lenin wrote: "There you have Trotsky! Always equal to himself = prevaricates, swindles, poses as a leftist, *helps* the rightists, insofar as he can."[16]

IN 1922 Trotsky published a two-volume work entitled *War and Revolution* with abundant selections from his diaries, articles, essays, and pamphlets of 1914–1917. In his introduction Trotsky acknowledged the differences between *Our Word* and Lenin's *Social-Democrat* but pointed out that after the Zimmerwald and Kienthal Conferences he, together with other members of the editorial board, had pushed the newspaper's policy to the Left. To be sure, they still did not accept Lenin's defeatist position with respect to the war, but *Our World* advocated socialist revolution in Russia whereas *Social-Democrat* advocated only the "democratic" dictatorship of the proletariat and peasantry. "The March revolution liquidated these disagreements."[17] This was Trotsky's way of asserting his priority in the crucial slogan of 1917. Here, Lenin finally came over to his point of view—the position he had taken already in 1905.

One article that did not appear in *War and Revolution* gives a truer picture of the hostility between the two men. In "Under the Burden of Objectivism," published in two issues of *Our World* (November 24–25, 1915) Trotsky put things rather bluntly:

> I do not have to point out that among Russian internationalists *Our World* is conducting an ideological *[ideinuiu]* struggle with the Leninists not as Marxists but as extremists. . . . I do not doubt . . . that *Our World* . . . will take the field against . . . above all the moderate, pacifist elements, but also in considerable measure against the disorganizational sectarianism of the extremists.[18]

Trotsky's diaries, articles, and essays of 1914–1917 clearly reveal both his proneness to Marxian illusions and his superiority as a writer and thinker about the war and its impact. He shared with Lenin and other Marxian political economists a vision of struggle among capitalists trying to divide the riches of the world through wars of imperialism. Like his cobelievers Trotsky thought that he was witnessing "history's mightiest convulsion of an economic system, perishing because of its own contradictions,"[19] and he therefore took an optimistic illusion as his point of departure. He believed that economic development had made national states anachronistic, that new proletarian republics forming a "United States" of Europe would be the foundation for global unity. As for the Russian Empire:

> The Russian bourgeoisie, right up to the radical intelligentsia, decisively corrupted by the huge surge of Russian industry during the past five years, concluded a bloody union with the dynasty. . . . The war of 1914 signifies the complete liquidation of Russian liberalism, makes the Russian proletariat the sole bearer of the struggle for liberation, and decisively transforms the Russian Revolution into a component part of the social revolution of the European proletariat. . . . The fate of the Russian revolution is . . . indissolubly bound up with the fate of European socialism.[20]

Trotsky tried to divine the psychological impact of the war on the proletariat. One of the major weaknesses in Marxism as a doctrine resided in its failure to examine closely the moral characteristics of an immiserized proletariat. The notion that the miserable and the oppressed will proceed to create a better world is, of course, inherently problematic. Now Marxists had to imagine socialist revolutions and a better world issuing from the worst carnage in human history. Viewing the war as a crucible for a great experiment, Trotsky sometimes made use of a typical Marxian and dialectical approach: the worse the better. In the article "The Proletariat in the War" he assumed that the war provided a better material basis for radical change than even factory conditions. The terrible material need connected with the war would push the proletariat into active struggle: "Almost the entire male population is sent to this school of war, which, through its terrible realism, formulates a new human type."[21] Yet he also recognized that the experiment might fail, that the war might destroy moral as well as material resources. Human culture might be set back decades. World War I might end like the Balkan War, with unresolved antagonisms, and yield still another bloody struggle. "Together with a great many other things, the progress toward socialism accomplished by two human generations might sink without a trace in rivers of blood."[22]

Trotsky, although a firm believer in the inevitable victory of socialism, imagined possible accelerations and retardations. His articles during the war reveal his anxiety that it would retard rather than accelerate progress, and this anxiety is expressed in the Zimmerwald Manifesto: "For decades and decades to come the cost of the war will devour the strength of peoples, imperil the work of social reform and hamper every step on the path of progress."[23] Trotsky's social, cultural, and economic realism and compassion for human suffering contended with his revolutionary drive and Marxian acceptance of history's harsh ways. One wonders if he had recourse to Engels' famous dictum that history was the most cruel of goddesses, whose triumphal chariot rode over heaps of corpses. Revolutionary optimism and imagination, of course, won out. On the anniversary of the Paris Commune in February 1915 he wrote:

> Four and one half decades ago the French proletariat . . . gave the world an experiment in . . . anticipation of the dictatorship of the proletariat on national principles. Now the problem of social revolution stands before us, if not as a world problem in a direct sense, then in any case as a European problem. . . . The main task . . . is the organization of the dictatorship of the proletariat on an all-European scale, that is, in the form of republics within a United States of Europe.[24]

Trotsky did not shrink from the colossal task of conducting a vast experiment in economic centralism, rational control over the world's economic resources, the creation of a world economy dealing justly with the backward nations. The corollary to this social and economic vision was organizational optimism—the belief that internationalists could overcome factional division and unite into a single party.

Lenin could produce equally visionary political literature. During the autumn and winter of 1916–1917 he began to work up material for the treatise *The State and Revolution*, where he took up the slogan of the dictatorship of the proletariat and the legend of the Paris Commune and applied it to the current moment. But Lenin would not trade his organization, however enfeebled, for the noblest vision or most stirring slogan. Lenin's works and correspondence for 1914–1917 show his familiar belligerence, his instinct for attack, even where the issues seem hardly worth the effort. He exaggerates differences between his positions and those not only of opponents but of allies on the left. He dins into the ears of his lieutenants the tried, old epithet "opportunism," some new ones—"social-chauvinists," "Kautskyans"—and the usual warnings against compromise; he tells them not to fear splits, berates them for their mistakes, and sends them to battle with almost the entire socialist world as well as with the traditional enemies, the feudal remnants and the bourgeoisie. Lenin prepared his still tiny band in the only way he knew how: He gave them an unambiguous, militant line embodied in clear slogans to follow; he gave them enemies to fight and revolutionary goals to achieve. Most important of all, now that he had repudiated all contemporary authoritative figures and institutions, he demanded that his followers do the same. Without faith in the leaders of the revolution he retained faith in revolution itself. Krupskaia summarized it well: "Never, I think was Vladimir Il'ich's mood so uncompromising as during the last months of 1916 and the early months of 1917. He was profoundly convinced that the revolution was imminent."[25]

The Eve of 1917

EVEN THE most habitual revolutionary optimist had to doubt western Europe's capacity to lead the world to socialism, but he could not express it directly. Lenin pronounced the following words at a speech commemorating Bloody Sunday on January 22, 1917:

> The present deathly quiet in Europe should not deceive us. Europe is pregnant *[chrevata]* with revolution. The monstrous horrors of the imperialist war, the tortures of inflation *dorogovizna]* are everywhere inspiring a revolutionary mood, and the ruling classes—the bourgeoisie and their henchmen—the governments, are increasingly getting themselves into a blind alley, from which they generally will not be able to find escape without the mightiest upheavals. . . . We of the older generation *[stariki]* will perhaps not live to see the decisive struggles of this approaching revolution. But I can, it seems to me, express with great certainty the hope that the younger generation . . . will have the joy not only of struggle, but of victory in the coming proletariat revolution.[26]

In their heart of hearts Russian revolutionaries doubted that Europe would lead the way. After all, it had been Russia in 1905 that had produced the mightiest proletarian upheaval in history.

Europe now made life difficult for them and their cause. The belligerent western nations, traditionally hospitable (despite cooperation of police agencies with the Okhrana) to professional revolutionaries and their journals, exercised censorship during wartime and began to expel foreign troublemakers. For some, the United States became an increasingly attractive base. Russian socialists, particularly Jewish ones after the pogroms connected with the 1905 revolution, had sometimes emigrated to the United States. They had established a number of journals, among them *The New World*. Lev Deutsch, one of the early Russian Marxists and Trotsky's sponsor during the *Iskra* period, had traveled to New York to become its editor in 1912. In 1917 it served both Mensheviks and Bolsheviks. Trotsky, expelled from France and denied haven in Spain, sailed from Barcelona at the end of December 1916. At that moment, like Lenin, he probably doubted that he would see a revolution launched from Europe.

After their arrival in New York on January 13, 1917, Trotsky, Sedova, and their two sons lived in the Bronx. That he expected to stay a while is suggested by the fact that they bought furniture on the installment plan. He became an instantaneous celebrity, a popular lecturer, and, if we are to believe the resentful memoirs of his former colleague, Ziv, showed more than a little self-importance and high-handedness.[27] Even Ziv attests to the power of his oratory, particularly to the brilliance of Trotsky's speech on the impact of the war delivered on January 25 to a "reception meeting" at the Cooper Union. He called it a "model of the orator's art" and a "colossal success."[28] Trotsky reviewed the negative impact of the war and even paraded atrocities (which were deleted from the version published in *The New World*), but exhorted socialists to action and drew optimistic conclusions:

> Crawling on your knees before the numbers and weight of authority is a pitiful and disgraceful blindness in this epoch, when the old foundations of life, the old authorities, the old methods are collapsing and new forces, new hidden tendencies arise. . . . A new human type is being created. People for whom the path between words and deeds is shorter, people of *daring*. This is a necessary precondition for revolution.[29]

Despite a busy lecture and interview schedule, Trotsky devoted his major efforts to *The New World*. There he worked with a talented group of publicists and experienced the usual frustrations connected with émigré publications. Trotsky got along famously with Bukharin, one of two Bolsheviks on the editorial board (all of whose members joined the party during 1917), but not with Kollontai, who sent critical reports to Lenin about him. Lenin's letters during this period reflected Kollontai's criticisms and later became a source of embarrassment to Trotsky, who placed the blame on Kollontai for misrepresenting his position.[30] Trotsky, of course, tended in retrospect to exaggerate all of those positions that brought him closer to Lenin, and one can indeed find such positions in speeches and articles published in *The New World*.

Trotsky's investment in revolution, like Lenin's, kept the image of the Paris Commune before his eyes and also evoked the Russian uprising of 1905. He summed up his wisdom about such things in one succinct sentence: "War and revolution often follow one another in history."[31] Like most students of revolutionary history Trotsky knew that once millions of men had arms in their hands, the constituted system might be threatened. Trotsky continued to take a political line separating him decisively from the Mensheviks. He repudiated the Kadets and other "bourgeois" parties. When the February Revolution began (March 8, 1917) Trotsky showed that he now viewed the situation in a spirit akin to Lenin's: Anyone who compromised with the Kadets was betraying the revolution. Instead of being allies, fellow socialists, leaders in the reborn Petrograd Soviet who supported the Kadets, became enemies. Like Lenin, Trotsky attacked the Provisional Government and its supporters. This new intolerance for compromise with fellow Social Democrats like Tsereteli and Chkeidze proved to be a more important turning point in Trotsky's political career than the theory of permanent revolution. All of Trotsky's former mentors and allies had strayed from the path. Aksel'rod, Martov, Parvus—there were no longer any leaders of stature among the Mensheviks. He was even less inclined to compromise with figures of lesser reputation, like his former collaborator on the Viennese *Pravda*, Skobelev. But in the spring of 1917 he still could not overcome his antipathy for Lenin's faction.

Neither the revolutionary optimism nor voluntarism nor vanguardism nor centralism nor repudiation of compromise that appear in Trotsky's works during 1914–1917 were sufficient to make him a Leninist. The evidence suggests that by 1917 Trotsky felt most comfortable as a revolutionary publicist freed from party infighting and intrigue. For all his inveighing against intelligentsia amateurism, he fit badly in *any* kind of organization, much less the kind created by Lenin. If anyone lacked the *psychology* appropriate to Leninism, it was Trotsky. He not only had to overcome his own "organizational Platonism," as his opponents called it, but to cross the psychological threshold that would permit him to overcome his antipathy for Lenin. The crucial factors were Trotsky's desire for an immediate socialist revolution, his willingness to improvise and adapt, his search for allies on the left, and, at last, his recognition that Lenin's organization was the most potent one. Trotsky still had not made that discovery in the spring of 1917, when he began his preparations to return to Russia.

THERE IS a letter, heretofore unused by Trotsky's biographers, which, if trustworthy, sheds new light on his state of mind on the eve of his departure. Written on January 11, 1936, by Roger William Riis to Quincy Howe, it was forwarded to Max Eastman and currently resides in his archives. Howe was an editor for Simon and Schuster, publishers of Trotsky's *History of the Russian Revolution,* which Eastman translated into English, and this, no doubt, explains the correspondence. Howe evidently had prior knowledge of the incident recounted below through discussion with Riis. In the spring of 1917 Riis was a reporter on the *New York Sun*. His editor assigned him to interview Trotsky about the Russian Revolution.[32] They used German as the lingua franca for the interview, although Riis's college German was barely up to the task.

> I found him in the basement of an old residence where his office was, wearing no coat or vest, with the sleeves of his shirt rolled down, and no collar or necktie. It was the kind of shirt that should have had a collar, and he had the neck buttoned up with the regular type of collar-button. He looked untidy and not attractive, but when he began to talk one forgot all this. . . .

I think all told I saw him three or four different times over a period of perhaps a month, and he always ended every interview with a statement, "Why should I tell you all this? Your capitalist paper will not print it." As a matter of fact, the *Sun* did and also printed that remark.

The specific incident to which you refer arose one day when he was turning the fires of his sarcasm on Kerensky. "What is going on in Russia," he said, "is not a revolution at all." Since it looked to my American eye like a pretty good one, I asked him what he meant by "revolution," and he straightened up in his chair, thumped his chest, and said, "*I—I* am the revolution." Strangely enough this remark from an unkempt little Hebrew in an East Side basement did not seem at all ridiculous.

There was one other curious recollection of him which I have which is very distinct and which I noted definitely at the time. He was one of the three people I have known of whom it could truly be said that their eyes flashed. The other two were Theodore Roosevelt and my father [Jacob August Riis]. As a matter of fact, the three were curiously alike physically—rather short stocky men of big torsos and immense personal fire and vigor.[33]

It is difficult to believe that Trotsky would have said anything of the sort in an interview with an American journalist representing a "capitalist" newspaper. Did he lose patience? Was he being heavily ironic? Trotsky's alleged remark presented in this manner sounds baldly egocentric, even megalomaniacal. By the rule of verisimilitude this document is problematic. But it should not be ignored either.

AFTER A sojourn of roughly two months in New York Trotsky began proceedings for his return to Russia. The dynasty had fallen. He, Natalia, and the two boys, one still convalescing after a bout with diphtheria, set sail on a Norwegian ship on March 27, 1917. It was Trotsky's misfortune to have attracted the attention of the British authorities, for when the boat docked at Halifax, Nova Scotia, for inspection on April 3, he, his family, and several other suspicious passengers were taken off the ship, not without a struggle. The British authorities interned him in a detention camp at Amherst with about eight hundred prisoners, most of them German sailors or workers. Trotsky spent his month there trying to convert them to the cause. In his own words, it "was like one continuous mass meeting."[34] The camp at Amherst gave Trotsky the opportunity to rehearse for the Cirque Moderne in Petrograd. Meanwhile he and the other Russians were suspected (or it was said they were suspected) of being German spies paid to overthrow the Provisional Government established in Russia as a consequence of the revolution. After experiencing the intense frustration of delay, Trotsky and his family were released on April 29, 1917. They set sail again for Europe, arriving on May 4(17), roughly six weeks later than Lenin. The situation of 1905 was reversed. Lenin got there first, this time.

23

1917: The Return of the Exiles

THE FEBRUARY Revolution, often described as a spontaneous revolution along the lines of 1905, actually had an ambiguous character. The urban insurrectionaries had long been exposed to revolutionary propaganda and agitation, and *narodniki* had worked patiently in the villages for decades. After 1905 mass-circulation legal newspapers, electoral campaigns, Social Democratic and *narodnik* representation in the Duma, trade unions, insurance councils—the list of forums and contacts could go on—yielded numerous converts, in both the cities and the countryside. For every active party worker there were many sympathizers and supporters. No one had planned an uprising on the day when the February Revolution began, although several thousand activists of different parties and factions had continued to operate in Petrograd during the war and had been actively involved in the growing strike movement on the eve of the revolution. Oddly enough, the unplanned character of the outburst on February 23 (March 8), 1917, worked to the advantage of the revolutionaries. The police, ordinarily well informed by their agents and ready for strikes and demonstrations, were caught unprepared. So were the party organizations. Those with wisdom about such things understood that revolutions could not be managed like committee meetings and immediately began to adjust to the new situation.

Decades of sacrifice by the revolutionary intelligentsia had not been expended in vain. When workers thronged the streets of Petrograd, they sang traditional revolutionary songs, marched under red banners, and, as the revolution progressed, looked to the well-known intelligentsia members of the socialist parties—the celebrities, so to speak, of the movement—for leadership. Although still riven by ideological disputes and power struggles, still relatively powerless to control the rhythms of mass movements, and still confronted by stubborn assertions of autonomy by worker groups, the revolutionary subculture and the party organizations created by the intelligentsia had established a form of hegemony over the mass labor movement. If this was not clear during the earliest phase of the February Revolution, it became strikingly apparent as the revolution unfolded.

One can hardly exaggerate the importance of the war for the revolutionary process. The war only temporarily interrupted a period of serious labor unrest. It also curtailed the regime's experiment in social engineering in the countryside at an awkward moment, when peasants were still experiencing acute land shortage and before they had adjusted to the disruptions and threats to their traditional way of life. Mass conscription on an unprecedented scale (15 million men under arms) as well as the pull of the factories during a period of labor shortages denuded the villages of the young and vigorous. Wartime dislocations, massive casualties, and military failures, scandals at the court, ministerial "leapfrog," acute shortages of staple goods, imbalance of the terms of trade between city and countryside, soaring prices, bread lines and rationing —in short, the government's incompetence and a disastrous military and economic situation—finally yielded an elemental upsurge of popular resentment. Triggered by women demanding bread, it exploded in the capital on International Women's Day. The alienation of the troops from their officers finally brought about the crucial transformation that the socialists had long worked for: the breakdown of discipline in the army. The mutiny of the garrison settled the issue in Petrograd. By March 2(15), 1917, the government had dissolved and Nicholas II had abdicated. The disposition of the troops would continue to play a major role in the ensuing revolutionary process.

A dual power structure emerged after the abdication of the tsar: the Provisional Government and the Petrograd Soviet. The Provisional Government, which engineered the abdication, included mainly leading figures of the Duma prorogued by the tsar before the collapse of the regime. Only one socialist joined, Alexandr Kerensky, an ambitious radical lawyer of *narodnik* leanings. The first Provisional Government was headed by the Kadet Party, whose commitment to Russia's war aims, respect for law and property, and relatively small, urban, educated constituency served it ill in the months following the February Revolution. Meanwhile, in view of recent repressions against the

Bolsheviks and the hesitancy of the Bolshevik leadership in the capital, mainly Menshevik and Socialist Revolutionary leadership presided over the resurrection of the Petrograd Soviet, which now contained soldiers' as well as workers' deputies. The leader of the Menshevik Duma faction, N. Chkeidze, became the first chairman of the Soviet, with cochairs M. Skobelev and Kerensky. Two Bolsheviks, A. Shliapnikov and P. Zalutskii, joined the first Executive Committee of the Soviet.

The acceptance of ministerial portfolios by top soviet leaders of the Menshevik and Socialist Revolutionary parties later complicated matters by blurring the boundaries between a presumably bourgeois institution and a socialist one. At first, socialists (with the exception of Kerensky) had shunned posts in a "bourgeois" government. Once the Mensheviks and SRs (both parties severely split) associated themselves with a "bourgeois" government and its policies, instead of winning more support for the Provisional Government, they made themselves a target for the left wings of their respective parties and for the anarchists, who enjoyed considerable popularity during 1917.

Pressure from both the left and the right finally thwarted the Provisional Government's efforts to preside over an orderly transition to a parliamentary regime representing a variety of interests, a "bourgeois-democratic" republic. The forging of links with mobilized mass constituencies through party organizations and radical slogans played a decisive role in the struggle for power. To be sure, the unstable chemistry of the mass movements put all parties in perilous positions. The leaders had to conduct experiments. The slogans of the revolutionary parties sometimes ran ahead of and sometimes lagged behind the demands of soldiers, workers, and peasants. For example, premature Bolshevik antiwar slogans and rumours that the Bolsheviks were in the pay of the Germans had almost fatal consequences for the party leadership in the summer of 1917. On the other hand, correct slogans, such as those embodying the agrarian program of the Socialist Revolutionary Party, could backfire unless put into practice. By October(November) 1917 the Bolsheviks proved to be most adept at formulating and spreading the correct slogans, recruiting and organizing radicalized workers, linking their agrarian demands with those of the popular Socialist Revolutionary Party, and putting into practice (at least temporarily) what other revolutionary parties only preached. No brief summary can capture the stormy events of those months or do justice to the fierce process of political selection for leaders with the greatest will to power and skills at adaptation and improvization.

NOT LENIN and the émigrés but party workers in Petrograd and internal exiles amnestied by the Provisional Government were the first to start rebuilding the shattered Bolshevik apparatus. Stalin returned from his long exile in the arctic tundra. Aside from some scanty memoir material and correspondence, Stalin's last years in exile (1913–1917) remain almost blank. We do know that his arrogant and sullen behavior and his unwillingness to adjust to the needs of others made him singularly unattractive to fellow exiles. Sverdlov, whose discreet letters do not detail the reasons for his difficulties living with Stalin, was happy to change domiciles after they had spent a short time together in the spring of 1914. During his self-isolation Stalin "went native," hunted and fished, lived with a peasant woman for part of the time, fathered a son, and deserted the two of them without a backward glance. One other event is worth mentioning: He was called up for military service and rejected as physically unfit in December 1916. After his examination in Krasnoiarsk he was permitted to settle at nearby Achinsk, where he joined, among others, Kamenev, former editor of *Pravda*, and M. K. Muranov, one of the five Bolshevik deputies expelled from the Fourth Duma. They all departed from Achinsk, conveniently located near the Trans-Siberian railway, and arrived in Petrograd on March 12(25), 1917, roughly three weeks before Lenin.

The leading Bolsheviks in Petrograd tried to take the situation in hand without Lenin's leadership. Despite superficial resemblances with 1905, the situation in most respects was quite different. The liberals, who had seen no enemies to the Left during the unfolding of the 1905 revolution, had become far warier of radicalism. Perhaps even more important, wartime patriotism strongly affected their fear of total breakdown precipitated by the Left. Although some workers also reflected the patriotic mood and cooperated with mobilized "society," other elements of the labor movement had become extremely radical after a series of defeats and repressions, and they were the moving force in strikes and demonstrations. Masses of workers were ready to march under radical slogans, whether provided by Social Democrats, Socialist Revolutionaries, or Anarchists.

In 1905 the Bolsheviks had at first mistrusted a broad, spontaneous movement that did not conform to their organizational ideas, then changed course, and finally resorted to desperate methods to keep the revolution alive. In the period 1906–1917 Lenin continued his flexibility about means and revised his political goals. He did whatever was necessary to maintain his faction's independence and his own preeminence as a theorist and tactician within it. As time went on, his faction had strengthened its position in the labor movement relative to that of the Mensheviks. The Bolsheviks were quite in tune with labor militancy in 1917 and even without Lenin had established themselves as a force in Petrograd, especially in the Vyborg district, one of the centers of revolutionary ferment. When Stalin and the other exiles arrived, they found *Pravda* already functioning and the Russian Bureau in a militant mood.

Stalin did not receive a warm reception from his colleagues. He was at first offered only an advisory vote on the Russian Bureau of the Central Committee at a meeting of March 12, 1917, a demotion from his previous position. Of the three returning exiles only Muranov was backed unanimously by the Bureau. At the time, *Pravda* and the Bureau were led by P. A. Zalutskii, A. Shliapnikov, and V. Molotov, all younger men, and Elena Stasova, a veteran of Lenin's generation.[1] The protocols of the portion of the meeting devoted to Stalin's status on the Bureau mentioned "certain personal qualities," no doubt a euphemism for the rude behavior that had alienated many of Stalin's colleagues. Kamenev, with whom Stalin had formed a kind of alliance during their last exile, was also admonished for his political sins, and his readmission to *Pravda* was made contingent on his explaining them. Nonetheless by March 15(28), 1917, both Stalin and Kamenev had joined the Bureau and the editorial board of *Pravda*.[2] The three exiles had successfully asserted their seniority. *Pravda* changed course.

Stalin's every political move between his return and the October Revolution has been subjected to very close scrutiny by a variety of biographers. His official biographers, of course, pictured him as Lenin's partner in struggle, an unwavering champion of Lenin's line. Trotsky, on the other hand, portrayed Stalin as a nonentity before 1917 and after his return as a helpless and confused party functionary, ill-equipped to play a leading role in Lenin's absence. In Trotsky's version the return of the exiles brought a change of course from a more militant line to one of compromise and conciliation — support for the Provisional Government, a rejection of Lenin's call for defeatism in the war, and de facto acceptance of the line taken by the left Mensheviks and SRs. He relies upon Shliapnikov's memoirs for his interpretation. However, Shliapnikov's memoirs also reveal awareness of the shifting character of the situation in Petrograd: "A movement, begun as a proletarian one under proletarian and popular revolutionary slogans, insofar as it expanded, assumed a more and more general character."[3] The radical Vyborg district committee had indeed inspired the Bureau of the Central Committee to produce a radical manifesto calling for a provisional revolutionary government on February 28 (March 13).[4] However, no one yet conceived of the revived Petrograd Soviet, which had held its first meeting on February 27(March 12), 1917, as a form of government and an alternative to the "bourgeois" Provisional Government. Rather, the Soviet was seen as an organ of revolutionary democracy, an instrument for creating a new government.[5] The early militancy of the Vyborg committee, although shared by other groups, did not catch hold generally. Support for the Provisional Government grew. The changes of tone in *Pravda* reflected the vicissitudes of an expanding movement and the changing mood in the capital.

Trotsky's retrospective criticism of Stalin's behavior from a Leninist point of view rings true to this extent: The behavior of the editors of *Pravda* both before and after Lenin's return on April 3(16), 1917, recalls their earlier evasions and subversions of Lenin's line. As in the earlier period (1912–1913), when they had flinched from Lenin's splitting tactic and responded to the desire for unity, the editors of *Pravda* reflected the mood in the capital. Although they can be accused of backing away from a more militant line, they can also be credited with a certain amount of political prudence. Furthermore, they would have had to have been clairvoyant in March to know that Lenin was going to call for all power to the soviets and for a socialist state akin to the Paris Commune of legend. When he did, they were stunned.

After Lenin presented his "April Theses" on April 4(17), 1917, it seemed to most Marxists, including many of his own followers, that he was raving, that he had abandoned "scientific" socialism, that he had become an anarchist. He revealed, in effect, his conversion to permanent (or uninterrupted) revolution by turning the bourgeois-democratic phase of the Russian Revolution into a sort of fiction. Lenin *believed* that his political maneuvers were guided by correct theory, but few others did. Marx and Engels, his only remaining authorities, provided him with an image of a commune state, a revolutionary dictatorship of the proletariat and—his own amendment—poor peasants. He had already established the international framework for socialist revolutions in *Imperialism, the Highest Stage of Capitalism.* Now he began to justify the creation of a new kind of power, a soviet state. Lenin knew that he had in hand a promising revolutionary situation and understood where to gather and direct power: in the streets and villages, barracks and naval bases, in the soviet movement. An experimenter in the workshop of politics, Lenin not only created his own tools, he also worked with whatever materials he found immediately available.

SENIOR BOLSHEVIKS like Kamenev and Stalin, caught between a younger generation aspiring to leadership and Lenin's surprising moves, struggled to maintain their position in the party. As they had in the past when confronted with a surprise maneuver, they temporized, subverted Lenin's most extreme positions, and hoped that he would come to his senses. During the months following his return, Lenin brought the rapidly growing Bolshevik organization under his control and tried to recruit the talent necessary to reach the vast revolutionary constituencies. Trotsky, who later so strongly condemned Stalin for not following the Leninist line, after his own arrival in Russia did not rush to offer his services to Lenin and the Bolsheviks. On his side, Lenin saw in Trotsky a useful instrument for revolution and soon offered him a powerful position in the party. Trotsky understood very well that if he became a Bolshevik he would have to submit to Lenin.

Lenin revealed himself to be a true *homo politicus* of a most ruthless variety in his response to 1917. He showed the willingness to take risks and decisiveness that distinguish revolutionary leaders of the first rank. This was already apparent in his five "Letters from Afar," written during the period between March 7(20) and March 26(April 8), 1917. Only one of them actually appeared in print in *Pravda* in 1917—and that one edited by his colleagues. It is impossible to say exactly what they censored, but given the extreme language of some parts of the version that survived their excisions, one can easily guess why they felt nervous about it. Lenin's letters contained, among other extreme positions, a merciless attack on the Provisional Government. He did not trust it to deal summarily with the dynasty, which he described as bloody, depraved, and monstrous. Perhaps the tsarist regime was only wounded; perhaps the beast would try to return. Even if the Tsar was finished, the "bourgeois" parties of the old Duma, whose leaders formed the Provisional Government, were instruments of the English and French capitalists and imperialists. Lenin's arguments pointed toward a single conclusion: Only the soviet, a government of workers, soldiers, and poor peasants, could be trusted to carry the revolution through decisively.

All of the essential features of the "April Theses" and *The State and Revolution* appear in the "Letters from Afar." Lenin saw the February Revolution as a transitional moment, to be followed quickly by continued class struggle and a shift in the correlation of forces to the soviet. The soviet would gather vast democratic forces and smash the professional state apparatus inherited and sustained by the Provisional Government. Democratic control over the production and distribution of goods and the nationalization of the landlords' estates would never take place if instruments of coercion remained in the hands of a government protecting the interests of landlords and factory owners. Although Lenin did not call for an end to the state as such, he offered a radical alternative to the existing state instruments of coercion: a popular militia of all adult men and women instead of professional police and army. Marx's teaching on the Paris Commune and his own experience in 1905 supported this radical conclusion. The soviet, even though presently dominated by Mensheviks and SRs, had vast potential as a revolutionary force, a force that could be used against the new bourgeois regime and serve as a new form of government. Equally important, the European proletariat would follow suit. Lenin's optimism about the Russian Revolution issued from internationalist assumptions. Everything depended upon the collapse of world capitalism predicted in *Imperialism, the Highest Stage of Capitalism.*

When he arrived at the Finland Station in Petrograd on April 3(16), 1917, Lenin had already made the most important decision of his revolutionary career: He would call for the destruction of the Provisional Government and the transfer of power to the soviet. His task was not an easy one. The proletariat, after all, had submitted meekly to the new power. Although the correlation of forces lay on the side of a huge population of peasants and workers, disoriented and unprepared during a moment of transition, they had listened to the petty-bourgois opportunitists, the right-wing Mensheviks and SRs. The betrayers of the working class had to be unmasked. The Bolsheviks themselves had sinned. Now they had to change course and explain patiently to the workers why defeatism was the correct war policy; why the revolution had to proceed to its next, democratic phase, to a soviet government; why only the soviet could be trusted to call a constituent assembly, which would then institutionalize the gains of the revolution. Lenin had not yet concluded that he could dispense with a constituent assembly.

The arrival of the Bolshevik leader was treated as a major event. Someone had commandeered a searchlight. A huge throng, including bands, military units, party members, an official delegation from the Soviet Executive Committee, led by Chkeidze and Shliapnikov, and the usual crowd of curious onlookers, greeted the train, even though it arrived shortly after eleven at night. All of this impromptu theater was out of keeping with Lenin's style—it was the sort of thing made for Trotsky—yet he rose to the occasion. Instead of acting in a bland ceremonial manner or feeling his way, he got down to work and immediately launched into the substance of his theses about the war and the world socialist revolution. After the playing of the *Marseillaise*, the official greetings, and his initial brief comment, Lenin climbed onto the roof of a car and made his first speech on Russian soil. It was followed by a triumphal midnight ride (accompanied by a band and a crowd of workers, soldiers, and ordinary citizens) through the streets of Petrograd in an armored vehicle, from which he delivered extemporaneous street oratory.

Lenin made his way to Bolshevik headquarters, the mansion of Nicholas II's former mistress, the ballerina Kshesinskaias. There he made more speeches from the second-floor balcony and finally presented his ideas at length to a gathering of his followers in the spacious reception room of the mansion. The impact of the speech was dramatically rendered by N. N. Sukhanov, at the time a leading figure in the Petrograd Soviet, whose eyewitness account of the events of the night of April 3–4(16–17) is the best single source for this extraordinary moment in history:

> I shall never forget that thunder-like speech, which startled and amazed not only me, a heretic [of Menshevik leanings] who had accidentally dropped in, but all the true believers. I am certain that no one had expected anything of the sort. It seemed all the elements had risen from their abodes, and the spirit of universal destruction, knowing neither barriers nor doubts, neither human difficulties nor human calculations, was hovering around Kshesinskaia's reception-room above the heads of the bewitched disciples.[6]

But as Sukhanov knew, the "bewitched" listeners came to their senses and, however ineffectually, tried to prevent Lenin from taking a position that might easily lead not only to the loss of Bolshevik influence but harm the soviet movement as well. Kamenev, who had assumed a leading role in formulating the policy of *Pravda*, was not enthralled. The triumphant scenes of April 3–4 quickly gave way to long months of struggle and, for Lenin, near disaster.

In the Tauride Palace, where the Petrograd Soviet and the Provisional Government shared separate chambers, Lenin delivered his historic speech of April 4(17), 1917, to a group of Bolsheviks serving in the Soviet and then spoke to a united session of Bolshevik and Menshevik deputies. The Bolsheviks and Mensheviks gathered in the Tauride Palace were there not just to greet Lenin. They were conducting the business of soviet and party conferences that had begun at the end of March. The joint Bolshevik-Menshevik session had been arranged by Stalin, among others. Lenin's speech to the Bolsheviks contained the ten programmatic points known as the "April Theses." Lenin set the stage for a struggle within the inner core of his faction and put the Bolsheviks as a whole in an embattled position. Indeed, he seemed to be intent on isolating his party. He held up the example of Karl Liebknecht, who had defied the German Social Democrats. The Bolsheviks would stand alone for the time being. History was on their side. What was needed was patient work at raising the level of consciousness of mass constituencies. In fact, Lenin believed that he had to change the consciousness of his own followers. He proposed that they even change their name to the "Communist Party" to separate themselves from the traitorous opportunists bearing the title "Social Democrats." Nothing is quite so telling as a change in symbolism. Lenin wanted to prevent any turning away from the course he had set. When he had split the RSDRP formally in 1912 in Prague, he had taken one radical step; his positions at Zimmerwald and Kienthal signified further movement in the direction of a break, now with the Second International; it remained to convince his party to go one more step along the path of total autonomy, to rename the party and make it the vanguard of a Third, Communist International.

Needless to say, the speech to the joint Bolshevik-Menshevik session was designed not to conciliate but to destroy whatever frail ties were in the process of formation. Whereas the Bolsheviks who had listened to Lenin's "ravings" had held their tongues, the Mensheviks spoke out candidly. According to the eyewitness Sukhanov, one of the Menshevik leaders of the Soviet, Tsereteli, said: "Lenin has now made himself a candidate for one European throne that has been vacant for thirty years—the throne of Bakunin! Lenin's new words echo something old—the superannuated truths of primitive anarchism."[7] Tsereteli was wrong. Lenin, of course, was far from being an anarchist. He was destroying in order to build an organizational weapon of his own design and under his own control.

LENIN'S DECISIVE actions, his symbolic burning of bridges, should be seen in the context of events in his family as well as political struggle. During the war, he had suffered two family losses: His mother-in-law, who had lived with him and Krupskaia almost continuously since their marriage, died in March 1915; and in July 1916, a few months before the momentous events of 1917, his own mother had died in Petrograd at the age of eighty-one. The dying out of the older generation of his immediate family created a divide in his life at a time of decisive political breaks with the past just before the end of his exile. Soon after his tumultuous welcome and the reception at Bolshevik headquarters, in the early morning of April 4 Lenin made his way to the apartment of his older sister, Anna, and her husband, Mark Elizarov. Their apartment became his home until July 1917. On that same day, the day when he presented his April theses, Lenin went to the Volkov cemetery to visit his mother's and Olga's graves. The return to Russia was also a return to his family. He would soon be working side by side in the offices of *Pravda* with his younger sister. Lenin now became the sole head of both his family and the party.

LENIN'S FACTION had awaited his arrival with both anticipation and apprehension. Now that he had arrived, they could no longer hold off his thunder and lightning but instead opposed him openly on the pages of *Pravda*. The decisive ceremonial moment for asserting hegemony over the party and setting the new party line came at the Petrograd Conference in mid-April and the Seventh All-Russian Conference of the RSDRP (Bolshevik), which convened three weeks after his arrival on April 24(May 7) and ended on April 29(May 12), 1917. Lenin threw down the gauntlet to the "Old Bolsheviks" in his opening statement at the Petrograd All-City Party Conference, demanding that they open their eyes to unexpected events and change their ways. This, of course, was not the first time party leaders had heard Lenin call for a change, and not all of them were ready to admit to the backwardness of which he accused them. Of the leading Bolsheviks, Kamenev showed the most zeal in opposing Lenin's formulations as deviations from Marxian analysis and dangerous for both the party and soviet movement. In essence Kamenev's critique accused Lenin of political irresponsibility and, although euphemistically, suggested that Lenin had lost touch with reality. However, in the end the Bolsheviks passed Lenin's main resolutions on the war and the Provisional Government at the Seventh Party Conference. Furthermore, Lenin had the political intelligence to use Kamenev rather than crush him, putting Kamenev on the commission for the drafting of the resolutions. Later, when Kamenev's candidacy to the Central Committee was questioned, Lenin was the first to speak for him and affirmed his importance to the party. Without Lenin's support no one's place was really secure, but Lenin could not accomplish his goals without cultivating and at least minimally propitiating his veteran cadres. By now a clear pattern of political manipulation had emerged. Lenin would roundly berate the veterans, "tactfully" reestablish their status, and then exact their obedience, however bogus.

STALIN'S EVOLUTION during the weeks between March 12 and April 29 is highly instructive. At first he accepted Kamenev's line with respect to the war and the Provisional Government and reasserted his prewar conciliationist position, now toward the left-wing Mensheviks who adhered to the Zimmerwald-Kienthal line against defensism. As a member of the Executive Committee of the Soviet after March 18(31), 1917, he simply receded into the background. Only in his articles in *Pravda* that call for a Central or All-Russian Soviet does one sense that Stalin's attitude toward the concentration of power made him a good Leninist. Stalin's initial deference to Kamenev certainly did not signify a moderate political attitude toward either the Provisional Government or the Soviet. Rather, Stalin was trying to adapt himself to his political context. He took an instrumental approach towards power quite in keeping with Leninism. In an article appearing in *Pravda* on March 18(31) he pronounced a plague on all houses. Neither the Provisional Government nor the present Soviet were up to the tasks of the revolution.

> What is needed is an all-Russian organ of revolutionary struggle of the democratic forces of all Russia, one authoritative enough to weld together the democratic forces of the capital and the provinces and to transform itself at the required moment from an organ of revolutionary *struggle* of the people into an organ of revolutionary *power*, which will mobilize all the vital forces of the people against counter-revolution. Only an All-Russian Soviet of Workers', Soldiers', and Peasants' Deputies can be such an organ.[8]

Stalin had learned some fundamental Leninist tactics. One could hold one's radical goals in abeyance and use whatever instruments came to hand while preparing for the next struggle. Meanwhile, Stalin continued to write on the nationalities problem and tried to sustain the Leninist line, although his own brutally centralist aims made him an odd candidate for the role. The idea of the centralization of power did not sit well with real tolerance for the rights of nationalities to self-determination in Stalin's mind. He would bide his time on this as on other matters.

Stalin's gravest "sins" against the Leninist line occurred at the end of March and the beginning of April 1917, when an All-Russian Conference of Bolsheviks convened in Petrograd. Trotsky, in his later efforts to correct Stalin's falsifications and editings of party history, produced the original drafts of the protocols for the sessions beginning with March 29. There is nothing particularly shocking or sinful there. Stalin, like the other Bolsheviks, was afraid to attack the Provisional Government in March. Kamenev and the Bureau of the CC wanted the Soviet to "control" it. It would take a fine talmudic mind to detect the substance of the differences among the resolutions presented. Stalin shifted his position during the debate. Nothing much can be learned from the verbal flailing about for a correct statement about the attitude of the party toward the Provisional Government at this time. Indeed, after radical workers, soldiers, and party members under the leadership of the Petrograd Committee did launch an abortive attack on the Provisional Government during the "April crisis" caused by Miliukov's annexationist policy as Foreign Minister, even Lenin had to denounce as "adventurism" the slogan "Down with the Provisional Government." The Executive Committee of the Soviet had asserted its authority and put an end to the massive demonstrations against the Provisional Government, but any intelligent political observer could see how volatile things were. Stalin's was a prudent waiting game in view of an unstable revolutionary situation. It was in fact the game Lenin was forced to play between April and October while the Bolsheviks gathered strength in the Soviet and the Provisional Government, now with Menshevik and SR representation, lost support.

Stalin's only real sin lay in his efforts at conciliation with the Mensheviks, who, following Martov, opposed defensism. Here he abetted Kamenev's efforts to forge an internationalist group in the Soviet in order to control the Provisional Government's war policy. In the session of April 1(14) Stalin played a decisive role in discussion and moved toward conciliation with the Menshevik-Internationalists. The entire effort was, of course, aborted by Lenin's arrival and his schismatic speech in the Tauride Palace on April 4(17). Stalin could hardly have enjoyed that moment. Like the other party leaders he was somewhat intimidated by Lenin, but neither he nor any of the other leading Bolsheviks became obedient extensions of Lenin's will. All of them had to resort to stratagems of concealment, evasion, and subversion in the face of Lenin's ability to dominate the faction. Stalin was a past master of all of these stratagems.

After reassessing the correlation of forces within the leadership, Stalin quickly reinstated himself as Lenin's henchman by attacking the idea of "control" over the Provisional Government in defense of Lenin's formulation. Stalin was sufficiently adroit not to criticize Kamenev, the main sponsor of "control" over the Provisional Government, in his attack, mentioning only

Bubnov, another advocate of "control." Then at the ninth session of the conference Stalin resumed his role as Lenin's mouthpiece on the nationalities problem. By the end of the conference, he had not only regained his old position as one of Lenin's whips but had established himself in the first rank of the party.

All of the resolutions, counterresolutions, and amendments presented at the Seventh All-Russian Conference were equally academic—and not just because of the fluidity of the situation. The real issue was leadership, not correct Marxian formulas or slogans. Like all such moments, the Seventh Party Conference was a test of Lenin's qualities as a leader and an opportunity for him to exercise his formidable political intelligence—his mastery of the idiom of revolutionary Marxism, his agility in debate, his ability in maneuvering his opponents into difficult positions, in putting them on the defensive and then coopting them. After a rocky beginning Lenin took things in hand, put together a commission including his main critics to draft the resolutions on war and the Provisional Government, and won the main battles without conceding any of his goals. Although he had placed his faction in a sort of limbo, neither in support of the Provisional Government nor in a position to launch a direct attack on it, he had achieved what he wanted: a clear boundary separating his party from the others, the creation of a small but expandable base for his leadership and for the conquest of power. What he did not get in April—a decisive break with the Second International and a renaming of the party—he would get later. All of his maneuvers separated him from the main body of Marxian revolutionaries. Lenin justified his actions in the idiom of scientific Marxism, but they are better understood in the light of the psychology of power and the art of politics. His opponents in the party had tried to stop him, but had failed. After April they could only ride out the rough trip that lay ahead and wait for an opportune moment to fight back.

Not a single member of the nine-man Central Committee elected at the Seventh Party Conference had made a mark as an outstanding figure in international socialism or even in the history of the RSDRP—besides Lenin himself. Lenin's right-hand man, chairman of the Petrograd All-City Conference, and Lenin's manager at the party conference, Zinov'ev, received only three fewer votes than Lenin. Stalin received four fewer than Zinov'ev. The next highest was Kamenev, with two votes less than Stalin. Not only their rank but the special tasks assigned them in April prefigured the roles the future triumvirate would continue to play under Lenin's sponsorship. Only Trotsky— still en route from the United States—was missing from the picture.

24

Trotsky and the Bolsheviks

TROTSKY'S INTERNMENT of roughly one month caused him to miss the April (first days of May) crisis. Roughly at the time of his arrival on May 4 (17), Miliukov was forced to resign as foreign minister. On May 5, 1917, five socialists joined the Provisional Government, among them, Skobelev, Trotsky's protégé on the Viennese *Pravda*, and Victor Chernov, a veteran SR, émigré, and theoretical leader of the right wing of the most popular revolutionary party in Russia. Alexander Kerensky became prime minister. Leading Mensheviks and SRs had made what proved to be a fatal commitment to orderly progress, to taming the increasingly tempestuous revolutionary process. Trotsky, on the other hand, reacted like an intrepid explorer. In his autobiography he uses the image of plunging into a whirlpool, the very same image he had used to capture his feelings in 1905.

Trotsky's reception was not uncomplicated. His opponents, like Lenin's, circulated rumors that he too had received German money. The British authorities knew that Trotsky might harm their interests, just as the Germans knew that Lenin might serve theirs, and there were more than a few machinations on the side of the belligerent powers and the Provisional Government in dealing with the two leaders. In Lenin's case rumors of German aid and treason annulled the temporary benefits of a relatively quick return and almost led to his political downfall. In Trotsky's, although the delay caused by the internment no doubt affected his political fortunes, it is impossible to measure the extent of the damage. The rumors about German aid had not only less substance but less effect on his reputation than those about Lenin.

Within a short time Trotsky had reestablished himself as an agitator of the first order. No Trotskyist organization as such existed in St. Petersburg, although for a few months in 1914 Trotsky had enjoyed an outlet in the capital, the newspaper *The Struggle*, an affiliate of the Viennese *Pravda*. The "Interdistrict Commission," an all-city organization founded in 1913 and joined by a variety of dropouts from the official factions, sustained the conciliationist, unifying spirit of 1912–1914, when Trotsky had striven vainly to create an alternative to the vicious factionalism of the period. However, it was by no means his organization. It had existed for more than three years without his direct participation under the leadership of I. Iurenev, a former Bolshevik-conciliator. The Interdistrict Commission had started from the following assumptions: The Russian Social Democratic Workers' Party no longer existed as a party; the factions were weak; the workers strongly wanted unity; the process of rebuilding had to come from below; the organizers would have to create a new unified party around a core of proletarian members.[1] When Trotsky and some of the other émigrés who had worked on *Our Word* and *The New World* returned, they found the Interdistrict Commission, which had survived the vicissitudes of the war period and played a significant left-wing role in the February Revolution, the most attractive arena for their activities.

The émigrés who joined the Interdistrict Commission, like those who founded it, represented splinter groups formerly affiliated with the Bolsheviks and Mensheviks. Even before Trotsky's arrival, the Bolshevik Petrograd Committee had proposed a merger with the IC, whose views were close to their own, without success. Trotsky's position on the merger later became a matter of some importance in party history.[2] The sparse documentation that has survived casts doubt on his later claim that he had immediately gravitated toward the Bolsheviks and pushed for a merger against the resistance of other Interdistrict leaders. Trotsky pictured himself as a Bolshevik avant la lettre trying to bring over a great prize to the party, but his behavior in April and May was at best ambiguous.

Lenin immediately realized how much talent and revolutionary élan had coalesced in the IC: not only Trotsky but Lunacharskii and other Bolshevik heretics of the post-1906 era—former god-seekers, recallists, and conciliationists—and Menshevik-Internationalists. All of them opposed the war (even if they avoided Lenin's unpopular defeatism); all took a militant position toward the Provisional Government and called for soviet power. Shortly after the Seventh Party Conference in April, Lenin again reconnoitered the possibility of joint action. Together with Zinov'ev and Kamenev, he attended the IC conference and proposed the following at a session held on May 10(23), 1917: one member of the IC would join *Pravda* and a new central organ; two delegates of the IC and, if possible, an unspecified number of Menshevik-Internationalists would enter an organization commission for the calling of a party congress to be convened in six weeks; there would be free discussion of all controversial matters in the Bolshevik press.

Given Lenin's long experience at engineering majorities on editorial boards and at congresses, he undoubtedly believed that the Bolsheviks would be able to dominate their partners. In mid-1917 the IC had roughly 4,000 members. The Menshevik-Internationalists did not have a large organization. Estimates of Bolshevik strength during this period are controversial, but they almost certainly had several times more people in their organization than the IC and Menshevik-Internationalists combined. The leaders of the Interdistrict Commission, Iurenev and Trotsky (according to Trotsky, D. Manuil'skii and Iurenev), had no desire to be swallowed up by the Bolsheviks or to contend with Lenin for power on editorial boards or precongress commissions. Rather, they called for the unification of the internationalist left-wing of the Social Democratic movement and all proletarian groups.

For Trotsky's personal response we have to rely upon Lenin's fragmentary notes on the meeting and Kamenev's editing of the volume of Lenin miscellany in which they are preserved. There are two sections of notes on Trotsky, suggesting that he spoke at least twice. But the notes are ambiguous, despite the editorial assessment that they contain the essential points and even precise language of Trotsky's speeches. If the notes under roman numeral I do refer to Trotsky's comments rather than Lenin's response to them, Trotsky evidently cautioned the Interdistrict Commission not to move too quickly toward a merger but to wait for a unification congress. Continuing with the same assumption, in his policy toward the war, although not an enthusiastic defeatist, Trotsky called defeat a lesser evil than pacifism.[3] Lenin's notes on Trotsky's attitude toward the current phase of the revolution—still proceeding under the assumption that the notes describe Trotsky's views—suggest the following: Trotsky believed that the revolution was presently on a "national-democratic, but not an international-proletarian plane; a dictatorship of the proletariat and peasantry (bourgeois) and not a proletarian socialist one."[4] Presumably, Trotsky wanted to move to the "international-proletarian plane" and to a proletarian socialist dictatorship.

Aside from their ambiguity, there is an interesting puzzle in Lenin's notes. At a certain point in his second speech Trotsky presumably said: "The Bolsheviks have de-Bolshevized [*razbol'shevichilis'*]—and I cannot call myself a Bolshevik."[5] If this is what Trotsky actually said, what can it possibly mean? Is it a play on words, signifying that the Bolsheviks had no claim to majority status? Is the part of the sentence after the conjunction connected by an implied "therefore" to the first, or not? The preceding sentence in the notes may shed light on it. There Trotsky (presumably) agreed entirely with Lenin's resolution but only insofar as "Russian Bolshevism internationalizes itself." Is this logically linked to the second sentence about de-Bolshevization? Was Trotsky referring to his initial remarks and implying that the Bolsheviks rested on the "national-democratic plane?" The meaning of "de-Bolshevization" is crucial, but if we cannot find any moment in Trotsky's career when he identified himself with Bolshevism, then we are forced to speculate. His use of the word makes complete sense if Trotsky was identifying himself with former Bolsheviks like Lunacharskii who had left Lenin earlier and now belonged to the Interdistrict Commission. They had "de-Bolshevized" and no longer called themselves Bolsheviks. Given Trotsky's long history of contention with Bolshevism, it would make better sense if Trotsky had said: *"Until* the remaining Bolsheviks have de-Bolshevized, I cannot make common cause with them." Alas, some documents only tantalize; their meanings evade our grasp. We are left with ambiguity.

As for the creation of an organization commission for the purpose of calling a conference, Trotsky wanted representation not only for the IC, Bolsheviks, and Menshevik-Internationalists, insofar as they detached themselves from the defensist wing of their party, but for the nationalities (Polish, Latvian) as well. Trotsky sought the broadest possible coalition of internationalists, probably with the hope of diluting the Bolsheviks. Like other members of the IC, he hoped that the old factional barriers would break down as all left-wing SD groups dissolved into a reconstructed Social Democratic Party founded on internationalist principles and goals. Trotsky would have been happy to see the word "Bolshevism," with the stubborn sectarianism it signified, disappear into oblivion.

One wonders how Lenin's courtship of Trotsky and the other outsiders sat with the Old Bolsheviks. Did they see Lenin's apparent moves toward unity of the internationalists shrewd tactical maneuvers? Or were the *komitetchiki* who had risen during the period 1912–1917 confronted with the painful prospect of diminished standing as Lenin turned to people like Trotsky, Lunacharskii, and even Martov for help? In all likelihood, they were forced into an ambivalent posture. Given the struggle shaping up, they had to take in new recruits and strengthen the party, but the evidence suggests that it was particularly galling for them to have to court Trotsky. All of the Old Bolsheviks knew very well that to Trotsky Bolshevism signified fraud, illegitimacy, splitting, and "substitutionism." Those who had suffered for their Bolshevism in tsarist prisons and Siberian exile could only be enraged at Trotsky's threat to the symbol of their identity as professional revolutionaries. Yet Lenin himself had suggested that the party rename itself "Communist."

When confronted by symbolic threats of this sort, men like Stalin, who had fought in the underground under the banner of Bolshevism for his entire adult life, must have felt more than a little bitterness. And the threats were not only symbolic: Kamenev, who had struggled with Trotsky on the Viennese *Pravda* and then become an editor of Lenin's *Pravda*, could not have looked forward to a renewal of the partnership with his overbearing brother-in-law; and Zinov'ev, who had functioned virtually as Lenin's clerk during the last years in exile and now had risen to the second position in the party, must have anxiously watched his leader's maneuvers. When Lenin began to offer positions on party organs to former heretics and Judas figures, even hard-bitten revolutionary politicians must have felt resentful. To be sure, during the mounting struggle between May and October Trotsky proved that he did not have "fake muscles," that his prominence in 1905 had not been a fluke, and that he was a crucial ally. Antagonisms were temporarily suppressed, but they erupted again after 1917 and became acute in 1923–1924.

TROTSKY'S RELATIONSHIP to the Bolshevik faction during the spring and summer of 1917 deserves careful scrutiny. His loyalty to Lenin and his Bolshevism or non-Bolshevism played an important role in the political infighting of the period 1923–1927. Both Trotsky and his opponents went over each step of the way between 1903 and October 1917 microscopically, although in each case the microscope had flawed lenses. The documentation is reasonably clear for Trotsky's position after his arrival. He saw himself as a Zimmerwaldist and wanted to revive the International on the principles of Zimmerwald. The World War had created the conditions for a social upheaval, but should Europe fail to rise to the historical occasion, then it was "destined to degenerate economically, to perish as a center of civilization, and only serve the curiosity of tourists, while the center of the revolutionary movement moves to America or Japan."[6] One can immediately see from the prediction that Trotsky had no faith in the victory of the revolution. Yet he saw no other way than to work for it: "We must go with our class, not knowing whether we will win, but knowing that there is no other way."[7]

Trotsky still held to the internationalist ideas he had formulated while writing for *Our Word* in Paris. He issued a pamphlet, *The Peace Program,* a reworking of his basic positions: international relations under capitalism could only duplicate the processes of the marketplace—the strong would dominate the weak; small nations would continue to lose their independence under capitalism; annexations were unavoidable in imperialist struggles; nations would be guaranteed self-determination only in a new world order of proletarian international relations. Trotsky sought a centralized economic order without boundaries and yet recognized the rights of small nations to their national-cultural identity and to secession from imperial structures. He revived his idea of a "United States" of Europe and reviewed Lenin's criticism of it: the objection that uneven development made it possible for socialism to conquer in a single country. Trotsky conceded the point, but argued that it was hopeless to assume that an isolated socialist nation could survive in a hostile capitalist world. He warned against messianism, the vain belief that a given nation might lead humanity to socialism.[8] On the other hand, he held up the example of the French army after the revolution. Once liberated from service to feudal aims, it had shown its heroic side. The increasingly mutinous Russian army, now cannon fodder for French and English imperialists, would show its mettle as a conscious instrument of revolutionary socialist liberation.

During the spring and summer of 1917 Trotsky believed it was premature to think about a seizure of power by the Soviet. Genuinely revolutionary Social Democrats would first have to forge a majority in the Soviet; meanwhile they would have to pursue a policy of no support but rather criticism of and vigilant control over the Provisional Government until the moment of transition of power.[9] Trotsky combined revolutionary commitment, adventurism, and tactical prudence, the latter informed by a first-rate sense of spectacle, a theatrical feel for the staging and timing of the symbolic moment of revolution. He operated well in both the symbolic and practical world of revolutionary politics: the lackeys of the capitalists and imperialists had to be unmasked, the Soviet taught to believe in its power and capacity to govern; radical constituencies such as that at the important naval base of Kronstadt had to be courted. He aimed, of course, to reestablish the leadership over the Petrograd Soviet that he had enjoyed in 1905, to wean it from the right-wing Mensheviks and SRs. While Trotsky exercised his charisma in the public arena, the party organizations fought for delegates to the Soviet.

Three organs—*Izvestiia*, the newspaper of the Soviet, *Vpered*, the newly established (at the beginning of June) newspaper of the Interdistrict Commission, and Maxim Gorky's *New Life* became Trotsky's journalistic outlets during the spring and summer of 1917, but his oratory probably had a greater impact than his writings upon the mood of the revolutionary throngs of Petrograd and Kronstadt. Trotsky addressed not only the Petrograd and Kronstadt Soviets, but the All-Russian Congress of Soviets convening in the capital during June 3(16)–24(July 7). It was dominated by the supporters of the Provisional Government and was less than friendly at times to Trotsky's oratory. His favorite hall was the Cirque Moderne, whose crowds he enthralled. There are eloquent testimonials to Trotsky's oratorical powers. Lunacharskii, Trotsky's closest colleague at the time, who addressed the same crowds at the Cirque Moderne, in his *Revolutionary Silhouettes* records in brief compass one of the most apt descriptions of Trotsky:

> I regard Trotsky as probably the greatest orator of our age. In my time I have heard all the greatest parliamentarians and popular tribunes of socialism and very many famous orators of the bourgeois world and I would find it difficult to name any of them, except Jaurès (Bebel I only heard when he was an old man), whom I would put in the same class as Trotsky. . . . His impressive appearance, his handsome, sweeping gestures, the powerful rhythm of his speech, his loud but never fatiguing voice, the remarkable coherence and literary skill of his phrasing, the richness of imagery, scalding irony, his soaring pathos, his logic, truly steely in its clarity—those are Trotsky's virtues as a speaker. He can speak in lapidary phrases, or throw off a few unusually well-aimed shafts and he can give a magnificent set-piece political speech of the kind that previously I had only heard from Jaurès. I have seen Trotsky speaking for two and a half to three hours in front of a totally silent, standing audience listening as though spellbound to his monumental political treatise. . . . His articles and books are, as it were, frozen speech—he was literary in his oratory and an orator in literature.[10]

Lunacharskii's book of character sketches contains more than a little Bolshevik hagiography, but some of his realistic observations and comparisons of Trotsky with Lenin make it one of the valuable sources on the personalities of the leaders. One finds in it hints that Trotsky had begun to overshadow Lenin as an on-the-spot leader during the spring and summer of 1917. At the time when Lunacharskii composed his sketches and even when later editions were published, it was still possible for prominent figures in the party to recognize that Lenin and Trotsky had led the Bolsheviks to victory in 1917 together, as a kind of team, and that Trotsky had strengths that Lenin lacked. Lenin could not match Trotsky's capacity for making contact with mass audiences. During May and June, after Trotsky's arrival, it looked as if he would soon eclipse Lenin, as he had eclipsed all other Social Democratic leaders in 1905. Trotsky sensed his own "organic" fitness for this moment. His description of his performances in the Cirque Moderne has the ring of authentic insight:

> I usually spoke in the Circus in the evening, sometimes quite late at night. My audience was composed of workers, soldiers, hard-working mothers, street urchins—the oppressed under-dogs of the capital. Every square inch was filled, every human body compressed to its limit. Young boys sat on their fathers' shoulders; infants were at their mothers' breasts. No one smoked. The balconies threatened to fall under the excessive weight of human bodies. I made my way to the platform through a narrow trench of bodies, sometimes borne on peoples' hands. The air, tense with breathing, exploded with shouts, with the peculiar passionate cries of the Cirque Moderne. Around and above me were densely compressed elbows, chests, heads. I spoke as if out of a warm cavern of human bodies. Whenever I made a sweeping gesture, I always brushed someone, and a grateful movement in response would let me understand that I should not worry, should not break off, but should continue. No kind of fatigue could resist the electric tension of this passionate human throng. At times it seemed as though you felt with your lips the insistent searching of this crowd that had fused into a whole. It wanted to know, to understand, to find its way. Then all the arguments and words outlined beforehand gave way, receded before the imperative pressure of sympathy, and from a secret place there came forth fully prepared other words, other arguments, unexpected by the orator but needed by the mass. And then it seemed as if you were listening to the orator yourself, just a little bit off to the side, trailing behind his thought and being anxious about only one thing, that he, like a somnambulist, might lurch from the edge of the roof from the sound of your reasoning.[11]

Trotsky places an image of wholeness, of fusion of the many into one and of himself with the people, at the center of his portrait of the revolutionary crowd. Actually, it is not so much a crowd as a family. A brilliant rhetorician, Trotsky also skillfully chose touching and evocative images in which several kinds of love are suggested, but the rhetoric no doubt also gives access to the meaning of peak moments in his life. Trotsky experienced such transcendent moments when he made unmediated contact with the body of the people. In his autobiography he uses the image of plunging into a whirlpool to describe his entry into the events of both 1905 and 1917.[12] In other of Trotsky's writings bodies of water symbolize the unconscious mind. At moments of total immersion in a turbulent medium and during fusion with the revolutionary crowd he believed he had access to native powers of intuition and a vast reservoir of instinctual energy, which, on the one hand, inspired his individual creativity and will-power and, on the other, connected him with the unconscious masses. One interesting passage suggests that a willful act of transgression was necessary on the part of both the individual and the masses in order for that connection to be made. Only then could latent instinctual powers supply the necessary force for a breakthrough to a revolutionary creativity.

> Marxism considers itself to be the conscious expression of an unconscious historical process . . . a process that coincides with its conscious expression only at its very highest points, when the masses with elemental force smash down the doors of social routine and give victorious expression to the deepest needs of historical development. The highest theoretical consciousness of an epoch at such moments merges with the immediate action of the lowest oppressed masses who are the farthest away from theory. The creative union of conscious-ness with the unconscious is what we usually call inspiration. Revolution is the violent inspiration of history. Every real writer knows moments of creativity, when someone else, stronger than he, guides his hand. Every genuine orator knows minutes, when something stronger than he speaks through his lips. This is "inspiration." It issues from the greatest creative tension of all one's powers. The unconscious climbs up from its deep lair and subjects the conscious effort of thought to itself, merging with it in some kind of higher unity. The latent *[podspudnye]* powers of the organism, its deepest instincts, its flair, inherited from animal ancestors, all of this rose up, smashed down the doors of psychic routine and—together with the highest historico-philosophical generalizations —stood in the service of revolution. Both of these processes, individual and mass, were based on the combination of consciousness with the unconscious, of instinct, the mainspring of will, with the highest forms of generalizing thought. [13]

Trotsky hardly seems like an orthodox Marxist in the above passages, even though he claims to use "unconscious" in the "historico-philosophical sense." He makes the release of primitive instinctual energy an essential part of both mass and individual creativity in history, just as he had made an "organic" faculty of intuition a sine qua non of revolutionary fitness in the face of turbulent and complex situations. Such qualities of leadership could not be taught. They were biological gifts that determined one's fitness in given con-texts. Trotsky believed that Lenin, too, had special gifts.

All of this is more Darwinian than Marxist, with unformulated Freudian elements as well. Translated into Freudian terms (with which he was undoubt-edly familiar), Trotsky's passages suggest that the leaders play the role of ego to the masses' id. Until their fusion on such occasions as the meetings in the Cirque Moderne, leaders and masses are closed off from each other, but when they do come together, they generate that creative, explosive force called revolution—the "violent inspiration of history." In short, for Trotsky, revolu-tion signified those moments of wholeness, when both the fittest individual leaders and the masses joined in the creative act. Trotsky saw himself as a lover (one can hardly avoid that conclusion, given the imagery of the above passage) and artist of revolution. [14] His somewhat romantic self-identity and modus operandi contrasts vividly with that of Lenin, who had very little unmediated contact with the masses and led his party, partly by choice and partly by necessity, as a revolutionary journalist and behind-the-scenes organizer. The Trotsky-Lenin combination recalls Trotsky's partnership with Parvus in 1905.

25

Lenin's First Bid for Power

ENIN ALSO engaged in speech-making during May and June, although this
was not his forte or his central activity. His most interesting sally
occurred at the first All-Russian Congress of Soviets on June 4(17).
When Tsereteli, who at that time held the position of Minister of Posts and
Telegraph, said in a speech, "In Russia at the present moment there is not a
single party that would say, 'Give us the power in our hands,' " Lenin shouted
from the floor, "There is!"[1] He then followed Tsereteli to the rostrum. The
following part of his roughly fifteen-minute speech amazed and amused the
curious but mainly hostile audience:

> If you want to make reference to *"revolutionary"* democracy, then you should
> distinguish this concept from *reformist* democracy under a capitalist ministry,
> because, finally, it is time to move from phrases about "revolutionary democ-
> racy," from congratulating each other about "revolutionary democracy," to a
> *class* characterization taught us by Marxism and in general by scientific social-

ism. What is proposed to us is a transition to a reformist democracy under a capitalist ministry. That, perhaps, would be marvelous from the point of view of the usual European models. At this very moment a whole row of nations is on the verge of perishing, and those practical measures, so seemingly complicated and difficult to introduce, and needing special working up, as suggested by the preceding orator, the citizen Minister of Posts and Telegraphs—these measures are quite clear. He said that there is not in Russia a political party, which would declare its readiness to take upon itself all the power *[tselikom na sebia]*. I answer: "There is! No party can refuse this, and our party does not refuse it: at any moment it is ready to seize all of the power." [Applause and laughter.][2]

Lenin delivered his speech to 822 delegates, only 105 of whom were Bolsheviks. The vast majority were right-wing SRs and Mensheviks. Although the Bolsheviks were growing in strength, particularly in the garrison and at the grass roots level in factory and shop committees, the idea that they could take power seemed ludicrous at the time. One can be certain that those who laughed outnumbered those who applauded.

THE ANGRY delegates, among whom were a large number of Lenin's old colleagues and bêtes noirs, hurled accusations of Bakuninism, Blanquism, and Jacobinism at him—of apostasy from Marxism and of a mindless, destructive approach to revolution. It was a reprise of many such moments in Lenin's life. Lenin's call for the arrest of fifty or one hundred of Russia's wealthiest citizens evoked images of revolutionary terror. Trotsky spoke in a more conciliatory tone than Lenin, but his backing for the slogan "All Power to the Soviets" and general support for what was seen as the Bolshevik line linked him with Lenin. According to Trotsky, the text of his resolution opposing the government's planned military offensive was substituted for Lenin's to represent the position of the Bolsheviks and Internationalists.[3] Speakers frequently mentioned Lenin and Trotsky in tandem when rebutting the Bolshevik position. After Lenin delivered his speech about the seizure of power, some of the remarks directed against him provoked Lenin to deliver an occasional indignant outburst from the floor. One can infer from the transcript of the sessions that Trotsky's oratory was received with greater enthusiasm, although he encountered a hostile audience when he spoke on the war during the evening session on June 9. The embattled position of the left wing of the Soviet Congress did not give a true indication of the tenor of the revolutionary movement in Petrograd. As Trotsky himself noted, the delegates' malicious laughter directed against Lenin's remarks was edged with anxiety.

For the Bolsheviks the seizure of power had become more than a laughing matter. The most intense pressure to move against the Provisional Government came from several quarters: from the sailors of the Kronstadt Soviet, from the restless troops in the Petrograd garrison led by the Bolshevik Military Organization, and from the restive, proletarian Vyborg district. In all of these areas, Anarchists supplied much of the radical inspiration and the actions of the Petrograd Federation of Anarcho-Communists played a significant role in pushing the Bolsheviks to the left. As the pressure to prevent the Provisional Government's planned military offensive increased, the Bolshevik Central Committee began to split, ostensibly over the correlation of forces and the dangers of premature action, in this case, an armed demonstration that might easily turn into a battle for which they were ill-prepared. Lenin wanted to prevent the launching of a successful military offensive by the Provisional Government and believed in the efficaciousness of a demonstration. Stalin zealously supported the idea,[4] whereas Zinov'ev and Kamenev played the role of principal brakemen for the party.[5]

On June 8, 1917, the Bolshevik Central Committee voted for a mass demonstration to be held on June 10, with the purpose of rallying the masses in the capital against the Provisional Government and in favor of Soviet power. They were supported by Anarchists and a part of the Interdistrict Commission, including Trotsky. The Soviet Congress, sensing a Bolshevik conspiracy to seize power, replied by voting on June 9 to ban all demonstrations for three days and taking measures to enforce the ban. Within a few hours of a CC decision to defy the ban on the night of June 9, the increasingly split Bolsheviks reversed themselves. Lenin (who actually abstained) and a rump of the CC made an awkward, eleventh-hour decision to cancel the demonstration. Stalin had become so committed to the planned course of action that he felt obligated to resign from the CC. His colleagues rejected the resignation.[6] One close student of Stalin's behavior in 1917 believes that Stalin had actually moved to the forefront as a Bolshevik leader in connection with the preparation for the June demonstrations and that his threatened resignation was a serious matter. It expressed a genuine rebellion against Lenin.[7] Although the resignation probably was merely a gesture, Stalin, like many leading Bolsheviks, had a quite ambivalent attitude toward Lenin. He acted like a dutiful subordinate in some contexts and like his own man in others.

No less than the others, Stalin was trying to negotiate the zigzag course laid down by Lenin and, to a greater extent during June and July, by the revolutionary masses themselves and the party groups in direct contact with them, such as the Bolshevik Military Organization. He attended the Soviet Congress as a delegate, but instead of orating, at which he was quite colorless, he worked with Sverdlov as a floor manager of the Bolshevik delegation. Even Trotsky had to credit him with effectiveness in that role.[8] Stalin was one of the thirty-five Bolsheviks elected to the All-Russian Central Executive Committee of the Soviet. Although under Lenin's leadership one could be either punished or rewarded for initiatives and humiliated and promoted in rapid succession, the upward trajectory of Stalin's career reinforced his sense that like the party itself he had emerged from a weak position and grown enormously in dignity and strength. Although he exhibited resentment in a variety of ways, he never lost his fierce political will to survive and grow stronger.

Meanwhile, each month, week, and day revealed to Trotsky that he could not ally himself with the left-wing Mensheviks, that the Interdistrict Commission alone could not provide a strong organizational base and support for his journalism, and that his political options were narrowing toward collaboration with the Bolsheviks. Aside from anarchist groups, only the Bolsheviks seemed willing to encourage the radical demands of workers, soldiers, and peasants. Bolshevik slogans alarmed the Provisional Government and moderate socialists, who began to use the word "anarchy" freely, but even more important, these slogans intensified the campaign of accusations and rumors, mainly against Lenin but against Trotsky as well, about German money and treason.

After the abortion of the demonstration planned for June 10(23) Trotsky collaborated with Kamenev in the composition of a Bolshevik statement read by V. P. Nogin at the evening session of the Soviet Congress on June 12(25), 1917.[9] Nogin was not permitted to complete the reading, and the delegates passed a resolution censuring the Bolsheviks, although the latter were not named specifically in the resolution. The tension had reached a point where some of the Bolsheviks walked out of the session. However, the break between the Bolsheviks and the leading parties in the Soviet was still not complete, and there is no indication yet that Trotsky himself wanted to make a clean break with those Mensheviks and SRs who would support an internationalist position. On the same evening, several Menshevik leaders of the Soviet decided to show the Bolsheviks where the true correlation of forces lay by organizing their own parade, a move that proved to be imprudent. The Mensheviks overestimated their ability to rally support and played into the hands of the Bolsheviks and Anarcho-Communists by giving them several days (June 12–18) to unleash a barrage of successful agitation among workers and soldiers.

Stalin could feel vindicated. A leaflet he had prepared for the aborted demonstration planned for June 10 appeared in slightly modified form in *Pravda* on June 17. A comparison of the two leaflets shows how an internationalist spirit, lacking in the first version, has been injected in the second one, apparently by Lenin.[10] The parade began on the morning of June 18, 1917. The vast majority of the more than 400,000 demonstrators marched under the slogans of the Left—for the most part, Bolshevik slogans. Stalin himself left a rather decent piece of journalism describing the event, but Sukhanov gave one of his usual vivid, literary accounts of the parade, and because he was not a Bolshevik, his testimony is more valuable:

> The situation was absolutely unambiguous. Here and there the chain of Bolshevik flags and columns was interrupted by specifically SR and official Soviet slogans. But they were submerged in the mass; they seemed to be exceptions, intentionally confirming the rule. Again and again, like the unchanging summons of the very depths of the revolutionary capital, like fate itself, like the fatal Burnham wood—there advanced towards us: "All Power to the Soviets!" "Down with the Ten Capitalist Ministers."[11]

Lenin's account of the parade showed understandable satisfaction. For him, the demonstration of June 18 revealed how far the popular mood had outstripped the policies of the Soviet:

> The eighteenth of June, in one way or the other, will go into the history of the Russian Revolution as one of its decisive moments. The mutual position of classes, their correlation in their struggle with one another, their strength,

especially by comparison with the strength of the party—all of this the Sunday demonstration revealed so vividly, so clearly, so inspirationally, that whatever the outcome and the tempo of the future development the gain in consciousness and clarity remains gigantic. The demonstration in a few hours shattered, like a heap of dust, the empty speeches about the Bolshevik-conspirators and showed with indisputable clarity that the vanguard of the working masses of Russia, the industrial proletariat of the capital, and its forces by an overwhelming majority march under slogans that our party has always defended.[12]

However, in the aftermath of the parade Lenin took a cautious approach and urged restraint rather than armed action against the Provisional Government. Despite the success of the demonstration, no one could be certain of the true correlation of forces, and Lenin seemed to lose some of the militancy he had expressed at the Soviet Congress. Furthermore, instead of intimidating it, the demonstration of June 18 stimulated the patriotic public to action. On June 19 patriotic citizens spontaneously filled the streets of Petrograd and organized their own demonstration. According to Miliukov:

> The next day, after the unsuccessful Bolshevik demonstration, the streets of Petrograd which had been half empty the day before were packed with dense crowds of people. . . . They did not pour into the streets at the behest of a party order for a "show of strength," but as an expression of the ecstacy [sic] which was seizing them. . . . Everyone who had felt the pressure of events in recent days now felt the possibility of and the need for straightening things out, and they resoundingly celebrated the recovery of the Russian national sense and the Russian Revolution that was now under way. That is why, without any prior arrangement, a public quite different from that which had demonstrated the previous day now overflowed into the streets. It improvised parades, large meetings, and in the speeches of well-known orators, one could detect a throbbing joy in which party considerations were put aside. Posters honoring Kerensky and the Provisional Government, animated demonstrations in front of the embassies of the allied powers—all of this was in such contrast to what had gone on in the streets the day before that an involuntary sense of disbelief was added to the feelings of jubilation. Was this something durable? Was this not just an episode which would pass without a trace? Or was it rather the beginning of a new change holding promise of a wonderful continuation?[13]

In June and July the government could still exploit a large reservoir of patriotism; accusations of treason still inspired rage and mobilized people of all classes. When such accusations issued from the Soviet leadership and not just the leaders of the bourgeois parties, they were taken more seriously. However, as Miliukov, writing his history of the revolution while in exile, well knew, the answer to the question, Was this something durable? was resoundingly negative. The apparent success and then failure of the Provisional Government's military offensive in June–July 1917 had the effect of widening the split between those who wanted to put an end to Russia's participation in the war immediately and those who sought scapegoats on the left for the deterioration of Russia's wartime position. Thus, alongside the Anarchists, who kept up an incessant clamor for insurrection, the Bolsheviks became the primary targets of an outburst of patriotic outrage. The reaction of the left to the government's attack on the Anarcho-Communists' headquarters on June 19 and the continuing pressure for action from grassroots Bolshevik constituencies and the Military Organization plagued the Bolshevik leadership.

The pressure became too great for Lenin. Suffering from sleeplessness, headaches, and exhaustion, he left Petrograd on June 27(July 10) in the company of his younger sister for Finland, where he stayed in Bonch-Bruev-ich's dacha. For several days he rested, swam, read lightly, acquainted himself with Bonch-Bruevich's work, and slowly came to himself. He missed the July all-city Bolshevik Party Conference in Petrograd and the beginning of the July uprising. Rousted out of bed by an emissary from Petrograd on the morning of July 4, he had to hurry back to the city to tend to his party during the crisis caused by the uprising.[14]

Lenin later described the July uprising and the April and June crises that had preceded it as significantly more than a demonstration and less than a revolution, an "explosion of the revolution and counterrevolution *together*."[15] It began on July 3(16), 1917. The First Machine Gun Regiment stationed in the radical Vyborg district of the capital led the revolt. Long infiltrated by Anarchist and Bolshevik agitators and under immediate pressure from the Provisional Government, which was transferring troops from the garrison to the front lines to prop up the failing offensive, the machinegunners decided to take things into their own hands. They held a meeting on July 2, with Trotsky and Lunacharskii, among others, invited as guest speakers. Although Trotsky's speech is not recorded and he gives no indication of what he said in his version of the July days, he evidently was willing to swim with the revolutionary tide.

During the first days of July, an all-city Bolshevik Party Commission convened, with 145 delegates representing more than 30,000 party members. The report of the Military Organization and Sverdlov's on the expansion of the party, its need for an updated program, its planned Sixth Congress later in the month, and its efforts to resolve differences with the Interdistrict Conference and Menshevik-Internationalists for purposes of merger (meaning absorption into the much larger Bolshevik faction) were at the center of discussion on the first day. Despite the fact that Sverdlov's authority emanated from Lenin, Volodarskii, a powerful personality in the Petrograd Committee, dominated the meeting. In fact, leadership for a time actually passed to figures like Volodar-sky, N. I. Podvoiskii, and V. I. Nevsky, whose contacts with the soldiers and workers of the Vyborg district gave them a crucial role. A strong majority supported the idea of creating a separate newspaper for the Petrograd Committee, a move that once again revealed the tension between the grassroots agitators and the Bolshevik Central Committee. At the concluding session on July 3 Volodarskii's motion to organize a delegation to the Central Executive Committee of the Soviet with a demand that it seize power in order to avert an armed insurrection received forty votes, but by that time events had overtaken the conference.[16] As in February and the earlier crises, important decisions were made at the grassroots level of the revolution, where agitators faced soldiers and workers. Many of the delegates rushed to the Vyborg district after an announcement by I. N. Ilinksii of the First Machine Gun Regiment that an attack on the cadets in the capital and on the Provisional Government was underway.[17]

During the July days the danger from the left, from Anarchists and Bolsheviks who agitated in the same military units and factories, forced the first rank leaders of the Bolsheviks on the defensive, and rendered them ineffective. Lenin found himself dragged into a whirlpool of events beyond his control. Trotsky, who wrote in his autobiography that in the "confusion of revolution . . . men and ideas distribute themselves naturally in new channels," when writing the *History of the Russian Revolution* provided a vivid example of someone else who expressed that faith to a far greater extent than even he. Despite the condescending tone, in the following description of the Anarcho-Communist, I. S. Bleikhman, who addressed the machinegunners on the morning of July 3, some of Trotsky's own features are evident:

> There appeared at this meeting the anarchist, Bleikhman, a small but colorful figure on the background of 1917, with a very modest equipment of ideas but a certain feeling for the masses — sincere in his limited and ever inflammable intelligence — his shirt open at the breast and curly hair flying on all sides. . . . By the end of June, Bleikhman was swimming in all these impromptu meetings like a fish in a river. His opinion he had always with him: *It is necessary to come out with arms in our hands.* Organization? "The street will organize us." The task? "To overthrow the Provisional Government, just as it overthrew the czar although no party was then demanding it." These speeches perfectly met the feelings of the machine-gunners at that moment — and not theirs alone. Many of the Bolsheviks did not conceal their satisfaction when the lower ranks pressed forward against their official admonition.[18]

All last-minute Bolshevik Central Committee efforts to stop the demonstration failed. When the soldiers appeared before Bolshevik headquarters on the evening of July 3, they flouted the efforts of the Bolshevik Military Organization, whose leaders tried to dissuade them from the balcony of Kshesinskaia's mansion, and marched to the Tauride Place to finish off the Provisional Government and hand power over to the Soviet. The leaders, caught between two fires, began to vacillate. On the morning of July 4 the Bolshevik Military Organization assumed responsibility for organizing the "demonstration," presumably in order to make it as peaceful and orderly as possible, but they failed. They were simply carried along.

In the absence of insistent urging from a party that would actually assume responsibility for governmental power, the soldiers, sailors, and workers simply menaced the proceedings of the Provisional Government and the Soviet. The Soviet leaders temporized. Trotsky and Zinov'ev made rousing speeches, yet counseled the demonstrators to disperse. At no moment during the history of the revolution was the significance of decisive leadership more clearly demonstrated. The insurrectionaries had sufficient forces to dispose of any resistance in the Tauride Palace itself, but no first-rank leader called for a seizure of power. It was an odd situation indeed. The bulk of the masses surrounding the Tauride Palace went home in the early hours of the morning, but only for a short pause.

Meanwhile, a Bolshevik leaflet produced for the occasion of the demonstration on July 4 called for "a peaceful, organized expression of the will of the workers, soldiers, and peasants of Petrograd."[19] But the moment had passed for a peaceful demonstration. The demonstrators had been fired upon and fired back. On July 4 not only soldiers but contingents from the naval fortress of Kronstadt added to the turmoil. However, the mood of the capital shifted on the night of July 4–5. The government's campaign to win support among the troops (which included circulation of rumors that Lenin was a German agent) and the actual arrival of loyal regiments at the Tauride Palace proved to be decisive.

Not only did Lenin's debilitated emotional and physical state at the end of June and beginning of July place him hors de combat at a moment of crisis, it undoubtedly affected the quality of his leadership after his return. According to his own account, he was still too ill on July 4 to make more than one brief speech from the balcony of the Bolshevik headquarters in Kshesinskaia's mansion.[20] Indeed, he only consented to speak after some pressure, at a moment when a contingent from Kronstadt was parading before the mansion. When he appeared on the balcony and spoke, his heart was not in it, but he got tumultuous applause anyway. He apologized for his brevity, greeted the demonstrators, affirmed the slogan "All Power to the Soviets," and avoided any but the most innocuous exhortation, proclaiming that the cause would prevail. It must have been a bitter moment for Lenin: thousands of armed soldiers, sailors, and workers parading before him—and he unable to offer fighting words. For all of his brave talk before the Soviet only a month earlier, on July 4, he was not ready to seize power.

After July 4 the Provisional Government quickly moved to the attack. Exploiting the arrival of troops from the front and the reaction to rumors circulated by the Minister of Justice, P. N. Pereverzev (rumors supported, by among others, one of Lenin's former colleagues, G. Aleksinskii), the Provisional Government forced Lenin deeper into hiding by putting out a warrant for his and Zinov'ev's arrest on the night of July 6–7. Trotsky claims to have spoken to Lenin on the morning of July 5, when it was already clear that the insurrection had failed. " 'Now they will shoot us down, one by one,' said Lenin. 'This is the right time for them.' "[21] Had Lenin been correct and had the Provisional Government acted more quickly, twentieth-century history would have been quite different.

Although the repression occurred, it did not take a ruthless or decisive form. On July 5–6 troops loyal to the government ransacked the printing offices of *Pravda*, and early on July 6 they surrounded the Bolshevik headquarters in the Kshesinskaia mansion. A few party workers trying to save the party files surrendered without a fight, but others had traversed the short distance to the Peter and Paul Fortress, where for moment it looked as if the Military Organization and a few hundred soldiers from Kronstadt might contest the formidable force sent against them. Stalin, a member of the Central Committee and ranking figure among those besieged, assumed responsibility for surrendering the fortress. He was also a member of the Central Executive Committee of the

Soviets, and this gave him added authority to negotiate with the military officer charged with liquidating opposition at Bolshevik headquarters and the fortress.[22] Although the insurgents were disarmed, they were not imprisoned. Stalin and Podvoiskii of the Military Organization were able to attend a meeting with Lenin, Zinov'ev, and Kamenev that evening.[23]

After the July uprising measures were taken to disarm soldiers and workers and disperse insurrectionary units in the army. The Provisional Government launched a temporarily successful propaganda campaign, but the support for the uprising in Petrograd was too broad and Bolshevik organizations too well rooted for the repression to succeed. The Petrograd Committee would report no significant losses in party membership at the all-city conference held shortly after the July days. Although there were warrants for the arrest of party leaders and a curtailment of the party press, party organizations remained intact and did not go underground. Furthermore, Kadets were leaving the cabinet and the military offensive was failing at the very moment when the Provisional Government was coping with internal rebellion. The government campaign after the July days only briefly interrupted the Bolsheviks' successes among the workers and soldiers of Petrograd. In August the threat from the right, in the form of General Lavr Kornilov, settled the issue.

Meanwhile, Lenin had to reassess the position of the party and its slogans. He had to reorient a party of roughly 200,000 after a stunning blow. Once again, he demonstrated his characteristic qualities of leadership: an instrumental and unsentimental approach to revolution, an unshakable faith in the correctness of his revolutionary line, and a fiercely combative spirit in the face of defeat. Lenin showed his usual flexibility about the means to achieve his ends. Now that it had failed him, he was ready to abandon the Soviet as the chosen vehicle of revolution.

Lenin saw a situation similar to that of 1912–1914 emerging. The Bolsheviks at that time had simply read their opponents out of the party and made use of whatever legal forums they could (the Duma, professional unions, insurance councils), but all the while they had prepared themselves for an armed insurrection against the tsarist government. At the present moment the Provisional Government was a counterrevolutionary military dictatorship. The Soviet, now dominated by "petit-bourgeois" parties (Mensheviks and Socialist Revolutionaries) had become an extension of that dictatorship. The party would have to find a more direct route to power—armed insurrection at the head of the revolutionary proletariat and poorest peasants. Of course, to their opponents armed insurrection is precisely what the Anarchists and Bolsheviks had already attempted. However, the participants in the July uprising had paraded ineffectually before an unresponsive Soviet instead of making a direct attack upon the government. When looking to the Bolshevik leaders for a call to battle, they had received mixed signals. Lenin's reorientation, therefore, was not merely symbolic. Previously he had allowed for power passing peacefully to the Soviet, but now he viewed it as a "fig leaf" for the counterrevolution. Until such time as it accepted the Bolshevik line, the Soviet, like the tsarist Duma before it, would serve only as a propaganda forum. But if not the Soviet, what democratic institution could serve as an organ of insurrection? Evidently, Lenin began to consider the factory committees, expressions of grassroots radicalism, for that role.[24] The Bolshevik leader took a flexible approach, indeed.

Lenin did not fully appreciate the difficulties of sudden reorientations—a flaw he had shown repeatedly in the past. The soviets had acquired a powerful mystique. Since the "April Theses" he had dinned into the ears of his followers," All Power to the Soviets," and they had spread the word to the revolutionary masses of Petrograd. It was no easy matter to call for abandonment of the slogan or the symbol. In any case, the need to stay underground prevented him from bringing direct pressure to bear upon his colleagues. For most of July, all of August and September, and most of October Lenin became, in effect, an exile. After July 6 he had to conduct business through intermediaries and by correspondence—a not uncommon situation for him and one that permitted his subordinates to alter or delay his policies. After his theses about the current situation were debated and modified by an expanded meeting of the Central Committee of the party and then rejected in the form of the CC's resolutions to an all-city Bolshevik conference, the slogan "All Power to the Soviets" was abandoned reluctantly and, as things turned out, only temporarily at the end of July at the Sixth Party Congress.

MEANWHILE, STALIN once again moved to the forefront of party affairs. When the time came for Lenin to make security arrangements, Stalin played a central role. On July 7 Lenin moved to the apartment of Stalin's future father-in-law, which Stalin had made into a safe apartment. At the time, Lenin had second thoughts about surrendering and permitting himself to be tried by the Provisional Government. Many Bolsheviks believed that he had to appear and answer the slanderous accusations and rumors, including a new one that he had been an agent provocateur for the tsarist police. Although the other slanders had no shock value, the last one shook Lenin and induced him to explore the possibility of a trial to clear his honor. Ordzhonikidze was commissioned to demand that the Central Executive Committee of the Soviet guarantee Lenin's and Zinov'ev's safety if they turned themselves in, but he did not negotiate seriously. Ordzhonikidze shared Stalin's views at the time, and Stalin predicted that Lenin would be killed before he could be brought to trial.[25] Given his belief in the treachery of others, Stalin advised Lenin to go into the deep underground. As Lenin's security agent, Stalin realized in a much more direct form than ever before his Koba identity. Fantasy and reality had merged. Furthermore, with Lenin and Zinov'ev in hiding and Kamenev under arrest, Stalin and Sverdlov had become Lenin's main executives in Petrograd, responsible for presenting the new party line.

The Bolshevik Central Committee and lower ranking committeemen, accustomed to subverting Lenin's most radical reorientations, dealt with this new one in the usual way. It would have been ill-considered at best for the

Bolsheviks, now branded as outlaws, to affirm their new status nakedly. With Lenin absent, it was far easier to vote against the unpopular resolutions put forward by his spokesmen. A case can be made that Stalin himself wanted to blunt the thrust of Lenin's latest policy, given his lame presentation of it at the Bolshevik all-city conference.[26] Moreover, the Petrograd Organization did not automatically accept the word handed down from Lenin. Volodarskii, as noted earlier, had considerable influence, and he opposed abandonment of the call for "All Power to the Soviets." The Bolsheviks were actually put in a sort of double bind: If they withdrew the slogan and replaced it with Lenin's call for armed insurrection, they would be pursuing an adventurist policy and provoke even stronger repressive measures by the government at a time when the government had the advantage; on the other hand, if they withdrew their fighting slogan, they might demoralize and lose those who had fought under it since April.

Moreover, the debate at the all-city Bolshevik conference in Petrograd on July 16–17 reveals how difficult it was to adjust to Lenin's new line at the ideological level. Many of the delegates found unacceptable the analysis of the correlation of forces and class antagonisms set forth by Stalin on behalf of Lenin and the Central Committee. Serious Marxists, some wondered what changes in either the internal lineup of classes or the international context justified a change of slogan. They directly challenged Stalin's analysis and offered numerous amendments to the CC's resolutions. Stalin's concluding remarks and rebuttal of criticisms were feeble, at best. His analysis of the international situation and the role of the peasantry did not bear close scrutiny. The real message was one of betrayal: The Mensheviks and SRs had delivered the Bolsheviks into the hands of the counterrevolutionary forces led by the Kadets. Only the Menshevik-Internationalists led by Martov and the left-wing SRs could be trusted as allies. (Interestingly, Stalin did not mention the Interdistrict Commission, which was preparing to merge with the Bolsheviks. Trotsky, of course, was their leading figure.) The Soviet could not therefore be regarded as a socialist body because its leading parties had betrayed socialism. Yet, even with these accusations Stalin did not call for withdrawal from and rebellion against the Soviet. Those Bolsheviks who remained in the Central Executive Committee of the Soviet would submit to its decisions. The Bolsheviks would strive for a majority, but until they achieved one, they could not call for all power to the soviets.

Thus, Stalin presented the essential Leninst strategy of 1912–1914 revised for the current situation. Even though almost isolated, the Bolsheviks would proclaim themselves the sole representatives of true socialism—the leaders of the proletariat and poorest peasants. They would use whatever means available, including the Soviet that had betrayed them, to present their views and continue to try to convert the Soviet into their instrument. However, in a moment of insight and candor, when replying to objections that Lenin's call for armed insurrection and a dictatorship of the proletariat and poorest peasants made little sense in the present context, Stalin replied:

Those comrades who say that the dictatorship of the proletariat is impossible because the proletariat constitutes a minority of the population interpret the strength of a minority mechanically. Even the Soviets represent only the 20,000,000 people they have organized, but thanks to their organization they have the following of the [whole] population. The whole population will follow an organized force that can break the shackles of economic disruption.[27]

This was the gist of the matter. The Bolsheviks had only to organize and mobilize a part of the population as a striking force at a time when the disruptions caused by the war made crises inevitable and governments perpetually vulnerable. Lenin's class analysis did not have to be correct. In the hands of those who sought power, Marxian concepts were sufficiently malleable to justify a wide range of tactics and could be made sufficiently cogent to inspire followers. Stalin's impatience with the comrades who kept on bringing up issues of the role of the petit-bourgeois peasants and the smallness of the forces who proposed to lead the entire country reflected a realistic grasp of the nature of power at that historical juncture. What mattered was organizing and mobilizing people under one's slogans. Stalin knew this intuitively and, unlike those whose Marxism was of a different sort, did not expend a great deal of effort defending formulations and slogans that were quite good enough to get on with the job. Furthermore, the idea that the Bolsheviks were isolated and surrounded by betrayers appealed to Stalin's longstanding sense of the embattled position of just avengers. Always just beneath the surface of his Marxian rhetoric lay deeper layers of motivation and Stalin's old models of heroism.

Any analyst removed from the emotions and rationalizations of the moment can see how murky the Bolshevik thinking about institutions and classes was. But it would be wrong to assume that Lenin was simply producing a great cloud of Marxian rhetoric to obscure his maneuvers. He genuinely wanted to provide a "scientific" analysis of the new situation and justification for his new line, even though the psychology of power-seeking underlay both. Each new tactic, formulation, and slogan tended to isolate the Bolsheviks from other political parties, on the one hand, yet put them into a position to strike for power, on the other. Stalin understood that very well.

26

The Bolsheviks in Extremis

WHEREAS LENIN and Stalin reverted to the traditions of the revolutionary underground in their efforts to survive the Provisional Government's repressive measures, Trotsky, as in 1905, exhibited more than a little quixotic courage during the July days and their aftermath. During a tense moment on July 4 the SR Minister of Agriculture, Victor Chernov, came out of the Tauride Palace to pacify the mob gathered in front. A contingent of sailors from Kronstadt began to abduct him, when Trotsky intervened. The Kadet leader Miliukov captured the moment in his memoirs:

> Chernov began a lengthy speech outlining the activities of the socialist ministers in general and his own as minister of agriculture in particular. As far as the Kadet ministers were concerned, he said—"good riddance to them." In answer, voices shouted "why didn't you say this before? Announce at once that the land is going to the toiling people and the power to the Soviets." A sturdy worker, waving his fist in front of the minister's face cried in a frenzy: "Take

power, you son of a bitch, when it is offered to you." Amid the mounting tumult several people grabbed Chernov and pulled him towards a car. Others pulled him toward the palace. After ripping his coat, some Kronstadt sailors pulled him into the car and announced that they would not release him until the Soviet had assumed full power. Some anxious workers broke into the meeting hall crying: Comrades, they are beating up Chernov. Amid the turmoil Chkeidze announced that Comrades Kamenev, Steklov, and Martov were delegated to liberate Chernov. He was freed, however, by Trotsky who had just arrived on the scene. The Kronstadt people listened to him. Accompanied by Trotsky, Chernov returned to the hall.[1]

Other accounts give a fuller if not entirely consistent picture of Trotsky's intervention. According to Sukhanov, he climbed onto the hood of the automobile and tried to calm the mob, but received a hostile response, the Kronstadters only sullenly acquiescing in Chernov's release.[2] The leader of the Kronstadt contingent, a sailor appropriately named Raskol'nikov, who later became a commander in the Red fleet and member of the Revolutionary War Council, gave a more heroic version, with an odor of hagiography about it. According to him, Trotsky, with consummate self-possession and commanding presence instantly quieted the mob, declared citizen Chernov free, and accompanied him into the Tauride Palace.[3] In every version, Trotsky plunged into the crowd while the others sent to aid Chernov faded into the background. All of his actions of the period reveal his penchant for taking center stage — and his willingness to risk his life in the process.

During the mounting campaign against the Bolsheviks, Trotsky decided on a theatrical and, to less dramatic souls, needlessly dangerous gesture of support for the Bolsheviks. Still a member of the Interdistrict Commission and not yet enrolled as a Bolshevik, Trotsky had pursued a policy similar to that of the Bolshevik leadership. Not only his theatrical bent but his duelist's sense of honor came to the fore during the slander campaign against Lenin and the Bolsheviks. He identified himself with them completely in their new position as victims of the machinations of the Kadets, Mensheviks, and SRs. It was an important psychological turning point for Trotsky. He wrote an open letter (dated July 10, 1917, and published in *New Life* three days later) to the Provisional Government in which he showed that the parallel and sometimes unified actions of the Bolsheviks and Interdistrict group were all designed to restrain the insurgents of July 3–4, to encourage an organized, peaceful demonstration. The letter announced Trotsky's continuing solidarity with the Bolsheviks and scotched rumors appearing in the newspapers of the capital that he had repudiated his affiliation with them. In fact, at no time in his life had Trotsky ever leapt to Lenin's defense with such alacrity. The oddest part of the letter is Trotsky's demand that he be included under the government order for the arrest of Lenin, Zinov'ev, and Kamenev. His wish was granted. The Provisional Government arrested Trotsky on the night of July 22, and his fellow Interdistrictite, Lunacharskii, to boot.

LUNACHARSKII'S BEHAVIOR during the period between the July uprising and his arrest raises some interesting questions. Sukhanov gives a relatively detailed account of a conversation with him on July 7 in which he allegedly outlined a conspiracy to seize power, an account Sukhanov himself admitted might be garbled.[4] Given Lunacharskii's denial and the absence of verification by any other source, it remains only a curiosity. Did Lenin have a secret plan to seize power if the opportunity arose? Were Trotsky and Lunacharskii privy to it, as Sukhanov claimed? Thus far, no verification of Sukhanov's story has appeared.

THE JULY days hastened the long-delayed merger of the two most consistently radical Social Democratic groups in the capital. Despite the initial failure of efforts at unification and the jailing or absence of the party leaders, the Interdistrict Commission and the Bolsheviks worked out a modus vivendi and carried off their joint congress. It went down in history as the Sixth Party Congress of the Communist Party of the Soviet Union. The Menshevik-Internationalists declined to accept the invitation to join the other two groups as part of a unified internationalist bloc. However, the Menshevik-Internationalist Iurii Larin attended the Congress and made a rousing speech. Sverdlov and Stalin played central roles at the Congress, the former as organizer and chairman and latter as reporter for the Central Committee and mover of the resolution on the political situation. Both men had assiduous knowledge of the party's modus operandi and prodigious memories. On July 26(August 8), 1917, the opening day of the Sixth Party Congress, those in attendance made honorary delegates of the absent leaders: Lenin, Zinov'ev, Kamenev, Trotsky, Kollontai (also under arrest), and Lunacharskii.

Two hundred and sixty-four delegates from all corners of the empire convened in Petrograd. There was a handful of party veterans with more than twenty years of service and a few youths still in their teens. On the whole, it was a youthful party, the average age of the delegates, twenty-nine. The oldest delegate was only forty-seven years old. Of the 171 who replied to a party questionnaire, ninety-two were Great Russian, but given the high proportion of minority nationalities, particularly Jews, in the Menshevik and SR parties, the Bolshevik Party, in some sense, was more ethnically Russian than the others.[5] The prominence of Jewish members at the summit of the party (Zinov'ev, Kamenev, Sverdlov, and Trotsky, for example) nonetheless made the Bolsheviks equally a target of Jew-baiting and the pogrom mentality. In fact, Lenin compared the Provisional Government's accusation that he and other Bolsheviks were German agents to the famous Dreyfus and Beilis affairs, both involving trumped up accusations against Jews. Twenty-nine of the delegates declared their nationality as Jewish. The questionnaire sent out to the delegates also tried to establish their occupations. In a nation in which the vast majority of the population worked in agriculture, not a single delegate gave farming as his or her occupation. As for gender, the record shows only ten women among the 171 delegates who filled in the questionnaire.

Just as at the Third All-City Petrograd Conference, here it was Stalin's responsibility to present Lenin's new political line and push through the resolution embodying it. At no time in his career had Stalin borne more responsibility or had a more central role. In the famous speech to the railway workers in Tbilisi, cited earlier, he declared 1917 to be the year when he became a "master workman" of the revolution. He may have had in mind his performance at the Sixth Party Congress. Stalin succeeded in his difficult task, which included the troublesome change of slogans, but not without serious challenges from the delegates. They both criticized the substance of the resolution, for which Lenin was responsible, and carped at its formulation. Here Stalin undoubtedly bore some personal responsibility. A committee was formed to redraft the resolution. Among the critics were men who would play important roles during Stalin's rise to power as allies, opponents, and, in the end, victims.

Stalin also raised the touchy issue of the circumstances under which Lenin and the other party leaders might appear for trial. Earlier he had taken an uncompromising position against their surrender. Now he suggested that they might appear before a "democratically organized" court under an "honorable" government, which would guarantee their security before trial. Here, too, he encountered critics, Bukharin among them. Far more theoretically sophisticated than Stalin, although nine years younger, Bukharin had risen to prominence within the increasingly powerful and assertive Moscow party organization. He quickly established himself at the Congress by successfully presenting his resolution protesting the Provisional Government's attempt to bring the party leaders to trial and dismissing any effort to reopen the question. It must have been an embarrassing moment for Stalin. Bukharin had stolen his thunder.

Stalin and Bukharin came into direct conflict again during the debate over the main resolution at the tenth session of the Congress on July 31(August 13). In reply to Stalin's report and some of the ensuing comments, Bukharin presented his own view of the correlation of forces and the correct Marxian deductions—and they did not coincide with Lenin's. Unlike Lenin, who believed that the poorest peasants would now join with the proletariat against the counterrevolutionary alliance of big and petit-bourgeoisie, Bukharin insisted that the revolution would occur in two phases: First, the peasants in typically petit-bourgeois fashion would satisfy their land hunger; then, in the next phase, the proletariat would join their European brethren in the long-awaited proletarian revolution. However, the second phase could virtually merge with the first. Bukharin proposed his own slogan for the present tactics: the organization of *revolutionary* soviets and the transfer of power to them. In more naked terms, Bukharin said that the most urgent practical concern was "the transfer of power to Bolshevik-dominated soviets and reelections in others."[6]

Stalin found Bukharin's criticism more substantive than the others' and spent most of his rebuttal attacking it. To his credit, Stalin did not flinch from the real problem: "The second stage, according to Comrade Bukharin, is a proletarian revolution supported by Western Europe, without the peasants, who have received their land and are satisfied. Then against whom is this revolution directed?"[7] Of course, Bukharin had in mind a second phase dominated by the revolution of the European proletariat against their bourgeoisie, a phase that was essential for the introduction of socialism in Russia as well. On the other hand, Stalin remained focused on the Russian Revolution and its future development. He would find his own bloody solution to the peasant problem somewhat later. For the present moment everyone tried to find a way to make that huge, mysteriously constructed social mass melt into an optimistic formula. All of the meaningful distinctions between a "democratic" phase and a revolutionary socialist phase tended to disappear as the delegates struggled to justify the seizure of power toward which Lenin relentlessly drove them against their Marxian scruples. Stalin proved to be a good spokesman for Lenin's revolutionary optimism and risk-taking. To Bukharin's substitute slogan about organizing revolutionary soviets, he replied:

> The main task is to propagandize the idea of the necessity of *overthrowing* the existing power. The workers, peasants, and soldiers must understand that without overthrowing the present power, they will receive neither freedom nor land! Therefore, the issue is not about the organization of power, but about its overthrow, and when we receive power in our hands, we will know how to organize it.[8]

Bukharin had been given responsibility for presenting the resolution on the relationship of the war to current events separately from Stalin's resolution on the political situation. His report preceded Stalin's at the ninth session of the Congress. Bukharin presented an eloquent statement of the internationalist position. International socialist revolution was the only acceptable outcome. In the event of the success of the Russian Revolution and economic recovery, they would engage in offensive revolutionary war. If recovery did not occur, they would conduct a defensive revolutionary war, but in the interest of the world proletariat.

> By means of such a revolutionary war we will ignite the conflagration of world socialist revolution. The only genuinely democratic way out of this blind alley, which the western Europeans have gotten into, and later the American countries, is international proletarian revolution, no matter how many sacrifices it would cost. There is no other solution to the problem. We are often reproached with setting too ambitious goals, with failing to set forth concrete steps, with this sort of reasoning: If we have a bird in hand, perhaps we should forget about the one in the bush. But no such bird in hand is possible. They forget that the political efforts to act on our government have failed. Therefore, the idea of an international socialist revolution must be supported to the utmost, as the only way out of the situation that has been created.[9]

Stalin clashed with Bukharin's internationalist point of view again, albeit indirectly, on August 3(16), 1917 at the last session of the Congress. As mover of the resolution Stalin was presenting it paragraph by paragraph and came to the ninth, which read:

The task of these revolutionary classes will then be to exert all of their might for seizing state power into their hands and, in alliance with the revolutionary proletariat of the advanced nations, to direct it towards peace and the socialist reconstruction *[perestroistva]* of society.[10]

E. A. Preobrazhenskii, later a prominent left-wing economist and ally of Trotsky during the debates over the New Economic Policy in the 1920s, offered an amendment. Preobrazhenskii believed that the ninth paragraph violated Bukharin's resolution on the war, which had been passed the day before, and suggested that the paragraph end with the following words: "for directing it [state power] towards peace and, in the presence of *[pri nalichii]* a proletarian revolution in the West, towards socialism."[11] Stalin countered with an unexpectedly eloquent reply. His enormous pride and grandiose self-image as an original thinker and leader broke through:

> I am against this ending of the resolution. The possibility is not excluded that precisely Russia will be the country paving the way for socialism. Until this very moment not a single country has enjoyed such freedom as has appeared in Russia, nor tried to realize workers' control over production. Besides, the base for our revolution is wider than in western Europe, where the proletariat stands face to face with the bourgeoisie in complete isolation. Our workers are supported by the poorest stratum of peasants. Finally, in Germany the state apparatus of power operates incomparably better than the imperfect apparatus of our bourgeoisie, which is itself a tributary of European capital. We must discard obsolete ideas that only Europe can show the way. There is dogmatic Marxism and creative Marxism. I stand on the latter ground.[12]

Like Lenin, Stalin understood that the old state apparatus stood in the way of an armed insurrection. The civil bureaucracy, the police, and the army—those agencies that administered and maintained power for regimes—were crucial. The opportunity for smashing the Russian state apparatus, now controlled by "counterrevolutionaries," had arrived. No such opportunity existed in the West. It was criminal to refrain from launching an attach upon a vulnerable counterrevolutionary government with a weak, disintegrating state apparatus supported by European capital. This was Lenin's message, and Stalin understood it well. Stalin also grasped that the seizure of power was the next priority. Like Lenin he had learned not to attach too great value to any institutional forms. What would come after the seizure of power? Stalin was determined to have a say in that. After smashing the old machine, one had to create a new one. Although the credit for that achievement belongs mainly to Lenin, Stalin learned how to master Lenin's machine and run it on new principles—perhaps it is better to say without them. The new *apparat* in Russia, an isolated "socialist" party-state, would be Stalin's bird in hand. Oddly enough, the ideologue who supplied the theoretical support for the new regime during Stalin's consolidation of power was Bukharin.

WHAT WE know of Stalin's psychology strongly suggests that he found the experience of debating in an open forum painful. His thin voice, heavy accent, and oddly stylized language, which evoked the contempt of accomplished rhetoricians like Trotsky, put him at a disadvantage. But in the later sessions of the Sixth Party Congress Stalin rose to the occasion and atoned for his absence at the deciding session of the Third All-City Conference. His nonappearance had contributed to the failure of the Central Committee's initial resolution. Now, with the help of a drafting committee and his own vigorous defense, he achieved better results. Once again, he emerged vindicated. After every fall, backed by Lenin's authority he had set himself even more firmly on his feet and gained in personal stature.

The Sixth Party Congress, like previous congresses, showed how little inclined Old Bolsheviks and new were to docile acceptance of their leaders' formulations. A genuine debate ensued in which all of the difficulties of Lenin's position were exposed. No one could be certain about the impact of the international situation; the huge mass of peasants, whose "poorest" layer Lenin now made a crucial component of his slogans, remained a puzzling factor. Astute critics could divine precisely what kind of dictatorship might emerge, just as they had after Lenin's performance at the Second Party Congress. But for all of the uneasiness expressed, the majority of delegates were swayed by the compromise Lenin had worked into the new line. After all, Lenin and the Central Committee, for which Stalin spoke, did not call for an attack upon the soviets as such or even withdrawal from them.

Lenin's prestige, Sverdlov's management of the Congress, and Stalin's presentation of the case were good enough to get the new line adopted. However, in retrospect the events seem like an exercise in party discipline and conditioning for battle. Lenin's slogans of the moment seem less important than the political psychology of Bolshevism. What mattered was Lenin's continual pressure upon his party, his tempering of their spirit. He forced them to stand virtually alone on the left flank of the socialist movement. This seemingly uncompromising radicalism confirmed his followers in their choice of leader and also won over people like Trotsky. On the other hand, it encouraged a left wing within the party inspired by an all-or-nothing approach Lenin did not at all have in mind.

Lenin's "all" turned out to be limited to the destruction of the old state apparatus and the seizure and retention of power. Ad hoc innovations, improvisations would determine the rest. Bukharin, distinctly internationalist in orientation, for a time was misled into thinking that the entire project depended upon international revolution. In 1918 he would be prepared to risk the revolutionary regime in Russia in an all-out revolutionary war and even contemplate arresting Lenin for obstructing it. Others, like Kollontai, took Lenin's ideas of 1917 as sanction for an anarcho-syndicalist turn. They later believed that the abandonment of the slogan of workers' control and the idea of a commune state, one of Lenin's most inspirational ideas during 1917, was tantamount to betrayal of the revolution. Stalin sometimes balked, sometimes subverted or sabotaged Lenin's improvisations, but he adapted himself to each change in the party line far more readily than the other leading figures.

WITH THE absorption of the Interdistrict Committee into the Bolshevik party at the Sixth Congress, Trotsky at last became a Bolshevik, and high-ranking one at that. He was voted a member of the Central Committee of the party. Only Lenin (134) and Zinov'iev (132) received more votes than Trotsky and Kamenev (each 131). All the while Trotsky resided in Kresty prison, where he remained until September 4(17), when he was liberated by the revolutionary upsurge provoked by General Kornilov's attempt at a coup. Lenin, meanwhile, took even greater precautions against arrest by moving to Finland. There, in a bucolic setting of the sort that always revived him, he completed his extraordinary treatise, *The State and Revolution*. As if in response to the doubts expressed by the delegates at the Sixth Party Congress, Lenin found scriptural support for smashing the old state apparatus and outlined the new kind of state that would replace it.

27

Lenin's Utopia

ENIN'S IMMERSION in the writing of *The State and Revolution* at a time
when he was calling for armed insurrection once again strikingly
illustrates the importance to him of justifying political practice by
means of Marxian theory. Not that his concern with what would follow the
smashing of the current state apparatus was new. Partly under the spur of
Bukharin's theoretical work, he had faced the problem of the state in contemporary Marxian theory in 1916 and continued to pursue it in the months that
followed.[1] He had reacted to Bukharin—and would continue to do so—in a
somewhat crabby manner. Lenin, like Plekhanov before him, still tended to
guard jealously his status as theoretician for his faction and then the party.
The upstart Bukharin's position on the national question, his excellent knowledge of modern sociological and economic theory, his striking work on the
theory of the modern state, and his systemic approach to dialectics, the last of
which owed a great deal to Lenin's old theoretical nemesis, Bogdanov, all

evoked aggressive responses in Lenin. His identity as proud theoretical *vozhd'* (leader) of the party showed prominently and not very graciously in Lenin's criticism of Bukharin in his "Testament," about which more will be said later. However, in 1917 Lenin clearly owed a great deal not only to Bukharin's stimulus but to his analysis of the modern state as well.[2] Lenin's debt to other thinkers for his theory of the state cannot be dealt with adequately here. Suffice to say, as with his theory of imperialism and "uninterrupted revolution," he relied heavily on the work of others. Most important of all, he dutifully grounded his theory of the state in the works of Marx and Engels and in historical revolutionary experience. Lenin drew genuine sustenance from the master works of the fathers and from the promise of 1905 and 1917.

He found in works such as Marx's *The Eighteenth Brumaire of Louis Bonaparte* a devastating portrayal of the modern state as parasite on the body of bourgeois society. When non-Marxian thinkers, less inclined to emphasize the supreme importance of class, dealt with the problem of the state, they proposed that this "parasitic" entity lived a life of its own at the expense of all classes of society. For many modern sociologists and students of politics, the notion that the state might have a relatively autonomous character entailed a rethinking, if not repudiation, of a fundament of Marxism. But to devoted Marxists, however impressive the modern Leviathan, it was still only an instrument of bourgeois class domination. In order for a socialist revolution to succeed, the hypertrophied state machine had to be smashed; the bureaucracy that managed it kicked out; the banks that financed it seized; the standing army and police force that protected it dissolved.

However, Marx and Engels were not anarchists and most certainly did not believe in small-scale socioeconomic structures. The centralization that had occurred under the bourgeoisie and fostered the monstrous state structures serving imperialist capitalism also had created the bases for socialist economies. Economic centralization was good; large-scale production units and huge labor forces massed in them were good; centralized banking systems were good. In short, the centralized and monopolistic forms taken by capital, summarized in the concept of state capitalism, would ease the task of the proletariat. The task was clear enough. Marx and Engels had taught that the historical dialectic would deliver into the hands of the proletariat the marvelous productive system created by the bourgeois hunger for profits. The time had now arrived, believed Lenin, to seize the wealth the international bourgeoisie had accumulated during centuries of exploitation. After smashing the bourgeois state, the proletariat would expropriate the expropriators. Then, matters became a bit more complicated.

Several questions issued from attempts of Marxists to imagine the form a successor state would take after the overthrow of the rule of the imperial bourgeoisie. Marx and Engels, had referred, although not very frequently, to a "dictatorship of the proletariat."[3] The idea first appears in Lenin's writings as early as the winter of 1902, in connection with the formulation of the program of the RSDRP at that time. Lenin wanted mention of the dictatorship of the proletariat to be inserted into the program drafted by Plekhanov and emphasized Marx's and Engels' position of 1847 that the proletariat was the only genuinely revolutionary class. In 1917 the idea of the dictatorship of the proletariat took on new luster. In fact, Lenin saw in it Marx's and Engels' essential teaching about the state and a key to understanding what would happen after the proletariat smashed the bourgeois state. Until the bourgeoisie disappeared, some repressive machinery would have to remain; but the dictatorship of the proletariat was presumably only a transitional form of state control until the advent of a classless society. Interestingly, Lenin did not make a single mention of the poorest peasantry, presumably the proletariat's class ally, in *The State and Revolution*.

What form would the dictatorship of the proletariat take? In post mortems of the revolutionary politics of the mid-nineteenth century and the Paris Commune of 1871 Marx and Engels provided some help. Their praise and critique of the Paris Commune, however mythical their version of it, gave Lenin one source of inspiration. Lenin's own experience with the revolution of 1905 and his recent experience of 1917, reviewed in the light of Marx's and Engel's analyses of the failed French revolutions, permitted him to develop a theory with an indisputable Marxian pedigree: the theory of a commune state as the appropriate form of the dictatorship of the proletariat, the form the state would take during the historical period when the proletariat still had to use repressive measures against the bourgeoisie.

One should note that Lenin's use of the word "dictatorship" had none of the connotations that the word later acquired during the height of totalitarian rule. For Lenin *all* rule of one class over another took the form of a dictatorship. He also used the phrase "dictatorship of the bourgeoisie." As noted above, the use of the word "dictatorship" to describe the rule of the bourgeoisie and the proletariat had appeared fairly early in Lenin's writings, and we may rest assured that the concept itself had no striking novelty for him. He had long ago studied the teachings of Marx and Engels on Louis Bonaparte and the Paris Commune and learned the lessons of 1905. One could not take half-measures. Without ruthlessly decisive actions a dictatorship by plebiscite or a de facto military dictatorship might snatch victory from the proletariat. The added "lessons" of February and July 1917 only strengthened a long-standing tendency in Lenin's thinking. It was not enough merely to seize power. The enemy's capacity to wage war had to be destroyed. This very useful bit of stark realism was imbedded in the distorted, wishful Marxian thinking surrounding the Paris Commune.

In 1917 Lenin had as well a sense of urgency, a belief that the end of the bourgeois era and the advent of the dictatorship of the proletariat could not be put off, and a need to describe precisely a transitional state form which would follow a seizure of power. Lenin had to convince himself and his followers that the proletariat could run things themselves, that they could go it alone without the civil servants of the old state, without a special police force and standing army. He minimized the complexity of modern statecraft and economics, both the quality of the skills and the quantity of personnel needed to staff the bureaus, financial institutions, security agencies, and armies of his new state.

The commune state visualized by Lenin had the following features: A popular militia with broad police powers would replace the old standing army and police; the bureaucrats, professionals, and managers of the old regime would be replaced by employees, who would be paid wages no higher than those of factory workers; all offices would be elective and all officials subject to recall; the workers would control production as well as own the means of production; the public would adapt the centralized banking system and its ready-made techniques of accounting and control to the needs of the new order. In short, Lenin pictured a thoroughly centralized, though democratized, state machine (an image seemingly at odds with the democratic spontaneity of a commune) made possible by the very achievements of the bourgeoisie. He followed Marx and Engels, who had assumed that capitalism would be destroyed precisely when it had given all that it had to offer historically. Their entire theory of progress depended upon the idea that capitalism's "progressive" features could be transferred intact to a socialist regime.

One might wonder at this point at Lenin's failure to understand either the workings of institutions or the motivations of people. Clearly, whether in more advanced nations or in Russia those people who had been educated or trained for their positions under the old regime—the paid servants of the bourgeoisie—might not want to serve under the new one. They might even seek to sabotage it. Even if one emphasized the extent to which procedures and techniques had been simplified, a quick seizure of power would entail a transitional period in which people brought up and trained under the old system would have to be pressed into service. Lenin had a rather simple but ominous solution, the coercive power of the revolutionary state—in short, state terror. The dictatorship of the proletariat would resort to "plebian" methods and not flinch from the use of force. However, the problem of retaining the service of "bourgeois specialists" in every area—in the army, in the bureaucracy, and in the financial sphere—would haunt the regime.

Lenin, like Marx, was a rather poor prophet. We know now that not proletarianization but the enormous expansion of the professional stratum working in a variety of institutional settings has issued from the long-term process of modernization. Lenin should not be criticized severely for not having foreseen this in 1917; and he can be forgiven for having failed to see that the heroic image of the proletariat created by Marx and sustained by succeeding generations of Marxists was not widely shared. The proletarian identity proved to be a relatively unappealing one, as mass education and economic and social change provided alternative identities to increasingly urbanized populations. Any modern economic system has to have highly trained and motivated managers and experts. In Lenin's state, as elsewhere, differential wage scales would have to be used to motivate specialists—the postrevolutionary "intelligentsia." What seems obvious now was far from Lenin's mind in 1917. He thought that the threat of starvation was quite enough to terrorize the "bourgeois specialists" and get them to perform.

Lenin also assumed that an immense amount of talent and creative energy locked up in hundreds of millions of formerly oppressed people would be released by the promise of a commune state. Here of course, he was at least partially correct. Like all revolutionary regimes his depended upon mass mobilization and ready acceptance of new tasks after the moment of liberation. In 1917 the promise of his type of commune state seemed to be a reasonable way to rally the broad masses of the population behind the leadership of his party. It made sense in the light of revolutionary experience. The revolutionary parties could rely upon the hatred and resentment of the masses: they hated the bureaucrats, the *chinovniki*, and the old intelligentsia; they hated the fat capitalist bankers, the factory owners, and the foremen; they hated the land-owners and their estate managers; they hated the police; and they hated the officers who humiliated them and drove them into machinegun fire. Their hatred could be converted into the force to smash the state machine. But aside from the fatal miscalculations about the historical process, very immediate and serious problems issued from a misreading of mass motivation. Even though previous and subsequent revolutionary history validated some of the Marxian revolutionaries' assumptions about class hatred and resentment, the vision of the future of proletarians and peasants in truth did not necessarily coincide with that of Marxian theoreticians. Even if it had, not all of the promises of the leaders could be fulfilled. Not only was *The State and Revolution* based upon false expectations, it created them.

Lenin's notion of a commune state was the utopian issue of both his faith in Marxian theory and his need to offer inspiration for struggle, just as his theory of the final stage of capitalism was an optimistic misreading (using the most generous evaluation possible, from a Marxian point of view) of the historical moment. Lenin's failure to foresee that leviathanism would issue quite naturally from the tasks of building and defending a new kind of centralized system in a world of unrepentant capitalist-imperialist states, whose end he had erroneously predicted, had enormous consequences in the years that followed the establishment of the "dictatorship of the proletariat."

He also had to reconcile the new state form with the Marxian prediction of the disappearance of the state. This was the most academic part of his work, but it at least clarified the issue of distribution and the broad Marxian slogan under which workers in the commune state would labor. During the transitional period of the dictatorship of the proletariat, the slogan "From each according to his ability, from each according to his work" would be the appropriate one. There would be an extension of bourgeois right—the right to appropriate a product on the basis of one's wage labor. A socialist commune state and dictatorship of the proletariat therefore did not imply complete leveling in the form of equalization of wages and appropriation of product. That would come only once the bourgeoisie had disappeared and full abundance had been achieved. At that point the slogan of communism would take effect, and the state, such as it was, would wither away. By emphasizing the need to maintain some sort of state and a form of production and distribution still marked by the bourgeois system, Lenin tried to dispel any notions that the utopia of the anarchists or the Marxist millenium was at hand, but his ideas were sufficiently utopian, in their own way.

ONCE THE Bolsheviks regained momentum, the soviets could serve as the institutional framework for the commune state. However, the role of the party in this new kind of state remained undefined. Lenin, of course, had minimized the function of leadership and expertise in *The State and Revolution* and maximized the spontaneous initiative and competency of mobilized masses. Hence, his treatise appealed to anarchist sentiments. One must credit Lenin with a good sense of the situation. It should be recalled that he had responded similarly in 1905, when the word "spontaneity" lost its negative connotations and Lenin became concerned about the unreceptivity of the Bolshevik committeemen to raw recruits. In 1917 Lenin sounded so much like an anarchist that he was at pains to distinguish his position from theirs, even while he stole their thunder. Only later would the crucial role of the party machine come to the fore and conscious leadership resume its position of preeminence. No one reading *The State and Revolution* would infer the dictatorship of the party from Lenin's inspirational image of the dictatorship of the proletariat—except those who knew Lenin well.

28

Reversal: On the Attack

WHILE LENIN recovered his health in Finland and placed the capstone on his theoretical edifice and Trotsky prepared for his trial (which never took place) in Kresty prison, a sudden turn of events reversed their fortunes dramatically. The period between the July repression and the October Revolution was punctuated on August 25, 1917, by General Kornilov's march on Petrograd, ending with his arrest on September 1. Kornilov was commander in chief of Russia's armed forces under Kerensky's regime. In retrospect, the personalities involved and their maneuvers seem to be of minor significance. Contemporaries with a sense of history and politics guessed that sooner or later a patriotic military man would try to overawe the squabbling parties with force. All of the leaders knew French revolutionary history well; all expected a man on a white horse to make an appearance at some point. No one imagined he would be so ineffectual. Kornilov's badly timed and quickly aborted move on the capital had the immediate effect of weakening the Provisional Government's efforts to hold off the radical left. The threat to the revolution now overshadowed the patriotic sentiments of July. The disposition of the army changed decisively under the impact of the failure of the July offensive and Kornilov's attempted coup. Kerensky, Prime Minister under the latest coalition, found himself dependent upon the ability of the left to mobilize armed resistance to Kornilov. Trotsky was actually visited in his prison cell by a delegation from Kronstadt to seek his advice: Should they not dispose of Kerensky right now, too? Trotsky wisely told them to deal with the immediate threat, Kornilov, and bide their time with Kerensky. Meanwhile, he defied the Provisional Government's judiciary. Like Lenin he compared the present regime's mood and judicial behavior to that of the French during the Dreyfus affair and to the Beilis scandal in Russia. Trotsky was far luckier than either Dreyfus or Beilis. The Provisional Government's judiciary released him on bail six weeks after his arrest. With the added glamour of martyrdom (however mild and temporary) his popularity in the Soviet increased.

After Kornilov, the slogan "All Power to the Soviets" gained even greater support. Lenin revived it as an official party slogan. The military collapse and failed coup played into the hands of the left-wing parties, primarily the Bolsheviks and left-SRs. During September and October their power grew significantly in the soviets, with peasant soldiers voting in larger numbers for the left-SRs and the Bolsheviks increasing their popularity among the urban workers. As the peasant movement gathered force, the parties that encouraged seizures of property naturally received the peasants' support. The left-SRs and Bolsheviks seemed to present a solid front in this respect. Polarization proceeded apace. Lenin had stated as a general formula that the situation in Russia could only yield either a counter-revolutionary dictatorship or the dictatorship of the proletariat and poor peasants. His either-or approach now gained cogency, whatever the real meaning and intent of his slogans.

On August 31 the Bolsheviks won a majority vote in the all-important Petrograd Soviet, but even this did not convince all of the Bolshevik leaders that the time was ripe for armed insurrection against the Provisional Government. The Bolsheviks grew in strength but the Central Committee acted cautiously, as if the lessons of July had made a greater impression on them than those of late August and September. Trotsky, once released from prison on September 4, quickly resumed his ascent to leadership in the Soviet and now in the Bolshevik party as well. A situation emerged in October in which Trotsky and Lenin finally combined in a joint effort with momentous historical consequences. On the other hand, Zinov'ev's, Kamenev's, and Stalin's failures to rise to the occasion left them with bitter feelings, which only increased as Trotsky and later Bukharin gained in status.

TROTSKY BECAME the key leader in September and October, partly because of Lenin's absence but largely because the fluid situation played to his strengths. He emerged from Kresty Prison a Bolshevik in good standing, a high-ranking member of the Central Committee. If he had designed his imprisonment to win favor in the party, it had worked — but only up to a point. At the August 4 (17) meeting of the Central Committee, a bare majority (eleven to ten) voted against making Trotsky an editor of *Pravda* (temporarily operating under the name, *The Workers' Way*) in the event of his release from prison, even though he stood head and shoulders above the others as a revolutionary journalist. Stalin, whose authority had increased at the Sixth Party Congress, received the highest number of votes (fifteen) and continued as an editor of the central organ of the party, now with G. Ia. Sokolnikov and V. P. Miliutin.[1] The CC voted to maintain the Interdistrict Commission's old journal, *Vpered*, so that Trotsky still had his own organ, but that should not have precluded work as editor of *Pravda*. As the ranking figure at the meeting, Stalin surely played some role in the rebuff of Trotsky.

Stalin became one of the field commanders of the party in Petrograd, now as a member of the *uzkii sostav*, a term awkward to translate that signifies a special body of eleven leaders within the CC itself. In mid-August he joined the editorial boards of *Vpered* and *Prosveshchenie*, the latter a theoretical journal. However, once Trotsky, Kamenev, and Lunacharskii got back into the swing of things, Stalin lost status as *teoretik*. The CC voted Trotsky an editor of *Pravda* and *Prosveshchenie*, removed Stalin from the editorial board of the latter, and shut down *Vpered*. In the absence of notes on the discussion surrounding the personnel changes, it is difficult to know exactly what this signified. The reappearance of the *teoretiki* always affected Stalin's status, and he knew it. Furthermore, the greater the influx into the party of turncoat intelligentsia from other factions, the more unpleasant it must have been for Stalin and other Old Bolsheviks.

Not only Trotsky but many other former Mensheviks or Social Democrats on the left, such as Iurii Larin, abandoned their "scientific" scruples, their critique of bolshevism, and followed Lenin. They were revolutionaries first of all, and Lenin had much to offer them: an internationalist orientation; an uncompromising attitude and impatience for the "real" revolution; the promise of establishing a commune state immediately; and an end to the war. Lenin's authoritarianism, his drive for exclusive power, remained a problem. However, as the revolutionary situation developed, Lenin increasingly looked like the lesser evil to Marxists on the left. Lenin thus polarized revolutionary politics on a national scale, just as he had earlier on the relatively trivial scale of émigré politics. Who would have known that the dramas acted out between 1903 and 1917 in emigration would be rehearsals for the real thing, telescoped into a period of less than six months? Who would have guessed that the arch-splitter and chronic sectarian of the RSDRP would be able to weld together a mass party capable of winning a majority in the Petrograd Soviet?

Trotsky's own motives for throwing in with Lenin were no doubt quite complex. Given his courtship of danger and the attractiveness of revolutionary martyrdom, Trotsky may have joined Lenin at least partly because Lenin now seemed so quixotic. At the same time Trotsky, like Lenin, understood that the power of the state had virtually disintegrated and that an organization of determined revolutionaries could direct a vast tide of popular rebellion against the pathetic remnants of organized force under Kerensky's command. Either outcome conformed to a heroic scenario. If Trotsky and Lenin lost, they would become revolutionary martyrs; if they won, a great adventure lay in store for them. Trotsky would not settle for anything in between.

Like most members of the intelligentsia in general and Marxists in particular, Trotsky retained an ambivalent attitude towards power. Unlike Lenin, he did not aspire to a position of control. He was more concerned with proving his astuteness as a Marxian prophet and his fitness as a leader at a turning point in history than with governing an organization—or a nation. It was an odd attitude indeed—one that guaranteed a tragic end to Trotsky's career. Part of it was that he did not believe—quite consciously, in this case—that a Jew should aspire to a position of prominence in a revolutionary government. Trotsky soon articulated that position, one that not he alone held. In politics one had to take into account mass prejudices. Finally, Trotsky had none of the characteristics of homo politicus. His aesthetic needs were too profound. He felt uncomfortable with the unharmoniousness and incompleteness of politics. If he could not be an artist of revolution, he would be a self-destructive prophet or a tribune flaying the mighty with words and merging with the spontaneous force of the people. He might gather up vast armies and propel them into action. He might believe that he had the *vision* to be the supreme leader; yet in the end he deferred to Lenin, who could deal with the mess of politics, the quotidian affairs of the party and state.

Lunacharskii, quite close to Trotsky throughout 1917, testified to Trotsky's change of attitude toward the man he had formally despised.

> Trotsky as a man is prickly and overbearing. However, after Trotsky's merger with the Bolsheviks, it was only in his attitude to Lenin that Trotsky always showed—and continues to show—a tactful pliancy which is touching. With the modesty of all truly great men he acknowledges Lenin's primacy.[2]

To everyone *except* Lenin, Trotsky persisted in his prickly and overbearing attitude, and Lunacharskii does not fail to note that Trotsky and Lenin continued to clash on policy matters. In 1917 joining the Bolsheviks signified less entry into an organization for Trotsky than fidelity to the revolution itself and to his own destiny. As the only revolutionary Marxist party dedicated to permanent revolution and the revival of international socialism, the Bolsheviks became the best vehicle for Trotsky's ambitions. Here again Lunacharskii is an excellent guide. He perceived that Trotsky's ambitions had a rather elevated character:

> It is usual to say of Trotsky that he is ambitious. This, of course, is utter nonsense. I remember Trotsky making a very significant remark in connection with Chernov's acceptance of a ministerial portfolio: "What despicable ambition—to abandon one's place in history in exchange for the untimely offer of a ministerial post." In that, I think, lay all of Trotsky. There is not a drop of vanity in him, he is totally indifferent to any title or to the trappings of power; he is, however, boundlessly jealous of his own role in history and in that sense he is ambitious. Here he is I think as sincere as he is in his natural love of power.[3]

Lenin, not nearly as astute as Lunacharskii in psychological matters (the latter correctly said of him that he could not see things from his opponent's point of view), probably never really understood Trotsky's motives or fully trusted him. More will be said about this later. Suffice it for the present to quote Lenin's remark to Angelica Balabanoff made in 1917 before Trotsky had joined the Bolsheviks:

> "Tell me, Vladimir Il'ich, what is the difference between the Bolsheviks and Trotsky? Why does he hold apart from your group and create another newspaper?" Lenin seemed both astonished and irritated by my naiveté, perhaps because he suspected that I was trying to tease him. "Now don't you know?" he answered curtly. "Ambition, ambition, ambition." [4]

What Lunarcharskii had noted in Trotsky was a transcendent kind of ambition, something of a higher order than love of the mere trappings of power. Lenin evidently had a less generous view of things. But the crux of the matter is that Trotsky felt comfortable with power only when it lay in the streets or in mass meetings or out on the battlefield in fluid, heroic revolutionary forms rather than in the cramped, rigid organizational forms it took behind closed doors. Trotsky believed that he would prevail in a struggle where a natural unity of consciousness and spontaneity could occur—a charismatic relationship of leader and led defined in terms both Marxian and biopsychological. In the years ahead Trotsky's *constructive* Marxism—his Promethean romance of the machine and penchant for social engineering—formed an odd contrast with his hatred for the party *apparat*. He tried to substitute a heroic kind of social engineering for the cowardly machinations of the *apparat* and to shape Bolshevism in his own Promethean image. But what looked heroic and appropriate on the revolutionary battlefield or in wartime took on a threatening, dictatorial character in its postrevolutionary forms. Trotsky could neither seek the less exalted goals of ordinary politics nor exercise mundane forms of power with any grace.

Trotsky's conversion to Bolshevism was a betrayal of his entire previous career: He betrayed the conciliationism that he had pursued more consistently than any other Russian Social Democratic leader; and he betrayed his own insights of 1903–1904 about Lenin and Bolshevism when he became a zealous Jacobin. Recognition of certain imperatives of revolutionary politics—centralized party organization, monolithic control, the repression of opposition—overwhelmed his earlier principles and insights. Although at the time he could not see it, in his own way he was acting like Chernov—the difference being that Chernov had thrown in with the losing side. Trotsky too had become a politician, someone interested in winning power. If victory could not be gained without a political organization and if the political organization that best served his politics happened to be Lenin's, then he would have to extol organizational forms and a style of leadership he had earlier anathematized. The allure of a great revolution, a full-blooded socialist revolution spreading from Russia to Europe, and he its great tribune was overwhelming.

TROTSKY'S LEADERSHIP of the Bolsheviks in the Soviet seemed for a moment to shift the party's center of gravity. His bold maneuvers brought things to a head within a few days of his return. On September 9 he pushed through a vote of no confidence in the Soviet Presidium, another clear signal of the Bolsheviks' growing strength in Petrograd. By September the party that stood for all power to the soviets had majorities in both Petrograd and Moscow. In mid-September Lenin, still in hiding in Finland, sent two letters to the Central Committee calling for a seizure of power. The letters sounded feverish. The CC feared that Lenin would subject the Bolsheviks to all of the misery of the July repression again by pursuing still another adventure.

Lenin was not only trying to catch the tide of Bolshevik popularity. He also feared that Kerensky's latest maneuvers might simply revise the forms of bourgeois hegemony. At the beginning of September Lenin had experienced a fleeting mood of reconciliation, when the successful cooperation of all socialists against Kornilov had inspired him to write "On Compromises." In this article he called for a return to the slogan "All Power to the Soviets" and for a government of Mensheviks and SRs responsible to the soviets. Only for the moment it might be possible to effect a peaceful transfer of power to the "petit-bourgeois" socialists. Even before he sent the article to press, Lenin added a final paragraph, suggesting that the moment had probably passed. In any case, Lenin did not hide his intentions. He wrote: "Our party, like any other political party, strives for political supremacy *for itself*. Our goal—is a dictatorship of the revolutionary proletariat."[5] Once he became convinced that Kerensky, the Mensheviks, and the SRs were conspiring to prevent such an outcome, his attitude shifted abruptly. Kerensky's reorganization of the government and the call for a Democratic Conference by the Mensheviks and the SRs triggered the response.

The Kornilov movement had pushed the Mensheviks and SRs to the left and created even greater divisions among them. They would no longer sit with the Kadets in the same government, yet they would fight Bolshevik ultrarevolutionism to the bitter end. Better Kerensky's new coalitions and political bric-a-brac than Lenin's deadly thrust for power. With each day their room for maneuvering decreased, and defections to bolshevism increased. The Menshevik and SR leadership decided upon an all-socialist Democratic Conference to be convened on September 14, the preliminary to a "pre-parliament" scheduled for October. To all appearances, these were steps towards an exclusively socialist government and therefore movement in the right direction from a Bolshevik point of view. However, by mid-September Lenin would no longer tolerate any efforts to snatch power away from the Bolsheviks. His call for immediate insurrection anticipated the outcome of the Democratic Conference. It did not yield the expected commitment to purely socialist government. Rather, it offered another improvisation, another evasion of Soviet power—the Council of the Republic or "pre-parliament."

The maneuvering at the Democratic Conference and the notion of a pre-parliament created new occasions for splits within the Bolshevik Central Committee. In another of those curious reversals of roles that occur so often in political careers (recalling the Trotsky-Kamenev fight on the Viennese *Pravda*), Kamenev now began to behave in a more conciliatory manner toward the Bolsheviks' "petit-bourgeois" opponents. In September Kamenev fended off Lenin's radical proposals, whereas Trotsky resumed his role as Lenin's big stick—the role that he had abandoned long ago in 1903. Lenin's two letters to the Central Committee ("The Bolsheviks Must Seize Power" and "Marxism and Insurrection"), initiated the end game of the revolution of 1917. They had such an inflammatory character—in the light of the experiences of July—that by a vote of six to four (with six of the sixteen present evidently abstaining) the CC decided to burn all but one copy of each letter. Although they voted against Kamenev's resolution rejecting Lenin's proposals and asking that Lenin support his ideas in a fuller statement about the current situation, Lenin's colleagues asserted their authority to prevent what he aimed at from occurring.

The minutes of the meeting of September 15 are very brief and devoid of the dramatic content provided by memoirs. The sixteen party leaders present (including Trotsky, Kamenev, Stalin, Sverdlov, and Bukharin, but not Zinov'ev) were stunned by Lenin's demands because they seemed to come at a moment when things were already moving in the right direction. The crucial part of the two letters was Lenin's demand that the Bolsheviks immediately begin agitation in the factories and barracks and his sketch of the process of insurrection itself—his plea that they treat insurrection as an art. Lenin had had enough of "parliamentary cretinism." His missives of September and October present a multitude of reasons for an immediate insurrection, some of which can be seen as quite realistic in retrospect, others a bit feverish. He presented the bogeyman of a separate peace, a German invasion, and the surrender of Petrograd (which, out of aversion for the Russian chauvinism implied in the change of name, he always referred to as "Peter") by the Kerensky regime, or possibly a new Kornilov. The results would be equally disastrous. On the other hand, he offered the glittering prospect of a truce with Germany in the event of a successful insurrection. Such arguments probably had little weight compared to Lenin's demand that they start an immediate insurrection at a moment when conciliation with the other socialist parties seemed possible. He believed that an immediate burst of agitation in the factories and barracks, plus an artfully executed insurrection, could carry the Bolsheviks to a virtually bloodless victory.

Although Lenin hurled thunderbolts against the Democratic Conference and pre-parliament, the Bolsheviks seemed to be charmed by parliamentary cretinism. As a new Bolshevik, Trotsky found himself caught between Lenin's demands and the CC's resistance to them, a rather difficult position for a new recruit. On September 21 Trotsky cast his lot with Lenin by opting for a boycott of the pre-parliament. He had no interest in supporting debating bodies other than the Soviet, where he held sway. Trotsky thus supported Lenin, but did not follow all of his prescriptions, a rather typical posture for Lenin's colleagues. When the mutual recriminations of the contenders for power broke out in 1923, they all had stories to tell about each other's sins against Lenin in 1917. The deep split in the CC shows dramatically in the 9 to 8 vote to boycott the pre-parliament, a vote in which Trotsky carried the majority. However, a solid majority of the Bolshevik delegates to the Democratic Conference supported Rykov and Kamenev, who were for participating, and Trotsky retreated to the position that the matter should be decided at the Second Congress of Soviets—once again revealing a desire to strengthen the authority of the Soviet.[6] In any case, Lenin appreciated his new ally's support for the boycott.

Trotsky's motives were no doubt different from Lenin's. As he rose to a position of leadership in the Petrograd Soviet—actually taking over the chairmanship, just as he had in 1905—Trotsky began to guard jealously the primacy of the Soviet as the vehicle for the legitimation of the revolution. In his speech to the Soviet on September 25, after the creation of the new Presidium, he sounded very little like a Bolshevik:

> We are all people with party affiliations, and in the conduct of our work we will no doubt cross swords more than once. But we will conduct the business of the Petrograd Soviet in a spirit of the rights and full freedom of all factions, and the hand of the Presidium will never suppress the minority.[7]

Although Trotsky's chivalric speech seems like a bogus gesture in retrospect, given Trotsky's conversion into a super-Bolshevik, at the time it was probably an authentic expression of his intentions, of his longstanding penchant for conciliation, not to speak of his sense of justice and fair procedures. Trotsky did not create an exclusively Bolshevik Presidium. In addition to three Bolsheviks, he appointed two SRs (Chernov, one of them) and a Menshevik, to Lenin's disgust. We can be certain that Trotsky was intent on demonstrating that he was too honorable to deal with opponents the way Bolsheviks had been dealt with by the Provisional Government after the July days. Perhaps Trotsky (although not fully conscious of it) also meant to communicate that he was not really a sectarian Bolshevik like Lenin. Whatever the case, later Trotsky in the service of the revolution betrayed the oath uttered on September 25. Revolutionary politics and chivalric codes are a particularly unsuitable match. It was easy to forget that, to feel a surge of romantic magnanimity as well as a secure sense of destiny, when assuming for the second time the mantle of Soviet authority.

It was as if history had created the Soviet especially for him, as his revolutionary stage. Trotsky would champion its role against Lenin's insistent demand that they bypass everything, go straight to the factories and barracks, and make a violent seizure of power the symbolic center of the revolution. Lenin had long ago lost his faith in deliberative bodies that he did not control. To the devil with parliamentary forms. Even the Bolshevik slogan calling for a constituent assembly was beside the point. Lenin *knew* that the majority of workers, soldiers, and poor peasants were for the Bolsheviks—that was enough. The Bolsheviks were going to take power at the head of the proletariat and poor peasantry. Nothing else really mattered. Trotsky, however, had in mind a revolutionary spectacle in which he, at the head of the Petrograd Soviet, would preside over the proletariat's assumption to power. The Second All-Russian Congress of Soviets, scheduled for October 20, would be exactly right for historical symbolism, for the climax of the revolutionary drama and Trotsky's apotheosis in it. Thus, even Trotsky abetted the delay of the insurrection. Kamenev, Zinov'ev, and others who feared a premature insurrection and still believed in conciliation with the other socialist parties tried to subvert Lenin's plans. Trotsky stalled in order to set the revolutionary stage properly for dramatic and symbolic purposes—and to assure himself a starring role.

In retrospect, Lenin's preferred method, an act of force against the latest coalition government, actually supplemented Trotsky's symbolism of Soviet legitimacy and power. Furthermore, Lenin had nothing to lose if things were to ripen at the moment of the convening of the Second All-Russian Congress of Soviets. It was he, after all, who had initially launched the campaign for all power to the soviets. His strong urge for a violent revolution, it turned out, might carry more meaning at the symbolic level than as a military action. An insurrection, if properly managed, could have much more symbolic value than a victory by ballot. Any revolutionary instinctively knew that without the seizure of some symbolic objective and the spilling of blood, the revolution would be somehow incomplete. In the weeks ahead Trotsky would be able to carry out his plan and Lenin's simultaneously. No one could wish for a finer conjunction of symbolisms than the one Trotsky would stage-manage in Lenin's behalf, but in late September and early October the delay infuriated Lenin.

TROTSKY'S APPROACH seemed to be winning out during the last days of September and the beginning of October. The October 20 date seemed close enough for most. After all, the slogan of all power to the soviets was already six months old. Why should a few weeks more matter? Time slipped by without any preparation for insurrection on the part of the Central Committee. Lenin bombarded them with invective-laden letters, articles, expansions and clarifications of his position, some of which were suppressed, edited, or had their publication delayed by the editors of the central organ—all familiar procedures for Lenin's colleagues when he went overboard. He tried to find alternative means to achieve his end. On September 29 he even tendered his resignation from the CC and threatened to agitate among the rank and file. Needless to say, it was a gesture designed for the maximum effect—but not merely a gesture. Although he did not follow through on his "resignation," Lenin did bypass the CC and stir up the ranks.[8] Such actions clarify Lenin's political modus operandi: No less than the Soviet, the party was an instrument. He would bypass the very institutions he had created and promoted if they would not serve him personally in a crucial matter. On October 3 the harrassed CC invited him to Petrograd. Finally, he decided to leave his hiding place in Finland and confront his colleagues directly.

Lenin's epistolary campaign succeeded to the extent that his desires became known to party circles beyond the Central Committee and Petrograd. Given the food shortages in the cities, anxieties about the war, and fear of another Kornilov-style attack, there was a considerable amount of flammable material for Lenin to ignite. Lenin's pressure began to work even before his arrival in

Petrograd on October 7.[9] Trotsky was probably galvanized as much by the Provisional Government's plan to abandon Petrograd for Moscow in view of German military pressure as by Lenin's impending arrival. Time might be growing short. With Lenin's footsteps near, on October 5 the CC decided to reverse itself and stage a dramatic walkout at the opening of the pre-parliament, for which Trotsky drafted a declaration. It was nothing less than a signal that in order to "defend" the revolution, the Bolsheviks were going directly to the people. On October 7 Trotsky read it to an incredulous and hostile audience.

The pre-parliament, a body of roughly 500 selected from the larger Democratic Conference, met in the Mariinskii Palace. The socialists commanded a majority, with the SRs having the largest single bloc, 120 delegates. The Bolsheviks had sixty-six delegates and the Mensheviks sixty. The "bourgeoisie" numbered 156, of which about one half were Kadets. The presence of nonsocialists no doubt eased Trotsky's task. His concluding words, the signal for the Bolshevik walkout, aroused a storm of indignation:

> Petrograd is in danger! The people is in danger! The government intensifies this danger. The ruling parties help it. Only the people by their own efforts can save themselves and the country. We turn to the people. All power to the Soviets! All land to the people! Long live a timely, honorable, and democratic peace! Long live the Constituent Assembly![10]

Trotsky's language actually avoided the most inflammatory Bolshevik slogans about a dictatorship of the proletariat and the poor peasants. He said not a word about insurrection. Indeed, he blunted the most extreme Leninist formulations by holding up the *legal* framework for popular power: the soviets and the long-awaited Constituent Assembly. Yet in that context Trotsky was also saying, "On guard! We are going into the factories and barracks." It was the symbolic point of no return. The Bolsheviks filed into the street, followed by the curses of the delegates.

Things now began to unfold rapidly. With each day some sort of attack upon Petrograd seemed closer. Now Lenin pled with his party to have the insurrection coincide with the meeting of the Congress of Soviets of the Northern Region, scheduled for October 11–13. However, even his presence in Petrograd did not achieve the desired outcome. Lenin met with his foot-dragging colleagues on the Central Committee on October 10–11, the famous meeting where they voted formally to recognize "that an armed insurrection is inevitable and has fully ripened."[11] In most respects the ten-to-two vote merely signified submission, for the die had already been cast. It did not yield a timetable or blueprint. It simply called for immediate practical measures. All of those present (including Trotsky and Stalin) but Kamenev and Zinov'ev voted for Lenin's resolution. Seven of the twelve entered a Political Bureau. Lenin wanted Zinov'ev and Kamenev on the Politburo, in spite of their rejection of his resolution. However, far from being coopted, they continued to campaign against the decision.

Lenin had demonstrated once again his personal preeminence in the party.

Even if he could not have an insurrection on command, with every man running to battle stations, he got something reasonably close to that. He reinvigorated the process of polarization among the socialist parties after his brief mood of compromise. For him compromise did not signify conciliation; it was a tactic for the moment, until the next struggle, the next polarization. Historians, alas, have no laboratory for measuring the impact of individuals on history. But all students of October are impressed by Lenin's singular importance, his role as revolutionary gadfly. All of the other actors, including Trotsky, had to react to his initiatives, whatever their merits. When writing the history of the revolution Trotsky gave Lenin his full due, and perhaps slighted his own contribution. In the days that followed Lenin went back into hiding, and Trotsky played the major role in organizing and executing the armed insurrection—an insurrection that might not have occurred without Lenin's prodding. It is now called the Great October Revolution.

29

October 1917

DURING THE period between the first days of October and the "storming" of the Winter Palace, the residence of the Provisional Government, Bolshevik party organizations sent their agitators into the field to test the mood of the workers, soldiers, and peasants. As usual, the reports were filtered through party operatives with their own sense of the situation, but information about the mood of workers, soldiers, or peasants seems less important than the will to power generated by Lenin's prodding. Bolshevik control of the major soviets played a crucial role in convincing waverers that the time had come to transfer power to the soviets. The situation was far better than it had been in July, when the Bolsheviks, then a minority in the soviets, tried to base their authority on street demonstrations. In October they controlled the Presidium of the Petrograd Soviet. Instead of having to win the Soviet over by demonstrations, as in July, the Bolsheviks through liaison with Trotsky could use it to further their plans. Finally, given the German military operations threatening the capital, the government's efforts to transfer troops from the garrison in the capital, and the threat of evacuation—all of which looked like maneuvers to aim a blow at the revolutionary nerve center of Russia—the actions of both the Bolsheviks and the soviets could be seen as much as *defense* of revolutionary Petrograd as preparation for a coup d'état. The spectacle of the defense of the revolution by its legitimate institutions gave Lenin's party a psychological advantage. The memory of the Kornilov episode helped immeasurably.

During October 11–13 Trotsky pulled out all stops in his rhetoric of defense in a series of speeches delivered at the Congress of Soviets of the Northern Region. In an un-Bolshevik gesture of complete openness, he intoned: "Our government can run from Petrograd, but the revolutionary people will not leave Petrograd; it will defend it to the last. Petrograd, as it is said in the Evangels, is 'a city on a hill,' there is for all to see. Everyone knows what we are thinking and doing."[1] There was only one way to forestall the machinations of the Provisional Government and save the revolution: a transfer of power to the soviets. The new soviet government would bring about a truce and then an honorable peace, transfer all of the landlords' estates to the peasants, and lay hold of the goods of the wealthy. It would convene the Constituent Assembly. However, Trotsky directed the attention of the delegates to the Second All-Russian Congress of Soviets. That, too, had to be defended against efforts to wreck it. Trotsky heightened the mystique of the upcoming Congress by portraying it as a target of evil designs.

The Petrograd Soviet had started to prepare itself for "defense" on October 9 by authorizing the creation of a Military Revolutionary Committee, which only began to function a week later. Trotsky, a persistent champion of legitimacy and procedures, now became associated with the armed force of the uprising. At first he did not seem to want to use that force to seize any particular objective. The Bolshevik plans (although no precise blueprint or timetable existed yet) for an "action" against the Provisional Government were an open secret, and now it was rumoured that the Petrograd Soviet would be involved. On October 18 Trotsky promised a session of the Petrograd Soviet that no decisions would be made in secret and that "no armed actions have been set by us."[2] To the amusement of the delegates, Trotsky read the Bolsheviks' alleged plan of battle published by Potresov in a Menshevik daily. For those who knew about Lenin's sketches toward the art of insurrection and discussions underway in the Bolshevik Military Organization, it was no joke. Trotsky reiterated his theme of defense. If the Soviet were *forced* into action by an attack, then the mass of workers and soldiers supporting it would reply with a "merciless" counterattack. Of course, Trotsky knew that the contest was already underway. It was a war of maneuver at this point. At some later moment defense might be transformed into offense. However, Trotsky evidently preferred not to launch an offensive.

Trotsky's openness and his defensive posture contrasted with Lenin's more conspiratorial and aggressive one, and after Lenin's death, when writing about his statement of October 18, Trotsky claimed that Lenin and he had discussed it afterwards at a meeting. The self-justifying account nonetheless admits that Lenin had been suspicious about Trotsky's posture. That is not surprising. Lenin trusted only himself to carry through the revolution in proper fashion. It is Trotsky's guilty conscience that is interesting.

> I remember that I was very curious to learn what had been Lenin's reaction to the "defensive" character of the speech I made at the session of the Petrograd Soviet. I had branded as false all the rumors according to which we were preparing an armed uprising for October 22 (which was "The Day of the Proletarian Soviet"); at the same time I had warned that we would meet every attack against us with a merciless and resolute counterattack. When I saw Vladimir Il'ich it struck me he was in a rather serene and confident mood, and, I would say, he was less suspicious. He not only had nothing critical to say about my speech, he even approved of it, considering its defensive tone useful as a means to lull the vigilance of the enemy. He, nevertheless, kept on shaking his head and asking: "Won't they forestall us? Won't they attack all of a sudden?" I was trying to prove that from now on everything would go on almost automatically. During that conversation, or at least part of it, Comrade Stalin was present, if I am not mistaken.[3]

Much of the evidence suggests that Trotsky was playing a double game. If he could simply overawe his opponents by thundering from the rostrum of the Soviet and displaying its growing military support, then he could avoid a bloody Bolshevik-led action against the Provisional Government. Power could be transferred smoothly; fewer non-Bolshevik socialists would be alienated. On the other hand, by working jointly with the Bolsheviks through the Military Revolutionary Committee of the Soviets, in the event of a Bolshevik coup he could satisfy Lenin that he had served the party well and claim that his earlier legalistic, defensive approach to Soviet power was merely a screen for the insurrection.[4] Trotsky had not completely abandoned his old ways. He knew how powerful the urge toward unity with other left-wing socialists remained, even among many Bolsheviks, and left open the possibility of conciliation with other socialists at the Second Congress of Soviets. However, if the Bolshevik method prevailed, he would be a good party member, serving the party behind the facade of Soviet openness and legality.[5]

During the period between October 10 and the meeting described by Trotsky, Lenin continued to berate his followers for failing to carry out the insurrection and demanded that they do so before the Second Congress of Soviets. He found himself directly subverted by Kamenev and Zinov'ev and indirectly by the entire Central Committee. The Military Organization, so zealous before the July days, now dragged its feet. Lenin began to recognize the value of connecting the uprising with the Soviet and not merely Bolshevik organizations. Once the Military Revolutionary Committee of the Soviet had been created, he understood that by connecting leading members of the Bolshevik Military Organization to the MRC, he would be in a position to put pressure on both to mount the insurrection. Against the prevailing opinion of most Bolsheviks, who were well attuned to the mood in the capital, Lenin wanted the destruction of the Provisional Government to be a fait accompli before the convening of the Second Congress of Soviets. He wanted the overthrow of the government to be seen as a Bolshevik victory and suspected all delaying tactics as forms of conciliationism. A great deal hinged on Trotsky's behavior. Lenin watched this former "Judas" and arch-conciliationist carefully. He remembered well the Second Party Congress in 1903. During the last days before the Second Congress of Soviets, now postponed until October 25, Trotsky showed the zeal of a man not only pursuing his own destiny but acting under the spur of another's will and the pressure of events.

Trotsky's feverish activity during the period October 18–25 made him the most prominent figure in the struggle between the Petrograd Soviet and the Provisional Government for control of the garrison and the strategic points in the city. Although he did everything to gain the loyalty of the troops and to arm Red Guards to defend the Soviet, he also carefully avoided the use of force. It was all done through Trotsky's powers of persuasion and the authority of the Soviet. No one knew the mood in the capital better than Trotsky; no one was in a better position to affect that mood. Preparation for the transfer of power occurred more or less as Trotsky had imagined it would: At crucial moments he appeared on the scene of action with a burst of oratory, which won over another constituency and placed more force at the disposal of the Soviet without a shot being fired.

In the final assessment, although Lenin provided the push, his own approach to the insurrection had little to commend it. From his hysterical calls for the arrest of the Democratic Conference to his efforts to plan an attack force from outside Petrograd, Lenin's behavior reveals a man not in his element. By contrast, Trotsky showed an extraordinary ability to exploit the circumstances as they arose. Trotsky played a key role in making the garrison an instrument of the Soviet: He acquired arms for the workers' militia and Red Guards; he achieved a bloodless capture of the Peter and Paul Fortress on the day before the uprising by the force of persuasion; and he inspired an almost religious fervor in the capital in service of Soviet power. During the days before October 24 Trotsky, Lunacharskii, Kollontai, Volodarskii, and others—the most popular agitators in Petrograd—preached Soviet power to huge crowds in the Cirque Moderne and the House of the People. Sukhanov captured one such moment, a speech delivered by Trotsky to a packed audience of 3,000 at the House of the People on October 22, the "Day of the Petrograd Soviet." It was one of those rapturous moments when Trotsky and his audience achieved a sort of fusion:

> All round me was a mood bordering on ecstasy. It seemed as though the crowd, spontaneously and of its own accord, would break into some religious hymn. Trotsky formulated a brief and general resolution, or pronounced some general formula like "we will defend the worker-peasant cause to the last drop of our blood." Who was—for? The crowd of thousands, as one man, raised their hands. I saw the raised hands and burning eyes of men, women, youths, soldiers, peasants, and—typically lower-middle-class faces. . . . Trotsky went on speaking. The innumerable crowd went on holding their hands up. Trotsky rapped out the words: "Let this vote of yours be your vow—with all your strength and at

any sacrifice to support the Soviet that has taken on itself the glorious burden of bringing to a conclusion the victory of the revolution and of giving land, bread, and peace!" The vast crowd was holding up its hands. It agreed. It vowed. . . . Throughout Petersburg more or less the same thing was going on. Everywhere there were final reviews and final vows. Thousands, tens of thousands and hundreds of thousands of people. . . . This, actually, was already an insurrection. Things had started . . .[6]

At few major turning points in history had so many people responded to the direct power of the spoken word. It made Lenin's emphasis upon military technique and the use of force seem beside the point. Lenin was right to this extent: There were indeed people who were ready to use any subterfuge in order to prevent the seizure of power. The SR leader, A. R. Gots, on the night of October 24 called for the dispatch of troops from the front in the name of the Presidium of the Central Executive Committee of the Soviet—a Presidium whose de facto authority no longer existed. It did not matter. Nor did it matter when the few reliable units at the disposal of the Provisional Government made their move against the Military Revolutionary Committee and the Bolsheviks during the early morning of October 24. Kerensky decided to stop the usurpation of power carried out in the name of the Soviet, but it was already too late. Trotsky, the MRC, and Bolshevik agitators, with help from the left-wing SRs and Anarchists, had won the minds of the soldiers, sailors, and workers in the areas crucial for a seizure of power. They took back what the government troops had seized on October 24 and accomplished a virtually bloodless takeover of the capital. The insurrection so far was occurring according to Trotsky's scenario—as a defensive action.

DURING THE late afternoon of October 24, still in hiding in the apartment of M. V. Fofanova, Lenin learned from her that the bridges in Petrograd were being raised. This alarming news inspired him to ask permission to leave hiding and go to Smol'nyi. Unaware that the insurrection was already underway, Lenin wrote an emotional letter revealing both his ignorance of the situation and his frantic mood and told Fofanova to deliver it to Krupskaia. On the very eve of the Second All-Russian Congress of Soviets, with the balance of force clearly in favor of the Soviets, Lenin was demanding an armed insurrection with undiminished ferocity, almost hysterically. It was not a matter of defending the Congress of Soviets—the people themselves had to be defended! He sent a letter to the district committees calling for immediate mobilization of all of the available military units to put pressure on the Military Revolutionary Committee of the Soviet and the Bolshevik Central Committee. It did not matter what institution seized power.

If we seized power today, it would not be against the Soviets but for them. The seizure of power is the business of insurrection; its political goal will be clarified after the seizure. It would be fatal or formalistic to await an uncertain vote on October 25; the people have the right and duty to decide such issues not by voting, but by force; the people have the right and duty at a critical moment of the revolution to direct its representatives, even its best representatives, and not to wait for them. The history of all revolutions has shown this, and it would be an immeasurable crime for revolutionaries to let slip the moment knowing that on them depends the *salvation of the revolution,* the offering of peace, the salvation of Peter [Petrograd], salvation from hunger, the transfer of land to the peasants. The government is wavering. It has to be finished off, come what may! Delaying the action is akin to death.[7]

Lenin sounds like a man who did not really believe in the correlation of social forces. Rather, he sounds like someone who believed that revolutionary situations were fragile, evanescent, and that armed bodies of men with correct military technique determined the fate of revolutions. He also showed little respect for the deliberative body in whose name the revolution was presumably occurring. His frantic desire to have the revolution before the Congress of Soviets makes it quite clear that the soviets had none other than instrumental value for him. To be sure, he had to appeal to something. In the absence of any reliable instrument he could always appeal to the armed people. According to Trotsky, the letter of October 24 was sent to the district committees. Thus, until the uprising itself Lenin used every means at his disposal to circumvent the Central Committee and simultaneously to put pressure on it. Not content with the letter alone and unsatisfied with the information he got from Fofanova and Krupskaia, Lenin decided to throw caution to the winds and leave for Smol'nyi despite the warnings of the Vyborg district committee. When Fofanova arrived with her last message for Lenin shortly before 11:00 P.M., she found a note he had left in her dark and empty apartment. Accompanied by his bodyguard, Rakh'ia, he was en route to Smoln'yi, the headquarters of the Bolsheviks and the home of the Petrograd Soviet.[8] Lenin arrived there near midnight to confront his field commanders.

As events unfolded on October 25, it was clear that the defensive approach worked quite well and that Trotsky had done an excellent job of avoiding precipitate action and bloodshed, but Lenin remained furious. It had to be done the right way—by the use of force. The Winter Palace had to be stormed, the government captured by troops under Lenin's command. And it should be done before the Second Congress of Soviets declared that it had taken power. One begins to wonder at Lenin's hysterical demands beginning on the morning of October 25, when he resorted to every possible threat to spur the military action against the Winter Palace. Did he sense that Trotsky was winning— that he had been pushed aside, his own role diminished by Trotsky's management of the revolutionary process at the crucial moment? Was he reliving the trauma of 1905? Did he fear that Trotsky would let victory slip away? Or was he expressing a professional revolutionary's sense of how to administer the coup de grace? Probably it was all of these.

SHORTLY AFTER his arrival at Smol'nyi Lenin had an impromptu meeting with roughly half the members of his Central Committee to discuss the formation of a new government. This meeting, about which little is known due to the absence of any stenographic notes or summary, determined the name of the future government: the Council of People's Commissars.[9] Trotsky's account of the meeting is brief, and only he and Lenin appear as dramatis personae.

> The power is taken over, at least in Petrograd. Lenin has not yet had time to change his collar, but his eyes are wide-awake, even though his face looks tired. He looks softly at me, with that sort of awkward shyness that with him indicates intimacy. "You know," he says hesitatingly, "from persecution and a life underground, to come so suddenly into power. . . ." He pauses for the right word. "*Es schwindelt*," [it's dizzying] he concludes, changing suddenly to German, and circling his hand around his head. We look at each other and laugh a little. All this takes only a minute or two; then a simple "passing to next business." The government must be formed. We number among us a few members of the Central Committee. A quick session opens over in a corner of the room. "What shall we call them?" asked Lenin, thinking aloud. "Anything but ministers—that's such a vile, hackneyed word." "We might call them commissars," I suggest, "but there are too many commissars just now. Perhaps 'supreme commissars'?" No, 'supreme' does not sound well, either. What about 'people's commissars'?" " 'People's commissars'? Well, that might do, I think," Lenin agrees. "And the government as a whole?" "A Soviet, of course . . . the Soviet of People's Commissars, eh?" Lenin picks it up. "That's splendid; smells terribly of revolution!"[10]

Not everyone present was delighted at the prospect of creating a new revolutionary government, whatever its title. Kamenev, submitting to party discipline, but in an ironic mood, allegedly said: "Well, if we were stupid enough to seize power, then we have to set up a ministry."[11] The Bolsheviks would undertake that task shortly. First, a number of other ceremonial and symbolic tasks—one of them military—had to be completed.

OCTOBER 25 (NOVEMBER 7) is celebrated as the anniversary of the Great October Revolution mainly because of Lenin's ardent wish to proclaim victory before the convening of the Second Congress of Soviets. Lenin engaged in a small ruse. At roughly 10:00 A.M. on October 25 he issued a statement, "To the Citizens of Russia," informing them that the Provisional Government had been overthrown and that power lay in the hands of an organ of the Soviet, the Military Revolutionary Committee. He had the good political sense to keep Soviet power at the symbolic center of things. However, the Winter Palace and the ministers of the Provisional Government convening there remained untouched. The MRC controlled the capital before Lenin succeeded on the morning of October 25 in getting his balky followers to attack the Winter Palace. Moreover, the "storming" of the Winter Palace, actually a fitful, limping occupation of Rastrelli's spacious monument, was not really completed until the early morning of October 26, when V. A. Antonov-Ovseenko arrested the ministers of the Provisional Government still in the palace. The Winter Palace had already been isolated. It had no significance as a military objective, and the main target, Kerensky, slipped away before the siege began. In any case, Lenin could rely upon the human desire for spectacle and the need to anchor symbolic moments in concrete images of authority, rebellion, struggle —and victory. However delayed and unheroic its capture, the Winter Palace became the Bastille of the Russian Revolution.

Trotsky acted quickly to insure the symbolic primacy of the Soviet at the magic moment of revolutionary victory. On October 25 he called an extraordinary session of the Petrograd Soviet, to which he announced at 2:35 P.M. the fall of the Provisional Government. Like Lenin he did it in the name of the Military Revolutionary Committee of the Soviet. To a thunder of applause Trotsky also announced the dispersal of the pre-parliament. He specifically noted that the Winter Palace had not yet fallen. It would fall any minute. No one was in any hurry to claim victory for the Bolsheviks, as such, in any official forum, but everyone understood whose victory it was. The Bolsheviks had prevented any possible peaceful resolution by means of coalition tactics with nonsocialist parties. There is profound tragedy imbedded in the proud lines that followed:

> They told us that the uprising of the garrison would cause a pogrom and drown the revolution in torrents of blood. For the moment everything has occurred bloodlessly. We do not know of a single casualty. I don't know of a single example in history of a revolutionary movement where such huge masses of people were involved and which took place so bloodlessly.[12]

Trotsky might take pride indeed in the bloodless seizure of power in Petrograd, for which he deserved a great deal of credit, but he and the Bolsheviks would fight a bloody civil war for three years. Trotsky would lose his aversion for bloodshed, and after the Civil War, the revolutionary process would continue and take an even bloodier turn, unforeseen by any of the present leaders.

When Trotsky announced that after the report of the MRC Lenin would speak on the question of power, a storm of sustained applause from the mainly Bolshevik audience interrupted his speech. Trotsky continued, but then another spontaneous burst of applause interrupted him, and he recognized Lenin. Lenin approached the rostrum while Trotsky eulogized his role in the revolutionary movement and ended with a warm greeting. Then Lenin addressed a Soviet gathering for the first time since his brave remarks of June 4, when, to the nervous laughter of the delegates to the First All-Russian Congress of Soviets, he had expressed the willingness of the Bolsheviks to take power. He made one reference to his party at the very beginning of his brief statement, but only claimed that the Bolsheviks had long championed the necessity of the very revolution that had just been completed: a workers' and peasants' revolution. Lenin closed with the words: "We must now set out to build a proletarian socialist state. Long live the world socialist revolution!" On this occasion no one laughed.

If Trotsky had any doubts as to who was perceived as the real leader of the revolution, the ovation Lenin received should have put them to rest. As a token of his submission to Lenin, Trotsky then informed the Soviet that revolutionary commissars would be sent to the front and throughout the country to spread word of the revolution. When someone objected from the floor that he was predetermining the will of the Congress of Soviets, Trotsky replied: "The will of the All-Russian Congress of Soviets was predetermined by the overwhelming fact of the insurrection of Petrograd workers and soldiers that occurred during the night. Now it remains only to consolidate our victory."[13] Just a few days earlier these would have been difficult words for Trotsky to speak; he had been forced beyond another psychological turning point into an even firmer commitment to Lenin's tactic. Lenin, after all, had won.

Lenin, however, would not face the Second Congress of Soviets until the Winter Palace had fallen. He remained anxious and furious throughout the day. According to accounts, he paced the floor of a side room in Smol'nyi like a caged animal, scrawled note after note demanding immediate action, and hurled exorbitant threats at his cowed colleagues.[14] To Lenin the delay seemed interminable. Trotsky's account of the capture of the Winter Palace in *The History of the Russian Revolution* leaves little doubt that common soldiers conspired to thwart Lenin's will. Few evidently wanted to participate in a bloody spectacle. The labyrinthine buildings swallowed up hundreds of occupiers without any resolution to the conflict. Only in the early hours of the morning of October 26 did Antonov-Ovseenko arrest the cabinet members in the Winter Palace.

The opening of the first session of the Second Congress of Soviets was delayed until 10:40 P.M. There were almost 400 Bolsheviks among the roughly 650 voting delegates. The noise of artillery bursts around the Winter Palace (the gunners only managed two hits—one wonders why) could be heard by the delegates in the crowded meeting hall. Odd though it may seem, given his "strike-breaking" activities against the insurrection, Kamenev presided. He had taken part in the Central Committee meeting called on the morning of October 24 to deal with the beginning of the Provisional Government's futile attack on the Bolsheviks and, as noted above, the impromptu session dealing with the question of a new government. Aside from advertising Kamenev's submission to Lenin, his appearance as chairman was a victory for the Old Bolsheviks in the CC and a sign that Lenin's wrath had peaked. Neither Lenin nor Trotsky was present at the beginning of the session. Both were exhausted and trying to snatch a moment of rest. As with the account of their meeting in the early morning, Trotsky, emphasized the intimacy of their new affiliation, their closeness, when he later recollected how he and Lenin lay side by side resting on the floor of one of the rooms in Smol'nyi during the first session of the Congress. Trotsky had to leave his place of rest to reply to the opposition, then returned. There were many interruptions; rest was impossible.

During that dramatic night Trotsky returned again to confront Martov in an episode that became one of the icons of the revolution and yielded Trotsky's most famous and oft-quoted words. A bit earlier in the session the moderate socialists, who saw the implications of Lenin's tactics, had protested the bombardment of the Winter Palace, among whose besieged were the socialist ministers in the Provisional Government. Some delegates walked out. Martov, farther to the left and the most cogent anti-Bolshevik in the assembly, tried desperately to appeal to socialist unity and the spirit of compromise to assure as broad a coalition of socialist parties as possible. The once influential émigré, for a time Lenin's closest colleague, had played an important role in pulling Trotsky away from Lenin in 1903. Then he had treated Trotsky condescendingly and ridiculed his later efforts at conciliation. Now it was Martov who was asking Trotsky, the leader of the Petrograd Soviet and Military Revolutionary Committee, a member of the Bolshevik Central Committee, and Lenin's partner in organizing the capture of Petrograd, for conciliation, for compromise. The powerful scene that took place had depths of meaning that few would plumb, but the deadly emotional charge behind it escaped no one. Trotsky confronted Martov on the rostrum. In the audience John Reed noted Trotsky's "pale, cruel face" and the cool contempt in his voice when he spoke:

> What has taken place is an insurrection, not a conspiracy. An insurrection of the popular masses needs no justification. We have tempered and hardened the revolutionary energy of the Petrograd workers and soldiers. We have openly forged the will of the masses to insurrection, and not conspiracy. . . . Our insurrection has conquered, and now you propose to us: Renounce your victory; make a compromise. With whom, I ask: With whom ought we to make a compromise? With that pitiful handful who just went out? . . . Haven't we seen them through and through? There is no longer anybody in Russia who is for them. Are the millions of workers and peasants represented in this congress, whom they are ready now as always to turn over for a price to the mercies of the bourgeoisie, are they to enter a compromise with these men? No, a compromise is no good here. To those who have gone out, and to all who make like proposals, we must say, "You are pitiful isolated individuals; you are bankrupts; your role is played out. Go where you belong from now on—into the rubbish-can of history."[15]

The clash climaxed fourteen years of revolutionary history, in which Trotsky had tried to create for himself an independent role against either Martov's or Lenin's leadership—and failed. To his ordinary sharpness in debate Trotsky now added a surcharge of cruelty. His crushing of Martov signified his adherence to a new creed: revolutionary power in its most ruthless form. He would be not only a Bolshevik, but an arch-Bolshevik. No one would accuse Trotsky of being a Judas, of failing to act as Lenin's obedient instrument on this occasion; no one would accuse him of softness or conciliationism. He would not repeat his mistake of 1903. Trotsky's description of the episode reveals a great deal about the identity he had repudiated as well as the one he had chosen. He called Martov the Hamlet of democratic socialism who "would make a step forward when the revolution fell back as in July; but now when the revolution was ready for a tiger's leap, Martov would fall back."[16] It was not just the revolution that took a tiger's leap but Trotsky, too. His decisiveness during a series of crises, his plunge into the fray, and his victory permitted him to think of himself as a successful predator. In fact, in the original Russian text Trotsky used the adjective derived from the word "lion" (l'vinyi skachok) rather than Max Eastman's "tiger's leap." Whether consciously or unconsciously playing on his own name, Trotsky affirmed the most primitively grandiose aspect of his identity when writing about his role in the Russian Revolution. Like Lenin he must have felt the intoxication of power during that momentous night.

TROTSKY'S SUCCESS and his new partnership with Lenin changed his orientation dramatically. Alliance with Lenin brought out Trotsky's most ruthless characteristics. However, behind his commanding posture lurked his old insecurities. He had submitted to Lenin reluctantly—there can be no doubt of that; he had preferred words to weapons. Was he really a beast of prey (in the service of revolution, of course) or merely dressed up as one? Did he have the right instincts for leadership? Or was he a "hero with fake muscles," as Stalin had put it years ago? His behavior had an exaggerated, stagey character that only those hypnotized by his eloquence and overcome by the mystique of his revolutionary role failed to see. His need to advertise his affiliation with Lenin hid anxiety about belonging with the Bolsheviks. He had to overcompensate in that area, too. When he assumed his new historical role as Lenin's big stick, Trotsky became a rather dangerous person. In power he would be as hard as he imagined Lenin wanted a Bolshevik to be and as merciless as History and the Revolution, his cruel goddesses, demanded. He would not be a Hamlet, like Martov, or as he himself had been at earlier, painful moments in his own career—moments of indecisiveness, inaction, and breakdown. He would try to be like Lenin, but, of course, he would fail.

STALIN'S ROLE during October was so modest compared to Trotsky's or to the part assigned him later by sycophantic Communist Party historians that it is easy to lose perspective and reduce it to insignificance or like Trotsky to accuse him of being politically "noncommittal." In the following passage in his biography of Stalin Trotsky probably projects some of his own motives, perhaps never fully conscious ones, onto Stalin:

> The cautious schemer preferred to stay on the fence at the crucial moment. He was waiting to see how the insurrection turned out before committing himself to a position. In the event of failure he could tell Lenin, and me and our adherents: "It's all your fault!" One must clearly recapture the red-hot temper of those days in order to appreciate according to its deserts the man's cool grit or, if you like, his insidiousness.[17]

Trotsky himself had stayed on the fence in his own way as long as he could before joining the Bolsheviks. Even after joining he had done everything possible to base the revolution on the Soviet rather than the party and to avoid armed clashes. That, too, was fence-sitting. To be sure, in his commitment to the revolution itself he acted boldly, and once he became a Bolshevik, he never looked back. But in this context, when Trotsky judged others—Martov, Stalin—he cannot be trusted to have judged them fairly, for they were foils for his own heroic role. Trotsky was a courageous man in his way, but not always a generous one. He certainly cannot be expected to have given Stalin his due when writing about October 1917.

In fact, Stalin was at the center of things—in his own way: He was responsible for the party's central organ; he had been named to the seven-man Political Bureau at the Central Committee meeting of October 10, although it never really functioned; at the CC meeting of October 16 he was made a member of a five-man center to deal with military matters, although this group had little significance compared to the MRC of the Soviet; through Rakh'ia he linked Lenin to the CC. Like the other members of the CC, during September and October Stalin had to cope with Lenin's excessive demands and try to keep the furious leader from subverting the CC itself and other party organizations. Like most of the others he voted for Lenin's resolutions and accepted assignments, but showed no haste in fulfilling Lenin's orders. Historians are forced to dwell on these matters because Communist Party historians on one extreme concocted legends of Stalin's partnership with Lenin, and Trotsky (and later others) ran to the other extreme by questioning Stalin's "commitment." The record shows nothing unusual. Stalin appears to be a rather sensible (within the terms of the revolutionary subculture to which he belonged) party man trying to cope with Lenin's demands and the realistic reports coming from party organizations. His behavior had a defensive rather than a noncommittal character.

Stalin did experience a vicarious threat to his own position when Lenin, now joined by Trotsky, attacked Stalin's old comrades in arms. It was like 1912–1914, when against the prevailing mood of conciliation Lenin had forced his party to stand alone. Then Kamenev and Stalin had worked together on *Pravda* to minimize Lenin's damage. But now the stakes were higher and people like Trotsky made things even worse. A dramatic moment occured at a CC meeting on October 20, when in one of his epistolary tirades Lenin (still hiding in Fofanova's apartment) demanded that Kamenev be prevented from sabotaging the plans for insurrection. Stalin tried to defend Kamenev by invoking procedures: They did not have a plenum—only nine members of the CC were present. Sverdlov insisted that the matter be settled immediately. At that meeting Trotsky nervously defended himself against the accusation that he had taken a position akin to Kamenev's in his speech to the Soviet on October 18. He claimed to be camouflaging the Bolshevik position, which Kamenev was exposing. Trotsky backed Lenin and demanded Kamenev's resignation from the CC.[18]

Stalin appealed to the spirit of unity, of *partiinost'*. Why not just demand submission? Why exclude veteran comrades like Kamenev and Zinov'ev from the CC? Stalin lost, Trotsky won. Those present voted in favor of Kamenev's resignation by a vote of 5 to 3, which Stalin took as a vote of no confidence and announced (once again) his resignation from the editorial board of the central organ. It was rejected, but Stalin clearly felt put down. At the next CC meeting on October 21 he tried to salvage what he could by helping to set the agenda for the Second Congress of Soviets. He proposed that Lenin speak on the issues of land, the war, power, Trotsky on the current situation, and he on the nationalities.[19] Stalin was notably deferential to Trotsky. The speaker on the current situation always had a position of prominence on the agenda. Not without tact when his position dictated it, Stalin could always retreat to his specialty: the nationalities problem. He knew how to survive.

Stalin was not present at the emergency CC meeting on the morning of October 24, the moment when the counterattack of the MRC and the party began to unfold in response to Kerensky's raid on the Bolshevik press. Much was later made of Stalin's absence at that meeting. Why was he not there when important tasks in connection with the insurrection were assigned to the party leaders? Was he sulking because of the meeting of October 20, when he had tendered his resignation as editor? This seems unlikely. He had recovered himself and seemed to be functioning as before at the meeting of October 21. He continued to perform his duties as editor. On the afternoon of October 24 he was at Smol'nyi with the other Bolshevik delegates preparing for the Second Congress of Soviets. Furthermore, he was there with the other leaders when Lenin arrived on the night of October 24. He took part in the discussion of the formation of a new government.[20] There seems to be nothing amiss here, except for Stalin's absence at the emergency meeting on the morning of October 24, and no particular significance can be attached to it in the light of Stalin's other activities.[21] His absence was too temporary to be meaningful. How was he to know that the events of October 24 would finish off the Provisional Government? At the very most, Stalin failed to understand how near the end was.

To be sure, Stalin was overshadowed by others and often insecure, but there was nothing new in this. Despite his heroic self-image and ambition, Stalin had learned to be patient about some things, realistic—even a bit stoic. He watched the theoretical titans of the party fall. *Everyone* was vulnerable. Comrades became enemies; enemies became comrades. Lenin was a hard leader to follow. When he lost touch with political reality, Stalin, like the others, disobeyed him. From past experience he knew that if you disobeyed Lenin and lost, he would forgive you so long as you submitted and repented. He not only accepted you back in the fold, he might even promote you. Stalin rode out such moments and always found himself either vindicated or forgiven.

Lenin reinstated his old comrades Kamenev and Zinov'ev, and they seemed almost instantaneously to recover their positions in the party hierachy. Stalin must have felt vindicated when he saw not Trotsky but Kamenev take over the chair at the Second Congress of Soviets. Kamenev, at least, was a Bolshevik of long standing, someone with whom Stalin could identify himself. For the time, at least, he seemed content to play familiar roles—working with the Bolshevik delegates to the Second Congress of Soviets, sustaining his position as the party's expert on the nationalities, editing the central organ, serving as Lenin's troubleshooter on various assignments. Throughout October Stalin remained a good comrade and dutiful party member, by Bolshevik standards.

THERE IS still another aspect to the problem of Stalin's role in October—the long-term psychological one. Did Stalin carry with him a sense of having failed to rise to the occasion in October? Did he envy Lenin and Trotsky their leading roles? Did his desire for an equally exalted place in history affect his later political behavior and inspire some of the monstrous decisions of the period 1929–1953? The answers are all undoubtedly affirmative. However, the events of the years between 1917 and 1927 were equally important in affecting Stalin's later political career. Lenin and Trotsky played a major role then, too. The perpetual insecurity of Stalin and the other veteran Bolsheviks, Lenin's humiliation of them in the so-called "Testament," and Trotsky's lame attempt (indeed, failure) to exploit it put the old Bolsheviks on the defensive. They had to fight off dishonor and political defeat. Perhaps any serious stain on his honor and any powerful rival would have inspired a similar reaction in Stalin. Be that as it may, it was Lenin who humiliated him and Trotsky who tried to exploit this situation. Of course, the Lenin cult that began to emerge even before Lenin's death forced Stalin to create the myth of his close partnership with Lenin. He simply couldn't push Lenin aside. But he would not exercise any such restraint with others.

Stalin would defeat Trotsky and a whole series of rivals, denude them of their achievements, and turn them into traitors and enemies of the people for good measure. Trotsky responded with many brilliant works, among them the monumental *History of the Russian Revolution* and his still useful biography of Stalin. Like Stalin he felt constrained to emphasize his partnership with Lenin. Thus, the rivalry between the two men had vast consequences for the revolution itself, for our image of the revolution, and for the cult of Lenin. Lenin became a magical figure, the source of all revolutionary legitimacy, all revolutionary honor.

30

The Travails of Power

WHEN LENIN and his colleagues got down seriously to the delegation of posts in the new government, they faced some difficult questions. Who had the skills to run a ministry, a bank, a postal service, a police force, an army? Would the proletarians and peasants (whose consciousness, after all, had not undergone a total transformation on October 25) tolerate Jews in high positions? What would foreign relations under a socialist regime be like? All they had to guide them was Lenin's optimism about a new kind of state akin to the Paris Commune and their faith in imminent socialist revolutions in Europe. Everything that they did (or that Lenin made them do) depended upon Marxian historical analysis, as amended by Lenin. Another, more immediate problem: What other parties would play a role in government? On the day of the formation of the Council of People's Commissars Lenin demanded that it be purely Bolshevik. At this point the left-wing Socialist Revolutionaries refused to participate in the new government anyway. They still wanted a coalition of all socialist parties. Of course, Lenin did not want the right Mensheviks and SRs in the government. They had betrayed the revolution. How could he trust them in his government? But he later accepted a coalition with the left SRs, whose agrarian program he had simply copied and who themselves decided to enter the government shortly after the Second Congress of Soviets. Then there was the ticklish question of the imminent elections to the Constituent Assembly. What if the Bolsheviks became a minority party again? Would they give up their power to their rivals in the Constituent Assembly and let them create a constitution for Russia, as had been promised since the February Revolution?

Not only did these vexing questions provide new occasions for splits in the party, the answers to them in the years 1918–1921 laid the basis for the increasing isolation of the Bolsheviks: isolation from other socialists; isolation as an international power; and finally, isolation from the peasantry. The Bolsheviks became urban-based revolutionaries clinging to power at all costs, stumbling from crisis to crisis, living from hand to mouth. That is not to deny the heroic side to their survival, to their tenacious grip on power. Very few contemporary observers believed that the Bolsheviks could govern alone, much less stay in power indefinitely. Lenin's remarkable feat of forming a Bolshevik government and keeping it functioning continues to have tremendous historical ramifications. In the end what emerged was not a more advanced kind of economic, social, and political order, but a novel—and exportable—mixture of revolutionary inspiration and developed methods of single-party dictatorship.

AT 3:00 A.M. on October 26 the delegates to the Second Congress of Soviets were informed that the Winter Palace had been captured. It fell to Kamenev to read the list of arrested ministers. The Congress immediately resolved to take power for the soviets. Lenin did not make his appearance until that night, when it held its final session. Before getting down to the task of his address and offering the first decree, according to John Reed, Lenin gripped the edge of the lectern for several minutes while waves of applause rolled through the densely packed hall and then said: "We shall now proceed to construct the Socialist order."[1] Before the Congress ratified the new government, Lenin presented the decrees on peace and on land. Again according to Reed: "His great mouth, seeming to smile, opened wide as he spoke; his voice hoarse— not unpleasantly so, but as if it had hardened that way after years and years of speaking—and went on monotonously, with the effect of being able to go on forever. . . . For emphasis he bent forward slightly. No gestures. And before him, a thousand simple faces looking up in intent adoration."[2] The decree on peace, designed as much as anything to signal the German proletarian soldiers and those of other belligerent nations that they had an alternative to dying in the trenches for their treacherous imperialist governments, was passed unanimously.

At that moment, all of the years of imprisonment and exile, of acrimonious splits and denunciations, of occasional suicide and frequent despair, of struggle and defeat and now victory were summed up in an impulse both exalted and solemn:

> Suddenly, by common impulse, we found ourselves on our feet, mumbling together into the smooth lifting unison of the *Internationale*. A grizzled old soldier was sobbing like a child. Alexandra Kollontai rapidly winked the tears back. The immense sound rolled through the hall. . . . "The war is ended! The war is ended!" said a young workman near me, his face shining. And when it was over, as we stood there in a kind of awkward hush, someone in the back of the room shouted, "Comrades! Let us remember those who have died for liberty!" So we began to sing the Funeral March.[3]

Sukhanov, retaining his reserve, still believing that the celebration of the revolution was premature, that its leaders had usurped power, nonetheless found himself moved, and he faithfully recorded the spiritual beginning of a new order:

> The whole Presidium, headed by Lenin, was standing up and singing, with excited, exalted faces and blazing eyes. But the delegates were more interesting: they were completely revivified. The overturn had gone more smoothly than most of them had expected; it already seemed consummated. Awareness of its success was spreading; the masses were permeated by the faith that all would go well in future too. They were beginning to be persuaded of the imminence of peace, land, and bread, and even beginning to feel some readiness to stand up positively for their newly acquired goods and rights.[4]

Following this Lenin presented the decree on land. What happened was curious and perhaps revealing of Lenin's psychological state. Lenin had to read the hand-written decree in its original and evidently none-too-neat form. He began to lose his place and, instead of recovering, got even more confused. Finally, he stopped altogether and was rescued by someone who continued the reading. Lenin, who had begun his career as a Marxian expert on agrarian economic and social change, must have experienced great misgivings when he read the land decree. Although the Bolsheviks in theory were nationalizing the land and preparing the way for its large-scale and collective cultivation, in practice they were simply giving it to the peasants to dispose of as they wished. Lenin's party had virtually no control over what happened.

Thousands of peasant villages, containing the vast majority of the population of the old empire, had already begun to seize and redistribute land that they had long coveted. The increase in the amount of land controlled by peasant communes signified an abandonment of the Bolshevik agrarian program. The peasants, led by the left SRs, were accomplishing some of the goals the *narodniki* had fought and died for unsuccessfully since the reign of Alexander II. Now, it was the peasants and the SRs who presented Lenin with the fait accompli. Small-scale, family farming would become more entrenched than ever. Perhaps that is why the decree at first had stuck in Lenin's throat. However, after the reading of the decree and the peasants' own "instruction [nakaz] on the land," an SR document based upon 242 local instructions from soviets of peasants' deputies, Lenin recovered. He made a small, remarkably eloquent and statesmanlike speech designed to placate the left SRs for stealing their thunder and to reassure the peasants.

> Some say that the decree and the instruction were composed by the Socialist Revolutionaries. So be it. . . . And even if the peasants continue to follow the Socialist Revolutionaries and even if they give this party a majority in the Constituent Assembly, then we will say: so be it. Life is the best teacher, and it will show who is right, and let the peasant from one end and we from the other solve this problem. Life will force us to fuse in a single stream of revolutionary creativity. . . . Russia is vast and has a variety of local conditions; we believe that the peasants themselves know better than we how to go about finding the correct solution to problems. Whether it is in the spirit of our program or the SR program—this is not the heart of the matter. The heart of it is that the peasants should be completely assured that the landlords are gone from the countryside, so that the peasants themselves solve all the problems, themselves arrange their own lives.[5]

One begins to sense how far Lenin would go to retain power. He would win the trust of all the peasants, but at the same time coopt his political opponents. Lenin, of course, had no intention of giving up power to the SRs. All of this would become clear in due time.

The last session of the Second Congress of Soviets, stretching well into the early morning of October 27, did not go entirely like a revival meeting. Objections were voiced, accusations made. There was even a vote cast against the land decree. Trotsky, like some revolutionary nemesis, struck down one opponent after another. John Reed described him as "calm and venomous, conscious of power."[6] Trotsky's last foray occurred after Kamenev officially proposed the new government to the Congress. Among the sixteen names were his own, as Commissar for Foreign Affairs, and Stalin's as Commissar for the Nationalities. More objections followed, more last-minute efforts to make the Bolsheviks and the other delegates see reason. Trotsky rose to give an eloquent speech that rendered further opposition hopeless, and toward its end he reiterated the article of faith upon which everything had been undertaken.

> We place all of our hope on this, that our revolution will unleash a European revolution. If the peoples of Europe do not crush the imperialists in an uprising, we will be crushed—that is without a doubt. Either the Russian Revolution raises the whirlwind of struggle in the West, or the capitalists of all countries will strangle our revolution. . . . It is important and necessary to define the method of struggle equally for both external and internal politics. A union of the oppressed anywhere and everywhere—that is our path. The Second Congress of Soviets has worked out an entire program of actions. The entire group, which wishes to realize this program and which in this critical moment is on this side of the barricades, will hear only one greeting from us: Welcome, dear comrades, we are brothers in arms and we are with you to the end.[7]

John Reed, who obviously detected something unwholesome in Trotsky ("confident and dominating, with that sarcastic expression about his mouth which was almost a sneer"), nonetheless gives him his due: "They greeted him with an immense crusading acclaim, kindling to the daring of it, with the thought of championing mankind. And from that moment there was something conscious and decided about the insurrectionary masses, in all their actions, which never left them."[8] When the list of candidates for posts in the new government was read, the names of Lenin and Trotsky received the greatest ovations. They seemed like equal partners to the politically uninformed. The dawn had already risen when the delegates left Smol'nyi. They had created a new government.

When Lenin had canvassed the party leadership in his search for People's Commissars during those hectic days of the Second Congress of Soviets, he found a surprising amount of doubt and hesitancy. Even the supremely self-assured Trotsky held back. His initial intoxication with power did not blur Trotsky's sense of reality to a point where he lost touch with his self-identity. In his autobiography he captured well both the psychological experience of post-victory depression and his coming realization of just who he was and what the situation demanded.

> The conquest of the power brought up the question of my government work. Strangely enough, I had never even given a thought to it; in spite of the experience of 1905, there was never an occasion when I connected the question of my future with that of power. From my youth on, or, to be more precise, from my childhood on, I had dreamed of being a writer. Later, I subordinated my literary work, as I did everything else, to the revolution. The question of the party's conquest of power was always before me. Times without number, I wrote and spoke about the program of the revolutionary government, but the question of my personal work after the conquest never entered my mind. And so it caught me unawares. After the seizure of power, I tried to stay out of the government, and offered to undertake the direction of the press. It is quite possible that the nervous reaction after the victory had something to do with that; the months that had preceded it had been too closely tied up with the preparatory work for the revolution. Every fiber of my entire being was strained to its limit. Lunacharskii wrote sometime in the papers that Trotsky walked about like an electric battery and that each contact brought forth a discharge. The twenty-fifth of October brought the let-down. I felt like a surgeon who has finished a difficult and dangerous operation—I must wash my hands, take off my apron, and rest.[9]

These recollections ring true. Essentially a Marxian critic, a man of letters, a practiced orator, and a dramatist and stage-manager of the October Revolution, Trotsky had not worked out a scenario for himself in power. He had already experienced a fusion of fantasy and reality that few are privileged to achieve, and he hadn't reached his fortieth year. However, the job was not done. Trotsky did not need Lenin to tell him that they were only barely in power, that great travails lay ahead, that the revolution remained in danger. Perhaps Lenin even tried to exploit his sense of duty. Lenin was not about to give up an instrument as useful as Trotsky. An anecdote recorded by Trotsky in his autobiography, although no doubt designed to enhance his status as Lenin's partner and heir, also sounds authentic. The exchange below occurred during February 1918.

"And what," Vladimir Il'ich once asked me quite unexpectedly, during those first days—"what if the White Guards kill you and me? Will Sverdlov and Bukharin be able to manage?" "Perhaps they won't kill us," I rejoined, laughing. "The devil knows what they might do," said Lenin, laughing in turn. [10]

Interestingly, Lenin seems to have had Sverdlov in mind as his replacement in the practical sphere of government and party organization, for Bukharin quite clearly would be the *teoretik* and head of the party press. It should be kept in mind that Lenin posed a question and did not give his own final assessment. As shall be seen, he remained highly ambivalent about Bukharin to the very end. At the very least, the anecdote dramatizes Lenin's refusal to let anti-Semitism affect his policies. Like Trotsky, Sverdlov was a Jew and, despite his Russian pseudonym, unmistakably so, if physical stereotypes that prevailed in that time and place are taken into account. Trotsky and other Bolsheviks, however, would not permit Lenin to ignore the implications of anti-Semitism for the new government and urged him to keep Jews out of sensitive positions. Why not avoid complications? According to Trotsky, on October 26, at the meeting of the Central Committee devoted to the creation of the new government, Lenin proposed that Trotsky become the Chairman of the Council of People's Commissars, since he had been at the head of the Petrograd Soviet when the seizure of power occurred. We have no minutes for that meeting, but, once again, Trotsky's version sounds authentic. Lenin signaled that he understood Trotsky's triumph and had the generosity to recognize Trotsky's work in 1917, as he had in 1905. It was a statesmanlike gesture Lenin could afford to make—although it probably inspired a moment of anxiety in some of those present. Trotsky's resolution to reject the proposal without debate carried. However, Lenin then proposed that Trotsky be given the Commissariat of the Interior, which in Russia traditionally signified internal security. Now it would mean fighting counterrevolution. Trotsky pointed out that his Jewish background would complicate matters. He won that argument too, although the man to whom Lenin entrusted the task of combatting counterrevolution, Felix Dzerzhinskii, was a Pole. In the end Trotsky took the Commissariat of Foreign Affairs, his first assignment on behalf of the new Soviet government headed by Lenin, but he remained Lenin's military troubleshooter during the first days after the revolutionary seizure of Petrograd.

The Council of People's Commissars, in Russian contraction the Sovnarkom, found itself immediately threatened. It was not clear that the rest of the country would support them. Things did not go as well in Moscow, where several hundred were killed in the struggle for the city. Military cadets seized the telephone exchange in Petrograd on October 29 before being crushed, and from south of the city on the next day Kerensky tried to launch an attack, which Trotsky quickly squelched. During the first weeks of Soviet rule the MRC continued to function in defense of the revolution. However, a more serious threat came from within the party's upper ranks. Lenin had seemingly beaten his own Central Committee into submission, but at the first opportunity several members tried to revive the idea of coalition. The heroic mood of October 25–26 not only faded, but was replaced by a sense of the grim reality of the situation: The new regime had isolated itself; no one knew who would support it or for how long. The powerful union of railroad workers threatened to paralyze communications if the Bolsheviks did not negotiate with the other socialists. Civil servants and white collars workers refused to work for the new government. Kamenev, the head of the Central Executive Committee of the Soviet, led the opposition within the CC of the party. The Bolshevik "conciliators" had well-founded anxieties about the course that lay ahead. Lenin and Trotsky had created the illusion of majority rule, but in fact had installed a minority government. They either would have to rule by terror or else bring other parties into a coalition government. After the brief intraparty struggle of October 29–November 2, five CC members—Kamenev, Zinov'ev, Rykov, Miliutin, and Nogin—resigned, and the latter three also resigned their positions in the government. In all, five of the original People's Commissars resigned. Sverdlov replaced Kamenev as the head of the Central Executive Committee of the Soviet.

Lenin's ruthlessness showed throughout. At a meeting of the Bolshevik Petrograd Committee on November 1 he frantically attacked his opposition. Now that they were going to be in a fight for power, Lenin's essential political approach came to the fore. He began to peel away the soft layers of support to get down to a hard core. He wanted people who would be willing to resort to state terror. If this meant reducing his base of support, so be it.

> In Paris, they used the guillotine while we will only take away the food cards of those who fail to obtain them from the trade unions. Thereby we fulfill our duty. And now, at such a moment, when we are in power, we are faced with a split. Zinov'ev and Kamenev say that we will not seize power [in the entire country]. I am in no mood to listen to this calmly. I view this as treason. What do they want? Do they want to plunge us into [spontaneous] knifeplay? Only the proletariat is able to lead the country.[11]

Lenin did not mince words. He was not interested in appealing to the "weary masses" but to the proletarian vanguard. In a sense, he was redefining "vanguard" to include only those who had a will to exclusive power. How could one trust the other parties? "Only we can create a plan of revolutionary work. Only we are capable of waging the struggle."[12] According to his estimate, 99 percent of the workers were behind them. If the CC revolted, he would "go to the sailors"—another signal that he would not hesitate to use force against his own party if it refused exclusive power. No one doubted Lenin's threats. Everyone knew from his past political behavior that he would reconstruct the party on a new basis if he felt it necessary. They also knew that if they submitted and served him well, things would be as before.

Meanwhile, Lenin would use the new people to full advantage. The neophytes would have to prove themselves and in the process would put pressure on the others. Trotsky became one of the "hard" members of the CC. He did not flinch from the notion of exclusive Bolshevik rule and seemed to take to the use of force quite naturally. Angelica Balabanoff, an astute observer, clearly understood how Trotsky, not only a neophyte in the party but a longstanding opponent of Lenin, had to "lean over backward to prove himself a good Bolshevik and an orthodox Leninist."[13] During the crisis over conciliationism at the meeting of November 1 Lenin praised Trotsky to the Petrograd Committee: "Trotsky long ago said that unification is impossible. Trotsky understood this, and from that time on *there has been no better Bolshevik* [Trotsky's italics]."[14] No better Bolshevik than Judas Trotsky! How unpleasant a thought to those who had worked with Lenin since the origin of the Bolshevik faction. The veterans, shamed, humiliated, would usually submit in the end and often return with renewed zeal. Lenin's methods created insecurities, overcompensations, resentments, and mistrust among subgroups within the party oligarchy and ultimately made Lenin the only one who could manage it. Given the crises and cruel decisions that lay ahead, even sometimes he failed to control the party leadership.

As the revolutionary process continued to unfold, Lenin forced all members of the oligarchy to violate what they believed were fundamental Marxian principles and to abandon the course that he himself had set. Always moving and changing, never showing complete trust or giving unqualified support to any of them, at one time or another Lenin alienated all of his colleagues—just as he had done before the revolution. Sverdlov, the supreme Bolshevik organization man, is the exception who proved the rule, though even he at times had to rein Lenin in. Yet the inner circle of the party remained remarkably stable. Trotsky was the only outsider to gain entry. On November 29, when the CC created one of its many ad hoc groups to deal with political emergencies, Lenin was joined by Trotsky, Sverdlov, and Stalin.

The Sovnarkom ruled by decree during the Smol'nyi period of Soviet rule —the period between October 26 and the transfer of the seat of government to Moscow in March 1918. Lenin converted some rooms into an apartment for himself in Smol'nyi and presided over Sovnarkom meetings in his office on the third floor of the former school for girls of the nobility, which between July and October had served as the home of the Petrograd Soviet, Bolshevik party headquarters, and the command post of the insurrection. Within a few weeks the legitimacy of the new regime was called into question. What the Bolsheviks had feared came to pass: the November elections to the Constituent Assembly returned a majority of Right SRs. Of the 707 delegates, 410 were SRs (370 Right SRs, forty Left SRs) and 175 were Bolsheviks.[15] Lenin found himself in a quandary. The revolution had occurred in a vast country with a largely peasant population. The SRs, whether of the Right or the Left, represented the peasants, although like the Marxists they had split over Russia's ripeness for a purely socialist regime. The Bolsheviks had given the peasants what the SRs had promised but failed to deliver. From the Bolshevik point of view—and that of the Left SRs—the delegates elected to the Constituent Assembly by the peasants did not represent the true correlation of forces in the country at the present moment. The Bolsheviks and Left SRs composed their differences on November 15 and then created a transient coalition government of the left, with seven SR members. This was as far as Lenin would go. He did not really trust the SRs; they did not trust him; each side had good reason to be mistrustful.

The dictatorship moved to a higher level during November with the outlawing of the Kadet Party as enemies of the people and the suppression of the oppositional press. It followed in December with the establishment of the Vecheka, better known as the Cheka, an "extraordinary" commission created to deal with sabotage, counterrevolution, and economic crimes under the heading, "speculation." A decisive moment, however, occurred when Lenin decided to disperse the Constituent Assembly after its first meeting on January 5, 1918, putting an end to the "parliamentary cretinism" of his rivals. Within the capital itself few came to the aid of the elected representatives of the people. The Bolshevik action signalled to its opponents that only civil war would decide the issue. The dispersal of the long-awaited Constituent Assembly thus had little immediate impact. Meanwhile, Lenin and his colleagues continued to issue decrees, to elaborate the institutions of the dictatorship, and to formulate their own Soviet constitution.

THE INITIAL decrees of the Soviet had not dealt with the factory workers as such. The regime's behavior toward the constituency in whose name the revolution had occurred deserves comment. Before the October Revolution the Bolsheviks had offered the factory proletariat, among other things, an eight-hour day and workers' control of the factories and had thereby gained the loyalty of a strategically placed constituency. The factory committees that sprang up after the February Revolution had gained de facto control of many factories even before the Soviet government came into being. Powerful anarchist influence had forced the Bolsheviks to move to the Left in order to compete for the allegiance of the workers. The Bolsheviks endorsed the slogan of workers' control during the struggle with the owners and the Provisional Government, but the meaning of "control" became clarified only after the revolution. When the Bolsheviks took power, the struggle between management and the factory committees became their problem instead of that of the factory owners. Lenin took the same instrumental approach to the grass roots workers' organization as to all else. When he had been desperately looking for an alternative to the soviets after the disaster of the July days, he had even suggested the factory committees as a possible instrument of insurrection. Now the factory committees had to be made to perform for the new state, for the Bolsheviks quickly began to nationalize large-scale industry. In keeping with a central tenet of Marxism, the Bolsheviks wanted to increase production. Lenin had no desire to give the workers managerial functions if they did not have the expertise to manage production rationally. Even the draft decree of November 3, which gave its blessing to workers' control, referred to the interests of the new socialist state. Although it would take a while to work out the theory of the new economic system and the structure of management, the handwriting was already on the wall so far as factory committees were concerned.

Very quickly the Bolshevik-controlled trade unions assumed the function of curbing the unruly factory committees, and the problem became one of the nature of the trade union movement, its relationship to the party-state. However, some party leaders in the trade union movement themselves had been infected by anarcho-syndicalist ideas, and they did not submit readily to the centralized managerial institutions created by Lenin and the party. Workers' control haunted the regime until the decisive struggle of 1920–1921 over the trade unions. Once the Soviet regime began to control the entire industrial process, the struggle between the workers and the factory owners backed by the force of the tsarist state became transformed into one between bureaucracies of the party-state headed by their chiefs in the party oligarchy. The workers' fate depended on the outcome. The concern of the party-state with production won out over the brief romance with workers' control, just as the realities of power won out over the idea of a commune state.

The regime would quickly show its willingness to resort to force against the workers themselves. Marxian class definitions became rather fluid. The decision as to who belonged to the vanguard, who had the correct consciousness, depended upon the current views of the party leadership. Party cadres, activists backed by armed men, quickly asserted their control over the factory labor force. Given the late onset of industrialization, its rapid pace, and the artificial speed-up connected with World War I, the Russian factory labor force had close ties with the villages. Many workers hastened to return to their villages after the revolution, some to take advantage of the redistribution of land, others to avoid the food shortages in the cities. A tremendous drop occurred in both the factory labor force and the urban population. Soon, the "class-conscious" Bolsheviks would be resorting to force to keep the workers who belonged to the category of "the weary masses" in the factories. That is not to say that the Bolsheviks alienated the urban proletariat. They continued to inspire their labor constituency and gave it sufficient privileges under the new order to be able to recruit from it a significant army of activists. Only by such recruitment would they, the vanguard, be able to control both the cities and the countryside —to rule the tens of millions who did not belong to the vanguard. The party could and did demand sacrifices in the name of proletarian power—great sacrifices.

31

Crisis: Brest-Litovsk

THE CHARACTER of the new regime became articulated with each day of struggle, each decision. The policy crisis that brought the political careers of both Lenin and Trotsky to abysmal depths in 1918 revolved around the issue of peace with Germany. Lenin, who had seemed like a wild gambler before the seizure of power, now began to think defensively: What strategy would best serve the retention of revolutionary power? To those who looked to Germany for the next phase of revolutionary struggle and proposed revolutionary war on its behalf, Lenin said: "But Germany is still only pregnant with revolution, and we have given birth to a completely healthy child—a socialist republic, which we might kill if we start a war."[1] He had a distinctly parental attitude toward the *Russian* Revolution, and it showed in his first conservative postrevolutionary policy. A sizable gulf began to develop between his theoretical commitments and his policy decisions, but that seemed to trouble him little. Each day that the Bolsheviks retained power represented a victory for Lenin.

The Russian armed forces were in a state of disintegration. Since the February Revolution the destruction of the authority of their officers and Bolshevik propaganda had rendered the army ineffective. Now the lure of the land redistribution powerfully affected the soldiers. Mass desertions occurred; the trenches emptied. Partial demobilization had begun in November. Even before the armistice of December 2 (15), 1917, between Russia and the Central Powers, Russia's military position was hopeless. Its diplomatic position was weak, especially after the dispersal of the Constituent Assembly. The Bolsheviks seemed to be usurpers with a frail and momentary grip on power. Only if the armed forces of the Central Powers showed signs of responding to Bolshevik propaganda, to the fraternization the Bolsheviks hoped would influence the German troops, might there be some hope.

In the absence of this and clear signs of revolution in Europe Lenin would have to make hard choices. He had understood the fragility of the power of the Provisional Government; he knew how vulnerable his own government was. In order to protect it, he would do what he had accused others of plotting: If necessary, Lenin would sign a separate peace; he would give up vast amounts of territory; and he would move the seat of government from its relatively exposed position in Petrograd to the interior, to Moscow. In pursuing these policies, Lenin mercilessly trod on the feelings of his followers. His unsentimental approach permitted him to abandon the city that had become the first base and symbol of Soviet power and to contemplate the dismemberment of the homeland. For Lenin there was no such thing as sacred ground. He would give up territory in order to gain the time needed to consolidate power.

Trotsky's less pragmatic and more pedantic approach made the growing discrepancy between theory and practice painful, but there were immediate reasons for discomfort. As Commissar of Foreign Affairs, Trotsky had responsibility for conducting negotiations with the Central Powers in the border town of Brest-Litovsk. Lenin was pressuring him to sign an immediate separate peace, even though the demands of the Central Powers seemed exorbitant: the detachment of Poland, Lithuania, and western Latvia. On the other hand, the militant faction of the Central Committee, led by Bukharin, believed that the continuation of the war would serve the international cause better. The ultra-revolutionism of the Left Bolsheviks had the same emotional charge as Trotsky's. It harmonized with theory, was more symmetrical with the revolutionary process, and expressed the optimism prevalent among party leaders after a series of victories. But Trotsky probably felt more nervous about opposing Lenin than the Old Bolsheviks did. As was his habit when caught in a double bind, Trotsky resorted to camouflage, to stalling tactics.

The Central Committee of the party began to debate the treaty in earnest on January 11, 1918, with Trotsky on furlough from Brest-Litovsk. The situation resembled October. Trotsky fought on the front line, quite literally in this case, while Lenin tried to direct things from afar. Lenin wanted immediate surrender. Trotsky and the others did not. Lenin feared the effects of decisive military action against the revolution, whereas the left wing of the party feared that the principles of the revolution would be compromised and the revolutionary process in the West curtailed. The Bolsheviks who opposed signing an immediate peace agreement had great faith in the power of revolutionary propaganda and theater. Once the German soldiers were exposed to it, they would go the way of General Kornilov's troops; and the European workers would not tolerate an imperialist attack on the cradle of the new socialist order. Any such assault on the infant Soviet state would inspire revolutionary uprisings in Europe, where worker unrest was already simmering. The spectacle of the revolution in danger would serve again, now on an international scale.

Trotsky pictured himself acting as the great tribune of the revolution, but this time on a world stage. He would convert Brest-Litovsk into an open courtroom in which he would expose the crimes of the imperialist powers. That is what he had done in 1905, when he had faced a tsarist tribunal. A stalling tactic would give Trotsky more time on the stage, more time to spread propaganda—and more time for the European proletariat to arrive at the level of consciousness already achieved in Petrograd. The Bolsheviks could incite the international revolutionary war from a defensive posture, just as they had in Petrograd in October. However, unlike Bukharin and the others, Trotsky did not oppose Lenin vehemently. He worked out a compromise solution in which the Soviet state would neither return to belligerent status nor accept the severe terms dictated by the Central Powers. Trotsky's compromise formula, "neither war nor peace," satisfied the Left, for it left open the possibility of revolutionary war. Even Lenin took heart from an upsurgence in the labor movement in Berlin and Vienna in January. Thus, Trotsky's stalling tactic served both wings of the party for the moment as well as his own tendency to turn revolution into theater. On January 11 his view prevailed in the CC by a close vote of nine to seven.

Between January 11 and Trotsky's return trip to Brest-Litovsk a few days later Lenin extracted from Trotsky a promise that he would sign a peace if it became clear that the Germans would resume military operations. Trotsky did not fulfill the promise—perhaps because he and Lenin had miscommunicated, but more likely because Trotsky, like others, found it unbearable to stand up to Lenin in personal exchange. They later rationalized their "betrayals." Lenin, in effect, wanted him to act in accordance with their private agreement, without party approval. Trotsky, however, decided not to take action without formal approval of the CC, and this would mean stalling until the Germans renewed hostilities and the party decided on a new policy.

Trotsky's approach rested on a calculated gamble that the Germans would not attack a defenseless opponent. If he proved wrong and the Germans resumed hostilities after the three-month armistice, the still-effective German army of more than fifty-eight divisions would be able to move virtually unimpeded from forward bases into the territory of the old Russian empire. Lenin was fully reconciled to the loss of Latvia, Estonia, and Finland. He was even willing to abandon Petrograd. However, the Ukraine, whose independence movement gave the Germans an additional excuse for their designs, presented an enormous problem. The grain supplies of the Ukraine, which the Germans coveted, were crucial for the survival of the new Soviet state. The stakes were very high. On January 28(February 10), 1918, Trotsky announced to the stunned representatives of the Central Powers that Russia was going to demobilize (this merely formalized what had already been going on in stages and was well known to his diplomatic and military opponents) but that he would not sign a peace treaty. On February 17 (all dates are now in the new style due to the change from the Julian to the Gregorian calendar on February 1, 1918) the Germans announced that they were renewing hostilities.

On February 18 the German attack moved forward unimpeded while the Central Committee debated its next move. Now Trotsky sparred with Lenin, still refusing to admit defeat, fending off Lenin's bitter criticism that he had made a game of war, trying to find new ways to win more time before signing a peace treaty. Bukharin defended Trotsky and received his portion of Lenin's anger. In the end, however, Trotsky honored his agreement and voted with Lenin for signing an immediate peace. So far as Lenin was concerned, Trotsky had betrayed him; so far as the left wing of the party was concerned, Trotsky had abandoned them. If Trotsky had voted against Lenin's resolution, the Central Committee would have remained deadlocked. On February 22 Trotsky tried another tack: He sounded the CC on Anglo-French assistance. In effect, he was suggesting that they take a small step toward de facto re-entry into the old alliance. When Bukharin countered that this was tantamount to colonial status and refused support from imperialist powers on principle, Trotsky justified his proposal with reasoning that would serve any unprincipled action: "The state is forced to do that which the party would never do."[2] Lenin showed the spirit of the moment when he inscribed in the meeting's protocols: "I cast my vote for taking potatoes and arms from the bandits of Anglo-French imperialism."[3] Even before the vote on his resolution (which he won by a vote of six to five) Trotsky resigned his post as Commissar of Foreign Affairs. Shortly thereafter, Bukharin in protest against the CC's decisions resigned from the CC and his post as editor of *Pravda*.

After the receipt of the German conditions and the calling of still another CC meeting on February 23 Trotsky continued to argue against Lenin. At each stage Lenin made him pay a bigger price in humiliation. Lenin accused him of revolutionary phrase-making—a cutting remark that recalled earlier insults hurled by the Bolsheviks against Trotsky—and demanded that they accept the German conditions, however severe, without delay or he would resign from the CC and the government. Lenin's ultimatum initially provoked a great deal of resentment, and, although he won, he did not even receive a majority vote. Instead of supporting Lenin, Trotsky abstained. The split in the party worsened. There were more resignations from the government. Trotsky again brought up his own resignation, but agreed to stay in his post until the peace delegation returned from Brest-Litovsk. The incomplete minutes of the CC meeting of February 23 reveal a spirit of acrimony accompanied by desperate efforts to keep the party from the open split Lenin would precipitate unless it submitted to him. Lenin had made it clear to Trotsky that he did not fear a split. He was confident that they would survive it—that the left wing of the party would reenter the fold. Lenin was correct, but in the short run he had to face an open rebellion by the left wing of the party, with Bukharin and the Moscow organization leading it.

On March 3, 1918, the Soviet delegation signed a peace treaty in which they accepted immense losses in territory, population, and resources—losses far worse than those initially demanded by the Central Powers. When Lenin addressed the extraordinary Seventh Party Congress on March 7, he justified the humiliating peace on behalf of the Central Committee. He replied in scathing terms to accusations that they were betraying the revolution and subjected Bukharin to merciless, ironic criticism. In addition, Lenin lashed Trotsky openly for pursuing a costly gamble. Trotsky in rebuttal openly advertised his self-sacrifice for the sake of party unity and suggested that Lenin had acted quite differently. Now, within the context of the Bolshevik party, Trotsky retreated to his old conciliationist stand—a sign of his weakness. Lenin would not permit Trotsky to amend the treaty in any way, all the while suspecting him (and rightly so) of looking for a way to return to the old position. Lenin won, but not without resistance. Trotsky's colleagues tried to defend him against Lenin's reproaches. They failed, but the Congress also refused to vote to condemn Trotsky's actions outright.

In the end he fared reasonably well and received as many votes as Lenin during the elections to the new CC. He had salvaged his honor, but Lenin had not made it easy for him. By emphasizing the stupidity of delay, Lenin burdened Trotsky with the blame for much of the disaster—the loss not only of the Baltic states and Finland but sizable territories in the western and southern part of the old empire. Trotsky obviously could not say openly all that was on his mind and on the minds of the left wing of the party: Lenin's ultimatums had been irresponsible; Lenin had endangered the revolution by using his authority to force the party in a direction in which it did not want to go; Lenin was destroying the chances for an international uprising of the proletariat. However, Trotsky and Bukharin had been unable to assume leadership at a moment when Lenin's authority had been most vulnerable. They failed a crucial test. Lenin passed it, and with each successful struggle he acquired greater credibility as a leader. Trotsky would later have to recant and make a low bow to Lenin's foresight—as would Bukharin.

AT THE fifth session of the Seventh Party Congress, at Lenin's urging they created a commission for revising the party program and changing its name. Since the outbreak of World War I and the disgrace of the German Social Democrats, he had tried unsuccessfully to make the symbolic break. Now he achieved it. There was something relentless about Lenin's pressure. Even when pursuing the unpopular policy of surrender to the Germans, he moved ahead on symbolic and ideological fronts. The Bolsheviks would no longer call themselves "Social Democrats" but "Communists." Lenin continued to show his proclivity for creating unambiguous boundaries around the community of the faithful—and, at least for the moment, both its symbolic and territorial boundaries had shrunk drastically.

With the evacuation of Petrograd on March 12, 1918, Lenin completed another symbolic burning of the bridges. Transporting the seat of government out of harm's way was a ruthlessly practical move. But he apparently had other motives as well. He seemed to want to put the Smol'nyi period of rule behind him and referred to it disparagingly. Trotsky, like the other Bolsheviks, had to accept Lenin's unsentimental approach, although they all had strong attachments to Petrograd. In fact, Trotsky remained behind for two weeks in order "to soften the impression that we were demoting the October capital."[4] When he arrived in Moscow, Trotsky was struck by the irony of the situation. The revolution had migrated from the most modern and Europeanized of Russian cities, a city that looked to the West, to old-fashioned Moscow, in the Volga heartland—where Lenin had spent more than twenty years of his life.

32

The Civil War: Trotsky Versus Stalin

AFTER THE move to Moscow Trotsky assumed his new post—Commissar for War. Stalin, although still bearing the major responsibility for designing a Soviet federation of nationalities, also became involved in military operations. All of the party leaders emerged from the critical struggle over Brest-Litovsk with wounds and grudges. The Civil War provided the new arena in which the hostility between the two men, which only showed occasionally at Central Committee meetings, erupted into open conflict. Trotsky, who had immense responsibilities for organizing the Red Army, selecting its staff, and deciding military priorities, found himself in a vulnerable position. Even a brief acquaintance with military history suggests both the perils and opportunities associated with commanding roles in wartime. Trotsky created a functioning military organization out of disparate and seemingly incompatible parts. Along the way he made ruthless and unpopular decisions. Although one can question his judgement in specific military decisions and personnel matters, on balance Trotsky's style of leadership provoked chronic resentment, a resentment magnified by the incipient rivalries within the party. Stalin was among those who suffered under Trotsky's imperious command and who began to engage in intrigues to undermine his position. Real differences in approach to the conduct of the war became mixed up with the personal rivalry between the two men. Lenin (often through Sverdlov) tried to manage the conflicts among the leaders from his office in the Kremlin, but his own style of leadership sometimes aggravated the wounds and grudges. It is also likely that the assassination attempt on Lenin's life on August 30, 1918, created anxieties among the oligarchs, who were forced to contemplate a successor to Lenin.

The Civil War raised to a higher level the leaders' need to establish their fitness to hold power. Trotsky, in an almost Nietzschean litany, repeatedly spoke of the Communists' need to show their will to power, which in that context meant that they had to show their toughness, their willingness to use violence. As the conflict escalated, so did the rhetoric of the leaders—and their use of violence as well. "Shoot them," exploded from the lips of Communist leaders throughout the period of the Civil War, and mass executions of both military and civilian personnel occurred. Trotsky, however, emerged with a distinctive reputation for ruthlessness and bloodthirstiness. It was no doubt partly associated with his Jewishness. The traditional idea that Jews were physically cowardly and averse to violence existed side by side with the suspicion that, given the chance, they would be terribly cruel. It was assumed that they had every reason to be cruel and vengeful. The vindictive feelings of the proletariat and peasants toward their oppressors had a different character than that of the Jews, who presumably had broader resentments. No matter on what side Trotsky erred—on that of clemency or cruelty—his failures would be seen in the light of his Jewishness. Isaac Babel's stories of a Jewish commissar attached to the Red cavalry during the Civil War vividly portray all of the underlying tensions and mistrust between Jews and the men under their command, all of the ways in which a bespectacled Jew had to prove himself to Cossacks born to the saddle. Trotsky greatly admired Babel's work. It is therefore little short of astonishing that in his autobiography he could write the following about "the question of race":

> It would seem that in military matters this consideration should have involved even greater complications than in civil administration. But Lenin proved to be right. In the years of the revolutionary *ascendancy*, this question never had the slightest importance. Of course, the Whites tried to develop anti-Semitic motifs in their propaganda in the Red army, but they failed signally. There are many testimonials to this, even in the White press. In "Archives of the Russian Revolution," published in Berlin, a White Guard writer relates the following episode: "A Cossack who came to see us was hurt by someone's taunt that he not only served under, but actually fought under the command of a Jew—Trotsky— and retorted with warm conviction: "Nothing of the sort. Trotsky is not a Jew. Trotsky is a fighter. He's ours . . . Russian! . . . It is Lenin who is a communist, a Jew, but Trotsky is ours, . . . a fighter . . . Russian . . . our own!" [1]

What is odd, Trotsky did not notice that his illustration hardly disproved the existence of anti-Semitism as a factor. It showed that anti-Semitism had been directed at Lenin, not at him. Trotsky proudly advertised that he had passed the Cossack's test for virility. No one would take *him* for a Jew. Furthermore, Trotsky believed that Lenin *was* Jewish—or at least partly so. In an article on Lenin written for the 1926 edition of *Encyclopedia Britannica*, when discussing Lenin's family background Trotsky mistakenly gave Maria Alexandrovna's maiden name as "Berg," a distinctly Jewish surname. In his later biography of Lenin he hinted at Lenin's Jewish background. His ambivalence toward Lenin (like me, Lenin is a Jew, but he seems more Jewish than I do) reflected his self-ambivalence. Trotsky assumed an exaggerated masculinity to prove that he was not one of *those* Jews.

However, it is extremely hard to weigh the relative importance of personal psychological factors in this particular context. Lenin relentlessly demanded that his colleagues show their ruthlessness. He knew very well what revolutionary power and the self-isolation of the Communists entailed. Lenin urged his colleagues to take whatever measures were necessary to retain power in the face of civil war and intervention. They would use the threat of starvation, forced labor, hostage-taking, summary executions, concentration camps—in short, terror—in clinging to power and expanding it. Trotsky became one of Lenin's more creative executives in the application of these methods. One might say that he distinguished himself. He provided theoretical justification for Communist terror and became an advocate of the use of military methods in civilian activities. When combined with his chronic overcompensations, his compulsive need for order and impatience with any kind of slovenliness, Trotsky's efforts on behalf of Communist power created a singularly threatening style of leadership. All of this, however, appealed to Lenin. He wanted executives who could exert pressure, who would not tolerate the pervasive Oblomovism and shirking that made his new state easy prey for class enemies.

The critics who pinned the label "Arakcheev" on Trotsky knew what they were talking about. Arakcheev, Minister of War and de facto Prime Minister under Alexander I, had appealed to the Tsar's love of rationality and order. After the Napoleonic Wars, with Alexander's backing he created military agricultural colonies. The short-lived colonies were designed to maintain the security of the empire at low cost, but the Russian term "Arakcheevshchina" long afterwards signified the ultimate intrusion of the military-administrative apparatus into the lives of Russia's citizens. In the Soviet parallel Trotsky's successes with military organization and his zeal for order and punctuality impressed Lenin. Lenin shared many of his convictions about centralization and scientific management, but had the political wisdom to oppose him when Trotsky's methods alienated much of the party. Trotsky carried the onus for the most extreme policies of the Civil War period. In a lecture in April 1918 he introduced a new metaphor for history in keeping with his mood at the beginning of the new period: "History is no indulgent, soft mother who will protect the working class: she is a wicked stepmother who will teach the workers through bloody experience how they must attain their aims."[2]

WITHIN MONTHS of the move to Moscow the new regime faced threats from several directions. Despite the treaty of Brest-Litovsk, the Germans might decide to take advantage of the Communists' weakness and strike again. White generals and Cossacks still loyal to the old regime threatened in the South. Both internal enemies and the imperialist powers established footholds on the periphery of the old Russian Empire. The most immediate threat, however, came from the East, from the Volga area and Western Siberia, where a variety of anti-Communist groups were coalescing. Trotsky decided in May to disarm the most combat-ready body of troops on Russian soil, forty-thousand Czecho-slovakian prisoners of war formed into a legion and making their way to Vladivostok for evacuation. The resistance of the Czech Legion along the Trans-Siberian railway actually triggered the campaign on the Volga, where SRs and Anarchists had established themselves. Then, in early July 1918 a group of Left SRs opposed to the Communist regime's war policy assassinated the German ambassador and tried to coordinate a series of military uprisings. They failed, but the crisis associated with the attempt revealed the perilous military position of the regime. Furthermore, SR assassins began to attack prominent Communists. Uritskii, at the time head of the Petrograd Cheka, was gunned down on August 30, 1918. On that very day a woman terrorist shot and wounded Lenin seriously. While Lenin lay wounded, the party leaders un-leashed the first major campaign of Red Terror. Meanwhile, in August–September 1918 at Sviazhsk, in the area of Kazan, where Lenin had spent much of his childhood and adolescence, Trotsky faced the major military crisis of the regime since the move to Moscow and exhibited his gifts as a leader under fire.

At Sviazhsk Trotsky began his career as military troubleshooter. He virtually lived on board a specially equipped train for two and one half years, speeding along interior lines from front to front, from crisis to crisis. Trotsky's train was eventually equipped with two locomotives, a garage for his automobiles, a radio transmitter, a telegraph station, an electric generator, a library, and a printing press, which issued the train's own newspaper, *En Route*. Trotsky's ability to inspire, to organize—and to intimidate—played a central role in the Red victory at Kazan and throughout the Civil War period. On August 14 he announced, in deadly earnest as it turned out, "I issue this warning: If any unit retreats without orders, the first to be shot will be the commissar, and the next the commander."[3] On the next day Trotsky threatened to shoot anyone who collaborated with the Czechs and White Guards. Lenin followed the fight for Kazan with great interest. On August 17 in a telegram he asked Trotsky if a convoy of barges under a Red Cross flag and with Red Cross officials aboard could pass through Red lines along the Volga for purposes of purchasing grain. Trotsky refused. He did not want Red Cross officials around when the "bourgeois districts" of Kazan and other Volga towns would be in flames. Then on August 21, as if to show *his* toughness, Lenin urged Trotsky not to quail before the destruction of Kazan: "There must be no question of taking pity on the town and putting matters off any longer, as merciless annihilation is . . . vital once it is established that Kazan is enclosed is an iron ring."[4] No war for the fainthearted, this.

What is surprising, Trotsky's actual use of a field court martial and executions on the spot on August 29, 1918—the decimation of a regiment that had deserted its post at Sviazhsk—haunted him throughout the war. The execution of the commissar of the regiment, Panteleev, caused a tremor in the party. Panteleev was a Communist. Trotsky was executing party members. Under attack by the "criminal clique of the Western Regional Executive Committee," Trotsky defended his action in a telegram of October 23, 1918 to Lenin and Sverdlov. (The latter had assumed many of Lenin's responsibilities during his period of convalescence.) However, he found himself on the defensive. Trotsky's callous treatment of party members (his low tolerance for their "tea parties"!) and his use of tens of thousands of "military specialists," former tsarist officers, only reinforced the feelings among some of the top leaders that Trotsky lacked genuine comradeliness. He finally had to demand a formal hearing in order to clear his name in connection with the Panteleev affair.

Trotsky's need to assert his superiority and to humiliate opponents in itself would have sufficiently complicated his life without the additional tasks of cannibalizing the usable parts of the old military machine and subjecting them to political control. He had major responsibility for a series of policy decisions with vast consequences for the "commune state" promised by Lenin. Trotsky's successful advocacy of a centralized command structure and traditional recruitment into the Red Army (after a brief experiment with a volunteer principle) inspired a reaction in the party—the Military Opposition. They deeply resented and feared his heavy reliance upon the talents of the old officers' corps. So far as the Military Opposition was concerned, Trotsky was opening the door to treason and sabotage. Furthermore, the professionalism of the officers, the style of command and warfare associated with Trotsky's policy, went counter to the spontaneity and "guerrillaism," as Trotsky labelled it, of the opposition. However, Lenin backed him. The two men were traveling the same course.

Trotsky's dramatic reversal of style, from that of a revolutionary artist whose consciousness had fused with the instinctive energy of the revolutionary masses in action to that of an arch-disciplinarian trying to impose order on the chaos, paralleled Lenin's abandonment of the ideas of *The State and Revolution*. Both men had to deal with a central paradox of revolutions from below: The liberated masses lacked the background to conduct modern military operations, to staff the apparatus of military or civilian command structures calling for both technical expertise and "habits of rule." To be sure, Trotsky promised that in the long run a new kind of military structure, a militia more in keeping with proletarian rule, would be created. However, for the time being he presented a list of desiderata that, presumably, class oppression had denied the average proletarian or peasant recruit: a capacity for systematic work, punctuality, conscientiousness, executive sense, orderliness, precision, technical knowledge, and perseverance. These virtues were close to Lenin's heart, too.

The people who possessed such virtues usually came from the old officers' corps and intelligentsia, privileged elements of the traditional order. They had functioned "both as mechanism of technical leadership and mechanism of class rule."[5] They naturally had tried to sabotage the workers' regime, but now that the power of the soviets was on a firm footing (this on March 28, 1918!), the military and civilian specialists had to be treated like the people's "national capital." Furthermore, they had to be given sufficient freedom to perform creatively. All of Trotsky's prescriptions entailed the rejection or modification of the revolution's early zeal for grassroots rule: no more elected officers; more centralization; and less collegial decision-making and control. Although Trotsky never failed to point out that the system of commissars—of political overseers—and various types of coercion would minimize the inevitable treason and sabotage one could expect from the mass use of unreliable elements, he could not placate guerrillaists like Stalin.

Stalin not only violently opposed in principle the extensive use of military specialists, he also distrusted Trotsky's specific judgements on personnel and military tactics and did everything possible to subvert his command. Stalin retained an element of romanticism, a durable aspect of his adolescent Koba identity, in military matters. Given responsibility at first for facilitating grain shipments, Stalin soon found a small band of like-minded men on the Southern Front. He quickly developed a grandiose image of himself as a military leader and organizer. Although it is not easy to plot his transformation, it may be that his mission to Tsaritsyn, the city on the Volga that became Stalingrad, marked a major turning point in his self-awareness. The man who had been described as appearing like "a grey blur" by Sukhanov retained fantasies of a heroic military career. The experience in Tsaritsyn and in other theaters of the Civil War fulfilled some of his longings and reinforced that component of his identity, but in view of Trotsky's threat to the fulfillment of his heroic role, he had to sharpen and deploy his special political skills. In the long run Stalin was a far greater success at waging guerrilla war against Trotsky within the party oligarchy than at conducting operations in the Civil War.

Only a master at intrigue could handle the complexities confronting Stalin. He had little respect for the other oligarchs, yet he had to work with them—in fact, use them against each other. Stalin must have been appalled at Lenin's willingness to let Trotsky play such a major role in military matters. Stalin had always had a strong self-identity as a fighting man. How could Lenin entrust the conduct of the war to a phrase-maker like Trotsky? Stalin found a willing accomplice in Zinov'ev in his efforts to discredit Trotsky. On the other hand, Lenin entrusted Petrograd's defense to the hysteria-prone and pusillanimous Zinov'ev. Stalin would have to come to his rescue and at the same time aggrandize himself in the defense of Petrograd in the spring of 1919. As he contemplated the possibility of Lenin's death in 1918, Stalin probably suffered greater anxiety about the succession than about Lenin's leaving the scene. Lenin kept on putting Jews in commanding positions—people who in Stalin's view could neither lead the party effectively in struggle nor command respect in a predominantly Russian state. Of course, Stalin had Lenin's ear, but Lenin did not always take his advice. Sverdlov (another Jew) seemed to be his closest adviser now, and there was little love lost between Sverdlov and Stalin. At some risk to his own position, during the course of the Civil War and after Stalin used both direct and indirect means to subvert Trotsky and his appointees and to elevate himself and his cronies to leading roles.

The first struggle with Trotsky occurred in the summer and autumn of 1918, during Stalin's mission to Tsaritsyn, where the Tenth Army held the southern line against General Krasnov's Cossacks. Shortly after he arrived, he unleashed a barrage of criticisms (both direct and indirect accusations of Trotsky), self-serving descriptions of how he was whipping things into shape, and inflated promises about the grain he would deliver to the center. He immediately began to criticize Trotsky's appointments in the South and shifted from grain supplies as such to military matters. Demanding military powers for himself, Stalin wrote impatiently: "I shall myself, without any formalities, dismiss army commanders and commissars who are ruining the work. The interests of the work dictate this, and, of course, not having a paper from Trotsky is not going to deter me."[6] Stalin refused to submit to Trotsky and told his underlings to disregard Trotsky's orders. It was simply impossible for Stalin to accept the idea that someone like Trotsky could be trusted to conduct a fight properly or that he, Stalin, should take commands from him. Unlike the Cossack in Trotsky's anecdote, Stalin had no illusions about Trotsky's ethnic background.

The Tsaritsyn clique immediately antagonized Trotsky by their insubordination and subversion of his policy of command. Trotsky had no confidence in the ability of the commander of the Tenth Army, K. E. Voroshilov, who had worked with Stalin during his days as a committeeman in Baku and with whom Stalin struck up a surprisingly durable friendship. Voroshilov was one of the few people from Stalin's past to survive the Great Purge. He no doubt survived at least partly because of their mutual suffering at Trotsky's hands. Voroshilov and Stalin agreed that officers should have impeccably Red credentials and advocated the kind of guerrillaism condemned by Trotsky. They were joined by Stalin's long-time colleague Ordzhonikidze, who served as political commissar for the Tenth Army, and S. M. Budenny, who later organized the Red Cavalry, became Marshal of the Soviet Union under Stalin, and also survived the Great Purge. Like Voroshilov, whom Stalin named Commander in Chief of Soviet forces in World War II, he rose to unexpected heights. Their careers shed light on Stalin's rise to power. All of them were survivors, clever and resourceful men who ultimately achieved positions and responsibilities beyond their capacities, as the history of World War II demonstrates. However, except for Budenny, they were not guerrilla fighters in any strict sense. Stalin requested vast military supplies directly from Lenin. At the end of August 1918 he asked for several light destroyers and two submarines! (Stalin's interest in submarine warfare seems quite in keeping with his political methods.) Rather, guerrillaism manifested itself in an insubordinate attitude and boorish behavior towards the central command structure and the military specialists and in the local usurpation of control of supplies and fighting units.

Stalin, with Voroshilov, made himself de facto ruler of Tsaritsyn and the area controlled by the Tenth Army. In connection with the attempt on Lenin's life he instituted "open and systematic mass terror" there on August 31, 1918, and acquired a reputation for Draconian severity. It is at Tsaritsyn that for the first time the lineaments of the future dictator appear. He learned how important it was to have *his* men in commanding positions. It was impossible to trust the higher-ups to make the right decisions. He and the real Communists were surrounded by enemies, who had to be replaced by reliable people. If Lenin could be so wrongheaded as to appoint Trotsky to such a crucial position, how could he, Stalin, be sure of anything? There was de facto treason, rot at the very center of the party. It followed, in Stalin's thinking, that his and the revolution's survival depended upon the total control of a handful of vigilant Communists acting, frequently, in a conspiratorial mode. This band of brothers would have the will and intelligence to destroy the traitors and turncoats and replace them by new, Red, loyal people.

For the time being Stalin had to submit. Lenin and Sverdlov took Trotsky's side and recalled Stalin to Moscow in October 1918. The men at the center tried to keep their irascible colleagues in the field from tearing at each other. They arranged a meeting between the two antagonists, with Sverdlov acting as mediator. Trotsky was on the way to Tsaritsyn, where he was going to deliver an ultimatum to Voroshilov. Trotsky provided the fullest account of the meeting, which occurred in a carriage on Trotsky's train.

> "Do you really wish to dismiss them all?" Stalin asked me, in a tone of exaggerated humility. "They are fine boys!" "Those fine boys will ruin the revolution, which can't wait for them to grow out of their adolescence," I answered him. "All I want is to draw Tsaritsyn into Soviet Russia."[7]

The episode does not enhance Trotsky's image as a leader, even if we grant that he was correct and review the relationship between the two men in the light of Stalin's later career. Trotsky's habitual arrogance, his inability to show any consideration for the feelings of his colleagues, showed in his refusal to make the slightest concession to Stalin. He made it perfectly clear that he had no use for Stalin or any of his cronies at Tsaritsyn. To Trotsky loyalty and Redness were not the real issues. Rather, the incompetence, obstinacy, boorishness, and insubordination of men like Stalin and Voroshilov threatened military operations. In October 1918 Trotsky signaled to Stalin what his fate would be should Trotsky ever succeed to the first position in the party. Stalin might easily infer that if Trotsky had his way, he would establish some sort of system in which expertise and skill would outweigh *partiinost'*—long-term loyalty and service to the party.

Stalin fell back upon his old skill at concealment. There was no defeating Trotsky, so he would appease Lenin and play the good party man by praising Trotsky in an article appearing in *Pravda* on November 6 to mark the first anniversary of the October Revolution. Of course, it appeared not long after

Stalin's recall from Tsaritsyn to Moscow and his unpleasant encounter with Trotsky. Trotsky later loved to quote it when unmasking Stalinist falsifications about the leadership of the October Revolution. Although Stalin put in first place the role of the Central Committee and Lenin (to have failed to mention the role of the CC in *Pravda*, the organ of the CC, would have been absurd and to have denied Lenin the primary political role would have been lèse majesté), he can hardly be accused of slighting Trotsky. Only two party members were mentioned by name in the article: Lenin and Trotsky.

> From beginning to end, the insurrection was inspired by the Central Committee of the party, with Comrade Lenin at its head. Lenin at that time lived in Petersburg on the Vyborg side in a secret apartment. On 24 October, in the evening, he was called out to Smol'nyi to assume general charge of the movement. All practical work in connection with the organization of the uprising was done under the immediate direction of Comrade Trotsky, the President of the Petrograd Soviet. It can be stated with certainty that the party is indebted primarily and principally to Comrade Trotsky for the rapid going over of the garrison to the side of the Soviet and the efficient manner in which the work of the Military Revolutionary Committee was organized.[8]

Stalin knew how to withdraw, how to avoid direct confrontations with someone in a superior position, and how to wait in ambush. His years of apprenticeship stood him in good stead.

Trotsky did not win all of his struggles during the Civil War, nor did Stalin always lose. On the eastern front at Perm in December 1918 the Red Army suffered a disastrous loss in a White counterattack. Stalin and Dzerzhinskii went to Perm at Lenin's behest to investigate the "Perm Catastrophe" and their report said not a word about Trotsky and his Commander in Chief, I. I. Vatsetis, but did implicitly accuse them. Stalin didn't always have to attack Trotsky directly. Zinov'ev and others sometimes played that role for him. It was, however, an excellent report and yielded an appropriate reorganization. Moreover, its recommendations led to the promotion of M. V. Frunze, who would later succeed Trotsky as the head of the Red Army. What is important, Lenin showed no loss of faith in Stalin as a consequence of Tsaritsyn. He continued to give him weighty assignments. If ever Lenin looked like a statesman in his party, it was during this period of confusion and doubt, when he had to judge heated accusations and panicky reports from several fronts and keep yoked together men who despised and mistrusted each other. Lenin got uneven performances from his troubleshooters, but their combined executive talents outweighed the costs of their personal rivalries.

Comparing himself to the other leaders, Stalin could still convince himself of his military prowess. When he was sent to Petrograd in May 1919 to assist the ineffectual Zinov'ev in organizing the city's defenses, he received an enormous boost in self-esteem. After the capture of two fortresses on the Gulf of Finland near Petrograd on June 16, 1919, Stalin telegraphed Lenin:

> Naval experts assert that the capture of Krasnaia Gorka from the sea runs counter to naval science. I can only deplore such so-called science. The swift capture of Gorka was due to the grossest interference in the operations by me

and civilians generally, even to the point of countermanding orders on land and sea and imposing our own. I consider it my duty to declare that I shall continue to act this way in the future, despite all my reverence for science.[9]

In Petrograd Stalin revealed clearly that the inflated, self-serving estimates of his achievements in Tsaritsyn issued not only from his rivalry with Trotsky but from a sense of his own superiority as a judge of enemies and as a military leader. Just as Trotsky believed in his special fitness to lead when masses of people created a revolutionary whirlpool, Stalin believed in his innate gifts in military matters. His reports from the field of combat to Lenin exude a sense of competency and decisiveness. Stalin portrayed himself as someone who knew how to unearth conspiracies, fight corruption, assess the relative dangers posed by different opponents and sectors of the front, and coolly disregard the advice of so-called experts in crucial matters, where his judgement was always superior to theirs. These attitudes and actions foreshadow the Stalin who would decapitate the armed forces in his massive purge of the officers' corps in 1937 and the man whose personal decisions, particularly those in the early phases of World War II, cost millions of Soviet lives.

In his later unmasking of Stalin, Trotsky jealously guarded his own preeminence in the defense of Petrograd in 1919. Stalin's measures had hardly saved the city. General Iudenich launched a far greater threat to the city in September–October 1919 than Stalin had anticipated. Zinov'ev reacted in his usual craven manner. Lenin was willing to sacrifice Petrograd in the struggle to prevent a breakthrough to Moscow from the South, where General Denikin was poised to thrust northward. In his retelling of this episode of the Civil War Trotsky does not fail to mention his violent disagreement with Lenin over the policy towards the city. Trotsky won. The city would be defended.

On October 16, 1919, Trotsky rushed from Moscow to the scene of his greatest triumphs. Through his efforts sufficient strength was mustered to defend the city, and he showed immense physical courage at the front. On October 18 he actually seized command of a regiment and on horseback chased the fleeing troops back into line. At no point in his life did he display greater romanticism, greater willingness to sacrifice his life in a dramatic gesture. Where Lenin seemed to write off Petrograd's value too easily, Trotsky exaggerated its strategic and military significance. Once again the rivalry between the two men affected their respective attitudes towards the defense of Petrograd. It was Trotsky's city; its heroic frenzy during the decisive battles of late October was his own. Both Trotsky and the crew of his train received the Order of the Red Banner for bravery under fire. No crueller cut could be aimed at Trotsky than renaming Petrograd Leningrad, evidently largely at Zinov'ev's instigation in 1924. For his efforts Trotsky had Gatchina, near Petrograd, named for him. It was called "Trotsk" until Stalin in 1929 decided to expunge its hated name from the map, just as he tried to erase the memory of all of Trotsky's other achievements from history.

ANOTHER REVEALING episode occurred at the end of the Civil War, when the Red Army, having all but defeated the White Armies and interventionists, at Lenin's behest invaded Poland. This moment in the early history of Soviet Russia reveals clearly Lenin's fidelity to internationalism and his willingness to gamble, once he sensed a position of strength. The Polish campaign reflected the change of mood that had occurred during the Civil War. Lenin had begun the Civil War in a desperate mood: Retreat was the only path to survival. By the end of the war the Red Army had 3 million men under arms. Lenin's native optimism about the possibilities of world revolution needed little encouragement, and he could satisfy the left wing of his party by seizing the opportunity to export the revolution. The moment seemed propitious. Germany seemed to be destabilized in the wake of defeat in World War I and, more immediately the Kapp putsch of March 1920. Furthermore, the attack on Poland seemed justified by Polish efforts to detach territories on the western border. The new Polish state had tried to extend earlier successes in the spring of 1920 by striking at Kiev, but the Red Army successfully counterattacked and even won back ground lost earlier. Should they advance farther into Poland, or stop? The idea of advancing was generally popular. Lenin was for it. Oddly enough, it was Trotsky who cautioned him not to "sound" Poland in 1920.

Stalin's position on the invasion of Poland and his role in the campaign led to his retirement from military duty in the wake of the disastrous battle of the Vistula, when the Western Army Group under Tukhachevskii advanced hastily toward Warsaw in August 1918 with its lines stretched thin and left flank inadequately protected. The Polish armies not only held but attacked the weak flank and threw Tukhachevskii's forces into disarray. Although the leadership, Lenin and Trotsky included, had to answer to the party as a whole for the debacle, Stalin found himself particularly vulnerable. First of all, he had opposed the idea of the invasion but then voted with Lenin for it. This is not in itself remarkable. The majority of the Politburo (which had become a permanent institution in 1919) and Central Committee backed Lenin. Zinov'ev, with whom Stalin was allied against Trotsky during the Civil War period, strongly supported Lenin. The politics of the situation tended to draw Stalin into the side opposite Trotsky's, even though Stalin initially opposed the "march on Warsaw." However, once the decision had been made in July 1920 and Tukhachevskii's forces committed, Stalin, the political commissar of the Southwestern Army Group and a member of the Revolutionary War Council, remained intent on capturing Lvov. Egerov, the military commander of the Southwestern Army, and Stalin refused to send Budenny's and Voroshilov's First Cavalry to support the Western Army at a critical moment in the Battle of the Vistula. It was the Tsaritsyn clique against the command structure again.

Trotsky's version of the catastrophe is particularly interesting, and not just because of his unmasking of Stalin's falsification of their mutual roles or his contribution to the historical record. Given Trotsky's sense of the role of individuals at historical turning points, the search for the reasons for the failure of the Polish campaign had larger implications. Just as he believed that Lenin and he had played crucial roles in the October Revolution, he conjectured that Stalin's delinquency had destroyed Tukhachevskii's chances to capture Warsaw. That failure, in turn, had struck a blow against the spread of the revolution to the West.[10] It should be added that Trotsky had earlier laid the blame at Lenin's door. Lenin, after all, was guilty of a serious error by calling for the campaign to seize Warsaw in the first place. It followed that both Lenin and Stalin, but not Trotsky, bore some share of the blame for the catastrophe. In his recollections of Lenin, Trotsky speculated about the consequences of the unfavorable Treaty of Riga, which followed the failure at Warsaw.

> Now we all know that the March on Warsaw was a very costly mistake, resulting not only in the conclusion of the Riga Treaty which cut us off from Germany, but also, together with other contemporary developments, helping tremendously in the consolidation of bourgeois Europe. The counterrevolutionary character of the Riga Treaty and its influence becomes quite obvious if one imagines the course events might have taken during one year only, during 1923, if we had had a common frontier with Germany. There are innumerable reasons to think that the German developments would have shaped themselves in an entirely different manner.[11]

The leaders were all aware of the magnitude of the defeat, although they might differ in their interpretation of its repercussions. Delegates at the Ninth Party Conference in late September 1920 demanded an explanation for the decision to send exhausted, poorly organized, and badly protected troops against Warsaw. All of those involved tried to shift the onus for the decision elsewhere. Stalin called for an investigation and tried to blame the command of the Western Army Group for misleading the Central Committee. At the evening session of September 22 Trotsky criticized Stalin, who, he pointed out, was guilty of the same sin. Stalin had given an overly optimistic estimate of Russian and Polish comparative strength by pointing to the supposedly high rate of desertion in the Polish army. He was mistaken. The CC relied upon Stalin's erroneous information, and so the mistake affected their policy in July.[12] Evidently Lenin accused Stalin of prejudice against the Western command during the crucial days of mid-August, although his remarks do not appear in the minutes of conference. The accusation can be inferred from Stalin's reply to both Lenin and Trotsky at the opening of the morning session of September 23:

> Comrades, some parts of yesterday's speechs of comrades Lenin and Trotsky could give you grounds to suspect me of the erroneous transmission *[sic]* of facts, therefore I consider it my duty to declare the following: In the first place, comrade Trotsky's declaration, that I portrayed the frontline position in a rosy light before the attack on Warsaw, does not correspond to reality. To the contrary, I was almost the only member of the Central Committee who in the press ridiculed the command to "march on Warsaw." If you want confirmation for the accuracy of my declaration, read my articles in *Pravda*. In the second place, comrade Trotsky's declaration that Stalin's calculations with respect to the seizure of Lvov were not borne out also do not correspond to reality. In the middle of August our troops stood eight versts from Lvov, and we would surely

have seized it but for the fact that at this moment the general command in order to rescue the Western front transferred Budenny to the Western front. In the third place, comrade Lenin's declaration that I was prejudiced against the command of the Western front, also does not correspond to reality. The fact that on the sixteenth we did not seize Warsaw — is a trifle. Rather, the whole point is that at that moment we were in no position to seize Warsaw, but were on the verge of collapse, the possibility of which the military command had not taken into account. If at that time the command had declared to the Central Committee that the condition of the front was poor, I do not doubt that the CC would have temporarily abandoned the policy of attack. This was not done. I repeat: it is a trifle that we did not seize Warsaw on the sixteenth. But that we unexpectedly found ourselves confronted with a catastrophe — that is due to the negligence of the command. That is why I demanded an inquest into the facts. I consider it necessary to put my present declaration into the written record. [13]

It is true that Stalin had warned against the march on Warsaw in articles in *Pravda* and *Kommunist,* but he had in the end voted with the others to invade. He obviously regretted his acquiescence. More important, Stalin would not tolerate any suggestion of malfeasance on his part in military matters. The accusations before 241 delegates by the two leading figures in the party embittered him — a bitterness reflected in the touchy, proud, and coldly angry tone of his declaration. This was neither the first nor the last time that he would stand his ground against Lenin and Trotsky together. He had to protect his self-identity as an eagle-eyed Caucasian mountaineer, who could see farther than the others. Trotsky and Lenin, on the other hand, wanted above all to control the damage and not to single out anyone for blame. They were forced to reprimand Stalin. The issue did not die at the Ninth Party Conference, but was discussed again at the Tenth Party Congress in 1921 at a closed session of which there is no written record. Although Trotsky is hardly an impartial judge of Stalin, his account of the later session is probably accurate. There Stalin tried to accuse the political commissar of the Western Front, evidently in terms similar to those of his declaration of September 23, 1920, but received no support. [14] Only after he had gained total power did Stalin manage to revise the history of the Civil War to suit him.

Any illusion that Stalin meekly submitted to Lenin in this period or consistently maintained the posture of a loyal subordinate is dispelled by the above incident and at least one other during the Civil War. When Lenin telegraphed Stalin to send reinforcements to the Caucasian Front in February 1920, Stalin objected to the additional burden on his command and provoked Lenin to reprimand him for quibbling about jurisdictional matters. [15] In short, Stalin's spirit of insubordination during the war did not express only his rivalry with Trotsky. He deeply believed that he knew the military role better than either Trotsky or Lenin. Thus, when it was decided to award Trotsky the Order of the Red Banner for his defense of Petrograd, Stalin evidently went into such a sulk that the party leadership decided to give him the award as well, although no one except insiders understood what it was for. The military role was so close to the core of his self-identity as a fighter that Stalin abandoned his usual strategy of concealment and clashed head on with his rivals, openly rejected their commands, and demanded that his achievement be recognized.

THE BALANCE sheet of the Civil War of 1918–1921 reveals a disaster of extraordinary magnitude alongside the indisputable victory of the new regime. However, from the point of view of the Communist Party, a luminous victory had been achieved. The somewhat mystifying attitude can only be understood by taking into account the party's starting point. The leaders were continually haunted by the ghosts of revolutionary history. They studied the post mortems of Marx and Engels and their own recent experience. First of all, there were the lessons of the French Revolution: the Jacobins, Thermidor, and then Napoleon. There followed the failed revolutions of 1848 and the eighteenth Brumaire of Louis Bonaparte. Finally, as exemplary experiments and models of revolutionary courage they had the Paris Commune of 1871, the St. Petersburg Soviet, and the Moscow insurrection of 1905. All of the previous efforts to consolidate a working-class revolution had failed. Lenin was determined to learn, to be prepared for the worst and to do whatever was necessary to survive. To his immense satisfaction the Communists did survive. In this sense—mere survival—in 1921 the Communists could boast that they had achieved what no revolutionary in history had. But when one begins to look at the price paid in lives and the characteristics of the social and economic order that emerged from the Civil War, the victory looks hollow indeed.[16]

The deaths in the Red and White armies alone probably totaled roughly 1 million, if one takes into account epidemic disease as well as military casualties. If the civilian victims of the Red Terror, epidemics connected with war conditions, war-induced famine, increased infant mortality, and the deficit in births caused by war and dislocation are factored in, it is impossible to avoid the tragic conclusion that the Civil War cost the Soviet people many more lives than World War I did. In that war Imperial Russia had lost roughly 2 million troops, but approximately 5 million people died in the famine of 1921–1922, which was connected with both warfare and economic disruption. Millions of homeless children roamed the cities and the countryside. It was a human disaster of enormous magnitude.

The economic data are no less disheartening. The measures generally grouped together under the term "War Communism" aggravated the economic consequences of the war. The regime's monetary policy led to a virtual barter economy. In every area of industry, now nationalized, 1921 production had generally dropped to less than one third, often less than one-fifth, and sometimes less than one-tenth of prewar levels. The system of transportation had virtually broken down. The Red Army took what it needed and the government desperately tried to sustain industrial production and urban life. This meant antagonizing and using force against the rural population by a system of grain requisitioning and subjecting the urban population to discriminatory forms of rationing—the distribution of supplies based upon class and occupation. The breakdown of trade between city and country and the requisitioning system led to grain hoarding, reduction of acreage under cultivation, more forceful forms of grain requisitioning, and finally peasant insurrections. Shortages and food rationing in cities led to economic crimes—speculation, a black market, and embezzlement. With the disruption of market mechanisms urban population center shrank to a fraction of their size. Roadblocks prevented the remaining factory workers from foraging in the countryside. Machine guns appeared in factories. Whose dictatorship was this?

33

War Communism

THE NEED to adapt Marxian theory to the kaleidoscopic postrevolutionary situation yielded new and unexpected formulations. At the beginning of the Civil War Lenin had toyed with the idea of state capitalism. Somehow, the new Communist state and the bourgeois factory owners would create a viable economic system together. In order to sustain a modern, centralized system of production, the regime would have to make use of the experience of the old owners and their specialists—engineers, accountants, managers. Lenin also proposed differential wage rates, with the bourgeoisie and their experts earning more than workers. The workers themselves would be induced to produce more by incentives. However, within a period of weeks in the spring of 1918 Lenin abandoned his scheme of a mixed system of state control and private enterprise and plunged recklessly into broad nationalization of industry and centralized control over production.

The Bolsheviks went far beyond the German system of wartime controls and economic centralization, the model that first attracted them. The "sabotage" of the bourgeoisie made it impossible to carry forward any such plan; and the pressure from the Left pushed the party into the policy of War Communism. Production continued to founder. In his rhetoric Lenin ominously referred to the proletariat as weary, exhausted, or dejected. Incapable of the roles assigned them in *The State and Revolution,* proletarians would have to submit to the dictatorship of the party and of individual managers in the process of production. Anarchy had to be overcome. Only the party and its agencies had the will and expertise to organize production. Lenin began to examine new forms of scientific management of labor, such as Taylorism. Lenin and Trotsky both wanted a high degree of control, planning, orderliness, and punctuality, and they despised the anarchy and lethargy they found in the workplace.

Every effort at centralized control and scientific management signified another step away from the ideal of a new type of commune state. The assumption of responsibility for production by the party-state stimulated the rapid proliferation of bureaucratic structures. Lenin, Trotsky, and others anxiously watched the bureaucratic explosion and issued warnings about its dangers for the proletarian cause, yet had no solution for it in 1918—or later. Lenin's jumping about from the idea of a commune state, to the notion of a system of state capitalism, and then to the dictatorship of a party-state that in practice resembled neither was not only symptomatic of the failure of his gamble and the inadequacy of his theoretical framework. His settling on dictatorship also seemed to issue naturally from his preferred style of leadership. Even if there had been no extended and destructive Civil War, it seems highly unlikely that Lenin could have tolerated the spontaneity of a commune state for very long or managed a modus vivendi with the class enemy. His style of leadership had always tended towards self-isolation, dictatorial control. Now that his party had power, it had to justify the gamble and somehow make good the catastrophe of virtual economic collapse. The Communist Party became a self-justifying dictatorship. Dialectics, formerly the "algebra of revolution," once again demonstrated its flexibility by serving as the apologetics of the partocracy. In justifying the disaster of War Communism, Lenin received help from his colleagues, who were quite adept at addressing the problems in a Marxian idiom.

Bukharin, one of the major theoreticians of the period of War Communism, seemed intent on making a virtue of disaster. Like most of Lenin's opponents in the upper ranks of the party, he had repented his error over Brest-Litovsk, returned to the fold, and resumed his position as hired pen. In *The Economics of the Transition Period* (1920) he produced what now seems to be a sinister rationalization for the economic disaster produced by revolution and civil war and the harsh measures of the new regime. He tried to show that the economics and politics of crisis and scarcity would be midwife to socialism. Like the earlier heretic Bogdanov, Bukharin used Marxian dialectical language to theorize about disruptions and the reestablishment of dynamic equilibrium in socioeconomic systems. In effect, he justified the utter ruin of one social and economic system so that a new and better one could be organized. Bukharin's

Economics of the Transition Period seems to be the perfect theoretical pendant to the historical impatience and essentially political character of Leninism and the spirit of command and coercion issuing from the Civil War. The new dynamic equilibrium would be organized from above, by the conscious efforts of the rulers of the new state.

> In the transition period, when one productive structure gives way to another, the midwife is revolutionary force. This revolutionary force must destroy the fetters on the development of society, i.e., on one side, the old forms of "concentrated force," which have become a counterrevolutionary factor—the old state and the old type of production relations. This revolutionary force, on the other side, must actively help in the formation of production relations, being a new form of "concentrated force," the state of the new class, which acts as the lever of economic revolution, altering the economic structure of society. Thus on one side force plays the role of a destructive factor; on the other, it is a force of cohesion, organization, and construction. The greater this "extra-economic" power is . . . the less will be "the costs" of the transition period (all other things being equal, of course), the *shorter* will be this transition period, the faster will a social equilibrium be established on a new foundation and the quicker will the . . . production curve begin to rise.[1]

The ad hoc theories of the leaders could put the best face on, but not hide the ugly truth: War Communism had virtually ruined industry, reduced agricultural production significantly, and forced the party-state to rule increasingly by force. The state budget was based largely upon confiscations of produce from tens of thousands of villages. This, too, issued partly from Marxian theory. Many peasants, after all, were petty-bourgeois class enemies consciously or unconsciously sabotaging the dictatorship of the proletariat. Presumably, the poor peasants, organized into committees, would side with the regime against their richer peasant neighbors, just as the peasants as a whole had against the gentry. In fact, the land redistribution and leveling that had occurred as a result of the revolution had turned Russia into a nation of small farms. The expected second stage of class struggle in the countryside of the poor peasants against the kulaks simply did not materialize. Even if it had, it would probably only have accelerated the ruin of the agricultural economy. Forcible gain procurements quickly brought the peasant to a desperate state. After the last White armies had been subdued, the Bolsheviks had to suppress large-scale peasant rebellions. Thus, the Civil War against the Whites and foreign intervention gave way to a war of the regime against the average peasant citizen and against the remaining intelligentsia opposition. Increasingly, the question became: How long could the party hold out against the majority of the population? The answer lay in retreat from the coercive policies of War Communism. Theoreticians like Bukharin would discover that there were other, better ways to raise the curve of production.

This honest recognition of the paramount role of the power of the state, the "superstructure," in the transition period is perhaps less significant than the central position of the value of production. Concern with restoring to health the crippled system of production took precedence over other Marxian values. For

Marx production in a socialist system would serve human needs. For the new Communist party-state, control over and expansion of production increasingly made workers mere appendages or instruments to be used according to the latest theories about the transition to socialism and the needs of the system of production. Even more ominous than references to the proletariat as weary and confused was the appearance of the economic concept of "primitive socialist accumulation." The theoreticians of the regime began to entertain the idea that they might have to act the way the capitalists of old had—as ruthless extractors of surplus value from working people. Of course, the Communists had a social end in mind rather than private appropriation. Hence, it would be "socialist" rather than capitalist accumulation. It remained to convince the workers that they were making the sacrifice on their own behalf. In this the regime was reasonably successful. During the first decades of Communist rule, the party learned how to use agitprop and cadres to good advantage. Relying not only on the full force of the mass media and trained activists for its mobilization campaigns, the party also used a variety of carrots and sticks of a traditional sort to keep the workers producing more and consuming less.

The Communist Party intelligentsia thus justified sacrifice of others as well as its own self-sacrifice. In spite of themselves, first-rank leaders like Lenin, Trotsky, and Bukharin had not really lost the old intelligentsia mentality, that mixture of pride and guilt that had inspired acts of great courage and self-sacrifice under the old regime. It simply expressed itself in new and ambivalent forms. Before, one had to sacrifice one's own career, one's own ego, in order to raise the consciousness of the people, who were less "developed" or less "conscious" than the intelligentsia. After decades of sacrifice the great moment had arrived. The masses had shown the requisite revolutionary consciousness in 1917 and played the historical role assigned by the dialectic of history. But now, during the Civil War, they were increasingly listening to the "petty-bourgeois" intelligentsia, the Mensheviks and SRs. The latter exploited the masses' weariness and confusion. Evidently, proletarian consciousness had a certain fragility. Like human virtue itself, it fell easy prey to a variety of temptations and corruptions. Now the party had to work with the deficient material bequeathed by the old order. It had to learn to shape this mass and temper it.

The party had undergone its own process of tempering, first in the revolutionary underground, then in the revolution itself, and finally in the Civil War. Its hard mentality distinguished it from the "petty-bourgeois" intelligentsia. The sheer experience of sacrifice and survival had given party membership a special mystique. Communists had earned their preeminence. They demanded nothing of others that they did not demand of themselves, and in addition, like all ruling groups, they took upon themselves the burden of cruel policies. The party now had to make painful "scientific" decisions for the good of the weary and confused masses, even if it meant forcing them to make sacrifices too. Of course, one had to continue to suppress one's own ego, one's own doubts and scruples when the party demanded it, for despite its flaws, the party had become the unique instrument of progress in a dialectical universe of cruel choices. The party had to be cruel in order to be kind. There was not yet any element of cynicism or *mere* power-seeking in the leaders. That would come later. Despite all of their many and significant personal differences, the founders all saw themselves as instruments of that cruel goddess, the dialectic of history. History spoke only through the party, and ultimately, Lenin determined the party line.

For Lenin, of course, sacrifice had become second nature. He had taken a ruthlessly instrumental attitude toward himself since his brother's death. He had been a conscious "hard" since 1900, after his confrontations with Plekhanov and Struve. Now he seemed willing to use an entire generation, if necessary, to keep advancing toward his goal. Along the way he had become the ultimate politician, developing an extraordinary repertoire, all of which served to keep him in a position of leadership during 1917–1922. He quickly adapted himself to the role of Chairman of the Sovnarkom. In the words of the foremost student of Lenin's government:

> It is remarkable, and perhaps unprecedented, that Lenin, a man approaching fifty who had spent his whole youth and adult life as a professional revolutionary, could apply himself so single-mindedly and persistently to such humdrum matters, especially when one recalls the critical and chaotic circumstances in which he did so. This relates, moreover, not only to his contribution to the creation and running of the Sovnarkom machine, but to his exercise of the 'prime-ministerial' role. In such matters as the management of agendas, the clarification of issues and judicious injection of his influence on them before they came up for formal consideration, the guidance, stimulation and focusing of discussion, and the crystallisation of clear decisions embodied in his summings-up, the use of standing and *ad hoc* committees, and the exercise of his executive authority in taking, facilitating or ensuring administrative decisions, Lenin quickly displayed a mastery that would have done credit to a politician who had served a long apprenticeship in a mature system of cabinet government.[2]

In fact, Lenin's career had not been that of the typical revolutionary. He had long been accustomed to getting business done on editorial boards, committees, conferences, and congresses. He had not only worked as a propagandist or agitator, but written programs, set agendas, chaired—in short, learned politics from the ground up. His professionalism had never been merely that of the underground revolutionary, even though he had championed conspiratorial methods and technique. He had long had the characteristics of a prime minister without portfolio. However, in his running of the Sovnarkom he showed his deep propensity to use others without fully trusting them. Hence, he never cultivated a replacement because he did not believe anyone could replace him.[3] The illusion of Soviet rather than party rule quickly dissipated during Lenin's illness in 1922.

Managing the party was the crucial matter for the leader of the Soviet state, and here too Lenin retained his mastery. The party might split into factions under his pressure and his zigzag course, but only Lenin knew how to work all levels of the organization, to thrust forward a surprising initiative and make it policy, to rebound from defeats, whether in committee, conference, or congress, and fashion majorities. He masterfully identified and named heresies, orchestrated campaigns, isolated his opponents of the moment, defeated them, tactfully offered them face-saving positions—but forced them to submit to party discipline and join the campaign against the next round of heresy. Today's allies became tomorrow's heretics; today's heretics, tomorrow's allies. Lenin knew how to steal an opponent's policy, reshape it a bit, and present it in a new guise as part of his own platform. Always inclined toward sectarianism, Lenin managed nonetheless to assimilate a great variety of people into the party by this rather painful technique of dividing, forming coalitions, appropriating his opponents' best ideas—and conquering.

Lenin, in some sense, became the reincarnation of Plekhanov, the only adult in the party. He thundered at the children. Sometimes he flew off the handle, and they would have to act behind his back or humor him. Sometimes they would squabble amongst themselves and only Lenin could manage the fight. If a group or groups refused to submit, he would decide which portion of the party remained within the family. Then he would resort to that painful last remedy—a purge. Lenin showed no hesitancy or doubt in his last years, no inclination to yield to others. However able his lieutenants, in his eyes not one of them had the requisite combination of Marxian theoretical acumen, political intelligence, and will to replace him. During the course of the Civil War the situation had not improved. In March 1919 the party suffered a great loss when Sverdlov, the party's premier personnel manager, died of the flu during the great epidemic of that time. He had served well, and in retrospect, his loss left the field free for Stalin to become the party's main organizer. But it is unlikely that Lenin could really conceive of Sverdlov playing *his* role. It now seems clear that Lenin could not really conceive of *anyone* playing his role. Ultimately, his style of leadership created the groundwork for disaster, and he showed no capacity for changing it, even on his deathbed.

34

Lenin Against Trotsky

DURING THE critical transition from war to peace in 1920–1922, Lenin and the party oligarchy engaged in a new series of policy conflicts. He had played a relatively irenic role when dealing with rivalries over military matters, possibly because he felt less competent and relatively remote from battlefield situations. However, when it came to the reorganization of the economy and the vast array of political and social issues facing the regime toward the end of the Civil War, Lenin showed his usual ruthlessness in conflict. During the policy debates of 1920–1922, instead of soothing over the rivalries among the oligarchs, Lenin used them for his own purposes. He often handled the top rank of leaders roughly, with little regard for their feelings. Lenin treated them as he always had, but in this new context his behavior had different meaning, greater impact. After all, Lenin's subordinates were now no longer merely undergrounders or players in the game of émigré politics. The stakes had changed. They were public figures with not only reputations to protect but even at this early stage their own fiefdoms or machines in the rapidly proliferating party and Soviet organizations. The oligarchs emerged from each conflict resentful of each other and of Lenin.

At a moment when he should have been smoothing over differences and easing the way for a successor, Lenin instead engaged in his last series of maneuvers. The coalitions that formed within the oligarchy were inherently unstable, for Lenin's style of leadership and the political culture in which the oligarchs had developed made it very likely that someone would emerge as first among equals. Today's ally might be tomorrow's opponent in a struggle for the top position. His military cachet gave Trotsky a temporary advantage, but his arrogant and insensitive treatment of his colleagues made him vulnerable. As noted earlier, several of the oligarchs, with Zinov'ev and Stalin in the lead, tried to undermine his reputation, but Lenin, in particular, weakened him in several ways: In 1920–1921, he undermined Trotsky's authority within the party by dealing with him harshly in policy debates; in 1919–1922 he strengthened Stalin by putting him at the head of the Worker-Peasant Inspectorate (Rabkrin), giving him a leading position in the Organizational Bureau of the party, and making him General Secretary of the Central Committee; then in 1922–1923, already deathly ill, he formed an alliance of convenience with Trotsky that had the effect of forcing the other contenders for leadership into defensive postures and diverted their anger against their moribund leader to Trotsky. Finally, instead of picking a successor, Lenin left his so-called "Testament," an odd document that damned all of his likely successors with faint praise and left them to fight it out amongst themselves.

Despite Lenin's essential agreement with Trotsky about the need to impose order upon the chaotic situation in the country at the end of the Civil War and to use military methods of discipline and organization in domestic matters, he ultimately sided with Trotsky's opponents. It is easy to see the political rationale for Lenin's positions, but one wonders whether other motives were at work as well. During 1919 and most of 1920 the two men seemed to be in full accord about the need for order, compulsory labor service, severe punishments for "desertion," whether from the army or the labor force, a unified command system, and the subordination of trade unions to the state apparatus. The proletariat's own organizations would function as recruitment centers in the process of labor conscription and help the government raise productivity. Trotsky even seemed to believe that military methods were the only ones that would prevent a cultural apocalypse.

> The imperialist war and its aftermath revealed that it is impossible for society to go on any longer on the basis of free labor. . . . If it were to turn out that the planned, and consequently compulsory, organization of labor which is replacing imperialism leads to a decline of the economy, that would mean the ruin of all our culture, a retrograde movement of mankind back to barbarism and savagery.[1]

Trotsky tried to counter accusations of Arakcheevism by emphasizing the subjective factor—the attitude of the workers during the labor process.

Militarization of labor when the working people are against it is Arakcheevism. Militarization of labor by the will of the working people themselves is socialist dictatorship. . . . Russian capitalism, owing to its belatedness, its lack of independence, and the parasitic features resulting from this, has been able to train the worker masses, to educate them technically and discipline them to the service of production, only to a much smaller extent than European capitalism did with its workers. This task now falls entirely upon the trade-union organizations of the proletariat.[2]

Trotsky invoked all of human historical experience to make his argument for the command economy and militarization. No human society had existed without organized labor; no labor force had worked without compulsion. Organized forms of compulsion might have to be ruthless in the new state, but they were nonetheless benign—not tokens of the submission of the proletariat to a ruling class but self-generated forms of discipline. Russia's low level of cultural development made a combination of military methods and Taylorism attractive ways to raise the general level of the nation. Trotsky became enchanted with the notion that wartime mobilization and scientific management together could lift the nation to new heights. In a speech of November 1920 on the militia system he cited a U.S. engineer, a student of Taylor and a socialist:

The engineer I have mentioned says that the Taylor system can be fully developed only under the socialist order. This idea must also be introduced into military technique, into the army of the socialist state. And, since an enemy threatens us, we shall imbue with this idea of military education, of precision and assiduity in behavior, the entire education of our children and youth— militarizing, in the best sense of the word, our entire country.[3]

What does militarizing mean? It means inculcating a sense of responsibility and, therefore, forming the best type of cultured person. . . . The petty-bourgeois individual egoism, the self-seeking which is encountered in the life of bourgeois society manifests itself in barbarously crude forms: a man locks himself in his room and everyone else can go to hell. . . . As I see it, a new religious bond between men will arise in our epoch, in the form of the spirit of solidarity—and it is with this idea that we must imbue the army, the people, the school, the factory and the village.[4]

All of this was in keeping with the spirit of War Communism. However, even Lenin's backing could not make Trotsky's position acceptable. The Communist trade union leaders almost unanimously rejected the policy of the militarization of labor in January 1920. Perhaps the knowledge that the system of militarization was identified with him personally—that he had become the dread Arakcheev of the regime—prompted Trotsky to seek an alternative to the unpopular labor armies, the hated system of grain requisitioning, and the statization of trade unions. He himself claimed that he was influenced by the army's morale and his observations of the state of the economy in the Urals during his trip there at Lenin's behest in the winter of 1920. In February 1920 Trotsky presented the CC with a proposal that, because never fully published, is a matter of scholarly controversy. He definitely called for an end to grain requisitioning in favor of a tax in kind and the restoration of incentives for peasants to produce a surplus.[5] Trotsky later claimed that his proposal anticipated Lenin's New Economic Policy (NEP) of 1921. Whatever its full content, Trotsky's proposal was rejected. To members of the CC still under the influence of the aggressive mentality of War Communism, it smacked of Menshevism and retreat to petty-bourgeois free trade. Despite the country's economic difficulties and the chaos caused by the party's economic policies, the CC of the party did not yet want to sound a retreat.

In view of the Central Committee's and Lenin's rejection of his proposal for a policy shift, Trotsky presented a program for economic recovery fully compatible with War Communism, including his unpopular position on trade unions, to the Ninth Party Congress in March–April 1920. As reporter on economic matters, Trotsky placed before the Congress the theses he had earlier submitted to the leadership, a four-stage approach toward economic revival and growth that placed the consumers' needs last on the agenda. First, the transport system and stockpiles of basic industrial materials such as fuel and ore had to be restored; second, emphasis would be placed upon the production of capital equipment, heavy machinery for expanding the transport system and mining; then the plan would move to consumer industries and yield capital equipment in that area; finally, they would produce goods for consumption. Bukharin supported Trotsky. Both of them seemed transfixed by a heroic image of industrial revival by military methods in Soviet Russia and an apocalyptic vision of European decline.[6]

Despite opposition, the Congress supported the policy, and throughout 1920 Lenin continued to use Trotsky as an economic trouble shooter. Lenin relied upon him to reorganize the transport system and to launch the experiment with labor armies in 1920, projects that only worsened Trotsky's reputation. It was Trotsky who embodied the spirit of dictatorship and state terror, Trotsky whose methods polarized the party, Trotsky who became the convenient scapegoat for the Communist Party's worst sins in domestic policy during the period of the Civil War. When Lenin decided to change course in favor of the trade unions in November 1920, not only Trotsky but half the CC forced a stalemate. Instead of soothing his colleagues, Lenin sided with Tomsky, the trade union head, against Trotsky. The CC then put Zinov'ev in charge of a subcommittee to explore the matter farther. All of this was designed to put Trotsky and his transport bureaucracy in its place. In the end Lenin emerged victorious and Trotsky humiliated but unrepentant. He refused to work on Zinov'ev's subcommittee, which inevitably would have endorsed Lenin's policy and squelched the debate behind closed doors. Bukharin, although not fully in accord with Trotsky and trying to act as "buffer" between the factions warring over the trade union issue, believed in public discussion of the issues. Trotsky saw no other way to prosecute his cause. Thus, Trotsky opened himself to the accusation of factionalism and Bukharin to Lenin's judgment that he only posed as a "buffer." On December 30, 1920, the conflict between Lenin and Trotsky and Bukharin erupted into a more public arena dramatically when Lenin denounced their "mistakes" to the Communists attending the Eighth Congress of Soviets.[7]

During the speech Lenin brought forward the notion that the trade unions would serve as "schools" for the proletariat—ultimately, schools of communism. This was simply a way of saying that the proletariat was too backward to exercise its power directly. It had to do so through its vanguard, the apparatus of the party-state. The trade unions linked the workers with the vanguard. Furthermore, Lenin now decided to bring the peasants back into the picture, foreshadowing his NEP, by counterposing to Trotsky's notion of a worker state the notion of a worker-peasant state. Bukharin, later the most zealous proponent of the worker-peasant alliance but presently Trotsky's ally, shouted from the auditorium, "What kind? Worker-peasant?"[8] The party theoreticians had dropped the "peasant" from the slogan after 1917, signifying the passage to a higher stage of the historical process. Now Lenin pointed out that theirs was not, in fact, a workers' state. He proceeded to ridicule Trotsky's "principled" positions and deride Bukharin's recent theoretical excursions. He signaled the retreat from War Communism and the dictatorship of the proletariat exercised through its vanguard.

Lenin knew that the factory proletariat had been decimated by the war, by the process of deurbanization, by industrial collapse, and by absorption into the apparatus. The original revolutionary proletariat had been used as the shock troops of the revolution and now survived only as a remnant. The party-state would have to renew the proletariat, reeducate it. Trotsky, too, believed this, but he refused to use euphemisms like "schools of Communism" or to hide the coercive aspects of Soviet rule in such inauspicious conditions. Lenin wanted to achieve statization of the unions without too much noise: "Speech is silver, silence is golden."[9] Lenin's tirade against Trotsky and Bukharin was simply another way of saying, "Trotsky and Bukharin should shut up; they should know their place." In the end Lenin turned Trotsky's critique of trade union bureaucracy against him, accusing Trotsky of bureaucratic harrassment of the trade unions.

TROTSKY'S REPUTATION in the Soviet Union today among a significant part of the intelligentsia is based largely upon his dictatorial methods during the period of War Communism and the belief that Stalin simply imitated them. The four-stage program presented to the Ninth Party Congress is seen as the forerunner of the Five-Year Plans. The contemporary Soviet intelligentsia divide over many issues, but they all seem to be united in their contempt for Trotsky. Those who despise Stalin believe that Trotsky would have behaved as badly as Stalin had he won and Stalin lost in the struggle for succession after Lenin's death. Those who still believe that Stalin's methods were the only ones that guaranteed the survival of the Soviet Union see Trotsky from Stalin's point of view. The former group forgive Lenin and Bukharin their sins during War Communism because they became advocates of a more pluralistic approach to economic development, the one currently popular among Soviet reformers. Trotsky, on the other hand, seemed wed to the methods of War Communism. Yet he had simply followed organizational imperatives laid down by previous policy decisions and had taken only the role of point man for a policy backed by both Lenin and Bukharin, the party's other premier theoreticians, and supported by the party's leading organs between 1918 and 1920.

In fact, all three men bore some share of the responsibility for the system that emerged full-blown under Stalin. However, the others cannot be held responsible for the new rules of the political game established by Stalin. It seems futile to pick through the rubble of their policies at different points between 1918 and 1924 to see what parts of them can be held up now as a sign of historical grace or a source of damnation. One can blame a great deal on the miseries of war, Civil War, and economic isolation. However, the centrality of the idea of large-scale production in Marxian theory, Lenin's decision to seize power, and the consequences issuing from his later decisions to maintain dictatorial power for himself and his party still remain the single most important causes of the agonizing policy debates that followed. Trotsky's program of 1919–1920 reflected earlier decisions made by Lenin and the party. He differed from Lenin and the others only in his merciless consequentiality—a good trait for a revolutionary, but a source of ruin for a politician.

LENIN, ACTING more like a politician trying to preserve his power than like a revolutionary zealot, in some respects repeated his retreat after the failure of the revolution of 1905. The parallel is a bit weak, in that now Lenin had to decide to call off an offensive and make compromises with his subjects rather than with the institutions of the autocracy. However, the retreat demoralized and split the party, as it had earlier. Lenin had to abandon the ultrarevolutionaries and utopians, those whom he had earlier encouraged. He proceeded to treat them like children, sprinkling his polemics with references to infantilism and exhortations to grow up, and accusations that his opponents did not know Marxism. Yet he could not admit that the Mensheviks and Socialist Revolutionaries had been right. Thus, he resolved to finish off the opposition outside the party as well as to purge the factions within it. Before the Tenth Party Congress he began to use the metaphor of illness in the party, a metaphor he had used before when preparing to purge it. Trotsky, for three years Lenin's ablest lieutenant, now became one of the sources of the "fever" in the party.

35

1921: Year of Crisis and Retreat

O NCE THE split in the Central Committee over the policy toward the trade unions became public, Lenin attacked Trotsky and Bukharin mercilessly and not always coherently. The article of January 19, 1921 in *Pravda* entitled "The Party Crisis" had a feverish tone reminiscent of Lenin's early polemical works signaling a major split. In this and other speeches and articles Lenin chewed over every step, every bit of incriminating evidence that showed that his opponents had fallen into serious sins, of which factionalism was only one. Lenin's rhetoric escalated to the point where he accused Trotsky not only of factionalism and "bureaucratic excesses" but of imperiling the very revolution and the dictatorship of the proletariat (meaning Communist rule) by precipitating the split. Trotsky, to be sure, had behaved tactlessly by talking about a "shake-up" of the trade unions, but Lenin's attack on him has the feel of a personal vendetta. When disagreeing in closed sessions, Lenin and Trotsky debated ruthlessly and intemperately—something hinted at even in Trotsky's later pious accounts of their relationship. After the debate broke into the party press, Trotsky and others blamed Lenin for attempting to intimidate and silence them, and this only incited Lenin to even angrier denunciations in public forums. He reacted bitterly and angrily to Trotsky's public criticisms of him even though Trotsky's had a far more temperate tone than his.

Furthermore, he now accused Bukharin of blundering over to the side of the syndicalists in the trade union debate, of supporting un-Marxist and un-Communist positions. Bukharin did not understand Marxism at all: "Politics is the concentrated expression of economics. . . . Politics must take precedence over economics. To argue otherwise is to forget the alphabet of Marxism. . . . By preaching a combined political and economic approach, Bukharin has fallen theoretically into *eclecticism*."[1] Lenin did everything in his power to humiliate his opponents publicly, including lecturing Bukharin, the party's outstanding theoretician, on dialectics. Lenin's lessons on dialectics recall the struggles with Bogdanov leading to his expulsion in 1908 and the publication of *Materialism and Empiriocriticism*. Bogdanov, now a member of the party, still inspired alarm as a powerful intellectual influence on Bukharin and among Left Communists. Lenin thus reacted vehemently to what he believed was a recrudescence of the dangerous heresies of the period 1907–1910. He even revived the antisyndicalist rhetoric of that period in the metaphor of a "child-hood disease."[2] Not idle rhetoric, his attacks signaled Lenin's deadly earnestness and his readiness to resort to a purge in order to cure the party's disease. But alongside his concern for the health of the party appears Lenin's anxiety about threats to his leadership. Lenin was incapable of separating the two.

It was no longer merely a matter of a young Russian party trying to acquire maturity in an international movement. Lenin, the leader of the Third International, the Communist International, now stood where Marx, Engels, and Kautsky had. As the elder statesman of revolutionary Marxism, he lectured to an international audience, but unlike his predecessors, he did so as modern history's most successful revolutionary tactician. In his influential pamphlet published in May 1920, *"Left-Wing" Communism, an Infantile Disorder*, Lenin sounded a note of self-affirmation, of political pride, when surveying the twists and turns, attacks and retreats, all of which had educated him and the party in political maneuvering, yielded revolutionary victory, and sustained them in power. The main point of the pamphlet was to prepare the movement for tactical retreat and compromise, to show that earlier retreats and compromises had not diminished the fighting spirit of the party or deterred victory. Quite the contrary, one sometimes had to use the institutions of the bourgeoisie, enter into alliances with opponents in order to defeat a common enemy and then turn against the erstwhile ally. Communists should support their temporary allies, as Lenin put it, "the way a rope supports the neck of a hanged man." Lenin asserted his mature understanding of dialectics—a method yielding knowledge of the nature of class struggle at a given historical moment and providing the utmost tactical flexibility.

In 1920–1921 Lenin believed that he had to steer a perilous course between the "bureaucratic excesses" and militarization of War Communism, on the one side, and, on the other, intemperate critiques of centralization and bureaucracy by the Democratic Centralists and the Workers' Opposition. The latter had great influence in the trade union movement and were infecting the proletariat with the more dangerous, from his point of view, childhood disease of syndicalism. It seems odd to call the Democratic Centralists and Workers' Opposition left-wing heresies, for what is involved is not so much a difference between Right and Left in ideological terms as "hard" and "soft" notions of leadership and organization: the "democratic centralism" of the Communist Party—meaning de facto rule by the Central Committee and centralized and single-person command in industry versus grassroots initiative and control exercised through collegial management; hierarchy versus egalitarianism; statism versus syndicalism; de facto dictatorship versus democracy. The platform of the Workers' Opposition was put most eloquently by Alexandra Kollontai in *The Workers' Opposition*, her critique of the bureaucratization of the party, the recruitment of bourgeois specialists into the managerial stratum in industry, and the principle of one-man management:

> The basis of the controversy is precisely this: whether we shall realize communism through workers or over their heads, by the hands of Soviet officials. And let us, comrades, ponder: Is it possible to attain and build a Communist economy by the hands and creative abilities of the scions from the other class who are imbued with their *routine of the past?* If we begin to think as Marxians, as people of science, we shall answer categorically and explicitly—no.[3]

The Workers' Opposition demanded that the Party expel all nonproletarian elements, that it remove all bourgeois specialists from the administration, that it reverse the regime of bureaucratic appointment from above and tap local workers' initiative. They demanded measures similar to those outlined in Lenin's own *The State and Revolution*.

Kollontai's critique had far more dangerous implications than Trotsky's. Quite clearly, slogans of Soviet rule and the dictatorship of the proletariat fit ill with the rule of a horde of bureaucrats and careerists, many of them former servants of the old ruling class with specialists' skills. The fact that the party gave its blessing to this stratum of political and economic managers made it all the more galling to the oppositionists. Trotsky had made himself the main protector, but those who were sufficiently astute understood what Trotsky himself knew all too well. He was Lenin's and the party's hired gun, faithfully trying to restore production and creating a technically competent managerial stratum. However, in Lenin's view the politics of the situation demanded, at the very least, a symbolic retreat of the hards and, by refusing to mouth the rhetoric of compromise, Trotsky had made himself a political liability. Lenin wielded a two-edged sword: In 1921 he savagely attacked both Trotsky and the Left Opposition. The bourgeois order had survived; the Soviet state was barely surviving. The proletariat had to regroup and with iron discipline hold what ground it could until the next opportunity for attack. It was a dangerous maneuver. Lenin's approach satisfied neither the hards nor the softs, for, although retreating from the economic program of War Communism, he strengthened the party's political dictatorship and maintained what the oppositionists called "bourgeois" forms of bureaucratic control over the proletariat.

THE REGIME felt its utter isolation, painfully brought home during 1920–1921 by massive peasant insurrections. Large-scale peasant uprisings assumed an especially menacing character now because masses of demobilized soldiers were available as recruits and leaders. The last coercive measures of War Communism, the breakdown of food supplies, and hunger in the cities also provoked a large-scale strike movement and the return of Petrograd to its rebellious mood of 1917—this time against the Communist regime. Months of mounting popular anguish and anger preceded the Kronstadt rebellion. Those who had passed through the experience of February 1917 could easily interpret the strikes in Petrograd of February–March 1921 and the Kronstadt rebellion as the beginning of a new phase of the revolution. The remaining Mensheviks and Socialist Revolutionaries in Soviet institutions raised a clamor of criticism against the policies of War Communism and fueled the atmosphere of rebellion. All of this occurred while the world press carried numerous stories of the imminent collapse of the Soviet regime. Finally, former stalwarts of 1917, Trotsky and Kollontai, stood up to Lenin and refused to submit to his notion of party discipline.

A leader with less political stamina, with a streak of fatalism and a less robust will to power, might have bowed his head and admitted defeat. Lenin showed utter ruthlessness and went over to the attack. The propaganda barrage used to discredit the rebels of Kronstadt and the Left Oppositionists within the party give some forewarning of Stalin's future campaigns. White generals, Menshevik and SR schemers, and émigré plotters were accused of conspiring with the Kronstadters. Although in a moment of candor Lenin admitted to the delegates of the Tenth Party Congress that the Kronstadters "do not want the White Guards, and they do not want our power either,"[4] he used the resurgence of opposition as an excuse for intimidating and muzzling his critics within the party. As in 1908, Lenin would not stop until he had excised from the body of the party the infected organs, even if it meant purging or executing those who had been in the forefront of the struggle during 1917–1920. It was a struggle between the principle of political organization and that of revolutionary purity embodied in the idea of workers' democracy and control.

The story of the Kronstadt rebellion cannot be told here. Although it fails to capture the angry mood and the bloody outcome of the rebellion, the following bit of inspired doggerel conveys the revolutionary hopes of the mutineers:

> O what a bright morn is dawning: Trotsky's fetters we're now throwing off!
> And Lenin the tsar we'll be toppling, As dictatorship comes crashing down! The
> toiler shall find a new freedom: Land and works will be labor's own. Free labor's
> the road to equality, To brotherhood now and forever, So let's do it now, or we'll
> never![5]

The Kronstadt rebellion set the stage for the defeat of the opposition. Trotsky and other oppositionists found themselves backed into a corner by Lenin and to an even greater extent by the situation. Petrograd and Kronstadt, with which Trotsky and Kollontai, both now seen as factionalists, had formed special relationships in 1917, had become centers of sedition and rebellion. Trotsky had become a hated taskmaster. Zinov'ev's efforts to diminish Trotsky's influence in the area had only aggravated the mistrust that had grown up between the sailors and the party regime. Lenin no doubt had a frank conversation with Trotsky during their meeting before his departure for Petrograd. Trotsky had to display his *partiinost'* by dealing as ruthlessly with his former favorites as he had with other enemies of the regime. On March 5 he issued an ultimatum to the sailors to lay down their arms, in vain. Zinov'ev authored a far harsher threat. But it was Trotsky who, as War Commissar and chairman of the Revolutionary War Council, had the real authority in suppressing the Kronstadt rebellion.

The assault on the naval fortress began on March 8, 1921, the day of the opening of the Tenth Party Congress, and ended only on March 18. Although Trotsky, unlike many delegates to the Congress, did not take part in the actual fighting, he had made plans with his military staff to use gas against the insurgents, if it proved necessary.[6] The author of a treatise on revolutionary terror, *Terrorism and Communism*, Trotsky had no compunctions about using whatever means he had at his disposal to achieve his end. Although he and his generals did not have to execute the planned gas attack, the siege and taking of the fortress probably cost the Red Army and the party, which contributed thousands of activists to the final assault, more than ten thousand casualties.[7] Between two and three hundred delegates left the Tenth Party Congress to take part in the assault, prominent among them leaders of the Workers' Opposition, whose infantile leftism, according to Lenin and Trotsky, had helped inflame the insurrectionaries. Alexandra Kollontai, no less than the other oppositionists at the Congress, had to protest the loyalty of her faction and boast of their role in the suppression of the Kronstadt rebellion—only to be derided by the delegates. Like Trotsky she had to accuse of "petty-bourgeois spontaneity" those whom she herself had inspired in 1917 with the promise of a new world.[8] One could not otherwise remain a member of Lenin's victorious party—of the vanguard of the proletariat.

One can only imagine the bitterness Trotsky felt as he contemplated the bombardment of the former citadel of the revolution with poison gas. Sailors and proletarians who had adored him now hated him. To be sure, Trotsky could console himself with the thought that the war had depleted the earlier heroic population of both the city and the naval base. Those who hated him were not the proletarians who had made the revolution. Furthermore, not he but Lenin and the party had brought things to this pass. Trotsky made his first speech at the Tenth Party Congress on March 14, with the siege of Kronstadt still in progress. He accused Lenin and the CC of having rejected his policy of retreat in February 1920. Now they presented it, almost word for word, as

NEP, but in far worse conditions, indeed, in the midst of a crisis. During the ensuing year relations with the peasants had seriously deteriorated.[9]

In the main Trotsky attacked the theses on the trade unions, defended his transport bureaucracy, and directed his fire at Zinov'ev, although Zinov'ev had only acted as Lenin's main executive in the struggle against Trotsky in the debate over the trade unions. Lenin replied in the most acid manner, accusing Trotsky of having instigated the entire controversy with his talk of a "shake-up" of the trade unions. Furthermore, Trotsky had publicly accused him, Lenin, of wrecking the discussion at the end of December 1920, when only a "blind man" could fail to see how much harm the open debate was causing. At these words Trotsky laughed bitterly and loudly and provoked Lenin to further revelations to the Congress. In December Trotsky had accused Lenin of exhibiting "diabolical rage," *osatanenie*; earlier, he had violated CC discipline by refusing to serve on Zinov'ev's subcommittee.[10] In short, Lenin berated Trotsky before the entire Congress as if he were scolding an errant schoolboy.

However, he did not silence him. Trotsky accused Lenin of giving a false account of the history of the debate and quoted some of the intemperate language Lenin had used against the leader of the trade union movement, Tomsky, when Lenin had been on the same side of the debate as Trotsky. Although Trotsky still attacked Zinov'ev, the accusation of double-dealing he hurled at him quite clearly referred to Lenin as well.[11] Zinov'ev had acted as Lenin's cudgel. They had shifted the policy suddenly, tried to make him the scapegoat, to silence him, and now were attempting to rewrite the history of the whole affair. To this Trotsky refused to submit without a fight, but the outcome was predetermined. The mood of retreat had won out. Nothing that Trotsky said could change the situation. The world that he had begun to build in 1917 had started to collapse. He had sacrificed his ego—so he thought— done the dirty work of the party, and now stood accused by Lenin of breaking discipline. Unlike Lenin, whose relentless will to power and struggle sustained him through the crisis, in March 1921 Trotsky suffered a psychological and political blow from which he never fully recovered.

The utter bankruptcy of revolutionary forecasts and feverish hopes inspired during 1918–1921 by the utopian dreams of economic planners and engineers, the failure of labor mobilization, the ruined state of both the economy and the urban labor force—all of this did not throw Lenin into utter despair. He knew only one way to operate: He would continue to struggle for his goals. Now he retreated to his earlier notion of state capitalism—a somewhat confused notion to be sure, but a far more fruitful approach to economic recovery than forced and militarized labor and grain requisitioning. However, Lenin's political psychology only increased the isolation of the "vanguard." Although he retreated significantly from the regime's efforts to create a command economy in the fullest sense, he simultaneously attacked on the political front. He laid what he believed was the groundwork for a more disciplined and less factious party. This new development, more than any, revealed once again that power mattered most to Lenin. He would compromise socialist principles—but neither his party's monopoly of power nor his personal control of the party.

Both measures, the retreat to NEP and the attack against the factions, had fatal flaws. The regime had created a great reservoir of mistrust in the countryside. It would have taken many years of free trade and agrarian recovery before the peasants would trust Communist intentions. The full recovery of trust, of course, never occurred. The mutual hostility of peasants and Communists and the party's own disagreements over economic development doomed both NEP and party unity. The party never hit upon a policy that could stabilize the terms of trade between factory and village, between the industrial sector and the agrarian one. It remained committed to maintaining the supremacy of the city over the countryside and clung to a philosophy of massive industrial expansion. Ultimately, this entailed the use of force against the peasants. However, during the first years of NEP the regime's failures served less as a trigger for a renewed struggle between the party and the peasants than as occasions for intraparty conflict and jockeying for position by the oligarchs.

36

Lenin's Last Campaigns

LENIN LIVED to see only the partial economic recovery of the Soviet state under the New Economic Policy and on numerous occasions revealed anxiety about the impact of his retreat. Toward the end of 1921 he began to abandon his Spartan work regime. A victim of advanced arteriosclerosis, Lenin probably suffered minute strokes, signaled by headaches and moments of utter exhaustion, long before his first serious stroke and incapacitation on May 25, 1922. More than four years of a murderous schedule and relentless stress in his roles as Chairman of the Sovnarkom and leader of the Communist Party, frequent fits of rage, and a hereditary disposition to arteriosclerosis doubtlessly all contributed to Lenin's deteriorating health and his death in January 1924.

AT THE beginning of 1922 things stood badly with the Soviet state. The famine of 1921–1922 had forced Lenin to turn to the bourgeois nations for economic assistance. The Western world expected the Soviet state either to collapse or else to return, by way of embourgeoisment, to the community of civilized nations. A less fiercely committed leader might have faltered during the period of transition to NEP, a period of disappointment and humiliation. Lenin, however, had no intentions of giving up what he had won on the political front. To the world's shock he instead returned to the attack. In a pattern now reasonably familiar to students of Leninist regimes, with fierce determination he showed the Communist Party's will to maintain its monopoly of power.

In a letter of February 20, 1922, Lenin exhorted D. I. Kurskii, Commissar of Justice, to bring his judicial policy into line with the NEP. The Commissariat of Justice now had to play the militant role formerly assumed by the military and the Cheka. For this purpose "model trials"—what we now call "show trials"—would be used to educate the popular masses, teach them how swiftly and powerfully the regime dealt with enemies. Trials staged in major cities (Moscow, Petrograd, Khar'kov, for example) would educate the masses about Menshevik and SR traitors, saboteurs, and terrorists and about the limits of NEP. Lenin would not permit capitalism to flourish outside the boundaries of the regime's state capitalism, however ill-defined the latter. In an accusatory tone he told his Commissar of Justice that despite all of the clamor in the press about the abuses occurring under NEP, nothing had been done yet to display the sins of the scoundrels trying to exploit the regime's retreat. The Communists' will to repress enemies should be exhibited in exemplary trials featuring merciless and swift punishments. They should not flinch from the death penalty. In effect, Lenin warned Kurskii that if they did not display sufficient energy and *shoot* enough people as examples, he would hold the judiciary responsible.[1] The judiciary obliged him with a show trial featuring the Socialist Revolutionaries.

If among the party oligarchs Trotsky had played the role of scapegoat for the failures of War Communism, and White generals and a host of other conspirators (including, not least of all, the SRs) had been blamed for the Kronstadt mutiny, in party propaganda for mass consumption the SRs had to carry the largest share of blame for the peasant uprisings, terrorism against Communist leaders, and the famine. True to his hard position on Kronstadt, Trotsky played a central role in the composition of the indictment against the SRs. He had long favored trials as a method of revolutionary propaganda. Courtroom drama and rhetoric suited Trotsky well, and in his memoirs he claimed that it was he who arrived at idea of making the death sentences conditional: The death sentence would not be enforced so long as the SRs did not engage in terrorist acts against the Soviet regime. In effect, the regime took the SR leaders hostage.[2] Bukharin observed party discipline (presumably against his personal convictions) and took a hard line, and although Stalin was involved in the preparation for the trial, it is not easy to determine exactly how. Lenin had spurred on this campaign, but his illness did not permit him to play a major role during the trial, which took place between June 8 and August 7, 1922, in Moscow.[3]

The trial of the SRs is of more than passing interest, for it can be seen as a predecessor of the show trials under Stalin and raises questions about Stalin's debt to Lenin for the methods he used during the Great Terror. The role of the 1922 trial seems clear enough: It was designed not only to teach but to intimidate and to destroy any hopes that the economic concessions to the peasants under NEP would be accompanied by the political revival of the party of the peasants—the SRs. Although the millions of voters who had supported the SRs in 1917 did not constitute an immediate political threat, Lenin decided that it was time to put an end to the political opposition both within the party and without, and there was no better way to combine political repression and propaganda against one's enemies than through a show trial.

To be sure, things did not go smoothly. The SRs knew how to play the game of accusing their accusers, of capturing the sympathy of the foreign intelligentsia. The rules of the political-judicial game in 1922 were far laxer and more humane those of the infamous Moscow Trials under Vyshinskii and Stalin, where confessions were extracted by torture and ritualized and the death penalty enforced. Thanks largely to the outcry among foreign intellectuals, the outcome in 1922 was also far milder for the twenty-four defendants—surprisingly mild in view of the mockery of ordinary judicial procedure and the frenzy whipped up by Communist agitators. No one was actually executed, despite the pronouncement of fifteen "conditional" death sentences.[4] The fact remains that Lenin initiated the Soviet practice (the tsarist regime's staging of trials of terrorists preceded it) of using the courts as political arenas. He wanted to show that the law of the revolutionary state took precedence over private rights, that civil rights would be subjected to "revolutionary legal consciousness."[5] Some of the foremost theoreticians of the regime as well as leading poets and artists contributed to the campaign. The utility of such a spectacle was hardly lost on Stalin, whatever his role in 1922.

THE SUPPRESSION of the SRs and Mensheviks only partly eased Lenin's worries about the condition of his regime. The health of the party itself remained his main concern during the last three years of his life. He continued to attack the oppositionists. Lenin presided over the purge of roughly one-fourth of the party in 1921 and when healthy in 1922 helped engineer the suppression of the Workers' Opposition and Democratic Centralists. The Workers' Opposition claimed to be the voice of a betrayed proletariat. To the oppositionists it mattered little that the party had repressed the SRs. The Communist Party itself now represented the interests of the petty-bourgeois peasants. Moreover, to the Workers' Opposition and the splinter groups that formed after the purge of 1921 the horde of bureaucrats, the "technical intelligentsia," served their own interests and those of the NEP bourgeoisie, of which they were a part, but neglected those of the factory proletariat. Unemployment and layoffs connected with the end of the Civil War and the beginning of NEP created enormous resentment in the factory labor force. Some defected from the party and formed clandestine workers' groups. Given the atmosphere of disillusionment and disarray, Lenin would not tolerate dissent. He reacted furiously to the opposition's futile appeal to the Comintern against his policies and even turned to Trotsky to help in his struggle against Kollontai, Shliapnikov, and S. P. Medvedev, the triumvirate leading the Workers' Opposition. Trotsky apparently returned once again to his old role of Lenin's "cudgel" in the Comintern in February 1922, although after his experiences of 1920–1921 he remained circumspect.

In 1921–1922 Lenin increasingly resorted to the organizational weapons which had distinguished him among the early Social Democratic leaders. Although formally in power, the party remained an island in a bourgeois sea. It could not afford the luxury of open discussion anymore; it could not tolerate dissent; it could not give its ubiquitous enemies the opportunity to destroy it. Now working mainly through Stalin and Molotov, Lenin cut off the opposition at its roots by extending the power of the central apparatus. Stalin proved to be a master of this technique, quickly discovering that the real levers of power could be exercised through the central party apparatus. At first operating through the Politburo and the Organizational Bureau (created in December 1919) of the Central Committee, Stalin became the prime mover of the *apparat* in April 1922, when the CC made him General Secretary of the Party. Appointments, purges, and the setting of the Central Committee's agenda became the basic methods for bringing the party to heel, lining up support at party congresses, and guiding policy. If we are to believe a man who claimed to be member of Stalin's own staff in 1923–1926, and a secretary of the Politburo in 1923–1924, Stalin soon installed a secret telephone line and could eavesdrop on the conversations of his colleagues.[6] Stalin had come to understand that the Worker-Peasant Inspectorate (Rabkrin), in which Lenin had invested his hopes for control over the abuses of the state bureaucracy, would not serve his purposes. Although he himself had encouraged Lenin to create such an organ, Stalin asked to be relieved of his position as head of Rabkrin once he assumed the post of General Secretary. His neglect of Rabkrin, however, opened him to Lenin's criticism, as shall be seen shortly.

After Sverdlov's death the Secretariat of the CC had passed to Stasova, then to Krestinskii, soon joined by Preobrazhenskii and Serebriakov, and in 1921 to Molotov chiefly, before Stalin took over. The failure of Sverdlov's successors to manage the *apparat's* affairs had led to successive reorganizations of the Secretariat. The last shifts to Molotov and Stalin were probably also symptomatic of the diminution of Trotsky's influence and the oligarchs' maneuvers to undermine his position. There is no indication that Lenin himself wished to restore Trotsky's strength in the party. At this moment of dangerous retreat Lenin would only place the most trusted insiders, those who knew the modus operandi of the party thoroughly and intimately, in positions that would influence the disposition of delegates to party congresses and engineer majorities for the party line. Still another watchdog organ, the Central Control Commission, became part of Stalin's arsenal in 1922. There can be no doubt that Lenin continued to place great trust and confidence in Stalin during the first months of 1922.

Already the most authoritative member of the Organizational Bureau, Stalin in 1921 used the mandate given him to struggle against the Workers' Opposition and the Democratic Centralists as a means of disposing of Trotsky's supporters as well. Lenin's complicity in this secret campaign against Trotsky cannot be documented, but it is difficult to believe that Stalin could have engineered the election of delegates to the Eleventh Party Congress without consultation with Lenin. Stalin, probably with Lenin's blessing, was therefore using the party's central organs to undermine Trotsky's support in 1921, even before he assumed the post of General Secretary.[7] However, the major task at hand was the destruction of the Workers' Opposition and the Democratic Centralists.

Although the opposition had less strength at the Eleventh than at the Tenth Party Congress, the new masters of the *apparat* still could not command the unanimity that Lenin now demanded. For example, in August 1921 it still was not possible to get the two-thirds majority necessary to expel Shliapnikov from the CC. The leadership was not able to prevent Shliapnikov from appearing at the Congress as a delegate or avoid criticisms from the floor. Lenin's health allowed him to participate only minimally in the Eleventh Party Congress, but his long speech on March 27, 1922, showed typical combativeness and to the oppositionists had sinister overtones. Lenin recommended the use of machine guns to keep a retreating army, the party, from a panicky and disorderly rout. Shliapnikov took this as a threat against the opposition within the party. In his rebuttal to Shliapnikov on March 28, Lenin defensively claimed that he meant the Mensheviks and SRs, but quickly went over to the attack, reminding the Congress that Shliapnikov had narrowly escaped expulsion from the party. He made a point of praising Trotsky's attack on the Workers' Opposition and also praised Stalin highly, as if prefiguring his letter to the Twelfth Party Congress, in which he designated Trotsky and Stalin the two outstanding leaders in the CC.

In his closing speech at the last session of the Eleventh Party Congress Lenin seemed to be trying to convince the delegates, and perhaps himself too, that things were going well. He ridiculed the party's enemies who claimed that the party was "growing old, losing its mental resiliency and the resiliency of the entire organism." Lenin, who had recovered sufficiently from his stroke in May to deliver a speech of almost two hours was referring whether consciously or unconsciously to himself as well as the party, but he could not really hide the truth about the gravity of his condition from himself for very long. He began to rearrange the affairs of the state and the party. Yet in the end he was incapable of yielding his preeminence and formulating an unambiguous testament.

DURING 1921 Lenin had kept Trotsky at a distance. He used him to attack the Left Opposition and the SRs in 1922, and several times in that same year he proposed that Trotsky be made one of three or four deputy chairmen of the Sovnarkom, a post which Trotsky rejected, to Lenin's chagrin. Evidently, not only Trotsky but other top leaders (in this instance, Rykov and Tomsky) objected to Lenin's administrative improvisations.[8] Although his health forced him to seek new arrangements, Lenin also seemed to be trying to use the most authoritative party members in different combinations in both party and state institutions in order to balance power among them and to avoid excessive concentrations of it in any given individual, duumvirate, or triumvirate. (Needless to say, in Stalin's case, he failed.) Assuming that he had benign intentions in encouraging collective leadership in both the party and state, Lenin's manipulations of top personnel also tended to keep him in a position of undisputed authority. No doubt resenting this, Trotsky persistently refused the job of deputy chair, and Stalin saw to it that he paid a big price for such delinquency. However, Lenin refused to be put off. He had more uses for Trotsky.

After the Eleventh Party Congress the machinery created to discipline the party and dispose of the remaining opposition quickly began to operate at Stalin's behest and sometimes against Lenin's will. All of Lenin's efforts to control the bureaucracy had yielded only more bureaucracy and greater problems; all of his organizational weapons fell into the hands of people whom he trusted only provisionally and whose actions now antagonized him. His praise of Stalin, as of others, proved to be hollow. Lenin grew anxious at the thought of other hands steering the party. During his extended illness, when his loss of power became apparent to him, he became increasingly critical of the way Stalin was using the party's organizational weapons. Lenin began to listen more attentively to Trotsky's criticisms of the party bureaucracy. In December 1922 he expressed a desire to form a "bloc" with Trotsky in order to put Stalin in his place. He operated, out of habit, in a quasiconspiratorial manner, and used his last remaining strength trying to show his lieutenants that he could still hold the reins of power. Lenin knew that his alliance with Trotsky would intimidate the others. He began to arrange his last political campaign.

Lenin waged his campaign against Stalin and the *apparat* on several fronts. The first skirmish occurred in May 1922 over the party's effort to change Lenin's policy on the government's monopoly of foreign trade. Two months earlier Lenin had expressed alarm at the thought of foreign capitalists penetrating the country and linking up with the mass of petty-bourgeois peasants. His attitude toward the monopoly of foreign trade issued from his anxiety that the strict boundaries of NEP and the defensive line established during the party's retreat might be breached. Lenin's adamant position was a symptom of his fierce desire to maintain the party's monopoly of power and to return to the attack as quickly as possible. In a letter to Kamenev of March 3, 1922, he had expressed his intentions in no uncertain terms: "It is the greatest mistake to think that NEP assumes an end to terror. We will resort to terror again and to economic terror."[9] The Politburo's proposed policy of relaxation, however consistent with the economic logic of NEP, might tempt both the foreign bourgeoisie and the peasants to exploit the regime's weakness.

Supporters of the monopoly—planners and those who believed in the quickest route to industrial recovery—predicted that the end to the monopoly of foreign trade would mean a flow of consumer goods to the peasants and a dearth of investment in heavy industry. Those who wanted to maintain and encourage currency stabilization and agricultural recovery sought ways to permit the foreigners to buy grain directly and to give peasants access to desired goods. The lines were being drawn for the long struggle between the "Left" (Trotsky, Preobrazhenskii, and others) and the "Right" (Stalin, Bukharin, and others) over economic policy. Lenin sided with the Left on the issue of the state monopoly over foreign trade—and won a temporary victory on May 22. His first paralytic stroke occurred three days later, and he did not recover sufficiently to return to his work schedule until October. The counterattack of the Right and its victory on October 6, 1922 (significantly, a day when Lenin could not attend a CC meeting because of illness), spurred Lenin, who soon thereafter recovered sufficiently to try his habitual political methods, to seek alliances. On October 11 he approached Trotsky.

Trotsky vaguely suggests in his autobiography that Stalin, too, had courted him in 1922, although he does not specify over what issue.[10] Clearly, to Stalin and a majority of the CC, Lenin was becoming more of a burden to the party in its conduct of NEP than an effective political leader. Lenin, no doubt sensing a change in attitude toward him, redoubled his efforts to retain control and to prove his capacity to lead. All of this led to an escalation of bad feeling between him and his recent allies in the oligarchy and his decision to rely more heavily upon Trotsky—to form a "bloc" with him. However, Trotsky, like the others, had grown accustomed to Lenin's maneuvers and knew that any alliance with him might easily end badly. Furthermore, in view of the state of Lenin's health, it would be doubly unwise for Trotsky to jeopardize his already precarious position with his colleagues in the party by joining Lenin in an alliance. Should he ally himself with a dying lion? Trotsky, as shall be seen, tried to have it both ways. He and Lenin agreed about the foreign trade monopoly, but Trotsky wanted to broaden the counterattack of the Left by getting Lenin's support for a strengthening of the State Planning Commission (Gosplan). Lenin did not want to proceed immediately on Gosplan, but nonetheless signaled enough backing to win Trotsky's support by December 15, 1922. All of Lenin's maneuvers came to a head at that time in preparation for a plenum of the CC.

Once again, Lenin won and continued to struggle despite a series of strokes in mid- to late December. On December 18, 1922, the CC annulled its decision of October 6 and reinstated Lenin's policy on the state monopoly of foreign trade. Three days later Lenin sent a celebratory letter to Trotsky. The prideful tone of the letter leaves little doubt as to Lenin's belief that he was overcoming the effects of the illness he had suffered shortly before the CC meeting. He had proven himself once again by achieving the ultimate in generalship. In Lenin's words, they had captured the position without having to fire a shot. The mere threat of their alliance had led the CC to surrender. However, on the night of December 22, not long after his victory, Lenin suffered another paralytic stroke. It seems remarkable that in spite of his illness, within a few days Lenin began to fulfill his part of the bargain with

Trotsky by sketching out a compromise that would strengthen Gosplan and possibly give it legislative force. However, during his ruminations about Gosplan Lenin revealed his reservations about Trotsky.

On December 23, as if in denial of the gravity of his illness, he began to dictate notes on a variety of issues in preparation for the Twelfth Party Congress.[11] One finds in the notes echoes of his famous remarks about Trotsky's "preoccupation with the purely administrative side of work" in the "Testament" of December 24–25, 1922. The "Testament" seems to be a sort of aside, a commentary on personnel matters, rather than a distinct, coherent statement with a definite purpose. Lenin's thoughts about Trotsky's one-sidedness in the "Testament" was clearly connected with the notes on Gosplan, where he expressed concerns about strengths and weaknesses of different types of administrators. The party needed people with both technical expertise and Communist commitment. Concern with the dichotomy of "Red" and "expert" triggered Lenin's anxiety about a new debate and possibly a split erupting in the party. He knew that Trotsky stood for "expert," meaning subservience to the bourgeois technical intelligentsia and insufficient *partiinost'*, and Stalin for "Red," signifying *partiinost'*, and class loyalty, but lack of respect for expertise.

Lenin found himself torn. When trying to imagine the ideal administrator, he found that both elements, Red and expert, had to be combined in some measure. Without scientific and technical expertise of the sort called for in the State Planning Commission, nothing could be accomplished toward a developed centralized economy. Yet such expertise could be found mainly in the intelligentsia of the old regime, a much despised and mistrusted stratum. Only Communist vigilance could keep it in check. Lenin decided to solve the problem by splitting functions: The party should create a watchdog political group, a presidium composed of Communists, to oversee the bourgeois experts. Furthermore, Gosplan and other Soviet bureaucracies needed administrators with strong scientific-technical background but also with breadth of experience and the capacity to enlist the loyalty of their colleagues. Lenin's notes implicitly condemned Trotsky, who did not possess the qualities Lenin called for. Trotsky and another leftist, G. L. Piatakov of Gosplan, belonged to that group of comrades Lenin criticized for exaggerating "the administrative side" of things. In Lenin's mind, three kinds of tensions—Red versus expert, administrative severity as opposed to the capacity to enlist the loyalty of coworkers, and emphasis upon administrative methods instead of political adaptability—created continuous dilemmas that could only be resolved by playing individuals and groups off against other. Trotsky's Arakcheevism, his arrogance, and his association with expertise rather than with *partiinost'* limited him as a top administrator in Lenin's mind, however much Lenin prized his capacity to get things done and his current "hard" positions. Thus, Lenin's notes on Gosplan, which were the stimulus for the "Testament" of December 24–25, 1922, suggest that he was looking for a way to fulfill his agreement with Trotsky without giving Trotsky or people like him a decisive role on Gosplan or in the party.

37

The "Testament"

LENIN'S RUMINATIONS about the characteristics of the ideal administrator at the end of December 1922 raised troubling questions about several of the oligarchs, including Stalin. The decisive and sometimes brutal characteristics of both Trotsky and Stalin had commended them to Lenin during 1917–1921, and he still found the two of them to be useful tools. Lenin had relied upon and promoted those who were not afraid to use "plebian methods." They would beat, shoot, terrorize in order to save the regime; they could be relied upon to smash through opposition and standard procedures in order to get a job done. Yet in his last notes and articles Lenin showed doubts about the administrative harshness of the two men whom he called "the two outstanding leaders of the present Central Committee." One searches in vain for any distinct positive signal from Lenin in his "Testament" of December 24–25, 1922. Lenin himself had recognized Stalin as a man of authority and had given him his power, but he now expressed doubts that Stalin was the kind of man who could use vast power with "sufficient caution" — a vast understatement.

Lenin's brief and unsystematic remarks on Trotsky, Stalin, Zinov'ev, Kamenev, Bukharin, and Piatakov do not make up a genuine political testament. They are a section of a draft of a letter to the Twelfth Party Congress summarizing Lenin's recommendations for Gosplan and calling for an expansion in the size of the CC. The remarks about the leaders of the party come haphazardly and are in line with his thoughts about Gosplan and the expansion of the CC. Lenin dictated his notes to M. A. Volodicheva, a member of his staff. He knew that they contained politically important material, for his last bout of stroke and paralysis on the night of December 22, 1922, had finally convinced him that he had to put his political and personal affairs in order. However, alongside these concerns one senses massive denial of the gravity of his illness. The notes he began to dictate reveal, more than anything else, ambivalent feelings and attitudes — mainly anxieties about the people to whom he had to entrust the future of the regime he had created and sustained by incredible exertions of political will and intelligence. According to Volodicheva, Lenin asked for five copies of all his last notes and articles and had them put in sealed envelopes. Only Lenin and, in the event of his death, Krupskaia had the right to open them. It is notable, however, that the notes on the characteristics of the leading candidates for leadership of the party were not separated from the others or treated with special care.[1]

It is clear from the "Testament" that Lenin trusted neither the Old Bolsheviks nor Trotsky. Stalin had dangerous characteristics. Zinov'ev and Kamenev had failed the political test of October. Nor could he rely on the younger generation. To be sure, Lenin called Bukharin and Piatakov "the outstanding talents" among the younger members of the CC and went on to call Bukharin the most valuable and most prominent theoretician in the party. However, he lapsed into his chronic, resentful, and, in this situation, unexpectedly peevish form of dogmatism. Lenin berated Bukharin for theoretical deviations from Marxism, scholasticism, and insufficient knowledge of dialectics. Piatakov suffered from Trotsky's failings: He was too "administrative" in his approach and could not be trusted with political decisions. Nothing in the "Testament" suggests that leaders from either generation had the qualities needed to head the party. Thus, in his "Testament" Lenin seems to have had in mind mainly institutional arrangements that would prevent abuses of power and authority by the oligarchs and minimize the effects of their rivalries.

Even after the stroke of December 22, 1922, with his healthy rapidly failing, Lenin could not bear to name a successor. Although he knew how to use people, he had limited faith in all of them. Trotsky's efforts to present himself as Lenin's heir and main ally in the struggle shaping up between Lenin and Stalin do not have much cogency. Lenin undoubtedly turned to Trotsky for help, and he was on the verge of breaking off personal relations with Stalin, but in neither case did he take a decisive step before he died. Lenin's methods during his last political battles are quite familiar. He used whomever he could against his foes of the moment. There is no reason to believe that he had in mind any enduring alliance. Had he wanted to name a successor or rank his heirs, he had quite enough time before his death to revise the notes of December 24–25 or to expand them. The notes in sketchy form reveal only what most people already knew and add nothing to the stature of a possible successor. Thus, we must look elsewhere for Lenin's testament.

STUDENTS OF Lenin's last letters, notes, and articles believe with greater justice that they, collectively, rather than his remarks about his colleagues, comprise whatever political testament Lenin left. An examination of these articles in the light of Lenin's last alliances and battles, particularly his efforts to circumvent and combat Stalin, at the very least suggests that Lenin had illuminations both about Stalin and the long-term tasks ahead of the party. Undoubtedly, Lenin's attitude toward Stalin had changed fairly dramatically during the winter of 1922–1923. He grew resentful at the CC's wardship over his health, and the CC had made Stalin the main warden. Stalin, to be sure, had at first shunned this role, but the fact that the CC saw him as the logical person for it is indicative of a general belief in Stalin's authority, his relative closeness to Lenin, and probably the confidence of the oligarchs that Stalin would keep a close watch and protect their common interests.

Lenin had always made life difficult for them. Every leading figure in the party had suffered Lenin's abuse or had found himself left in the lurch after one of Lenin's policy reversals. But however much his past humiliations of them rankled, all of them recognized his political genius. As practical politicians of a particularly tough breed, they had been willing to pay a personal price for his remarkably effective leadership. Lenin had given them all a special place in history. Yet now Lenin lay ill. He was failing and not always coherent. Could they let the ramblings of a dying man damage the edifice they had all built together? Ominously, Lenin was scheming with Trotsky—who in their eyes had exploited the party's success in Petrograd, who would have been just another popular agitator had he not joined the party and used its resources at a critical moment, whom even now many of them saw as more a functionary of the state than of the party. Lenin had used Trotsky against them when they had doubted Lenin's slogan of "All Power to the Soviets" and his feverish call for insurrection. He had given Trotsky the lion's share of glory in the Civil War by putting him at the head of the military forces. But Lenin had given Trotsky a political lesson in the trade union debate and brought him down several pegs. It is unlikely that the oligarchs believed that Lenin really wanted to promote Trotsky. More likely, they all had had enough of the political scheming of an invalid and were afraid that it might unduly benefit Trotsky should Lenin die at the wrong moment.

The behavior of the oligarchs suggests that they tried to keep Lenin from engaging in political activity not only because of concern for his health but for the above reasons. Although Stalin's arrangements for spying on Lenin have never been fully brought to light (and perhaps never will be), they almost certainly existed. In a way, spying on Lenin was superfluous, for despite the procedure of concealing his last writings, he did not hide his political intentions. Nonetheless, quick intelligence saved the oligarchs time and trouble. They needed to react immediately, and a sick Lenin might do something unpredictable. During the last months (December 1922–March 1923), when he sustained the will to carry on the political struggle, he stubbornly and sometimes successfully fought the regime set by his doctors and the CC and enforced by Krupskaia and his secretaries. However, the oligarchs could take measures to control any damage issuing from his last political maneuvers and writings. To this end they were willing to resort not only to spying but to deception. Stalin and the others had circumvented Lenin's unreasonable demands and deceived him before. It seemed all the more important to do so now.

Stalin behaved quite unsentimentally and ruthlessly in his dealings with his political mentor and model. Ironically, this was the political modus operandi Lenin himself had encouraged. The party had flourished, so Lenin thought, because executives like Stalin would do whatever was necessary to gain a political goal. Now, Stalin treated Lenin himself as a political liability and fought the sick and dying man, first over the state monopoly of foreign trade and then over the nationalities policy in general and the struggle of the Georgians for autonomy in particular. Moreover, the political struggle took unpleasant personal forms. When Stalin learned that Krupskaia had taken Lenin's dictation for the letter of December 21, 1922, to Trotsky, he expressed his frustration and anger by unleashing a tirade against her, the only opportune target, on December 22, 1922. When Lenin in turn learned about this incident, he took it as a personal affront and was on the verge of a personal break with Stalin. Suddenly, Lenin became acutely aware of the personal style in which his own picked men were conducting affairs of the party and state. The rough plebian manners Lenin had prized seemed sinister, now that they were being used in ways that offended him. Both the incident with Krupskaia and the Georgian affair, which involved Ordzhonikidze and Dzerzhinskii as well, forced Lenin to reexamine his personal and political affairs in a new light.

Lenin and Trotsky Against Stalin

THE GEORGIAN affair resembled many other political struggles between Lenin and his lieutenants. He would give them jurisdiction over a difficult problem or area, support their initiatives up to a point, and when confronted with their "administrative" extremes, not only remove his support but attack them. Thus, Lenin's treatment of Stalin in the debate over the nationalities bears some resemblance to his treatment of Trotsky during the trade union debate. Stalin did not yield immediately to all of Lenin's attacks, and he showed considerable resentment as well as stubborn resistance (up to a point) when Lenin reversed policies in areas where Stalin considered himself to be the expert. This was particularly true with the nationalities policy, an area Lenin had entrusted to Stalin long ago. In 1922 when given responsibility for drafting a constitution for a federation of socialist republics, Stalin, whose conversion to a Great Russian point of view had occurred relatively early in his revolutionary career, expressed his preference in no uncertain terms. He revived in Soviet form the traditional arrangement in which the dominant nationality in a multinational grouping subjected its "younger brothers" to its hegemony. Such an arrangement accorded well with Stalin's respect for power and his realism about relations based upon power. He remains one of history's striking examples of a leader from a "marginal" nationality who identified himself with the oppressor—the dominant nationality in an imperial structure. Thus, Stalin and Lenin clashed over Stalin's handling of the Georgian Communists who felt that Stalin was betraying his own people.

Lenin, to be sure, remained a centralist and sought ways to keep the territories of the old Russian Empire under his party's rule. However, within his own regime he abhorred policies or behavior that smacked of Great Russian chauvinism. He showed no less outrage against such chauvinism as the head of the Soviet state than he had when assailing the tsarist regime's Jew-baiting. Lenin's preference for men of minority background in leading roles in the party and government remains a striking fact. The silence of family or other memoirs about the impact of his own ethnic background on his outlook permits only speculation that personal resentment of Great Russian arrogance toward minorities sometimes lay behind his choices. In the article on the nationalities issue, which he dictated on December 30–31, 1922, Lenin did refer to his personal experience in the Volga area. He bitterly remembered how the Russians showed their contempt for other nationalities by stigmatizing them with humiliating nicknames: Poles were "little Poles," Tatars were always called "Prince," Ukrainians *khokhols* (a reference to the old Cossack hair style).[2] Needless to say, the prominent position of "marginals" in revolutionary parties, particularly in leadership roles, has to be taken into account. As noted earlier, the Bolsheviks, although more Great Russian than other revolutionary parties, still had a misproportionate number of leaders from minority nationalities. One need only to survey the membership of the party's central organs during the period 1917–1924 in order to appreciate this. Lenin clearly identified himself with the victims of Great Russian oppression. However, he was guided by political calculation as well. Appealing to the pride and sense of justice of all nationalities subjected to oppression and discrimination by dominant nationalities in multinational empires, Lenin calculated that exemplary Soviet treatment of minor nationalities would trigger movements for national liberation against the remaining imperial powers.

Although Stalin had mouthed Lenin's views in numerous articles, he evidently thought of them mainly as propaganda and sustained his own traditionalist attitude toward centralization and Russian power. It appeared in his policy of "autonomization." As the head of the committee charged with redesigning the Soviet federal constitution, Stalin sought to make the Ukraine, Belorussia, Azerbaijan, Armenia, and Georgia (the last three united in a Transcaucasian Federation) "autonomous" republics of the Russian Soviet Federated Socialist Republic (RSFSR). Although Stalin's solution did not take the most extreme Great Russian centralist form—simple absorption of the smaller republics into a Russian Soviet Republic—it would have deprived the lesser republics of equal legal status within the RSFSR. In effect, they would be governed from Moscow, the capital of the RSFSR. On the other hand, Lenin clearly wanted to internationalize the Soviet state symbolically by removing from its title any national designation. Hoping that his Soviet state would be a political magnet for others, he suggested the rather cosmopolitan and nationally neutral title "Union of Soviet Republics of Europe and Asia."

During the first months of 1922 Lenin had shown great confidence in Stalin, making him de facto head of the party apparatus. Then, after Lenin's stroke in late May 1922, Stalin had played the privileged role of liaison between Lenin and the party. It must have been something of a slap in the face when Lenin, on September 26, 1922, in an open letter to Kamenev for forwarding to the Politburo specifically urged him and Zinov'ev to busy themselves with the nationalities issue and serve as his watchdogs over Stalin during the discussion of the new federation.[3] Hoping that the others might share his resentment of an invalid's attempts to control them,[4] Stalin criticized Lenin's amendments to his plan and called Lenin's position "national liberalism." However, when he realized that the CC planned to back Lenin's amendments, Stalin acquiesced. He sullenly submitted in the nationalities debate, just as he yielded to Lenin and Trotsky in the struggle over the state monopoly of foreign trade. Thus, in two policy debates Lenin defeated Stalin and his allies of the moment by using the services of the three men who seemingly had the strongest claims to leadership after his death: Trotsky, Kamenev, and Zinov'ev.

In the course of the long debate over nationalities policy the Georgian party, vehemently opposed to autonomization, appealed to high-ranking party members about Stalin's and Ordzhonikidze's methods. Lenin, to be sure, had encouraged the creation of the Transcaucasian Federation, and Ordzhonikidze, the party's chief executive in Transcaucasia, thought like Stalin that he was carrying out centralization under Lenin's auspices in 1921–1922. At first Lenin supported Stalin and Ordzhonikidze against their Georgian critics. He did not back the Georgians' efforts to enter the new Union as a separate republic rather than as part of the Transcaucasian Federation. However, he remained wary of his lieutenants' motives and behavior. In late November 1922, the struggle between Stalin, Ordzhonikidze, and the dissident Georgians took an ugly turn when Ordzhonikidze struck one of them, A. Kobakhidze, during a heated conversation.[5] The incident took place in the presence of Lenin's emissary, Rykov. Lenin impatiently awaited a full report on the incident from Rykov and Dzerzhinskii, who had been commissioned by the CC to investigate the Georgian situation, and when he received it on December 12, he became extremely agitated.[6] The upshot was Lenin's memorandum on the nationalities, which he dictated to his secretary, Volodicheva, on December 30–31, 1922. It became part of the political testament Lenin's staff took down between December 1922 and March 1923. Finally, at the beginning of March 1923 Lenin turned to Trotsky, among others, for help in his campaign against Stalin, Ordzhonikidze, and Dzerzhinskii.

TROTSKY'S ACCOUNT of his role in Lenin's campaign is at odds with most accepted versions, both Soviet and non-Soviet, and thus deserves special scrutiny. Despite Trotsky's portrayal of himself as Lenin's major ally and by implication heir, his reluctance to form an alliance with Lenin can be inferred from his own version of events. Granting its untrustworthiness, the account is nonetheless valuable for its revelations of the attitude of Stalin and probably the other oligarchs towards Lenin during his last months. It also sheds light on the ease with which the other party leaders disposed of a rival as apparently formidable as Trotsky. Finally, Trotsky gives us numerous clues to his own inner turmoil—debilitating ambivalences toward Lenin and the party that were both a symptom and a cause of his political weakness.

There are manifest and latent components to Trotsky's version of the events of March 1923. When he tells the story of Lenin's efforts to form an alliance and his own response, Trotsky, probably not at all consciously, expresses his ambivalence toward Lenin and his anxiety about stepping decisively into a role of leadership in the party. Trotsky, like others, found Lenin's example so powerful that he began to imitate him in some respects. Like Lenin he became an outdoorsman, cultivating a taste for hunting and fishing, and it is likely that when he discusses his outdoor activities in conjunction with political events, Trotsky is putting in symbolic form both his identification with Lenin and his fitness for leadership. In the chapter on Lenin's illness in his autobiography Trotsky describes a hunting and fishing expedition of May 1922. While fishing in the old channel of the Moscow River, Trotsky slipped and injured the ligaments in one foot. The injury forced him to cut short his holiday and convalesce for a few days. On the third day Bukharin visited him and told him about Lenin's paralytic stroke, which had occurred at the same time as Trotsky's accident.[7] Trotsky goes on to surmise that Stalin had concealed the news of Lenin's illness from him. Thus, the story links the two leaders, portrays them as lying helpless while Stalin, Zinov'ev, and Kamenev schemed to seize power.

There may be another, unconscious level to Trotsky's story. It calls to mind earlier stories in his autobiography in which Trotsky is laid low because he is an unwitting impostor and transgressor: the one about the school uniform when he was nine and entering St. Paul's *realschule;* the story of the night at the opera with Lenin, when he had borrowed Lenin's shoes and suffered when they proved too tight. It also prefigures a later story of an accident in October 1923, when he stepped into a bog while on a hunting trip, got his feet wet, caught cold, and developed a "cryptogenic fever." His illness immobilized him at a critical moment during the struggle developing among the party oligarchs. Still another illness occurred roughly a year later, at the time of Lenin's death, preventing his attendance at Lenin's funeral.[8] There seems to be an underlying message in the stories and symbols: Trotsky's false position in the party and his inherent inability to play Lenin's role led to injuries and illnesses. The hunting and fishing accidents suggest self-defeating maneuvers (missteps), cowardice (cold feet), and immersion in a political mess (a bog).

Trotsky's story of Lenin's last effort to form an alliance with him contains similar symbolic elements. At the beginning of March, just before Lenin suffered the stroke that definitively ended his political career, Trotsky once again found himself.abed, this time with lumbago, "separated from Lenin by the enormous courtyard of the Kremlin."[9] According to both Trotsky and a recent Soviet account, in a telephone conversation of March 5, 1923, Volodicheva informed Trotsky that Lenin wanted him to attack Stalin's, Ordzhonikidze's, and Dzerzhinskii's handling of the Georgian affair. On the same day Trotsky received in written form the request that had been read to him over the telephone. It informed him that he might signify his refusal by returning the documents. According to the Soviet account, the next morning Lenin asked about Trotsky's reply, and Volodicheva told him that Trotsky had refused the commission on grounds of illness. Trotsky, however, claimed that two days after he had received the documents Lenin's health had deteriorated. They therefore did not have the opportunity to discuss or resolve the matter. Some time later, M. I. Gliasser, another member of Lenin's staff, demanded the documents, and Trotsky returned them, but not before he had made copies of them. (According to Trotsky, Gliasser had also been the intermediary who had ascertained for Lenin that he and Trotsky shared the same position before Lenin's decision of March 5.) However, the most interesting aspect of Trotsky's account touches upon his relations with the other oligarchs in connection with this episode.

After receiving the documents concerning the Georgian affair and the nationalities issue, Trotsky spoke to Fotieva and asked her if he could show them to Kamenev. Within a quarter hour she conveyed Lenin's opinion:

> "Vladimir Il'ich says: 'Kamenev will immediately show everything to Stalin, and Stalin will make a rotten compromise and then deceive us.' " "Then the thing has gone so far that Vladimir Il'ich no longer thinks we can compromise with Stalin even on the right line?" "Yes, he does not trust Stalin, and wants to come out against him openly before the entire party. He is preparing a bomb."[10]

Only an hour later Fotieva returned, this time carrying a note from Lenin addressed to P. G. Mdivani and F. E. Makharadze (and others), Stalin's ardent opponents over the Georgian issue: "I am following your case with all my soul. I am upset by Ordzhonikidze's rudeness and Stalin's and Dzerzhinskii's connivances. I am preparing notes and a speech for you."[11] The note is dated March 6, 1923, and copies to Trotsky and Kamenev are indicated in the text. Lenin had reversed himself dramatically by including Kamenev in the campaign against Stalin.

Assuming that Trotsky is telling the truth about this incident, it appears that Lenin did not trust Trotsky to do his bidding and, as he often did, changed the character of his maneuver. Trotsky, once again unwittingly, reveals a lack of mutual confidence between himself and Lenin. Furthermore, Trotsky engaged in maneuvering, although it was presumably only to thwart the party leaders who were scheming against him and Lenin. Once he received confirmation from Fotieva that Lenin had changed his mind about Kamenev, Trotsky requested a meeting with him. Kamenev appeared at Trotsky's bedside within a short time and, after being shown the manuscript on the nationalities issue, told Trotsky that he had learned from Krupskaia that on the previous day Lenin had dictated a letter to Stalin "saying he breaks off all relations with him." [12] This account does not accurately describe Lenin's letter, as shall be seen from the document below. It is not clear whether Trotsky misremembered what Kamenev told him, whether Kamenev had made the error, or whether Krupskaia, who had told Kamenev both about the incident of December 22, when Stalin had berated her, and the letter of March 5 to Stalin, had herself transmitted erroneous information. In any case, Lenin did not actually break off relations, but only threatened to do so. The complete text reads as follows:

> To Comrade Stalin
> Strictly secret Personal
> Copies to Comrades Kamenev and Zinov'ev
> Esteemed Comrade Stalin,
> You had the rudeness to call my wife to the telephone and abuse her. Although she agreed to forget what was said, that fact nonetheless became known to Zinov'ev and Kamenev through her. I am not inclined so readily to forget what was perpetrated against me for, needless to say, I consider what was perpetrated against my wife as perpetrated against me too. Therefore, I ask you to inform me whether you agree to take back what was said and to apologize or whether you prefer to break off relations between us.
> Respectfully, Lenin
> 5th March 23 [13]

As the story unfolds, we learn that Krupskaia herself had turned to the people she believed to be closest to Lenin and highest in the party leadership. On December 23, 1922, Krupskaia had dictated a letter to Kamenev asking him to protect her from Stalin's threat that she would be hauled before the Control Commission for violating the conditions of Lenin's medical regime. [14] This might explain why Lenin had dictated his famous undelivered note of January 4, 1923, which is reproduced below.

> Stalin is too rude, and this defect, which is quite acceptable in a Communist milieu and in our mutual contacts, is intolerable in the post of gensek [General Secretary]. Therefore, I propose that the comrades think of a way to transfer Stalin from this post and to appoint in his place another person, who in all other respects distinguishes himself from comrade Stalin by precisely one superiority, namely, [he is] more patient, more loyal, more polite, and more attentive to comrades, less capricious, etc. This circumstance can seem like an insignificant trifle. But I think that from the point of view of taking precautions against a split and from the point of view of what I have written above [the letter of December 24, 1922] about the mutual relationship of Stalin and Trotsky, this is not a trifle, or it is the sort of trifle that could have decisive significance. [15]

Lenin's letter of January 4, 1923, which itself is somewhat garbled after "who in all other respects," becomes clearer in the light of the letter of March 5, 1923. It is possible that Lenin learned about Stalin's behavior through Kamenev rather than from Krupskaia herself. Kamenev could have gotten word to Lenin between December 23 and January 4, although exactly how and when is not known. The standard biographical chronicle and the secretaries' log shed no light on any event that might have precipitated either the note of January 4 asking for Stalin's removal from his post as General Secretary (officially designated "An Addendum to the Letter of December 24, 1922") or the letter of March 5 to Stalin demanding an apology for the insult. In the Soviet version it is inferred rather than shown that Krupskaia had, for reasons not given, decided to tell Lenin about Stalin's behavior in March 1923, more than two months after she had been insulted.

What is more likely, Krupskaia decided to let Kamenev handle the matter. By her action she gave Kamenev what appeared to be a tremendous advantage over Stalin. If Kamenev, Zinov'ev, and Trotsky combined against Stalin in the nationalities issue and now in this matter with Krupskaia, his position might indeed be undermined. However, Stalin no doubt convinced his comrades that this was another of those tempests in a teapot. He could, and did, present himself as someone burdened with the miserable task of trying to keep Lenin from behaving foolishly. In order to prevent the worst, Stalin had to discipline the members of Lenin's staff, including Krupskaia, who had complicity in Lenin's delinquencies. He probably presented Krupskaia as the guilty one and himself as the victim. Stalin, in fact, asked to be relieved of his duties as Lenin's warder in February 1923.[16] His colleagues were content to let him carry the burden. Stalin had working to his advantage not least of all the fear inspired in the other oligarchs by Trotsky.

Thus, after March 5, 1923, Kamenev and Trotsky, together with Zinov'ev, only appeared to have Stalin's political fate in their hands. Through Krupskaia, Kamenev presumably had learned that Zinov'ev was also privy to the letter, but there is no indication that Trotsky was aware that a copy had gone to Zinov'ev. It did not matter. Trotsky could not really form a coalition with Zinov'ev and Kamenev. At best, he might use Kamenev to help him improve his position in the party. According to Trotsky's own account, he himself made a gesture of conciliation. Knowing Kamenev's anxiety about a shake-up, he would not press for severe punishments for Stalin, Ordzhonikidze, and Dzerzhinskii. However, he demanded a "firmer policy in matters of industrialization," a revision of the nationalities policy, "a discontinuance of the administrative oppression of the party," acceptance of Lenin's policy toward the Georgians, the apology to Krupskaia demanded by Lenin, and—in a moment of unusual naiveté—no more intrigues! Kamenev later brought word that Stalin had accepted all of Trotsky's terms and written an apology to Krupskaia that very day, March 6, 1923.[17] Within the next few days, however, the situation changed dramatically.

LENIN'S HEALTH deteriorated rapidly on the night of March 6, and on March 10, 1923, he suffered a decisive stroke, which paralyzed his right side, caused a serious speech impairment, and ended his political career. Although he staged still another recovery, he never felt well enough to resume real work and never fully recovered his faculties. Yet his "Testament" remained as a political factor. It made all of his lieutenants politically vulnerable and gave no one either the support or encouragement to replace him in the role of leadership. Trotsky's claim that Lenin's last campaign had been in his behalf carries no conviction.

MEANWHILE, KAMENEV traveled to Georgia, presumably to carry out Lenin's wishes, but (according to Trotsky) instead sustained Stalin's position. In Trotsky's version of party history, with Lenin incapacitated and no longer a threat to them, the "epigones" conspired to remove him as well. Trotsky later judged that they were trying to set him up for a fall by encouraging him to replace Lenin as the political reporter at the Twelfth Party Congress, scheduled for April. Anyone who tried to wear Lenin's mantle would surely become a target for the rest. Trotsky's Napoleonic image remained. He least of all should make the first move, and thus refused the assignment. Stalin at first flattered him and tried to win his confidence, but then struck suddenly in mid-April, shortly before the opening of the Twelfth Congress. The occasion was Lydia Fotieva's "revelation" of Lenin's dealings with Trotsky over the nationalities issue.

On April 16, 1923, Fotieva, the senior secretary on Lenin's staff, called Trotsky and wrote a personal letter to Kamenev informing him about the article on the nationalities problem dictated by Lenin on December 31 and Lenin's wish that it be published. She told Kamenev something that he already knew —that Lenin had given the article to Trotsky and wanted Trotsky to present their position. It is difficult to say who had inspired Fotieva's action, but it precipitated a series of maneuvers. On the same day Trotsky, who received a copy of the letter to Kamenev, wrote to the entire Central Committee that he possessed a copy of the article and other pertinent materials. He had used them for his own discussion of the nationalities problem in *Pravda* and for corrections to Stalin's theses. Trotsky also revealed what they all undoubtedly already knew—that the article contained sharp criticisms of three members of the CC (Stalin, Ordzhonikidze, and Dzerzhinskii). He justified his own silence about the article by saying that as long as he had the slightest hope that Lenin himself would recover and deal with the matter at the Twelfth Party Congress, he himself should not go forward with it. Furthermore, Trotsky implied that he had remained silent in order to minimize the damage the document might have caused.[18] Now, however, it was clear that the article should be handed over to the CC for publication.

All of this was designed to make Trotsky appear the good party man. He wanted reconciliation, not acrimony. Rather than acting alone, he had left the matter for the party to decide. Stalin would not let the matter rest and on April 16 issued a statement asking Trotsky to explain his handling of Lenin's request. It is not clear whether Stalin had been apprised of the contents of the article. The information might have been leaked to him by someone on Lenin's staff or by Kamenev. It did not matter to Stalin that he had been unmasked by Lenin to the other oligarchs. They had all suffered at Lenin's hands and all wanted to minimize the damage to their collective interests. Some of Lenin's most telling judgments of his colleagues therefore had no significant impact in 1923.

Lenin understood the psychological mechanism that converted victims of a dominant nationality into great power chauvinists. He accused his lieutenants of precisely this failing. Furthermore, the *apparat* had taken on some characteristics of the old ruling class, the arrogant bureaucrats of the old regime. Stalin and Ordzhonikidze had acted in the old unenlightened way. In Lenin's words: "I think that in this instance Stalin's passion for administrative measures and his haste played a fatal role, and also his resentment towards the notorious 'social-nationalism.' In general, resentment usually plays the most harmful role in politics. . . . That Georgian who . . . casually hurls accusations of 'social chauvinism' (when he himself is not only a real and true 'social-chauvinist' but a crude great Russian bully), that Georgian, in essence, violates the interests of proletarian class solidarity."[19] To the casual reader of Lenin's prose there could hardly be a more damaging criticism of an opponent, much less a political colleague. However, already inured to Lenin's intemperate denunciations, the CC had no desire to take action against either Stalin or his accomplices in the Georgian affair.

Stalin decided to harass Trotsky by issuing a statement making him the delinquent party, the one who had not carried out Lenin's commission, and who now had to answer to the CC for failing to inform it about Lenin's article on the nationalities. It was a calculated risk: Stalin assumed that the damaging article, about which rumours were already spreading, would be stopped before it reached a wider audience and that Trotsky would not carry the struggle farther than the CC.[20] Trotsky replied in full to Stalin's statement of April 16 in a letter of April 17, 1923, saying that he had been told not to mention the article to anyone, that Lenin had fallen ill before they had come to any agreement about it, and that it had been demanded back by one of Lenin's secretaries "some time" later, but not before he had made a copy. The matter then rested in the hands of Krupskaia, Maria Il'inichna, and Lenin's staff. If Lenin had given them no special instructions, then any decision about the article should place political expediency first. Trotsky pointed out that he had acted immediately on April 16, once he had known that no provision had been made for publication of the article, and offered to have his conduct scrutinized by the conflict commission or any special commission of the imminent party congress.[21] Trotsky's explanation was accepted by the CC and Stalin, who evidently promised Trotsky that he would write a new statement absolving Trotsky of any wrongdoing. Stalin, however, did not act immediately.

On April 18 Trotsky wrote directly to Stalin and demanded immediate action on the matter. He was concerned that delegates to the Twelfth Party Congress would be misled by Stalin's statement of April 16. Trotsky threatened that in the absence of a statement issued that very day to the CC to the effect that he had acted properly, he would have the affair duly investigated at the Congress and ended: "You better than anyone can appreciate that if I have not done this up to now, then it was hardly because it could harm my interests."[22] Stalin complied, but he had achieved his aim: He had forced Trotsky on the defensive and cast doubt once again on his loyalty to Lenin and his *partiinost'*. Not least of all, he had forced Trotsky to confront his own vulnerability to the procedures of the *apparat*.

The Oligarchs Alone

DESPITE LENIN'S attack upon Stalin, Trotsky's situation was far more perilous than that of the other oligarchs. By turning to Trotsky for help, Lenin had only provoked the resentment of the others. Hardly an adept schemer, Trotsky awkwardly tried to conspire with Lenin to further his notion of a planned economy, to enhance the role of experts and weaken that of the party *apparat*. Trotsky was caught in a double bind. If he acted too vigorously as Lenin's agent, he would be suspected, as he later put it, "of casting dice for Lenin's chasuble" and further inflame the resentment of the other leaders; yet if he did not use Lenin's mandate decisively against the *apparat*, he might be overcome by it. He produced one of his painful compromises: On the one hand, he used Lenin's authority to further his cause; on the other, he suppressed those aspects of Lenin's last commission that would harm the others. The compromise, he later admitted, proved to be a disastrous mistake.

In the last days before the Twelfth Party Congress, Trotsky did not prepare an attack on Zinov'ev, Kamenev, and Stalin. Although Stalin incorporated Trotsky's amendments to the theses on the nationalities to be presented to the Congress, the CC decided not to publish Lenin's manuscripts.[23] The treatment of Lenin's last writings reveals how far his last maneuvers had alienated the leaders of the party. Even before the suppression with Trotsky's complicity of the article on the nationalities, the oligarchs had contemplated suppressing Lenin's article, "Better Fewer, But Better" (dictated between February 1 and 9, 1923), which contained still another implied attack upon Stalin, this time for his maladministration of Rabkrin. Trotsky on this occasion had refused to go along with the bizarre idea of producing a single issue of *Pravda* in order to deceive and pacify Lenin.[24] He zealously promoted publication, and the article was finally published in *Pravda* on March 4, 1923. Thus, in April Trotsky went farther in his efforts at compromise with his rivals than he had in February and early March, no doubt because Lenin's latest illness had convinced him that he had no other choice.

Trotsky's compromise bought him at least the formal support of his colleagues. There followed the strange spectacle of Trotsky and Stalin thrusting each other forward as political reporter at the Congress, with neither accepting the role of Lenin's substitute. Zinov'ev, the most keenly ambitious of the group, took it, and paid the price. Trotsky and Stalin had shown sounder political instincts in refusing to try to step into Lenin's shoes on this occasion. The party had tolerated Zinov'ev's pretensions to leadership when they knew he was really only one of Lenin's factotums. As a candidate for Lenin's position he appeared in a different light. Lenin himself had not been able to subdue the opposition within the party; Zinov'ev only provoked it. Trotsky received as his reward for restraint and the the appearance of solidarity with the others something that he cherished, the report on industry and the authorship of the theses on industry. Once again Trotsky placed faith in his powers of persuasion in open debate before a massed hall. He at once overestimated the power of his personal prestige and oratory and underestimated the day-to-day workings of the political machine, over which Stalin continued to extend his control despite all of his formal concessions to Lenin's wishes and Trotsky's ostensible authority.

ALTHOUGH TROTSKY'S heirship to Lenin seemed perfectly natural to contemporaries, collective leadership was the only tolerable solution during Lenin's remaining eight months of life and even for some time after his death. Each of the oligarchs watched with delight the injuries inflicted on the others by Lenin or by intraparty intrigues. However, they all had an overriding interest to preserve the illusion of solidarity and to fend off the more unruly oppositionists in the party. They lived in an insecure world, one that became even more insecure with each day of Lenin's absence, with each sign that he would not be able to return to political life. Contemporary observers (and later, historians) believed that Trotsky missed a supreme moment of opportunity, but the constraints upon him suggest otherwise.

Max Eastman, aspiring during 1923 and 1924 to be Trotsky's Boswell, with both regret and an undertone of malice picked out his subject's failings: Trotsky did not know how to plan a series of maneuvers against his main rivals Zinov'ev, Kamenev, and Stalin; he did not know how to use Lenin's commissions. Eastman astutely described some of Trotsky's seeming renunciation of power as an overreaction to his own egoism.[25] However, Eastman failed to take into account the long-term resentment of the Old Bolsheviks and their continuing doubts about the nature of Trotsky's commitment to the party and to them. Only Lenin's sponsorship (unreliable though it was) had sustained his position in the top rank of the party leadership. Trotsky surely understood this at some level, although circumstance and possibly a certain amount of self-deception led Trotsky to create the legend of his partnership with Lenin. No one could be Lenin's partner in any strict sense; nor had he cultivated anyone to be his successor. The reading of his "Testament" in small, closeted sessions of the Thirteen Party Congress in May 1924 would make that quite clear. All that the oligarchs could do for the present was to keep an eye on each other as well as on Lenin. Thus, Trotsky's behavior in April 1923, although not astute, was so constrained by circumstance that one can hardly imagine him taking advantage of Lenin's "gifts."

The alleged whispering campaigns conducted against Trotsky no doubt played a role, but one difficult to measure. The fear of a Bonaparte assuredly hurt Trotsky more than the other oligarchs. The party leaders exploited the Napoleonic legend. They assumed a posture of redoubled vigilance against the appearance of a military leader of outstanding ability and personality who would crush opposition and rely upon administrative measures to rule. However, all too much has been made of the dissemination of such rumors.

Offsetting these was the barrage of favorable press building up the images of the leaders, including Trotsky. Greetings from the delegations at the Twelfth Party Congress frequently placed Trotsky alongside Lenin or just after him. His popularity remained considerable, although in view of the rejection of a proposal to announce the number of votes cast at the end of the Congress for membership on the CC, it is difficult to know how the delegates ranked him. Neither a decline in popularity nor any decision of the moment defeated Trotsky. He was defeated by his past and his persona. The maneuvers in the highest organs of the party against both Lenin and Trotsky during 1922–1923 limited both the damage either of them could do to the other oligarchs and Trotsky's ability to seize the initiative.

Trotsky could not carry out his main goals, the strengthening of Gosplan and the rapid development of heavy industry, because no one, including Lenin, would entrust to him and his allies the administration of the economy. The events of 1923–1924 simply confirmed what had become evident by the end of the period of War Communism: The majority of party leaders would no longer tolerate Trotsky in a leading role in either the military or the economy.[26] At best, they would try to use him in their intrigues against each other or, if possible, as a tool in the execution of their policies.

The debates over the best path to economic recovery and administrative reform were thus intertwined with the rivalries and political maneuvers of the oligarchs. They carried over into the Twelfth Party Congress, where Trotsky used his report on industry to assail the trends toward a market economy under NEP and the neglect of planning and investment in industry in favor of the peasants' petty agriculture. The adoption of his theses (heavily amended, to be sure) obscured the extent of his political weakness at the Congress. He had little room in which to maneuver. Trotsky, no less than the others, repudiated the more militant left opposition. As a centralizer and a member of the oligarchy he would stand to lose much more than he might gain by a strengthening of the opposition. The struggle against the *apparat* was for him a struggle against those who controlled it and its present character, not against the principles of centralized control as such. Thus, Trotsky was caught in another double bind: An outsider to the Old Bolsheviks and party oligarchy and an opponent of the present *apparat*, he nonetheless could not join with the rebels of the left opposition who openly attacked the oligarchs. While decked out with the trappings of power, he was slipping into a political abyss.

Trotsky's failure to lead the opposition at the Twelfth Party Congress appears to be a fatal failure of will and political intelligence only later, in the light of Stalin's triumph. But in 1923 Stalin could not have been Trotsky's central target. The greetings of delegates to the Congress made it quite clear that they saw Trotsky, Zinov'ev, and Kamenev as the top leaders. Only those who understood the political uses of the *apparat* divined how much Stalin's personal power had grown. To Trotsky at the time Stalin was not so much a direct rival for leadership of the party as an obstacle to his plans. Trotsky took a rather straightforward approach: He would not attack Stalin and the others involved in the Georgian affair; he would permit Stalin to preside over the organizational reforms suggested by Lenin; he would close ranks in exchange for the opportunity to place his own economic platform before the delegates. Of the top leaders only Bukharin obliquely attacked Stalin over the Georgian affair.[27] The need to secure the collective leadership in Lenin's absence remained an overriding imperative. During the Twelfth Party Congress Trotsky had no intention of jeopardizing the status quo by making a decisive move against the oligarchy.

Within a few months, however, Trotsky feared that time might be running out—that the regime might not survive the crises of NEP. The failure of the party to deal with the "scissors crisis" (Trotsky's term describing the diagram for the eight-month period between August 1922 and April 1923 showing an ascending curve of industrial prices juxtaposed against plummeting agricultural prices) yielded unacceptable terms of exchange for agricultural products, a crisis of grain marketing, and hyperinflation. In his voluminous report on industry Trotsky had placed on the agenda "primitive socialist accumulation," a term he attributed to V. S. Smirnov, one of his allies on Gosplan. It became widely used by the left economists, who presented a rather unattractive image of the peasants as an economic colony to be exploited as a source of capital by the industrial sector. To the opponents of the left-wing economists any such arrangement would threaten the alliance of the proletariat and peasants upon which NEP rested. Trotsky, to be sure, did not characterize his program as anti-peasant. He imagined a situation in which the planned socialist sector would coexist with, but eventually absorb the private, market-regulated one. Presumably, this would happen without resort to coercive measures. Given the state of affairs during and after 1921, the last assumption seems unrealistic. The peasants, with their self-sustained economy, could offer both active and passive resistance. They could cripple fiscal efforts to make them pay for industrialization a second time. They had paid once under the Tsars. Who, then, would pay, if not the factory workers? Trotsky, as usual, demanded austerity, discipline, and heroic effort of the vanguard of the revolution, the workers themselves. His message was inspiring and ceremonially apt, but politically ineffectual.

Trotsky's report and the passage of his theses on industry mattered little compared to the election and appointment of new members to both the party's leading organs and lower levels. His base of support within the *apparat* narrowed; that of the triumvirate of Zinov'ev, Kamenev, and most distinctly, Stalin, expanded. As the difficulties of NEP increased along with the oligarchs' intrigues and power, Trotsky became desperate. When the others tried to draw him into their combinations, he expressed disgust. During the months after the Twelfth Party Congress, they measured each other's political resources. Each tried to keep the others from accumulating too much strength in any given area. Not at all capable of behind-the-scenes activity of this nature, Trotsky was the first to break down. In a clear sign of desperation, in the autumn of 1923 he sought an escapist solution: He would smuggle himself into Germany to lead the revolution presumably ripening there because of the French occupation of the Ruhr. When his colleagues rejected this quixotic yet threatening gesture, he offered his resignation as Commissar of War, member of the Military Revolutionary Council, and member of the Central Committee. They rejected these too. The oligarchs understood that Trotsky's extravagant moves signaled his sense of superiority to them and his desire to find some way to gain leverage against them. However, while undermining his power, they needed to sustain the facade of unity and stability. Trotsky himself would be forced to make the decisive move.

38

Trotsky's "New Course"

THWARTED IN his political efforts, such as they were, Trotsky turned his main energy for a while to other outlets. He began to outline the characteristics of the culture befitting citizens of a new socialist world. During the mid-1920s, before his final defeat, he used to show his contempt for the proceedings of the Politburo by reading French novels while his colleagues droned on. Trotsky's speeches and essays of the period of Lenin's illness and those of the mid-1920s reveal the workings of a still brilliant mind. However, it could not content itself with cultural criticism and propaganda for the new order. Trotsky's peculiar psychology did not permit him either to eschew political struggle or to play the game of politics in a routine way. In the autumn of 1923 he reentered the game without having in the slightest improved his chances for victory. The last half-hearted alliance with Lenin had rebounded against him. The recognition given to him in the party press, the praise and stormy applause of the delegates to Twelfth Party Congress had only increased the jealousy and anxiety of the oligarchs and strengthened their determination to weaken his position.

In September 1923, at the very meeting of the Central Committee where in desperation he tried to resign his posts in the government and party and volunteered to go to Germany, Trotsky suffered another defeat. The oligarchs reduced his power in the Military Revolutionary Council. Underemployed and suffering from the knowledge that his political opponents were continually strengthening their position through the *apparat,* Trotsky began a new series of maneuvers in October 1923. He decided to ally himself with a group of high-ranking dissidents in the party. Max Eastman, one of the best-informed observers of these events, believed that Trotsky acted only when the revolution seemed threatened. He had remained silent while the party machine deprived him of his own power—"a miracle of submission to discipline."[1] However, it is more likely that Trotsky's position on bureaucracy issued less from principle than from political considerations of the moment. The wrong people—his political opponents—controlled the *apparat.* Trotsky only made common cause with some oppositionists when no other course remained open to him.

A large-scale strike movement in several cities during the summer of 1923 and the growth of offshoots from the old Workers' Opposition provided the background for the appearance of what became known as the Left Opposition. Perhaps sensing that the new intraparty security measures proposed by Dzerzhinskii to squelch the opposition would work against him as well, Trotsky assailed the oligarchs. They in turn attacked him for violating the unity he had supported at the Twelfth Congress. The next shot in the new round of struggle came on October 8, 1923, when Trotsky wrote a scathing letter to the CC denouncing the state of affairs since the Twelfth Party Congress.[2] Trotsky's letter bewailed the party's violation of his and Lenin's program of economic recovery—the fiscal policies that led to discontent among peasants, strikes among workers, and dissension in the party. Alongside his attack on economic policy Trotsky directed a blast against Stalin's system of appointments and the "party secretary psychology" that had developed. Appointments were made not with an eye to competence but in order to strengthen the regime—the *apparat* and the oligarchs. From the CC down to the factory cells the Secretariat and Orgburo held sway. In short, the party had become bureaucratized, and rank-and-file members who did not belong to the *apparat* had little to do but obey it.

Trotsky brought up other grievances: against his violent opposition they had tried to revive the state vodka trade in order to increase state revenues; they were reorganizing the Revolutionary Military Council in order to weaken him. Personal pleading breaks through the entire document, yet in the end Trotsky appealed to principle: to party democracy. The threat was not to his policies, his power, but to the "ossification and degeneration" of the party. The party would not be prepared to take advantage of the revolutionary opportunity in Germany nor to deal with the internal crisis of NEP. Thus, Dzerzhinskii's methods for dealing with intraparty dissent had little to commend them, for they only treated the symptoms. Rather, the party could only solve the current crisis by getting at the causes of the malaise, extending discussion beyond the inner circle, and increasing party democracy.

The nascent opposition quickly followed Trotsky's letter of October 8, 1923 with the so-called "Platform of the Forty-Six." The signatories to the document (dated October 15, 1923) included high-ranking officials in the party and government—industrial and military executives—as well as chronic opposi- tionists. Aside from attacking the oligarchs' economic policy, their platform accurately described the circular flow of power from the General Secretary down to the lowest levels of the hierarchy and back again through delegates to party conferences and congresses. A regime governed by such principles of recruitment and appointment would not be able to respond flexibly to the crises looming ahead. It had already discredited itself by its bungling in recent months. In language stronger than Trotsky's, the Forty-Six characterized the regime as a faction within the party created to meet the emergency of 1921, but no longer serving any useful purpose.[3] This might be read as an implicit criticism of Lenin, the architect of the ban on factions at the Tenth Party Congress and the purge in 1921. More important, the signatories to the "Platform of the Forty-Six" urged the oligarchs to abolish the regime they had created between March 1921 and October 1923 and to begin by opening discussions about reform.

The oligarchs responded firmly, at first. A joint meeting of the Central Committee and Central Control Commission condemned Trotsky's "serious political mistake" and accused the Forty-Six of factionalism. Using the strate- gies of a regime that controls everything but public opinion, the oligarchs moved on two fronts: On the one hand, they began to weaken the organized opposition by removing its leaders from positions of authority; on the other, they made gestures of conciliation by opening up discussion and even endors- ing oppositional views about party democracy. The last maneuver of the oligarchs only multiplied the dangers. For every member of the organized opposition there were numerous potential oppositionists, especially in the younger generation, who were encouraged by the quickening of discussion and criticism of the regime. Thus, the autumn of 1923 witnessed the rise of an apparently vigorous left opposition.

While the opposition as well as the attacks upon him gained momentum, Trotsky succumbed to illness after one of his seemingly trivial hunting "acci- dents," this one on October 23.

> There was a light frost that night [in Zabolote] I sat in the tent in felt boots. But in the morning the sun was warm and the bog thawed. . . . From the canoe to the automobile I had to walk about a hundred steps, not more. But the moment I stepped onto the bog in my felt boots my feet were in cold water. By the time I leaped up to the automobile, my feet were quite cold. . . . I took off my boots and tried to warm my feet by the heat of the motor. But the cold got the better of me. I had to stay in bed. After the influenza, some cryptogenic fever set in. The doctors ordered me to stay in bed, and thus I spent the rest of the autumn and winter. This means that through all the discussion of "Trotskyism" in 1923, I was ill. One can foresee a revolution or war, but it is impossible to foresee the

> consequences of an autumn shooting-trip for wild ducks. . . . Lenin was laid
> up at Gorkii; I was in the Kremlin. The epigones were widening the circle of
> conspiracy.[4]

The story suggests, once again, that Trotsky's fate was linked with Lenin's.
The two of them lay helpless before the machinations of the triumvirate.
Trotsky wrote to his colleagues on October 24 that not they, but he carried on
Lenin's last policies. If it came to an open struggle, he hinted that he could
make public extremely embarrassing actions on the part of the Politburo—
revelations, for example, of machinations to suppress publication of Lenin's
last articles and circumvent his wishes. The oligarchs, of course, read all of
Trotsky's moves as personal ambition and political blackmail, but still did not
feel they could bring him down immediately. What seems bizarre in retrospect,
the Politburo began to meet in Trotsky's apartment, in his very study. In an
odd charade they all tried to maintain the semblance of unity, but each meeting
led to a struggle between Trotsky and the rest, after which he would go to bed
feverish and drained.

   While struggling with Trotsky, the oligarchs formulated their compromise
with the opposition, an ostensible "New Course," a renewal of open discussion
within the party. They began a campaign to undercut the opposition in November 1923 by stealing their thunder—their antibureaucratic rhetoric—but the
oligarchs' experiment with open discussion revealed the extent of the opposition. Threatened, they began to remove dissidents from strategic positions,
especially in Communist youth organizations. A still bedridden Trotsky amended
the Politburo's New Course and voted together with his opponents to adopt a
"Resolution on Workers' Democracy" as policy on December 5, 1923. However, he reserved the right to continue to agitate for pressure "from below"
against the bureaucratic regime.[5] Trotsky correctly assumed that his opponents
were only trying to throw sops to the opposition, to pacify it. He did not trust
them to implement the new policy. The oligarchs, on their side, assumed that
Trotsky's antibureaucratic position was simply a tactic, an attempt to exploit
both the oppositionists and the less conscious elements in the party and use
them against the legitimate leadership. Hence, the formal gesture of conciliation, the signing of the resolution, only signaled the weakness of both sides:
Trotsky and the oppositionists did not feel strong enough to make a clean break
from the party; the oligarchs had learned in November how fragile their own
reputations were and held back from an open and sustained attack on Trotsky
and the other oppositionists.

   Trotsky quickly provided his opponents with the opportunity to accuse him
of a variety of sins by writing an open letter on December 8 to his party local,
whose meetings he could not attend because of his illness. In the letter,
published after a delay of three days in *Pravda*, Trotsky appealed to the
younger generation to sustain its militancy against an ossifying Old Guard—
the leaders of the *apparat*. During the delay Trotsky learned that certain
comrades had seen dangers in the letter and added a postscript replying to
their fear that he might encourage a conflict of generations in the party. His
logic was quite easy to follow: Insofar as the New Course represented a true

change and a weakening of the oligarchs who controlled the *apparat,* the younger generation could unanimously support the policy handed down from the center. In other words, Trotsky wanted to agitate the young into militant support for his policy and active resistance against the *apparat.* The clear suggestion that the Old Bolsheviks were at the root of the problem, that they were causing a "dead calm" in both the international revolutionary process (he cited the precedent of European Social Democracy, naming the epigones of Marx and Engels) and internal development by retarding planned economic development, only inflamed the resentment of the other leaders. Trotsky was now openly agitating, placing himself at the head of a large and dangerous constituency. He was calling for nothing less than a purge of the Old Guard and their replacement by new forces.

The series of articles which Trotsky published as a pamphlet in mid-January 1924 under the title of *The New Course* contained a new interpretation of the revolutionary process. Trotsky, although not in strident tones, consigned the Old Bolsheviks and their methods of leadership to the rubbish heap of history. Because the oligarchs had officially embraced his policy, he could only accuse them on the grounds of their inability to implement it. Their continuing leadership, already costly, would guarantee the degeneration of the party at a moment when history demanded that it take a leap forward. Unlike Lenin, who attributed a great many of the flaws of Soviet bureaucratism to the tsarist heritage, Trotsky laid it at the door of history. History had posed a new problem, which the Old Bolsheviks had not solved: The leaders had to avoid merging the dictatorship of the party of the proletariat with the administrative methods of the state bureaucracy, something that would lead to the degeneration of the party itself. But they had failed. Of course, similar accusations had been hurled at Trotsky. His opponents in the party *apparat* had long seen him as a creature of the state *apparat*—someone of doubtful loyalty—and an arch-bureaucrat. Trotsky now turned the accusation around, raised the intraparty squabble to a new theoretical level, and gave the political rhetoric of bureaucratic degeneration a new significance. "Bureaucratic dictatorship", "bureaucratic degeneration," and "bureaucratic factionalism" became catchwords for the betrayal of the revolution by the Old Bolsheviks, the leaders of the party *apparat.*

Trotsky found the durable rhetoric that would permit him to affirm the revolution and the party—to make himself the voice of the revolution and the party against the bureaucratic factionalism of the *apparat.* Lenin had prepared the way by attacking the evils of bureaucracy in his last articles. The left opposition had provided many of the arguments and much of the rhetoric, but Lenin's authority had greater weight. Trotsky, no less than his opponents, tried to appropriate Lenin's authority and Lenin's style of leadership for his cause. The time had come for a sharp turn, a courageous reorientation in the manner of Lenin's audacious maneuvers. For Trotsky this was the essence of Leninism, and it contrasted dramatically with the tendency of the Old Bolsheviks to hold back, to stagnate. The party had to shake off the husk of Old Bolshevik tradition. Only those who truly followed the New Course, who interpreted it the way Trotsky did, who understood Leninism the way Trotsky did, could revitalize the Party.

Anyone who knew party history and Lenin's methods understood the implicit threat in *The New Course*. Skillfully—that is, selectively—reviewing the past, Trotsky both defended his relationship to Lenin and the party and presented himself as the true interpreter and champion of Leninism. He was trying to abscond with the party. By suggesting that Lenin's more obedient lieutenants (he also showed that they had not been obedient at crucial moments) might be too docile to lead with Lenin's audacity and foresight, Trotsky cut to the quick. When one subtracts for rhetoric and selective remembering in his own behalf, Trotsky's substantive message in *The New Course* amounts to a prescription for revitalized leadership and mobilization of untapped energy. Above all, the party needed a leader *like* Lenin. The implication was clear: Trotsky was such a leader; Trotsky should lead the party. But in the autumn and winter of 1923–1924 Trotsky lay abed, immobilized by his probably psychosomatic illness. He could not even lead the oppositionists' struggle, except as a journalist. On January 18, 1924, with the Thirteenth Party Conference and the destruction of the opposition underway, Trotsky, at the advice of his doctor, left the scene of battle and travelled with Natalia Sedova to Sukhumi on the Black Sea.

39

Lenin's Death and Trotsky's Decline

IN MID-DECEMBER 1923 Zinov'ev and Stalin began an immense barrage of propaganda and agitation against the opposition in general and Trotsky in particular. The contenders for power began to drag up their opponents' pasts and to promote their own political genealogies. The oligarchs had more than enough material from the past with which to smear Trotsky. In an article of December 15, 1923, in *Pravda*, Stalin, citing Lenin, warned of the infiltration of the party by Mensheviks, who had joined opportunistically and developed protective coloring. Any reader with knowledge of Trotsky's political past would have no difficulty understanding the otherwise puzzling appearance of the reference to the Mensheviks in Stalin's article. To be sure, Stalin did not dwell upon Trotsky's past sins. The article was the merest hint of things to come. Between the publication of Trotsky's letter against the Old Guard on December 11, 1923, and the Thirteenth Party Congress, at the end of May, 1924, the oligarchs demolished the opposition by the most underhanded machine politics (including falsifying votes) and successfully appropriated their dead leader's mystique. They marshaled sufficient strength to force Trotsky to a gesture of submission. Although Trotsky did not truly submit or repent, the events of 1923–1924 exposed both his incapacities as a political leader and the power of the *apparat*.

Stalin's personal power grew with that of the *apparat*, something that Zinov'ev tried to counteract—to no avail. However, it was not merely possession of an organizational weapon that determined Stalin's victory. His rivals had their own. Careful students of the debates of the 1920s have shown how personal rivalries led all of the oligarchs, including Trotsky, to line up on one side or other. Behind all of the rhetoric of the moment supporting a "principled" position, one can discern calculation about power—maneuverings to promote political allies and damage opponents. Aside from using his powers of appointment brutally and effectively, Stalin maneuvered more successfully within the oligarchy than the others. He forged his final victory by choosing an alliance with Bukharin and the right rather than with Zinov'ev and Kamenev, making fewer mistakes than his opponents did, and benefiting from the fact that his most formidable rivals on the road to power were Jews. Finally, Stalin's relatively modest self-presentation stood him in good stead. Unlike Trotsky, at the outset he tried to present himself not as someone with Lenin's genius, but as Lenin's disciple, someone who knew Leninist scriptures and served the Central Committee faithfully.

THE OLIGARCHY defeated the opposition decisively at the Thirteenth Party Conference, which completed its business three days before Lenin's final illness and death on January 21, 1924. The left oppositionists had attacked on several fronts: They had paraded the failures of NEP, the blundering policy of the Comintern; they had analyzed the bureaucratization of the party as both a symptom and cause of the decline of revolutionary momentum. In his report on the immediate tasks before the party on January 17, Stalin presented his version of recent history, the sins of the opposition, and a litany of Trotsky's errors: He had opposed the CC by publishing the open letters that made up part of *The New Course;* he had behaved ambiguously (an interesting accusation, in the mouth of Stalin), coming out clearly neither for the CC nor the opposition; his attack on the *apparat* had an "anarcho-Menshevik" character; he had accused the party of degenerating like the German Social Democratic party; he had encouraged a generational split.

Stalin ridiculed Trotsky's notion (rather, a notion he attributed to Trotsky) that it was permissible to form a "group" rather than a faction. In fact, Trotsky had stated that in the absence of correct leadership "ideological and organic" groupings would inevitably appear. Trotsky's essential weakness issued from his acceptance in principle of the party's ban against factions. All of his distinctions sounded like rhetorical ploys, for under Lenin's presumably correct leadership factions and "groupings" had flourished. Everyone knew that the real issues were power and leadership. Nothing had changed, except that instead of attacking Lenin, the leaders of the different factions attacked each other in the name of Lenin. Under Stalin's leadership the Conference resolved to publish the secret seventh clause of Lenin's resolution at the Tenth Party Congress condemning both factions and groups and providing for the demotion and expulsion of CC members guilty of factionalism.

In Trotsky's absence Preobrazhenskii took the lead for the opposition, but was no match for the General Secretary. Stalin made oblique references to Trotsky's Menshevik past, but attacked him directly for his un-Bolshevik behavior and his numerous refusals of Lenin's and the party's commissions. Appealing to the organizational tradition of bolshevism, the very tradition Trotsky had deviated from and fought during his earlier career, Stalin cast more than a little doubt on Trotsky's loyalty. Closing his final speech at the Thirteenth Party Conference with a clear threat, Stalin quoted the words of a Menshevik émigré who expressed thanks to the opposition for exposing the "horrifying moral cesspool that goes by the name of the Russian Communist Party."[1]

Successfully appealing both to the party's pride and the traditional bolshevik fear of subversion, Stalin carried the day rhetorically. Exploiting the image of Trotsky carefully nurtured by the *apparat's* agitators, he intoned: "Trotsky's error consists in the fact that he has set himself up in opposition to the CC and imagines himself to be a superman standing above the CC, above its laws, above its decisions, thereby providing a certain section of the Party with a pretext for working to undermine confidence in the CC."[2] In the end the Conference resolved that the oppositionists were guilty not only of revising Bolshevism and Leninism, but of propagating a petty-bourgeois deviation. The party threatened them with the application of the seventh clause: unless they ceased their deviationism and splitting activities and submitted to party discipline, they would be expelled from the party. Only 3 of the 128 voting delegates opposed the resolution. The *apparat* had predetermined the victory by packing the Conference with loyalists. Thus, the bitter controversy over the New Course ended with a crushing defeat for Trotsky and the opposition.

Lenin died three days after the Thirteenth Conference of the Russian Communist Party. Trotsky learned about it by telegram on January 21 in Tbilisi, while en route to Sukhumi. Instead of making a strenuous effort to return to Moscow, he followed the advice that he tend to his own health. In his memoirs Trotsky claimed that he had been deceived about the date of the funeral and in later accounts embellished his reasons for not making a greater effort to attend. Psychological incapacitation rather than the machinations of the oligarchs no doubt played the greatest role in Trotsky's political paralysis. Instead of racing to Moscow, he wired a brief and touching eulogy. During the days ahead he evidently revived himself by strengthening the conviction, at least at a conscious level, that he and Lenin had truly been partners. He resolved his ambivalence about Lenin at this dramatic and pressure-laden moment by forming a partial identification with him and putting himself in a state of mind to revise the history of the party. Knowing that he could never work with the oligarchs or function in the party as it was, Trotsky redefined

Leninism to suit his purposes, to show that only he could be Lenin's true heir. But for a few months he would have to temporize. Lenin's death, the anxieties precipitated by it, not least of all those aroused by his "Testament," and the ceremonies of the moment forced the leaders to refashion, however briefly, the facade of unity. They all gathered at the Thirteenth Party Congress to hear Lenin's "Testament" and to advertise their solidarity.

It is not certain when Stalin and the others first read what Lenin had dictated on December 24–25, 1922 and January 4, 1923. According to a recent Soviet account, Fotieva was guilty of delivering some of the material on or before December 29, 1922.[3] Trotsky claimed in his biography of Stalin that Stalin knew about the "Testament" beforehand because Krupskaia had transmitted the text to him. Without naming his source, Trotsky asserted that upon being apprised of its contents, Stalin broke into cursing in the presence of his personal secretary, L. Z. Mekhlis and S. I. Syrtsov, a secretary of the CC.[4] In an unpublished letter of June 7, 1933, Trotsky wrote that Stalin exploded: "Lenin has shit on himself and shit on us."[5] The "Testament" was not officially made public until May 21, 1923, when it was discussed at a CC plenum, which decided not to publish it, but to read it to the heads of the provincial delegations to the Congress the next day. A rather poorly kept secret, the "Testament" proved to be more a personal nuisance to all of them than a genuine poilitical bomb. The most embarrassing comments about Stalin were glossed over. He was said to have taken Lenin's criticism to heart.[6]

Trotsky's version of the emotions swirling around the "Testament" calls for careful scrutiny. It is impossible to know what he really felt about the "Testament" after he first heard it. In 1932 he wrote his fullest description of the events of May 1924. According to this account, Radek was seated next to him at the reading of the "Testament." Radek leaned toward him and said: "Now they won't laugh at you." Trotsky replied: "Quite the contrary, now they will have to get to the end more quickly."[7] Thus, Trotsky claimed that he assumed the "Testament" would catastrophically accelerate the intraparty struggle because it praised him and denigrated the other oligarchs. Is it possible that at the time Trotsky's own powerful defenses against Lenin's obvious criticisms did not permit him to see clearly, much less to admit openly, that Lenin had not really made him the heir? Did he project his own anger against Lenin upon Stalin so that he could get on with the task of reconciling himself to Lenin, identifying himself with Lenin's political genius, and forming an image of Lenin that would allow him to affirm his own political choice in 1917? Trotsky's later career suggests that distortions issuing from defense mechanisms rather than outright prevarication account for his version of the "Testament."

Although we may never know what Stalin really said, the language attributed to him by Trotsky might easily be his, and it is unlikely that he alone felt bitter about the "Testament." To men struggling to maintain their power (in a situation, some no doubt still believed, largely created by Lenin's and Trotsky's adventurousness in 1917), the condescension in the "Testament" could only reopen old wounds and create new ones. On May 22 it was read to the heads of the provincial delegations and then in closed sessions to each delegation. However, all agreed not to take notes, and (against Krupskaia's wishes) the document was not read before a plenum of the Congress. According to Trotsky, the oligarchs had carefully prepared the leaders of the delegations, who, when they read the "Testament," emphasized some passages, "swallowed" others, and added their own glosses, pointing out that Lenin had been ill and surrounded by intriguers when he wrote it.[8] Despite such machinations and efforts to keep discussion of the document at a minimum, Lenin's criticisms and faint praise of the oligarchs achieved sufficient publicity to humiliate them. Even after his death Lenin had once again put them in their place.

Despite it all, the expressions of grief surrounding the death of their leader, the oligarchs' deep sense of loss cannot be doubted. Most of them had learned politics at Lenin's knee. However, it is no less certain that Lenin's style of leadership had produced powerfully ambivalent feelings. Those who had most benefited from his political acumen had also suffered the most from his wrath. Lenin had alternately lifted them up and hurled them down. If they loved him in any sense of the word, it was with a love akin to that of the children of a capricious patriarch, who might praise them one day and unleash his wrath upon them the next. Perhaps Lenin's death forced some of them actually to *repress* the resentment they felt toward him. Others, like Stalin, still furious about Lenin's meddling in party affairs during his illness, were not only relieved by his death but provoked to rage by the "Testament." What could it be other than an ill-conceived and peevish thrust at his closest comrades, a last insult, the opposite of a statesmanlike gesture? Under the circumstances, they could only vent their rage privately, like Stalin, blame the "Testament" on Lenin's illness and Trotsky's machinations, or else suppress their rage against Lenin and look for some other convenient target.

Stalin's two eulogies of Lenin in late January show the other side of the ambivalence. The first, delivered at the Second All-Union Congress of Soviets on January 26, 1924, had a more ceremonial character and consisted of a series of oaths to Lenin. Using military imagery and biblical cadences to give solemnity to his vows, Stalin revealed a great deal about his own mentality. He had never lost his romantic self-identity as a fighter—a knight of the revolution —nor his sense of consecration to a cause. He derived much of his dignity from long association and tempering in an army created by another man. Now a general in his own right, Stalin would never forget that Lenin alone had persevered and held the army—the party—together. On the occasion of his second eulogy of Lenin, delivered at the Kremlin Military School on January 28, he showed keen appreciation of Lenin's skills as a political survivor and leader. Stalin emphasized Lenin's hatred of whining intellectuals—those who lost heart during defeat—his ability to regroup his forces or, if necessary, to stand alone until the future proved him right. Now Stalin would try to show that he was a worthy member of Lenin's general staff, a student of the master. In April and May, shortly before the convening of the Thirteenth Party Congress, he gave a series of lectures at Sverdlov University, later published as *The Foundations of Leninism*. With these lectures Stalin served notice that he saw himself as Lenin's heir in the area of theoretical guidance as well as a staff officer maintaining the unity and fighting mettle of Lenin's army. Now he would be for the party the "mountain eagle" he had wanted Lenin to be during his revolutionary apprenticeship — not a long-winded theoretician in a three-piece suit, but a plain man, a Bebel, or more aptly, a Koba who had risen from the underground to lofty heights.

Trotsky's Political Invalidism

IN THE months preceding Lenin's death and the period following it, Trotsky became the perfect scapegoat for the anger of the oligarchs. None of them really wanted another Lenin. Life under Lenin had been uncertain. He had expected them to be as perpetually mobilized and vigilant as he was; his continual demands and harsh criticism had made them continually insecure. Now Trotsky threatened to step into Lenin's role, to disrupt the modicum of stability they had achieved. Like Lenin he liked to apply pressure, to push them forward against their will into new and even less promising adventures. Furthermore, he was not one of them. He was a Menshevik who had made use of Lenin's organization to promote himself and had tried to use Lenin against them when the old man's mind and judgment were already impaired by disease. Clinging to power in the midst of economic instability, they saw Trotsky as their arch-enemy, but, although still popular and dangerously disruptive, neither as ruthless as Lenin nor as politically tenacious. To Stalin, Trotsky was surely still a "hero with fake muscles." The oligarchs would be able to revenge themselves upon Trotsky not only for his arrogance, for the humiliations he had inflicted on them, but for those Lenin had inflicted as well. Yet, as good students of Lenin, they practiced the political arts: They used their opponents even while preparing their demise. So long as a man of Trotsky's talents could serve the cause, they would keep him in harness, in some fashion. Thus, they made no move to precipitate a final split and watched with malicious pleasure when Trotsky awkwardly and unconvincingly bowed to *partiinost'* in May 1924 at the Thirteenth Party Congress.

Trotsky did not give in without having his say, despite the results of the Thirteenth Party Conference. Demoted from his position as the major speaker on industrialization at the last Congress, Trotsky listened in silence as his opponents delivered their reports on the state of the economy, international relations, and organizational matters. Zinov'ev assumed responsibility for the political report, which Lenin traditionally delivered, and Stalin reported on the party's organizations. After Zinov'ev's and Stalin's lengthy presentations of the party's achievements during the second and third sessions of the Congress, Trotsky took the floor on May 26, 1924, to present his defense of the opposition, stigmatized as a petty-bourgeois deviation. He tried to resurrect the resolution of December 5, 1923, and return the party to the point at which the Central Committee had bowed to the New Course; he tried to turn the accusation around, to show that the bureaucratization of the party *apparat* reflected petty-bourgeois influences. In the end, however, Trotsky provided the terms of his own surrender:

Comrades, none of us wants to be or can be right against his party. The party, in the last analysis, is always right, because the party is the only historical instrument given to the proletariat for the solution of its basic problems. . . . I know that it is impossible to be right against the party. It is possible to be right only with the party and through the party, for history has created no other paths for the realization of rightness. The English have a historical saying: My country right or wrong. With considerably greater historical justification we can say: My party, right or wrong in particular concrete issues, at particular moments. . . . Not only individual members of the party, but the party itself can make particular mistakes; such, for example, were the particular decisions of the last conference. . . . But if the party passes a resolution, which one or another of us considers unjust, then he says: My party, just or unjust, and I will take responsibility for its decision to the end.[9]

Very basic, long-term flaws—Trotsky's weaknesses as a political organizer, his savage attacks upon Lenin during their years of open enmity, his late entry into the party, and his personal arrogance, which did not permit him to maneuver within the oligarchy—all contributed to his downfall. The psychological mechanisms that prevented him from acting decisively in an organizational context, even when he felt himself to be the legitimate heir, also show through in this final, dramatic submission. Trotsky had made defeat and death, whether on the barricades or before the party in some sort of duel, an acceptable scenario for his political career. He had always courted martyrdom. Now, he gambled that the pathos of his submission would win him the good will of the party. It was a grave mistake. Trotsky's reputation in the upper ranks of the party suffered irreparable harm. Stalin, who knew how to bide his time, gather his forces, and strike against his opponents at the first opportunity, had his day. Now, in open forum, before more than 700 delegates to the Thirteenth Party Congress, he, Zinov'ev, and Kamenev had the joy of humiliating Trotsky.

One speaker after another rose to denounce Trotsky. To a cry of "Right!" from the auditorium and applause, Uglanov accused Trotsky of not knowing the party, of issuing confusing commands, something unforgivable in one of the party's leading officers. Others denounced Trotsky for the insincerity and ambiguity of his remarks. Kamenev accused him of trying to incite a revolution in the party, for putting the party in a state of fever for three months—for making the party ill, like Trotsky himself. Krupskaia rose in defense of party unity and appeared to take the side of Zinov'ev, Stalin, and Kamenev against Trotsky, but subtly criticized as "psychologically impossible" Zinov'ev's demand that the opposition admit its mistakes to the Congress. She urged them to get on with more important matters. Stalin and Zinov'ev, however, refused to deny themselves the pleasure of twisting the knife a bit more. Stalin opened the next session with a round denunciation of Trotsky and Preobrazhenskii, a lengthy review of their sins, and refutation of their positions. Ominously, he extolled the use of the purge as a weapon. It threatened only whining intellectuals and those who had grown accustomed to privilege:

Comrade Lenin taught us that the Party can strengthen itself only if at each step it rids itself of the unstable elements that penetrate, and will continue to penetrate, the Party. We would be going against Leninism if we were to repudiate Party purges in general. As for the present purge, what is wrong with it? . . . The chief thing about the purge is that it makes people of that sort feel that there exists a master *[khoziain]*, who can call them to account for sins against the Party. I think that sometimes it is imperative that the master take a broom and make a sweep of the ranks of the Party.[10]

Stalin ended by demanding that the "minority" submit to the "majority" and show that they really wanted party unity. He made a show of mercy and for some time continued to restrain the other oligarchs from reducing Trotsky to the ranks immediately. It was not beyond Stalin to keep an enemy around so he could enjoy his discomfiture. The delegates to the Thirteenth Congress dutifully returned Trotsky to his seat on the CC. In a sense, party history had come full circle. The oligarchs championed the party machine against usurpers, who would open the party to "soft" elements, here called "unstable." Stalin knew the history of the party well. Lenin had built it up by continually moving forward, exploiting opportunities, but after each concession to "spontaneity," had pared away the party until he had a hard core of "conscious" workers, a tempered organization. When necessary, Lenin had called a small group of his followers—really no more than a faction—"the Party." Stalin, Zinov'ev, and Kamenev could now call the *apparatchiki*, the 20,000 to 30,000 officials controlling the party (swollen to more than 670,000 by the recent "Lenin enrollment" of 200,000), "the majority." In the years ahead Stalin, the master of the *apparat*, would control not only the party but wield unprecedented power—the power to mobilize, inspire, imprison, and kill on a massive scale.

Trotsky and others had long before deduced the logical outcome of Lenin's conception of the party. They had prophesied the emergence of a dictator. Although in 1924 Stalin could not yet claim that role, he had converted the post of General Secretary into the control center of the party. Trotsky, for all of the brilliance of his contributions to the revolutions of 1905 and 1917 and the civil war, lost the battle for power. However, in the years ahead he made a brave and highly successful effort to win with his pen what he had lost in intraparty duels: Trotsky created a picture of the revolution and his role in it that guaranteed his place in history despite all of Stalin's efforts to erase it. As a historian of revolution, as a dramatist of one of the turning points in human history, Trotsky had no peer in his time. He convinced millions of readers that he, not Stalin, understood the dialectic of history, that he, not the *apparatchiki*, would sustain the ideal proclaimed by Marx and Engels and embodied in the first workers' state by Lenin. Furthermore, despite Stalin's superiority to him in organizational fights, Trotsky finally used his tormenter well. Stalin obligingly played the role of murderous tyrant and provided the tragic ending to Trotsky's career—the only appropriate ending.

Notes

1. The Ul'ianovs

1. Discrepancies in the census and tax records and disagreements among Soviet researchers make it difficult to establish Nikolai's precise age. Nikolai's and Anna's ethnic origins are also in doubt. Marietta Shaginian, whose researches in the 1930s broke new ground in the history of Lenin's family, suggested Kalmyk origins for both Ul'ianov and Smirnov. Other Soviet historians, however, maintain that Il'ia was ethnically Russian on his father's side. For many of the details of family history below, I am indebted to the labors of the Soviet historian, Zhores A. Trofimov, who has written or co-authored numerous recent studies of the Ul'ianovs.

2. For a reasonably detailed discussion of Vasilii, see A. S. Markov, *Ul'ianovy v Astrakhani* [The Ul'ianovs in Astrakhan] (Volgograd: Nizhne-Volozhskoe izdatel'stvo, 1970), pp. 40–44.

3. *Ibid.*, p. 70.

4. A. I. Elizarova-Ul'ianova, "A. I. Ul'ianov," *Proletarskaia revoliutsiia* [Proletarian revolution] (1927), 1(60):76.

5. Rolf Theen, *Lenin, Genesis, and the Development of a Revolutionary* (Philadelphia: Lippincott, 1973), p. 25.

6. V. Arnol'd, *Sem'ia Ul'ianovykh v Samare* [The Ul'ianov Family in Samara] (Kuibyshev: Kuibyshevskogo knizhnoe izdatel'stvo, 1979), pp. 6–7.

7. A. Ivanskii, ed., *Zhizn' kak fakel'* [A Luminous Life] (Moscow: Izdatel'stvo politicheskoi literatury, 1966), p. 27.

8. B. Eklof, *Russian Peasant Schools* (Berkeley: University of California Press, 1986), p. 127.

9. Elizarova-Ul'ianova, "A I. Ul'ianov," p. 85.

10. *Ibid.*, pp. 86–89.

11. *Ibid.*, p. 89.

12. L. Trotsky, *The Young Lenin* (Garden City, N.Y.: Doubleday, 1977), pp. 77–78.

2. Alexander Ul'ianov, Terrorist

1. Elizarova-Ul'ianova, "A. I. Ul'ianov," p. 75.

2. Quoted in Trotsky, *The Young Lenin*, p. 38.

3. Ivanskii, ed., *Comet in the Night*, T. Kapustin, trans. (Moscow: Progress Publishers, 1968), p. 164.

4. Ivanskii, ed., *Zhizn' kak fakel'*, p. 329.

5. *Ibid.*, pp. 89–91.

6. Elizarova-Ul'ianova, "A. I. Ul'ianov," pp. 102–103.

7. *Ibid.*, pp. 96–97.

8. Norman M. Naimark, *Terrorists and Social Democrats* (Cambridge: Harvard University Press, 1983), pp. 130–53.

9. Ivanskii, *Comet in the Night*, pp. 266–267.

10. *Ibid.*, p. 268.

11. Trotsky, *The Young Lenin*, p. 25.

12. Rosa Luxemburg, *The Russian Revolution and Leninism or Marxism?* Bertram Wolfe, trans. (Ann Arbor: University of Michigan Press, 1961), p. 107.

13. Ivanskii, *Comet in the Night*, p. 246.

14. *Ibid.*, p. 78.

15. *Ibid.*, pp. 228–29.

16. *Ibid.*, p. 332.

17. *Ibid.*, p. 278.

3. Vladimir Ul'ianov, Substitute Revolutionary

1. Elizarova-Ul'ianova, "A. I. Ul'ianov," p. 285.

2. V. V. Kashkadamova, "Semeistvo V. I. Ul'ianova-Lenina v Simbirske," [V. I. Ul'ianov's Family in Simbirsk] in *Izvesten vsei Rossii, I. N. Ul'ianov* [Known Throughout Russia, I. N. Ul'ianov] (Saratov: Privolzhskoe knizhnoe izdatel'stvo, Ul'ianovskoe otdelenie, 1974), pp. 293–94.

3. D. I. Ul'ianov "Liubov' k myzyke," [Love of Music] in G. N. Golikov et al., ed., *Vospominaniia o Vladimire Il'iche Lenine* [Reminiscences about Vladimir Il'ich Lenin] 5 vols. (Moscow: Izdatel'stvo politicheskoi literatury, 1969), 1:109.

4. Elizarova-Ul'ianova, "A. I. Ul'ianov," p. 232.

5. M. I. Ul'ianova, "V gymnazii," [In the Gymnasium] in *Vospominaniia o Vladimire Il'iche Lenine*, 1:138.

6. Trotsky, *The Young Lenin*, p. 118.

7. *Ibid.*, pp. 116–17.

8. "Kazan' i Samara," [Kazan' and Samara] *Krasnyi arkhiv*, [Red Archive] (1934), no. 1, p. 55.

9. G. S. Zhuk, ed., *Lenin i Tatariia* [Lenin and Tartary] (Kazan': Tatarskoe knizhnoe izdatel'stvo, 1970), p. 280.

10. A. Ivanskii, ed., *Molodoi Lenin* [Young Lenin] (Moscow: Izdatel'stvo politicheskoi literatury, 1964), pp. 419–23.

11. *Ibid.*, p. 406.

12. Lenin had told Valentinov that he had read Chernyshevskii without appreciating him when he was fourteen.

13. Ivanskii, *Molodoi Lenin*, p. 357.

14. Golikov et al., eds., *Vospominaniia o Vladimire Il'iche Lenine*, 1:28.

4. Moratorium and Apprenticeship

1. L. Trotsky, *The Young Lenin*, pp. 125–31.

2. Ivanskii, *Molodoi Lenin*, p. 500.

3. N. M. Mor, ed., *Vospominaniia o Vladimire Il'iche Lenine*, 3 vols. (Moscow: Gosudarstvennoe izdatel'stvo politicheskoi literatury, 1956–1960), 1:16.

4. Trotsky, *The Young Lenin*, p. 153.

5. Ivanskii, *Molodoi Lenin*, p. 640.

6. Trotsky had astutely observed this when he was collecting material for his biography of Lenin. Among his notes there is an excerpt from Krupskaia's memoirs in which she describes the behavior noted above and quotes Lenin's dismissive remark. Trotsky noted alongside it, in red pencil, *otets* (father). Trotsky Archives, T3801, Houghton Library, Harvard University.

7. Ivanskii, *Molodoi Lenin*, p. 671.

8. The following article contains a scathing attack on those responsible for the publication of Beliakov's memoirs: N. Valentinov, "O predkakh Lenina i ego biografiakh" [About Lenin's Ancestors and His Biographers], *Novyi zhurnal* [New Journal] (1960), 61–62:232–35.

9. Trotsky, *The Young Lenin*, pp. 130–31.

10. G. N. Golikov et al., eds., *Vospominaniia o Lenine*, 1:35.

11. V. I. Lenin, *Collected Works*, 4th ed. (Moscow: Foreign Languages Publishing, 1960), 1:298.

12. *Ibid.*

13. R. Pipes, *Struve, Liberal on the Left, 1870–1905*, (Cambridge: Harvard University Press, 1970), pp. 137–39.

14. P. B. Aksel'rod and G. V. Plekhanov, *Perepiska G. V. Plekhanova i P. B. Aksel'roda* [The Correspondence of G. V. Plekhanov and P. B. Aksel'rod] (Moscow: Izdanie, P. M. Plekhanovoi, 1925), pp. 269–75.

15. *Ibid.*, p. 274.

16. P. N. Lepeshinskii, "Po sosedstvy s Vladimirom Il'ichem" [With Vladimir Il'ich], in *Ob Il'iche, vospominaniia pitertsev* [About Lenin, Reminiscences of St. Petersburg] (Leningrad: Leninzdat, 1970), p. 65. Lepeshinskii had met G. M. Krzhizhanovskii, V. V. Starkov, Martov, A. A. Vaneev, and P. K. Zaparozhets (Gutsul) in 1897.

17. I. Getzler, *Martov* (Cambridge: Cambridge University Press, 1967), p. 29.

5. Exile and Emigration

1. See Robert H. McNeal, *Bride of the Revolution, Krupskaya and Lenin* (Ann Arbor: University of Michigan Press, 1972).

2. In V. I. Lenin *Collected Works*, 4th ed., (London: Lawrence and Wishart, 1960), 4:173.

3. The protest was published in Plekhanov's attack on economism and revisionism, the collection *Vademecum* (March 1900), to be discussed in chapters 5 and 6.

6. Lenin and Plekhanov

1. His entire family had become involved in the revolutionary movement. By 1900 both Dmitrii and Maria had become Social Democrats and subjected to arrest and imprisonment. Anna and her husband, Mark Elizarov, were already veterans of social democracy. Maria Alexandrovna continually petitioned the authorities on behalf of her children, looked after their material welfare, and moved her household as they pursued both education and revolution.

2. A. Ascher, *Pavel Akselrod and the Development of Menshevism* (Cambridge: Harvard

University Press, 1972), pp. 111 ff. Ascher's study is an excellent source for insight into the clashes of personalities and their connections with the development of Russian Marxism. For the best early study of the connection of personality and political behavior see L. H. Haimson, *The Russian Marxists and the Origins of Bolshevism* (Cambridge: Harvard University Press, 1955).

3. V. I. Lenin, *Collected Works*, 4th ed., (London) 4:340–42.

4. *Ibid.*, p. 343.

5. *Ibid.*, p. 344.

6. *Ibid.*, p. 346–48.

7. V. I. Lenin, *Polnoe sobranie sochinenii* [Complete Collected Works], 5th ed., 55 vols. (Moscow: Gosudarstvennoe izdatel'stvo politicheskoi literatury, 1958–1965), 4:386.

7. The Emergence of Leninism

1. *Protokoly i stenograficheskie otchety s'ezdov i konferentsii kommunisticheskoi partii sovetskogo soiuza. Vtoroi s'ezd RSDRP* [The Protocols and Stenographic Accounts of the Congresses and Conferences of the Communist Party of the Soviet Union. The Second Congress of the RSDRP] (Moscow: Gosudarstvennoe izdatel'stvo politicheskoi literatury, 1959), p. 178.

2. J. L. H. Keep, *The Rise of Social Democracy in Russia* (Oxford: Clarendon Press, 1963), p. 127.

3. *Ibid.*, pp. 126–28.

4. Reproduced in Getzler, *Martov*, pp. 93.

5. Okhrana Archives, XVII-a (Box 293-a), no. 5086, April 1904, Hoover Institution Archives, Stanford University.

6. Golikov et al., eds., *Vospominaniia o V. I. Lenine*, 2:77.

7. Lenin and V. D. Bonch-Bruevich, one of the Bolshevik faithful, organized a printing venture toward the end of the summer. During this period Bonch-Bruevich and M. S. Ol'minskii were his major literary collaborators.

8. V. I. Lenin, *Polnoe sobranie sochineniia*, 46:414.

9. *Ibid.*, 9:152.

10. *Ibid.*, 9:205.

8. 1905

1. V. I. Lenin, *Polnoe sobranie sochinenii*, 10:127, 129.

2. *Ibid.*, p. 163.

3. Rossiiskaia sotsial-demokraticheskaia rabochaia partiia. *Protokoly tret'ego s'ezda RSDRP* (Moscow: Partizdat TsK, VKP[b], 1937), p. 349.

4. N. K. Krupskaia, *Reminiscences of Lenin* (Moscow: Foreign Languages Publishing House, 1959), pp. 124–25.

5. *Protokoly tret'ego s'ezda RSDRP*, p. 354.

6. For a good summary, see Keep, *The Rise of Social Democracy in Russia*, pp. 210–13.

9. The Bronsteins

1. Okhrana Archives, XIIIc, folder 1, "Lev Trotsky."

2. Boris Nicolaevsky Collection, Trotsky Papers, Box 312 (manuscript of *My Life*, "Detstvo," p. 3), Hoover Institution Archives, Stanford University.

3. The Okhrana includes another child, Evsei, in its report on Trotsky, but he is evidently David's nephew. Okhrana Archives, XIIIc, folder 1.

4. For a contrary view see Eastman Archive, M. F. Shpentser, Ms. Lilly Library, Indiana University. Shpentser's memoirs suggest that as a child Trotsky was closer to his mother and had little respect for his father. He appreciated his father's gifts much later. But Shpentser (who, after all, was Anna's nephew) might have inferred closeness with Anna because Lev's academic gifts brought him closer to his mother's side of the family—the more cultured side—

and as a boy of nine (when he went to live with the Shpentsers in Odessa) he already had difficulty identifying himself with a father who could neither read, write, nor keep accounts.

5. There is no reason to doubt Trotsky's own memories about this, but one should add that Max Eastman, who devoted a small book to Trotsky's childhood and youth, believed that the lack of affection and respect for his mother in Trotsky's adult recollections probably obscured a deep childhood attachment to Anna. See M. Eastman, *Leon Trotsky: The Portrait of a Youth* (New York: Greenberg, 1925), p. 7. In 1923 Eastman interviewed Trotsky, some of Trotsky's relatives, his first wife, and several others close to Trotsky during his school years and early career. The stenographic accounts taken by Eastman and Trotsky's replies to some of his questions preserved in Eastman's archive are the only surviving primary sources about Trotsky's childhood other than the autobiography. Given Eastman's exposure to Freud and the theory of the oedipus complex, it is not surprising that he questioned Trotsky's version of his childhood.

6. L. Trotsky, *My Life* (New York: Pathfinder Press, 1970), p. 36.

7. *Ibid.*, p. 39. For a fuller description than the brief mention in *My Life*, see the manuscript of the autobiography, Nicolaevsky Collection, Trotsky Papers, Box 312 (29); Trotsky Mss., "Otvet na voprosy t. Istmena" [Answer to Comrade Eastman's question], February 26, 1923 Lilly Library, Indiana University.

8. Trotsky, *My Life*, p. 40.

10. The Impostor

1. L. Trotsky, *My Life*, p. 43.

2. According to one of his close schoolmates, identified only as Rozenshtein on the typed manuscript, his own parents held up Trotsky as a model to him, causing some resentment. Other schoolmates also resented Trotsky for his achievements and princely bearing. Rozenshtein Ms., Trotsky Mss., Lilly Library.

3. M. Eastman, *Leon Trotsky*, p. 15.

4. I have used the manuscript of Trotsky's answers to Max Eastman's questionnaire, as well as the version in the autobiography. Trotsky Mss., "Otvet na voprosy t. Istmena," Lilly Library.

5. *Ibid.*

6. Trotsky, *My Life*, p. 149.

7. *Ibid.*, p. 73.

8. Rozenshtein Ms. Rozenshtein is probably the "Kostya R." referred to on p. 69 of *My Life*. Trotsky refers to him here as his best friend, and in the manuscript cited Rozenshtein refers to Trotsky as one of his best friends.

9. Trotsky, *My Life*, pp. 66–70.

10. Skorcheletti Ms., Trotsky Mss., Lilly Library, Indiana University. Trotsky mentions Kologrivov in his autobiography, but in connection with completely different matters.

11. Trotsky, *My Life*, pp. 70, 72.

12. *Ibid.*, pp. 90, 96.

13. *Ibid.*, p. 95.

14. Dikshtein Ms., Trotsky Mss., Lilly Library, Indiana University.

15. According to Dikshtein, he planned to enroll in the St. Petersburg Technological Institute after completing his seventh year of the *realschule* in Nikolaev. *Ibid.*

11. Lev Bronstein's Two Conversions

1. M. Eastman, *Leon Trotsky*, p. 33.

2. Trotsky to Eastman, February 11, 1923, p. 3., Trotsky Mss., Lilly Library.

3. Eastman, *Leon Trotsky*, p. 33.

4. L. Trotsky, *My Life*, p. 99.

5. Dikshtein Ms., pp. 1–2.

6. Eastman, *Leon Trotsky*, p. 36.

7. Trotsky to Eastman, February 11, 1923, p. 3., Trotsky Mss., Lilly Library.

8. G. A. Ziv, *Trotskii: Kharakteristika* [Trotsky: A Description] (New York: Knigoizdatel'stvo "Narodopravstvo," 1921), p. 9.

9. In a version not found in any other source, one of Trotsky's revolutionary colleagues, Shatunovskii, claimed that the younger Shvigovskii had been expelled from the *realschule* because of his brother's political unreliability. The younger brother had refused to move out of the cottage when requested by the local police. Trotsky then moved in with the Shvigovskiis in protest, but was not expelled. Shatunovskii Ms., p. 2., Trotsky Mss., Lilly Library, Indiana University.

10. Dikshtein Ms., p. 2.; Eastman, *Leon Trotsky*, p. 39.

11. Vegman Ms., p. 1., Trotsky Mss., Lilly Library, Indiana University.

12. Aleksandra Sokolovskaia Ms., p. 2., Trotsky Mss., Lilly Library, Indiana University.

13. Eastman, *Leon Trotsky*, pp. 32, 54.

14. Vegman Ms., p. 1.

15. Sokolovskaia Ms., pp. 2–3.

16. Skorcheletti Ms., p. 2., Trotsky Mss., Lilly Library, Indiana University.

17. Ziv, *Trotskii*, p. 12.

18. Eastman, *Leon Trotsky*, pp. 17–18.

19. Shatunovskii Ms., p. 2.

20. Dikshtein Ms., p. 2.

21. Trotsky, *My Life*, pp. 99–102.

22. *Ibid.*, p. 100.

23. Vegman Ms., p. 2.

24. Eastman, *Leon Trotsky*, pp. 57–58.

25. One of those employees, Shatunovskii, described his own conversion by Trotsky. Shatunovskii Ms., p. 1.

26. Trotsky to Eastman, February 11, 1923, p. 7., Trotsky Mss., Lilly Library. The version in this document is fuller than Trotsky's account in his autobiography and is reinforced by Vegman's memoirs concerning the same period.

27. Vegman Ms., p. 2. Trotsky's account of his activities in Odessa during the autumn of 1896 does not include mention of this episode. He only says that he tutored private pupils. Trotsky, *My Life*, p. 103.

28. *Ibid.*, p. 3.

29. See Sokolovskaia Ms., p. 2.

30. Trotsky to Eastman, February 11, 1923, p. 5. Trotsky Mss., Lilly Library.

31. Vegman Ms., p. 4.

32. Sokolovskaia Ms., p. 3.

33. *Ibid.*, p. 4.

34. Trotsky to Eastman, February 26, 1923, pp. 6–7., Trotsky Mss., Lilly Library; Vegman Ms., p. 3.

35. Trotsky, *My Life*, pp. 105–106.

36. Trotsky to Max Eastman, March 29, 1923, Trotsky Mss., Lilly Library.

37. Vegman Ms., p. 4.

38. Sokolovskaia Ms., p. 1.

39. Vegman Ms., p. 1.

40. L. Trotsky, *My Life*, p. 111. In Trotsky's reply of February 26, 1923, to Max Eastman's questionnaire, cited above, he refers to the composition of this "constitution" and adds that it actually contained a program, but describes it in only the vaguest terms. In Eastman's biography the rules of the organization are outlined and some proclamations quoted. See M. Eastman, *Leon Trotsky*, pp. 81–83.

41. Ziv, *Trotskii*, p. 26.

42. N. Valentinov, *Encounters with Lenin*, Paul Rosta and Brian Pearce, trans. (New York: Oxford University Press, 1968), pp. 43–45.

43. I. Deutscher, *The Prophet Armed*, p. 56.

44. Robert Wistrich, *Trotsky, Fate of a Revolutionary* (London: Robson Books, 1979), p. 23.

45. Eastman, *Leon Trotsky*, p. 143.

46. Trotsky to Eastman, March 15, 1923, p. 6., Trotsky Mss., Manuscripts Department, Lilly Library, Indiana University.

47. Deutscher, *The Prophet Armed: Trotsky, 1879–1921* (New York: Oxford University Press, 1954), pp. 22–23.

48. Trotsky, *Trotsky's Notebooks, 1933–35: Writings on Lenin, Dialectics, and Evolutionism* (New York: Columbia University Press, 1986), pp. 90–91, 101.

49. Trotsky, *My Life*, pp. 122–23.

12. Leon Trotsky, Romantic Exile

1. According to Eastman, she was six years older than Trotsky. See M. Eastman, *Leon Trotsky*, p. 44. Ziv, on the other hand, wrote that she was at least ten years older. See Ziv, *Trotskii*, p. 35.

2. Eastman, *Leon Trotsky*, p. 119. David Bronstein vehemently and stubbornly opposed the marriage. Ziv mentions Trotsky's youth compared to his bride as one reason for David's opposition. See Ziv, *Trotskii*, p. 35. Furthermore, David could only see his son's marriage to another political criminal as a disaster. David had gotten the Minister of the Interior to stop the marriage in Odessa, but could not keep up with them in Moscow.

3. Ziv, *Trotskii*, p. 40.

4. Trotsky claims that they moved to Verkholensk, but Sokolovskaia describes the new place of exile as Nizhne-Lamsk.

5. In her memoirs, Sokolovskaia reveals that Zina lived with Trotsky's parents until the age of nine and then with Sokolovskaia's sister, but that Nina had remained with her almost the entire time.

6. The story of Zina's descent into mental illness is told in I. Deutscher, *The Prophet Outcast, Trotsky: 1929–1940* (New York: Oxford University Press, 1963), pp. 146–151, 176–178, 195–198. Deutscher had access to the family correspondence in the closed (until 1980) section of Trotsky's archives in the Houghton Library at Harvard but did not have access to the materials, only recently unearthed, in the Hoover Institution. Further correspondence between Trotsky and Leon Sedov preserved in the Nicolaevsky Collection in the Hoover Institution (for example, a letter of November 21, 1931) reveals Trotsky's doubts about the value of psychoanalysis as a therapy, even though he respected its theoretical findings. Trotsky's anxiety about Zina and his main prescription for her—reintegration into society and work, which would only be possible if she returned to the Soviet Union—punctuate his correspondence with his older son.

7. L. Trotsky, *Lenin, Notes for a Biographer*, Tamara Deutscher, trans. (New York: Putnam, 1971), p. 66.

8. L. Trotsky, *Sochineniia*, 21 vols, (Moscow-Leningrad: Gosudarstvennoe izdatel'stvo, 1924–1927), 20:78.

9. *Ibid.*, pp. 202–204.

10. In Eastman's account, Trotsky spent two months in Paris with Natalia Sedova. See Eastman, *Leon Trotsky*, pp. 152–53. Although Trotsky testifies to the factual accuracy of Eastman's book, in his own autobiography he creates the impression that his first meeting with Natalia Sedova occurred *after* his trip to London, when he was sent on a lecture tour that took him back to Paris. Krupskaia places Trotsky's time of arrival in London in early October.

11. N. Krupskaia, *Reminiscences of Lenin*, p. 82. A letter of January 27, 1903, to Krzhizhanovskii suggests that Lenin may have merely acquiesced because he recognized that Trotsky did not want to go. See V. I. Lenin, *Polnoe sobranie sochinenii*, 46:259. Deutscher suggests that Lenin's letter to Krzhizhanovskii was merely a subterfuge. See Deutscher, *The Prophet Armed*, p. 71.

12. Trotsky, *My Life*, pp. 144–45. Trotsky also wrote that the "prospect of working in the Russian organization of *Iskra* was tempting, but nevertheless I was very glad to be able to stay abroad a little longer." *Ibid.*, pp. 146–47. This probably understates Trotsky's ambitions and entirely omits his relationship with Natalia Sedova. In any case, it is unlikely that someone of Trotsky's drive and self-esteem would have settled for less than a leading role.

13. Trotsky, *My Life*, p. 149. The incident is not mentioned in any other source.

14. Trotsky, *Lenin, Notes for a Biographer*, p. 49.

15. Trotsky, *My Life*, p. 155. Krupskaia's memoirs contain a similar version of the matter, but she omits the fact that Lenin tried to coopt Trotsky. She mentions instead a decision to coopt P. N. Krasikov until the Second Party Congress. See Krupskaia, *Reminiscences of Lenin*, p. 88.

16. V. I. Lenin, *Polnoe sobranie sochinenii*, 8:42; Getzler, *Martov*, p. 74 fn. 66. Getzler's speculation that this incident may have contributed to Trotsky's defection at the Second Party Congress is quite plausible.

17. Lenin, *Polnoe sobranie sochinenii*, 46:241, 277–78.

18. Trotsky, *My Life*, p. 160.

19. *Ibid.*, pp. 161–62. Of course, for political reasons (at the very least) Trotsky in 1929 had to add that Lenin was correct and that he was too immature to grasp the logic of Lenin's position.

20. Trotsky evidently never understood the complex relationship of Plekhanov and Lenin. He believed that Lenin "won over" Plekhanov at the Congress and did not know that despite their differences, both of them had strong affinities for Jacobinism. See Trotsky, *Lenin, Notes for a Biographer*, p. 69.

13. Trotsky Against Lenin

1. V. I. Lenin, *Polnoe sobranie sochinenii*, 7:435.

2. *Ibid.*, 8:5.

3. L. Trotsky, *Lenin, Notes for a Biographer*, pp. 67–68. Trotsky was mistaken about Spinoza's occupation. He was a lens grinder.

4. Trotsky, *Trotsky's Notebooks, 1933–35*, pp. 83, 95.

5. Trotsky, *My Life*, p. 184.

6. For a full discussion of the report, see Baruch Knei-Paz, *The Social and Political Thought of Leon Trotsky* (Oxford: Clarendon Press, 1978), pp. 176–85.

7. N. Trotsky, *Nashi politicheskie zadachi* [Our Political tasks] (Geneva: Tipografiia partii, 1904), p. 54. Trotsky used the initial "N" as part of his pseudonym during this phase of his career.

8. *Ibid.*, p. 59.

9. *Ibid.*, p. 74.

10. Trotsky, *Trotsky's Notebooks, 1933–35*, p. 33.

14. Trotsky in 1905

1. According to Trotsky, he had "ceased being an active member" of the Menshevik group in April 1904 and "formally renounced membership" in September. See L. Trotsky, *My Life*, p. 165.

2. Z. A. B. Zeman and W. B. Scharlau, *The Merchant of Revolution, the Life of Alexander Israel Helphand (Parvus), 1867–1924* (London: Oxford University Press, 1965).

3. N. Trotsky, *Do deviatogo janvaria* [Before the ninth of January] (Geneva: Tipografiia partii, 1905), p. 63. Deutscher mistakenly believes that the quoted material appeared in a separate publication, *After the Petersburg Insurrection*. See Deutscher, *The Prophet Armed*, p. 114. The original pamphlet contained a section composed after the events of January 9, 1905. In Trotsky's *Sochineniia* this section is presented in such a way that it might be mistaken as a separate publication, but the "2." in front of the title should have suggested that it was the second part of the pamphlet.

4. Quoted and translated in Deutscher, *The Prophet Armed*, pp. 110–11.

5. Trotsky, *My Life*, pp. 172–73. Also, see *Protokoly tret'ego s'ezda RSDRP*, pp. 208–10.

6. Trotsky, p. 174.

7. For two thorough studies, see Victoria E. Bonnell, *Roots of Rebellion, Workers' Politics, and Organizations in St. Petersburg and Moscow, 1900–1914* (Berkeley: University of California

Press, 1983), chs. 1 and 2; David Lane, *The Roots of Russian Communism* (Assen: Van Gorcum, 1969), ch. 3.

8. For a thorough account of the Shidlovskii Commission, see Solomon M. Schwarz, *The Russian Revolution of 1905* (Chicago: University of Chicago Press, 1967), ch. 2.

9. Trotsky, *My Life*, pp. 179, 185.

10. *Ibid.*, p. 182.

11. L. Trotsky, *1905*, (New York: Vintage Books, 1972), p. 117.

12. Trotsky, *My Life*, pp. 181–82.

13. *Ibid.*, pp. 190–91.

14. Trotsky, *1905*, p. 406.

15. Lenin at Loose Ends

1. A footnote states that the manuscript was only found "in the autumn of 1940." V. I. Lenin, *Polnoe sobranie sochinenii*, 12:443–44.

2. V. I. Lenin, *Collected Works*, (Moscow, 1962) 10:21, 22.

3. L. Trotsky, *Sochineniia*, vol. 2, part 1, pp. 298–99. The editors did say that they had not established the authorship of all the materials in the volume with total certainty.

4. L. Trotsky, *My Life*, p. 181.

5. *Vospominaniia o V.I. Lenine* (1969), 2:122–23.

6. *Ibid.*, p. 29. For a fuller description of the meeting, see the reminiscences of A. G. Shlichter in *Ob Il'iche, vospominaniia pitertsev*, pp. 156–61.

7. N. K. Krupskaia, *Reminiscences of Lenin*, p. 149.

8. Lenin, *Collected Works*, (Moscow, 1962) 10:69–70.

9. *Ibid.*, 10:32.

10. Lenin, *Polnoe sobranie sochinenii*, 12:130.

11. *Ibid.*, 13:376–77.

16. Iosif Dzhugashvili Becomes Koba

1. Unauthenticated stories circulated in the Gulag and among émigrés as well as in Georgia have been given credence. Imaginative writers of considerable reputation, such as Faizel Iskander and Anatolii Rybakov, and a recent biographer, Alexander De Jonge, have all relied upon oral tradition.

2. According to the most detailed account, it happened on January 6, Epiphany, when the boy was singing with the church choir on a narrow street near the Okonskaia Church. A phaeton bore down on them, and Soso (diminutive of Iosif) failed to escape the onrushing vehicle. The injury kept him from attending school for two weeks. See V. Kaminskii and I. Vereshchagin, "Detstvo i iunost' vozhdei," [The Leader's Childhood and Youth] *Molodaia gvardiia* [The Young Guard] (1939), no. 12, pp. 31–34.

3. In the Okhrana files Stalin's height was recorded in traditional Russian measures: the *arshin* (two) and *vershok* (seven and three-fourths). This is equal to exactly five feet three and seven-eighths inches.

4. The Russified transliterations of their names are used here for purposes of simplifaction. This is the way the names are encountered in most texts. Apologies for those of Georgian nationality are called for.

5. Vano, Vissarion's father, tended a vineyard but traded in town. Vano's other son, George, was killed by bandits, leaving Vissarion without family. His mother is not mentioned. See, Kaminskii and Vereshchagin, "Detstvo i iunost' vozhdei," p. 24.

6. See I. V. Stalin, *Sochineniia* [Works], 13 vols. (Moscow: Godudarstvennoe izdatel'stvo politicheskai literatury, 1946–1951), 1:314–15. In his essay "Anarchism or Socialism?" Stalin tries to reconstruct the transformation of the consciousness of a shoemaker. Given what we know of his career, Vissarion remained at the petit-bourgeois stage.

7. Kaminski and Vereshchagin, "Detstvo i iunost' vozhdei," p. 45.

8. See Svetlana Allilueva, *Twenty Letters to a Friend*, Priscilla Johnson McMillan, trans.

(New York: Harper and Row, 1967), p. 153 fn. Another version has Vissarion surviving until 1909, when he is probably killed in a drunken brawl. See Robert H. McNeal, *Stalin: Man and Ruler* (New York: New York University Press, 1988), p. 336, n. 15.

9. Kaminski and Vereshchagin, p. 25.

10. Allilueva, *Twenty Letters*, p. 153.

11. *Ibid.*

12. Stalin's neglect of his mother is attested to by Svetlana Allilueva and by Ekaterina Georgievna herself. In an interview published in the *New York Evening Post* on December 1, 1930, she said: "I visited the Kremlin once. Just once I've been in Moscow. I lived with my son there. . . . Oh yes, he comes often to Georgia. But he seldom gets farther than Sochi, over there on the coast. Soso came to see me once in 1921 and once three years ago."

13. Allilueva, *Twenty Letters*, pp. 153–54.

14. According to one oral tradition presented in Faizel Iskander's novel, *Sandro of Chegem*, as a boy Stalin was humiliated and felt terrible resentment because his mother's putatively loose morals were whispered about by the local men.

15. S. Allilueva, *Only One Year* (New York: Harper and Row, 1969), p. 360.

16. Quoted in Robert C. Tucker, *Stalin as Revolutionary, 1879–1929* (New York: Norton, 1973), p. 73.

17. Soso's official date of entry in the school is 1888, but it seems likely that he did not spend much time there until 1890, when the family problems were resolved. All of this is speculation, but the school had a four-year curriculum, and it is otherwise difficult to understand why it took the boy six years.

18. J. Iremaschwili, *Stalin und die Tragödie Georgiens* [Stalin and the Georgian Tragedy] (Berlin, 1932), p. 5. Iremaschwili's account was written in 1932, more than forty years after the event, but such events are etched into one's memory.

19. For example, D. Gogokhiia ("Na vsiu zhizn' Zapomnilis eti dni," p. 10) noted that Soso was the only boy in the school in Gori with a monthly stipend. G. Elisabedashvili ("Gody v uchilishche," p. 22) noted that he was one of the neediest students. See *Rasskazy starykh rabochikh zakavkaz'ia o velikom Staline* [Stories of old Caucasian workers about mighty Stalin] (Moscow, 1937), pp. 10, 22.

20. Ekaterina worked for the school and the teachers, for which she received ten roubles a month in addition to the three-rouble stipend given Iosif. See Kaminskii and Vereshchagin, "Detstvo i iunost' vozhdei," p. 34.

21. Allilueva, *Only One Year*, p. 361.

22. According to Iremaschwili, this included school supplies, shoes, clothing, and laundry. See, Iremaschwili, *Stalin*, p. 16. Another source describes his award as a "half pension." See Kaminski and Vereshchagin, "Detstvo i iunost' vozhdei," p. 64.

23. Quoted in L. Trotsky, *Stalin*, Charles Malamuth, trans. (New York: Grosset and Dunlap, 1941), p. 14.

24. The poems are printed in Russian. See E. Kelendrzheridze, "Stikhi iunogo Stalina" [Young Stalin's poems], in *Rasskazy o velikom Staline* [Stories about mighty Stalin] (Tbilisi: Zaria vostoka, 1941), pp. 67–70. Three are published in English translation in Robert Payne, *The Rise and Fall of Stalin* (New York: Simon and Schuster, 1965), pp. 47–51. Stalin also published in *Kvali* (1896), no. 32, and in 1899 his verse appeared in honor of Eristavi. See, Kaminskii and Vereshchagin, "Detstvo i iunost' vozhdei," p. 69. For new English translations see D. Rayfield, "Stalin the Poet," in *Poetry and Nation Review*, no. 41 (Manchester, England: 1984), pp. 44–47.

25. Iremaschwili, *Stalin*, p. 18.

26. *Ibid.*, p. 18. Iremaschwili, relying upon a faulty memory, got the name of the novel and its plot wrong. Trotsky relied upon Iremaschwili's account in his own description of the novel in his biography of Stalin and thus repeated the erroneous version.

27. Aleksandr Kazbegi, *Izbrannoe*, [Selected works] F. Tvaltvadze and A. Kochetkova, trans. (Tbilisi: Izdatel'stovo Merani, 1974), p. 218.

28. *Ibid.*, p. 208.

29. *Ibid.*, p. 201.

17. Koba: From Apprentice to Journeyman

1. J. V. Stalin, *Works*, 13 vols. (Moscow: Foreign Languages Publishing House, 1952–1955), 8:183.

2. According to one source, Stalin informed on others in order to get them expelled from the Seminary. See R. Arsenidze, "Iz vospominaniia o Staline," [From Reminiscences about Stalin] *Novyi zhurnal* [New Journal] (1963), no. 2, p. 224.

3. For another version, see *ibid.*, pp. 227–28.

4. L. Trotsky, *Stalin*, p. 30.

5. Robert H. McNeal, *Stalin's Works. An Annotated Bibliography* (Stanford: Hoover Institution on War, Revolution and Peace, Stanford University, 1967), p. 21–22. The Georgian texts and Russian translations are in *Batumskaia demonstratsiia 1902 goda* (Moscow: Partizdat, 1937), pp. 27–33.

6. H. Barbusse, *Stalin*, Vyvyan Holland, trans. (New York: Macmillan, 1935), p. 21.

7. Trotsky, *Stalin*, p. 22.

8. *Ibid.*, p. 34.

9. For different versions, see A. Ulam, *Stalin, the Man and His Era* (New York: Viking, 1973), p. 49; Edward Ellis Smith, *The Young Stalin* (New York: Farrar, Straus, and Giroux, 1967), ch. 5.

10. Stalin, *Works*, 6:54–55.

11. The letters are published in Stalin, *Works*, 1:55–62. For a plausible account of this incident see Robert C. Tucker, *Stalin as Revolutionary, 1879–1929* (New York: Norton, 1973), pp. 122–25. Tucker believes that Stalin had probably responded with enthusiasm to Lenin's *Letter to a Comrade on Our Organizational Tasks*, June 1903, which had been circulated among Siberian exiles and had retrospectively (and wishfully) turned it into a personal communication. According to Tucker's view, Stalin was already attuned to the ideas in Lenin's *Letter* and can be counted a Leninist in 1903.

12. The most recent scholarly biography of Stalin gives 1905 as the year of his marriage to Ekaterina Svanidze. According to the same source, she gave birth to Iakov in Tbilisi in March 1907 and died only a few months later, in October 1907. See Robert H. McNeal, *Stalin: Man and Ruler*, pp. 13–14. Iremaschwili also gives 1907 as the year of Ekaterina's death and he was an eye-witness to the funeral. See Iremaschwili, p. 39. Iremaschwili, however, places the marriage as early as 1903. See *ibid.*, p. 30.

13. Tucker, *Stalin as Revolutionary*, p. 107.

14. Quoted in Smith, *The Young Stalin*, p. 128.

15. Trotsky, *Stalin*, p. 66.

16. *Ibid.*, p. 67.

17. *Ibid.*, p. 51.

18. Aleksandr Rusov, "Memuary. Arkhivy. Svidetel'stva" [Memoirs. Archives. Evidence] *Znam'ia* [The Banner] (1987) no. 9, p. 135.

19. See, for example, Smith's contention, based upon N. Zhordania's memoirs, that Stalin had sold out Stepan Shaumian. Smith, *The Young Stalin*, p. 143.

20. Tucker, *Stalin as Revolutionary*, pp. 134–37. Here Tucker argues that Stalin saw Lenin as the incarnation of the Shamil of Kazbegi's novel *Parricide*. He relies heavily upon Stalin's stylized language, his use of the expression "mountain eagle" in his description of Lenin, and assumes that the identification with Lenin was decisive for Stalin's development. By contrast, Smith, using the same document surmises that Stalin's *hatred* of Lenin may have begun in Tammerfors. See Smith, *The Young Stalin*, pp. 152–53.

21. Stalin, *Works*, 6:56.

22. *Ibid.*

23. In the speech of January 28, 1924, Stalin claimed that Lenin had delivered a speech on the agrarian question that had "roused the whole conference to a pitch of stormy enthusiasm." *Ibid.*, p. 57.

24. See his two articles on the agrarian question in Stalin, *Works*, 1:216–37.

25. *Ibid.*, 8:183.

26. For a concise discussion of both the doctrines and actions of Russian anarchists in this period, see Paul Avrich, *The Russian Anarchists* (Princeton: Princeton University Press, 1967), chs. 2–4.

27. Stalin, *Works*, 1:301.

28. For a discussion of the scholarly controversies surrounding the suspicion that Stalin was a double agent, see Tucker, *Stalin as Revolutionary*, pp. 108–14. In my own contacts with members of the Soviet intelligentsia I have found a surprising consensus. A prominent writer who has written historical novels dealing with double agents and studied their psychology believes that Stalin was clearly of their type. Several people with whom I spoke in March 1987 believed that Stalin's purges were motivated by a desire to remove everyone who knew about his shady past. This is a revival of Isaac Don Levine's venerable thesis of 1956, presented in *Stalin's Great Secret* (New York: Coward-McCann, 1956).

29. For a good recent account of the period of expropriations see Robert C. Williams, *The Other Bolsheviks* (Bloomington: Indiana University Press, 1986), ch. 6.

30. Trotsky, *Stalin*, p. 109.

31. This phrase is taken from the title of R. G. Suny's study of Stalin in Baku: "A Journeyman for the Revolution: Stalin and the Labour Movement in Baku, June 1907–May 1908," *Soviet Studies* (1972), 23:373–94.

32. Stalin, *Works*, 2:51–52.

33. Arsenidze, "Iz vospominaniia o Staline," p. 221.

34. Stalin, *Works*, 2:148.

18. The Travails of Russian Social Democracy

1. *Piatyi (Londonskii) s'ezd RSDRP* [The Fifth (London) Congress of the RSDRP] (Moscow: Gosudarstvennoe izdatel'stvo politicheskoi literatury, 1963), p. 266.

2. *Ibid.*, p. 402.

3. *Ibid.*, p. 443.

4. V. I. Lenin, *Polnoe sobranie sochinenii*, 47:137.

5. L. Trotsky, *Stalin*, p. 90. Trotsky believed that Stalin's presence in London could be explained only on conspiratorial grounds, in connection with the expropriations being planned.

19. Philosophical Interlude

1. V. I. Lenin, *Materialism and Empirio-Criticism* (Moscow: Progress Publishers, 1970), p. 217.

2. *Ibid.*, p. 156.

3. *Ibid.*, p. 176.

4. *Ibid.*, p. 177.

5. *Ibid.*, pp. 312, 315.

6. Bogdanov has attracted a great deal of scholarly attention in recent years. Aside from R. C. Williams's book, *The Other Bolsheviks*, one should mention Z. Sochor, *Revolution and Culture: The Bogdanov-Lenin Controversy* (Ithaca: Cornell University Press, 1988).

7. Williams, *The Other Bolsheviks*, pp. 69–70.

8. V. I. Lenin, *Polnoe sobranie sochinenii*, 47:203–204.

9. N. K. Krupskaia, *Reminiscences of Lenin*, p. 208.

10. Lenin, *Polnoe sobranie sochinenii*, 47:18.

11. *Ibid.*, p. 209.

12. *Ibid.*, p. 335, fn. 204.

13. Williams, *The Other Bolsheviks*, p. 153.

14. See his article "Na partiinuiu dorogu," [On the Party Road] in *Pravda* (Vienna), February 12 (25), 1910, no. 10. Cited in Getzler, *Martov*, p. 132, fn. 9.

15. According to a version found only in his autobiography, Trotsky accidentally encountered Lenin at an unspecified train station on the way from Vienna to Copenhagen. During the course of their conversation, Trotsky told Lenin about the article, "Die Russische Sozialdemok-

ratie" ["Russian Social Democracy"], *Vorwärts*, no. 201, Aug. 28, 1910 and, alarmed by what he heard, Lenin asked him if it was possible to stop publication. Not only was it impossible to do so (the conversation allegedly occurred on the very day of publication), but Trotsky believed in the correctness of his article at the time, although in his autobiography he repented. Trotsky described the controversy surrounding the article and Lenin's efforts to get the Russian delegation to condemn it as "the sharpest conflict with Lenin in my whole life." See Trotsky, *My Life*, p. 218. Either Trotsky's memory had failed him or the article had appeared a bit later than he had thought. According to the standard biographical chronicle, Lenin was in transit on August 23 and 26, but was already in Copenhagen on August 28 (new style), when the article appeared.

 16. A. Ascher, *Pavel Axelrod and the Development of Menshevism*, p. 287.

20. The Death and Rebirth of Bolshevism

 1. R. C. Williams, *The Other Bolsheviks*, pp. 158–60.

 2. V. I. Lenin, *Polnoe sobranie sochinenii*, 47:249.

 3. M. A. Tsiavlovskii, ed., *Bol'sheviki, Dokumenty po istorii bol'shevizma c 1903 po 1916 god. byvsh. Moskovskogo Okhrannago Otdeleniia* [The Bolsheviks: Documents on the History of Bolshevism from 1903 through 1916, compiled by the Moscow Okhrana Section] (Moscow: Zadruga, 1918), p. 44.

 4. *Ibid.*, p. 58.

 5. "Protokoly VI (Prazhskoi) vserossiiskoi konferentsii RSDRP," in *Voprosy istorii KPSS*, July 1988, no. 7, pp. 33ff.

 6. Although this piece is signed by the "editorial board," Trotsky's authorship is almost certain. The author's participation in *Vpered*'s school is mentioned in the article.

 7. S. Vereshchak, "Stalin v tiur'me (vospominaniia politischeskogo zakliuchennogo)," [Stalin in Prison (reminiscences of a political prisoner)] *Dni*, January 24, 1928, no. 1306, p. 2.

 8. Quoted in Trotsky, *Stalin*, p. 119.

 9. Williams, *The Other Bolsheviks.* pp. 119–21.

 10. Trotsky, *Stalin*, pp. 130–31. For the Russian text, see I. Dubinskii-Mukhadze, *Ordzhonikidze* (Moscow: Molodaia gvardiia), p. 92, fn. 1.

 11. V. T. Loginov, *Lenin i Pravda, 1912–1914 godov* [Lenin and *Pravda*, 1912–1914] (Moscow: Gosudarstvennoe izdatel'stvo politicheskoi literatury, 1962), p. 36 fn. 1.

 12. Trotsky is seconded in this assessment by Adam Ulam in his biography of Stalin, *Stalin, the Man and His Era*, pp. 105–106. Even Soviet authorities during the period of de-Stalinization resurrected Stalin's sins of this period.

 13. Stalin had sent a letter to the editorial board of *The Proletarian* in which he had defended Mach and Avenarius. See I. Dubinskii-Mukhadze, *Shaumian* (Moscow: Molodaia gvardiia, 1965), p. 156. Robert Tucker speculates that Lenin not only knew of Stalin's criticisms, but that he might have communicated a reproach to Stalin by way of Ordzhonikidze. See Tucker *Stalin as Revolutionary*, pp. 149–50.

 14. Trotsky, *My Life*, p. 154.

 15. Loginov, *Lenin i Pravda*, p. 95, 112. Stalin had opposed the decision. See P. N. Pospelov, ed., *V. I. Lenin, a Biography* (Moscow: Progress Publishers, 1965), p. 203.

 16. The bizarre deals made by the Okhrana with the Socialist-Revolutionary terrorist Azev, who was permitted to arrange the assassination of some officials so long as he would protect others and secure the safety of the royal family, suggests how strange politics had become in Russia toward the end of the old regime. Azev had been unmasked in 1909.

 17. Bonnell, *Roots of Rebellion*, pp. 428, 434.

 18. N. K. Krupskaia, *Reminiscences of Lenin*, p. 226.

 19. *Ibid.*, p. 248.

 20. It should be noted that his right-hand men in this period, Stalin and Sverdlov, conducted their work while on brief liberties from prison and exile. Stalin spent less than two years out of nine at large between March 1908 and March 1917.

21. Trotsky, *Stalin*, pp. 145–51. It is suggested elsewhere that Krupskaia's dislike of Stalin may have been behind the decision to send him to Vienna. See Ulam, *Stalin*, p. 119.

22. Krupskaia, *Reminiscences of Lenin*, p. 262. In the Russian text Krupskaia used the verb *stolkovyvat'sia*, which connotes not merely discussion but a difference of views or bargaining before arriving at an agreement. See also R. C. Elwood, "Lenin and *Pravda*," *Slavic Review* (1972), 31(2):364ff.

23. B. Wolfe, *Three Who Made a Revolution* (New York: Dell Publishing Co., Inc., 1964) pp. 581–86.

24. Lenin, *Polnoe sobranie sochinenii*, 48:162.

25. Ulam, *The Bolsheviks* (New York: Collier Books, 165), p. 293.

26. R. C. Tucker, *Stalin as Revolutionary*, pp. 152–56; McNeal, *Stalin's Works*, pp. 42–44.

27. Stalin, *Works*, 2:330.

28. *Ibid.*, p. 376.

29. *Ibid.*, p. 208.

30. *Ibid.*, p. 212.

21. Lenin in Isolation

1. Okhrana agents noted this with some anxiety. See M. A. Tsiavlovskii, ed. *Bol'sheviki*, pp. 143–48.

2. V. I. Lenin, *Polnoe sobranie sochinenii*, 25:403.

3. For a recent and scholarly account of the Brussels Conference, see R. C. Elwood, "Lenin and Brussels," *The Russian Review* (1980), 39:32–49.

4. See, for example, V. I. Lenin, "Edinstvo rabochii i 'techeniia' intelligentov" [Unity of the workers and "currents" of the intellectuals], *Polnoe sobranie sochinenii*, 25:151–54.

5. Lenin, *Polnoe sobranie sochinenii*, 25:202–203.

6. *Pravda*, April 23(May 6), 1912, no. 25.

22. Lenin, Trotsky, and World War I

1. For a good discussion, see Neil Harding, *Lenin's Political Thought*, 2 vols. (New York: St. Martin's Press), 2:41–70.

2. V. I. Lenin, *Polnoe sobranie sochinenii*, 26:354–55.

3. *Ibid.*, 30:133.

4. Quoted in Deutscher, *The Prophet Armed*, p. 238.

5. Lenin, *Polnoe sobranie sochinenii*, 49:259.

6. *Pravda*, April 23(May 6), 1912, no. 25.

7. Letter to Aksel'rod of April 29, 1912, Nicolaevsky Collection, series no. 16 (42–48), Box 3.

8. Nicolaevsky Collection, XVII-C, Box 940, no. 97359.

9. Trotsky, *Sochineniia*, 20:336.

10. *Ibid.*, pp. 340–41.

11. Deutscher, *The Prophet Armed*, p. 210.

12. In slightly different English translation in Stalin, *Works*, 2:288. Deutscher mistakenly believed that Stalin first used his pseudonym "K. Stalin" in this very article ("The Elections in St. Petersburg"), published in *Social-Democrat* on January 12(25), 1913. The first use of the Stalin pseudonym according to the most reliable source occurred a full year earlier, in *Pravda*, December 1, 1912. See McNeal, *Stalin's Works*, p. 42, item 134. See also Robert Himmer, "On the Origin and Significance of the Name Stalin," in *The Russian Review* (1986), 45: 269–86.

13. Letter to Aksel'rod, July 20, 1912, Nicolaevsky Collection, Series 16, Box 3 (42–48).

14. For an English translation of the Zimmerwald Manifesto, see O. H. Gankin and H. H. Fisher, *The Bolsheviks and the World War* (Stanford: Stanford University Press, 1940), pp. 329–33.

15. S. Iu. Bagotskii, "V. I. Lenin v Krakove i Poronine," [V. I. Lenin in Cracow and Poronin] in G. N. Golikov et al., eds., *Vospominaniia o V. I. Lenine*, 2:325.

16. Lenin, *Polnoe sobranie sochinenii*, 49:390.

17. L. Trotsky, *Voina i revoliutsiia*, [War and Revolution] 2 vols., 2d ed., (Moscow: Gosudarsvennoe izdatel'stvo, 1923), 1:27.

18. L. Trotsky *Nashe slovo* [Our Word] November 25, 1915, no. 249. "Pod bremenem ob'ektivizma [Under the Burden of Objectvism].

19. L. Trotsky, *Golos* [The Voice], November 20, 1914, no. 59.

20. L. Trotsky, *Golos*, November 21, 1914, no. 60.

21. L. Trotsky, *Golos*, November 27, 1914, no. 65. "Proletariat v voine" [The Proletariat in the War].

22. *Golos*, November 28, 1914, no. 66 (conclusion of "Proletariat vo voine").

23. O. H. Gankin and H. H. Fisher, *The Bolsheviks and the World War*, p. 330.

24. L. Trotsky, "Nash politicheskii lozung," [our Political Slogan] *Nashe slovo* [our word], February 24, 1915, no. 23.

25. G. N. Golikov et al, eds., *Vospominaniia o Vladimire Il'iche Lenine*, 1:430.

26. Lenin, *Polnoe sobranie sochinenii*, 30:327–28. The speech was delivered to an audience of young socialists. Hence, the reference to their victory was quite appropriate to the occasion.

27. Ziv, *Trotskii*, p. 74.

28. *Ibid.*, pp. 69–73.

29. Trotsky, *Voina i revoliutsiia*, 2:365, 367.

30. Trotsky, *My Life*, p. 274.

31. *Ibid.*, p. 412.

32. Riis's description of the encounter, recollected more than nineteen years later, contains at least one historical inaccuracy. He claims that it took place in April 1917 at the editorial offices of *Novyi mir* (New World), whereas Trotsky and his family sailed from New York on March 27. Riis also claims that his interview with Trotsky was published in *The New York Sun*, but I have not been able to locate the article.

33. Letter from R. W. Riis to Quincy Howe, June 11, 1936, Trotsky Mss., Lilly Library.

34. Trotsky, *My Life*, p. 282.

23. 1917: The Return of the Exiles

1. One can be certain that Lenin was well informed about the situation. His younger sister, Maria Il'inichna, had joined the editorial board of *Pravda* and attended the Bureau's sessions. A. I. Elizarova, his old sister, also attended.

2. The minutes of the meetings of March 13 and 15—there are none for March 14—do not permit accurate reconstruction of the reasons for the reversal of the decisions of March 12.

3. A. Shliapnikov, *Semnadtsatyi god* [The Year 1917], 4 vols. (Moscow: Gosudarstvennoe izdatel'stvo, 1923–1931), 1:204.

4. See E. N. Burzhdalov, *The February 1917 Uprising in Petrograd*, Donald J. Raleigh, ed. and trans. (Bloomington: Indiana University Press, 1987), pp. 229–31; T. Hasegawa, *The February Revolution: Petrograd, 1917* (Seattle: University of Washington Press), p. 333.

5. Burzhdalov, *The February 1917 Uprising*, pp. 234–37.

6. N. N. Sukhanov, *The Russian Revolution of 1917*, Joel Carmichael, ed., abr., and trans. (Princeton: Princeton University Press, 1984), p. 280.

7. *Ibid.*, p. 287.

8. Stalin, *Works*, 3:14.

24. Trotsky and the Bolsheviks

1. I. Iurenev, "Mezhraionka" [The Interdistrict Commission], *Proletarskaia revoliutsiia* (1924), 1(24):116.

2. L. Trotsky, *The Stalin School of Falsification*, 3d ed. (New York: Pathfinder Press, 1972), p. 5. Trotsky's version appears in his voluminous "Letter to the Bureau of Party History" of

October 21, 1927. There he asserts that he learned about the Interdistrict Commission only after his arrival at the Finland Station and that the organization's leaders postponed their decision to merge with the Bolsheviks until discussing the matter with him. Trotsky no doubt underplays his differences with Lenin and the Bolsheviks and exaggerates his efforts to bring about the fusion.

3. In other works, Trotsky uses "the lesser evil" to refer to the position of social-patriotism, which, of course, he rejected. Thus, there may be crucial omissions in the notes and they may be misleading.

4. *Leninskii sbornik* (Moscow: Instituta Lenina Ts. K.P.K.P.(b), 1925), 4:301.

5. *Ibid.*, p. 303.

6. Trotsky, *Sochineniia*, 3:43.

7. *Ibid.*, p. 48.

8. *Ibid.*, pp. 70–92.

9. *Ibid.*, p. 49.

10. A. V. Lunacharsky, *Revolutionary Silhouettes*, Michael Glenny, trans. (London: Penguin, 1967), p. 65. I have reproduced Mr. Glenny's translation with a small modification of "his rigid logic, clear as polished steel."

11. Trotsky, *My Life*, pp. 295–96. Although I largely follow the translation in the text cited, I have modified it somewhat following the published Russian text: Trotsky, *Moia zhizn'*, 2 vols. (Berlin, 1930), 2:15–16. The same modified translation appears in Trotsky, *Trotsky's Notebooks, 1933–35*, p. 69.

12. See Trotsky, *My Life*, pp. 184, 287.

13. Trotsky, *Moia zhizn'*, 2:56.

14. In a manuscript version of his autobiography preserved in the Houghton Library, Trotsky had crossed out the words "you physically felt in your entire body," then replaced it with "on your lips the physical pressure," before settling on "you felt with your lips the insistent searching . . ." He seems to have begun with phallic imagery—Trotsky himself—and transmuted it into a maternal image, in that he goes on to compare the crowd to infants sucking at the breast of the revolution. In any case, no psychoanalyst would have much difficulty finding psychosexual content in the images conjured up when Trotsky recalled his performances in the Cirque Moderne. See the Trotsky Archives, T3264 (2 of 6, p. 15), Houghton Library.

25. Lenin's First Bid for Power

1. L. Trotsky, *The History of the Russian Revolution*, 3 vols. (New York: Simon and Schuster, 1932), 1:479.

2. Lenin, *Polnoe sobranie sochinenii*, 32:266–67.

3. Trotsky, *Lenin, Notes for a Biographer*, p. 80. For the document itself, see Trotsky, *Sochineniia*, 3:136–37. Lenin did make a speech about the war on June 9. See Lenin, *Polnoe sobranie sochinenii*, 32:277–91. The original versions of both Trotsky's and Lenin's speeches on the war are in *Pervyi vserossiiskii s'ezd sovetov R. i S. D.* [The First All-Russian Congress of Soviets of Workers' and Soldiers' Deputies] 2 vols. (Moscow: Gosudarstevennoe izdatel'stvo, 1930).

4. Robert M. Slusser, *Stalin in October* (Baltimore: Johns Hopkins University Press, 1987), pp. 119–21.

5. Alexander Rabinowitch, *Prelude to Revolution* (Bloomington: Indiana University Press, 1968), pp. 56–57.

6. Slusser, *Stalin in October*, p. 124. Stalin's behavior during the June days received scant attention from Trotsky. See Trotsky, *Stalin*, p. 207.

7. Slusser, *Stalin in October*, p. 134. The resignation was first revealed in 1966. See A. M. Sovokin, "K istorii iiun'skoi demonstratsii 1917 g.," *Voprosy istorii KPSS* (1966), no. 5, pp. 45–54.

8. Trotsky, *Stalin*, p. 207.

9. Trotsky, *Lenin, Notes for a Biographer*, p. 81.

10. Slusser's careful study of the two texts can be found in *Stalin in October*, pp. 125–27.

11. N. N. Sukhanov, *The Surrian Revolution*, pp. 416–17.

12. Lenin, *Polnoe sobranie sochinenii*, 32:360.

13. P. N. Miliukov, *The Russian Revolution*, Richard Stites, ed., Tatyana and Richard Stites, trans. (Gulf Breeze, Florida: Academic International Press, 1978), pp. 186–87.

14. V. D. Bonch-Bruevich, *Vospominaniia o Lenine* [Reminiscences about Lenin] (Moscow: Izdatel'stvo politicheskoi literatury, 1969), pp. 96–106. According to Lenin's own account, he left Petrograd on June 29, (*Polnoe sobranie sochinenii*, 34:21) but Bonch-Bruevich records the date as June 27 and even notes the precise time of Lenin's arrival—five P.M. I take Bonch-Bruevich's date, which was published in memoirs written after the Revolution, as the correct one, because Lenin's dating of his departure from Petrograd, given in reply to attacks on him in late July, may very well have been falsified for conspiratorial reasons.

15. Lenin, *Polnoe sobranie sochinenii*, 32:430.

16. In Rabinowitch's translation, the demand *(trebovanie)* is called an ultimatum and rendered "take power now or face an armed uprising." See Rabinowitch, *Prelude to Revolution*, p. 159.

17. *Vtoraia i tret'ia Petrogradskie obshegorodskie konferentsii bol'shevikov v iiule i sentiabre 1917 g.* [The Second and Third All-City Petrograd Conferences of Bolsheviks in July and September 1917] (Moscow: Gosudarstevennoe izdatel'stvo, 1927), pp. 52, 142 fn. 52. For Trotsky's version of these events, see *The History of the Russian Revolution*, 2:32.

18. *Ibid.*, 2:25–26.

19. The leaflet is attributed to Stalin by Rabinowitch, although it does not appear in his works. Slusser, another close student of this period, is not convinced that it was Stalin's work. See Rabinowitch, *Prelude to Revolution*, p. 175; Slusser, *Stalin in October*, pp. 144–45.

20. Lenin, *Polnoe sobranie sochinenii*, 32:22.

21. Trotsky, *My Life*, p. 313.

22. Stalin's account of the events, delivered at the Third All-City Bolshevik Conference on July 16 (29), 1917 is reproduced in his *Works*, 3:118.

23. Rabinowitch, *Prelude to Revolution*, pp. 215–216.

24. G. K. Ordzhonikidze, "Il'ich v iiul'skie dni," [Il'ich in the July Days] *Vospominaniia o V. I. Lenine*, (1969), 2:416.

25. *Ibid.*, pp. 414–15. At the Third All-City Bolshevik Conference in Petrograd on July 16 Stalin claimed that he had been involved in the negotiations with the Central Executive Committee of the Soviet without mentioning Ordzhonikidze. See *Vtoraia i tret'ia Petrogradskie obshchegorodskie konferentsii bol'shevikov*, p. 56.

26. See Slusser, *Stalin in October*, pp. 168–71; Trotsky, *Stalin*, pp. 214–17.

27. The translation, while not exact, is adequate. It is from Stalin, *Works*, 3:132.

26. The Bolsheviks in Extremis

1. Miliukov, *The Russian Revolution*, 1:202. Sukhanov claims that Kamenev, Martov, Lunacharskii, and Trotsky were delegated. See Sukhanov, *The Russian Revolution*, p. 445.

2. *Ibid.*, p. 446.

3. Quoted in Trotsky, *My Life*, p. 312.

4. Sukhanov, *The Russian Revolution*, pp. 479–81.

5. The assumption here is that the nonreporting delegates were distributed in roughly the same way as the reporting ones. Obviously, such an assumption can be challenged. In a pioneering but speculative study, *The Roots of Russian Communism*, David Lane showed that even earlier the Bolsheviks had become more ethnically Russian than the other socialist parties.

6. *Shestoi s'ezd RSDRP (bol'shevikov), protokoly* [The Sixth Conference of the RSDRP (bolsheviks), Protocols] (Moscow: Gosudarstvennoe izdatel'stvo politicheskoi literatury, 1958), p. 138.

7. *Ibid.*, p. 143.

8. *Ibid.*

9. *Ibid.*, p. 105.

10. *Ibid.*, p. 250.
11. *Ibid.*
12. *Ibid.*

27. Lenin's Utopia

1. Neil Harding, *Lenin's Political Thought*, 1:92ff. Harding provides an excellent account of both Bukharin's and Lenin's debt to Rudolph Hilferding.

2. Not only Harding but Stephen Cohen in his earlier biography of Bukharin makes this point at length. See Stephan F. Cohen, *Bukharin and the Bolshevik Revolution* (New York: Oxford University Press, 1980), pp. 34–43.

3. The phrase itself appears in a letter from Marx to Josef Weydemeyer written in 1852, but published for the first time in 1907. Lenin found an earlier version of the same idea, without the terminology, in *The Communist Manifesto* (1847) and later in the writings of Marx and Engels analyzing the Paris Commune.

28. Reversal: On the Attack

1. *Protokoly tsentral'nogo komiteta RSDRP(b), Avgust 1917–Fevral' 1918*, [Protocols of the Central Committee of the RSDRP(b) August 1917–February 1918] p. 4.

2. Lunacharsky, *Revolutionary Silhouettes*, p. 66.

3. *Ibid.*, p. 67.

4. Angelica Balabanoff, *My Life as a Rebel* (New York: Harper, 1938), pp. 155–56.

5. Lenin, *Polnoe sobranie sochinenii*, 34:134.

6. *Protokoly tsentral'nogo komiteta RSDRP(b), Avgust 1917–Fevral' 1918*, pp. 65, 262, fn. 100.

7. Trotsky, *Sochineniia*, vol. 3, part 1, p. 314.

8. A. Rabinowitch, *The Bolsheviks Come to Power* (New York: Norton, 1976), pp. 195ff; Robert V. Daniels, *Red October* (New York: Scribner's, 1967), p. 65–67; Trotsky, *The History of the Russian Revolution*, 3:137–38.

9. This is the generally accepted date, although Lenin's conspiratorial methods made it difficult to establish it with any certainty.

10. Trotsky, *Sochineniia*, vol. 3, part 1, p. 323.

11. *Protokoly tsentral'nogo komiteta RSDRP(b), Avgust 1917–Fevral' 1918*, p. 86.

29. October 1917

1. Trotsky, *Sochineniia*, vol. 3, part 2, p. 5.

2. *Ibid.*, p. 31.

3. Trotsky, *Lenin, Notes for a Biographer*, pp. 94–95.

4. This is what Lenin evidently believed. See Lenin, *Polnoe sobranie sochinenii*, 34:423.

5. Robert V. Daniels' view is on the mark. See Daniels, *Red October*, p. 217.

6. N. N. Sukhanov, *The Russian Revolution*, pp. 584–85.

7. Lenin, *Polnoe sobranie sochinennii*, 34: 436. The letter is erroneously addressed to the Central Committee in Lenin's collected works. Both Trotsky and E. Rakh'ia, Lenin's bodyguard in September–October, testify to the fact that it was sent to the district committees.

8. M. V. Fofanova, "Il'ich Pered Oktiabrem" [Lenin Before October], in G. N. Golikov et al., eds., *Vospominaniia o Vladimire Il'iche Lenine*, 2:445–46. Stalin claims that Lenin was "called to Smol'nyi" in *Works*, 4:157.

9. Trotsky refers to the meeting in his autobiography without giving it a time, but from his narrative one would get the impression that the CC met later than the night of October 24–25. Eino Rakh'ia claims in his memoirs that they met after Lenin's statement to the Petrograd Soviet, which took place roughly twelve hours later. The weight of the evidence collected by Soviet scholars places the meeting in the wee hours of the morning of October 25. For a recent

Soviet attempt to reconstruct the meeting, although without reference to Trotsky's memoirs, see E. A. Lutskii, "Zasedanie TsK RSDRP(b) noch'iu 24–25 Oktiabria 1917 g." [The Session of the CC of the RSDRP(b) of the Night of October 24–25, 1917], *Voprosy istorii KPSS* (1986), no. 11, pp. 81–90.

10. Trotsky, *My Life*, pp. 337–38. In other memoirs, Trotsky's contribution is limited to providing the world "people's."

11. *Istochnikovedenie. Teoreticheskie i metodicheskie problemy* [Source Book. Theoretical and Methodological Problems] (Moscow: Izdatel'stvo nauka, 1969), p. 372.

12. Trotsky, *Sochineniia*, vol. 3, part 2, p. 56.

13. *Ibid.*, p. 58.

14. See, for example, N. I. Podvoiskii's memoirs in *Vospominaniia o V.I. Lenine*, 2:450.

15. Trotsky, *The History of the Russian Revolution*, 3:306.

16. *Ibid.*

17. Trotsky, *Stalin*, p. 234.

18. For a recent Soviet article on Lenin's struggle with Zinov'ev and Kamenev, Trotsky's position, and Stalin's maneuvering, see V. I. Startsev, "Lenin v Oktiabre 1917 g.," [Lenin in October 1917] *Voprosy istorii* (1987), no. 10, pp. 86–101.

19. *Protokoly tsentral'nogo komiteta RSDRP(b), Avgust 1917–Fevral' 1918*, p. 118. Stalin also recommended that Miliutin speak on workers' control.

20. A. Rabinowitch, *The Bolsheviks Come to Power*, p. 272; Slusser, *Stalin in October*, pp. 244–45.

21. Slusser speculates that Sverdlov and Trotsky played some role in this. Perhaps they failed to notify Stalin of the emergency session. Neither of them liked him or had much confidence in him. See Slusser, *Stalin in October*, p. 246.

30. The Travails of Power

1. John Reed, *Ten Days That Shook the World* (New York: Boni and Liveright, 1919), p. 126.

2. *Ibid.*, p. 127.

3. *Ibid.*, p. 132.

4. N. N. Sukhanov, *The Russian Revolution*, p. 659.

5. V. I. Lenin, *Polnoe sobranie sochinenii*, 35:27.

6. Reed, *Ten Days*, p. 135.

7. Trotsky, *Sochineniia*, vol. 3, part 2, pp. 66–67.

8. Reed, *Ten Days*, p. 143.

9. Trotsky, *My Life*, pp. 339–40.

10. *Ibid.*, p. 338. For a slightly different version, see Trotsky, *Lenin, Notes for a Biographer*, p. 124.

11. Trotsky, *The Stalin School of Falsification*, p. 110.

12. *Ibid.*, p. 111.

13. A. Balabanoff, *My Life as a Rebel*, p. 157.

14. Trotsky, *The Stalin School of Falsification*, p. 110.

15. These bare figures do not give a true picture of Bolshevik and Left SR strength in the country relative to the other parties represented in the Constituent Assembly; nor do they give a strategic map of the areas of Bolshevik strength.

31. Crisis: Brest-Litovsk

1. *Protokoly tsentral'nogo komiteta RSDRP(b), Avgust 1917–Fevral' 1918*, p. 168.

2. *Ibid.*, p. 207.

3. *Ibid.*

4. Trotsky, *My Life*, p. 350.

32. The Civil War: Trotsky Versus Stalin

1. Trotsky, *My Life*, pp. 360–61.
2. Trotsky, *The Military Writings and Speeches of Leon Trotsky: How the Revolution Armed*, Brian Pearce, trans. and annot., 5 vols. (London: New Park Publications, 1979), 1:58.
3. A. Lunacharskii, *Revoliutsionnye siluety*, p. 313.
4. L. Trotsky, *The Trotsky Papers: 1917–1922*, J. M. Meijer, ed., 2 vols. (London: Mouton, 1964, 1971), 1:91.
5. Trotsky, *Military Writings and Speeches*, 1:32.
6. Stalin, *Works*, 4:123.
7. Trotsky, *My Life*, p. 442.
8. Quoted in I. Deutscher, *Stalin: A Political Biography*. (New York: Vintage, 1960), p. 206.
9. Stalin, *Works*, 4:271.
10. Trotsky, *Stalin*, p. 332.
11. Trotsky, *Lenin, Notes for a Biographer*, pp. 107–108.
12. *Deviataia konferentsiia RKP(b), Sentiabr' 1920 goda, protokoly* [The Ninth Conference of the RCP(b), September 1920, Protocols] (Moscow: Izdatel'stvo politicheskoi literatury, 1972), p. 77.
13. *Ibid.*, p. 82. The stenographic account of the session of September 22 is obviously incomplete. What is surprising is that the record of Stalin making a speech against a united Lenin and Trotsky survived.
14. Trotsky, *Stalin*, p. 329.
15. *Ibid.*, p. 326.
16. For recent estimates, see E. Mawdsley, *The Russian Civil War* (Boston: Allen and Unwin), pp. 285–90.

33. War Communism

1. Quoted in Cohen, *Bukharin and the Bolshevik Revolution*, p. 92.
2. T. H. Rigby, *Lenin's Government* (London: Cambridge University Press, 1979), p. 226.
3. *Ibid.*, p. 228.

34. Lenin Against Trotsky

1. Trotsky, *Military Writings and Speeches*, 3:110.
2. *Ibid.*, pp. 113–14.
3. *Ibid.*, 2:181.
4. *Ibid.*, p. 188.
5. It is not completely clear whether Trotsky actually proposed free trade or merely "uncoerced exchange" between city and countryside. See Thomas Remington's article and Richard Day's comment, "Trotsky, War Communism, and the Origin of NEP," *Studies in Comparative Communism* (Spring/Summer 1977), 10:44–68.
6. In August 1919 Trotsky's sense of Europe's failure was so strong, that he suggested shifting the "center of gravity" of revolutionism to the East. The Urals would be made a center of "military-industrial operations" for an Asian campaign. See *The Trotsky Papers*, 1:627.
7. For a good discussion of the debate, see Daniels, *The Conscience of the Revolution: Communist Opposition in Soviet Russia* (Cambridge: Harvard University Press, 1960), ch. 5.
8. Lenin, *Polnoe sobranie sochinenii*, 42:208.
9. *Ibid.*, p. 212.

35. 1921: Year of Crisis and Retreat

1. V. I. Lenin, *Polnoe sobranie sochinenii*, 42:278–79.
2. R. C. Williams, *The Other Bolsheviks*, pp. 176–77.
3. Quoted in R. V. Daniels, ed. and trans., *A Documentary History of Communism*, 2 vols.

(Hanover and London: University Press of New England, 1984), 1:134. I have altered the translation slightly.

4. V. I. Lenin, *Polnoe sobranie sochinenii*, 43:72.

5. Quoted in I. Getzler, *Kronstadt 1917–21* (London: Cambridge University Press, 1983), p. 234.

6. Paul Avrich, *Kronstadt 1921* (Princeton: Princeton University Press, 1970), pp. 211–12.

7. *Ibid.*, p. 211.

8. *Protokoly s'ezdov i konferentsii vsesoiuznoi kommunisticheskoi partii(b). Desiatyi s'ezd RKP(b)* [Protocols of the Congresses and Conferences of the All-Union Russian Communist Party(b): The Tenth Congress of the RCP(b)] (Moscow: Partiinoe izdatel'stvo, 1933), pp. 300–303.

9. *Ibid.*, p. 352.

10. *Ibid.*, p. 381.

11. *Ibid.*, pp. 392–95.

36. Lenin's Last Campaigns

1. V. I. Lenin, *Polnoe sobranie sochinenii*, 44:396–400.

2. L. Trotsky, *My Life*, p. 75. Elsewhere, Kamenev is given credit for proposing the idea of the conditional death sentence against Trotsky's proposal that if the accused did not promise to sever their ties to the Socialist Revolutionary Party within twenty-four hours, they would be executed immediately. It they agreed, then they would serve five years of forced labor. See Marc Jansen, *A Show Trial Under Lenin* (The Hague: Martinus Nijhoff, 1982), p. 135.

3. The most thorough study of the trial questions R. Medvedev's attempts to absolve Lenin and Bukharin completely and to place the main blame on Stalin for the organization of the trial. See *ibid.*, pp. 134–40.

4. For the fate of the defendants, see, Jansen, *A Show Trial Under Lenin*, ch. 10.

5. Lenin, *Polnoe sobranie sochinenii*, 44:398.

6. B. Bazhanov, *Vospominaniia byvshego sekretaria Stalina* (France: Tret'ia vol'na, 1980), pp. 56–59. For a close analysis of Bazhanov as a source, see N. E. Rosenfeldt, *Knowledge and Power* (Copenhagen: Rosenkilde and Bagger, 1978), pp. 40–41.

7. Robert Service, *The Bolshevik Party in Revolution, 1917–1923* (New York: Harper and Row, 1979), p. 182.

8. Robert H. McNeal, *Stalin: Man and Ruler*, p. 76.

9. Lenin, *Polnoe sobranie sochinenii*, 44:428.

10. Trotsky, *My Life*, p. 477.

37. The "Testament"

1. Lenin, *Polnoe sobranie sochinenii*, 45:592–93.

2. *Ibid.*, p. 359.

3. *Ibid.*, p. 211.

4. He tried to bring Kamenev over to his side, without success. See M. Lewin, *Lenin's Last Struggle*, A. M. Sheridan Smith, trans. (New York: Monthly Review Press, 1968) pp. 51–52.

5. R. C. Tucker, *Stalin as Revolutionary*, p. 260.

6. L. A. Fotieva, *Iz zhizni V. I. Lenina* [From the Life of V. I. Lenin] (Moscow: Izdatel'stvo politicheskoi literatury, 1967), p. 251.

7. Trotsky's memory betrayed him. He recalls his injury and Lenin's stroke as taking place in early May. Lenin's stroke took place on May 25.

8. In this case too, Trotsky accused Stalin of scheming to prevent him from attending.

9. Trotsky, *My Life*, p. 482.

10. *Ibid.*, p. 484.

11. Lenin, *Polnoe sobranie sochinenii*, 54:330.

12. Trotsky, *My Life*, p. 485.

13. Lenin, *Polnoe sobranie sochinenii*, 54:329–30.

14. *Ibid.*, pp. 674–75.

15. *Ibid.*, 45:346.

16. Lewin, *Lenin's Last Struggle*, p. 95.

17. Trotsky, *My Life*, p. 486. On the apology, see also Lenin, *Polnoe sobranie sochinenii*, 54:675.

18. Trotsky to all members of the Central Committee, April 16, 1923. See Trotsky Archives, bMsRuss13 T794, Houghton Library.

19. Lenin, *Polnoe sobranie sochinenii*, 45:357, 360.

20. Actually, the contents of the article were known by some of the delegates to the Congress who were already in Moscow. Inside information about the struggle among the oligarchs was also leaked to Menshevik émigrés. N. Valentinov is one of the best sources on the April events.

21. Trotsky Archives, bMsRuss13 T795, Houghton Library.

22. *Ibid.*, T796.

23. They were not published until 1956, under Khrushchev.

24. Max Eastman, *Since Lenin Died* (London: Labour Publishing, 1925), p. 25.

25. *Ibid.*, p. 18.

26. For a detailed discussion of the maneuvers against Trotsky before the Twelfth Party Congress, see Richard B. Day, *Leon Trotsky and the Politics of Economic Isolation* (Cambridge: Cambridge University Press, 1973), pp. 75–81.

27. *Protokoly i stenograficheskie otchety s'ezdov i konferentsii Kommunisticheskoi Partii Sovetskogo Soiuza. Dvenadtsatyi s'ezd RKP(b) 17–25 aprelia 1923 goda* [Protocols and Stenographic Accounts of the Congresses and Conferences of the All-Union Russian Communist Party(b): The Twelfth Congress of the RCP(b)] (Moscow: Izdatel'stvo politecheskoi literatury, 1968), pp. 611–15.

38. Trotsky's "New Course"

1. M. Eastman, *Since Lenin Died*, pp. 36–37.

2. Like Stalin's letter of April 16, 1923, it found its way to the Mensheviks, who published excerpts in their émigré journal, *Sotsialisticheskii vestnik* (Berlin), May 28, 1924. The letter of October 8, 1923 (in the form printed in Berlin in 1924) is reprinted in English translation in L. Trotsky, *The Challenge of the Left Opposition (1923–25)* (New York: Pathfinder Press, 1980), pp. 51–58.

3. It should be noted that only three of three of the forty-six signators, no doubt the main authors, endorsed the document in its entirety. The remaining signators added qualifications or claimed to adhere only in general to the document.

4. L. Trotsky, *My Life*, p. 498.

5. Eastman, *Since Lenin Died*, p. 38.

39. Lenin's Death and Trotsky's Decline

1. J. V. Stalin, *Works*, 6:46.

2. *Ibid.*, p. 14.

3. V. P. Naumov, "Leninskoe zaveshchanie," [Lenin's Testament] in *Pravda*, February 26, 1988, p. 3. For another, less authoritative version, see B. Bazhanov, *Vospominaniia byvshego sekretaria Stalina*, pp. 106–7.

4. L. Trotsky, *Stalin*, p. 375.

5. Trotsky to Max Eastman, June 7, 1933, Trotsky Mss., Lilly Library. Trotsky recounted the incident in a reply to Eastman's letter of May 24, 1933, in which Eastman asked: "Would you mind telling me privately what is the 'winged phrase' that Stalin used when he learned about Lenin's attitude toward him in the last days?" Eastman's letter is also contained in the Trotsky Mss., Lilly Library. Bazhanov gives another version of Stalin's reaction, allegedly told to him by Mekhlis. See "Stalin Closely Observed," in G. R. Urban, ed., *Stalinism* (Cambridge: Harvard University Press, 1986), p. 17.

6. V. P. Naumov, "Leninskoe zaveshchanie," p. 4.

7. L. Trotsky, "Zaveshchanie Lenina," [Lenin's Testament] *Obozrenie* [Review] (July 1984), 10:44.

8. *Ibid.*, pp. 42–44.

9. *Trinadtsatyi s'ezd rossiiskoi kommunisticheskoi partii (bol'shevikov). Stenograficheskii otchet, 23–31 maia 1924 g.* [The Thirteenth Congress of the Russian Communist Party (Bolsheviks), Stenographic Accounts, May 23–31, 1924] (Moscow: Izdatel'stvo "Krasnaia Nov," 1924), pp. 166–68.

10. *Ibid.*, p. 245.

Index